POETRY
IN
ENGLISH

THE MACMILLAN COMPANY

POETRY
SECOND EDITION *IN*
ENGLISH

WARREN TAYLOR
Oberlin College

DONALD HALL
The University of Michigan

Acknowledgments

Thanks are due the following copyright owners and publishers for permission to reprint certain poems in this anthology:

ATHENEUM HOUSE, Inc.—for "Behold the Lilies of the Field" from the book *The Hard Hours* by Anthony Hecht, published by Atheneum, copyright © 1961, 1967 by Anthony E. Hecht. Reprinted by permission of Atheneum. The poem appeared originally in the *Hudson Review*.

ROBERT BLY—for "A Man Writes to Part of Himself" and "Taking the Hands . . ." by Robert Bly from *From Silence in the Snowy Fields*, published by Wesleyan University Press; poems copyright by Robert Bly.

CITY LIGHTS BOOKS—for "America" from *Howl* by Allen Ginsberg, copyright © 1956, 1959 by Allen Ginsberg, reprinted by permission of City Lights Books.

THE CLARENDON PRESS, OXFORD—for "The Salutation" and "Wonder" from *Poems* by Thomas Traherne, by permission of The Clarendon Press, Oxford; for "Low Barometer," "London Snow," and "ΕΡΩΣ," from *The Poems of Robert Bridges*, by permission of The Clarendon Press, Oxford.

COLLINS-KNOWLTON-WING, INC.—for "Apples and Water," "Warning to Children," "In Broken Images," "The White Goddess," "Counting the Beats," and "To Juan at the Winter Solstice" by Robert Graves. Reprinted by permission of Collin-Knowlton-Wing, Inc. Copyright © 1955 by Robert Graves.

CRITERION BOOKS, INC.—for "Epistle I" and "Epitaph for the Poet," from *Collected Poems 1930–1955* by George Barker, copyright © 1957 by George Granville Barker and reprinted by permission of the publisher, Criterion Books, Inc.

CURTIS BROWN, LTD.—for "How Beastly the Bourgeois Is," from *Pansies* by D. H. Lawrence, copyright 1929 by Frieda Lawrence Ravagli, reprinted by permission of the author's estate.

ANDRE DEUTSCH, LTD.—for "Orpheus and Eurydice," from *For the Un-Fallen* by Geoffrey Hill, reprinted by permission of the publishers.

DOUBLEDAY & COMPANY, INC.—for "Cuttings (Later)," copyright 1948 by Theodore Roethke; "Dolor," copyright 1947 by Theodore Roethke; "The Visitant," copyright 1950 by Theodore Roethke; "I Knew a Woman," copyright 1954 by Theodore Roethke; "The Meadow Mouse" and "The Rose," copyright © 1963 by Beatrice Roethke as Administratrix of the Estate of Theodore Roethke, from *The Collected Poems of Theodore Roethke*, reprinted by permission of Doubleday & Company, Inc.

FABER AND FABER LIMITED—for "The Strangled Prayer," reprinted from *The Death Bell* by Vernon Watkins.

FARRAR, STRAUS & CUDAHY, INC.—for "Skunk Hour" from *Life Studies* by Robert Lowell, copyright © 1956, 1959 by Robert Lowell, reprinted by permission of Farrar, Straus & Cudahy, Inc.

GROVE PRESS, INC.—for "The Island," "The Labyrinth," and "The Three Mirrors," from *Collected Poems 1921–1951* by Edwin Muir, copyright © 1957 by Edwin Muir; "The Horses" and "The Incarnate One," from *One Foot in Eden* by Edwin Muir; for "Heat," from *Selected Poems* by H. D., copyright © 1957 by Norman Holmes Pearson; all reprinted by permission of the publishers, Grove Press, Inc.

HARCOURT, BRACE & WORLD, INC.—for "Poem, Or Beauty Hurts Mr. Vinal" and "next to of course god america i," copyright 1926 by Horace Liveright, copyright 1954 by E. E. Cummings; "i sing of Olaf glad and big," copyright 1931, 1959 by E. E. Cummings; "my father moved through dooms of love," copyright 1940 by E. E. Cummings, all from *Poems 1923–1954* by E. E. Cummings, reprinted by permission of Harcourt, Brace and World, Inc.; for "The Quaker Graveyard in Nantucket" by Robert Lowell, from *Lord Weary's Castle*, copyright 1944, 1946 by Robert Lowell, reprinted by permission of Harcourt, Brace & World, Inc.; for "Museum Piece," copyright 1948, 1949, 1950 by Richard Wilbur; "Juggler" and "Years-End," copyright 1949 by Richard Wilbur, from *Ceremony and Other Poems* by Richard Wilbur, reprinted by permission of Harcourt, Brace & World, Inc.; for "Mind," © 1956 by Richard Wilbur, from *Things of This World* by Richard Wilbur, reprinted by permission of Harcourt, Brace & World, Inc.; for "Villanelle," "Missing Dates," and "Let It Go" by William Empson, from *Collected Poems of William Empson*, copyright 1935, 1940, 1949 by William Empson, reprinted by permission of Harcourt, Brace & World, Inc.; for "Gerontian," "The Love Song of J. Alfred Prufrock," "La Figlia Che Piange," "Journey of the Magi," "Marina," and "Whispers of Immortality," from *Colleced Poems 1909–1935* by T. S. Eliot, copyright 1936 by Harcourt, Brace & World, Inc.; for "Little Gidding," from *Four Quarters*, copyright 1943 by T. S. Eliot and reprinted by permission of Harcourt, Brace & World, Inc.

HARPER & ROW—for "Thrushes," from *Lupercal* by Ted Hughes, copyright © 1959 by Ted Hughes; for "The Retired Colonel" from *Lupercal* by Ted Hughes, copyright © 1960 by Ted Hughes; for "Wodwo" from *Wodwo* by Ted Hughes, copyright © 1962 by Ted Hughes; for "Romans Angry About the Inner World" from *The Light Around the Body* by Robert Bly, copyright, © 1967 by Robert Bly; and for the following poems from *After Experience* by W. D. Snodgrass: "Lobsters in the Window," copyright © 1963 by W. D. Snodgrass, originally appeared in *The New Yorker;* "Mementos, 1," copyright © 1960 by W. D. Snodgrass. All of these poems are reprinted by permission of Harper & Row, Publishers.

RUPERT HART-DAVIS LIMITED—for "Death of a Peasant" and "The Country Clergy" by R. S. Thomas, reprinted by permission of the publisher.

HARVARD UNIVERSITY PRESS—for poems #67, 130, 249, 303, 341, 465, 536, 564, 575, 640, 712, 769, 986, 1461, 1593, and 1760, reprinted by permission of the publishers, from *The Poems of Emily Dickinson* edited by Thomas H. Johnson, The Belknap Press of Harvard University Press, copyright 1951, 1955 by The President and Fellows of Harvard College.

HOLT, RINEHART AND WINSTON, INC.—for "Birches," "To Earthward," "Acquainted with the Night," "The Gift Outright," "The Most of It," "Come In," "The Silken Tent," "Design," "Desert Places," "Tree at my Window," and " 'Out, Out—' " from *Complete Poems of Robert Frost,* copyright 1916, 1921, 1923, 1928 by Holt, Rinehart and Winston, Inc., copyright 1936, 1942 by Robert Frost, copyright renewed 1944, 1951, © 1956 by Robert Frost, reprinted by permission of Holt, Rinehart and Winston, Inc.; for "Ends" from *In the Clearing* by Robert Frost, copyright © 1962 by Robert Frost, reprinted by permission of Holt, Rinehart and Winston, Inc.; for "To an Athlete Dying Young," " 'Farewell to barn and stack and tree,' " and "On Wenlock Edge," from "A Shropshire Lad," authorized edition, from *Complete Poems* by A. E. Housman, copyright © 1959 by Holt, Rinehart and Winston, Inc., reprinted by permission of Holt, Rinehart and Winston, Inc.; for "Eight O'Clock" and "Epitaph on an Army of Mercenaries," from *Complete Poems* by A. E. Housman, copyright 1922 by Holt, Rinehart and Winston, Inc., copyright renewed 1950 by Barclay's Bank Ltd., reprinted by permission of Holt, Rinehart and Winston, Inc.; for "Chicago," from *Chicago Poems* by Carl Sandburg, copyright 1916 by Holt, Rinehart and Winston, Inc., copyright renewed 1944 by Carl Sandburg, reprinted by permission of Holt, Rinehart and Winston, Inc.

HOUGHTON MIFFLIN COMPANY—for "You, Andrew Marvell" and "The End of the World" by Archibald MacLeish; for "The Monument" by Elizabeth Bishop; for "The Bear" by Galway Kinnell from *Body Rags,* copyright © 1967 by Galway Kinnell; all reprinted by permission of the publisher, Houghton Mifflin Company.

INDIANA UNIVERSITY PRESS—for "Dirge," from *Poems New and Selected* by Kenneth Fearing, reprinted by permission of the Indiana University Press.

ALFRED A. KNOPF, INC.—for "The Course of a Particular," from *Opus Posthumous* by Wallace Stevens, copyright 1957 by Elsie Stevens and Holly Stevens, reprinted by permission of Alfred A. Knopf, Inc.; for "The Snow Man," "The Emperor of Ice Cream," Disillusionment of Ten O'Clock," "Sunday Morning," "Anecdote of the Jar," "The Idea of Order at Key West," "Man Carrying Thing," and "Final Soliloquy of the Interior Paramour," from *The Collected Poems of Wallace Stevens,* copyright 1923, 1931, 1935, 1936, 1947, 1951, 1954 by Wallace Stevens, reprinted by permission of Alfred A. Knopf, Inc.; for "Bells for John Whiteside's Daughter," "Captain Carpenter," "Painted Head," and "Janet

Waking," from *Selected Poems* by John Crowe Ransom, copyright 1924, 1927, 1934, 1945 by Alfred A. Knopf, Inc., reprinted by permission of Alfred A. Knopf, Inc.

PHILIP LARKIN—for "Mr. Bleaney," reprinted by permission of the author, who holds copyright.

LITTLE, BROWN & COMPANY—for #341, 564, 575, 769, and 1461, from *The Poems of Emily Dickinson,* copyright 1914, 1929, 1942 by Martha Dickinson Bianchi, copyright © 1957 by Mary L. Hampson, reprinted by permission of Little, Brown & Company.

LIVERIGHT PUBLISHING CORPORATION—for "Repose of Rivers," "At Melville's Tomb," "Voyages I, II, III," "Royal Palm," "The Air Plant," "Poem: To Brooklyn Bridge," and "The Broken Tower," from *The Collected Poems of Hart Crane,* copyright © 1961 by Liveright Publishing Corporation, reprinted by permission of Liveright Publishing Corporation.

THE MACMILLAN COMPANY—for "Nature's Questioning," "Afterwards," "The Darkling Thrush," "The Man He Killed," "Weathers," "The Master and the Leaves," "The Dark Eyed Gentleman," "Channel Firing," "The Oxen," "Transformations," and "During Wind and Rain," copyright 1925 by The Macmillan Company, and for "Epitaph on a Pessimist," copyright 1925 by The Macmillan Company, copyright 1953 by Lloyd's Bank Ltd., all from *Collected Poems* by Thomas Hardy, reprinted by permission of The Macmillan Company; for "Eros Turannos," "The Poor Relation," and "Hillcrest," copyright 1916 by The Macmillan Company, copyright 1944 by Ruth Nivison; and for "The Dark Hills" and "The Mill," copyright 1920 by The Macmillan Company, copyright 1948 by Ruth Nivison, all from *Collected Poems* by Edwin Arlington Robinson, reprinted by permission of The Macmillan Company; for "When You Are Old" and "Who Goes with Fergus," copyright 1906 by The Macmillan Company, copyright 1934 by Willian Butler Yeats; for "No Second Troy," copyright 1912 by The Macmillan Company, copyright 1940 by Bertha Georgie Yeats; for "September 1913" and "The Magi," copyright 1916 by The Macmillan Company, copyright 1944 by Bertha Georgie Yeats; for "The Wild Swans at Coole," copyright 1919 by The Macmillan Company, copyright 1946 by Bertha Georgie Yeats; for "Easter 1916" and "The Second Coming," copyright 1924 by The Macmillan Company, copyright 1952 by Bertha Georgie Yeats; for "Sailing to Byzantium," "Two Songs from a Play," "Leda and the Swan," and "Among School Children," copyright 1928 by The Macmillan Company, copyright 1956 by Bertha Georgie Yeats; for "Byzantium" and "Crazy Jane Talks with the Bishop," copyright 1933 by The Macmillan Company, copyright 1961 by Bertha Georgie Yeats; and for "Lapis Lazuli," "Long-Legged Fly," "The Circus Animal's Desertion," copyright 1940 by Bertha Georgie Yeats, and "The Apparitions," copyright 1940 by Georgie Yeats, renewed 1968 by Bertha Georgie Yeats, Michael Butler Yeats, and Anne Yeats; all from *Collected Poems* by W. B. Yeats, reprinted by permission of The Macmillan Company; for "Poetry," "Silences," "A Grave," and "Sojourn in the Whale," copyright 1935 by Marianne Moore, and for "Rigorists," copyright 1941 by Marianne Moore, all from *Collected Poems* by Marianne Moore, reprinted by permission of The Macmillan Company; for "Reason," "The Birdcatcher," and "The Bells of Heaven," from *Poems* by Ralph Hodgson, copyright 1917 by The Macmillan Company, copyright 1945 by Ralph Hodgson, reprinted by permission of The Macmillan Company; for "The Flower-Fed Buffaloes" and "Factory Windows Are Always Broken," from *Collected Poems* by Vachel Lindsay, copyright 1913, 1914, 1916, 1917, 1919, 1920, 1923, 1925 by The Macmillan

ACKNOWLEDGMENTS [ix]

versity Press, Inc.; for "The Groundhog," "I Walked Out to the Graveyard to See the Dead," and "The Fury of Aerial Bombardment," from *Collected Poems 1930–1960* by Richard Eberhart, © 1960 by Richard Eberhart, reprinted by permission of Oxford University Press, Inc.; for "Wessex Guidebook" and "The Sunlight on the Garden," from *Eighty-Five Poems* by Louis MacNeice, © 1959 by Louis MacNeice, reprinted by permission of Oxford University Press, Inc.; for "The Wall" and "The Truisms," from *Solstices* by Louis MacNeice, © 1961 by Louis MacNeice, reprinted by permission of Oxford University Press, Inc.

RANDOM HOUSE, INC.—for "A Negro Woman," from *Journey to Love* by William Carlos Williams, copyright © 1955, by William Carlos Williams, reprinted by permission of Random House, Inc.; for "Shine, Perishing Republic," from *The Selected Poetry of Robinson Jeffers*, copyright 1925, renewed 1953 by Robinson Jeffers, reprinted by permission of Random House, Inc.; for "Musée des Beaux Arts" and "In Memory of W. B. Yeats," copyright 1940 by W. H. Auden, and for "Petition" and "O Where Are You Going," copyright 1934, renewed 1961 by W. H. Auden, from *The Collected Poetry of W. H. Auden*, reprinted by permission of Random House, Inc.; for "In Praise of Limestone," from *Nones* by W. H. Auden, copyright 1951 by W. H. Auden, reprinted by permission of Random House, Inc.; for "I Think Continually of Those Who Were Truly Great" and "What I Expected, Was," from *Collected Poems 1928–1953* by Stephen Spender, copyright 1934, renewed 1961 by Stephen Spender, reprinted by permission of Random House, Inc.; for "Buick," copyright 1941 by Karl Jay Shapiro, and for "Glass Poem," copyright 1946 by Karl Jay Shapiro, from *Poems 1940–1953* by Karl Shapiro, reprinted by permission of Random House, Inc.; for "Spell of Creation," from *The Collected Poems of Kathleen Raine*, copyright © 1956 by Kathleen Raine, reprinted by permission of Random House, Inc.

RANDOM HOUSE, INC.—ALFRED A. KNOPF, INC.—for "Of Mere Being," © copyright 1957 by Elsie Stevens and Holly Stevens, reprinted from *Opus Posthumous*, by Wallace Stevens, by permission of Alfred A. Knopf, Inc.; for "Piazza Piece," copyright 1927 by Alfred A. Knopf, Inc., and renewed 1955 by John Crowe Ransom, reprinted from *Selected Poems*, Revised Edition, by John Crowe Ransom, by permission of the publisher; for "At the Party," © copyright 1965 by W. H. Auden, reprinted from *About the House*, by W. H. Auden, by permission of Random House, Inc.

THEODORE ROETHKE—for "My Papa's Waltz," from *The Lost Son and Other Poems*, reprinted by permission of the author.

ST. MARTIN'S PRESS INCORPORATED—for "The Hammers," from *The Last Blackbird and Other Lines* by Ralph Hodgson, reprinted by permission of the author, Allen and Unwin, Ltd., and St. Martin's Press, Inc.

CHARLES SCRIBNER'S SONS—for "Ode to the Confederate Dead," from *Poems* by Allen Tate, copyright 1932 by Charles Scribner's Sons, renewal copyright © 1960 by Allen Tate, reprinted by permission of Charles Scribner's Sons; for "Early in the Morning," from *Good News of Death and Other Poems* by Louis Simpson, in *Poets of Today II*, copyright 1955, by Louis Simpson, reprinted by permission of Charles Scribner's Sons; for "Luke Havergal," from *The Children of the Night* by Edwin Arlington Robinson, reprinted by permission of Charles Scribner's Sons.

KARL SHAPIRO—for "A Garden in Chicago," reprinted by permission of the author.

ALAN SWALLOW, PUBLISHER—for "To the Holy Spirit" and "A Fragment," from *Collected Poems* by Yvor Winters, by permission of the publisher, Alan Swallow, copyright, 1952, by Yvor Winters; for "August Hail," "Montana Pastoral," "On the Calculus," "In Whose Will Is Our Peace," "On a Cold Night," and "Horoscope," from *The Exclusions of a Rhyme: Poems and Epigrams* by J. V. Cunningham, copyright, 1942, 1947, 1950, 1960, by J. V. Cunningham.

MRS. EDWARD THOMAS—for "The Sign Post," "The Owl," "The Combe," "In Memoriam (Easter, 1915)," and "The Long Small Room" by Edward Thomas, reprinted by permission of Helen Thomas.

THE UNIVERSITY OF CHICAGO PRESS—for "Storm Windows," from *New and Selected Poems* by Howard Nemerov, © 1960 by The University of Chicago, reprinted by permission of The University of Chicago Press; for "In Santa Maria del Populo," from *My Sad Captains* by Thom Gunn, © 1961 by Thom Gunn, reprinted by permission of The University of Chicago Press.

UNIVERSITY OF MICHIGAN PRESS—for "Hogwash" by Robert Francis, reprinted from *Come Out Into the Sun* by permission of the University of Massachusetts Press and Robert Francis, copyright by Robert Francis.

THE VIKING PRESS, INC.—for "Ecce Puer" and "Tilly," from *Collected Poems* by James Joyce, all rights reserved, reprinted by permission of The Viking Press, Inc.; for "Song of a Man Who Has Come Through," "Cherry Robbers," and "Piano," from *Collected Poems* by D. H. Lawrence, copyright 1929 by Jonathan Cape and Harrison Smith, Inc., copyright 1957 by Frieda Lawrence Ravagli, reprinted by permission of The Viking Press, Inc.; for "Bavarian Gentians" and "Whales Weep Not!," from *Last Poems* by D. H. Lawrence, copyright 1933 by Frieda Lawrence, reprinted by permission of The Viking Press, Inc.; for "How Beastly the Bourgeois Is" from *The Complete Poems of D. H. Lawrence*, Volume I, edited by Vivian de Sola Pinto and F. Warren Roberts, copyright 1929 by Frieda Lawrence Ravagli, all rights reserved, reprinted by permission of The Viking Press, Inc.; and for "City Life" from *The Complete Poems of D. H. Lawrence*, Volume II, edited by Vivian de Sola Pinto and F. Warren Roberts, copyright 1933 by Frieda Lawrence, all rights reserved, reprinted by permission of The Viking Press, Inc.

WESLEYAN UNIVERSITY PRESS—for "Farm Boy After Summer," "Hide-and-Seek," and "Epitaph," from *The Orb Weaver* by Robert Francis, copyright 1945, 1946, 1947, 1948, 1949, 1950, 1953, 1954, 1955, 1956, 1959, 1960 by Robert Francis, reprinted by permission of the Wesleyan University Press; for "Birch" and "In the Suburbs," copyright © 1963 by Louis Simpson, reprinted from *At the End of the Open Road*, by Louis Simpson, by permission of Wesleyan University Press.

WILLIS KINGSLEY WING—for "Apples and Water," "Warning to Children," "In Broken Images," "To Juan at the Winter Solstice," and "The White Goddess," copyright © 1955 by International Authors N.V., and "Counting the Beats," copyright © 1950 by International Authors N.V., from *Collected Poems 1955* by Roberts Graves, reprinted by permission of Willis Kingsley Wing.

৳ PREFACE

This is a book of poems. We have included as many poems and as little commentary as possible. We have selected poems showing the richness and variety of verse in English from the age of Chaucer to the present.

Personal preferences are always reflected in choices. We have not sought to avoid them, but we are mindful of the multiple variations in genres, styles, and motives in the writing of poetry across several centuries. We have tried to leave no significant movement unrepresented, although we have placed first emphasis on the quality of the particular poems selected.

The order in which the poems occur is the indisputable one of chronology. We have let each stand on its own merit, without reference to genre, style, age, or school. For most readers, at any time, contemporary poetry is immediately inviting and intensely relevant. For this reason, and because ours is an age that has been particularly mindful of poetry, the verse of the twentieth century is fully represented. A thorough understanding of its achievement, however, will rest only on a knowledge of English poetry as a whole.

For verse of the centuries before ours we have included the date of first publication, when known, to facilitate historical perspective and thus assist understanding. We have also attempted to serve the real needs of college students by footnoting words and allusions not found in good abridged dictionaries.

Both editors have agreed on the inclusion of each poem. Donald Hall, however, has been primarily responsible for the selections grouped under the Twentieth Century and for those from the poetry of Gerard Manley Hopkins. Warren Taylor selected the work chosen to represent the earlier centuries. Poets born in the nineteenth century who lived well into the twentieth have been placed in the twentieth.

In the second edition of *Poetry in English,* we have added fifty poems. Although the additions appear everywhere except in Part I, we have tried particularly to stress the contemporary, both extending the previous selections of modern poets and adding six contemporary poets who were not in the earlier edition. Many teachers find it useful to make contact with their young students by assigning contemporary poetry. We believe that the condition of the art of poetry in this latter half of the twentieth century is encouraging, and that to stress the contemporary is consistent with our standard.

W. T.

D. H.

✒ CONTENTS

PART 1
The Fourteenth and Fifteenth Centuries

PART 2
The Sixteenth Century

FRANCIS BACON

SAMUEL DANIEL

MICHAEL DRAYTON

MARK ALEXANDER BOYD

CHRISTOPHER MARLOWE

WILLIAM SHAKESPEARE

THOMAS NASHE

THOMAS CAMPION

JOHN WEBSTER

GEORGE WITHER

ROBERT HERRICK

GEORGE HERBERT

THOMAS CAREW

EDMUND WALLER

JOHN MILTON

PART 4
The Eighteenth Century

PART 5

The Nineteenth Century

ROBERT BROWNING

JONES VERY

CHRISTOPHER PEARSE CRANCH

EMILY BRONTË

ARTHUR HUGH CLOUGH

WALT WHITMAN

HERMAN MELVILLE

FREDERICK GODDARD TUCKERMAN

MATTHEW ARNOLD

GEORGE MEREDITH

DANTE GABRIEL ROSSETTI

EMILY DICKINSON

ROBERT LOUIS STEVENSON

FRANCIS THOMPSON

PART 6

The Twentieth Century

THOMAS HARDY

ROBERT BRIDGES

A. E. HOUSMAN

ERRATA

In the Contents, page xxxiv has been omitted; in its proper place page xxiv was substituted for a second time. This slip contains the missing page xxxiv.

[xxxiv]   CONTENTS

PART *1*
The
Fourteenth
and
Fifteenth
Centuries

❧ GEOFFREY CHAUCER (1340–1400)

From *The Canterbury Tales*

THE PROLOGUE

 Whan that Aprill with his shoures soote [1]
The droghte [2] of March hath perced [3] to the roote,
And bathed every veyne [4] in swich licour,[5]
Of which vertu [6] engendred is the flour; [7]
Whan Zephyrus eek [8] with his sweete breeth   5
Inspired hath in every holt and heeth
The tendre croppes,[9] and the yonge sonne
Hath in the Ram his halfe cours yronne,
And smale foweles [10] maken melodye
That slepen al the nyght with open yë [11]—   10
So priketh hem Nature in hir corages [12]—
Thanne longen folk to goon on pilgrimages,
And palmeres for to seken straunge strondes [13]
To ferne halwes,[14] kouthe [15] in sondry londes;
And specially from every shires ende   15
Of Engelond to Caunterbury [16] they wende,
The holy blisful martir for to seke
That hem [17] hath holpen whan that they were seeke.

 Bifel that in that seson on a day,
In Southwerk [18] at the Tabard [19] as I lay,   20
Redy to wenden on my pilgrymage
To Caunterbury with ful devout corage,
At nyght was come into that hostelrye
Wel nyne and twenty in a compaignye
Of sondry folk, by aventure yfalle   25
In felaweshipe, and pilgrimes were they alle
That toward Caunterbury wolden ryde.
The chambres and the stables weren wyde,[20]
And wel we weren esed [21] atte [22] beste.
And shortly, whan the sonne was to reste,   30

[1] sweet showers   [2] drought   [3] pierced
[4] vein   [5] such liquid   [6] power   [7] flower   [8] also   [9] shoots   [10] birds   [11] eye
[12] hearts   [13] shores   [14] far-off shrines
[15] well-known   [16] pilgrimages were
made there to the shrine of the martyr,
Thomas à Becket (1170 A.D.) [17] them
[18] in London, south of the Thames
[19] an inn   [20] roomy   [21] accommodated
[22] at the best

3

So hadde I spoken with hem everichon [23]
That I was of hir felaweshipe anon,
And made forward [24] erly for to ryse
To take oure way ther-as I yow devyse. [25]
    But nathelees, whil I have tyme and space,   35
Er that I ferther in this tale pace,
Me thynketh it acordaunt to resoun [26]
To telle yow al the condicioun
Of ech of hem, so as it semed me,
And whiche they weren, and of what degree,   40
And eek in what array that they were inne;
And at a knyght than wol I first bigynne.
    A Knyght ther was, and that a worthy man,
That fro the tyme that he first bigan
To riden out, he loved chivalrye,   45
Trouthe [27] and honour, fredom [28] and curteisye.
Full worthy was he in his lordes werre,
And therto hadde he riden, no man ferre,[29]
As wel in Cristendom as in hethenesse,[30]
And evere honoured for his worthynesse.   50
At Alisaundre he was whan it was wonne.
Ful ofte tyme he hadde the bord bigonne [31]
Aboven alle nacions in Pruce;
In Lettow had he reysed,[32] and in Ruce,
No Cristen man so ofte of his degree.   55
In Gernade at the seege eek hadde he be
Of Algezir, and riden in Belmarye.
At Lyeys was he, and at Satalye
Whan they were wonne; and in the Grete See
At many a noble armee [33] hadde he be.   60
At mortal batailles hadde he been fiftene,
And foughten for oure feith at Tramyssene
In lystes thries, and ay [34] slayn his foo.
    This ilke [35] worthy knyght hadde been also
Somtyme with the lord of Palatye   65
Agayn another hethen in Turkye.
And everemoore he hadde a sovereyn prys; [36]
And though that he were worthy,[37] he was wys,[38]
And of his port as meeke as is a mayde.

---

[23] everyone   [24] had an agreement   at the head of the table   [32] campaigned
[25] describe to you   [26] reasonable   [33] armed expedition   [34] always
[27] fidelity   [28] liberality   [29] farther   [35] same   [36] a high reputation   [37] of
[30] heathendom   [31] as an honor placed   high rank   [38] wise

He nevere yet no vileynye ne sayde 70
In al his lyf unto no maner wight.[39]
He was a verray,[40] parfit, gentil knyght.
But for to tellen yow of his array,
His hors were goode, but he was nat gay.[41]
Of fustian [42] he wered a gypon [43] 75
Al bismotered [44] with his habergeon,[45]
For he was late ycome from his viage [46]
And wente for to doon his pilgrymage.
       With him ther was his sone, a yong Squier,[47]
A lovere and a lusty bacheler,[48] 80
With lokkes crulle [49] as they were leyd in presse.
Of twenty yeer of age he was, I gesse.
Of his stature he was of evene lengthe,
And wonderly delyvere,[50] and of greet strengthe.
And he hadde been som tyme in chivachye [51] 85
In Flaundres, in Artoys, and Picardye,
And born him wel as of so litel space,[52]
In hope to stonden [53] in his lady grace.
Embrouded was he as it were a meede,
Al ful of fresshe floures whyte and reede. 90
Syngynge he was, or floytynge, al the day;
He was as fressh as is the month of May.
Short was his gowne, with sleves longe and wyde.
Wel koude he sitte on hors and faire ryde;
He koude songes make and wel endite,[54] 95
Juste and eek daunce, and wel purtreye [55] and write.
So hote he lovede that by nyghtertale [56]
He slepte namoore than dooth a nyghtyngale.
Curteis he was, lowely, and servysable,
And carf biforn his fader at the table. 1C
       A Yeman hadde he and servantz namo
At that tyme, for hym liste [57] ride so,
And he was clad in cote and hood of grene.
A sheef of pecok arwes, bright and kene,
Under his belt he bar ful thriftily; 105
Wel koude he dresse his takel yemanly:
His arwes drouped noght with fetheres lowe.

---

[39] no manner of person [40] true
[41] gaily dressed [42] coarse cotton cloth
[43] a vest [44] stained [45] coat of chain
mail [46] voyage [47] a candidate for
knighthood [48] joyous bachelor [49] curled locks of hair [50] active [51] cavalry expedition [52] for the short time in
service [53] stand [54] compose lyrics and
music [55] draw [56] nighttime [57] it
pleased him

And in his hand he bar a myghty bowe.
A not heed [58] hadde he with a broun visage.
Of wodecraft wel koude [59] he al the usage.   110
Upon his arm he bar a gay bracer,
And by his syde a swerd and a bokeler,
And on that oother syde a gay daggere,
Harneised wel and sharpe as point of spere;
A Cristophre on his brest of silver sheene.   115
An horn he bar, the bawdryk [60] was of grene;
A forster was he soothly, as I gesse.
    Ther was also a Nonne, a Prioresse,
That of hir smylyng was ful symple and coy.
Hir gretteste ooth was but by Seint Loy;   120
And she was cleped Madame Eglentyne.
Ful wel she soong the service dyvyne,
Entuned in hir nose ful semely;
And Frenssh she spak ful faire and fetisly,[61]
After the scole of Stratford atte Bowe,[62]   125
For Frenssh of Parys was to hire unknowe.
At mete wel ytaught was she with alle: [63]
She leet no morsel from hir lippes falle,
Ne wette hir fyngres in hir sauce depe;
Wel koude she carie a morsel, and wel kepe   130
That no drope ne fille upon hir brest.
In curteisie was set ful muchel hir lest.[64]
Hir over-lippe wyped she so clene
That in hir coppe [65] ther was no ferthyng [66] sene
Of grece, whan she dronken hadde hir draughte;   135
Ful semely after hir mete she raughte.[67]
And sikerly she was of greet desport,
And ful plesaunt, and amyable of port,
And peyned hire to countrefete cheere
Of court,[68] and to been estatlich of manere,   140
And to been holden digne of reverence.
But for to speken of hir conscience,
She was so charitable and so pitous
She wolde wepe if that she sawe a mous
Caught in a trappe, if it were deed or bledde.   145
Of smale houndes hadde she that she fedde

---

[58] head with closely cropped hair [59] understood [60] carrying strap [61] clearly and carefully [62] a convent near London [63] moreover [64] To be courteous was greatly her wish [65] cup [66] bit [67] reached [68] took pains to follow courtly manners

With rosted flessh, or milk and wastel-breed; [69]
But soore wepte she if oon of hem were deed,
Or if men smoot it with a yerde smerte;
And al was conscience and tendre herte.   150
Ful semely hir wympel pynched was,
Hir nose tretys,[70] hir eyen greye as glas,
Hir mouth ful smal, and ther to softe and reed;
But sikerly she hadde a fair forheed;
It was almoost a spanne brood, I trowe,   155
For hardily, she was nat undergrowe.
Ful fetys [71] was hir cloke, as I was war;
Of smal coral aboute hir arm she bar
A peire of bedes, gauded al with grene,
And theron heng a brooch of gold ful sheene,   160
On which ther was first write a crowned A,
And after *Amor vincit omnia.*[72]
    Another Nonne with hire hadde she,
That was hire chapeleyne and preestes thre.
    A Monk ther was, a fair for the maistrie,[73]   165
An outridere [74] that lovede venerye,
A manly man, to been an abbot able.
Ful many a deyntee [75] hors hadde he in stable,
And whan he rood, men myghte his brydel heere
Gynglen in a whistlynge wynd as cleere   170
And eek as loude as dooth the chapel belle.
Ther as this lord was kepere of the celle,
The reule of Seint Maure or of Seint Beneit,
By cause that it was old and somdel streit,[76]
This ilke Monk leet olde thynges pace,   175
And heeld after the newe world the space.
He yaf nat of that text a pulled hen
That seith that hunters been nat holy men,
Ne that a monk, whan he is recchelees,
Is likned til a fissh that is waterlees—   180
This is to seyn, a monk out of his cloystre.
But thilke text heeld he nat worth an oystre;
And I seyde his opinion was good.
What sholde he studie and make hymselven wood,
Upon a book in cloystre alwey to poure,   185

[69] fine white bread   [70] well-formed   [74] overseer of the monastery's lands
[71] handsome   [72] Love conquers all.   [75] valuable   [76] somewhat strict
[73] a fair one, surpassing all others

Or swynken [77] with his handes and laboure,
As Austyn bit? How shal the world be served?
Lat Austyn have his swynk to him reserved!
Therfore he was a prikasour [78] aright.
Grehoundes he hadde as swift as fowel in flight;   190
Of prikyng and of huntyng for the hare
Was al his lust, for no cost wolde he spare.
I seigh his sleves purfiled [79] at the hond
With grys,[80] and that the fyneste of a lond;
And for to festne his hood under his chyn,   195
He hadde of gold yroght a ful curious pyn;
A love-knotte [81] in the gretter ende ther was.
His heed was balled, that shoon as any glas,
And eek his face, as he hadde been enoynt.
He was a lord ful fat and in good poynt.   200
His eyen stepe, and rollynge in his heed,
That stemed as a forneys of a leed,[82]
His bootes souple, his hors in greet estaat,
Now certeinly he was a fair prelaat.
He was nat pale as a forpyned [83] goost;   205
A fat swan loved he best of any roost.
His palfrey was as broun as is a berye.
      A Frere ther was, a wantowne and a merye,
A lymytour,[84] a ful solempne man.
In alle the ordres foure is noon that kan   210
So muche of daliaunce and fair langage.
He hadde maad ful many a mariage
Of yonge wommen at his owene cost.[85]
Unto his ordre he was a noble post.
Ful wel biloved and famulier was he   215
With frankeleyns over al in his contree,
And eek with worthy wommen of the toun;
For he hadde power of confessioun,
As seyde hymself, moore than a curat,
For of his ordre he was licenciat.   220
Ful swetely herde he confession,
And plesaunt was his absolucion.
He was an esy man to yeve penaunce
Ther as he wiste to have a good pitaunce;

[77] work or toil   [78] a hard rider   [83] tormented   [84] a friar licensed to beg
[79] trimmed, purfled   [80] a costly gray fur   within set limits   [85] He found hus-
[1] an intertwined device   [82] glowed   bands for women he had seduced.
[3] a furnace under a large kettle

For unto a povre ordre for to yive   225
Is signe that a man is wel yshryve;
For if he yaf, he dorste make avaunt [86]
He wiste that a man was repentaunt;
For many a man so hard is of his herte,
He may nat wepe althogh hym soore smerte.   230
Therfore, instede of wepynge and prayeres,
Men moote yeve silver to the povre freres.
His typet was ay farsed [87] ful of knyves
And pynnes, for to yeven faire wyves.
And certeinly he hadde a murye note;   235
Wel koude he synge and pleyen on a rote;
Of yeddynges [88] he baar outrely the pris.
His nekke whit was as the flour-de-lys;
Therto he strong was as a champioun.
He knew the tavernes wel in every toun,   240
And every hostiler and tappestere,
Bet than a lazar or a beggestere.
For unto swich a worthy man as he
Acorded nat, as by his facultee,
To have with sike lazars aqueyntaunce.   245
It is nat honeste, it may nat avaunce,
For to deelen with no swich poraille,[89]
But al with riche, and selleres of vitaille.
And over al ther as profit sholde arise,
Curteis he was, and lowely of servyse;   250
Ther nas no man man nowher so vertuous.
He was the beste beggere in his hous,
For thogh a wydwe hadde noght a sho,
So plesaunt was his *In principio* [90]
Yet wolde he have a ferthyng er he wente.   255
His purchas [91] was wel bettre than his rente.[92]
And rage [93] he koude as it were right a whelpe;
In love-dayes ther koude he muchel helpe,
For ther he was nat lyk a cloysterer
With a thredbare cope, as is a povre scoler,   260
But he was lyk a maister or a pope.
Of double worstede was his semycope,
And rounded as a belle out of the presse.

[86] He dared boast [87] stuffed [88] songs
[89] poor people [90] The New Testament: John 1:1: "In the beginning
[was the word]," held by friars to have
a magical power [91] what he got by
begging or fraud [92] regular income
or rent turned in to the monastery
[93] frolic

Somwhat he lipsed for his wantownesse,
To make his Englissh sweete upon his tonge;   265
And in his harpyng, whan that he hadde songe,
His eyen twynkled in his heed aryght
As doon the sterres in the frosty nyght.
This worthy lymytour was cleped Huberd.
        A Marchant was ther with a forked berd,   270
In mottelee, and hye on horse he sat;
Upon his heed a Flaundryssh bevere hat,
His bootes clasped faire and fetisly.
His resons [94] he spak ful solempnely,
Sownynge [95] alway th'encrees of his wynnyng.   275
He wolde the see were kept for any thing [96]
Betwixen Middelburgh and Orewelle.
Wel koude he in eschaunge sheeldes selle. [97]
This worthy man ful wel his wit besette:
Ther wiste no wight that he was in dette,   280
So estatly was he of his governaunce,
With his bargaynes, and with his chevyssaunce. [98]
For sothe he was a worthy man with alle,
But, sooth to seyn, I noot how men hym calle.
        A Clerk [99] ther was of Oxenford also,   285
That unto logyk hadde longe ygo.
As leene was his hors as is a rake,
And he nas nat right fat, I undertake,
But looked holwe, and therto sobrely.
Ful thredbare was his overeste courtepy, [100]   290
For he hadde geten hym yet no benefice,
Ne was so worldly for to have office. [101]
For hym was levere have at his beddes heed
Twenty bookes, clad in blak or reed,
Of Aristotle and his philosophie,   295
Than robes riche, or fithele, [102] or gay sautrie. [103]
But al be that he was a philosophre,
Yet hadde he but litel gold in cofre;
But al that he myghte of his freendes hente, [104]
On bookes and on lernynge he it spente,   300
And bisily gan for the soules preye
Of hem that yaf him wherwith to scoleye.

[94] opinions   [95] relating to   [96] kept
free from pirates at all costs   [97] profit
illegally from exchange of French coins,
shields   [98] borrowing, lending   [99] a
student in religious orders; an ecclesi-
astic   [100] outer coat   [101] secular employment   [102] fiddle   [103] harp, psaltery
[104] get

Of studie took he moost cure and moost heede.
Noght o word spak he moore than was neede,
And that was seyd in forme and reverence,   305
And short and quyk, and ful of hy sentence;
Sownynge in [105] moral vertu was his speche,
And gladly wolde he lerne and gladly teche.

       .   .   .   .   .

   A good Wif was ther of biside Bathe,   445
But she was somdel deef, and that was scathe.[106]
Of clooth-makyng she hadde swich an haunt,[107]
She passed hem of Ypres and of Gaunt.
In al the parisshe wif ne was ther noon
That to the offrynge bifore hire sholde goon;   450
And if ther dide, certeyn so wrooth was she,
That she was out of alle charitee.
Hir coverchiefs ful fyne were of ground; [108]
I dorste swere they weyeden ten pound
That on a Sonday weren upon hir heed.   455
Hir hosen weren of fyn scarlet reed,
Ful streite yteyd, and shoes ful moyste and newe.
Boold was hir face and fair and reed of hewe.
She was a worthy womman al hir lyve:
Housbondes at chirche dore she hadde fyve,   460
Withouten oother compaignye in youthe—
But therof nedeth nat to speke as nowthe.
And thries hadde she been at Jerusalem;
She hadde passed many a straunge strem;
At Rome she hadde been, and at Boloigne,   465
In Galice at Seint Jame, and at Coloigne;
She koude muche of wandrynge by the weye.
Gat-tothed was she, soothly for to seye.
Upon an amblere esily she sat,
Ywympled wel, and on hir heed an hat   470
As brood as is a bokeler or a targe;
A foot-mantel aboute hir hipes large,
And on hir feet a paire of spores sharpe.
In felaweshipe wel koude she laughe and carpe.
Of remedies of love she knew per chaunce,   475
For she koude of that art the olde daunce.

       .   .   .   .   .

[105] inclining to   [106] a pity   [107] skill
[108] texture

A Somnour [109] was ther with us in that place,
That hadde a fyr-reed cherubynnes face,
For sawcefleem [110] he was, with eyen narwe.   625
And hoot he was, and lecherous as a sparwe,
With scaled browes blake and piled [111] berd;
Of his visage children were aferd.
Ther nas quyksilver, lytarge,[112] ne brymstoon,
Boras, ceruce, ne oille of tartre noon,   630
Ne oinement that wolde clense and byte,
That hym myghte helpen [113] of his whelkes white,
Nor of the knobbes [114] sittynge on his chekes.
Wel loved he garlek, oynons, and eek lekes,
And for to drynken strong wyn reed as blood.   635
Thanne wolde he speke and crye as he were wood; [115]
And whan that he wel dronken hadde the wyn,
Thanne wolde he speke no word but Latyn.
A fewe termes hadde he, two or thre,
That he had lerned out of som decree—   640
No wonder is, he herde it al the day,
And eek ye knowen wel how that a jay
Kan clepen "Watte" [116] as wel as kan the Pope—
But whoso koude in oother thyng hym grope,
Thanne hadde he spent al his philosophie;   645
Ay *Questio quid juris* [117] wolde he crie.
He was a gentil harlot [118] and a kynde;
A bettre felawe sholde men noght fynde;
He wolde suffre, for a quart of wyn,
A good felawe [119] to have his concubyn   650
A twelf monthe, and excuse hym atte fulle.
Ful prively a fynch eek koude he pulle.[120]
And if he foond owher a good felawe,
He wolde techen him to have noon awe
In swich caas of the Ercedekenes curs,   655
But if a mannes soule were in his purs,
For in his purs he sholde ypunysshed be.
"Purs is the Ercedekenes helle," saide he.
But wel I woot he lyed right in dede;
Of cursyng oghte ech gilty man him drede,   660

---

[109] one who served summonses to an ecclesiastical court   [110] pimpled   [111] scanty   [112] white lead ointment   [113] rid him   [114] pimples   [115] mad   [116] Jays were then taught to say "Walter" as parrots may now be taught to say "Polly."   [117] "The question is: What part of the law applies?"   [118] rascal   [119] slang for disreputable fellow   [120] To pull a finch, to seduce

For curs wol slee right as assoillyng [121] savith,
And also war him of a *Significavit*.[122]
In daunger [123] hadde he at his owene gise [124]
The yonge girles [125] of the diocise,
And knew hir conseil, and was al hir reed.   665
A gerland hadde he set upon his heed
As greet as it were for an ale-stake; [126]
A bokeler hadde he maad him of a cake.

    With hym ther rood a gentil Pardoner [127]
Of Rouncival, his freend and his compeer,   670
That streight was comen fro the court of Rome.
Ful loude he soong, "Com hider, love, to me!"
This Somnour bar to hym a stif burdoun; [128]
Was nevere trompe of half so greet a soun.
This Pardoner hadde heer as yelow as wex,   675
But smothe it heeng as dooth a strike of flex;
By ounces henge his lokkes that he hadde,
And therwith he his shuldres overspradde;
But thynne it lay, by colpons,[129] oon and oon.
But hood for jolitee wered he noon,   680
For it was trussed up in his walet;
Hym thoughte he rood al of the newe jet; [130]
Dischevelee save his cappe he rood al bare.
Swiche glarynge eyen hadde he as an hare,
A vernycle [131] hadde he sowed upon his cappe.   685
His walet lay biforn hym in his lappe,
Bretful of pardon, comen from Rome al hoot.
A voys he hadde as smal as hath a goot;
No berd hadde he, ne nevere sholde have;
As smothe it was as it were late yshave;   690
I trowe he were a geldyng or a mare.
But of his craft, fro Berwyk into Ware,
Ne was ther swich another pardoner.
For in his male [132] he hadde a pilwe-beer,[133]
Which that he seyde was Oure Lady veyl;   695
He seyde he hadde a gobet of the seyl
That Seint Peter hadde whan that he wente

---

[121] absolution [122] the opening word of a writ remanding an excommunicated person to prison [123] control [124] way [125] persons of either sex [126] a pole extending over the door of an alehouse which supported a garland, the sign of a drinking place [127] one who sold papal indulgences [128] a bass accompaniment [129] strands [130] fashion [131] a veronica [132] bag [133] pillowcase

Upon the see, til Jhesu Crist hym hente.
He hadde a croys of laton,[134] ful of stones,
And in a glas he hadde pigges bones.   700
But with thise relikes whan that he fond
A povre person [135] dwellynge upon lond,
Upon a day he gat hym moore moneye
Than that the person gat in monthes tweye;
And thus with feyned flaterye and japes,   705
He made the person and the peple his apes.
But trewely to tellen atte laste,
He was in chirche a noble ecclesiaste;
Wel koude he rede a lesson or a storie,
But alderbest he song an offertorie;   710
For wel he wiste whan that song was songe,
He moste preche and wel affile his tonge
To wynne silver, as he ful wel koude;
Therefore he song the murierly and loude.

Now have I told you soothly, in a clause,   715
Th'estaat, th'array, the nombre, and eek the cause
Why that assembled was this compaignye
In Southwerk at this gentil hostelrye
That highte the Tabard, faste by the Belle.
But now is tyme to yow for to telle   720
How that we baren us that ilke nyght,
Whan we were in that hostelrie alyght;
And after wol I telle of our viage
And al the remenaunt of oure pilgrimage.
But first I pray yow of youre curteisye,   725
That ye n'arette it nat my vileynye,[136]
Thogh that I pleynly speke in this matere,
To telle yow hir wordes and hir cheere,
Ne thogh I speke hir wordes proprely.
For this ye knowen al so wel as I: 730
Who so shal telle a tale after a man,
He moot reherce, as neigh as evere he kan,
Everich a word, if it be in his charge,
Al speke he never so rudeliche and large,
Or ellis he moot telle his tale untrewe,   735
Or feyne thyng, or fynde wordes newe.
He may nat spare althogh he were his brother;

---

[134] a metal compounded of copper and zinc
[135] parson   [136] blame it not on ill breeding

He moot as wel seye o word as another.
Crist spak hymself ful brode in holy writ,
And wel ye woot no vileynye is it. 740
Eek Plato seith, whoso kan him rede,
The wordes mote be cosyn to the dede.
Also I pray yow to foryeve it me,
Al have I nat set folk in hir degree
Here in this tale as that they sholde stonde. 745
My wit is short, ye may wel understonde.
    Greet cheere made oure Hoost us everichon,
And to the soper sette he us anon.
He served us with vitaille at the beste;
Strong was the wyn, and wel to drynke us leste. 750
A semely man oure Hooste was withalle
For to been a marchal in an halle.
A large man he was, with eyen stepe;
A fairer burgeys was ther noon in Chepe,
Boold of his speche, and wys, and wel ytaught, 755
And of manhood hym lakkede right naught.
Eek therto he was right a murye man,
And after soper pleyen he bigan,
And spak of myrthe amonges othere thynges,
Whan that we hadde maad oure rekenynges, 760
And seyde thus, "Now, lordynges, trewely,
Ye been to me right welcome, hertely;
For by my trouthe, if that I shal nat lye,
I saugh nat this yeer so murye a compaignye
At ones in this herberwe as is now. 765
Fayn wolde I doon yow myrthe, wiste I how.
And of a myrthe I am right now bythoght
To doon yow ese, and it shal coste noght.
Ye goon to Caunterbury—God yow speede;
The blisful martir quite yow youre meede. 770
And wel I woot as ye goon by the weye,
Ye shapen yow to talen and to pleye,
For trewely, confort ne myrthe is noon
To ride by the weye domb as a stoon;
And therfore wol I maken yow disport, 775
As I seyde erst, and doon yow som confort.
And if yow liketh alle, by oon assent,
For to stonden at my juggement,
And for to werken as I shal yow seye,
Tomorwe whan ye riden by the weye, 780

Now by my fader soule that is deed,
But ye be murye I wol yeve yow myn heed!
Hoolde up youre hondes withouten moore speche."
    Oure conseil was nat longe for to seche;
Us thoughte it was nat worth to make it wys,[137]   785
And graunted hym withouten moore avys,
And bad him seye his voirdit as hym leste.
    "Lordynges," quod he, "now herkneth for the beste;
But taak it nought, I prey yow, in desdeyn.
This is the poynt, to speken short and pleyn,   790
That ech of yow, to shorte with oure weye
In this viage, shal telle tales tweye—
To Caunterbury-ward, I mene it so—
And homward he shal tellen othere two,
Of aventures that whilom have bifalle;   795
And which of yow that bereth hym best of alle—
That is to seyn, that telleth in this caas
Tales of best sentence and moost solaas—
Shal have a soper at oure aller cost,
Here in this place, sittynge by this post,   800
Whan that we come agayn fro Caunterbury.
And for to make yow the moore mury,
I wol myselven goodly with yow ryde,
Right at myn owene cost, and be youre gyde;
And who so wole my juggement withseye   805
Shal paye al that we spenden by the weye.
And if ye vouche sauf that it be so,
Tel me anon, withouten wordes mo,
And I wol erly shape me therfore."
    This thyng was graunted and oure othes swore   810
With ful glad herte, and preyden hym also
That he wolde vouche sauf for to do so,
And that he wolde been oure governour,
And of oure tales juge and reportour,
And sette a soper at a certeyn pris,   815
And we wol reuled been at his devys
In heigh and lowe; and thus by oon assent
We been acorded to his juggement.
And therupon the wyn was fet anon;
We dronken and to reste wente echon,   820
Withouten any lenger taryynge.

[137] to deliberate

Amorwe whan that day bigan to sprynge,
Up roos oure Hoost and was oure aller cok,
And gadred us togidre in a flok,
And forth we riden, a litel moore than paas,   825
Unto the wateryng of Seint Thomas;
And there oure Hoost bigan his hors areste,
And seyde, "Lordynges, herkneth if yow leste.
Ye woot youre forward and I it yow recorde;
If even-song and morwe-song accorde,   830
Lat see now who shal telle the firste tale.
As evere mote I drynke wyn or ale,
Who so be rebel to my juggement
Shal paye for al that by the wey is spent.
Now draweth cut [138] er that we ferrer twynne;   835
He which that hath the shorteste shal bigynne.
Sire Knyght," quod he, "my mayster and my lord,
Now draweth cut, for that is myn accord.
Cometh neer," quod he, "my lady Prioresse,
And ye, sire Clerk, lat be youre shamefastnesse,   840
Ne studieth noght. Ley hond to, every man!"
Anon to drawen every wight bigan,
And shortly for to tellen as it was,
Were it by aventure or sort or cas,
The sothe is this, the cut fil to the Knyght,   845
Of which ful blithe and glad was every wight,
And telle he moste his tale, as was resoun,
By forward and by composicioun,
As ye han herd. What nedeth wordes mo?
And whan this goode man saugh that it was so,   850
As he that wys was and obedient
To kepe his forward by his free assent,
He seyde, "Syn I shal bigynne the game,
What, welcome be the cut, a Goddes name!
Now lat us ryde, and herkneth what I seye."   855
And with that word we ryden forth oure weye,
And he bigan with right a murye cheere
His tale anon, and seyde as ye may heere.   (c. *1387*)

[138] draw lots

The Pardoner's Tale

In Flaundres whilom was a compaignye
Of yonge folk that haunteen [1] folye,
As riot, hasard,[2] stewes, and tavernes,
Where as with harpes, lutes, and gyternes,
They daunce and pleye at dees bothe day and nyght,   5
And ete also and drynken over hir myght,
Thurgh which they doon the devel sacrifise
Withinne that develes temple in cursed wise
By superfluytee abhomynable.
Hir othes been so grete and so dampnable   10
That it is grisly [3] for to heere hem swere.
Oure blessed Lordes body they totere,— [4]
Hem thoughte that Jewes rente hym noght **ynough**;
And ech of hem at otheres synne lough.
And right anon thanne commen tombesteres [5]   15
Fetys [6] and smale, and yonge frutesteres,
Syngeres with harpes, baudes, wafereres,
Whiche been the verray develes officeres
To kyndle and blowe the fyr of lecherye
That is annexed unto glotonye.   20
The holy writ take I to my witnesse
That luxurie [7] is in wyn and dronkenesse.
     Lo, how that dronken Loth, unkyndely,
Lay by his doghtres two unwityngly;
So dronke he was he nyste what he wroghte.   25
     Herodes, who so wel the stories soghte,
Whan he of wyn was repleet at his feste,
Right at his owene table he yaf his heste [8]
To sleen the Baptist John, ful giltelees.
     Senek seith a good word doutelees: 30
He seith he kan no difference fynde
Bitwix a man that is out of his mynde
And a man which that is dronkelewe,
But that woodnesse,[9] yfallen in a shewe,
Persevereth lenger than dooth dronkenesse.   35
     O glotonye, ful of cursednesse!
O cause first of oure confusion!

---

[1] habitually practiced   [2] a game played   [5] dancing girls   [6] graceful   [7] lechery
with dice   [3] horrible   [4] tore to pieces   [8] command   [9] madness

O original of oure dampnacion,
Til Crist hadde boght us with his blood agayn!
Lo, how deere, shortly for to sayn,   40
Aboght was thilke cursed vileynye!
Corrupt was al this world for glotonye:
Adam oure fader and his wyf also
Fro Paradys to labour and to wo
Were dryven for that vice, it is no drede.[10]   45
For whil that Adam fasted, as I rede,
He was in Paradys; and whan that he
Eet of the fruyt defended on a tree,
Anon he was out cast to wo and peyne.
O glotonye, on thee wel oghte us pleyne!   50
O, wiste a man how manye maladies
Folwen of excesse and of glotonyes,
He wolde been the moore mesurable
Of his diete, sittyng at his table.
Allas, the shorte throte, the tendre mouth,   55
Maketh that est and west and north and south,
In erthe, in eyr, in water, men to swynke [11]
To gete a gloton deyntee mete and drynke!
Of this matere, O Paul, wel kanstow trete:
"Mete unto wombe,[12] and wombe eek unto mete,   60
Shal God destroyen bothe," as Paulus [13] seith.
Allas, a foul thyng is it, by my feith,
To seye this word, and fouler is the dede,
Whan man so drynketh of the white and rede
That of his throate he maketh his pryvee   65
Thurgh thilke cursed superfluitee.
     The Apostle [14] wepyng seith ful pitously,
"Ther walken manye of whiche yow toold have I—
I seye it now wepyng with pitous voys—
That they been enemys of Cristes croys,   70
Of whiche the ende is deeth; wombe is hir god!"
O wombe! O bely! O stynkyng cod,[15]
Fulfilled of dong and of corrupcioun!
At either ende of thee foul is the soun.
How greet labour and cost is thee to fynde!   75
Thise cookes, how they stampe and streyne and grynde,
And turnen substaunce [16] into accident,[17]

---

[10] doubt   [11] toil   [12] belly   [13] I Corin-   [15] stomach   [16] reality   [17] appearance
thians 6:13   [14] Philippians 30:18–19

To fulfille al thy likerous talent! [18]
Out of the harde bones knokke they
The mary, for they caste noght awey   80
That may go thurgh the golet softe and soote.
Of spicerie of leef and bark and roote
Shal been his sauce ymaked by delit,
To make hym yet a newer appetit.
But certes, he that haunteth swiche delices   85
Is deed whil that he lyveth in tho vices.
        A lecherous thyng is wyn, and dronkenesse
Is ful of stryvyng and of wrecchednesse.
O dronke man, disfigured is thy face!
Sour is thy breeth! foul artow to embrace!   90
And thurgh thy dronke nose semeth the soun
As though thou seydest ay "Sampsoun Sampsoun."
And yet, God woot, Sampsoun drank nevere no wyn.
Thou fallest as it were a stiked swyn;
Thy tonge is lost, and al thyn honeste cure;   95
For dronkenesse is verray sepulture
Of mannes wit and his discrecion.
In whom that drynke hath dominacion
He kan no conseil kepe, it is no drede.
Now kepe yow fro the white and fro the red,   100
And namely fro the white wyn of Lepe,
That is to selle in Fisshstrete or in Chepe.
This wyn of Spaigne crepeth subtilly
In othere wynes groyng faste by,
Of which ther riseth swich fumositee   105
That whan a man hath dronken draughtes thre
And weneth [19] that he be at hoom in Chepe,
He is in Spaigne, right at the toune of Lepe,
Nat at The Rochele ne at Burdeux toun;
And thanne wol he seyn "Sampsoun, Sampsoun."   110
        But herkneth, lordynges, o word I yow preye,
That alle the sovereyn actes, dar I seye,
Of victories in the Olde Testament,
Thurgh verray God that is omnipotent,
Were doon in abstinence and in prayere.   115
Looketh the Bible and ther ye may it leere.
        Looke, Attilla, the grete conquerour,
Deyde in his sleep with shame and dishonour,

[18] gluttonous appetite   [19] thinks

Bledyng at his nose in dronkenesse.
A capitayn sholde lyve in sobrenesse.   120
And over al this, avyseth yow right wel
What was comaunded unto Lamuel—
Nat Samuel, but Lamuel, seye I—
Redeth the Bible and fynde it expresly
Of wyn-yevyng to hem that han justise.   125
Namoore of this, for it may wel suffise.
  And now that I have spoken of glotonye,
Now wol I yow defenden hasardrye.[20]
Hasard is verray moder of lesynges,[21]
And of deceite, and cursed forswerynges,   130
Blaspheme of Crist, manslaughtre, and wast also
Of catel and of tyme; and forthermo,
It is repreeve and contraire of honour
For to ben holde a commune hasardour.
And ever the hyer he is of estaat   135
The moore is he yholden desolaat.[22]
If that a prynce useth hasardrye,
In alle governance and policye
He is, as by commune opinion,
Yholde the lasse in reputacion.   140
  Stilbon, that was a wys embassadour,
Was sent to Corynthe in ful greet honour
Fro Lacedomye to make hir alliaunce;
And whan he cam, hym happede parchaunce
That alle the gretteste that were of that lond,   145
Pleiyng atte hasard he hem fond.
For which, as soone as it mighte be,
He stal hym hoom agayn to his contree,
And seyde, "Ther wol I nat lese my name,
N'I wol nat take on me so greet defame   150
Yow for to allie unto none hasardours.
Sendeth othere wise embassadours,
For, by my trouthe, me were levere dye
Than I yow sholde to hasardours allye.
For ye, that been so glorious in honours,   155
Shal nat allyen yow with hasardours
As by my wyl, ne as by my tretee."
This wise philosophre, thus seyde he.
  Looke eek that to the kyng Demetrius,

---

[20] gambling   [21] lying   [22] dissolute

The kyng of Parthes, as the book seith us,   160
Sente him a paire of dees of gold in scorn,
For he hadde used hasard ther-biforn;
For which he heeld his glorie or his renoun
At no value or reputacioun.
Lordes may fynden oother maner pley   165
Honeste ynough to dryve the day awey.
    Now wol I speke of othes false and grete
A word or two, as olde bookes trete.
Greet sweryng is a thyng abhominable,
And fals sweryng is yet moore reprevable.   170
The heighe God forbad sweryng at al—
Witnesse on Mathew; but in special
Of sweryng seith the holy Jeremye,
"Thou shalt swere sooth thyne othes and nat lye,
And swere in doom, and eek in rightwisnesse";   175
But ydel sweryng is a cursednesse.
Bihoold and se that in the firste table
Of heighe Goddes hestes honurable
How that the seconde heste of hym is this:
"Take nat my name in ydel or amys."   180
Lo, rather he forbedeth swich sweryng
Than homycide, or many a cursed thyng;
I seye that as by ordre thus it standeth;
This knoweth that his hestes [23] understandeth,
How that the seconde heste of God is that.   185
And forther over, I wol thee telle al plat,[24]
That vengeance shal nat parten from his hous
That of his othes is to outrageous.
"By Goddes precious herte!" and "By his nayles!"
And "By the blood of Crist that is in Hayles,[25]   190
Sevene is my chaunce, and thyn is cynk [26] and treye!"
"By Goddes armes, if thou falsly pleye
This daggere shal thurghout thyn herte go!"—
This fruyt cometh of the bicched bones [27] two,
Forsweryng, ire, falsnesse, homycide.   195
Now, for the love of Crist, that for us dyde,
Lete [28] youre othes bothe grete and smale.
But sires, now wol I telle forth my tale.
    Thise riotoures thre of whiche I telle,

---

[23] commandments   [24] plainly   [25] in a   [27] cursed bones, dice   [28] cease
phial in the abbey of Hayles   [26] five

Longe erst er prime [29] rong of any belle,   200
Were set hem in a taverne for to drynke,
And as they sat, they herde a belle clynke
Biforn a cors was caried to his grave.
That oon of hem gan callen to his knave:
"Go bet," quod he, "and axe redily   205
What cors is this that passeth heer forby;
And looke that thou reporte his name weel."
      "Sire," quod this boy, "it nedeth neveradeel;
It was me told er ye cam heer two houres.
He was, pardee, an old felawe of youres,   210
And sodeynly he was yslayn to-nyght,
Fordronke, as he sat on his bench upright.
Ther cam a privee [30] theef men clepeth Deeth,
That in this contree al the peple sleeth,
And with his spere he smoot his herte atwo,   215
And wente his wey withouten wordes mo.
He hath a thousand slayn this pestilence.
And, maister, er ye come in his presence,
Me thynketh that it were necessarie
For to be war of swich an adversarie;   220
Beth redy for to meete hym everemoore;
Thus taughte me my dame; I sey namoore."
      "By Seinte Marie," seyde this taverner,
"The child seith sooth, for he hath slayn this yeer,
Henne over a mile, withinne a greet village,   225
Bothe man and womman, child, and hyne, and page;
I trowe his habitacion be there.
To been avysed [31] greet wisdom it were,
Er that he dide a man a dishonour."
      "Ye, Goddes armes!" quod this riotour,   230
"Is it swich peril with hym for to meete?
I shal hym seke by wey and eek by strete,
I make avow to Goddes digne bones!
Herkneth, felawes, we thre been al ones;
Lat ech of us holde up his hand til oother,   235
And ech of us bicomen otheres brother,
And we wol sleen this false traytour Deeth.
He shal be slayn, he that so manye sleeth,
By Goddes dignitee, er it be nyght!"

[29] before nine in the morning   [30] secret
[31] forewarned

Togidres han thise thre hir trouthes plight 240
To lyve and dyen ech of hem for oother,
As though he were his owene ybore brother.
And up they stirte, al dronken in this rage,
And forth they goon towardes that village
Of which the taverner hadde spoke biforn. 245
And many a grisly ooth thanne han they sworn,
And Cristes blessed body they torente:
Deeth shal be deed if that they may hym hente!

Whan they han goon nat fully half a mile,
Right as they wolde han troden over a stile, 250
An old man and a povre with hem mette.
This olde man ful mekely hem grette,
And seyde thus, "Now lordes, God you see!"

The proudeste of thise riotoures three
Answerde agayn, "What, carl, with sory grace! 255
Why artow al forwrapped save thy face?
Why lyvestow so longe in so greet age?"

This olde man gan looke in his visage,
And seyde thus: "For I ne kan nat fynde
A man, though that I walked into Inde, 260
Neither in citee ne in no village,
That wolde chaunge his youthe for myn age;
And therfore moot I han myn age stille,
As longe tyme as it is Goddes wille.
Ne Deeth, allas, ne wol nat han my lyf. 265
Thus walke I lyk a restelees caytyf,
And on the ground, which is my modres gate,
I knokke with my staf bothe erly and late,
And seye, 'Leeve moder, leet me in!
Lo, how I vanysshe, flessh and blood and skyn! 270
Allas, whan shal my bones been at reste?
Moder, with yow wolde I chaunge my cheste
That in my chambre longe tyme hath be,
Ye, for an heyre clowt to wrappe in me.'
But yet to me she wol nat do that grace, 275
For which ful pale and welked is my face.

But sires, to yow it is no curteisye
To speken to an old man vileynye,
But he trespasse in word or elles in dede.
In Holy Writ ye may yourself wel rede: 280
'Agayns an old man, hoor upon his heed,
Ye sholde arise.' Wherfore I yeve yow reed,

Ne dooth unto an old man noon harm now,
Namoore than that ye wolde men did to yow
In age, if that ye so longe abyde.   285
And God be with yow, wher ye go or ryde;
I moot go thider as I have to go."
    "Nay, olde cherl, by God thou shalt nat so,"
Seyde this oother hasardour anon.
"Thou partest nat so lightly, by Seint John!   290
Thou spak right now of thilke traytour Deeth,
That in this contree alle oure freendes sleeth;
Have here my trouthe, as thou art his espye,
Telle wher he is, or thou shalt it abye,[32]
By God and by the holy sacrament!   295
For soothly thou art oon of his assent
To sleen us yonge folk, thou false theef!"
    "Now sires," quod he, "if that ye be so leef
To fynde Deeth, turne up this croked wey,
For in that grove I lafte hym, by my fey,   300
Under a tree, and ther he wol abyde;
Nat for youre boost he wol hym no thyng hyde.
Se ye that ook? Right ther ye shal hym fynde.
God save yow, that boghte agayn mankynde,
And yow amende." Thus seyde this olde man.   305
And everich of thise riotoures ran
Til he cam to that tree, and ther they founde
Of floryns fyne of gold ycoyned rounde
Wel ny an eighte busshels, as hem thoughte.
Ne lenger thanne after Deeth they soughte,   310
But ech of hem so glad was of the sighte,
For that the floryns been so faire and brighte,
That doun they sette hem by this precious hoord.
The worste of hem he spak the firste word:
    "Brethren," quod he, "taak kepe [33] what that I seye;   315
My wit is greet, though that I bourde [34] and pleye.
This tresor hath Fortune unto us yiven,
In myrthe and jolitee oure lyf to lyven,
And lightly as it comth, so wol we spende.
Ey! Goddes precious dignitee! who wende   320
Today that we sholde han so fair a grace?
But myghte this gold be caried fro this place
Hoom to myn hous—or elles unto youres—

[32] atone for it   [33] hear well   [34] jest

For wel ye woot that al this gold is oures—
Thanne were we in heigh felicitee.   325
But trewely, by daye it may nat be;
Men wolde seyn that we were theves stronge,
And for oure owene tresor doon us honge.
This tresor moste ycaried be by nyghte,
As wisely and as slyly as it myghte.   330
Wherfore I rede that cut among us alle
Be drawe, and lat se wher the cut wol falle;
And he that hath the cut with herte blithe
Shal renne to the town, and that ful swithe,[35]
And brynge us breed and wyn ful pryvely.   335
And two of us shal kepen subtilly
This tresor wel; and if he wol nat tarie,
Whan it is nyght we wol this tresor carie
By oon assent wher as us thynketh best."
That oon of hem the cut broghte in his fest   340
And bad hem drawe and looke wher it wol falle;
And it fil on the yongeste of hem alle,
And forth toward the toun he wente anon.
And also sonne as that he was agon,
That oon of hem spak thus unto that oother: 345
"Thow knowest wel thow art my sworen brother;
Thy profit wol I telle thee anon:
Thou woost wel that oure felawe is agon,
And heere is gold, and that ful greet plentee,
That shal departed been among us thre.   350
But nathelees, if I kan shape it so
That it departed were among us two,
Hadde I nat doon a freendes torn to thee?"
        That oother answerde, "I noot how that mey be.
He woot wel that the gold is with us tweye.   355
What shal we doon? What shal we to hym seye?"
        "Shal it be conseil?"[36] seyde the first shrewe,[37]
"And I shall tellen in a wordes fewe
What we shal doon, and brynge it wel aboute."
        "I graunte," quod that oother, "out of doute,   360
That, by my trouthe, I wol thee nat biwreye."
        "Now," quod the firste, "thou woost wel we be tweye,
And two of us shul strenger be than oon.
Looke whan that he is set, that right anoon

[35] quickly   [36] secret   [37] scoundrel

Arys as though thou woldest with hym pleye, 365
And I shal ryve hym thurgh the sydes tweye
Whil that thou strogelest with hym as in game,
And with thy daggere looke thou do the same;
And thanne shal al this gold departed be,
My deere freend, bitwixen me and thee. 370
Thanne may we bothe oure lustes al fulfille,
And pleye at dees right at oure owene wille."
And thus acorded been thise shrewes tweye
To sleen the thridde, as ye han herd me seye.

    This yongeste, which that wente to the toun, 375
Ful ofte in herte [38] he rolleth up and doun
The beautee of thise floryns newe and brighte.
"O Lord!" quod he, "if so were that I myghte
Have al this tresor to myself allone,
Ther is no man that lyveth under the trone 380
Of God that sholde lyve so murye as I!"
And atte laste the feend, oure enemy,
Putte in his thought that he sholde poyson beye,
With which he myghte sleen his felawes tweye;
Forwhy the feend foond hym in swich lyvynge 385
That he hadde leve hym to sorwe brynge;
For this was outrely his ful entente,
To sleen hem bothe, and nevere to repente.
And forth he gooth—no lenger wolde he tarie—
Into the toun unto a pothecarie, 390
And preyed hym that he hym wolde selle
Som poyson that he myghte his rattes quelle; [39]
And eek ther was a polcat in his hawe [40]
That, as he seyde, his capons hadde yslawe,
And fayn he wolde wreke hym if he myghte 395
On vermyn that destroyed hym by nyghte.
    The pothecarie answerde, "And thou shalt have
A thyng that, also God my soule save,
In al this world ther is no creature,
That ete or dronke hath of this confiture 400
Nat but the montance of a corn of whete,
That he ne shal his lif anon forlete; [41]
Ye, sterve [42] he shal, and that in lasse while
That thou wolt goon a paas [43] nat but a mile,

---

[38] mind [39] kill [40] yard [41] lose
[42] die [43] walk

The poysoun is so strong and violent."   405
    This cursed man hath in his hond yhent
This poyson in a box, and sith he ran
Into the nexte strete unto a man,
And borwed of hym large botels thre,
And in the two his poyson poured he;   410
The thridde he kepte clene for his drynke,
For al the nyght he shoop [44] hym for to swynke [45]
In cariyng of the gold out of that place.
And whan this riotour, with sory grace,
Hadde filled with wyn his grete botels thre,   415
To hise felawes agayn repaireth he.
    What nedeth it to sermone of it moore?
For right as they hadde cast his deeth bifore,
Right so they han hym slayn, and that anon.
And whan that this was doon, thus spak that oon: 420
"Now lat us sitte and drynke and make us merye,
And afterward we wol his body berye."
And with that word it happed hym, par cas,[46]
To take the botel ther the poyson was,
And drank, and yaf his felawe drynke also,   425
For which anon they storven bothe two.
    But certes I suppose that Avycen
Wroot nevere in no canon ne in no fen [47]
Mo wonder signes of empoisonyng
Than hadde thise wrecches two er hir endyng.   430
Thus ended been thise homicides two,
And eek the false empoysonere also.
    O cursed synne of alle cursednesse!
O traytours homicide! O wikkednesse!
O glotonye, luxurie, and hasardrye!   435
Thou blasphemour of Crist with vileynye
And othes grete of usage and of pride!
Allas, mankynde, how may it bitide
That to thy Creatour, which that thee wroghte,
And with his precious herte blood thee boghte,   440
Thou art so fals and so unkynde, allas?
    Now goode men, God foryeve yow youre trespas,
And ware yow fro the synne of avarice.
Myn holy pardon may yow alle warice.[48]

---

[44] planned   [45] toil   [46] by chance   medicine)   [48] save
[47] chapter (in Avicenna's treatise on

So that ye offre nobles or sterlynges, 445
Or elles silver broches, spoones, rynges.
Boweth youre heed under this holy bulle!
Cometh up, ye wyves, offreth of youre wolle!
Youre names I entre here in my rolle anon;
Into the blisse of hevene shul ye gon. 450
I yow assoille,[49] by myn heigh power—
Yow that wol offre—as clene and eek as cleer
As ye were born.—And lo, sires, thus I preche.
And Jesu Crist that is oure soules leche [50]
So graunte yow his pardon to receyve, 455
For that is best; I wol yow nat deceyve.
     "But sires, o word forgat I in my tale:
I have relikes and pardon in my male
As faire as any man in Engelond,
Whiche were me yeven by the Popes hond. 460
If any of yow wol, of devocion,
Offren and han myn absolucion,
Com forth anon, and kneleth here adoun,
And mekely receyveth my pardoun;
Or elles taketh pardon as ye wende, 465
Al newe and fressh at every miles ende—
So that ye offren alwey newe and newe
Nobles or pens whiche that be goode and trewe.
It is an honour to everich that is heer
That ye mowe have a suffisant pardoner 470
T'assoille yow in contree as ye ryde,
For aventures whiche that may bityde.
Paraventure ther may falle oon or two
Doun of his hors and breke his nekke atwo.
Looke which a seuretee is it to yow alle 475
That I am in youre felaweship yfalle,
That may assoille yow, bothe moore and lasse,
Whan that the soule shal fro the body passe.
I rede that oure Hoost heere shal bigynne,
For he is moost envoluped in synne. 480
Com forth, sire Hoost, and offre first anon,
And thou shalt kisse the relikes everychon,
Ye, for a grote! unbokele anon thy purs."
     "Nay, Nay," quod he, "thanne have I Cristes curs!
Lat be," quod he, "it shal nat be, so theech! 485

[49] absolve   [50] physician

Thow woldest make me kisse thyn olde breech
And swere it were a relyk of a seint,
Though it were with thy fundement [51] depeint!
But, by the croys which that seint Eleyne fond,
I wolde I hadde thy coillons [52] in myn hond   490
In stede of relikes or of seintuarie.
Lat kutte hem of, I wol thee helpe hem carie;
They shul be shryned in an hogges toord!"
    This Pardoner answerde nat a word;
So wrooth he was, no word ne wolde he seye.   495
    "Now," quod oure Hoost, "I wol no lenger pleye
With thee, ne with noon oother angry man."
But right anon the worthy Knyght bigan,
Whan that he saugh that al the peple lough,
"Namoore of this, for it is right ynough!   500
Sire Pardoner, be glad and murye of cheere;
And ye, sir Hoost, that been to me so deere,
I pray yow that ye kisse the Pardoner.
And Pardoner, I pray thee, draw thee neer,
And as we diden lat us laughe and pleye."   505
Anon they kiste and ryden forth hir weye.   (c. 1390?)

Balade de Bon Conseyl

Flee from the prees,[1] and dwelle with sothfastness,[2]
    Suffice unto thy good, though it be small;
For hord [3] hath hate, and climbing tikelnesse,[4]
    Prees hath envye, and wele blent [5] overall;
Savour no more than thee bihove shall;   5
    Reule well thyself, that other folk canst rede;
    And trouthe thee shall deliver, it is no drede.

Tempest thee noght all croked to redresse,
In trust of hir [6] that turneth as a ball:
Gret reste stant in little besinesse;   10
Be ware also to sporne [7] ayeyns an al; [8]
Stryve not, as doth the crokke [9] with the wall,

---

[51] excrement   [52] testicles   [5] blinds   [6] Fortune   [7] kick   [8] awl
                                         [9] crockery

[1] crowd   [2] truth   [3] wealth   [4] instability

Daunte [10] thyself, that dauntest otheres dede;
And trouthe thee shall deliver, it is no drede.

That thee is sent, receive in buxumness,[11]   15
The wrastling for this world axeth a fall.
Her is non hoom, her nis but wildernesse:
Forth, pilgrim, forth! Forth, beste, out of thy stall!
Know thy countree, look up, thank God of all;
Hold the heye way, and lat thy ghost thee lede;   20
And trouthe thee shall deliver, it is no drede.

Envoi

Therefore, thou vache,[12] leave thyn old wrecchednesse;
Unto the worlde, leve [13] now to be thrall;
Crye him mercy, that of his hy goodnesse
Made thee of noght, and in especial   25
Draw unto him and pray in general
For thee, and eek for other, levenlich mede; [14]
And trouthe thee shall deliver, it is no drede.   (*1390–1400?*)

The Compleynt of Chaucer to His Purse

To you, my purse, and to noon other wyght
    Compleyne I, for ye be my lady dere!
I am so sorry now that ye been light;
    For, certes, but ye make me hevy chere,[1]
    Me were as leef be leyd upon my bere,[2]   5
For whiche unto your mercy thus I crye—
Beth [3] hevy ageyn, or elles mot [4] I dye!

Now voucheth sauf [5] this day, or hit [6] be nyght,
    That I of you the blisful soun [7] may here,[8]
Or see your colour lyk the sonne bright,   10
    That of yelownesse hadde never pere.[9]
    Ye be my lyf! ye be myn hertes stere! [10]
Quene of comfort and of good companye!
Beth hevy ageyn, or elles mot I dye!

[10] subdue   [11] submissively   [12] cow, beast   [13] cease   [14] reward

[1] unless you take on a heavy counte-nance   [2] I would as soon be laid on my bier   [3] be   [4] must   [5] vouchsafe   [6] before it   [7] sound   [8] hear   [9] peer   [10] guide

Now, purse, that be to me my lyves light   15
   And saveour, as doun [11] in this worlde here,
Out of this toun help me throgh your myght,
   Syn [12] that ye wole not been my tresorere; [13]
   For I am shave as nye as is a frere.[14]
But yet I pray unto your curtesye,   20
Beth hevy ageyn, or elles mot I dye!

L'Envoye De Chaucer

O conquerour of Brutes Albioun,[15]
Which that by lyne and free eleccioun
   Ben verray kyng, this song to you I sende,
   And ye that mowen [16] al myn harm amende,   25
Have mynde upon my supplicacioun!   (1399)

---

[11] down [12] since [13] treasurer [14] hard pinched, shaved close as a friar [15] Henry IV; Brutus was a legendary king of England, Albion [16] are able (to amend)

EARLY ANONYMOUS LYRICS: RELIGIOUS AND SECULAR

I Sing of a Maiden

I sing of a maiden
    That is makeles; [1]
King of all kings
    To her son she ches.[2]

He came al so still   5
    Where his mother was,
As dew in April
    That falleth on the grass.

He came al so still
    To his mother's bower,   10
As dew in April
    That falleth on the flower.

He came al so still
    Where his mother lay,
As dew in April   15
    That falleth on the spray.[3]

Mother and maiden
    Was never none but she;
Well may such a lady
    Goddes mother be.   20

Lully, Lulley, Lully, Lulley

Lully, lulley! lully, lulley!
The faucon [1] hath borne my make away!

He bare him up, he bare him down,
He bare him into an orchard brown.

[1] matchless and without a mate   [2] chose   [3] foliage

[1] falcon

In that orchard there was an halle,   5
That was hanged with purple and pall [2]

And in that hall there was a bed,
It was hanged with gold sa red.

And in that bed there lith a knight,
His woundes bleeding day and night.   10

At that bed's foot there lith a hound,
Licking the blood as it runs down.

By that bed-side kneeleth a may, [3]
And she weepeth both night and day.

And at that bed's head standeth a stone,   15
Corpus Christi written thereon.

Lully, lulley! lully, lulley!
The faucon hath borne my make away.

Adam Lay I-Bowndyn

Adam lay i-bowndyn,
    Bowndyn in a bond—
Fowre thousand wynter
    Thoght he not too long;
And al was for an appil,   5
    An appil that he tok,
As clerkes fynden,
    Writen in here [1] book.

Ne hadde [2] the appil takë ben,
    The appil taken ben,   10
Ne haddë never our lady
    A ben [3] hevenë quene.
Blyssid be the tyme
    That appil takë was,
Ther fore we mown [4] syngyn   15
    Deo Gracias.

[2] velvet   [3] a maid

[1] their   [2] had not   [3] have been   [4] must

The Divine Paradox

A God and yet a man?
    A mayde and yet a mother?
Witt wonders what witt can
    Conceave this or the other.

A God, and can he die?
    A dead man, can he live?
Whatt witt can well replie?
    What reason reason give?

God, truth itselfe, doth teach it.
    Mans witt senckis [1] too farr under
By reasons power to reach it.
    Beleeve and leave to wonder.

I Have a Young Sister

I have a young sister
    Far beyond the sea;
Many be the drowryis
    That che sente me.

Che sente me the cherye   5
    With-outyn ony ston,
And so che ded the dowe [1]
    With-outyn ony bon.

Sche sente me the brer
    With-outyn ony rynde; [2]   10
Sche bad me loue my lemman
    With-oute longgyng.

How xuld ony cherye
    Be with-oute ston?
And how xuld only dowe   15
    Ben with-oute bon?

[1] sinks

---

[1] dove   [2] branch

How xuld ony brer
    Ben with-oute rynde?
How xuld love myn lemman
    With-oute longyng?   20

When the cherye was a flour,
    Than hadde it non ston.
Whan the dowe was an ey,[3]
    Than hadde it non bon.

When the brer was on-bred,[4]   25
    Then hadde it non rynd.
When the maydyn hayt that che louit,
    Che is with-out longing.

Westron Winde, When Will Thou Blow

Westron winde, when will thou blow,
The smalle raine downe can raine?
Crist, if my love wer in my armis,
And I in my bed againe.

Sumer Is Icumen In

Sumer is icumen in,
    Lhude sing cuccu;
Groweth sed and bloweth med
    And springth the wude nu.
        Sing cuccu!   5
Awe [1] bleteth after lomb,
    Lhouth [2] after calve cu;
Bulluc sterteth,[3] bucke verteth; [4]
    Murie sing cuccu.
        Cuccu, cuccu,   10
    Wel singes thu, cuccu,
    Ne swik thu naver nu.
Sing cuccu nu! Sing cuccu!
Sing cuccu! Sing cuccu nu!

[3] egg   [4] in seed

[1] ewe   [2] loweth   [3] springs   [4] breaks wind

BALLADS

Edward

"Why dois your brand sae drap wi bluid,
  Edward, Edward,
Why dois your brand sae drap wi bluid,
  And why sae sad gang yee O?"
"O I hae killed my hauke sae guid,   5
  Mither, mither,
O I hae killed my hauke sae guid,
  And I had nae mair but hee O."

"Your haukis bluid was nevir sae reid,
  Edward, Edward,   10
Your haukis bluid was nevir sae reid,
  My deir son I tell thee O."
O I hae killed my reid roan steed,
  Mither, mither,
O I hae killed my reid roan steid,   15
  That erst was sae fair and free O."

"Your steid was auld, and ye hae gat mair,
  Edward, Edward,
Your steid was auld, and ye hae gat mair,
  Sum other dule ¹ ye drie ² O."   20
"O I hae killed my fadir deir,
  Mither, mither,
O I hae killed my fadir deir,
  Alas, and wae is mee O!"

"And whatten penance wul ye drie for that,   25
  Edward, Edward?
And whatten penance wul ye drie for that?
  My deir son, now tell me O."
"Ile set my feet in yonder boat,
  Mither, mither,   30
Ile set my feet in yonder boat,
  And Ile fare ovir the sea O."

"And what wul ye doe wi your towirs and your ha,
  Edward, Edward?

¹ grief ² suffer

37

And what wul ye doe wi your towirs and your ha,   35
    That were sae fair to see O?"
"Ile let thame stand tul they doun fa,
    Mither, mither,
Ile let thame stand tul they doun fa,
    For here nevir mair maun I bee O."   40

"And what wul ye leive to your bairns and your wife,
    Edward, Edward?
And what wul ye leive to your bairns and your wife,
    Whan ye gang ovir the sea O?"
"The warldis room, let them beg thrae life,   45
    Mither, mither,
The warldis room, let them beg thrae life,
    For thame nevir mair wul I see O."

"And what wul ye leive to your ain mither deir?
    Edward, Edward?   50
And what wul ye leive to your ain mither deir?
    My deir son, now tell me O."
"The curse of hell frae me sall ye beir,
    Mither, mither,
The curse of hell frae me sall ye beir,   55
    Sic counseils ye gave to me O."

The Wife of Usher's Well

There lived a wife at Usher's Well,
    And a wealthy wife was she;
She had three stout and stalwart sons,
    And sent them o'er the sea.

They hadna been a week from her,   5
    A week but barely ane,
Whan word came to the carline [1] wife
    That her three sons were gane.

They hadna been a week from her,
    A week but barely three,   10
Whan word came to the carline wife
    That her sons she'd never see.

[1] an old woman

"I wish the wind may never cease,
    Nor fashes [2] in the flood,
Till my three sons come hame to me,   15
    In earthly flesh and blood."

It fell about the Martinmas,
    When nights are lang and mirk,
The carline wife's three sons came home,
    And their hats were o the birk.   20

It neither grew in syke nor ditch,
    Nor yet in ony sheugh; [3]
But at the gates o' Paradise,
    That birk grew fair eneugh.

"Blow up the fire, my maidens,   25
    Bring water from the well;
For a' my house shall feast this night,
    Since my three sons are well."

And she has made to them a bed,
    She's made it large and wide,   30
And she's taen her mantle her about,
    Sat down at the bed-side.

Up then crew the red, red cock,
    And up and crew the gray;
The eldest to the youngest said,   35
    " 'T is time we were away."

The cock he hadna crawd but once,
    And clappd his wings at a',
When the youngest to the eldest said,
    "Brother we must awa.   40

"The cock doth craw, the day doth daw,
    The channerin [4] worm doth chide;
Gin [5] we be mist out o our place,
    A sair [6] pain we maun bide.

"Fare ye weel, my mother dear!   45
    Fareweel to barn and byre!
And fare ye weel, the bonny lass
    That kindles my mother's fire!"

[2] troubles   [3] furrow   [4] grumbling   [5] if
[6] sore

Sir Patrick Spens

The king sits in Dumferling toune,
    Drinking the blude-reid wine:
'O whar will I get guid sailor,
    To sail this schip of mine?'

Up and spak an eldern knicht,   5
    Sat at the kings richt kne:
'Sir Patrick Spens is the best sailor
    That sails upon the se.'

The king has written a braid letter,
    And signd it wi his hand,   10
And sent it to Sir Patrick Spens,
    Was walking on the sand.

The first line that Sir Patrick red,
    A loud lauch lauched he;
The next line that Sir Patrick red,   15
    The teir blinded his ee.

'O wha is this has don this deid,
    This ill deid don to me,
To send me out this time o' the yeir,
    To sail upon the se!   20

'Mak hast, mak haste, my mirry men all,
    Our guid schip sails the morne.'
'O say na sae, my master deir,
    For I feir a deadlie storme.

'Late late yestreen I saw the new moone,   25
    Wi the auld moone in hir arme,
And I feir, I feir, my deir master,
    That we will cum to harme.'

O our Scots nobles wer richt laith
    To weet their cork-heild schoone;   30
Bot lang owre a' the play wer playd,
    Thair hats they swam aboone.

O lang, lang may their ladies sit,
    Wi thair fans into their hand,
Or eir they se Sir Patrick Spens   35
    Cum sailing to the land.

O lang, lang may the ladies stand
 Wi thair gold kems in their hair,
Waiting for thair ain deir lords,
 For they'll se thame na mair.   40

Haf owre, haf owre to Abedour,
 It's fiftie fadom deip,
And thair lies guid Sir Patrick Spens,
 Wi the Scots lords at his feit.

Get Up and Bar the Door

It fell about the Martinmas time,
 And a gay time it was then,
When our goodwife got puddings to make,
 And she's boild them in the pan.

The wind sae cauld blew south and north, 5
 And blew into the floor;
Quoth our goodman to our goodwife,
 "Gae out and bar the door."

"My hand is in my hussyfskap,[1]
 Goodman, as ye may see;   10
It shoud nae be barrd this hundred year,
 If it's to be barrd by me!"

They made a paction [2] tween them twa,
 They made it firm and sure,
That the first word whae'er shoud speak, 15
 Should rise and bar the door.

Then by there came two gentlemen,
 At twelve o'clock at night,
And they could neither see house nor hall,
 Nor coal nor candle-light.   20

"Now whether is this a rich man's house,
 Or whether it is a poor?"
But neer a word would ane o them speak,
 For barring of the door.

---

[1] housework [2] pact

And first they ate the white puddings,   25
    And then they ate the black;
Tho muckle ³ thought the goodwife to hersel,
    Yet neer a word she spake.

Then said the one unto the other,
    "Here, man, tak ye my knife;   30
Do ye tak off the auld man's beard,
    And I'll kiss the goodwife."

"But there's nae water in the house,
    And what shall we do than?"
"What ails ye at the pudding-broo,⁴   35
    That boils into the pan?"

O up then started our goodman,
    An angry man was he:
"Will ye kiss my wife before my een,
    And scald me wi pudding-bree?"   40

Then up and started our goodwife,
    Gied three skips on the floor:
"Goodman, you've spoken the foremost word,
    Get up and bar the door!"

Greensleeves

Greensleeves was all my joy,
    Greensleeves was my delight;
Greensleeves was my heart of gold,
    And who but Lady Greensleeves.

Alas, my Love! ye do me wrong   5
    To cast me off discourteously:
And I have lovéd you so long,
    Delighting in your company.
        Greensleeves was all my joy . . .

I have been ready at your hand,   10
    To grant whatever you would crave.
I have both wagéd life and land,
    Your love and good will for to have.
        Greensleeves was all my joy . . .

³ much   ⁴ brew

I bought thee kerchers to thy head,   15
     That were wrought fine and gallantly:
I kept thee both at board and bed,
     Which cost my purse well favouredly.
         Greensleeves was all my joy . . .

I bought thee petticoats of the best,   20
     The cloth so fine as fine might be:
I gave thee jewels for thy chest,
     And all this cost I spent on thee.
         Greensleeves was all my joy . . .

Thy smocks of silk, both fair and white,   25
     With gold embroidered gorgeously:
Thy petticoat of sendal right:
     And thus I bought thee gladly.
         Greensleeves was all my joy . . .

Thy girdle of gold so red,   30
     With pearls bedecked sumptuously:
The like no other lasses had,
     And yet thou wouldst not love me.
         Greensleeves was all my joy . . .

Thy purse and eke thy gay gilt knives,   35
     Thy pincase gallant to the eye,
No better wore the burgess wives,
     And yet thou wouldst not love me.
         Greensleeves was all my joy . . .

Thy crimson stockings all of silk,   40
     With gold all wrought above the knee;
Thy pumps as white as was the milk,
     And yet thou wouldst not love me.
         Greensleeves was all my joy . . .

Thy gown was of the grassie green,   45
     Thy sleeves of satin hanging by,
Which made thee be our harvest queen,
     And yet thou wouldst not love me.
         Greensleeves was all my joy . . .

Thy garters fringed with the gold,   50
     And silver aglets hanging by,
Which made thee blithe for to behold,
     And yet thou wouldst not love me.
         Greensleeves was all my joy . . .

My gayest gelding I thee gave,   55
    To ride wherever liked thee;
No lady ever was so brave,
    And yet thou wouldst not love me.
        Greensleeves was all my joy . . .

My men were clothéd all in green,   60
    And they did ever wait on thee:
All this was gallant to be seen,
    And yet thou wouldst not love me.
        Greensleeves was all my joy . . .

They set thee up, they took thee down,   65
    They served thee with humility;
Thy foot might not once touch the ground,
    And yet thou wouldst not love me.
        Greensleeves was all my joy . . .

For every morning when thou rose,   70
    I sent thee dainties orderly,
To cheer thy stomach from all woes,
    And yet thou wouldst not love me.
        Greensleeves was all my joy . . .

Thou couldst desire no earthly thing   75
    But still thou hadst it readily:
Thy music still to play and sing,
    And yet thou wouldst not love me.
        Greensleeves was all my joy . . .

And who did pay for all this gear   80
    That thou didst spend when pleaséd thee?
Even I that am rejected here,
    And thou disdain'st to love me.
        Greensleeves was all my joy . . .

Well, I will pray to God on high,   85
    That thou my constancy mayst see,
And that yet once before I die,
    Thou wilt vouchsafe to love me.
        Greensleeves was all my joy . . .

Greensleeves, now farewell! adieu!   90
    God I pray to prosper thee:
For I am still thy lover true—
    Come once again and love me.

Greensleeves was all my joy,
    Greensleeves was my delight;
Greensleeves was my heart of gold,
    And who but Lady Greensleeves.

95

Lord Randal

"O where hae ye been, Lord Randal, my son?
"O where hae ye been, my handsome young man?"
"I hae been to the wild wood; mother, make my bed soon,
For I'm weary wi hunting, and fain wald lie down."

"Where gat ye your dinner, Lord Randal, my son?
Where gat ye your dinner, my handsome young man?"
"I din'd wi my true-love; mother, make my bed soon,
For I'm weary wi hunting, and fain wald lie down."

"What gat ye to your dinner, Lord Randal, my son?
What gat ye to your dinner, my handsome young man?"
"I gat eels boiled in broo; mother, make my bed soon,
For I'm weary wi hunting, and fain wald lie down."

"What became of your bloodhounds, Lord Randal, my son?
What became of your bloodhounds, my handsome young man?"
"O they swelld and they died; mother, make my bed soon,
For I'm weary wi hunting, and fain wald lie down."

"O I fear ye are poisond, Lord Randal, my son!
O I fear ye are poisond, my handsome young man!"
"O yes! I am poisond; mother, make my bed soon,
For I'm sick at the heart, and I fain wald lie down."

5

10

15

20

The Unquiet Grave

"The wind doth blow today, my love,
    And a few small drops of rain;
I never had but one true-love,
    In cold grave she was lain.

"I'll do as much for my true-love   5
    As any young man may;
I'll sit and mourn at her grave
    For a twelvemonth and a day."

The twelvemonth and a day being up,
    The dead began to speak: 10
"Oh who sits weeping on my grave,
    And will not let me sleep?"

" 'Tis I, my love, sits on your grave,
    And will not let me sleep;
For I crave one kiss of your clay-cold lips,   15
    And that is all I seek."

"You crave one kiss of my clay-cold lips;
    But my breath smells earthy strong;
If you have one kiss of my clay-cold lips,
    Your time will not be long.   20

" 'Tis down in yonder garden green,
    Love, where we used to walk,
The finest flower that e'er was seen
    Is withered to a stalk.

"The stalk is withered dry, my love,   25
    So will our hearts decay;
So make yourself content, my love,
    Till God calls you away."

The Bitter Withy

As it fell out on a Holy day,
    The drops of rain did fall, did fall,
Our Saviour asked leave of His mother Mary
    If He might go play at ball.

"To play at ball, my own dear Son,   5
    It's time you was going or gone,
But be sure let me hear no complaint of You
    At night when You do come hone."

It was upling scorn and downling scorn,
    Oh, there He meet three jolly jerdins: [1]   10
Oh, there He asked the three jolly jerdins
    If they would go go play at ball.

"Oh, we are lords' and ladies' sons,
    Born in bower or in hall,
And You are but some poor maid's child   15
    Born'd in an ox's stall."

"If you are lords' and ladies' sons,
    Born'd in bower or in hall,
Then at the very last I'll make it appear
    That I am above you all."   20

Our Saviour built a bridge with the beams of the sun,
    And over He gone, He gone He,
And after followed the three jolly jerdins,
    And drowned they were all three.

It was upling scorn and downling scorn,   25
    The mothers of them did whoop and call,
Crying out, "Mary mild, call home your Child,
    For ours are drownded all."

Mary mild, Mary mild, called home her Child,
    And laid Our Saviour across her knee,   30
And with a whole handful of bitter withy [2]
    She gave Him lashed three.

Then He says to His Mother, "Oh! the withy, oh! the withy,
    The bitter withy that causes me to smart, to smart,
Oh! the withy it shall be the very first tree   35
    That perishes at the heart."

.

[1] meaning unknown   [2] willow twig

PART 2
The Sixteenth Century

JOHN SKELTON (1460?–1529)

To Mistress Isabell Pennell

By Saint Mary, my lady,
Your mammy and your dady,
Brought forth a godely baby!
    My fair Isabell,
Reflaring rosabell,   5
The flagrant camamell;
    The ruddy rosary,
The soveraine rosemary,
The praty strawbery;
    The columbine, the nepte,[1]   10
The jeloffer [2] well set,
The propre violet;
    Enuwid [3] your coloure
Is like the dasy flowre
After the Aprill showre;   15
    Sterre of the morow gray,
The blossom on the spray,
The fresshest flowre of May;
    Maidenly demure,
Of womanhode the lure;   20
Wherfore I make you sure
    It were an hevenly helth,
It were an endless welth,
A life for God himselfe,
    To here this nightingale,   25
Amonge the birdes smale,
Warbelinge in the vale,
    Dug, dug,
    Jug, jug,
Good yere and good luk,   30
With chuk, chuk, chuk, chuk!   (c. 1520)

[1] mint   [2] gillyflower   [3] fresh, renewed

To Mistress Margaret Hussey

Mirry Margaret,
As midsomer flowre,
Jentill as faucoun
Or hawke of the towre;
    With solace and gladnes,   5
Moche mirthe and no madnes,
All good and no badnes,
So joyously,
So maidenly,
So womanly   10
Her demening
In every thinge,
Far, far passinge
That I can endight,
Or suffice to wright   15
Of mirry Margarete,
As midsomer flowre,
Jentill as facoun
Or hawke of the towre;
    As pacient and as still,   20
And as full of good will,
As faire Ysaphill; [1]
Coliaunder, [2]
Swete pomaunder,
Good Cassaunder; [3]   25
Stedfast of thought,
Wele made, wele wrought;
Far may be sought
Erst that ye can finde
So corteise, so kinde   30
As mirry Margarete,
This midsomer flowre,
Jentill as faucoun
Or hawke of the towre.   (*c. 1520*)

[1] a princess of Lemnos who saved her father, the king Thoas, when the women killed all the men on the island [2] coriander [3] Cassandra

Upon a Dead Man's Head

Sent to him from an honourable gentlewoman for a token, he devised this ghostly meditation in English covenable, in sentence commendable, lamentable, lacrimable, profitable for a soul.

Your ugly token
My mind hath broken
From worldly lust:
For I have discust
We are but dust,   5
And die we must.
    It is general
To be mortal:
I have well espied
No man may him hide   10
From Death hollow-eyed,
With sinews withered,
With bones shivered,
With his worm-eaten maw,
And his ghastly jaw   15
Gasping aside,
Naked of hide,
Neither flesh nor fell.
    Then, by my counsell,
Look that ye spell   20
Well this gospell:
For whereso we dwell
Death will us quell,
And with us mell.
    For all our pampered paunches   25
There may be no fraunchis,
Nor worldly bliss,
Redeem us from this:
Our days be dated
To be check-mated   30
With draughtes of death
Stopping our breath:
Our eyen sinking,
Our bodies stinking,
Our gummes grinning,   35

Our soules brinning.[1]
To whom, then, shall we sue,
For to have rescue,
But to sweet Jesu
On us then for to rue?   40
  O goodly Child
Of Mary mild,
Then be our shield!
That we be not exiled
To the dun dale   45
Of bootless bale,
Nor to the lake
Of fiendes blake.
  But grant us grace
To see thy Face,   50
And to purchase
Thine heavenly place,
And thy palace
Full of solace
Above the sky   55
That is so high,
Eternally
To behold and see
The Trinitie!
  Amen.   60
Myrres vous y.[2]

A Prayer to the Father of Heaven

O radiant luminary of light interminable
  Celestial Father, potential God of might,
Of heaven and earth, O Lord incomparable,
  Of all perfections the essential most perfite!
  O maker of mankind, that formëd day and night,   5
Whose power imperial comprehendeth every place:
  Mine heart, my mind, my thought, my whole delight
Is after this life to see thy glorious face.

[1] burning   [2] see yourself in it

Whose magnificence is incomprehensible,
 All arguments of reason which far doth exceed,   10
Whose deity doubtless is indivisible,
 From whom all goodness and virtue doth proceed;
 Of thy support all creätures have need:
Assist me, good Lord, and grant me thy grace
 To live to thy pleasure in word, thought, and deed,   15
And after this life to see thy glorious face.   (1568)

Lullay, Lullay, Like a Child

 With lullay, lullay, like a child,
 Thou sleep'st too long, thou art beguiled.

"My darling dear, my daisy floure,
 Let me," quod he, "lie in your lap."
"Lie still," quod she, "my paramoure,   5
 Lie still hardlie,[1] and take a nap."
 His head was heavy, such was his hap,
All drowsy dreaming, drowned in sleep,
That of his love he took no keep,
 With hey lullay, lullay, like a child,   10
 Thou sleep'st too long, thou art beguiled.

With ba,[2] ba, ba! and bas, bas, bas!
 She cherished [3] him both cheek and chin,
That he wist never where he was:
 He had forgotten all deadly sin.   15
 He wanted wit her love to win:

He trusted her payment and lost all his pay;
She left him sleeping and stole away,
 With hey lullay, lullay, like a child,
 Thou sleep'st too long, thou art beguiled.   20

The rivers rough, the waters wan,
 She spared not to wet her feet;
She waded over, she found a man
 That halsed [4] her heartily and kissed her sweet:
 Thus after her colds he caught a heat.   25

[1] with confidence   [2] kiss   [3] kissed
[4] embraced

My love, she said, routeth [5] in his bed;
Ywis [6] he hath an heavy head,
    With hey lullay, lullay, like a child,
    Thou sleep'st too long, thou art beguiled.

What dream'st thou, drunkard, drowsy pate?   30
    Thy lust and liking is from thee gone;
Thou blinkard blowboll,[7] thou wakest too late,
    Behold thou liest, luggard, alone!
    Well, may thou sigh, well may thou groan,
To deal with her so cowardly: 35
Ywis, pole hatchet,[8] she bleared thine eye.[9]

[5] snores   [6] certainly   [7] a sot   [8] a   person   [9] deceived him
wielder of a poll-axe, a contemptuous

WILLIAM DUNBAR (1460?–1530?)

Lament for the Makaris [1]
Quhen He Wes Seik

I that in heill [2] wes and gladness,
Am trublit now with gret seiknes,
And feblit with infermite;
    Timor mortis conturbat me. [3]

Our plesance heir is all vane glory,   5
This fals warld is bot transitory,
The flesche is brukle, [4] the Fend is sle; [5]
    Timor mortis conturbat me.

The stait of man dois change and vary,
Now sound, now seik, now blith, now sary,   10
Now dansand mery, now like to dee;
    Timor mortis conturbat me.

No stait in erd [6] heir standis sickir; [7]
As with the wynd wavis the wickir,
Wavis this warldis vanite;   15
    Timor mortis conturbat me.

On to the ded [8] gois all Estatis,
Princis, Prelotis, and Potestatis,
Baith riche and pur of al degree;
    Timor mortis conturbat me.   20

He takis the knychtis in to feild,
Anarmit under helme and scheild;
Victour he is at all mellie;
    Timor mortis conturbat me.

That strang unmercifull tyrand   25
Takis on the moderis breist sowkand, [9]
The bab, full of benignite;
    Timor mortis conturbat me.

He takis the campion in the stour, [10]
The capitane closit in the towr,   30

[1] makers, poets [2] health [3] the fear of   [7] secure [8] death [9] nursing [10] battle
death shakes me. [4] frail [5] sly [6] earth

The lady in bowr full of bewte;
Timor mortis conturbat me.

He sparis no lord for his piscence,[11]
Na clark for his intelligence;
His awful strak may no man fle;   35
Timor mortis conturbat me.

Art, magicianis, and astrologgis,
Rethoris, logicianis, and theologgis,
Thame helpis no conclusions sle; [12]
Timor mortis conturbat me.   40

In medicyne the most practicianis,
Lechis, surrigianis and phisicianis,
Thame self fra ded may not supple; [13]
Timor mortis conturbat me.

I se that makaris amang the laif [14]   45
Playis heir ther pageant, syne [15] gois to graif;
Sparit is nocht ther faculte; [16]
Timor mortis conturbat me.

He hes done petuously devour,
The noble Chaucer, of makaris flour,
The Monk of Bery, [17] and Gower, all thre;   50
Timor mortis conturbat me.

The gude Syr Hew of Eglintoun,
And aik Heryot, and Wyntoun,
He hes tane out of this cuntre;   55
Timor mortis conturbat me.

That scorpion fell hes done infek [18]
Maister Johne Clerk, and James Afflek,
Fra balat making and tragidie;
Timor mortis conturbat me.   60

Holland and Barbour he hes berevit;
Allace! that he nocht with us levit
Schir Mungo Lokert of the Le;
Timor mortis conturbat me.

Clerk of Tranent eik he has tane,   65
That maid the Anteris [19] of Gawane;

[11] puissance [12] sly reasonings [13] res- [17] John Lydgate [18] infected [19] adven-
cue [14] rest [15] then [16] profession tures

Schir Gilbert Hay endit hes he;
    Timor mortis conturbat me.

He has Blind Hary and Sandy Traill
Slaine with his schour of mortall haill,   70
Quhilk Patrik Johnestoun mycht nocht fle;
    Timor mortis conturbat me.

He hes reft Merseir his endite,[20]
That did in luf so lifly write,
So schort, so quyk, of sentence hie;   75
    Timor mortis conturbat me.

He hes tane Roull of Edberdene,
And gentill Roull of Corstorphin;
Two bettir fallowis did no man se;
    Timor mortis conturbat me.   80

In Dumfermelyne he hes done roune [21]
With Maister Robert Henrisoun;
Schir Johne the Rose enbrast hes he;
    Timor mortis conturbat me.

And he hes now tane, last of aw,   85
Gud gentill Stobo and Quintyne Schaw,
Of quham all wichtis [22] hes pete: [23]
    Timor mortis conturbat me.

Gud Maister Walter Kennedy
In poynt of ded lyis veraly,   90
Gret reuth it wer that so suld be;
    Timor mortis conturbat me.

Sen he hes all my brether tane,
He will nocht lat me lif alane,
On forse I man [24] his nyxt pray be;   95
    Timor mortis conturbat me.

Sen for the deid remeid is none,
Best is that we for dede dispone,[25]
Eftir our deid that lif may we;
    Timor mortis conturbat me.   (1508)

[20] writing   [21] whispered   [22] beings
[23] pity   [24] must   [25] dispose

❧ THOMAS WYATT (1503–1542)

I Find No Peace [1]

DESCRIPTION OF THE CONTRARIOUS PASSIONS IN A LOVER

I find no peace, and all my war is done;
I fear and hope, I burn, and freeze like ice;
I fly aloft, yet can I not arise;
And nought I have, and all the world I seize on,
That locks nor loseth, holdeth me in prison,
And holds me not, yet can I scape no wise:
Nor letteth me live, nor die, at my devise,
And yet of death it giveth me occasion.
Without eye I see; without tongue I plain:
I wish to perish, yet I ask for health;
I love another, and I hate myself;
I feed me in sorrow, and laugh in all my pain.
Lo, thus displeaseth me both death and life,
An my delight is causer of this strife.

They Flee from Me

They flee from me, that sometime did me seek,
With naked foot, stalking [1] in my chamber.
I have seen them, gentle, tame, and meek,
That now are wild, and do not remember
That sometime they put themselves in danger   5
To take bread at my hand; and now they range,
Busily seeking with a continual change.

Thankèd be fortune, it hath been otherwise
Twenty times better; but once, in special,
In thin array, after a pleasant guise,   10
When her loose gown from her shoulders did fall,
And she me caught in her arms long and small,

---

[1] translated from Petrarch, *Sonnetto in Vita*, 90

---

[1] working furtively

Therewithal sweetly did me kiss,
And softly said, "Dear heart, how like you this?"

It was no dream; I lay broad waking.   15
But all is turned, thorough my gentleness,
Into a strange fashion of forsaking;
And I have leave to go, of her goodness,
And she also to use new-fangledness.[2]
But since that I so kindely [3] am served,   20
I would fain know what she hath deserved.   (1557)

And Wilt Thou Leave Me Thus?

And wilt thou leave me thus?
    Say nay! say nay! for shame!
    To save thee from the blame
    Of all my grief and grame.[1]
And wilt thou leave me thus?   5
    Say nay! say nay!

And wilt thou leave me thus,
    That hath loved thee so long
    In wealth and woe among?
    And is thy heart so strong   10
As for to leave me thus?
    Say nay! say nay!

And wilt thou leave me thus,
    That hath given thee my heart
    Never for to depart   15
    Neither for pain nor smart?
And wilt thou leave me thus?
    Say nay! say nay!

And wilt thou leave me thus,
    And have no more pity   20
    Of him that loveth thee?
    Alas! thy cruelty!
And wilt thou leave me thus?
    Say nay! say nay!

[2] fickleness   [3] naturally

[1] anger

Forget Not Yet

Forget not yet the tried intent
Of such a truth as I have meant;
My great travail so gladly spent,
     Forget not yet!

Forget not yet when first began   5
The weary life we know, since whan
The suit, the service none tell can;
     Forget not yet!

Forget not yet, the great assays,
The cruel wrong, the scornful ways,   10
The painful patience in delays,
     Forget not yet!

Forget not! O, forget not this,
How long ago hath been, and is
The mind that never meant amiss—   15
     Forget not yet!

Forget not then thine own approved
The which so long hath thee so loved,
Whose steadfast faith yet never moved—
     Forget not this!   20

Who So List to Hount

Who so list to hount, I knowe where is an hynde,
 But as for me, helas, I may no more:
 The vayne travaill hath weried me so sore.
 I ame of theim that farthest commeth behinde;
Yet may I by no meanes my weried mynde
 Drawe from the Diere: but as she fleeth afore,
Faynting I folowe. I leve of therefore,
 Sins in a nett I seke to hold the wynde.
Who list her hount, I put him owte of dowbte,
 As well as I may spend his tyme in vain:
 And, graven with Diamonds, in letters plain
There is written her faier neck rounde abowte:
 Noli me tangere,[1] for Cesars I ame;
 And wylde for to hold, though I seme tame.

[1] Do not touch me.

HENRY HOWARD, EARL OF SURREY
(1517?–1547)

Spring

The soote [1] season, that bud and bloom forth brings,
With green hath clad the hill and eke the vale:
The nightingale with feathers new she sings;
The turtle to her make [2] hath told her tale.
Summer is come, for every spray now springs;
The hart hath hung his old head on the pale;
The buck in brake his winter coat he flings;
The fishes float with new repairéd scale;
The adder all her slough away she slings;
The swift swallow pursueth the flies smale;
The busy bee her honey now she mings; [3]
Winter is worn that was the flowers' bale.
    And thus I see among these pleasant things
    Each care decays; and yet my sorrow springs.   (1557)

Martial, the Things for to Attain

Martial,[1] the things for to attain
The happy life be these, I find:
The riches left, not got with pain;
The fruitful ground; the quiet mind;
The equal friend; no grudge, no strife;   5
No charge of rule nor governance;
Without disease, the healthful life;
The household of continuance;
The mean diet, no delicate fare;
Wisdom joined with simplicity;   10
The night discharged of all care.
Where wine may bear no sovereignty;

---

[1] sweet   [2] turtle dove to her mate   [3] remembers

---

[1] a translation of one of Martial's epigrams: X, 47

The chaste wife, wise, without debate;
Such sleeps as may beguile the night;
Contented with thine own estate,   15
Neither wish death, nor fear his might.

Complaint That His Ladie After She Knew of His Love Kept Her Face Alway Hidden from Him

I never sawe my Layde laye apart
Her cornet [1] blacke, in colde nor yet in heate,
Sith first she knew my griefe was growen so great,
Which other fansies driveth from my hart
That to my selfe I do the thought reserve,
The which unwares did wounde my wofull brest:
But on her face mine eyes mought never rest,
Yet, sins she knew I did her love and serve
Her golden tresses cladde alway with blacke,
Her smilynge lokes that hid thus evermore,
And that restraines whiche I desire so sore.
So doth this cornet governe me alacke:
In somer, sunne: in winter breath, a frost:
Wherby the light of her faire lokes I lost.   (1557)

[1] a head-dress

❧ BARNABE GOOGE (1540–1594)

Out of Sight, Out of Mind

The oftener seen, the more I lust,
The more I lust, the more I smart,
The more I smart, the more I trust,
The more I trust, the heavier heart;
The heavy heart breeds mine unrest,   5
Thy absence, therefore, like I best.

The rarer seen, the less in mind,
The less in mind, the lesser pain,
The lesser pain, less grief I find,
The lesser grief, the greater gain,   10
The greater gain, the merrier I,
Therefore I wish thy sight to fly.

The further off, the more I joy,
The more I joy, the happier life,
The happier life, less hurts annoy,   15
The lesser hurts, pleasure most rife:
Such pleasures rife shall I obtain
When distance doth depart us twain.   (1563)

Gascoigne's Lullaby

Sing lullaby, as women do,
Wherewith they bring their babes to rest,
And lullaby can I sing too,
As womanly as can the best.
With lullaby they still the child,   5
And if I be not much beguiled,
Full many wanton babes have I,
Which must be stilled with lullaby.

First lullaby my youthful years,
It is now time to go to bed,   10
For crooked age and hoary hairs
Have won the haven within my head:
With lullaby then, youth, be still,
With lullaby content thy will,
Since courage quails and comes behind,   15
Go sleep, and so beguile thy mind.

Next lullaby my gazing eyes,
Which wonted were to glance apace.
For every glass may now suffice
To show the furrows in my face: 20
With lullaby then wink awhile,
With lullaby your looks beguile:
Let no fair face, nor beauty bright,
Entice you eft with vain delight.

And lullaby my wanton will,   25
Let reason rule, now rein thy thought,
Since all too late I find by skill
How dear I have my fancies bought:
With lullaby now take thine ease,
With lullaby thy doubts appease: 30
For trust to this, if thou be still,
My body shall obey thy will.

Eke lullaby my loving boy,
My little Robin, take thy rest,
Since age is cold and nothing coy,   35

Keep close thy coign, for so is best:
With lullaby be thou content,
With lullaby thy lusts relent,
Let others pay which hath more pence,
Thou art too poor for such expense.   40

Thus lullaby my youth, mine eyes,
My will, my ware, and all that was,
I can no more delays devise,
But welcome pain, let pleasure pass:
With lullaby now take your leave,   45
With lullaby your dream deceive,
And when you rise with waking eye,
Remember Gascoigne's lullaby.

Ever or never   (*1573*)

EDWARD DYER (1540?–1607)

My Mind to Me a Kingdom Is

My mind to me a kingdom is,
    Such present joys therein I find
That it excels all other bliss
    That earth affords or grows by kind:
Though much I want which most would have,   5
Yet still my mind forbids to crave.

No princely pomp, no wealthy store,
    No force to win the victory,
No wily wit to salve a sore,
    No shape to feed a loving eye;   10
To none of these I yield as thrall:
For why? My mind doth serve for all.

I see how plenty surfeits oft,
    And hasty climbers soon do fall;
I see that those which are aloft   15
    Mishap doth threaten most of all;
They get with toil, they keep with fear:
Such cares my mind could never bear.

Content to live, this is my stay;
    I seek no more than may suffice;   20
I press to bear no haughty sway;
    Look, what I lack my mind supplies:
Lo, thus I triumph like a king,
Content with that my mind doth bring.

Some have too much, yet still do crave;   25
    I little have, and seek no more.
They are but poor, though much they have,
    And I am rich with little store:
They poor, I rich; they beg, I give;
They lack, I leave; they pine, I live.   30

I laugh not at another's loss;
    I grudge not at another's pain;
No worldly waves my mind can toss;
    My state at one doth still remain:

I fear no foe, I fawn no friend; 35
I loathe not life, nor dread my end.

Some weigh their pleasure by their lust,
    Their wisdom by their rage of will;
Their treasure is their only trust;
    A cloaked craft their store of skill: 40
But all the pleasure that I find
Is to maintain a quiet mind.

My wealth is health and perfect ease;
    My conscience clear my chief defence;
I neither seek by bribes to please, 45
    Nor by deceit to breed offence:
Thus do I live; thus will I die;
Would all did so as well as I! (1588)

Prometheus When First from Heaven

Prometheus when first from heaven high
    He brought down fire, ere then on earth not seen,
    Fond of delight, a satyr, standing by,
    Gave it a kiss, as it like sweet had been.

Feeling forthwith the other burning power, 5
    Wood with the smart, with shouts and shrieking shrill
    He sought his ease in river, field, and bower,
    But for the time his grief went with him still.

So silly I, with that unwonted sight,
    In human shape an angel from above, 10
    Feeding mine eyes, the impression there did light,
    That since I run and rest as pleaseth love.
        The difference is, the satyr's lips, my heart,
        He for a while, I evermore, have smart. (1598)

⁊❦ NICHOLAS BRETON (1545?–1626?)

Come, Little Babe

Come, little babe, come, silly soul,
Thy father's shame, thy mother's grief,
Born as I doubt to all our dole,
And to thyself unhappy chief:
  Sing lullaby, and lap it warm,   5
  Poor soul that thinks no creature harm.

Thou little think'st and less dost know
The cause of this thy mother's moan;
Thou want'st the wit to wail her woe,
And I myself am all alone: 10
  Why dost thou weep? why dost thou wail?
  And know'st not yet what thou dost ail.

Come, little wretch—ah, silly heart!
Mine only joy, what can I more?
If there be any wrong thy smart,   15
That may the destinies implore:
  'Twas I, I say, against my will,
  I wail the time, but be thou still.

And dost thou smile? O, thy sweet face!
Would God Himself He might thee see!—   20
No doubt thou wouldst soon purchase grace,
I know right well, for thee and me:
  But come to mother, babe, and play,
  For father false is fled away.

Sweet boy, if it by fortune chance   25
Thy father home again to send,
If death do strike me with his lance,
Yet mayst thou me to him commend:
  If any ask thy mother's name,
  Tell how by love she purchased blame.   30

Then will his gentle heart soon yield:
I know him of a noble mind:
Although a lion in the field,
A lamb in town thou shalt him find:

70

Ask blessing, babe, be not afraid,   35
His sugar'd words hath me betray'd.

Then mayst thou joy and be right glad;
Although in woe I seem to moan,
Thy father is no rascal lad,
A noble youth of blood and bone: 40
    His glancing looks, if he once smile,
    Right honest women may beguile.

Come, little boy, and rock asleep;
Sing lullaby and be thou still;
I, that can do naught else but weep,   45
Will sit by thee and wail my fill:
    God bless my babe, and lullaby
    From this thy father's quality.   (*1593–1594*)

Say That I Should Say

Say that I should say I love ye,
    Would you say 'tis but a saying?
But if love in prayers move ye,
    Will you not be moved with praying?

Think I think that love should know ye,   5
    Will you think 'tis but a thinking?
But if love the thought do show ye,
    Will ye lose your eyes with winking?

Write that I do write you blessed,
    Will you write 'tis but a writing?   10
But if truth and love confess it,
    Will ye doubt the true inditing?

No: I say, and think, and write it,—
    Write, and think, and say your pleasure.
Love and truth and I indite it,   15
    You are blessed out of measure.   (*1600*)

EDMUND SPENSER (1552?–1599)

From *Amoretti*

34

Like as a ship that through the ocean wide
By conduct of some star doth make her way
Whenas a storm hath dimmed her trusty guide
Out of her course doth wander far astray,
So I whose star, that wont with her bright ray,
Me to direct, with clouds is overcast,
Do wander now in darkness and dismay,
Through hidden perils round about me plast.
Yet hope I well, that when this storm is past,
My Helice the lodestar of my life
Will shine again, and look on me at last,
With lovely light to clear my cloudy grief.
    Till then I wander careful comfortless,
    In secret sorrow and sad pensiveness.

55

So oft as I her beauty do behold,
And therewith do her cruelty compare,
I marvel of what substance was the mould
The which her made at once so cruel-fair.
Not earth; for her high thoughts more heavenly are:
Not water; for her love doth burn like fire:
Not air; for she is not so light or rare:
Not fire; for she doth freeze with faint desire.
Then needs another element inquire
Whereof she might be made; that is, the sky.
For to the heaven her haughty looks aspire,
And eke her love is pure immortal high.
    Then since to heaven ye likened are the best,
    Be like in mercy as in all the rest.

67

Like as a huntsman after weary chase,
Seeing the game from him escaped away,
Sits down to rest him in some shady place,
With panting hounds, beguiléd of their prey:

So, after long pursuit and vain assay,
When I all weary had the chase forsook,
The gentle deer return'd the self-same way,
Thinking to quench her thirst at the next brook.
There she, beholding me with milder look,
Sought not to fly, but fearless still did bide,
Till I in hand her yet half trembling took,
And with her own good-will her firmly tied.
    Strange thing, me seemed, to see a beast so wild
    So goodly won, with her own will beguiled.   (*1595*)

Prothalamion

Calm was the day, and through the trembling air
Sweet-breathing Zephyrus did softly play
A gentle spirit, that lightly did delay
Hot Titan's beams, which then did glister fair;
When I (whom sullen care,   5
Through discontent of my long fruitless stay
In prince's court, and expectation vain
Of idle hopes, which still do fly away,
Like empty shadows, did afflict my brain,)
Walk'd forth to ease my pain   10
Along the shore of silver streaming Thames;
Whose rutty ¹ bank, the which his river hems,
Was painted all with variable ² flowers,
And all the meads adorn'd with dainty gems,
Fit to deck maidens' bowers,   15
And crown their paramours,
Against the bridal day, which is not long:
    Sweet Thames! run softly, till I end my song.

There, in a meadow, by the river's side,
A flock of Nymphs I chancéd to espy,   20
All lovely daughters of the Flood thereby,
With goodly greenish locks, all loose untied,
As each had been a bride;
And each one had a little wicker basket,
Made of fine twigs, entailéd curiously,   25
In which they gather'd flowers to fill their flasket,³

¹ rooty   ² various   ³ a shallow basket

And with fine fingers cropt full feateously [4]
The tender stalks on high.
Of every sort, which in that meadow grew,
They gather'd some; the violet, pallid blue,   30
The little daisy, that at evening closes,
The virgin lily, and the primrose true,
With store of vermeil roses,
To deck their bridegrooms' posies
Against the bridal day, which was not long: 35
    Sweet Thames! run softly, till I end my song.

With that I saw two Swans of goodly hue
Come softly swimming down along the Lee;
Two fairer birds I yet did never see;
The snow, which doth the top of Pindus strew,   40
Did never whiter shew,
Nor Jove himself, when he a swan would be
For love of Leda, whiter did appear;
Yet Leda was (they say) as white as he,
Yet not so white as these, nor nothing near;   45
So purely white they were
That even the gentle stream, the which them bare,
Seem'd foul to them, and bade his billows spare
To wet their silken feathers, lest they might
Soil their fair plumes with water not so fair,   50
And mar their beauties bright,
That shone as heaven's light,
Against their bridal day, which was not long:
    Sweet Thames! run softly, till I end my song.

Eftsoons, the Nymphs, which now had flowers their fill,   55
Ran all in haste to see that silver brood,
As they came floating on the crystal flood;
Whom when they saw, they stood amazéd still,
Their wond'ring eyes to fill;
Them seem'd they never saw a sight so fair,   60
Of fowls, so lovely, that they sure did deem
Them heavenly born, or to be that same pair
Which through the sky draw Venus' silver team;
For sure they did not seem
To be begot of any earthly seed,   65
But rather angels, or of angels' breed;
Yet were they bred of Summer's heat, they say,

[4] neatly

In sweetest season, when each flower and weed
The earth did fresh array;
So fresh they seem'd as day,   70
Ev'n as their bridal day, which was not long:
    Sweet Thames! run softly, till I end my song.

Then forth they all out of their baskets drew
Great store of flowers, the honour of the field,
That to the sense did fragrant odours yield,   75
All which upon those goodly birds they threw,
And all the waves did strew,
That like old Peneus' waters they did seem,
When down along by pleasant Tempe's shore,
Scattered with flowers, through Thessaly they stream,   80
That they appear, through lilies' plenteous store,
Like a bride's chamber floor.
Two of those Nymphs, meanwhile, two garlands bound
Of freshest flowers which in that mead they found,
The which presenting all in trim array,   85
Their snowy foreheads therewithal they crown'd,
Whilst one did sing this lay,
Prepar'd against that day,
Against their bridal day, which was not long:
    Sweet Thames! run softly, till I end my song.   90

Ye gentle Birds! the world's fair ornament,
And heaven's glory, whom this happy hour
Doth lead unto your lovers' blissful bower,
Joy may you have, and gentle heart's content
Of your love's couplement;   95
And let fair Venus, that is Queen of Love,
With her heart-quelling son upon you smile,
Whose smile, they say, hath virtue to remove
All love's dislike, and friendship's faulty guile
For ever to assoil.[5]   100
Let endless peace your steadfast hearts accord
And blessed plenty wait upon your board;
And let your bed with pleasures chaste abound,
That fruitful issue may to you afford,
Which may your foes confound,   105
And make your joys redound
Upon your bridal day, which is not long:
    Sweet Thames! run softly, till I end my song.

[5] absolve

So ended she; and all the rest around
To her redoubled that her undersong,[6]   110
Which said, their bridal day should not be long:
And gentle Echo from the neighbour ground
Their accents did resound.
So forth those joyous Birds did pass along
Adown the Lee, that to them murmur'd low,   115
As he would speak, but that he lack'd a tongue,
Yet did by signs his glad affection show,
Making his stream run slow.
And all the fowl which in his flood did dwell
Gan flock about these twain, that did excel   120
The rest, so far as Cynthia doth shend [7]
The lesser stars. So they, enrangéd well,
Did on those two attend,
And their best service lend
Against their wedding day, which was not long: 125
    Sweet Thames! run softly, till I end my song.

At length they all to merry London came,
To merry London, my most kindly nurse,
That to me gave this life's first native source,
Though from another place I take my name,   130
An house of ancient fame:
There when they came, whereas those bricky towers [8]
The which on Thames' broad aged back do ride,
Where now the studious lawyers have their bowers,
There whilome wont the Templar Knights to bide,   135
Till they decay'd through pride;
Next whereunto there stands a stately place,[9]
Where oft I gainéd gifts and goodly grace
Of that great lord, which therein wont to dwell,
Whose want too well now feels my friendless case;   140
But ah! here fits not well
Old woes, but joys, to tell
Against the bridal day, which is not long:
    Sweet Thames! run softly, till I end my song.

Yet therein now doth lodge a noble peer,[10]   145
Great England's glory, and the world's wide wonder,
Whose dreadful name late through all Spain did thunder,

---

[6] echo   [7] surpass   [8] the Temple
[9] Leicester House   [10] Essex

And Hercules' two pillars standing near
Did make to quake and fear:
Fair branch of honour, flower of chivalry!   150
That fillest England with thy triumph's fame,
Joy have thou of thy noble victory,
And endless happiness of thine own name
That promiseth the same;
That through thy prowess, and victorious arms,   155
Thy country may be freed from foreign harms,
And great Eliza's glorious name may ring
Through all the world, fill'd with thy wide alarms,
Which some brave Muse may sing
To ages following,   160
Upon the bridal day, which is not long:
    Sweet Thames! run softly, till I end my song.

From those high towers this noble lord issuing,
Like radiant Hesper, when his golden hair
In th' ocean billows he hath bathéd fair,   165
Descended to the river's open viewing,
With a great train ensuing.
Above the rest were goodly to be seen
Two gentle Knights of lovely face and feature,
Beseeming well the bower of any queen,   170
With gifts of wit, and ornaments of nature,
Fit for so goodly stature,
That like the twins of Jove [11] they seem'd in sight,
Which deck the baldric of the heavens bright;
They two, forth pacing to the river's side,   175
Receiv'd those two fair Brides, their love's delight;
Which at th' appointed tide,
Each one did make his bride,
Against their bridal day, which is not long:
    Sweet Thames! run softly, till I end my song.   (1596)

[11] Castor and Pollux

The Passionate Man's Pilgrimage

Give me my scallop-shell of quiet;
My staff of faith to walk upon;
My scrip of joy, immortal diet;
My bottle of salvation;
My gown of glory, hope's true gage;   5
And thus I'll take my pilgrimage.
Blood must be my body's balmer—
No other balm will there be given—
Whilst my soul, like a white palmer,
Travels to the land of Heaven;   10
Over the silver mountains,
Where spring the nectar fountains,—
And there I'll kiss
The bowl of bliss,
And drink my eternal fill   15
On ever milken hill:
My soul will be a-dry before,
But after it will ne'er thirst more.
And by the happy blissful way,
More peaceful pilgrims I shall see,   20
That have shook off their gowns of clay,
And go apparelled fresh like me:
I'll bring them first
To slake their thirst,
And then to taste those nectar suckets,   25
At the clear wells
Where sweetness dwells,
Drawn up by saints in crystal buckets.
And when our bottles and all we
Are filled with immortality,   30
Then the holy paths we'll travel,
Strewed with rubies thick as gravel.
Ceilings of diamonds, sapphire floors,
High walls of coral, and pearl bowers.
From thence to Heaven's bribeless hall,   35
Where no corrupted voices brawl;
No conscience molten into gold;

Nor forged accusers bought and sold;
No cause deferred; nor vain-spent journey;
For there Christ is the King's Attorney,　　　　　　　40
Who pleads for all without degrees,
And he hath angels, but no fees.
When the grand twelve million jury
Of our sins and sinful fury,
'Gainst our souls black verdicts give,　　　　　　　45
Christ pleads his death, and then we live.
Be thou my speaker, taintless Pleader,
Unblotted Lawyer, true Proceeder!
Thou movest salvation even for alms,
Not with a bribed lawyer's palms.　　　　　　　　50
And this is my eternal plea
To him that made heaven, earth, and sea.
Seeing my flesh must die so soon,
And want a head to dine next noon,—
Just at the stroke, when my veins start and spread,　　55
Set on my soul an everlasting head:
Then am I ready, like a palmer fit,
To tread those blest paths which before I writ.　　(1604)

The Lie

Go, Soul, the body's guest,
Upon a thankless arrant:
Fear not to touch the best;
The truth shall be thy warrant:
Go, since I needs must die,　　　　　5
And give the world the lie.

Say to the court, it glows
And shines like rotten wood;
Say to the church, it shows
What's good, and doth no good:　　　10
If church and court reply,
Then give them both the lie.

Tell potentates, they live
Acting by others' action;

Not loved unless they give,   15
Not strong but by a faction:
If potentates reply,
Give potentates the lie.

Tell men of high condition,
That manage the estate,   20
Their purpose is ambition,
Their practice only hate:
And if they once reply,
Then give them all the lie.

Tell them that brave it most,   25
They beg for more by spending,
Who, in their greatest cost,
Seek nothing but commending:
And if they make reply,
Then give them all the lie.   30

Tell zeal it wants devotion;
Tell love it is but lust:
Tell time it is but motion;
Tell flesh it is but dust:
And wish them not reply,   35
For thou must give the lie.

Tell age it daily wasteth;
Tell honour how it alters;
Tell beauty how she blasteth;
Tell favour how it falters: 40
And as they shall reply,
Give every one the lie.

Tell wit how much it wrangles
In tickle ¹ points of niceness;
Tell wisdom she entangles   45
Herself in over-wiseness:
And when they do reply,
Straight give them both the lie.

Tell physic of her boldness;
Tell skill it is pretension;   50
Tell charity of coldness;
Tell law it is contention:

¹ delicate

And as they do reply,
So give them still the lie.

Tell fortune of her blindness;   55
Tell nature of decay;
Tell friendship of unkindness;
Tell justice of delay:
And if they will reply,
Then give them all the lie.   60

Tell arts they have no soundness,
But vary by esteeming;
Tell schools they want profoundness,
And stand too much on seeming:
If arts and schools reply,   65
Give arts and schools the lie.

Tell faith it's fled the city;
Tell how the country erreth;
Tell manhood shakes off pity
And virtue least preferreth: 70
And if they do reply,
Spare not to give the lie.

So when thou hast, as I
Commanded thee, done blabbing
—Although to give the lie   75
Deserves no less than stabbing—
Stab at thee he that will,
No stab the soul can kill.   (1608)

To His Son

Three things there be that prosper all apace,
    And flourish while they are asunder far;
But on a day, they meet all in a place,
    And when they meet, they one another mar.

And they be these: the Wood, the Weed, the Wag.
    The Wood is that that makes the gallows tree;
The Weed is that that strings the hangman's bag;
    The Wag, my pretty knave, betokens thee.

Now mark, dear boy—while these assemble not,
    Green springs the tree, hemp grows, the wag is wild;
But when they meet, it makes the timber rot,
    It frets the halter, and it chokes the child.

God bless the Child!   *(1618?)*

What Is Our Life? [1]

What is our life? a play of passion;
Our mirth, the music of division; [2]
Our mothers' wombs the tiring-houses [3] be
Where we are dressed for this short comedy.
Heaven the judicious sharp spectator is,   5
That sits and marks still [4] who doth act amiss;
Our graves that hide us from the searching sun
Are like drawn curtains when the play is done.
Thus march we playing to our latest rest;
Only we die in earnest—that's no jest.   10

Verses

WRITTEN THE NIGHT BEFORE HIS EXECUTION

Even such is time, that takes in trust
Our youth, our joys, our all we have,
And pays us but with age and dust;
Who in the dark and silent grave,
When we have wandered all our ways,   5
Shuts up the story of our days:
But from this earth, this grave, this dust,
My God shall raise me up, I trust.   *(1618)*

[1] Set to music by Orlando Gibbons, 1612.   [2] variations on a theme   [3] dressing rooms   [4] constantly

FULKE GREVILLE (1554–1628)

From *Caelica*

87

When as man's life, the light of human lust,
In socket of his earthly lanthorne burns,
That all this glory unto ashes must,
And generation to corruption turns—
    Then fond desires that only fear their end,
    Do vainly wish for life, but to amend.

But when this life is from the body fled,
To see itself in that *eternal glass,*
Where time doth end, and thoughts accuse the dead,
Where all to come is one with all that was;
    Then living men ask how he left his breath,
    That while he lived never thought of death.

99

Downe in the depth of mine iniquity,
That ugly center of infernall spirits;
Where each sinne feeles her owne deformity,
In these peculiar torments she inherits,
    Depriv'd of humane graces, and divine,   5
    Even there appeares this *saving God* of mine.

And in this fatall mirrour of transgression,
Shewes man as fruit of his degeneration,
The errours ugly infinite impression,
Which beares the faithlesse downe to desperation;   10
    Depriv'd of humane graces and divine,
    Even there appeares this *saving God* of mine.

In power and truth, Almighty and eternall,
Which on the sinne reflects strange desolation,
With glory scourging all the Sprites infernall,   15
And uncreated hell with unprivation;
    Depriv'd of humane graces, not divine,
    Even there appeares this *saving God* of mine.

For on this sp'rituall Crosse condemned lying,
To paines infernall by eternal doome,   20
I see my Saviour for the same sinnes dying,
And from that hell I fear'd, to free me, come;
  Depriv'd of humane graces, not divine,
  Thus hath his death rais'd up this soule of mine.

Chorus from *Mustapha*

Oh wearisome condition of humanity!
Born under one law, to another bound,
Vainly begot, and yet forbidden vanity,
Created sick, commanded to be sound.
What meaneth Nature by these diverse laws?   5
Passion and reason self-division cause.
Is it the mark or majesty of Power
To make offences that it may forgive?
Nature herself doth her own self deflower,
To hate those errors she herself doth give.   10
For how should man think that he may not do
If Nature did not fail and punish too?
Tyrant to others, to herself unjust,
Only commands things difficult and hard;
Forbids us all things which it knows we lust,   15
Makes easy pains, unpossible reward.
If Nature did not take delight in blood
She would have made more easy ways to good.
We that are bound by vows and by promotion,
With pomp of holy sacrifice and rites,   20
To preach belief in God and stir devotion,
To preach of heaven's wonders and delights.
Yet when each of us in his own heart looks
He finds the God there far unlike his books.   (*1609*)

ఆ PHILIP SIDNEY (1554–1586)

From *Astrophel and Stella*

1

Loving in truth, and fain in verse my love to show,
That she, dear she, might take some pleasure of my pain,
Pleasure might cause her read, reading might make her know,
Knowledge might pity win, and pity grace obtain,—
I sought fit words to paint the blackest face of woe;
Studying inventions fine, her wits to entertain,
Oft turning others' leaves to see if thence would flow
Some fresh and fruitful showers upon my sun-burned brain.
But words came halting forth, wanting invention's stay;
Invention, nature's child, fled step-dame Study's blows,
And others' feet still seemed but strangers in my way.
Thus, great with child to speak, and helpless in my throes,
    Biting my truant pen, beating myself for spite,
    Fool, said my muse to me, look in thy heart and write.

31

With how sad steps, O Moon! thou climb'st the skies!
How silently, and with how wan a face!
What! may it be, that even in heavenly place
That busy archer his sharp arrows tries?
Sure, if that long-with-love-acquainted eyes
Can judge of love, thou feel'st a lover's case;
I read it in thy looks; thy languish'd grace,
To me that feel the like, thy state descries.
Then, even of fellowship, O Moon, tell me,
Is constant love deem'd there but want of wit?
Are beauties there as proud as here they be?
Do they above love to be loved, and yet
    Those lovers scorn whom that love doth possess?
    Do they call virtue there ungratefulness?

39

Come, Sleep! O Sleep, the certain knot of peace,
The baiting-place of wit, the balm of woe,
The poor man's wealth, the prisoner's release,
The indifferent judge between the high and low;

With shield of proof shield me from out the prease
Of those fierce darts Despair at me doth throw:
Oh, make in me those civil wars to cease;
I will good tribute pay, if thou do so.
Take thou of me smooth pillows, sweetest bed,
A chamber deaf to noise and blind to light,
A rosy garland and a weary head:
And if these things, as being thine by right,
    Move not thy heavy grace, thou shalt in me,
    Livelier than elsewhere, Stella's image see.   (*1591*)

A Litany

Ring out your bells, let mourning shows be spread;
For Love is dead.
    All Love is dead, infected
With plague of deep disdain;
    Worth, as nought worth, rejected,   5
And Faith fair scorn doth gain.
    From so ungrateful fancy,
    From such a female franzy,
        From them that use men thus,
        Good Lord, deliver us!   10

Weep, neighbors, weep! do you not hear it said
That Love is dead?
    His death-bed, peacock's folly;
His winding-sheet is shame;
    His will, false-seeming holy;   15
His sole executor, blame.
    From so ungrateful fancy,
    From such a female franzy,
        From them that use men thus,
        Good Lord, deliver us!   20

Let dirge be sung and trentals rightly read,
For Love is dead.
    Sir Wrong his tomb ordaineth
My mistress Marble-heart,
    Which epitaph containeth,   25
"Her eyes were once his dart."

From so ungrateful fancy,
From such a female franzy,
   From them that use men thus,
   Good Lord, deliver us!   30

Alas! I lie, rage hath this error bred;
Love is not dead.
   Love is not dead, but sleepeth
In her unmatchèd mind,
   Where she his counsel keepeth,   35
Till due desert she find.
   Therefore from so vile fancy,
   To call such wit a franzy,
      Who love can temper thus,
      Good Lord, deliver us.   (1598)

Leave Me, O Love

Leave me, O love which reachest but to dust;
And thou, my mind, aspire to higher things;
Grow rich in that which never taketh rust,
Whatever fades but fading pleasure brings.
Draw in thy beams, and humble all thy might
To that sweet yoke where lasting freedoms be;
Which breaks the clouds and opens forth the light,
That doth both shine and give us sight to see.
O take fast hold; let that light be thy guide
In this small course which birth draws out to death,
And think how evil becometh him to slide,
Who seeketh heav'n, and comes of heav'nly breath.
Then farewell, world; thy uttermost I see;
Eternal Love, maintain thy life in me.   (1598)

THOMAS LODGE (1557-8–1625)

Rosalind

Like to the clear in highest sphere
   Where all imperial glory shines,
Of selfsame colour is her hair
   Whether unfolded, or in twines:
      Heigh ho, fair Rosalind!   5
Her eyes are sapphires set in snow,
   Refining heaven by every wink;
The Gods do fear whenas they glow,
   And I do tremble when I think
      Heigh ho, would she were mine!   10

Her cheeks are like the blushing cloud
   That beautifies Aurora's face,
Or like the silver crimson shroud
   That Phoebus' smiling looks doth grace;
      Heigh ho, fair Rosalind!   15
Her lips are like two budded roses
   Whom ranks of lilies neighbour nigh,
Within which bounds she balm encloses
   Apt to entice a deity:
      Heigh ho, would she were mine!   20

Her neck is like a stately tower
   Where Love himself imprison'd lies,
To watch for glances every hour
   From her divine and sacred eyes:
      Heigh ho, for Rosalind!   25
Her paps are centres of delight,
   Her breasts are orbs of heavenly frame,
Where Nature moulds the dew of light
   To feed perfection with the same:
      Heigh ho, would she were mine!   30

With orient pearl, with ruby red,
   With marble white, with sapphire blue
Her body every way is fed,
   Yet soft in touch and sweet in view:
      Heigh ho, fair Rosalind!   35

Nature herself her shape admires;
    The Gods are wounded in her sight;
And Love forsakes his heavenly fires
    And at her eyes his brand doth light:
        Heigh ho, would she were mine!   40

Then muse not, Nymphs, though I bemoan
    The absence of fair Rosalind,
Since for a fair there's fairer none,
    Nor for her virtues so divine:
        Heigh ho, fair Rosalind;   45
Heigh ho, my heart! would God that she were mine!

            (1592)

Rosalind's Madrigal

Love in my bosom like a bee
    Doth suck his sweet;
Now with his wings he plays with me,
    Now with his feet.
Within mine eyes he makes his nest,   5
His bed amidst my tender breast,
My kisses are his daily feast,
And yet he robs me of my rest—
    Ah, wanton, will ye?

And if I sleep, then percheth he   10
    With pretty flight,
And makes his pillow of my knee
    The livelong night.
Strike I my lute, he tunes the string,
He music plays if so I sing,   15
He lends me every lovely thing,
Yet cruel he my heart doth sting—
    Whist, wanton, still ye!

Else I with roses every day
    Will whip you hence,   20
And bind you, when you long to play,
    For your offence.
I'll shut mine eyes to keep you in,

I'll make you fast it for your sin,
I'll count your power not worth a pin; 25
Alas! what hereby shall I win
    If he gainsay me?

What if I beat the wanton boy
    With many a rod?
He will repay me with annoy, 30
    Because a god.
Then sit thou safely on my knee,
And let thy bower my bosom be,
Lurk in mine eyes, I like of thee,
O Cupid, so thou pity me, 35
    Spare not, but play thee!   (1592)

Accurst Be Love!

Accurst be Love, and those that trust his trains!
He tastes the fruit whilst others toil;
He brings the lamp, we lend the oil;
He sows distress, we yield him soil;
He wageth war, we bide the foil. 5

Accurst be Love, and those that trust his trains!
He lays the trap, we seek the snare;
He threat'neth death, we speak him fair;
He coins deceits, we foster care;
He favoureth pride, we count it rare. 10

Accurst be Love, and those that trust his trains!
He seemeth blind, yet wounds with art;
He vows content, he pays with smart;
He swears relief, yet kills the heart;
He calls for truth, yet scorns desart. 15
Accurst be Love, and those that trust his trains!
Whose heaven is hell, whose perfect joys are pains.   (1593)

GEORGE PEELE (1557?–1596)

From *Polyhymnia*

His [1] golden locks time hath to silver turned;
O time too swift, O swiftness never ceasing!
His youth 'gainst time and age hath ever spurned,
But spurned in vain; youth waneth by increasing:
Beauty, strength, youth, are flowers but fading seen; 5
Duty, faith, love, are roots, and ever green.

His helmet now shall make a hive for bees;
And, lovers' sonnets turned to holy psalms,
A man-at-arms must now serve on his knees,
And feed on prayers, which are age his alms: 10
But though from court to cottage he depart,
His saint is sure of his unspotted heart.

And when he saddest sits in homely cell,
He'll teach his swains this carol for a song,—
"Blest be the hearts that wish my sovereign well, 15
Curst be the souls that think her any wrong."
Goddess, allow this aged man his right,
To be your beadsman now that was your knight. (*1590*)

---

[1] Sir Henry Lee (1530–1610)

✄ CHIDIOCK TICHBORNE (1558?–1586)

His Elegy

WRITTEN BEFORE HIS EXECUTION

My prime of youth is but a frost of cares;
    My feast of joy is but a dish of pain;
My crop of corn is but a field of tares;
    And all my good is but vain hope of gain:
The day is past, and yet I saw no sun;   5
And now I live, and now my life is done.

My tale was heard, and yet it was not told;
    My fruit is fall'n, and yet my leaves are green;
My youth is spent, and yet I am not old;
    I saw the world, and yet I was not seen: 10
My thread is cut, and yet it is not spun;
And now I live, and now my life is done.

I sought my death, and found it in my womb;
    I looked for life, and saw it was a shade;
I trod the earth, and knew it was my tomb;   15
    And now I die, and now I was but made:
My glass is full, and now my glass is run;
And now I live, and now my life is done.   (*1586*)

ROBERT GREENE (1560?–1592)

Sephastia's Song to Her Child

Weep not, my wanton, smile upon my knee;
When thou art old there's grief enough for thee.
 Mother's wag, pretty boy,
 Father's sorrow, father's joy.
 When thy father first did see   5
 Such a boy by him and me,
 He was glad, I was woe:
 Fortune changèd made him so,
 When he left his pretty boy,
 Last his sorrow, first his joy.   10

Weep not, my wanton, smile upon my knee;
When thou art old there's grief enough for thee.
 Streaming tears that never stint,
 Like pearl drops from a flint,
 Fell by course from his eyes,   15
 That one another's place supplies:
 Thus he grieved in every part,
 Tears of blood fell from his heart,
 When he left his pretty boy,
 Father's sorrow, father's joy.   20

Weep not, my wanton, smile upon my knee;
When thou art old there's grief enough for thee.
 The wanton smiled, father wept;
 Mother cried, baby lept;
 More he crowed, more we cried;   25
 Nature could not sorrow hide.
 He must go, he must kiss
 Child and mother, baby bliss;
 For he left his pretty boy,
 Father's sorrow, father's joy.   30

Weep not, my wanton, smile upon my knee;
When thou art old there's grief enough for thee. (1590)

ROBERT SOUTHWELL (1561?–1595)

The Burning Babe

As I in hoary winter's night stood shivering in the snow,
Surprised I was with sudden heat, which made my heart to glow;
And lifting up a fearful eye to view what fire was near,
A pretty Babe all burning bright, did in the air appear,
Who scorched with excessive heat, such floods of tears did shed,   5
As though His floods should quench His flames which with His tears
    were fed;
Alas! quoth He, but newly born, in fiery heats I fry,
Yet none approach to warm their hearts or feel my fire but I!
My faultless breast the furnace is, the fuel wounding thorns,
Love is the fire, and sighs the smoke, the ashes shame and scorns;   10
The fuel Justice layeth on, and Mercy blows the coals,
The metal in this furnace wrought are men's defiled souls,
For which, as now on fire I am to work them to their good,
So will I melt into a bath to wash them in My blood:
With this He vanished out of sight, and swiftly shrank away,   15
And straight I called unto mind that it was Christmas-day.

(c. 1605)

94

❧ FRANCIS BACON (1561–1626)

In Vitam Humanam [1]

The world's a bubble, and the life of man
 Less than a span:
In his conception wretched, from the womb
 So to the tomb;
Curst from his cradle, and brought up to years   5
 With cares and fears.
Who then to frail mortality shall trust,
But limns on water, or but writes in dust.

Yet since with sorrow here we live oppressed,
 What life is best?   10
Courts are but only superficial schools
 To dandle fools:
The rural parts are turned into a den
 Of savage men:
And where's a city from all vice so free,   15
But may be termed the worst of all the three?

Domestic cares afflict the husband's bed,
 Or pains his head:
Those that live single, take it for a curse,
 Or do things worse: 20
Some would have children; those that have them, moan
 Or wish them gone:
What is it, then, to have, or have no wife,
But single thraldom, or a double strife?

Our own affections still at home to please   25
 Is a disease:
To cross the seas to any foreign soil,
 Perils and toil:
Wars with their noise affraight; when they cease,
 We're worse in peace;—   30
What then remains, but that we still should cry
Not to be born, or, being born, to die?   (1629)

---

[1] Against Human Life

From *Delia*

30

My cares draw on mine everlasting night,
In horror's sable clouds sets my live's sun;
My live's sweet sun, my dearest comfort's light,
Will rise no more to me, whose day is done.
I go before unto the myrtle shades,
To attend the presence of my world's dear,
And there prepare her flowers that never fades,
And all things fit against her coming there.
If any ask me why so soon I came,
I'll hide her sin, and say it was my lot;
In life and death I'll tender her good name,
My life nor death shall never be her blot.
Although this world may seem her deed to blame,
The Elysian ghosts shall never know the same.

54

Care-charmer Sleep, son of the sable Night,
Brother to Death, in silent darkness born,
Relieve my languish, and restore the light,
With dark forgetting of my cares return.
And let the day be time enough to mourn
The shipwreck of my ill-adventured youth;
Let waking eyes suffice to wail their scorn,
Without the torment of the night's untruth.
Cease, dreams, the images of day-desires,
To model forth the passions of the morrow;
Never let rising sun approve you liars,
To add more grief to aggravate my sorrow.
Still let me sleep, embracing clouds in vain;
And never wake to feel the day's disdain.   (*1594*)

Are They Shadows That We See?

Are they shadows that we see?
 And can shadows pleasure give?
Pleasures only shadows be,
 Cast by bodies we conceive,
And are made the things we deem   5
In those figures which they seem.

But these pleasures vanish fast
 Which by shadows are expressed:
Pleasures are not, if they last,—
 In their passing is their best: 10
Glory is most bright and gay
In a flash, and so away.

Feed apace, then, greedy eyes,
 On the wonder you behold;
Take it sudden as it flies,   15
 Though you take it not to hold:
When your eyes have done their part,
Thought must length it in the heart. *(1610)*

Love Is a Sickness

Love is a sickness full of woes,
 All remedies refusing;
A plant that with most cutting grows,
 Most barren with best using.
   Why so?   5
More we enjoy it, more it dies;
If not enjoyed, it sighing cries
   Heigh ho!

Love is a torment of the mind,
 A tempest everlasting;   10
And Jove hath made it of a kind
 Not well, nor full, nor fasting.
   Why so?
More we enjoy it, more it dies;
If not enjoyed, it sighing cries   15
   Heigh ho! *(1615)*

❧ MICHAEL DRAYTON (1563–1631)

From *Idea*

Sonnet 37

Dear, why should you command me to my rest,
When now the night doth summon all to sleep?
Methinks this time becometh lovers best;
Night was ordained together friends to keep.
How happy are all other living things,
Which though the day disjoin by several flight,
The quiet evening yet together brings,
And each returns unto his love at night!
Oh thou that art so courteous else to all,
Why shouldst thou, Night, abuse me only thus,
That every creature to his bind dost call,
And yet 'tis thou dost only sever us?
Well could I wish it would be ever day,
If when night comes you bid me go away.   (*1602*)

Sonnet 61

Since there's no help, come let us kiss and part;
Nay, I have done, you get no more of me;
And I am glad, yea, glad with all my heart,
That thus so cleanly I myself can free.
Shake hands for ever, cancel all our vows,
And when we meet at any time again,
Be it not seen in either of our brows
That we one jot of former love retain.
Now at the last gasp of love's latest breath,
When, his pulse failing, passion speechless lies,
When faith is kneeling by his bed of death,
And innocence is closing up his eyes,
Now if thou wouldst, when all have given him over,
From death to life thou might'st him yet recover.   (*1619*)

MARK ALEXANDER BOYD (1563–1601)

Fra Bank to Bank

Fra bank to bank, fra wood to wood I rin,
    Ourhailit [1] with my feeble fantasie;
    Like til a leaf that fallis from a tree,
Or til a reed ourblawin with the win'.
Twa gods guides me; the ane of them is blin',
    Yea and a bairn brocht up in vanitie;
    The next a wife ingenrit [2] of the sea,
And lichter nor a dauphin [3] with her fin.

Unhappy is the man for evermair
    That tills the sand and sawis [4] in the air;
    But twice unhappier is he, I lairn,
That feedis in his hairt a mad desire,
And follows on a woman throw the fire,
    Led by a blind and teachit [5] by a bairn.

[1] moved, blown   [2] engendered   [3] dolphin   [4] sows   [5] taught

CHRISTOPHER MARLOWE (1564–1593)

The Passionate Shepherd to His Love

Come live with me and be my love,
And we will all the pleasures prove
That hills and valleys, dale and field,
And all the craggy mountains yield!

There will we sit upon the rocks   5
And see the shepherds feed their flocks,
By shallow rivers, to whose falls
Melodious birds sing madrigals.

There will I make thee beds of roses
With a thousand fragrant posies;   10
A cap of flowers, and a kirtle
Embroider'd all with leaves of myrtle;

A gown made of the finest wool
Which from our pretty lambs we pull;
Fair lined slippers for the cold,   15
With buckles of the purest gold;

A belt of straw and ivy buds,
With coral clasps and amber studs:
And if these pleasures may thee move,
Come live with me and be my love!   20

Thy silver dishes, for thy meat
As precious as the gods do eat,
Shall on an ivory table be
Prepared each day for thee and me.

The shepherd swains shall dance and sing   25
For thy delight each May morning.
If these delights thy mind may move,
Then live with me and be my love!   (1600)

❧ WILLIAM SHAKESPEARE (1564–1616)

From *The Sonnets*

18

Shall I compare thee to a summer's day?
Thou art more lovely and more temperate:
Rough winds do shake the darling buds of May,
And summer's lease hath all too short a date:
Sometime too hot the eye of heaven shines,
And often is his gold complexion dimm'd;
And every fair from fair sometime declines,
By chance or nature's changing course untrimm'd:
But thy eternal summer shall not fade
Nor lose possession of that fair thou ow'st,
Nor shall Death brag thou wand'rest in his shade,
When in eternal lines to time thou grow'st;
 So long as men can breathe or eyes can see,
 So long lives this and this gives life to thee.

29

When, in disgrace with fortune and men's eyes,
I all alone beweep my outcast state
And trouble deaf heaven with my bootless cries
And look upon myself and curse my fate,
Wishing me like to one more rich in hope,
Featured like him, like him with friends possess'd,
Desiring this man's art and that man's scope,
With what I most enjoy contented least;
Yet in these thoughts myself almost despising
Haply I think on thee, and then my state,
Like to the lark at break of day arising
From sullen earth, sings hymns at heaven's gate;
 For thy sweet love remember'd such wealth brings
 That then I scorn to change my state with kings.

30

When to the sessions of sweet silent thought
I summon up remembrance of things past,
I sigh the lack of many a thing I sought,
And with old woes new wail my dear time's waste:

Then can I drown an eye, unus'd to flow,
For precious friends hid in death's dateless night,
And weep afresh love's long since cancell'd woe,
And moan the expense of many a vanish'd sight:
Then can I grieve at grievances foregone,
And heavily from woe to woe tell o'er
The sad account of fore-bemoaned moan,
Which I new pay as if not paid before.
　　But if the while I think on thee, dear friend,
　　All losses are restor'd and sorrows end.

64

When I have seen by Time's fell hand defaced
The rich proud cost of outworn buried age;
When sometime lofty towers I see down-razed,
And brass eternal slave to mortal rage:
When I have seen the hungry ocean gain
Advantage on the kingdom of the shore,
And the firm soil win of the watery main,
Increasing store with loss and loss with store:
When I have seen such interchange of state,
Or state itself confounded to decay;
Ruin hath taught me thus to ruminate—
That Time will come and take my love away.
　　This thought is as a death, which cannot choose
　　But weep to have that which it fears to lose.

65

Since brass, nor stone, nor earth, nor boundless sea,
But sad mortality o'er-sways their power,
How with this rage shall beauty hold a plea,
Whose action is no stronger than a flower?
O how shall summer's honey breath hold out
Against the wrackful siege of batt'ring days,
When rocks impregnable are not so stout,
Nor gates of steel so strong, but Time decays?
O fearful meditation! where, alack,
Shall Time's best jewel from Time's chest lie hid?
Or what strong hand can hold his swift foot back?
Or who his spoil of beauty can forbid?
　　O, none, unless this miracle have might,
　　That in black ink my love may still shine bright.

66

Tir'd with all these, for restful death I cry:
As to behold desert a beggar born,
And needy nothing trimm'd in jollity,
And purest faith unhappily forsworn,
And gilded honour shamefully misplac'd,
And maiden virtue rudely strumpeted,
And right perfection wrongfully disgrac'd,
And strength by limping sway disabled,
And art made tongue-tied by authority,
And folly, doctor-like, controlling skill,
And simple truth miscall'd simplicity,
And captive good attending captain ill:
 Tir'd with all these, from these would I be gone,
 Save that to die, I leave my love alone.

71

No longer mourn for me when I am dead
Than you shall hear the surly sullen bell
Give warning to the world that I am fled
From this vile world with vilest worms to dwell.
Nay, if you read this line, remember not
The hand that writ it, for I love you so
That I in your sweet thoughts would be forgot
If thinking on me then should make you woe.
O if, I say, you look upon this verse
When I perhaps compounded am with clay,
Do not so much as my poor name rehearse,
But let your love even with my life decay,
 Lest the wise world·should look into your moan
 And mock you with me after I am gone.

73

That time of year thou mayst in me behold
When yellow leaves, or none, or few, do hang
Upon those boughs which shake against the cold,
Bare ruin'd choirs, where late the sweet birds sang:
In me thou seest the twilight of such day
As after sunset fadeth in the west;
Which by and by black night doth take away,
Death's second self, that seals up all in rest:

In me thou seest the glowing of such fire
That on the ashes of his youth doth lie,
As the death-bed whereon it must expire,
Consumed with that which it was nourish'd by.
This thou perceiv'st, which makes thy love more strong,
To love that well which thou must leave ere long.

94

They that have power to hurt and will do none,
That do not do the thing they most do show,
Who, moving others, are themselves as stone,
Unmovéd, cold, and to temptation slow,—
They rightly do inherit heaven's graces
And husband nature's riches from expense;
They are the lords and owners of their faces,
Others but stewards of their excellence.
The summer's flower is to the summer sweet,
Though to itself it only live and die:
But if that flower with base infection meet,
The basest weed outbraves his dignity:
For sweetest things turn sourest by their deeds;
Lilies that fester smell far worse than weeds.

104

To me, fair friend, you never can be old,
For as you were when first your eye I ey'd,
Such seems your beauty still. Three winters cold
Have from the forests shook three summers' pride,
Three beauteous springs to yellow autumn turn'd
In process of the seasons have I seen,
Three April perfumes in three hot Junes burn'd,
Since first I saw you fresh, which yet are green.
Ah! yet doth beauty, like a dial-hand,
Steal from his figure and no pace perceiv'd;
So your sweet hue, which methinks still doth stand,
Hath motion, and mine eye may be deceiv'd:
For fear of which, hear this, thou age unbred:
Ere you were born was beauty's summer dead.

106

When in the chronicle of wasted time
I see descriptions of the fairest wights,
And beauty making beautiful old rhyme,

In praise of ladies dead and lovely knights,
Then, in the blazon of sweet beauty's best,
Of hand, of foot, of lip, of eye, of brow,
I see their antique pen would have expressed
Even such a beauty as you master now.
So all their praises are but prophecies
Of this our time, all you prefiguring;
And, for they looked but with divining eyes,
They had not skill enough your worth to sing:
 For we, which now behold these present days,
 Have eyes to wonder, but lack tongues to praise.

107

Not mine own fears, nor the prophetic soul
Of the wide world dreaming on things to come,
Can yet the lease of my true love control,
Supposed as forfeit to a confined doom.
The mortal moon hath her eclipse endured,
And the sad augurs mock their own presage;
Incertainties now crown themselves assured,
And peace proclaims olives of endless age.
Now with the drops of this most balmy time
My love looks fresh, and Death to me subscribes,
Since, spite of him, I'll live in this poor rhyme,
While he insults o'er dull and speechless tribes.
 And thou in this shalt find thy monument,
 When tyrants' crests and tombs of brass are spent.

116

Let me not to the marriage of true minds
Admit impediments. Love is not love
Which alters when it alteration finds,
Or bends with the remover to remove.
O no, it is an ever-fixed mark
That looks on tempests and is never shaken;
It is the star to every wand'ring bark,
Whose worth's unknown, although his height be taken.
Love's not Time's fool, though rosy lips and cheeks
Within his bending sickle's compass come;
Love alters not with his brief hours and weeks,
But bears it out even to the edge of doom.
 If this be error and upon me proved,
 I never writ, nor no man ever loved.

129

The expense of spirit in a waste of shame
Is lust in action; and till action, lust
Is perjur'd, murd'rous, bloody, full of blame,
Savage, extreme, rude, cruel, not to trust:
Enjoy'd no sooner but despised straight,
Past reason hunted, and no sooner had,
Past reason hated, as a swallowed bait
On purpose laid to make the taker mad;
Mad in pursuit and in possession so;
Had, having, and in quest to have, extreme;
A bliss in proof, and prov'd, a very woe;
Before, a joy propos'd; behind a dream.
    All this the world well knows; yet none knows well
    To shun the heaven that leads men to this hell.

130

My mistress' eyes are nothing like the sun;
Coral is far more red than her lips' red;
If snow be white, why then her breasts are dun;
If hairs be wires, black wires grow on her head.
I have seen roses damask'd, red and white,
But no such roses see I in her cheeks;
And in some perfumes is there more delight
Than in the breath that from my mistress reeks.
I love to hear her speak, yet well I know
That music hath a far more pleasing sound;
I grant I never saw a goddess go;
My mistress, when she walks, treads on the ground:
    And yet, by heaven, I think my love as rare
    As any she belied with false compare.

146

Poor soul, the centre of my sinful earth,
Thrall to these rebel powers that thee array,
Why dost thou pine within and suffer dearth,
Painting thy outward walls so costly gay?
Why so large cost, having so short a lease,
Dost thou upon thy fading mansion spend?
Shall worms, inheritors of this excess,
Eat up thy charge? Is this thy body's end?
Then, soul, live thou upon thy servant's loss,

And let that pine to aggravate thy store;
Buy terms divine in selling hours of dross
Within be fed, without be rich no more:
 So shalt thou feed on Death, that feeds on men,
 And Death once dead, there's no more dying then.   (1609)

Songs from the Plays

from TWO GENTLEMEN OF VERONA

Who Is Silvia?

Who is Silvia? what is she,
 That all our swains commend her?
Holy, fair, and wise is she;
 The heaven such grace did lend her,
That she might admirèd be.   5

Is she kind as she is fair?
 For beauty lives with kindness.
Love doth to her eyes repair,
 To help him of his blindness;
And, being helped, inhabits there.   10

Then to Silvia let us sing,
 That Silvia is excelling;
She excels each mortal thing
 Upon the dull earth dwelling;
To her let us garlands bring.   (1594–5)

from LOVE'S LABOUR'S LOST

Spring

When daisies pied and violets blue,
And lady-smocks all silver-white,
And cuckoo-buds of yellow hue
Do paint the meadows with delight,
The cuckoo then on every tree
Mocks married men; for thus sings he,
   Cuckoo;
Cuckoo, cuckoo: O word of fear,
Unpleasing to a married ear!

When shepherds pipe on oaten straws   10
And merry larks are ploughmen's clocks,
When turtles tread, and rooks, and daws,
And maidens bleach their summer smocks,
The cuckoo then on every tree,
Mocks married men; for thus sings he,   15
            Cuckoo;
Cuckoo, cuckoo: O word of fear,
Unpleasing to a married ear!

Winter

When icicles hang by the wall,
    And Dick the shepherd blows his nail,
And Tom bears logs into the hall,
    And milk comes frozen home in pail,
When blood is nipp'd, and ways be foul,   5
Then nightly sings the staring owl,
                        Tu-who;
Tu-whit, tu-who—a merry note,
While greasy Joan doth keel the pot.

When all aloud the wind doth blow,   10
    And coughing drowns the parson's saw,
And birds sit brooding in the snow,
    And Marian's nose looks red and raw,
When roasted crabs hiss in the bowl,
Then nightly sings the staring owl,   15
                        Tu-who;
Tu-whit, tu-who—a merry note,
While greasy Joan doth keel the pot.   (1594–5)

from AS YOU LIKE IT

Blow, Blow, Thou Winter Wind!

Blow, blow, thou winter wind!
Thou art not so unkind
As man's ingratitude;
Thy tooth is not so keen
Because thou art not seen,   5
Although thy breath be rude.
Heigh ho! sing heigh ho! unto the green holly:

Most friendship is feigning, most loving mere folly:
  Then, heigh ho! the holly!
  This life is most jolly.   10

  Freeze, freeze, thou bitter sky,
  Thou dost not bite so nigh
  As benefits forgot:
  Though thou the waters warp,
  Thy sting is not so sharp   15
  As friend remembered not.
Heigh ho! sing heigh ho! unto the green holly:
Most friendship is feigning, most loving mere folly:
  Then, heigh ho! the holly!
  This life is most jolly. (*1599–1600*)

from TWELFTH NIGHT

When That I Was

When that I was and a little tiny boy,
  With hey, ho, the wind and the rain,
A foolish thing was but a toy,
  For the rain it raineth every day.

But when I came to man's estate   5
  With hey, ho, the wind and the rain,
'Gainst knaves and thieves men shut the gate,
  For the rain it raineth every day.

But when I came, alas! to wive,
  With hey, ho, the wind and the rain, 10
By swaggering could I never thrive,
  For the rain it raineth every day.

But when I came unto my beds,
  With hey, ho, the wind and the rain,
With toss-pots still had drunken heads, 15
  For the rain it raineth every day.

A great while ago the world begun,
  With hey, ho, the wind and the rain,
But that's all one, our play is done,
  And we'll strive to please you every day. (*1599–1600*)

from MEASURE FOR MEASURE

Take, O! Take Those Sweet Lips Away

Take, O! take those lips away,
    That so sweetly were forsworn,
And those eyes, the break of day,
    Lights that do mislead the morn;
But my kisses bring again,
        Bring again,
Seals of love, but sealed in vain,
        Sealed in vain.   (1604–5)

from CYMBELINE

Hark, Hark! The Lark

Hark, hark! the lark at heaven's gate sings,
And Phoebus gins arise,
His steeds to water at those springs
On chaliced flowers that lies;
And winking Mary-buds begin
To ope their golden eyes:
With everything that pretty is,
My lady sweet, arise;
Arise, arise!

Fear No More

Fear no more the heat o' the sun,
    Nor the furious winter's rages;
Thou thy worldly task hast done,
    Home art gone, and ta'en thy wages;
Golden lads and girls all must,   5
As chimney-sweepers, come to dust.

Fear no more the frown o' the great,
    Thou art past the tyrant's stroke:
Care no more to clothe and eat;
    To thee the reed is as the oak: 10
The sceptre, learning, physic, must
All follow this, and come to dust.

Fear no more the lightning-flash,
    Nor the all-dread thunder-stone;

Fear not slander, censure rash; 15
    Thou hast finished joy and moan;
All lovers young, all lovers must
Consign to thee, and come to dust.

No exorciser harm thee!
    Nor no witchcraft charm thee! 20
Ghost unlaid forbear thee!
    Nothing ill come near thee!
Quiet consummation have;
And renowned be thy grave! (*1609–10*)

from THE TEMPEST

Full Fathom Five

Full fathom five thy father lies;
    Of his bones are coral made:
Those are pearls that were his eyes:
    Nothing of him that doth fade,
But doth suffer a sea-change
Into something rich and strange.
Sea-nymphs hourly ring his knell:
              Ding-dong.
Hark! now I hear them, —ding-dong, bell.

Come Unto These Yellow Sands

Come unto these yellow sands,
    And then take hands:
Curtsied when you have and kiss'd
    The wild waves whist:
Foot it featly here and there, 5
    And sweet sprites bear
The burthen. Hark, hark!
    The watch dogs bark
    Hark, hark! I hear
The strains of strutting Chanticleer 10
    Cry cock-a-diddle-dow (*1611–12*)

✑ THOMAS NASHE (1567–1601)

Spring

Spring, the sweet spring, is the year's pleasant king;
Then blooms each thing, then maids dance in a ring,
Cold doth not sting, the pretty birds do sing:
Cuckoo, jug-jug, pu-we, to-witta-woo!

The palm and may make country houses gay,
Lambs frisk and play, the shepherds pipe all day,
And we hear aye birds tune this merry lay:
Cuckoo, jug-jug, pu-we, to-witta-woo!

The fields breathe sweet, the daisies kiss our feet,
Young lovers meet, old wives a-sunning sit,
In every street these tunes our ears do greet:
Cuckoo, jug-jug, pu-we, to-witta-woo!   (1600)

Adieu! Farewell Earth's Bliss! [1]

Adieu! farewell earth's bliss!
This world uncertain is:
Fond are life's lustful joys,
Death proves them all but toys.
None from his darts can fly: 5
I am sick, I must die.
          Lord, have mercy on us!

Rich men, trust not in wealth!
Gold cannot buy you health;
Physic himself must fade;   10
All things to end are made;
The plague full swift goes by;
I am sick, I must die.
          Lord, have mercy on us!

[1] believed to have been written in London in time of plague, 1592–1594

Beauty is but a flower 15
Which wrinkles will devour:
Brightness falls from the air;
Queens have died young and fair;
Dust hath closed Helen's eye;
I am sick, I must die. 20
       Lord, have mercy on us!

Strength stoops unto the grave:
Worms feed on Hector brave;
Swords may not fight with fate;
Earth still holds ope her gate; 25
'Come! come!' the bells do cry.
I am sick, I must die.
       Lord, have mercy on us!

Wit with his wantonness
Tasteth death's bitterness: 30
Hell's executioner
Hath no ears for to hear
What vain art can reply:
I am sick, I must die.
       Lord, have mercy on us! 35

Haste, therefore, each degree,
To welcome destiny:
Heaven is our heritage,
Earth but a player's stage:
Mount we unto the sky. 40
I am sick, I must die.
       Lord, have mercy on us!   (1600)

✌ THOMAS CAMPION (1567–1620)

Rose-Cheeked Laura

Rose-cheeked Laura, come,
Sing thou smoothly with thy beauty's
Silent music, either other
    Sweetly gracing.

Lovely forms do flow   5
From concent [1] divinely framèd;
Heaven is music, and thy beauty's
    Birth is heavenly.

These dull notes we sing
Discords need for helps to grace them;   10
Only beauty purely loving
    Knows no discord,

But still moves delight,
Like clear springs renewed by flowing,
Ever perfect, ever in them-   15
    Selves eternal.   (1602)

What If a Day

What if a day, or a month, or a year
Crown thy delights with a thousand sweet contentings?
Cannot a chance of a night or an hour
Cross thy desires with as many sad tormentings?
    Fortune, honor, beauty, youth   5
    Are but blossoms dying;
    Wanton pleasure, doting love
    Are but shadows flying.
    All our joys are but toys,
    Idle thoughts deceiving;   10
    None have power of an hour
    In their lives' bereaving.

[1] harmony of sounds or voices

114

Earth's but a point to the world, and a man
Is but a point to the world's compared centure;
Shall then the point of a point be so vain   15
As to triumph in a seely point's adventure?
    All is hazard that we have,
    There is nothing biding;
    Days of pleasure are like streams
    Through fair meadows gliding.   20
    Weal and woe, time doth go,
    Time is never returning;
    Secret fates guide our states,
    Both in mirth and mourning.   (1606)

Cherry-Ripe

There is a garden in her face
Where roses and white lilies grow;
A heavenly paradise is that place
Wherein all pleasant fruits do flow.
    There cherries grow which none may buy,   5
    Till "Cherry Ripe" themselves do cry.

Those cherries fairly do enclose
Of orient pearl a double row,
Which when her lovely laughter shows,
They look like rosebuds filled with snow;   10
    Yet them nor peer nor prince can buy,
    Till "Cherry Ripe" themselves do cry.

Her eyes like angels watch them still,
Her brows like bended bows do stand,
Threatening with piercing frowns to kill   15
All that attempt with eye or hand
    Those sacred cherries to come nigh,
    Till "Cherry Ripe" themselves do cry.   (c. 1617)

HENRY WOTTON (1568–1639)

The Character of a Happy Life

How happy is he born or taught
　　That serveth not another's will,
Whose armor is his honest thought,
　　And simple truth his highest skill;

Whose passions not his masters are;　　　　　5
　　Whose soul is still prepared for death,
Untied unto the world with care
　　Of prince's grace or vulgar breath;

Who envies none whom chance doth raise,
　　Or vice; who never understood　　　　　10
The deepest wounds are given by praise,
　　By rule of state but not of good;

Who hath his life from rumors freed,
　　Whose conscience is his strong retreat,
Whose state can neither flatterers feed　　　15
　　Nor ruins make accusers great;

Who God doth late and early pray
　　More of his grace than goods to send,
And entertains the harmless day
　　With a well-chosen book or friend.　　　20

This man is free from servile bands
　　Of hope to rise or fear to fall,
Lord of himself, though not of lands,
　　And having nothing, yet hath all.　　*(1651)*

◄§ BARNABE BARNES (1569?–1609)

From *Parthenophil and Parthenophe*

Sonnet 31

I burn, yet am I cold; I am a-cold, yet burn.
In pleasing, discontent; in discontentment, pleased.
Diseased, I am in health; and healthful, am diseased.
In turning back, proceed; proceeding, I return.
In mourning, I rejoice; and in rejoicing, mourn.
In pressing, I step back; in stepping back, I pressed.
In gaining, still I lose; and in my losses, gain.
Grounded, I waver still; and wavering, still am grounded.
Unwounded, yet not sound; and being sound, am wounded.
Slain, yet am I alive; and yet alive, am slain.
Hounded, my heart rests still; still resting, is it hounded.
In pain, I feel no grief; yet void of grief, in pain.   (*1593*)

Sonnet 66

Ah, sweet Content! where is thy mild abode?
Is it with shepherds and light-hearted swains
Which sing upon the downs and pipe abroad,
Tending their flocks and cattle on the plains?
Ah, sweet Content! where dost thou safely rest?
In heaven with angels which the praises sing
Of Him that made, and rules at His behest,
The minds and hearts of every living thing?
Ah, sweet Content! where doth thine harbor hold?
Is it in churches, with religious men
Which please the gods with prayers manifold,
And in their studies meditate it then?
Whether thou dost in heaven or earth appear,
Be where thou wilt, thou wilt not harbor here.   (*1593*)

PART 3
The Seventeenth Century

—

ᴈᶘ JOHN DONNE (1572–1631)

Song

Go and catch a falling star,
 Get with child a mandrake [1] root,
Tell me where all past years are,
 Or who cleft the devil's foot;
Teach me to hear mermaids singing,   5
Or to keep off envy's stinging,
   And find
   What wind
Serves to advance an honest mind.

If thou be'st born to strange sights,   10
 Things invisible to see,
Ride ten thousand days and nights
 Till age snow white hairs on thee;
Thou, when thou return'st, wilt tell me
All strange wonders that befell thee,   15
   And swear
   No where
Lives a woman true, and fair.

If thou find'st one, let me know;
 Such a pilgrimage were sweet.   20
Yet do not; I would not go,
 Though at next door we might meet.
Though she were true when you met her,
And last, till you write your letter,
   Yet she   25
   Will be
False, ere I come, to two, or three.   (1633)

[1] then believed to resemble the human form and to suggest a link between the vegetable, animal, and human worlds; it was also believed to shriek when uprooted.

The Sun Rising

Busy old fool, unruly Sun,
    Why dost thou thus,
Through windows, and through curtains, call on us?
Must to thy motions lovers' seasons run?
        Saucy pedantic wretch, go chide   5
        Late school-boys and sour prentices,
    Go tell court-huntsmen that the king will ride,
    Call country ants to harvest offices;
Love, all alike, no season knows nor clime,
Nor hours, days, months, which are the rags of time.   10

Thy beams so reverend and strong
    Why shouldst thou think?
I could eclipse and cloud them with a wink,
But that I would not lose her sight so long.
        If her eyes have not blinded thine,   15
        Look, and tomorrow late tell me,
    Whether both th' Indias of spice and mine
    Be where thou left'st them, or lie here with me.
Ask for those kings whom thou saw'st yesterday,
And thou shalt hear, "All here in one bed lay."   20

She's all states, and all princes I;
    Nothing else is.
Princes do but play us; compared to this,
All honor's mimic, all wealth alchemy.[1]
        Thou, Sun, art half as happy as we,   25
        In that the world's contracted thus;
    Thine age asks ease, and since thy duties be
    To warm the world, that's done in warming us.
Shine here to us, and thou art everywhere;
This bed thy centre is, these walls thy sphere.   (1633)

The Ecstasy

Where, like a pillow on a bed,
    A pregnant bank swelled up, to rest
The violet's reclining head,
    Sat we two, one another's best.

[1] base metal, false gold

Our hands were firmly cémented   5
 With a fast balm, which thence did spring;
Our eye-beams twisted, and did thread
 Our eyes upon one double string.
So to entergraft [1] our hands, as yet
 Was all the means to make us one;   10
And pictures in our eyes to get
 Was all our propagation.
As, 'twixt two equal armies, Fate
 Suspends uncertain victory,
Our souls—which to advance their state,   15
 Were gone out—hung 'twixt her and me.
And whilst our souls negotiate there,
 We like sepulchral statues lay;
All day, the same our postures were,
 And we said nothing all the day.   20
If any, so by love refined,
 That he soul's language understood,
And by good love were grown all mind,
 Within convenient distance stood,
He—though he knew not which soul spake,   25
 Because both meant, both spoke the same—
Might thence a new concoction take,
 And part far purer than he came.
This ecstasy doth unperplex
 (We said) and tell us what we love;   30
We see by this, it was not sex;
 We see, we saw not, what did move:
But as all several souls contain
 Mixture of things they know not what,
Love these mixed souls, doth mix again,   35
 And makes both one, each this and that.
A single violet transplant,
 The strength, the color, and the size—
All which before was poor and scant—
 Redoubles still, and multiplies.   40
When love with one another so
 Interinanimates two souls,
That abler soul, which thence doth flow,
 Defects of loneliness controls.
We then, who are this new soul, know,   45
 Of what we are composed and made,

---

[1] entwine

For th' atomies of which we grow
    Are souls, whom no change can invade.
But, O alas! so long, so far,
    Our bodies why do we forbear? 50
They are ours, though they're not we; we are
    Th' intelligences, they the spheres.
We owe them thanks, because they thus
    Did us, to us, at first convey,
Yielded their forces, sense, to us, 55
    Nor are dross to us, but allay.
On man heaven's influence works not so,
    But that it first imprints the air;
So soul into the soul may flow,
    Though it to body first repair. 60
As our blood labors to beget
    Spirits, as like souls as it can,
Because such fingers need to knit
    That subtle knot, which makes us man:
So must pure lovers' souls descend 65
    To affections, and to faculties,
Which sense may reach and apprehend,
    Else a great prince in prison lies.
To our bodies turn we then, that so
    Weak men on love reveal'd may look; 70
Love's mysteries in souls do grow,
    But yet the body is his book.
And if some lover, such as we,
    Have heard this dialogue of one,
Let him still mark us, he shall see 75
    Small change when we're to bodies gone.   (1633)

The Good Morrow

I wonder, by my troth, what thou and I
Did, till we loved? were we not weaned till then?
But sucked on country pleasures, childishly?
Or snorted we in the Seven Sleepers' den? [1]
'Twas so; but this, all pleasures fancies be; 5
If ever any beauty I did see,

[1] the cave in which seven Christian youths, fleeing the Decian persecution, remained asleep for more than two centuries

Which I desired, and got, 'twas but a dream of thee.
And now good morrow to our waking souls,
Which watch not one another out of fear;
For love all love of other sights controls, 10
And makes one little room an everywhere.
Let sea-discoverers to new worlds have gone;
Let maps to other, worlds on worlds have shown;
Let us possess one world; each hath one, and is one.
My face in thine eye, thine in mine appears, 15
And true plain hearts do in the faces rest;
Where can we find two better hemispheres
Without sharp north, without declining west?
Whatever dies, was not mix'd equally;
If our two loves be one, or thou and I 20
Love so alike that none can slacken, none can die. (1633)

The Canonization

For Godsake hold your tongue, and let me love,
Or chide my palsy, or my gout,
My five grey hairs, or ruined fortune flout;
With wealth your state, your mind with arts improve,
Take you a course, get you a place, 5
Observe his Honor, or his Grace;
Or the king's real, or his stamped face [1]
Contemplate; what you will, approve,
So you will let me love.

Alas, alas, who's injured by my love? 10
What merchant's ships have my sighs drowned?
Who says my tears have overflowed his ground?
When did my colds a forward spring remove?
When did the heats which my veins fill
Add one more to the plaguy bill? [2] 15
Soldiers find wars, and lawyers find out still
Litigious men, which quarrels move,
Though she and I do love.

Call us what you will, we are made such by love;
Call her one, me another fly, 20

[1] stamped on coins [2] the list of those
dead from the plague

We're tapers too, and at our own cost die,
  And we in us find the eagle and the dove.
    The phœnix riddle hath more wit
    By us; we two being one are it.
So to one neutral thing both sexes fit,   25
  We die and rise the same, and prove
  Mysterious by this love.

We can die by it, if not live by love,
  And if unfit for tomb or hearse
Our legend be, it will be fit for verse;   30
  And if no piece of chronicle we prove,
    We'll build in sonnets pretty rooms;
    As well a well-wrought urn becomes
The greatest ashes, as half-acre tombs,
  And by these hymns all shall approve   35
  Us canonized for love:

And thus invoke us; You, whom reverend love
  Made one another's hermitage;
You, to whom love was peace, that now is rage;
  Who did the whole world's soul contract, and drove   40
    Into the glasses of your eyes
    So made such mirrors, and such spies,
That they did all to you epitomize,
  Countries, towns, courts: beg from above
  A pattern of your love!   (1633)

A Valediction Forbidding Mourning

As virtuous men pass mildly away,
  And whisper to their souls to go,
Whilst some of their sad friends do say,
  The breath goes now, and some say, No:

So let us melt, and make no noise,   5
  No tear-floods, nor sigh-tempests move;
'Twere profanation of our joys
  To tell the laity our love.

Moving of th' earth brings harms and fears,
  Men reckon what it did, and meant;   10
But trepidation of the spheres,
  Though greater far, is innocent.

Dull sublunary lovers' love
  —Whose soul is sense—cannot admit
Absence, because it doth remove   15
  Those things which elemented [1] it.

But we by a love so much refined
  That ourselves know not what it is,
Inter-assuréd of the mind,
  Care less eyes, lips and hands to miss.   20

Our two souls therefore, which are one,
  Though I must go, endure not yet
A breach, but an expansion,
  Like gold to airy thinness beat.

If they be two, they are two so   25
  As stiff twin compasses are two;
Thy soul, the fix'd foot, makes no show
  To move, but doth, if th' other do.

And though it in the centre sit,
  Yet, when the other far doth roam,   30
It leans, and hearkens after it,
  And grows erect, as that comes home.

Such wilt thou be to me, who must,
  Like th' other foot, obliquely run;
Thy firmness makes my circle just,   35
  And makes me end where I begun.   (1633)

From *Holy Sonnets*

At the round earth's imagined corners, blow
Your trumpets, angels, and arise, arise
From death, you numberless infinities
Of souls, and to your scattered bodies go;
All whom the flood did, and fire shall o'erthrow;
All whom war, dearth, age, agues, tyrannies,
Despair, law, chance, hath slain, and you whose eyes
Shall behold God, and never taste death's woe.

[1] composed

But let them sleep, Lord, and me mourn a space,
For, if above all these, my sins abound,
'Tis late to ask abundance of Thy grace,
When we are there; here on this lowly ground,
Teach me how to repent; for that's as good
As if Thou hadst sealed my pardon with Thy blood.

If poisonous minerals, and if that tree
Whose fruit threw death on else immortal us,
If lecherous goats, if serpents envious
Cannot be damned, Alas! why should I be?
Why should intent or reason, born in me,
Make sins, else equal, in me more heinous?
And mercy being easy, and glorious
To God, in his stern wrath why threatens he?
But who am I, that dare dispute with thee,
O God? O! of thine only worthy blood,
And my tears, make a heavenly Lethean flood,
And drown in it my sin's black memory;
That thou remember them, some claim as debt,
I think it mercy, if thou wilt forget.

Death, be not proud, though some have called thee
Mighty and dreadful, for thou are not so;
For those whom thou think'st thou dost overthrow
Die not, poor Death; nor yet canst thou kill me.
From rest and sleep, which but thy picture be,
Much pleasure; then from thee much more must flow;
And soonest our best men with thee do go—
Rest of their bones and souls' delivery!
Thou'rt slave to fate, chance, kings, and desperate men,
And dost with poison, war, and sickness dwell;
And poppy or charms can make us sleep as well
And better than thy stroke. Why swell'st thou then?
One short sleep past, we wake eternally,
And Death shall be no more: Death, thou shalt die.

Batter my heart, three-personed God; for you
As yet but knock, breathe, shine, and seek to mend.

That I may rise and stand, o'erthrow me and bend
Your force to break, blow, burn, and make me new.
I, like an usurped town, to another due,
Labor to admit you, but, oh, to no end;
Reason, your viceroy in me, me should defend,
But is captived and proves weak or untrue.
Yet dearly I love you and would be loved fain,
But am betrothed unto your enemy:
Divorce me, untie or break that knot again,
Take me to you, imprison me, for I,
Except you enthrall me, never shall be free,
Nor ever chaste, except you ravish me.   (1633–1669)

Good Friday, 1613. Riding Westward

Let man's soul be a sphere, and then, in this
The intelligence that moves, devotion is;
And as the other spheres, by being grown
Subject to foreign motion, lose their own,
And being by others hurried every day   5
Scarce in a year their natural form obey,
Pleasure or business, our souls admit
For their first mover, and are whirled by it.
Hence is't that I am carried towards the west
This day, when my soul's form bends towards the east.   10
There I should see a sun, by rising set,
And by that setting, endless day beget;
But that Christ on this cross did rise and fall,
Sin had eternally benighted all.
Yet dare I' almost be glad I do not see   15
That spectacle of too much weight for me.
Who sees God's face, that is self life, must die;
What a death were it then to see God die!
It made his own lieutenant, nature, shrink;
It made his footstool crack, and the sun wink.   20
Could I behold those hands which span the poles
And tune all spheres at once, pierced with those holes?
Could I behold that endless height, which is
Zenith to us and our antipodes,
Humbled below us? or that blood which is   25

The seat of all our souls, if not of his,
Made dirt of dust, or that flesh which was worn
By God for his apparel, ragg'd and torn?
If on these things I durst not look, durst I
Upon his miserable mother cast mine eye,   30
Who was God's partner here, and furnished thus
Half of that sacrifice which ransomed us?
Though these things, as I ride, be from mine eye,
They'are present yet unto my memory,
For that looks towards them; and thou look'st towards me,   35
O Savior, as thou hang'st upon the tree;
I turn my back to thee but to receive
Corrections, till thy mercies bid thee leave.
Oh, think me worth thine anger, punish me,
Burn off my rusts, and my deformity;   40
Restore thine image, so much, by thy grace,
That thou mayst know me, and I'll turn my face.   (1635–1669)

Hymn to God, My God, in My Sickness

Since I am coming to that holy room,
   Where, with thy choir of saints for evermore,
I shall be made thy music; as I come
   I tune the instrument here at the door,
   And what I must do then, think here before.   5

Whilst my physicians by their love are grown
   Cosmographers, and I their map, who lie
Flat on this bed, that by them may be shown
   That this is my south-west discovery
   Per fretum febris,[1] by these straits to die,   10

I joy, that in these straits, I see my west;
   For though their currents yield return to none,
What shall my west hurt me? As west and east
   In all flat maps (and I am one) are one,
   So death doth touch the Resurrection.   15

Is the Pacific Sea my home? Or are
   The eastern riches? Is Jerusalem?

---

[1] through the raging of fever

Anyan,[2] and Magellan, and Gibraltar,
    All straits, and none but straits, are ways to them,
    Whether where Japhet dwelt, or Cham, or Shem.   20

We think that Paradise and Calvary,
    Christ's cross, and Adam's tree, stood in one place;
Look, Lord, and find both Adams met in me;
    As the first Adam's sweat surrounds my face,
    May the last Adam's blood my soul embrace.   25

So, in his purple wrapp'd, receive me, Lord,
    By these his thorns give me his other crown;
And as to others' souls I preach'd thy word,
    Be this my text, my sermon to mine own,
    Therefore that he may raise, the Lord throws down.   30
                    (1635–1669)

A Hymn to God the Father

Wilt Thou forgive that sin where I begun,
    Which was my sin, though it were done before?
Wilt Thou forgive that sin, through which I run,
    And do run still, though still I do deplore?
        When Thou hast done, Thou hast not done,   5
        For I have more.

Wilt Thou forgive that sin which I have won
    Others to sin, and made my sin their door?
Wilt Thou forgive that sin which I did shun
    A year or two, but wallowed in a score?   10
        When Thou hast done, Thou hast not done,
        For I have more.

I have a sin of fear, that when I have spun
    My last thread, I shall perish on the shore;
But swear by Thyself, that at my death Thy Son   15
    Shall shine as he shines now, and heretofore;
        And, having done that, Thou hast done;
        I fear no more.   (1633–1669)

[2] Bering Strait

ᴥᶴ BEN JONSON (1572–1637)

On My First Son

Farewell, thou child of my right hand, and joy;
My sin was too much hope of thee, loved boy.
Seven years thou wert lent to me, and I thee pay,
Exacted by thy fate, on the just day.
O, could I lose all father now. For why   5
Will man lament the state he should envy?
To have so soon 'scaped world's, and flesh's, rage,
And if no other misery, yet age?
Rest in soft peace, and, asked, say here doth lie
Ben Jonson, his best piece of poetry.   10
For whose sake, henceforth, all his vows be such,
As what he loves may never like too much.   (1616)

Epitaph on Elizabeth, L.H.

Would'st thou hear, what man can say
   In a little? Reader, stay.
Underneath this stone doth lie
   As much beauty as could die;
Which in life did harbor give   5
   To more virtue than doth live.
If at all she had a fault,
   Leave it buried in this vault.
One name was Elizabeth,
   Th'other let it sleep with death;   10
Fitter, when it died, to tell.
   Than that it liv'd at all. Farewell.   (1616)

Song: That Women Are But Men's Shadows

Follow a shadow, it still flies you;
   Seem to fly it, it will pursue:
So court a mistress, she denies you,
Let her alone, she will court you.

Say, are not women truly, then,   5
    Styl'd but the shadows of us men?
At morn, and even, shades are longest;
    At noon, they are or short, or none:
So men at weakest, they are strongest,
    But grant us perfect, they're not known.   10
Say, are not women truly then
    Styl'd but the shadows of us men?   (1616)

To Celia

Drink to me only with thine eyes,
    And I will pledge with mine;
Or leave a kiss but in the cup
    And I'll not look for wine.
The thirst that from the soul doth rise   5
    Doth ask a drink divine;
But might I of Jove's nectar sup,
    I would not change for thine.

I sent thee late a rosy wreath,
    Not so much honoring thee   10
As giving it a hope that there
    It could not withered be;
But thou thereon didst only breathe
    And sent'st it back to me;
Since when it grows, and smells, I swear,   15
    Not of itself but thee!

To Heaven

Good and great God! can I not think of Thee,
    But it must straight my melancholy be?
Is it interpreted in me disease,
    That, laden with my sins, I seek for ease?
O be Thou witness, that the reins dost know   5
    And hearts of all, if I be sad for show;
And judge me after, if I dare pretend
    To aught but grace, or aim at other end.
As Thou art all, so be Thou all to me,
    First, midst, and last, converted One and Three!   10

My faith, my hope, my love; and, in this state,
    My judge, my witness, and my advocate!
Where have I been this while exiled from Thee,
    And whither rapt, now Thou but stoop'st to me?
Dwell, dwell here still! O, being everywhere,   15
    How can I doubt to find Thee ever here?
I know my state, both full of shame and scorn,
    Conceived in sin, and unto labor born,
Standing with fear, and must with horror fall,
    And destined unto judgment, after all.   20
I feel my grief too, and there scarce is ground
    Upon my flesh t'inflict another wound;
Yet dare I not complain or wish for death
    With holy Paul, lest it be thought the breath
Of discontent; or that these prayers be   25
    For weariness of life, not love of Thee.

It Is Not Growing Like a Tree

To the Immortal Memory and Friendship of that Noble Pair, Sir
Lucius Cary and Sir H. Morrison

It is not growing like a tree
In bulk, doth make man better be;
Or standing long an oak, three hundred year,
To fall a log at last, dry, bald, and sere:
      A lily of a day   5
      Is fairer far in May,
    Although it fall and die that night;
    It was the plant and flower of light.
In small proportions we just beauties see;
And in short measures life may perfect be.   (*1616*)

To the Memory of My Beloved, The Author Mr. William Shakespeare: and What He Hath Left Us

To draw no envy, Shakespeare, on thy name,
Am I thus ample to thy book and fame;

While I confess thy writings to be such
As neither man nor Muse can praise too much.
'Tis true, and all men's suffrage. But these ways   5
Were not the paths I meant unto thy praise;
For silliest ignorance on these may light,
Which, when it sounds at best, but echoes right;
Or blind affection, which doth ne'er advance
The truth, but gropes, and urgeth all by chance;   10
Or crafty malice might pretend this praise,
And think to ruin, where it seemed to raise.
These are, as some infamous bawd or whore
Should praise a matron. What could hurt her more?
But thou art proof against them, and, indeed,   15
Above the ill fortune of them, or the need.
I therefore will begin. Soul of the age!
The applause, delight, the wonder of our stage!
My Shakespeare, rise! I will not lodge thee by
Chaucer, or Spenser, or bid Beaumont lie   20
A little further, to make thee a room;
Thou art a monument without a tomb,
And art alive still while thy book doth live
And we have wits to read and praise to give.
That I not mix thee so, my brain excuses,   25
I mean with great, but disproportioned Muses;
For if I thought my judgment were of years,
I should commit thee surely with thy peers,
And tell how far thou didst our Lyly outshine,
Or sporting Kyd, or Marlowe's mighty line.   30
And though thou hadst small Latin and less Greek,
From thence to honor thee, I would not seek
For names; but call forth thundering Aeschylus,
Euripides, and Sophocles to us;
Pacuvius, Accius, him of Cordova [1] dead,   35
To life again, to hear thy buskin tread,
And shake a stage; or, when thy socks were on,
Leave thee alone for the comparison
Of all that insolent Greece or haughty Rome
Sent forth, or since did from their ashes come.   40
Triumph, my Britain, thou hast one to show
To whom all scenes of Europe homage owe.

[1] the third Roman tragedian named in
this line, Seneca

He was not of an age, but for all time!
And all the Muses still were in their prime,
When, like Apollo, he came forth to warm   45
Our ears, or like a Mercury to charm!
Nature herself was proud of his designs
And joyed to wear the dressing of his lines!
Which were so richly spun, and woven so fit,
As, since, she will vouchsafe no other wit.   50
The merry Greek, tart Aristophanes,
Neat Terence, witty Plautus, now not please,
But antiquated and deserted lie,
As they were not of Nature's family.
Yet must I not give Nature all; thy art,   55
My gentle Shakespeare, must enjoy a part.
For though the poet's matter Nature be,
His art doth give the fashion; and, that he
Who casts to write a living line, must sweat
(Such as thine are) and strike the second heat   60
Upon the Muses' anvil; turn the same
(And himself with it) that he thinks to frame,
Or, for the laurel, he may gain a scorn;
For a good poet's made, as well as born.
And such wert thou! Look how the father's face   65
Lives in his issue; even so the race
Of Shakespeare's mind and manners brightly shines
In his well turned, and true filed lines;
In each of which he seems to shake a lance,
As brandished at the eyes of ignorance.   70
Sweet Swan of Avon! what a sight it were
To see thee in our waters yet appear,
And make those flights upon the banks of Thames,
That so did take Eliza, and our James!
But stay, I see thee in the hemisphere   75
Advanced, and made a constellation there!
Shine forth, thou star of poets, and with rage
Or influence, chide or cheer the drooping stage,
Which, since thy flight from hence, hath mourned like night,
And despairs day, but for thy volume's light.   (*1635*)

Songs from the Plays

from CYNTHIA'S REVELS

Echo's Song

Slow, slow, fresh fount, keep time with my salt tears;
    Yet slower, yet; O faintly, gentle springs;
List to the heavy part the music bears,
    Woe weeps out her division when she sings.
        Droop, herbs and flowers;   5
        Fall, grief, in showers,
        Our beauties are not ours;
            O, I could still,
Like melting snow upon some craggy hill,
        Drop, drop, drop, drop,   10
Since nature's pride is now a withered daffodil.   *(1601)*

from THE SILENT WOMAN

Clerimont's Song

    Still to be neat, still to be drest
    As you were going to a feast:
    Still to be powdered, still perfumed:
    Lady, it is to be presumed,
    Though art's hid causes are not found,   5
    All is not sweet, all is not sound.

    Give me a look, give me a face
    That makes simplicity a grace;
    Robes loosely flowing, hair as free:
    Such sweet neglect more taketh me,   10
    Than all the adulteries of art,
    That strike mine eyes, but not my heart.   *(1609)*

from THE POETASTER

Hermogenes's Song

If I freely may discover,
What would please me in my lover:
    I would have her faire and witty,

Savouring more of court than city;
A little proud, but full of pity: 5
Light and humorous in her toying.
Oft building hopes and soon destroying,
Long, but sweet in the enjoying,
Neither too easy, nor too hard:
All extremes I would have barred.   10

She should be allowed her passions,
So they were but us'd as fashions;
Sometimes froward, and then frowning,
Sometimes sickish, and then swowning,
Every fit, with change, still crowning.   15
Purely jealous, I would have her,
Then only constant when I crave her.
'Tis a virtue should not save her.
Thus, nor her delicates would cloy me,
Neither her peevishness annoy me.   (1616)

from THE SAD SHEPHERD

Karolin's Song

Though I am young, and cannot tell,
Either what death, or love is well,
Yet I have heard, yet both bear darts,
And both do aim at human hearts:
And then again, I have been told   5
Love wounds with heat, as death with cold;
So that I fear, they do but bring
Extremes to touch, and mean one thing.

As in a ruin, we it call
One thing to be blown up, or fall;   10
Or to our end, like way may have,
By a flash of lightning, or a wave:
So love's inflamed shaft, or brand,
May kill as soon as death's cold hand;
Except love's fires the virtue have   15
To fright the frost out of the grave.   (1641)

✑§ JOHN WEBSTER (1580?–1630?)

Songs from the Plays

from THE WHITE DEVIL

Cornelia's Song

Call for the robin-redbreast, and the wren,
Since o'er shady groves they hover.
And with leaves and flowers do cover
The friendless bodies of unburied men.
Call unto his funeral dole   5
The ant, the field-mouse, and the mole,
To rear him hillocks that shall keep him warm,
And, when gay tombs are robbed, sustain no harm;
But keep the wolf far thence, that's foe to men,
For with his nails he'll dig them up again.   (*c. 1608*)

from THE DEVIL'S LAW CASE

Speech by Romelio

All the flowers of the spring
Meet to perfume our burying;
These have but their growing prime,
And man doth flourish but his time:
Survey our progress from our birth;   5
We are set, we grow, we turn to earth.
Courts adieu, and all delights,
All bewitching appetites.
Sweetest breath and clearest eye,
Like perfumes, go out and die;   10
And consequently this is done
As shadows wait upon the sun.
Vain the ambition of kings
Who seek by trophies and dead things
To leave a living name behind,   15
And weave but nets to catch the wind.   (*1623*)

✒ GEORGE WITHER (1588–1667)

Shall I Wasting in Despair

Shall I wasting in despair,
Die because a woman's fair?
Or make pale my cheeks with care,
Cause another's rosy are?
Be she fairer than the day,   5
Or the flowery meads in May,
    If she be not so to me,
    What care I how fair she be?

Should my heart be grieved or pined,
Cause I see a woman kind?   10
Or a well disposéd nature,
Joinéd with a lovely feature?
Be she meeker, kinder, than
Turtle-dove, or pelican,
    If she be not so to me,   15
    What care I how kind she be?

Shall a woman's virtues move
Me to perish for her love?
Or, her well-deserving known,
Make me quite forget mine own?   20
Be she with that goodness blest,
Which may gain her, name of Best,
    If she be not such to me,
    What care I how good she be?

Cause her fortune seems too high,   25
Shall I play the fool, and die?
Those that bear a noble mind,
Where they want of riches find,
Think what with them, they would do,
That without them, dare to woo.   30
    And, unless that mind I see,
    What care I, though great she be?

Great, or good, or kind, or fair,
I will ne'er the more despair,
If she love me, this believe,   35
I will die, ere she shall grieve.
If she slight me when I woo,
I can scorn, and let her go.
    For, if she be not for me,
      What care I for whom she be?   (1622)

A Sonnet upon a Stolen Kiss

Now gentle sleep hath closëd up those eyes
Which waking kept my boldest thoughts in awe,
And free access unto that sweet lip lies,
From whence I long the rosy breath to draw;
Methinks no wrong it were if I should steal
From those two melting rubies one poor kiss;
None sees the theft that would the thief reveal,
Nor rob I her of aught which she can miss;
Nay, should I twenty kisses take away,
There would be little sign I had done so;
Why then should I this robbery delay?
Oh! she may wake and therewith angry grow.
    Well, if she do, I'll back restore that one,
    And twenty hundred thousand more for loan.   (1622)

ROBERT HERRICK (1591–1674)

The Argument of His Book

I sing of brooks, of blossoms, birds, and bowers,
Of April, May, of June and July flowers.
I sing of Maypoles, hock-carts,[1] wassails, wakes,
Of bridegrooms, brides, and of their bridal-cakes.
I write of youth, of love, and have access
By these to sing of cleanly wantonness.
I sing of dews, of rains, and, piece by piece,
Of balm, of oil, of spice, and ambergris.
I sing of times trans-shifting, and I write
How roses first came red and lilies white.
I write of groves, of twilights, and I sing
The court of Mab and of the fairy king.
I write of hell; I sing (and ever shall)
Of heaven, and hope to have it after all.   (*1648*)

Delight in Disorder

A sweet disorder in the dress
Kindles in clothes a wantonness:
A lawn about the shoulders thrown
Into a fine distraction;
An erring lace, which here and there
Enthralls the crimson stomacher;
A cuff neglectful, and thereby
Ribands to flow confusedly;
A winning wave, deserving note,
In the tempestuous petticoat;
A careless shoe-string, in whose tie
I see a wild civility,—
Do more bewitch me, than when art
Is too precise in every part.   (*1648*)

[1] The hocking cart hauled home the
last load during harvest.

To the Virgins, to Make Much of Time

Gather ye rosebuds while ye may:
    Old Time is still a-flying,
And this same flower that smiles to-day
    To-morrow will be dying.

The glorious lamp of heaven, the sun,   5
    The higher he's a-getting,
The sooner will his race be run,
    And nearer he's to setting.

That age is best which is the first,
    When youth and blood are warmer;   10
But, being spent, the worse, and worst
    Times, still succeed the former.

Then be not coy, but use your time,
    And while ye may, go marry:
For having lost but once your prime,   15
    You may for ever tarry.   (1648)

The Night-Piece, to Julia

Her eyes the glow-worm lend thee,
The shooting stars attend thee;
    And the elves also,
    Whose little eyes glow
Like the sparks of fire, befriend thee.   5

No will-o'-th'-wisp mislight thee;
Nor snake, or slow-worm bite thee:
    But on, on thy way,
    Not making a stay,
Since ghost there's none to affright thee.   10

Let not the dark thee cumber;
What though the moon does slumber:
    The stars of the night
    Will lend thee their light,
Like tapers clear without number.   15

Then, Julia, let me woo thee,
Thus, thus to come unto me:
    And when I shall meet
    Thy silv'ry feet,
My soul I'll pour into thee.   (1648)

Upon Julia's Clothes

Whenas in silks my Julia goes,
Then, then, methinks, how sweetly flows
The liquefaction of her clothes.

Next, when I cast mine eyes, and see
That brave vibration, each way free,
O, how that glittering taketh me!   (1648)

Corinna's Going A-Maying

Get up, get up for shame! The blooming morn
Upon her wings presents the god unshorn.
See how Aurora throws her fair
Fresh-quilted colours through the air:
    Get up, sweet slug-a-bed, and see   5
    The dew bespangling herb and tree!
Each flower has wept and bow'd toward the east
Above an hour since, yet you not drest;
    Nay! not so much as out of bed?
    When all the birds have matins said   10
    And sung their thankful hymns: 'tis sin,
    Nay, profanation, to keep in,
Whenas a thousand virgins on this day
Spring sooner than the lark, to fetch in May.

Rise and put on your foliage, and be seen   15
To come forth, like the spring-time, fresh and green,
    And sweet as Flora. Take no care
    For jewels for your gown or hair:
    Fear not; the leaves will strew
    Gems in abundance upon you: 20
Besides, the childhood of the day has kept,

Against you come, some orient pearls unwept.
    Come, and receive them while the light
    Hangs on the dew-locks of the night:
    And Titan on the eastern hill   25
    Retires himself, or else stands still
Till you come forth! Wash, dress, be brief in praying:
Few beads are best when once we go a-Maying.

Come, my Corinna, come; and coming, mark
How each field turns a street, each street a park,   30
    Made green and trimm'd with trees! see how
    Devotion gives each house a bough
    Or branch! each porch, each door, ere this,
    An ark, a tabernacle is,
Made up of white-thorn neatly interwove,   35
As if here were those cooler shades of love.
    Can such delights be in the street
    And open fields, and we not see't?
    Come, we'll abroad: and let's obey
    The proclamation made for May,   40
And sin no more, as we have done, by staying;
But, my Corinna, come, let's go a-Maying.

There's not a budding boy or girl this day
But is got up and gone to bring in May.
    A deal of youth ere this is come   45
    Back, and with white-thorn laden home.
    Some have dispatch'd their cakes and cream,
    Before that we have left to dream:
And some have wept, and woo'd, and plighted troth,
And chose their priest, ere we can cast off sloth: 50
    Many a green-gown has been given,
    Many a kiss, both odd and even:
    Many a glance too has been sent
    From out the eye, love's firmament:
Many a jest told of the keys betraying   55
This night, and locks pick'd: yet we're not a-Maying!

Come, let us go, while we are in our prime,
And take the harmless folly of the time!
    We shall grow old apace, and die
    Before we know our liberty.   60
    Our life is short, and our days run
    As fast away as does the sun.

And, as a vapour or a drop of rain,
Once lost, can ne'er be found again,
   So when or you or I are made   65
   A fable, song, or fleeting shade,
   All love, all liking, all delight
     Lies drown'd with us in endless night.
Then, while time serves, and we are but decaying,
Come, my Corinna, come, let's go a-Maying.   (1648)

To Daffodils

Fair daffodils, we weep to see
   You haste away so soon:
As yet the early-rising sun
   Has not attain'd his noon.
      Stay, stay,   5
     Until the hasting day
       Has run
     But to the evensong,
And, having prayed together, we
    Will go with you along.   10

We have short time to stay as you,
   We have as short a spring,
As quick a growth to meet decay,
   As you, or anything,
      We die,   15
     As your hours do, and dry
       Away,
     Like to the summer's rain,
Or as the pearls of morning's dew,
    Ne'er to be found again.   (1648)

GEORGE HERBERT (1593–1633)

The Pulley

When God at first made Man,
Having a glass of blessings standing by;
Let us (said He) pour on him all we can:
Let the world's riches, which dispersèd lie,
     Contract into a span.   5

So strength first made a way;
Then beauty flow'd, then wisdom, honour, pleasure:
When almost all was out, God made a stay,
Perceiving that alone, of all His treasure,
     Rest in the bottom lay.   10

For if I should (said He)
Bestow this jewel also on My creature,
He would adore My gifts instead of Me,
And rest in Nature, not the God of Nature:
     So both should losers be.   15

Yet let him keep the rest,
But keep them with repining restlessness:
Let him be rich and weary, that at least,
If goodness lead him not, yet weariness
     May toss him to My breast.   (1633)

The Collar

I struck the board, and cried, No more.
     I will abroad.
What? shall I ever sigh and pine?
My lines and life are free; free as the road,
    Loose as the wind, as large as store.   5
     Shall I be still in suit?
Have I no harvest but a thorn
To let me blood, and not restore
What I have lost with cordial fruit?
     Sure there was wine   10

Before my sighs did dry it: there was corn
    Before my tears did drown it.
  Is the year only lost to me?
    Have I no bays to crown it?
  No flowers, no garlands gay? all blasted?   15
      All wasted?
  Not so, my heart: but there is fruit,
    And thou hast hands.
  Recover all thy sigh-blown age
On double pleasures: leave thy cold dispute   20
Of what is fit and not; forsake thy cage,
    Thy rope of sands,
  Which petty thoughts have made, and made to thee
    Good cable, to enforce and draw,
      And be thy law,   25
  While thou didst wink and would not see.
    Away; take heed:
    I will abroad.
Call in thy death's-head there: tie up thy fears.
    He that forbears   30
  To suit and serve his need,
    Deserves his load.
But as I rav'd and grew more fierce and wild
    At every word,
  Methought I heard one calling, *Child;*   35
    And I replied, *My Lord.*   (1633)

Church Monuments

While that my soul repairs to her devotion,
Here I intomb my flesh, that it betimes
May take acquaintance of this heap of dust;
To which the blast of death's incessant motion,
Fed with the exhalation of our crimes,   5
Drives all at last. Therefore I gladly trust

My body to this school, that it may learn
To spell his elements, and find his birth
Written in dusty heraldry and lines:
Which dissolution sure doth best discern,   10
Comparing dust with dust, and earth with earth.
These laugh at jet and marble, put for signs,

To sever the good fellowship of dust,
And spoil the meeting. What shall point out them
When they shall bow, and kneel, and fall down flat   15
To kiss those heaps, which now they have in trust?
Dear flesh, while I do pray, learn here thy stem
And true descent, that when thou shalt grow fat,

And wanton in thy cravings, thou mayst know,
That flesh is but the glass which holds the dust   20
That measures all our time; which also shall
Be crumbled into dust. Mark here below
How tame these ashes are, how free from lust—
That thou mayst fit thyself against thy fall.   (1633)

The Rose

Press me not to take more pleasure
    In all this world of sugared lies,
And to use a larger measure
    Than my strict yet welcome size.

First, there is no pleasure here: 5
    Coloured griefs indeed there are,
Blushing woes that look as clear
    As if they could beauty spare.

Or if such deceits there be—
    Such delights I meant to say—   10
There are no such things to me,
    Who have passed my right away.

But I will not much oppose
    Unto what you now advise;
Only take this gentle rose,   15
    And therein my answer lies.

What is fairer than a rose?
    What is sweeter? yet it purgeth.
Purgings enmity disclose,
    Enmity forbearance urgeth.   20

If then all that worldlings prize
    Be contracted to a rose,

Sweetly there indeed it lies,
    But it biteth in the close.

So this flower doth judge and sentence   25
    Worldly joys to be a scourge;
For they all produce repentance,
    And repentance is a purge.

But I health, not physic, choose:
    Only, though I you oppose,   30
Say that fairly I refuse,
    For my answer is a rose.   (1633)

Virtue

Sweet day, so cool, so calm, so bright,
The bridal of the earth and sky,
The dew shall weep thy fall to-night;
        For thou must die.

Sweet rose, whose hue angry and brave   5
Bids the rash gazer wipe his eye,
Thy root is ever in its grave,
        And thou must die.

Sweet spring, full of sweet days and roses,
A box where sweets compacted lie,   10
My music shows ye have your closes,[1]
        And all must die.

Only a sweet and virtuous soul,
Like season'd timber, never gives;
But though the whole world turn to coal,   15
        Then chiefly lives.   (1633)

Death

Death, thou wast once an uncouth hideous thing,
    Nothing but bones,
    The sad effect of sadder groans;
Thy mouth was open, but thou couldst not sing.

---

[1] conclusion of a phrase in music

For we consider'd thee as at some six   5
      Or ten years hence,
   After the loss of life and sense,
Flesh being turn'd to dust, and bones to sticks.

We lookt on this side of thee, shooting short;
      Where we did find   10
   The shells of fledge souls left behind,
Dry dust, which sheds no tears, but may extort.

But since our Saviour's death did put some blood
      Into thy face,
   Thou art grown fair and full of grace,   15
Much in request, much sought for as a good.

For we do now behold thee gay and glad,
      As at dooms-day;
   When souls shall wear their new array,
And all thy bones with beauty shall be clad.   20

Therefore we can go die as sleep, and trust
      Half that we have
   Unto an honest faithful grave,
Making our pillows either down or dust.   (*1633*)

THOMAS CAREW (1595?–1639?)

The Spring

Now that the winter's gone, the earth hath lost
Her snow-white robes; and now no more the frost
Candies the grass, or casts an icy cream
Upon the silver lake or crystal stream:
But the warm sun thaws the benumbed earth,   5
And makes it tender; gives a sacred birth
To the dead swallow; wakes in hollow tree
The drowsy cuckoo and the humble-bee.
Now do a choir of chirping minstrels bring,
In triumph to the world, the youthful spring: 10
The valleys, hills, and woods in rich array
Welcome the coming of the long'd-for May.
Now all things smile: only my love doth lower,
Nor hath the scalding noon-day sun the power
To melt that marble ice, which still doth hold   15
Her heart congeal'd, and makes her pity cold.
The ox, which lately did for shelter fly
Into the stall, doth now securely lie
In open fields; and love no more is made
By the fire-side, but in the cooler shade   20
Amyntas [1] now doth with his Chloris sleep
Under a sycamore, and all things keep
    Time with the season: only she doth carry
    June in her eyes, in her heart January.   (1640)

A Song

    Ask me no more where Jove bestows,
    When June is past, the fading rose;
    For in your beauty's orient deep
    These flowers, as in their causes, sleep.

[1] a shepherd in pastoral stories: Tasso's *Aminta*; Alexander Barclay's *Eclogues*, V; Samuel Daniel's *The Queen's Ar-* *cadia*; Spenser's *Colin Clouts Come Home Again*

Ask me no more whither do stray 5
The golden atoms of the day;
For, in pure love, heaven did prepare
Those powders to enrich your hair.

Ask me no more whither doth haste
The nightingale, when May is past; 10
For in your sweet dividing throat
She winters, and keeps warm her note.

Ask me no more where those stars light
That downwards fall in dead of night;
For in your eyes they sit, and there 15
Fixed become, as in their sphere.

Ask me no more if east or west
The phœnix builds her spicy nest;
For unto you at last she flies,
And in your fragrant bosom dies.   (1640)

Disdain Returned

He that loves a rosy cheek,
    Or a coral lip admires,
Or from star-like eyes doth seek
    Fuel to maintain his fires;
As old Time makes these decay, 5
So his flames must waste away.

But a smooth and steadfast mind,
    Gentle thoughts and calm desires,
Hearts with equal love combined,
    Kindle never-dying fires. 10
Where these are not, I despise
Lovely cheeks, or lips, or eyes.

No tears, Celia, now shall win
    My resolv'd heart to return;
I have searched thy soul within, 15
    And find nought but pride and scorn;
I have learned thy arts, and now
Can disdain as much as thou.
Some power, in my revenge convey
That love to her I cast away.   (1640)

EDMUND WALLER (1606–1687)

On a Girdle

That which her slender waist confined
Shall now my joyful temples bind;
No monarch but would give his crown
His arms might do what this has done.

It was my heaven's extremest sphere,
The pale which held that lovely deer;
My joy, my grief, my hope, my love
Did all within this circle move.

A narrow compass! and yet there
Dwelt all that's good, and all that's fair.
Give me but what this ribband bound,
Take all the rest the sun goes round.   (1664)

Song

    Go, lovely Rose!
Tell her, that wastes her time and me,
    That now she knows,
When I resemble her to thee,
How sweet and fair she seems to be.   5

    Tell her that's young
And shuns to have her graces spied,
    That hadst thou sprung
In deserts, where no men abide,
Thou must have uncommended died.   10

    Small is the worth
Of beauty from the light retired;
    Bid her come forth,
Suffer herself to be desired,
And not blush so to be admired.   15

    Then die! that she
The common fate of all things rare
    May read in thee:
How small a part of time they share
That are so wondrous sweet and fair!   (1664)

❧ JOHN MILTON (1608–1674)

Lycidas

Yet once more, O ye laurels, and once more
Ye myrtles brown, with ivy never-sere,
I come to pluck your berries harsh and crude;
And, with forc'd fingers rude,
Shatter your leaves before the mellowing year.   5
Bitter constraint, and sad occasion dear,
Compels me to disturb your season due:
For Lycidas is dead, dead ere his prime,
Young Lycidas, and hath not left his peer:
Who would not sing for Lycidas? He knew   10
Himself to sing, and build the lofty rhyme.
He must not float upon his watery bier
Unwept, and welter to the parching wind,
Without the mead of some melodious tear.
    Begin then, Sisters of the sacred well,[1]   15
That from beneath the seat of Jove doth spring;
Begin, and somewhat loudly sweep the string.
Hence with denial vain, and coy excuse:
So may some gentle Muse
With lucky [2] words favour my destin'd urn;   20
And, as he passes, turn,
And bid fair peace be to my sable shroud.
    For we were nurs'd upon the self-same hill,
Fed the same flock by fountain, shade, and rill.
Together both, ere the high lawns appear'd   25
Under the opening eye-lids of the morn,
We drove afield, and both together heard
What time the grey-fly winds her sultry horn,
Battening our flocks with the fresh dews of night,
Oft, till the star, that rose, at evening, bright,   30
Toward heaven's descent had slop'd his westering wheel.
Meanwhile the rural ditties were not mute,
Temper'd to the oaten flute;
Rough Satyrs danc'd, and Fauns with cloven heel

[1] the fountain of Aganippe, on Mount Helicon, sacred to the nine muses   [2] auspicious

From the glad sound would not be absent long;   35
And old Damœtas [3] lov'd to hear our song.
    But, O the heavy change, now thou art gone,
Now thou art gone, and never must return!
Thee, Shepherd, thee the woods, and desert caves
With wild thyme and the gadding vine o'ergrown,   40
And all their echoes mourn:
The willows, and the hazel copses green,
Shall now no more be seen
Fanning their joyous leaves to thy soft lays.
As killing as the canker to the rose,   45
Or taint-worm to the weanling herds that graze,
Or frost to flowers, that their gay wardrobe wear,
When first the white-thorn blows;
Such, Lycidas, thy loss to shepherd's ear.
    Where were ye, Nymphs, when the remorseless deep   50
Clos'd o'er the head of your lov'd Lycidas?
For neither were ye playing on the steep,[4]
Where your old Bards, the famous Druids, lie,
Nor on the shaggy top of Mona [5] high,
Nor yet where Deva [6] spreads her wizard stream: 55
Ay me! I fondly dream!
Had ye been there—for what could that have done?
What could the Muse herself that Orpheus bore,
The Muse herself, for her enchanting son,
Whom universal Nature did lament,   60
When, by the rout that made the hideous roar,
His gory visage down the stream was sent,
Down the swift Hebrus to the Lesbian shore?
    Alas! what boots it with incessant care
To tend the homely, slighted shepherd's trade,   65
And strictly meditate the thankless Muse?
Were it not better done, as others use,
To sport with Amaryllis in the shade,
Or with the tangles of Neæra's hair?
Fame is the spur that the clear spirit doth raise   70
(That last infirmity of noble mind)
To scorn delights, and live laborious days;
But the fair guerdon when we hope to find,

[3] As Lycidas is a pastoral name for Milton's friend, Edward King, drowned in the Irish Sea in 1637, so Damoetas is perhaps William Chappell, a tutor at Cambridge or another friend there. [4] the Druid sepulchers at Kerig y Druidion in Denbighshire [5] Anglesey [6] the Dee

And think to burst out into sudden blaze,
Comes the blind Fury [7] with the abhorred shears,   75
And slits the thin-spun life. 'But not the praise',
Phœbus replied, and touch'd my trembling ears;
'Fame is no plant that grows on mortal soil,
Nor in the glistering foil
Set off to the world, nor in broad rumour lies;   80
But lives and spreads aloft by those pure eyes,
And perfect witness of all-judging Jove;
As he pronounces lastly on each deed,
Of so much fame in heaven expect thy meed.'
    O fountain Arethuse [8] and thou honour'd flood,   85
Smooth-sliding Mincius, crown'd with vocal reeds.
That strain I heard was of a higher mood:
But now my oat proceeds,
And listens to the herald of the sea [9]
That came in Neptune's plea;   90
He ask'd the waves, and ask'd the felon winds,
What hard mishap hath doom'd this gentle swain?
And question'd every gust of rugged wings
That blows from off each beaked promontory:
They knew not of his story;   95
And sage Hippotades [10] their answer brings,
That not a blast was from his dungeon stray'd;
The air was calm, and on the level brine
Sleek Panope[11] with all her sisters play'd.
It was that fatal and perfidious bark,   100
Built in the eclipse, and rigg'd with curses dark,
That sunk so low that sacred head of thine.
    Next Camus,[12] reverend sire, went footing slow,
His mantle hairy, and his bonnet sedge,
Inwrought with figures dim, and on the edge   105
Like to that sanguine flower [13] inscrib'd with woe.
'Ah! Who hath reft (quoth he) my dearest pledge?'
Last came, and last did go,
The pilot of the Galilean lake;
Two massy keys he bore of metals twain,   110
(The golden opes, the iron shuts amain),
He shook his mitred locks, and stern bespake:
'How well could I have spar'd for thee, young swain,

[7] one of the Fates: Atropos   [8] in Sicily   Nereus   [12] a personification of the river
[9] Triton   [10] Aeolus   [11] a daughter of   Cam   [13] the hyacinth

Enow of such, as for their bellies' sake,
Creep, and intrude, and climb into the fold!   115
Of other care they little reckoning make,
Than how to scramble at the shearers' feast,
And shove away the worthy bidden guest;
Blind mouths! that scarce themselves know how to hold
A sheep-hook, or have learn'd aught else the least   120
That to the faithful herdman's art belongs!
What recks it them? What need they? They are sped;
And when they list, their lean and flashy songs
Grate on their scrannel pipes of wretched straw;
The hungry sheep look up, and are not fed,   125
But, swoln with wind and the rank mist they draw,
Rot inwardly, and foul contagion spread:
Besides what the grim wolf [14] with privy paw
Daily devours apace, and nothing said:
But that two-handed engine at the door [15]   130
Stands ready to smite once, and smite no more.'
     Return Alpheus,[16] the dread voice is past,
That shrunk thy streams; return, Sicilian Muse,
And call the vales, and bid them hither cast
Their bells, and flowerets of a thousand hues.   135
Ye valleys low, where the mild whispers use
Of shades, and wanton winds, and gushing brooks,
On whose fresh lap the swart star sparely looks;
Throw hither all your quaint enamell'd eyes,
That on the green turf suck the honied showers,   140
And purple all the ground with vernal flowers.
Bring the rathe [17] primrose that forsaken dies,
The tufted crow-toe, and pale jessamine,
The white pink, and the pansy freak'd with jet,
The glowing violet,   145
The musk-rose, and the well-attir'd woodbine,
With cowslips wan that hang the pensive head,
And every flower that sad embroidery wears:
Bid Amaranthus all his beauty shed,
And daffodillies fill their cups with tears,   150
To strew the laureat herse where Lycid lies.
For, so to interpose a little ease,
Let our frail thoughts dally with false surmise;

[14] perhaps selfish prelates   [15] possibly   river in Greece   [17] early
the two houses of Parliament   [16] a

Ay me! Whilst thee the shores and sounding seas
Wash far away, where'er thy bones are hurl'd,   155
Whether beyond the stormy Hebrides,
Where thou perhaps, under the whelming tide,
Visit'st the bottom of the monstrous world;
Or whether thou, to our moist vows denied,
Sleep'st by the fable of Bellerus [18] old,   160
Where the great Vision of the guarded Mount [19]
Looks towards Namancos and Bayona's hold;
Look homeward, Angel, now, and melt with ruth:
And, O ye dolphins, waft the hapless youth.
 Weep no more, woful Shepherds, weep no more,   165
For Lycidas your sorrow is not dead,
Sunk though he be beneath the watery floor;
So sinks the day-star in the ocean bed,
And yet anon repairs his drooping head,
And tricks his beams, and with new-spangled ore   170
Flames in the forehead of the morning sky:
So Lycidas sunk low, but mounted high,
Through the dear might of Him that walk'd the waves;
Where, other groves and other streams along,
With nectar pure his oozy locks he laves,   175
And hears the unexpressive nuptial song,
In the blest kingdoms meek of joy and love.
There entertain him all the saints above,
In solemn troops, and sweet societies,
That sing, and, singing, in their glory move,   180
And wipe the tears for ever from his eyes.
Now, Lycidas, the shepherds weep no more;
Henceforth thou art the Genius of the shore,
In thy large recompense, and shalt be good
To all that wander in that perilous flood.   185
 Thus sang the uncouth [20] swain to the oaks and rills,
While the still morn went out with sandals grey;
He touch'd the tender stops of various quills,
With eager thought warbling his Doric lay:
And now the sun had stretch'd out all the hills,   190
And now was dropt into the western bay:
At last he rose, and twitch'd his mantle blue:
To-morrow to fresh woods, and pastures new.   (1637)

[18] fabled Bellerium, a Latin name for Land's End in Cornwall [19] The archangel Michael was said, in legend, once to have appeared on St. Michael's Mount, opposite Penzance. [20] unknown, as was Milton in 1637

From *The Sonnets*

7: *On Being Arrived at the Age of Twenty-Three*

How soon hath time, the subtle thief of youth,
    Stolen on his wing my three-and-twenti'th year!
    My hasting days fly on with full career,
    But my late spring no bud or blossom shew'th.
Perhaps my semblance might deceive the truth,
    That I to manhood am arriv'd so near;
    And inward ripeness doth much less appear,
    That some more timely-happy spirits indu'th.
Yet be it less or more, or soon or slow,
    It shall be still in strictest measure ev'n
    To that same lot, however mean, or high,
Toward which time leads me, and the will of heav'n;
    All is, if I have grace to use it so,
    As ever in my great Task-Master's eye.   (1631)

18: *On the Late Massacre in Piedmont* [1]

Avenge, O Lord, thy slaughtered saints, whose bones
Lie scattered on the Alpine mountains cold;
Ev'n them who kept thy truth so pure of old,
When all our fathers worshipped stocks and stones,
Forget not: in thy book record their groans
Who were thy sheep, and in their ancient fold
Slain by the bloody Piedmontese, that rolled
Mother with infant down the rocks. Their moans
The vales redoubled to the hills, and they
To heav'n. Their martyred blood and ashes sow
O'er all th' Italian fields, where still doth sway
The triple [2] Tyrant that from these may grow
A hundredfold, who, having learnt thy way,
Early may fly the Babylonian woe.[3]   (1655)

19: *On His Blindness*

When I consider how my light is spent
Ere half my days in this dark world and wide,
And that one talent which is death to hide

---

[1] Refusing to accept the state religion, the Protestant Waldenses were crushed in southern France in 1655. [2] papal tiara [3] Revelation 27:8

Lodged with me useless, though my soul more bent
To serve therewith my Maker, and present
My true account, lest He returning chide.
"Doth God exact day-labor, light denied?"
I fondly ask. But Patience, to prevent
That murmur, soon replies, "God doth not need
Either man's work or his own gifts. Who best
Bear His mild yoke, they serve Him best. His state
Is kingly: thousands at His bidding speed,
And post o'er land and ocean without rest;
They also serve who only stand and wait."   (1652?)

22: To Cyriack Skinner, Upon His Blindness

Cyriack, this three-years-day these eyes, though clear
   To outward view of blemish or of spot,
   Bereft of light, their seeing have forgot;
   Nor to their idle orbs doth sight appear
Of sun, or moon, or star, throughout the year,
   Or man, or woman. Yet I argue not
   Against heav'n's hand or will, nor bate one joy
Or heart or hope; but still bear up, and steer
Right onward. What supports me, dost thou ask?
   —The conscience,[1] friend, to have lost them overpli'd
   In liberty's defence, my noble task,
Of which all Europe rings from side to side.
   This thought might lead me through this world's vain mask,
   Content, though blind, had I no better guide.   (1655?)

From *Paradise Lost*

Book III

Hail, holy Light, offspring of Heaven first-born,
Or of th' Eternal Coeternal beam
May I express thee unblam'd? since God is light,
And never but in unapproached light
Dwelt from eternity, dwelt then in thee,   5
Bright effluence of bright essence increate.
Or hear'st thou rather pure ethereal stream,

---

[1] consciousness

Whose fountain who shall tell? Before the Sun,
Before the Heavens thou wert, and at the voice
Of God, as with a mantle didst invest   10
The rising world of waters dark and deep,
Won from the void and formless infinite.
Thee I revisit now with bolder wing,
Escap'd the Stygian Pool, though long detain'd
In that obscure sojourn, while in my flight   15
Through utter and through middle darkness borne,
With other notes than to th' Orphean lyre
I sung of Chaos and eternal Night,
Taught by the heav'nly Muse to venture down
The dark descent, and up to reascend,   20
Though hard and rare: thee I revisit safe,
And feel thy sovran vital lamp; but thou
Revisit'st not these eyes, that roll in vain
To find thy piercing ray, and find no dawn;
So thick a drop serene hath quencht their orbs,   25
Or dim suffusion veil'd. Yet not the more
Cease I to wander where the Muses haunt
Clear spring, or shady grove, or sunny hill,
Smit with the love of sacred song; but chief
Thee Sion and the flowery brooks beneath,   30
That wash thy hallow'd feet, and warbling flow,
Nightly I visit: nor sometimes forget
Those other two equal'd with me in fate,
So were I equal'd with them in renown,
Blind Thamyris and blind Maeonides,   35
And Tiresias and Phineus prophets old.
Then feed on thoughts, that voluntary move
Harmonious numbers; as the wakeful bird
Sings darkling, and in shadiest covert hid
Tunes her nocturnal note. Thus with the year   40
Seasons return, but not to me returns
Day, or the sweet approach of ev'n or morn,
Or sight of vernal bloom, or summer's rose,
Or flocks, or herds, or human face divine;
But cloud instead, and ever-during dark   45
Surrounds me, from the cheerful ways of men
Cut off, and for the book of knowledge fair
Presented with a universal blank
Of Nature's works to me expung'd and ras'd
And wisdom at one entrance quite shut out.   50

So much the rather thou, Celestial Light,
Shine inward, and the mind through all her powers
Irradiate, there plant eyes; all mist from thence
Purge and disperse, that I may see and tell
Of things invisible to mortal sight.   55

    · · · · ·

Book IV

    · · · · ·

Now came still evening on, and twilight gray
Had in her sober livery all things clad;
Silence accompanied, for beast and bird,   600
They to their grassy couch, these to their nests
Were slunk, all but the wakeful nightingale;
She all night long her amorous descant sung;
Silence was pleas'd: now glow'd the firmament
With living sapphires: Hesperus, that led   605
The starry host, rode brightest, till the moon
Rising in clouded majesty, at length
Apparent queen unveiled her peerless light,
And o'er the dark her silver mantle threw.

    · · · · ·

With thee conversing, I forget all time,
All seasons, and their change, all please alike.   640
Sweet is the breath of morn, her rising sweet,
With charm of earliest birds; pleasant the sun,
When first on this delightful land he spreads
His orient beams, on herb, tree, fruit, and flower,
Glistering with dew; fragrant the fertile earth   645
After soft showers; and sweet the coming-on
Of grateful evening mild; then silent night,
With this her solemn bird, and this fair moon,
And these the gems of heaven, her starry train.
But neither breath of morn, when she ascends   650
With charm of earliest birds; nor rising sun
On this delightful land; nor herb, fruit, flower,
Glistering with dew; nor fragrance after showers;
Nor grateful evening mild; nor silent night,
With this her solemn bird; nor walk by moon,   655
Or glittering starlight, without thee is sweet.
But wherefore all night long shine these? for whom
This glorious sight, when sleep hath shut all eyes?

    · · · · ·

Book XII

. . . . .

      . . . now too nigh
Th' archangel stood, and from the other hill   625
To their fixed station, all in bright array
The cherubim descended; on the ground
Gliding meteorous, as ev'ning mist
Ris'n from a river o'er the marish glides,
And gathers ground fast at the laborer's heel   630
Homeward returning. High in front advanc'd
The brandished sword of God before them blaz'd
Fierce as a comet; which with torrid heat,
And vapour as the Libyan air adust,
Began to parch the temperate clime; whereat   635
In either hand the hastning angel caught
Our lingring parents, and to th' eastern gate
Led them direct, and down the cliff as fast
To the subjected plain; then disappear'd.
They looking back, all th' eastern side beheld   640
Of paradise, so late their happy seat,
Wav'd over by that flaming brand, the gate
With dreadful faces throng'd and fiery arms:
Some natural tears they dropp'd, but wip'd them soon;
The world was all before them, where to choose   645
Their place of rest, and providence their guide:
They hand in hand with wandring steps and slow,
Through Eden took their solitary way. (*1667*)

JOHN SUCKLING (1609–1642)

Song: Why So Pale and Wan, Fond Lover?

Why so pale and wan, fond lover?
    Prithee why so pale?
Will, when looking well can't move her,
    Looking ill prevail?
    Prithee why so pale?   5

Why so dull and mute, young sinner?
    Prithee why so mute?
Will, when speaking well can't win her,
    Saying nothing do't?
    Prithee why so mute?   10

Quit, quit, for shame; this will not move,
    This cannot take her;
If of herself she will not love,
    Nothing can make her:
    The devil take her!   (1646)

Song: No, No, Fair Heretic

No, no, fair heretic, it needs must be
    But an ill love in me,
    And worse for thee.
For were it in my power
To love thee now this hour   5
    More than I did the last,
I would then so fall,
    I might not love at all.
Love that can flow, and can admit increase,
Admits as well an ebb, and may grow less.   10

True love is still the same; the torrid zones,
    And those more frigid ones,
    It must not know;
For love, grown cold or hot,

Is lust or friendship, not   15
    The thing we have;
For that's a flame would die,
    Held down or up too high.
Then think I love more than I can express,
And would love more, could I but love thee less.   (*1646*)

Out Upon It! I Have Loved

Out upon it! I have loved
    Three whole days together;
And am like to love three more,
    If it prove fair weather!

Time shall moult away his wings,   5
    Ere he shall discover
In the whole wide world again
    Such a constant lover.

But the spite on't is, no praise
    Is due at all to me: 10
Love with me had made no stays,
    Had it any been but she.

Had it any been but she,
    And that very face,
There had been at least ere this   15
    A dozen dozen in her place!   (*1659*)

RICHARD LOVELACE (1618–1658)

To Althea, from Prison

When Love with unconfined wings
    Hovers within my gates,
And my divine Althea brings
    To whisper at the grates;
When I lie tangled in her hair   5
    And fetter'd to her eye,
The gods that wanton in the air
    Know no such liberty.

When flowing cups run swiftly round
    With no allaying Thames,   10
Our careless heads with roses crown'd,
    Our hearts with loyal flames;
When thirsty grief in wine we steep,
    When healths and draughts go free—
Fishes that tipple in the deep   15
    Know no such liberty.

When, like committed linnets, I
    With shriller throat shall sing
The sweetness, mercy, majesty
    And glories of my King;   20
When I shall voice aloud how good
    He is, how great should be,
Enlargéd winds, that curl the flood,
    Know no such liberty.

Stone walls do not a prison make,   25
    Nor iron bars a cage;
Minds innocent and quiet take
    That for an hermitage:
If I have freedom in my love
    And in my soul am free,   30
Angels alone, that soar above,
    Enjoy such liberty.   (1649)

To Lucasta, Going to the Wars

Tell me not, Sweet, I am unkind
    That from the nunnery
Of thy chaste breast and quiet mind
    To war and arms I fly.

True, a new mistress now I chase,   5
    The first foe in the field;
And with a stronger faith embrace
    A sword, a horse, a shield.

Yet this inconstancy is such
    As you too shall adore;   10
I could not love thee, Dear, so much,
    Loved I not Honour more.   (1649)

Lucasta Weeping

Lucasta wept, and still the bright
    Enamored god of day
With his soft handkercher of light
    Kissed the wet pearls away.

But when her tears his heat o'er came   5
    In clouds he quenched his beams,
And griev'd, wept out his eye of flame
    So drowned her sad streams.

At this she smil'd, when straight the sun
    Clear'd, with her kind desires;   10
And by her eyes reflection
    Kindled again his fires.   (1649)

ANDREW MARVELL (1621–1678)

The Garden

How vainly men themselves amaze
To win the palm, the oak, or bays;
And their incessant labours see
Crowned from some single herb or tree,
Whose short and narrow-vergéd shade   5
Does prudently their toils upbraid;
While all flowers and all trees do close
To weave the garlands of repose.

    Fair Quiet, have I found thee here,
And Innocence, thy sister dear!   10
Mistaken long, I sought you then
In busy companies of men.
Your sacred plants, if here below,
Only among the plants will grow:
Society is all but rude   15
To this delicious solitude.

    No white nor red was ever seen
So amorous as this lovely green.
Fond lovers, cruel as their flame,
Cut in these trees their mistress' name: 20
Little, alas, they know or heed,
How far these beauties hers exceed!
Fair trees! wheres'e'er your barks I wound,
No name shall but your own be found.

    When we have run our passion's heat,   25
Love hither makes his best retreat.
The gods, that mortal beauty chase,
Still in a tree did end their race:
Apollo hunted Daphne so,
Only that she might laurel grow;   30
And Pan did after Syrinx speed,
Not as a nymph, but for a reed.

    What wondrous life in this I lead!
Ripe apples drop about my head;

The luscious clusters of the vine   35
Upon my mouth do crush their wine;
The nectarine, and curious peach,
Into my hands themselves do reach;
Stumbling on melons, as I pass,
Ensnared with flowers, I fall on grass.   40

Meanwhile the mind, from pleasure less,
Withdraws into its happiness:
The mind, that ocean where each kind
Does straight its own resemblance find;
Yet it creates, transcending these,   45
Far other worlds, and other seas;
Annihilating all that's made
To a green thought in a green shade.

Here at the fountain's sliding foot,
Or at some fruit-tree's mossy root,   50
Casting the body's vest aside,
My soul into the boughs does glide:
There like a bird it sits and sings,
Then whets, and combs its silver wings;
And, till prepared for longer flight,   55
Waves in its plumes the various light.

Such was that happy garden-state,
While man there walked without a mate:
After a place so pure and sweet,
What other help could yet be meet?   60
But 'twas beyond a mortal's share
To wander solitary there:
Two Paradises 'twere in one,
To live in Paradise alone.

How well the skilful gardener drew   65
Of flowers and herbs this dial new!
Where, from above, the milder sun
Does through a fragrant zodiac run;
And, as it works, the industrious bee
Computes its time as well as we.   70
How could such sweet and wholesome hours
Be reckoned but with herbs and flowers?   (1681)

The Definition of Love

My love is of a birth as rare
As 'tis for object strange and high:
It was begotten by Despair
Upon Impossibility.

Magnanimous Despair alone   5
Could show me so divine a thing,
Where feeble Hope could ne'er have flown
But vainly flapped its tinsel wing.

And yet I quickly might arrive
Where my extended soul is fixed,   10
But Fate does iron wedges drive,
And always crowds itself betwixt.

For Fate with jealous eye does see
Two perfect loves, nor lets them close:
Their union would her ruin be,   15
And her tyrannic power depose.

And therefore her decrees of steel
Us as the distant poles have placed,
(Though love's whole world on us doth wheel)
Not by themselves to be embraced,   20

Unless the giddy heaven fall,
And earth some new convulsion tear,
And, us to join, the world should all
Be cramped into a planisphere.

As lines, so loves oblique may well   25
Themselves in every angle greet;
But ours, so truly parallel,
Though infinite, can never meet.

Therefore the love which us doth bind,
But fate so enviously debars,   30
Is the conjunction of the mind,
And opposition of the stars.   (*1681*)

To His Coy Mistress

Had we but world enough, and time,
This coyness, Lady, were no crime.
We would sit down, and think which way
To walk, and pass our long love's day.
Thou by the Indian Ganges' side   5
Shouldst rubies find; I by the tide
Of Humber would complain. I would
Love you ten years before the Flood;
And you should, if you please, refuse
Till the conversion of the Jews.   10
My vegetable ¹ love should grow
Vaster than empires, and more slow.
An hundred years should go to praise
Thine eyes, and on thy forehead gaze;
Two hundred to adore each breast;   15
But thirty thousand to the rest:
An age, at least, to every part,
And the last age should show your heart.
For, Lady, you deserve this state;
Nor would I love at lower rate.   20
      But, at my back, I always hear
Time's winged chariot hurrying near:
And yonder, all before us lie
Deserts of vast eternity.
Thy beauty shall no more be found;   25
Nor, in thy marble vault, shall sound
My echoing song. Then worms shall try
That long preserved virginity:
And your quaint honour turn to dust;
And into ashes all my lust.   30
The grave's a fine and private place,
But none, I think, do there embrace.
      Now, therefore, while the youthful hue
Sits on thy skin like morning dew,
And while thy willing soul transpires   35
At every pore with instant fires,
Now let us sport us while we may;
And now, like amorous birds of prey,

¹ vegetative

Rather at once our time devour,
Than languish in his slow-chapt power.   40
Let us roll all our strength, and all
Our sweetness, up into one ball;
And tear our pleasures, with rough strife,
Through the iron gates of life.
    Thus, though we cannot make our sun   45
Stand still, yet we will make him run.   (*1681*)

The Fair Singer

To make a final conquest of all me,
Love did compose so sweet an enemy,
In whom both beauties to my death agree,
Joining themselves in fatal harmony;
That while she with her eyes my heart does bind,   5
She with her voice might captivate my mind.

I could have fled from one but singly fair;
My disentangled soul itself might save,
Breaking the curlèd trammels of her hair.
But how should I avoid to be her slave,   10
Whose subtle art invisibly can wreathe
My fetters of the very air I breathe?

It had been easy fighting in some plain,
Where victory might hang in equal choice,
But all resistance against her is vain,   15
Who has th' advantage both of eyes and voice;
And all my forces needs must be undone,
She having gainèd both the wind and sun.   (*1681*)

HENRY VAUGHAN (1622–1695)

The Retreat

Happy those early days! when I
Shined in my angel-infancy.
Before I understood this place
Appointed for my second race,
Or taught my soul to fancy aught   5
But a white, celestial thought;
When yet I had not walked above
A mile or two from my first love,
And looking back, at that short space
Could see a glimpse of his bright face;   10
When on some gilded cloud or flower
My gazing soul would dwell an hour,
And in those weaker glories spy
Some shadows of eternity;
Before I taught my tongue to wound   15
My conscience with a sinful sound,
Or had the black art to dispense
A several sin to every sense,
But felt through all this fleshly dress
Bright shoots of everlastingness.   20
    Oh, how I long to travel back,
And tread again that ancient track!
That I might once more reach that plain,
Where first I left my glorious train;
From whence the enlightened spirit sees   25
That shady city of palm trees;
But ah! my soul with too much stay
Is drunk, and staggers in the way.
Some men a forward motion love,
But I by backward steps would move;   30
And when this dust falls to the urn,
In that state I came, return.   (1655)

The World

I saw Eternity the other night,
Like a great ring of pure and endless light,
    All calm, as it was bright;
And round beneath it, Time in hours, days, years,
    Driven by the spheres   5
Like a vast shadow moved; in which the world
    And all her train were hurled.
The doting lover in his quaintest strain
    Did there complain;
Near him, his lute, his fancy, and his flights,   10
    Wit's sour delights;
With gloves, and knots, the silly snares of pleasure,
    Yet his dear treasure,
All scattered lay, while he his eyes did pour
    Upon a flower.   15

The darksome statesman, hung with weights and woe,
Like a thick midnight-fog, moved there so slow,
    He did not stay, nor go;
Condemning thoughts—like sad eclipses—scowl
    Upon his soul,   20
And clouds of crying witnesses without
    Pursued him with one shout.
Yet digged the mole, and lest his ways be found,
    Worked underground,
Where he did clutch his prey; but one did see   25
    That policy.
Churches and altars fed him; perjuries
    Were gnats and flies;
It rained about him blood and tears, but he
    Drank them as free.   30

The fearful miser on a heap of rust
Sat pining all his life there, did scarce trust
    His own hands with the dust,
Yet would not place one piece above, but lives
    In fear of thieves.   35
Thousands there were as frantic as himself,
    And hugged each one his pelf;
The downright epicure placed heav'n in sense,
    And scorned pretence;

While others, slipped into a wide excess,   40
      Said little less;
The weaker sort slight, trivial wares enslave,
      Who think them brave;
And poor, despised Truth sat counting by
      Their victory.   45

Yet some, who all this while did weep and sing,
And sing and weep, soared up into the ring;
      But most would use no wing.
Oh, fools—said I—thus to prefer dark night
      Before true light!   50
To live in grots and caves, and hate the day
      Because it shows the way;
The way, which from this dead and dark abode
      Leads up to God;
A way where you might tread the sun, and be   55
      More bright than he!
But as I did their madness so discuss,
      One whispered thus,
'This ring the Bridegroom did for none provide,
      But for His bride.'   (*1658*)

They Are All Gone

They [1] are all gone into the world of light!
      And I alone sit lingering here;
Their very memory is fair and bright,
      And my sad thoughts doth clear.

It glows and glitters in my cloudy breast,   5
      Like stars upon some gloomy grove,
Or those faint beams in which this hill is dressed,
      After the sun's remove.

I see them walking in an air of glory,
      Whose light doth trample on my days;   10
My days, which are at best but dull and hoary,
      Mere glimmering and decays.

[1] spirits, heavenly beings, dead friends,
good people now dead

O holy Hope! and high Humility!
    High as the heavens above!
These are your walks, and you have showed them me,   15
      To kindle my cold love.

Dear beauteous Death! the jewel of the just,
    Shining nowhere but in the dark;
What mysteries do lie beyond thy dust,
      Could man outlook that mark!   20

He that hath found some fledged bird's nest may know
    At first sight if the bird be flown;
But what fair well [2] or grove he sings in now,
      That is to him unknown.

And yet, as angels in some brighter dreams   25
    Call to the soul when man doth sleep,
So some strange thoughts transcend our wonted themes,
      And into glory peep.

If a star were confined into a tomb,
    Her captive flames must needs burn there;   30
But when the hand that locked her up gives room,
      She'll shine through all the sphere.

O Father of eternal life, and all
    Created glories under Thee!
Resume Thy spirit from this world of thrall   35
      Into true liberty.

Either disperse these mists, which blot and fill
    My perspective still as they pass;
Or else remove me hence unto that hill
      Where I shall need no glass.   *(1655)*

---

[2] spring or pool

ᵉᔒ JOHN DRYDEN (1631–1700)

Mac Flecknoe

All human things are subject to decay,
And, when Fate summons, monarchs must obey.
This Flecknoe found, who, like Augustus, young
Was called to empire, and had governed long;
In prose and verse, was owned without dispute,   5
Through all the realms of Nonsense, absolute.
This aged prince, now flourishing in peace,
And blest with issue of a large increase,
Worn out with business, did at length debate
To settle the succession of the state;   10
And, pondering which of all his sons was fit
To reign and wage immortal war with wit,
Cried, " 'Tis resolved, for Nature pleads that he
Should only rule who most resembles me.
Shadwell [1] alone my perfect image bears,   15
Mature in dulness from his tender years;
Shadwell alone of all my sons is he
Who stands confirmed in full stupidity.
The rest to some faint meaning make pretence,
But Shadwell never deviates into sense.   20
Some beams of wit on other souls may fall,
Strike through, and make a lucid interval;
But Shadwell's genuine night admits no ray,
His rising fogs prevail upon the day.
Besides, his goodly fabric fills the eye   25
And seems designed for thoughtless majesty,
Thoughtless as monarch oaks that shade the plain,
And, spread in solemn state, supinely reign.
Heywood and Shirley were but types of thee,
Thou last great prophet of tautology.   30
Even I, a dunce of more renown than they,
Was sent before but to prepare thy way,
And coarsely clad in Norwich drugget came
To teach the nations in thy greater name.

[1] Thomas Shadwell, "Son of Flecknoe,"
a dull poet

178

My warbling lute, the lute I whilom strung,   35
When to King John of Portugal [2] I sung,
Was but the prelude to that glorious day
When thou on silver Thames didst cut thy way,
With well-timed oars before the royal barge,
Swelled with the pride of thy celestial charge,   40
And, big with hymn, commander of an host;
The like was ne'er in Epsom blankets [3] tossed.
Methinks I see the new Arion [3] sail,
The lute still trembling underneath thy nail.
At thy well-sharpened thumb from shore to shore   45
The treble squeaks for fear, the basses roar;
Echoes from Pissing Alley Shadwell call,
And Shadwell they resound from Aston Hall.
About thy boat the little fishes throng,
As at the morning toast that floats along.   50
Sometimes, as prince of thy harmonious band,
Thou wield'st thy papers in thy threshing hand.
St. André's [4] feet ne'er kept more equal time,
Not even the feet of thy own *Psyche's* rhyme:
Though they in number as in sense excel,   55
So just, so like tautology, they fell
That, pale with envy, Singleton [5] forswore,
The lute and sword which he in triumph bore,
And vowed he ne'er would act Villerius [6] more."
Here stopped the good old sire and wept for joy,   60
In silent raptures of the hopeful boy.
All arguments, but most his plays, persuade
That for anointed dulness he was made.
     Close to the walls which fair Augusta bind,
(The fair Augusta much to fears inclined,)   65
An ancient fabric raised to inform the sight
There stood of yore, and Barbican it hight;
A watch-tower once, but now, so fate ordains,
Of all the pile an empty name remains;
From its old ruins brothel-houses rise,   70
Scenes of lewd loves, and of polluted joys,

---

[2] Flecknoe had visited Portugal.
[3] Shadwell entitled one of his plays *Epsom Wells;* in another, *The Virtuoso,* a character was blanketed. The voyage image continues with the legendary Greek musician and poet, Arion, carried to shore by dolphins. [4] a French dancing master [5] an opera singer [6] a leading character in Davenant's operatic play, *The Siege of Rhodes*

Where their vast courts the mother-strumpets keep,
And, undisturbed by watch, in silence sleep.
Near these a Nursery [7] erects its head
Where queens are formed and future heroes bred,   75
Where unfledged actors learn to laugh and cry,
Where infant trulls their tender voices try,
And little Maximins [8] the gods defy.
Great Fletcher never treads in buskins here,
Nor greater Jonson dares in socks appear;   80
But gentle Simkin [9] just reception finds
Amidst this monument of vanished minds;
Pure clinches [10] the suburbian muse affords,
And Panton [11] waging harmless war with words.
Here Flecknoe, as a place to fame well known,   85
Ambitiously designed his Shadwell's throne.
For ancient Dekker prophesied long since
That in this pile should reign a mighty prince,
Born for a scourge of wit and flail of sense,
To whom true dulness should some *Psyches* [12] owe,   90
But worlds of *Misers* [12] from his pen should flow;
Humorists [12] and hypocrites it should produce,
Whole Raymond [13] families and tribes of Bruce.[13]
    Now Empress Fame had published the renown
Of Shadwell's coronation through the town.   95
Roused by report of fame, the nations meet
From near Bunhill and distant Watling-street.
No Persian carpets spread the imperial way,
But scattered limbs of mangled poets lay;
From dusty shops neglected authors come,   100
Martyrs of pies, and relics of the bum.
Much Heywood, Shirley, Ogleby there lay,
But loads of Shadwell almost choked the way.
Bilked stationers for yeomen stood prepared,
And Herringman [14] was captain of the guard.   105
The hoary prince in majesty appeared,
High on a throne of his own labors reared.
At his right hand our young Ascanius sat,
Rome's other hope, and pillar of the State.

---

[7] a theatre for training boys and girls for the stage [8] Maximin, in Dryden's *Tyrannic Love,* defies the gods [9] any simpleton. [10] puns [11] a contemporary writer [12] titles of works by Shadwell [13] two of Shadwell's characters [14] a contemporary publisher

His brows thick fogs, instead of glories, grace,   110
And lambent dulness played around his face.
As Hannibal did to the altars come,
Sworn by his sire a mortal foe to Rome;
So Shadwell swore, nor should his vow be vain,
That he till death true dullness would maintain;   115
And, in his father's right and realm's defense,
Ne'er to have peace with wit nor truce with sense.
The king himself the sacred unction made,
As king by office and as priest by trade.
In his sinister hand, instead of ball,   120
He placed a mighty mug of potent ale;
"Love's Kingdom" [15] to his right he did convey,
At once his scepter and his rule of sway;
Whose righteous lore the prince had practiced young
And from whose loins recorded "Psyche" sprung.   125
His temples, last, with poppies were o'erspread,
That nodding seemed to consecrate his head.
Just at that point of time, if fame not lie,
On his left hand twelve reverend owls did fly.
So Romulus, 'tis sung, by Tiber's brook,   130
Presage of sway from twice six vultures took.
The admiring throng loud acclamations make
And omens of his future empire take.
The sire then shook the honors of his head,
And from his brows damps of oblivion shed   135
Full on the filial dulness. Long he stood,
Repelling from his breast the raging god;
At length burst out in this prophetic mood:
"Heavens bless my son! from Ireland let him reign
To far Barbadoes on the western main;   140
Of his dominion may no end be known
And greater than his father's be his throne;
Beyond 'Love's Kingdom' let him stretch his pen!"
He paused, and all the people cried "Amen."
Then thus continued he: "My son, advance   145
Still in new impudence, new ignorance.
Success let others teach, learn thou from me
Pangs without birth and fruitless industry.
Let 'Virtuosos' in five years be writ,
Yet not one thought accuse thy toil of wit.   150

[15] a play by Flecknoe

Let gentle George [16] in triumph tread the stage,
Make Dorimant betray, and Loveit rage;
Let Cully, Cockwood, Fopling,[17] charm the pit,
And in their folly show the writer's wit.
Yet still thy fools shall stand in thy defense   155
And justify their author's want of sense.
Let them be all by thy own model made
Of dullness and desire no foreign aid,
That they to future ages may be known,
Not copies drawn, but issue of thy own.   160
Nay, let thy men of wit, too, be the same,
All full of thee and differing but in name.
But let no alien Sedley [18] interpose
To lard with wit thy hungry Epsom prose.
And when false flowers of rhetoric thou wouldst cull,   165
Trust nature, do not labor to be dull;
But write thy best and top, and in each line
Sir Formal's [19] oratory will be thine.
Sir Formal, though unsought, attends thy quill
And does thy northern dedications fill.[20]   170
Nor let false friends seduce thy mind to fame
By arrogating Jonson's hostile name;
Let father Flecknoe fire thy mind with praise
And uncle Ogleby [21] thy envy raise.
Thou art my blood, where Jonson has no part.   175
What share have we in nature or in art?
Where did his wit on learning fix a brand
And rail at arts he did not understand?
Where made he love in Prince Nicander's [22] vein
Or swept the dust in Psyche's humble strain?   180
Where sold he bargains, 'whip-stitch, kiss my arse,'
Promised a play and dwindled to a farce?
When did his muse from Fletcher scenes purloin.
As thou whole Etherege dost transfuse to thine?
But so transfused as oil on waters flow,   185
His always floats above, thine sinks below.
This is thy province, this thy wondrous way,
New humors to invent for each new play;

---

[16] George Etherege [17] characters in his plays [18] Charles Sedley wrote the prologue to Shadwell's *Epsom Wells*. [19] a character given to affected speech in Shadwell's *The Virtuoso* [20] Shadwell dedicated his books to the Duke of Newcastle. [20] a contemporary poet, also dull [22] a character in Shadwell's *Psyche*

This is that boasted bias of thy mind,
By which one way to dullness 'tis inclined, 190
Which makes thy writings lean on one side still,
And, in all changes, that way bends thy will.
Nor let thy mountain belly make pretense
Of likeness; thine's a tympany of sense.
A tun of man in thy large bulk is writ, 195
But sure thou'rt but a kilderkin of wit.
Like mine, thy gentle numbers feebly creep;
Thy tragic Muse gives smiles, thy comic sleep.
With whate'er gall thou setst thyself to write,
Thy inoffensive satires never bite; 200
In thy felonious heart though venom lies,
It does but touch thy Irish pen, and dies,
Thy genius calls thee not to purchase fame
In keen Iambics, but mild Anagram.
Leave writing plays, and choose for thy command 205
Some peaceful province in Acrostic land.
There thou mayest wings display and altars raise,
And torture one poor word ten thousand ways;
Or, if thou wouldst thy different talents suit,
Set thy own songs, and sing them to thy lute." 210
He said, but his last words were scarcely heard,
For Bruce and Longville [23] had a trap prepared,
And down they sent the yet declaiming bard.
Sinking, he left his drugget robe behind,
Borne upward by a subterranean wind. 215
The mantle fell to the young prophet's part
With double portion of his father's art. (1682)

A Song for Saint Cecilia's Day, November 22, 1687

From harmony, from heavenly harmony
    This universal frame began;
   When Nature underneath a heap
    Of jarring atoms lay,
   And could not heave her head, 5

[23] characters in Shadwell's plays

The tuneful voice was heard from high,
    Arise, ye more than dead.
Then cold and hot and moist and dry [1]
    In order to their stations leap,
      And Music's power obey   10
From harmony, from heavenly harmony
    This universal frame began;
      From harmony to harmony
Through all the compass of the notes it ran,
The diapason closing full in Man.   15

What passion cannot Music raise and quell?
    When Jubal [2] struck the corded shell,
    His listening brethren stood around,
      And, wondering, on their faces fell
    To worship that celestial sound.   20
Less than a god they thought there could not dwell
    Within the hollow of that shell,
    That spoke so sweetly, and so well.
What passion cannot Music raise and quell?

    The trumpet's loud clangor   25
      Excites us to arms
    With shrill notes of anger
      And mortal alarms.
    The double, double, double beat
      Of the thundering drum   30
      Cries, "Hark! the foes come;
Charge, charge, 'tis too late to retreat!"

    The soft complaining flute
    In dying notes discovers
    The woes of hopeless lovers,   35
Whose dirge is whispered by the warbling lute.

    Sharp violins proclaim
Their jealous pangs and desperation,
Fury, frantic indignation,
Depth of pains and height of passion,   40
    For the fair, disdainful dame.

    But, oh! what art can teach,
    What human voice can reach

[1] Mediaeval physics held that every- elements. [2] Genesis 4:21
thing was compounded of these four

The sacred organ's praise?
Notes inspiring holy love,   45
Notes that wing their heavenly ways
To mend the choirs above.

Orpheus could lead the savage race,
And trees unrooted left their place,
Sequacious of the lyre;   50
But bright Cecilia raised the wonder higher;
When to her organ vocal breath was given,
An angel heard, and straight appeared,
Mistaking earth for heaven.

As from the power of sacred lays   55
The spheres began to move,
And sung the great Creator's praise
To all the blest above;
So when the last and dreadful hour
This crumbling pageant shall devour,   60
The trumpet shall be heard on high,
The dead shall live, the living die,
And Music shall untune [3] the sky.

To the Memory of Mr. Oldham [1]

Farewell, too little and too lately known,
Whom I began to think and call my own;
For sure our souls were near allied, and thine
Cast in the same poetic mould with mine.
One common note on either lyre did strike,   5
And knaves and fools we both abhorred alike.
To the same goal did both our studies drive:
The last set out the soonest did arrive.
Thus Nisus [2] fell upon the slippery place,
Whilst his young friend performed and won the race.   10
O early ripe! to thy abundant store
What could advancing age have added more?
It might (what nature never gives the young)

---

[3] when the trumpet for the last judgment sounds

---

[1] John Oldham (1653–1683), a contemporary satirist   [2] Nisus and Eurya-
lus, young Trojan warriors, *Aeneid,* v

Have taught the numbers of thy native tongue.
But satire needs not those, and wit will shine 15
Through the harsh cadence of a rugged line.
A noble error, and but seldom made,
When poets are by too much force betrayed.
Thy gen'rous fruits, though gathered ere their prime,
Still shewed a quickness; and maturing time 20
But mellows what we write to the dull sweets of rhyme.
Once more, hail, and farewell! farewell, thou young
But ah! too short, Marcellus [3] of our tongue!
Thy brows with ivy and with laurels bound;
But fate and gloomy night encompass thee around. (1684)

Songs from the Plays

from THE INDIAN-QUEEN

Poor Mortals

Poor mortals that are clog'd with earth below
    Sink under love and care,
    While we that dwell in air
Such heavy passions never know.
    Why then shou'd mortals be 5
    Unwilling to be free
    From blood, that sullen cloud
    Which shining souls does shroud?
      Then they'l shew bright,
      And like us light 10
When leaving bodies with their care
    They slide to us and air. (1665)

from SECRET-LOVE

I Feed a Flame Within

I feed a flame within which so torments me
That it both pains my heart, and yet contents me:
'Tis such a pleasing smart, and I so love it,
That I had rather die, than once remove it.

[3] His early death was lamented by
Virgil, *Aeneid*, vi: 861–87

Yet he for whom I grieve shall never know it,   5
My tongue does not betray, nor my eyes show it:
Not a sigh nor a tear my pain discloses,
But they fall silently like dew on roses.

Thus to prevent my love from being cruel,
My heart's the sacrifice as 'tis the fuel: 10
And while I suffer this to give him quiet,
My faith rewards me love, though he deny it.

On his eyes will I gaze, and there delight me;
While I conceal my love, no frown can fright me:
To be more happy I dare not aspire;   15
Nor can I fall more low, mounting no higher.   (1668)

from TYRANNIC LOVE

Ah How Sweet It Is to Love

Ah how sweet it is to love,
Ah how gay is young desire!
And what pleasing pains we prove
When we first approach love's fire!
    Pains of love be sweeter far   5
    Than all other pleasures are.

Sighs which are from lovers blown
Do but gently heave the heart:
Ev'n the tears they shed alone
Cure, like trickling balm their smart.   10
    Lovers when they lose their breath,
    Bleed away in easy death.

Love and time with reverence use,
Treat 'em like a parting friend:
Nor the golden gifts refuse   15
Which in youth sincere they send:
    For each year their price is more,
    And they less simple than before.

Love, like spring tides full and high,
Swells in every youthful vein: 20
But each tide does less supply,
Till they quite shrink in again:
    If a flow in age appear,
    'Tis but rain, and runs not clear.   (1670)

Song to a Fair Young Lady
Going Out of Town in the Spring

Ask not the cause, why sullen spring
    So long delays her flow'rs to bear;
Why warbling birds forget to sing,
    And winter storms invert the year?
Chloris [1] is gone; and fate provides   5
To make it spring, where she resides.

Chloris is gone, the cruel fair;
    She cast not back a pitying eye:
But left her lover in despair;
    To sigh, to languish, and to die: 10
Ah, how can those fair eyes endure
To give the wounds they will not cure!

Great god of love, why hast thou made
    A face that can all hearts command,
That all religions can invade,   15
    And change the laws of ev'ry land?
Where thou hadst plac'd such pow'r before,
Thou shou'dst have made her mercy more.

When Chloris to the temple comes,
    Adoring crowds before her fall;   20
She can restore the dead from tombs,
    And ev'ry life but mine recall.
I only am by love design'd
To be the victim for mankind.   (1693)

---

[1] a personification of spring

THOMAS TRAHERNE (1637?–1674)

The Salutation

These little limbs,
These eyes and hands which here I find
This panting heart wherewith my life begins;
Where have ye been? Behind
What curtain were ye from me hid so long?   5
Where was, in what abyss, my new-made tongue?

When silent I
So many thousand thousand years
Beneath the dust did in a chaos lie,
How could I smiles, or tears,   10
Or lips, or hands, or eyes, or ears perceive?
Welcome ye treasures which I now receive.

I that so long
Was nothing from eternity,
Did little think such joys as ear and tongue   15
To celebrate or see:
Such sounds to hear, such hands to feel, such feet
Such eyes and objects, on the ground to meet.

New burnisht joys!
Which finest gold and pearl excell!   20
Such sacred treasures are the limbs of boys
In which a soul doth dwell:
Their organised joints and azure veins
More wealth include than the dead world contains.

From dust I rise   25
And out of nothing now awake;
These brighter regions which salute mine eyes
A gift from God I take:
The earth, the stars, the light, the lofty skies,
The sun and stars are mine; if these I prize.   30

A stranger here
Strange things doth meet, strange glory see;
Strange treasures lodg'd in this fair world appear,

Strange all and new to me:
But that they are mine should be who nothing was,   35
That strangest is of all, yet brought to pass.

Wonder

How like an angel came I down!
    How bright are all things here!
When first among His works I did appear,
    O how their glory me did crown!
The world resembled His eternity,   5
        In which my soul did walk;
    And everything that I did see
        Did with me talk.

The skies in their magnificence,
    The lively, lovely air,   10
Oh, how divine, how soft, how sweet, how fair!
    The stars did entertain my sense;
And all the works of God so bright and pure,
        So rich and great did seem
    As if they ever must endure   15
        In my esteem.

A native health and innocence
    Within my bones did grow;
And while my God did all his glories show,
    I felt a vigor in my sense   20
That was all spirit: I within did flow
        With seas of life like wine;
    I nothing in the world did know
        But 'twas divine.

Harsh, ragged objects were concealed: 25
    Oppressions, tears, and cries,
Sins, griefs, complaints, dissensions, weeping eyes
    Were hid, and only things revealed
Which heavenly spirits and the angels prize.
        The state of innocence   30
    And bliss, not trades and poverties,
        Did fill my sense.

The streets were paved with golden stones;
    The boys and girls were mine:
Oh, how did all their lovely faces shine!   35
    The sons of men were holy ones;
In joy and beauty they appeared to me;
    And everything which here I found,
    While like an angel I did see,
        Adorned the ground.   40

    Rich diamond and pearl and gold
      In every place was seen;
Rare splendors, yellow, blue, red, white, and green,
    Mine eyes did everywhere behold.
Great wonders clothed with glory did appear;   45
      Amazement was my bliss;
    That and my wealth was everywhere;
      No joy to this!

    Cursed and devised proprieties,
      With envy, avarice,   50
And fraud (those fiends that spoil even Paradise)
    Flew from the splendor of mine eyes;
And so did hedges, ditches, limits, bounds:
      I dreamed not aught of those,
    But in surveying all men's grounds   55
      I found repose.

    For property itself was mine,
      And hedges, ornaments:
Walls, houses, coffers, and their rich contents
    To make me rich combine.   60
Clothes, costly jewels, laces, I esteemed
      My wealth by others worn;
    For me they all to wear them seemed
      When I was born.

PART 4
The Eighteenth Century

ANNE FINCH, COUNTESS OF WINCHILSEA (1661–1720)

To the Nightingale

Exert thy voice, sweet harbinger of spring!
 This moment is thy time to sing,
 This moment I attend to praise,
And set my numbers to thy lays.
 Free as thine shall be my song;   5
 As thy music, short, or long.
Poets, wild as thee, were born,
 Pleasing best when unconfin'd,
 When to please is least design'd,
Soothing but their cares to rest;   10
 Cares do still their thoughts molest,
 And still th'unhappy poet's breast,
Like thine, when best he sings, is plac'd against a thorn.
She begins, let all be still!
 Muse, thy promise now fulfill!   15
Sweet, oh! sweet, still sweeter yet
Can thy words such accents fit,
Canst thou syllables refine,
Melt a sense that shall retain
Still some spirit of the brain,   20
Till with sounds like these it join.
 'Twill not be! then change thy note;
 Let division shake thy throat.
Hark! division now she tries;
Yet as far the Muse outflies.   25
 Cease then, pr'ythee, cease thy tune;
 Trifler, wilt thou sing till June?
Till thy bus'ness all lies waste,
And the time of building's past!
 Thus we poets that have speech,   30
Unlike what thy forests teach,
 If a fluent vein be shown
 That's transcendent to our own,
Criticize, reform, or preach,
Or censure what we cannot reach.   (1713)

౿ MATTHEW PRIOR (1664–1721)

An Epitaph

Stet quicunque volet potens Aulæ culmine lubrico, &c.
Seneca.[1]

Interr'd beneath this marble stone,
Lie saunt'ring Jack, and idle Joan.
While rolling threescore years and one
Did round this globe their courses run;
If human things went ill or well;   5
If changing empires rose or fell;
The morning pass'd, the evening came,
And found this couple still the same.
They walk'd and eat, good folks: what then?
Why then they walk'd and eat again: 10
They soundly slept the night away:
They did just nothing all the day:
And having buried children four,
Would not take pains to try for more.
Nor sister either had, nor brother: 15
They seem'd just tallied for each other.
    Their moral and economy
Most perfectly they made agree:
Each virtue kept its proper bound,
Nor trespass'd on the other's ground.   20
Nor fame, nor censure they regarded:
They neither punish'd, nor rewarded.
He car'd not what the footmen did:
Her maids she neither prais'd, nor chid:
So ev'ry servant took his course;   25
And bad at first, they all grew worse.
Slothful disorder fill'd his stable;
And sluttish plenty deck'd her table.
Their beer was strong; their wine was port;
Their meal was large; their grace was short.   30
They gave the poor the remnant-meat,
Just when it grew not fit to eat.

---

[1] Anyone who wishes power at court
stands on slippery ground.

They paid the church and parish rate;
And took, but read not the receipt;
For which they claim'd their Sunday's due,   35
Of slumb'ring in an upper pew.
　　No man's defects sought they to know;
So never made themselves a foe.
No man's good deeds did they commend;
So never rais'd themselves a friend.   40
Nor cherish'd they relations poor:
That might decrease their present store:
Nor barn nor house did they repair:
That might oblige their future heir.
　　They neither added, nor confounded: 45
They neither wanted, nor abounded.
Each Christmas they accompts did clear;
And wound their bottom [2] round the year.
Nor tear, nor smile did they employ
At news of public grief, or joy.   50
When bells were rung, and bonfires made,
If ask'd, they ne'er denied their aid:
Their jug was to the ringers carried,
Whoever either died, or married.
Their billet at the fire was found,   55
Whoever was depos'd, or crown'd.
　　Nor good, nor bad, nor fools, nor wise;
They would not learn, nor could advise:
Without love, hatred, joy, or fear,
They led—a kind of—as it were: 60
Nor wish'd nor car'd, nor laugh'd, nor cried:
And so they liv'd; and so they died.   (*1718*)

[2] thread

JONATHAN SWIFT (1667–1745)

A Description of the Morning

Now hardly here and there an hackney-coach
Appearing, show'd the ruddy morn's approach.
Now Betty from her master's bed had flown,
And softly stole to discompose her own;
The slip-shod 'prentice from his master's door   5
Had par'd the dirt, and sprinkled round the floor.
Now Moll had whirl'd her mop with dextrous airs,
Prepar'd to scrub the entry and the stairs.
The youth with broomy stumps began to trace
The kennel's edge, where wheels had worn the place.   10
The small-coal [1] man was heard with cadence deep,
Till drown'd in shriller notes of chimney-sweep:
Duns at his lordship's gate began to meet;
And brickdust Moll had scream'd through half the street.
The turnkey now his flock returning sees,   15
Duly let out a-nights to steal for fees:
The watchful bailiffs take their silent stands,
And schoolboys lag with satchels in their hands.   (1709)

A Description of a City Shower

Careful observers may foretell the hour
(By sure prognostics) when to dread a show'r.
While rain depends, the pensive cat gives o'er
Her frolics, and pursues her tail no more.
Returning home at night, you'll find the sink   5
Strike your offended sense with double stink.
If you be wise, then go not far to dine;
You'll spend in coach-hire more than save in wine.
A coming show'r your shooting corns presage,
Old a-ches throb, your hollow tooth will rage: 10
Saunt'ring in coffee-house is Dulman seen;
He damns the climate, and complains of spleen.

[1] charcoal

Meanwhile the South, rising with dabbled wings,
A sable cloud athwart the welkin flings,
That swill'd more liquor than it could contain,   15
And, like a drunkard, gives it up again.
Brisk Susan whips her linen from the rope,
While the first drizzling show'r is borne aslope:
Such is that sprinkling, which some careless quean
Flirts on you from her mop, but not so clean: 20
You fly, invoke the gods; then turning, stop
To rail; she singing, still whirls on her mop.
Not yet the dust had shunn'd th' unequal strife,
But, aided by the wind, fought still for life,
And wafted with its foe by vi'lent gust,   25
'Twas doubtful which was rain, and which was dust.
Ah! where must needy poet seek for aid,
When dust and rain at once his coat invade?
Sole coat, where dust cemented by the rain
Erects the nap, and leaves a cloudy stain.   30
Now in contiguous drops the flood comes down,
Threat'ning with deluge this *devoted* town.
To shops in crowds the daggled females fly,
Pretend to cheapen goods, but nothing buy.
The Templar spruce, while ev'ry spout's abroach,   35
Stays till 'tis fair, yet seems to call a coach.
The tuck'd-up sempstress walks with hasty strides,
While streams run down her oil'd umbrella's sides.
Here various kinds, by various fortunes led,
Commence acquaintance underneath a shed.   40
Triumphant Tories, and desponding Whigs,
Forget their feuds, and join to save their wigs.
Box'd in a chair the beau impatient sits,
While spouts run clatt'ring o'er the roof by fits,
And ever and anon with frightful din   45
The leather sounds; he trembles from within.
So when Troy chairmen bore the wooden steed,
Pregnant with Greeks impatient to be freed
(Those bully Greeks, who, as the moderns do,
Instead of paying chairmen, ran them through),   50
Laocoön struck the outside with his spear,
And each imprison'd hero quak'd for fear.
Now from all parts the swelling kennels flow,
And bear their trophies with them as they go:
Filth of all hues and odour seem to tell   55

What street they sail'd from, by their sight and smell.
They, as each torrent drives with rapid force,
From Smithfield [1] to St. Pulchre's shape their course,
And in huge confluence join'd at Snowhill ridge,
Fall from the conduit prone to Holborn bridge.   60
Sweeping from butchers' stalls, dung, guts, and blood,
Drown'd puppies, stinking sprats, all drench'd in mud,
Dead cats, and turnip-tops, come tumbling down the flood.

(1710)

The Furniture of a Woman's Mind

A set of phrases learnt by rote;
A passion for a scarlet coat;
When at a play to laugh, or cry,
Yet cannot tell the reason why:
Never to hold her tongue a minute;   5
While all she prates has nothing in it.
Whole hours can with a coxcomb sit,
And take his nonsense all for wit:
Her learning mounts to read a song;
But half the words pronouncing wrong;   10
Has ev'ry repartee in store,
She spoke ten thousand times before.
Can ready compliments supply
On all occasions, cut and dry.
Such hatred to a parson's gown,   15
The sight will put her in a swown.
For conversation well endu'd;
She calls it witty to be rude;
And, placing raillery in railing,
Will tell aloud your greatest failing;   20
Nor makes a scruple to expose
Your bandy leg, or crooked nose.
Can at her morning tea run o'er
The scandal of the day before.
Improving hourly in her skill,   25
To cheat and wrangle at quadrille.

[1] a London center for marketing and
slaughtering cattle

In choosing lace a critic nice,
Knows to a groat the lowest price;
Can in her female clubs dispute
What lining best the silk will suit;   30
What colours each complexion match:
And where with art to place a patch.
      If chance a mouse creeps in her sight,
Can finely counterfeit a fright;
So sweetly screams if it comes near her,   35
She ravishes all hearts to hear her.
Can dextrously her husband tease,
By taking fits whene'er she please:
By frequent practice learns the trick
At proper seasons to be sick;   40
Thinks nothing gives one airs so pretty;
At once creating love and pity.
If Molly happens to be careless,
And but neglects to warm her hair-lace,
She gets a cold as sure as death;   45
And vows she scarce can fetch her breath—
Admires how modest woman can
Be so robustious like a man.
      In party, furious to her pow'r;
A bitter Whig, or Tory sour;   50
Her arguments directly tend
Against the side she would defend:
Will prove herself a Tory plain,
From principles the Whigs maintain;
And, to defend the Whiggish cause,   55
Her topics from the Tories draws.
      Oh yes! If any man can find
More virtues in a woman's mind,
Let them be sent to Mrs. Harding; [1]
She'll pay the charges to a farthing: 60
Take notice, she has my commission
To add them in the next edition;
They may outsell a better thing;
So, holla boys; God save the King.   (1727)

[1] a contemporary printer

✑§ JOSEPH ADDISON (1672–1719)

Ode

The spacious firmament on high,
With all the blue ethereal sky,
And spangled heavens, a shining frame,
Their great Original proclaim.
The unwearied sun from day to day   5
Does his Creator's power display,
And publishes to every land
The work of an Almighty hand.

Soon as the evening shades prevail,
The moon takes up the wondrous tale,   10
And nightly to the listening earth
Repeats the story of her birth;
Whilst all the stars that round her burn,
And all the planets in their turn,
Confirm the tidings as they roll,   15
And spread the truth from pole to pole.

What though in solemn silence, all
Move round this dark terrestrial ball?
What though nor real voice nor sound
Amidst their radiant orbs be found?   20
In Reason's ear they all rejoice,
And utter forth a glorious voice,
Forever singing as they shine:
"The hand that made us is divine!"   (1712)

ALEXANDER POPE (1688–1744)

Ode on Solitude

Happy the man, whose wish and care
    A few paternal acres bound,
Content to breathe his native air,
        In his own ground.

Whose herds with milk, whose fields with bread,   5
    Whose flocks supply him with attire,
Whose trees in summer yield him shade,
        In winter fire.

Blest, who can unconcern'dly find
    Hours, days, and years slide soft away,   10
In health of body, peace of mind,
        Quiet by day,

Sound sleep by night; study and ease,
    Together mixed; sweet recreation;
And innocence, which most does please   15
        With meditation.

Thus let me live, unseen, unknown,
    Thus unlamented let me die,
Steal from the world, and not a stone
        Tell where I lie.   (1726)

An Essay on Criticism

Part II

Of all the causes which conspire to blind
Man's erring judgment, and misguide the mind,
What the weak head with strongest bias rules,
Is pride, the never-failing vice of fools,
Whatever nature has in worth denied,   5
She gives in large recruits of needful pride;
For as in bodies, thus in souls, we find
What wants in blood and spirits, swelled with wind.

Pride, where wit fails, steps in to our defense,
And fills up all the mighty void of sense.   10
If once right reason drives that cloud away,
Truth breaks upon us with resistless day.
Trust not yourself; but your defects to know,
Make use of every friend—and every foe.
    A little learning is a dangerous thing;   15
Drink deep, or taste not the Pierian spring.
There, shallow drafts intoxicate the brain,
And drinking largely sobers us again.
Fired at first sight with what the Muse imparts,
In fearless youth we tempt the heights of arts,   20
While from the bounded level of our mind
Short views we take, nor see the lengths behind;
But more advanced, behold with strange surprise
New distant scenes of endless science [1] rise!
So pleased at first the towering Alps we try,   25
Mount o'er the vales, and seem to tread the sky,
Th' eternal snows appear already past,
And the first clouds and mountains seem the last;
But, those attained, we tremble to survey
The growing labors of the lengthened way,   30
Th' increasing prospect tires our wandering eyes,
Hills peep o'er hills, and Alps on Alps arise!
    A perfect judge will read each work of wit
With the same spirit that its author writ;
Survey the whole, nor seek slight faults to find   35
Where nature [2] moves, and rapture warms the mind;
Nor lose, for that malignant dull delight,
The generous pleasure to be charmed with wit.
But in such lays as neither ebb nor flow,
Correctly cold, and regularly low,   40
That shunning faults, one quiet tenor keep,
We cannot blame indeed—but we may sleep.
In wit, as nature, what affects our hearts
Is not th' exactness of peculiar parts;
'Tis not a lip, or eye, we beauty call,   45
But the joint force and full result of all.
Thus when we view some well-proportioned dome,
(The world's just wonder, and even thine, O Rome!)

[1] all knowledge   [2] permanence, order,
and design in the world, man, and art

No single parts unequally surprise,
All comes united to th' admiring eyes;   50
No monstrous height, or breadth, or length appear;
The whole at once is bold and regular.
    Whoever thinks a faultless piece to see,
Thinks what ne'er was, nor is, nor e'er shall be.
In every work regard the writer's end,   55
Since none can compass more than they intend;
And if the means be just, the conduct true,
Applause, in spite of trivial faults, is due.
As men of breeding, sometimes men of wit,
T' avoid great errors, must the less commit;   60
Neglect the rules each verbal critic lays,
For not to know some trifles is a praise.
Most critics, fond of some subservient art,
Still make the whole depend upon a part;
They talk of principles, but notions prize,   65
And all to one loved folly sacrifice.
    Once on a time, La Mancha's knight,[3] they say,
A certain bard encountering on the way,
Discoursed in terms as just, with looks as sage,
As e'er could Dennis,[4] of the Grecian stage;   70
Concluding all were desperate sots and fools,
Who durst depart from Aristotle's rules.
Our author, happy in a judge so nice,
Produced his play, and begged the knight's advice;
Made him observe the subject, and the plot,   75
The manners, passions, unities, what not?
All which, exact to rule, were brought about,
Were but a combat in the lists left out.
"What! leave the combat out?" exclaims the knight;
Yes, or we must renounce the Stagirite.   80
"Not so, by heaven!" (he answers in a rage).
"Knights, squires, and steeds must enter on the stage."
So vast a throng the stage can ne'er contain.
"Then build a new, or act it in a plain."
    Thus critics, of less judgment than caprice,   85
Curious not knowing, not exact but nice,
Form short ideas; and offend in arts,
(As most in manners) by a love to parts.

[3] Don Quixote   [4] John Dennis, author
of *Appius and Virginia* (1709)

Some to conceit alone their taste confine,
And glittering thoughts struck out at every line;   90
Pleased with a work where nothing's just or fit;
One glaring chaos and wild heap of wit.
Poets like painters, thus unskilled to trace
The naked nature and the living grace,
With gold and jewels cover every part,   95
And hide with ornaments their want of art.
True wit is nature to advantage dressed,
What oft was thought, but ne'er so well expressed;
Something, whose truth convinced at sight we find,
That gives us back the image of our mind.   100
As shades more sweetly recommend the light,
So modest plainness sets off sprightly wit.
For works may have more wit than does them good,
As bodies perish through excess of blood.
    Others for language all their care express,   105
And value books, as women men, for dress;
Their praise is still—the style is excellent;
The Sense, they humbly take upon content.
Words are like leaves; and where they most abound,
Much fruit of sense beneath is rarely found: 110
False Eloquence, like the prismatic glass,
Its gaudy colours spreads on every place;
The face of Nature we no more survey,
All glares alike, without distinction gay:
But true expression, like th' unchanging Sun,   115
Clears and improves whate'er shines upon,
It gilds all objects, but it alters none.
Expression is the dress of thought, and still
Appears more decent, as more suitable;
A vile conceit in pompous words expressed,   120
Is like a clown in regal purple dressed:
For different styles with different subjects sort,
As several garbs with country, town, and court.
Some by old words to fame have made pretence,
Ancients in phrase, mere moderns in their sense;   125
Such laboured nothings, in so strange a style,
Amaze th' unlearn'd, and make the learnèd smile.
Unlucky, as Fungoso [5] in the play,

---

[5] in Jonson's *Every Man Out of His Humour*

These sparks with awkward vanity display
What the fine gentleman wore yesterday;   130
And but so mimic ancient wits at best,
As apes our grandsires, in their doublets drest.
In words, as fashions, the same rule will hold;
Alike fantastic, if too new, or old:
Be not the first by whom the new are tried,   135
Nor yet the last to lay the old aside.
    But most by *Numbers* [6] judge a Poet's song;
And smooth or rough, with them is right or wrong:
In the bright Muse, though thousand charms conspire,
Her voice is all these tuneful fools admire;   140
Who haunt Parnassus but to please their ear,
Not mend their minds; as some to Church repair,
Not for the doctrine, but the music there.
These equal syllables alone require,
Tho' oft the ear the open vowels tire;   145
While expletives their feeble aid do join;
And ten low words oft creep in one dull line·
While they ring round the same unvaried chimes,
With sure returns of still expected rhymes;
Where-e'er you find "the cooling western breeze,"   150
In the next line, it "whispers through the trees":
If crystal streams "with pleasing murmurs creep,"
The reader's threatened (not in vain) with "sleep":
Then, at the last and only couplet fraught
With some unmeaning thing they call a thought,   155
A needless Alexandrine ends the song,
That, like a wounded snake, drags its slow length along.
Leave such to tune their own dull rhymes, and know
What's roundly smooth or languishingly slow;
And praise the easy vigor of a line,   160
Where Denham's strength, and Waller's sweetness join.
True ease in writing comes from art, not chance,
As those move easiest who have learned to dance.
'Tis not enough no harshness gives offence:
The sound must seem an echo to the sense.   165
Soft is the strain when Zephyr gently blows,
And the smooth stream in smoother numbers flows;
But when loud surges lash the sounding shore,
The hoarse, rough verse should like the torrent roar.

[6] metrical rhythm in poetry

When Ajax strives some rock's vast weight to throw,   170
The line, too, labors, and the words move slow.
Not so when swift Camilla [7] scours the plain,
Flies o'er th' unbending corn, and skims along the main.
Hear how Timotheus' [8] varied lays surprise,
And bid alternate passions fall and rise!   175
While, at each change, the son of Libyan Jove [9]
Now burns with glory, and then melts with love;
Now his fierce eyes with sparkling fury glow,
Now sighs steal out, and tears begin to flow:
Persians and Greeks like turns of nature found,   180
And the world's victor stood subdued by sound!
The power of music all our hearts allow,
And what Timotheus was, is Dryden now.
      Avoid extremes; and shun the fault of such
Who still are pleased too little or too much,   185
At every trifle scorn to take offence;
That always shows great pride, or little sense;
Those heads, as stomachs, are not sure the best,
Which nauseate all, and nothing can digest.
Yet let not each gay turn thy rapture move;   190
For fools admire,[10] but men of sense approve:
As things seem large which we through mists descry,
Dullness is ever apt to magnify.
      Some foreign writers, some our own despise;
The Ancients only, or the Moderns prize.   195
Thus Wit, like Faith, by each man is applied
To one small sect, and all are damned beside.
Meanly they seek the blessing to confine,
And force that sun but on a part to shine,
Which not alone the southern wit sublimes,   200
But ripens spirits in cold northern climes;
Which from the first has shone on ages past,
Enlights the present, and shall warm the last;
Tho' each may feel increases and decays,
And see now clearer and now darker days.   205
Regard not then if Wit be old or new,
But blame the false, and value still the true.
      Some ne'er advance a Judgment of their own,
But catch the spreading notion of the Town;

[7] a maiden-warrior ally of Turnus in the *Aeneid,* VII [8] Greek poet and mu-sician [9] See Dryden's "Alexander's Feast." [10] wonder at

They reason and conclude by precedent,   210
And own stale nonsense which they ne'er invent.
Some judge of author's names, not works, and then
Nor praise nor blame the writings, but the men.
Of all this servile herd the worst is he
That in proud dullness joins with Quality: 215
A constant Critic at the great man's board,
To fetch and carry nonsense for my Lord.
What woful stuff this madrigal would be,
In some starved hackney sonneteer, or me?
But let a Lord once own the happy lines,   220
How the wit brightens! how the style refines!
Before his sacred name flies every fault,
And each exalted stanza teems with thought!
    The Vulgar thus through Imitation err;
As oft the Learn'd by being singular;   225
So much they scorn the crowd, that if the throng
By chance go right, they purposely go wrong;
So Schismatics the plain believers quit,
And are but damned for having too much wit.
Some praise at morning what they blame at night;   230
But always think the last opinion right.
A Muse by these is like a mistress used,
This hour she's idolized, the next abused;
While their weak heads, like towns unfortified,
'Twixt sense and nonsense daily change their side.   235
Ask them the cause; they're wiser still, they say;
And still tomorrow's wiser than today.
We think our fathers fools, so wise we grow;
Our wiser sons, no doubt, will think us so.
Once school-divines this zealous isle o'erspread;   240
Who knew most sentences, was deepest read;
Faith, gospel, all, seem'd made to be disputed,
And none had sense enough to be confuted:
Scotists and Thomists, now, in peace remain,
Amidst their kindred cobwebs in Duck Lane.[11]   245
If faith itself has diff'rent dresses worn,
What wonder modes in wit should take their turn?
Oft, leaving what is natural and fit,
The current folly proves the ready wit;

[11] a London center for dealers in old
books

And authors think their reputation safe,   250
Which lives as long as fools are pleas'd to laugh.
      Some, valuing those of their own side or mind,
Still make themselves the measure of mankind:
Fondly we think we honor merit then,
When we but praise ourselves in other men.   255
Parties in wit attend on those of state,
And public faction doubles private hate.
Pride, malice, folly, against Dryden rose,
In various shapes of parsons, critics, beaux; [12]
But sense survived, when merry jests were past;   260
For rising merit will buoy up at last.
Might he return, and bless once more our eyes,
New Blackmores and new Milbourns [13] must arise:
Nay should great Homer lift his awful head,
Zoilus [14] again would start up from the dead.   265
Envy will merit, as its shade, pursue;
But like a shadow, proves the substance true;
For envied Wit, like Sol eclipsed, makes known
Th' opposing body's grossness, not its own,
When first that sun too powerful beams displays,   270
It draws up vapours which obscure its rays;
But even those clouds at last adorn its way,
Reflect new glories, and augment the day.
      Be thou the first true merit to befriend;
His praise is lost, who stays till all commend.   275
Short is the date, alas, of modern rhymes,
And 'tis but just to let them live betimes.
No longer now that golden age appears,
When Patriarch-wits survived a thousand years:
Now length of Fame (our second life) is lost,   280
And bare threescore is all even that can boast;
Our sons their fathers' failing language see;
And such as Chaucer is, shall Dryden be.
So when the faithful pencil has designed
Some bright Idea of the master's mind,   285
Where a new world leaps out at his command,
And ready Nature waits upon his hand;
When the ripe colours soften and unite,

---

[12] a reference to *The Rehearsal,* which ridiculed Dryden   [13] Richard Blackmore and Luke Milbourne, dull writers, had both attacked Dryden.   [14] a critic of Homer

And sweetly melt into just shade and light;
When mellowing years their full perfection give,   290
And each bold figure just begins to live,
The treacherous colours the fair art betray,
And all the bright creation fades away!
    Unhappy Wit, like most mistaken things,
Atones not for that envy which it brings.   295
In youth alone its empty praise we boast,
But soon the short-lived vanity is lost:
Like some fair flower the early spring supplies,
That gaily blooms, but even in blooming dies.
What is this Wit, which must our cares employ?   300
The owner's wife, that other men enjoy;
Then most our trouble still when most admired,
And still the more we give, the more required;
Whose fame with pains we guard, but lose with ease,
Sure some to vex, but never all to please;   305
'Tis what the vicious fear, the virtuous shun,
By fools 'tis hated, and by knaves undone!
    If Wit so much from Ignorance undergo,
Ah let not Learning too commence its foe!
Of old, those met rewards who could excel,   310
And such were praised who but endeavoured well:
Tho' triumphs were to generals only due,
Crowns were reserved to grace the soldiers too.
Now, they who reach Parnassus' lofty crown,
Employ their pains to spurn some others down;   315
And while self-love each jealous writer rules,
Contending wits become the sport of fools:
But still the worst with most regret commend,
For each ill Author is as bad a Friend.
To what base ends, and by what abject ways,   320
Are mortals urged thro' sacred lust of praise!
Ah ne'er so dire a thirst of glory boast,
Nor in the Critic let the Man be lost.
Good-nature and good-sense must ever join;
To err is human, to forgive, divine.   325
    But if in noble minds some dregs remain
Not yet purged off, of spleen and sour disdain;
Discharge that rage on more provoking crimes,
Nor fear a dearth in these flagitious times.
No pardon vile Obscenity should find,   330
Tho' wit and art conspire to move your mind;

But Dulness with Obscenity must prove
As shameful sure as Impotence in love.
In the fat age of pleasure, wealth, and ease,
Sprung the rank weed, and thrived with large increase: 335
When love was all an easy Monarch's care;
Seldom at council, never in a war:
Jilts ruled the state, and statesmen farces writ;
Nay Wits had pensions, and young Lords had wit:
The Fair sat panting at a Courtier's play,   340
And not a Mask went unimproved away:
The modest fan was lifted up no more,
And Virgins smiled at what they blushed before.
The following licence of a Foreign reign
Did all the dregs of bold Socinus drain;   345
Then unbelieving priests reformed the nation,
And taught more pleasant methods of salvation;
Where Heaven's free subjects might their rights dispute,
Lest God himself should seem too absolute:
Pulpits their sacred satire learned to spare,   350
And Vice admired to find a flatterer there!
Encouraged thus, Wit's Titans braved the skies,
And the press groaned with licensed blasphemies.
These monsters, Critics! with your darts engage,
Here point your thunder, and exhaust your rage!   355
Yet shun their fault, who, scandalously nice,
Will needs mistake an author into vice;
All seems infected that th' infected spy,
As all looks yellow to the jaundiced eye.   (*1711*)

From *An Essay on Man*

Epistle I

.   .   .   .   .

Lo, the poor Indian! whose untutored mind
Sees God in clouds, or hears him in the wind;   100
His soul, proud science never taught to stray
Far as the solar walk, or milky way;
Yet simple nature to his hope has given,
Behind the cloud-topped hill, an humbler Heaven;

Some safer world in depths of woods embraced,   105
Some happier island in the watery waste,
Where slaves once more their native land behold,
No fiends torment, no Christians thirst for gold.
To be, contents his natural desire,
He asks no angel's wing, no seraph's fire;   110
But thinks, admitted to that equal sky,
His faithful dog shall bear him company.
Go, wiser thou! and in thy scale of sense
Weigh thy opinion against Providence;
Call imperfection what thou fanciest such,   115
Say, "Here he gives too little, there too much";
Destroy all creatures for thy sport or gust,
Yet cry, "If man's unhappy, God's unjust";
If man alone engross not Heaven's high care,
Alone made perfect here, immortal there,   120
Snatch from his hand the balance and the rod,
Re-judge his justice, be the god of God.
In pride, in reasoning pride, our error lies;
All quit their sphere, and rush into the skies.
Pride still is aiming at the blest abodes,   125
Men would be angels, angels would be gods.
Aspiring to be gods, if angels fell,
Aspiring to be angels, men rebel;
And who but wishes to invert the laws
Of order, sins against the Eternal Cause.   130
Ask for what end the heavenly bodies shine,
Earth for whose use? Pride answers, " 'Tis for mine.
For me kind nature wakes her genial power,
Suckles each herb, and spreads out every flower;
Annual for me, the grape, the rose renew   135
The juice nectareous, and the balmy dew;
For me, the mine a thousand treasures brings;
For me, health gushes from a thousand springs;
Seas roll to waft me, suns to light me rise;
My footstool earth, my canopy the skies."   140
        But errs not Nature from this gracious end,
From burning suns when livid deaths descend,
When earthquakes swallow, or when tempests sweep
Towns to one grave, whole nations to the deep?
No ('tis replied), the first Almighty Cause   145
Acts not by partial, but by general laws;
Th' exceptions few; some change, since all began

And what created perfect?—Why then man?
If the great end be human happiness,
Then nature deviates; and can man do less?   150
As much that end a constant course requires
Of showers and sunshine, as of man's desires;
As much eternal springs and cloudless skies,
As men forever temperate, calm, and wise.
If plagues or earthquakes break not Heaven's design,   155
Why then a Borgia, or a Cataline?
Who knows but he, whose hand the lightning forms,
Who heaves old Ocean, and who wings the storms;
Pours fierce Ambition in a Cæsar's mind,
Or turns young Ammon loose to scourge mankind?   160
From pride, from pride, our very reasoning springs;
Account for moral, as for natural things:
Why charge we Heaven in those, in these acquit?
In both, to reason right is to submit.
    Better for Us, perhaps, it might appear,   165
Were there all harmony, all virtue here;
That never air or ocean felt the wind;
That never passion discomposed the mind.
But ALL subsists by elemental strife;
And Passions are the elements of Life.   170
The general ORDER, since the whole began,
Is kept in Nature, and is kept in Man.
                          . . . . . .

What if the foot, ordained the dust to tread,
Or hand to toil, aspired to be the head?   260
What if the head, the eye, or ear repined
To serve mere engines to the ruling mind?
Just as absurd for any part to claim
To be another, in this general frame;
Just as absurd, to mourn the tasks or pains   265
The great directing Mind of all ordains.
    All are but parts of one stupendous whole,
Whose body nature is, and God the soul;
That, changed through all, and yet in all the same;
Great in the earth, as in th' ethereal frame;   270
Warms in the sun, refreshes in the breeze,
Glows in the stars, and blossoms in the trees,
Lives through all life, extends through all extent,
Spreads undivided, operates unspent;
Breathes in our soul, informs our mortal part,   275

As full, as perfect, in a hair as heart;
As full, as perfect, in vile man that mourns,
As the rapt seraph that adores and burns.
To him no high, no low, no great, no small;
He fills, he bounds, connects, and equals all.   280

Cease then, nor order imperfection name;
Our proper bliss depends on what we blame.
Know thy own point: this kind, this due degree
Of blindness, weakness, Heaven bestows on thee.
Submit. In this, or any other sphere,   285
Secure to be as blest as thou canst bear;
Safe in the hand of one disposing Power,
Or in the natal, or the mortal hour.
All nature is but art, unknown to thee;
All chance, direction, which thou canst not see;   290
All discord, harmony not understood;
All partial evil, universal good;
And, spite of pride, in erring reason's spite,
One truth is clear, whatever is, is right.

Epistle II

Know then thyself, presume not God to scan:
The proper study of mankind is man.
Placed on this isthmus of a middle state,
A being darkly wise and rudely great;
With too much knowledge for the sceptic side,   5
With too much weakness for the stoic's pride,
He hangs between; in doubt to act, or rest;
In doubt to deem himself a god or beast;
In doubt his mind or body to prefer;
Born but to die, and reasoning but to err;   10
Alike in ignorance, his reason such,
Whether he thinks too little or too much:
Chaos of thought and passion, all confused;
Still by himself abused, or disabused;
Created half to rise, and half to fall;   15
Great lord of all things, yet a prey to all;
Sole judge of truth, in endless error hurled;
The glory, jest, and riddle of the world!
    Go, wondrous creature; mount where science guides,
Go, measure earth, weigh air, and state the tides: 20

Instruct the planets in what orbs to run,
Correct old Time, and regulate the sun; [1]
Go, soar with Plato to th' empyreal sphere,
To the first good, first perfect, and first fair;
Or tread the mazy round his followers trod,   25
And quitting sense call imitating God;
As eastern priests in giddy circles run,
And turn their heads to imitate the sun.
Go, teach Eternal Wisdom how to rule—
Then drop into thyself, and be a fool!   30
    Superior beings, when of late they saw
A mortal man unfold all nature's law,
Admired such wisdom in an earthly shape,
And showed a Newton, as we show an ape.
    Could he, whose rules the rapid comet bind,   35
Describe or fix one movement of his mind?
Who saw its fires here rise, and there descend,
Explain his own beginning or his end?
Alas! what wonder! Man's superior part
Unchecked may rise, and climb from art to art;   40
But when his own great work is but begun,
What reason weaves, by passion is undone.
    Trace science, then, with modesty thy guide;
First strip off all her equipage of pride;
Deduct what is but vanity or dress,   45
Or learning's luxury, or idleness,
Or tricks to show the stretch of human brain,
Mere curious pleasure, or ingenious pain;
Expunge the whole, or lop th' excrescent parts
Of all our vices have created arts;   50
Then see how little the remaining sum,
Which served the past, and must the times to come!
    Two principles in human nature reign;
Self-love to urge, and reason to restrain;
Nor this a good, nor that a bad we call,   55
Each works its end to move or govern all;
And to their proper operation still
Ascribe all good; to their improper, ill.
    Self-love, the spring of motion, acts the soul;
Reason's comparing balance rules the whole.   60

[1] Since the calendar had fallen several in England in 1751.
days behind the sun, it was reformed

Man, but for that, no action could attend,
And, but for this, were active to no end;
Fixed like a plant on his peculiar spot,
To draw nutrition, propagate, and rot;
Or, meteor-like, flame lawless through the void,   65
Destroying others, by himself destroyed.
     Most strength the moving principle requires;
Active its task, it prompts, impels, inspires;
Sedate and quiet, the comparing lies,
Formed but to check, deliberate, and advise.   70
Self-love still stronger, as its objects nigh,
Reason's at distance and in prospect lie;
That sees immediate good by present sense;
Reason, the future and the consequence.
Thicker than arguments, temptations throng,   75
At best more watchful this, but that more strong.
The action of the stronger to suspend,
Reason still use, to reason still attend.
Attention, habit and experience gains;
Each strengthens reason, and self-love restrains.   80
     Let subtle schoolmen teach these friends to fight,
More studious to divide than to unite;
And grace and virtue, sense and reason split,
With all the rash dexterity of wit.
Wits, just like fools, at war about a name,   85
Have full as oft no meaning, or the same.
Self-love and reason to one end aspire,
Pain their aversion, pleasure their desire;
But greedy that, its object would devour,
This taste the honey, and not wound the flower;   90
Pleasure, or wrong or rightly understood,
Our greatest evil or our greatest good.   (1733–1734)

Epistle to Dr. Arbuthnot [1]

P. SHUT, shut the door, good John! [2] fatigu'd, I said,
Tie up the knocker, say I'm sick, I'm dead.
The Dog-star [3] rages! nay 't is past a doubt,

[1] Dr. John Arbuthnot, physician to
queen Anne and friend of Swift and
Pope   [2] John Searl, servant to Pope
[3] Sirius, connoting midsummer madness

All Bedlam, or Parnassus, is let out:
Fire in each eye, and papers in each hand,   5
They rave, recite, and madden round the land.
      What walls can guard me, or what shade can hide?
They pierce my thickets, thro' my Grot [4] they glide;
By land, by water, they renew the charge;
They stop the chariot, and they board the barge.   10
No place is sacred, not the Church is free;
Ev'n Sunday shines no Sabbath-day to me;
Then from the Mint [5] walks forth the Man of rhyme,
Happy to catch me just at Dinner-time.
      Is there a Parson, much bemus'd in beer,   15
A maudlin Poetess, a rhyming Peer,
A Clerk, foredoom'd his father's soul to cross,
Who pens a Stanza, when he should *engross*?
Is there, who, lock'd from ink and paper, scrawls
With desp'rate charcoal round his darken'd walls?   20
All fly to TWIT'NAM, and in humble strain
Apply to me, to keep them mad or vain.
Arthur,[6] whose giddy son neglects the Laws,
Imputes to me and my damn'd works the cause:
Poor Cornus [7] sees his frantic wife elope,   25
And curses Wit, and Poetry, and Pope.
      Friend to my Life! (which did not you prolong,
The world had wanted many an idle song)
What *Drop* [8] or *Nostrum* can this plague remove?
Or which must end me, a Fool's wrath or love?   30
A dire dilemma! either way I'm sped,
If foes, they write, if friends, they read me dead.
Seiz'd and tied down to judge, how wretched I!
Who can't be silent, and who will not lie.
To laugh, were want of goodness and of grace,   35
And to be grave, exceeds all Pow'r of face.
I sit with sad civility, I read
With honest anguish, and an aching head;
And drop at last, but in unwilling ears,
This saving counsel, "Keep your piece nine years." [9]   40
      "Nine years!" cries he, who high in Drury-lane,

[4] a tunnel under the London road which separated Pope's garden and house on the Thames at Twickenham   [5] where debtors gathered, free from arrest on Sundays   [6] Arthur Moore, father to a poet Pope often ridiculed, James Moore-Smythe   [7] Sir Robert Walpole   [8] a quack medicine   [9] Horace, *Ars Poetica,* V, 386

Lull'd by soft Zephyrs thro' the broken pane,
Rhymes ere he wakes, and prints before *Term* ends,[10]
Oblig'd by hunger, and request of friends: [11]
"The piece, you think, is incorrect? why, take it,   45
I'm all submission, what you'd have it, make it."
    Three things another's modest wishes bound,
My Friendship, and a Prologue, and ten pound.
    Pitholeon [12] sends to me: "You know his Grace,
I want a Patron; ask him for a Place."   50
'Pitholeon libell'd me,'—"but here's a letter
Informs you, Sir, 't was when he knew no better.
Dare you refuse him? Curll [13] invites to dine,
He'll write a *Journal*,[14] or he'll turn Divine."
    Bless me! a packet.—" 'T is a stranger sues,   55
A Virgin Tragedy,[15] an Orphan Muse."
If I dislike it, "Furies, death and rage!"
If I approve, "Commend it to the Stage."
There (thank my stars) my whole Commission ends,
The Play'rs and I are, luckily, no friends,   60
Fir'd that the house reject him, " 'Sdeath I'll print it,
And shame the fools—Your Int'rest, Sir, with Lintot!" [16]
'Lintot, dull rogue! will think your price too much:'
"Not, Sir, if you revise it, and retouch."
All my demurs but double his Attacks;   65
At last he whispers, "Do; and we go snacks."
Glad of a quarrel, straight I clap the door,
"Sir, let me see your works and you no more."
    'T is sung, when Midas' Ears began to spring,
(Midas, a sacred person and a king)   70
His very Minister who spy'd them first,
(Some say his Queen) was forc'd to speak, or burst.
And is not mine, my friend, a sorer case,
When ev'ry coxcomb perks them in my face?
A. Good friend, forbear! you deal in dang'rous things.   75
I'd never name Queens, Ministers, or Kings;
Keep close to Ears, and those let asses prick;
'T is nothing— P. Nothing? if they bite and kick?

---

[10] prints while law courts were in session and many people in London [11] actual and expressed reasons for publication here contrasted [12] a bad poet of ancient Rhodes, hence any bad poet [13] Edmund Curll, a notorious printer [14] support Walpole's government, as did the *London Journal* [15] R. Barford, who imitated Pope, wrote *The Virgin Queen* [16] Bernard Lintot, Pope's publisher

Out with it, DUNCIAD! let the secret pass,
That secret to each fool, that he's an Ass: [17]   80
The truth once told (and wherefore should we lie?)
The Queen of Midas slept, and so may I.
    You think this cruel? take it for a rule,
No creature smarts so little as a fool.
Let peals of laughter, Codrus! [18] round thee break,   85
Thou unconcern'd canst hear the mighty crack:
Pit, Box, and gall'ry in convulsions hurl'd,
Thou stand'st unshook amidst a bursting world.
Who shames a Scribbler? break one cobweb thro',
He spins the slight, self-pleasing thread anew: 90
Destroy his fib or sophistry, in vain,
The creature 's at his dirty work again,
Thron'd in the centre of his thin designs,
Proud of a vast extent of flimsy lines!
Whom have I hurt? has Poet yet, or Peer,   95
Lost the arch'd eye-brow, or Parnassian sneer?
And has not Colley [19] still his Lord, and whore?
His Butchers Henley,[20] his free-masons Moore? [21]
Does not one table Bavius [22] still admit?
Still to one Bishop [23] Philips [24] seem a wit?   100
Still Sappho [25]— A. Hold! for God's sake—you'll offend,
No Names!—be calm!—learn prudence of a friend!
I too could write, and I am twice as tall;
But foes like these— P. One Flatt'rer 's worse than all.
Of all mad creatures, if the learn'd are right,   105
It is the slaver kills, and not the bite.
A fool quite angry is quite innocent:
Alas! 't is ten times worse when they *repent*.
    One dedicates in high heroic prose,
And ridicules beyond a hundred foes: 110
One from all Grubstreet will my fame defend,
And more abusive, calls himself my friend.
This prints my *Letters*, that expects a bribe,
And others roar aloud, "Subscribe, subscribe."

---

[17] His talent is as visible as Midas's ass's ears. [18] a bad poet, satirized by Juvenal [19] Another bad poet, Colley Cibber, poet laureate [20] John Henley, who preached in Newport Market and Butcher Row [21] James Moore-Smythe frequently headed processions of Free-masons. [22] a bad Roman poet [23] Hugh Boulter, Archbishop of Armagh [24] Ambrose Philips, friend to Bishop Boulter, his patron [25] any woman poet, perhaps Lady Mary Wortley Montagu

There are, who to my person pay their court: 115
I cough like *Horace,* and, tho' lean, am short,
Ammon's great son [26] one shoulder had too high,
Such *Ovid's* nose, and "Sir! you have an Eye"—
Go on, obliging creatures, make me see
All that disgrac'd my Betters, met in me. 120
Say for my comfort, languishing in bed,
"Just so immortal *Maro* [27] held his head:"
And when I die, be sure you let me know
Great *Homer* died three thousand years ago.

Why did I write? what sin [28] to me unknown 125
Dipt me in ink, my parents', or my own?
As yet a child, nor yet a fool to fame,
I lisp'd in numbers,[29] for the numbers came.
I left no calling for this idle trade,
No duty broke, no father disobey'd.[30] 130
The Muse but serv'd to ease some friend, not Wife,
To help me thro' this long disease, my Life,
To second, ARBUTHNOT! thy Art and Care,
And teach the Being you preserv'd, to bear.

But why then publish? *Granville* [31] the polite, 135
And knowing *Walsh,* would tell me I could write;
Well-natur'd *Garth* inflam'd with early praise;
And *Congreve* lov'd, and *Swift* endur'd my lays;
The courtly *Talbot, Somers, Sheffield,* read;
Ev'n mitred *Rochester* would nod the head, 140
And *St. John's* self (great *Dryden's* friends before)
With open arms receiv'd one Poet more.
Happy my studies, when by these approv'd!
Happi ⁀ their author, when by these belov'd!
From these the world will judge of men and books, 145
Not from the *Burnets, Oldmixons,* and *Cookes.*[32]

Soft were my numbers; who could take offence,
While pure Description held the place of Sense?
Like gentle *Fanny's* [33] was my flow'ry theme,
A painted mistress,[34] or a purling stream.[35] 150

---

[26] Alexander the Great [27] Virgil
[28] John 9:2 [29] Verses [30] Pope's
father, difficult to please, required him
to write and rewrite verses. [31] He
and others immediately named were
patrons and admirers of Dryden.
[32] Gilbert Burnet, John Oldmixon, and
Thomas Cooke, here grouped as violent party writers [33] verse of any
insipid poet, like that of John, Lord
Hervey, friend of Lady Montagu
[34] a reference to Pope's *The Rape of
the Lock* [35] a reference to *Windsor
Forest,* also by Pope

Yet then did *Gildon* [36] draw his venal quill;—
I wish'd the man a dinner, and sat still.
Yet then did *Dennis* [37] rave in furious fret;
I never answer'd—I was not in debt.
If want provok'd, or madness made them print,   155
I wag'd no war with *Bedlam* or the *Mint*.
    Did some more sober Critic come abroad;
If wrong, I smil'd; if right, I kiss'd the rod.
Pains, reading, study, are their just pretence,
And all they want is spirit, taste, and sense.   160
Commas and points they set exactly right,
And 't were a sin to rob them of their mite.
Yet ne'er one sprig of laurel grac'd these ribalds,
From slashing *Bentley* [38] down to pidling *Tibalds*: [39]
Each wight, who reads not, and but scans and spells,   165
Each Word-catcher, that lives on syllables,
Ev'n such small Critics some regard may claim,
Preserv'd in *Milton's* or in *Shakespeare's* name.
Pretty! in amber to observe the forms
Of hairs, or straws, or dirt, or grubs, or worms!   170
The things, we know, are neither rich nor rare,
But wonder how the devil they got there.
    Were others angry: I excus'd them too;
Well might they rage, I gave them but their due.
A man's true merit 't is not hard to find;   175
But each man's secret standard in his mind,
That Casting-weight pride adds to emptiness,
This, who can gratify? for who can *guess?*
The Bard [40] whom pilfer'd Pastorals renown,
Who turns a Persian tale for half a Crown,   180
Just writes to make his barrenness appear,
And strains, from hard-bound brains, eight lines a year;
He, who still wanting, tho' he lives on theft,
Steals much, spends little, yet has nothing left:
And He, who now to sense, now nonsense leaning,   185
Means not, but blunders round about a meaning:
And He, whose fustian 's so sublimely bad,
It is not Poetry, but prose run mad:
All these, my modest Satire bade *translate,*

[36] Charles Gildon, a critic who had attacked Pope   [37] John Dennis, another critic   [38] Richard Bentley, a classical scholar who had *slashed* the text of *Paradise Lost*   [39] Louis Theobald, a pedantic editor of Shakespeare   [40] Ambrose Philips, earlier mentioned (l. 100), author of *Persian Tales*

And own'd that nine such Poets made a *Tate*.[41]   190
How did they fume, and stamp, and roar, and chafe!
And swear, not ADDISON himself was safe.
    Peace to all such! but were there One whose fires
True Genius kindles, and fair Fame inspires;
Blest with each talent and each art to please,   195
And born to write, converse, and live with ease:
Should such a man, too fond to rule alone,
Bear, like the Turk, no brother near the throne.
View him with scornful, yet with jealous eyes,
And hate for arts that caus'd himself to rise;   200
Damn with faint praise, assent with civil leer,
And without sneering, teach the rest to sneer;
Willing to wound, and yet afraid to strike,
Just hint a fault, and hesitate dislike;
Alike reserv'd to blame, or to commend,   205
A tim'rous foe, and a suspicious friend;
Dreading ev'n fools, by Flatterers besieg'd,
And so obliging, that he ne'er oblige'd;
Like *Cato,* give his little Senate laws,
And sit attentive to his own applause;   210
While Wits and Templars ev'ry sentence raise,[42]
And wonder with a foolish face of praise:—
Who but must laugh, if such a man there be?
Who would not weep, if ATTICUS [43] were he?
    What tho' my Name stood rubric on the walls   215
Or plaister'd posts, with claps,[44] in capitals?
Or smoking forth, a hundred hawkers' load,
On wings of winds came flying all abroad?
I sought no homage from the Race that write;
I kept, like *Asian* Monarchs, from their sight: 220
Poems I heeded (now be-rhym'd so long)
No more than thou, great GEORGE! [45] a birth-day song.
I ne'er with wits or witlings pass'd my days,
To spread about the itch of verse and praise;
Nor like a puppy, daggled thro' the town,   225
To fetch and carry sing-song up and down;
Nor at Rehearsals sweat, and mouth'd, and cry'd,
With handkerchief and orange at my side;

[41] Nahum Tate, a poet laureate, 1690–1715, without talent   [42] exalt   [43] a friend to Cicero; the name had been applied earlier to Addison   [44] placards   hung on doorposts   [45] George II, not interested in the poor birthday odes Colley Ciber, line 97, wrote for him

But sick of fops, and poetry, and prate,
To *Bufo* [46] left the whole *Castalian* state.   230
    Proud as *Apollo* on his forked hill,
Sat full-blown *Bufo,* puff'd by ev'ry quill;
Fed with soft Dedication all day long,
Horace and he went hand in hand in song.
His Library (where busts of Poets dead   235
And a true *Pindar* stood without a head,[47])
Receiv'd of wits and undistinguish'd race,
Who first his judgment ask'd, and then a place:
Much they extoll'd his pictures, much his seat,
And flatter'd ev'ry day, and some days eat: 240
Till grown more frugal in his riper days,
He paid some bards with port, and some with praise;
To some a dry rehearsal was assign'd,
And others (harder still) he paid in kind.
Dryden alone (what wonder?) came not nigh,   245
Dryden alone escap'd this judging eye:
But still the *Great* have kindness in reserve,
He help'd to bury whom he help'd to starve.
    May some choice patron bless each gray goose quill!
May ev'ry *Bavius* have his *Bufo* still!   250
So, when a Statesman wants a day's defence,
Or Envy holds a whole week's war with Sense,
Or simple pride for flatt'ry makes demands,
May dunce by dunce be whistled off my hands!
Blest be the *Great!* for those they take away,   255
And those they left me; for they left me GAY;
Left me to see neglected Genius bloom,
Neglected die, and tell it on his tomb:
Of all thy blameless life the sole return [48]
My Verse, and QUEENSB'RY [49] weeping o'er thy urn.   260
    Oh let me live my own, and die so too!
(To live and die is all I have to do:)
Maintain a Poet's dignity and ease,
And see what friends, and read what books I please;
Above a Patron, tho' I condescend   265
Sometimes to call a minister my friend.
I was not born for Courts or great affairs;

---

[46] any patron, perhaps Lord Halifax [47] Pope is ridiculing affectation for antiquarian sculpture. [48] John Gay had died the preceding year. [49] The Duke of Queensbury, friend to Pope and Gay

I pay my debts, believe, and say my pray'rs;
Can sleep without a Poem in my head;
Nor know, if *Dennis* be alive or dead.   270
    Why am I ask'd what next shall see the light?
Heav'ns! was I born for nothing but to write?
Has Life no joys for me? or, (to be grave)
Have I no friend to serve, no soul to save?
"I found him close with *Swift*"—'Indeed? no doubt,   275
(Cries prating *Balbus* [50]) 'something will come out.'
'T is all in vain, deny it as I will.
'No, such a Genius never can lie still;'
And then for mine obligingly mistakes
The first Lampoon Sir *Will.* [51] or *Bubo* [52] makes.   280
Poor guiltless I! and can I choose but smile,
When ev'ry Coxcomb knows me by my *Style?*
    Curst be the verse, how well soe'er it flow,
That tends to make one worthy man my foe,
Give Virtue scandal, Innocence a fear,   285
Or from the soft-eyed Virgin steal a tear.
But he who hurts a harmless neighbour's peace,
Insults fall'n worth, or Beauty in distress,
Who loves a Lie, lame Slander helps about,
Who writes a Libel, or who copies out: 290
That Fop, whose pride affects a patron's name,
Yet absent, wounds an author's honest fame:
Who can *your* merit *selfishly* approve,
And show the *sense* of it without the *love;*
Who has the vanity to call you friend,   295
Yet wants the honour, injur'd, to defend;
Who tells whate'er you think, whate'er you say,
And, if he lie not, must at least betray:
Who to the *Dean,* and *silver bell* can swear,[53]
And sees at *Canons* what was never there;   300
Who reads, but with a lust to misapply,
Make Satire a Lampoon, and Fiction, Lie.
A lash like mine no honest man shall dread,
But all such babbling blockheads in his stead.
    Let *Sporus* [54] tremble— A. What? that thing of silk,   305

---

[50] The Earl of Kinnoul, hated by Pope and Swift   [51] any titled writer of doggerel, perhaps Sir William Yonge   [52] Latin for *owl,* perhaps Bubb Doddington,   later   Lord   Melcombe

[53] Pope's *Epistle on Taste* had been said to ridicule the Duke of Chandos.   [54] a homosexual at Nero's court, usually taken to allude here to Lord Hervey

Sporus, that mere white curd of Ass's milk?
Satire or sense, alas! can *Sporus* feel?
Who breaks a butterfly upon a wheel?
P. Yet let me flap this bug with gilded wings,
This painted child of dirt, that stinks and stings;   310
Whose buzz the witty and the fair annoys,
Yet wit ne'er tastes, and beauty ne'er enjoys:
So well-bred spaniels civilly delight
In mumbling of the game they dare not bite.
Eternal smiles his emptiness betray,   315
As shallow streams run dimpling all the way.
Whether in florid impotence he speaks,
And, as the prompter breathes, the puppet squeaks;
Or at the ear of *Eve,*[55] familiar Toad,
Half froth, half venom, spits himself abroad,   320
In puns, or politics, or tales, or lies,
Or spite, or smut, or rhymes, or blasphemies.
His wit all see-saw, between *that* and *this,*
Now high, now low, now master up, now miss,
And he himself one vile Antithesis.   325
Amphibious thing! that acting either part.
The trifling head or the corrupted heart,
Fop at the toilet, flatt'rer at the board,[56]
Now trips a Lady, and now struts a Lord.
Eve's tempter thus the Rabbins have exprest,   330
A Cherub's face, a reptile all the rest;
Beauty that shocks you, parts that none will trust;
Wit that can creep, and pride that licks the dust.
    Not Fortune's worshipper, nor fashion's fool,
Not Lucre's madman, nor Ambition's tool,   335
Not proud, or servile;—be one Poet's praise,
That, if he pleas'd, he pleas'd by manly ways:
That Flatt'ry, ev'n to Kings, he held a shame,
And thought a Lie in verse or prose the same.
That not in Fancy's maze he wander'd long,   340
But stoop'd to Truth, and moraliz'd his song:
That not for Fame, but Virtue's better end,
He stood [57] the furious foe, the timid friend,
The damning critic, half approving wit,
The coxcomb hit, or fearing to be hit;   345

[55] *Paradise Lost,* IV, 799 ff.; Eve may   council table   [57] withstood
refer here to queen Caroline   [56] the

Laugh'd at the loss of friends he never had,
The dull, the proud, the wicked, and the mad;
The distant threats of vengeance on his head,
The blow unfelt, the tear he never shed; [58]
The tale reviv'd, the lie so oft o'erthrown,   350
Th' imputed trash, and dulness not his own;
The morals blacken'd when the writings scape,
The libell'd person, and the pictur'd shape;
Abuse, on all he lov'd, or lov'd him, spread,
A friend in exile, or a father, dead;   355
The whisper, that to greatness still too near,
Perhaps, yet vibrates on his SOV'REIGN's ear:
Welcome for thee, fair *Virtue!* all the past;
For thee, fair Virtue! welcome ev'n the *last!*
    A. But why insult the poor, affront the great?   360
P. A knave's a knave, to me, in ev'ry state:
Alike my scorn, if he succeed or fail,
Sporus at court, or *Japhet* [59] in a jail,
A hireling scribbler, or a hireling peer,
Knight of the post corrupt, or of the shire;   365
If on a Pillory, or near a Throne,
He gain his Prince's ear, or lose his own.
    Yet soft by nature, more a dupe than wit,
Sappho can tell you how this man was bit;
This dreaded Sat'rist *Dennis* will confess   370
Foe to his pride, but friend to his distress:
So humble, he has knock'd at *Tibbald's* door,
Has drunk with *Cibber,* nay has rhym'd for *Moore.*
Full ten years slander'd, did he once reply?
Three thousand suns went down on *Welsted's* lie.[60]   375
To please a Mistress one aspers'd his life;
He lash'd him not, but let her be his wife.
Let *Budgel* [61] charge low *Grubstreet* on his quill,
And write whate'er he pleas'd, except his Will;
Let the two *Curlls* of Town and Court,[62] abuse   380
His father, mother, body, soul, and muse.
Yet why? that Father held it for a rule,
It was a sin to call our neighbour fool:

---

[58] a pamphlet, A Pop upon Pope, reported that Pope had cried from pain when beaten in Ham Walks.   [59] Japhet Crook, imprisoned for forgery   [60] a charge in print that Pope had occasioned the death of a lady   [61] Eustace Budgell, said to have forged a will   [62] Curll the publisher and Lord Hervey, the "Curll of Court"

That harmless Mother thought no wife a whore:
Hear this, and spare his family, *James Moore!* [63]   385
Unspotted names, and memorable long!
If there be force in Virtue, or in Song.

    Of gentle blood (part shed in Honour's cause,
While yet in *Britain* Honour had applause)
Ere parent sprung—A. What fortune, pray?—P. Their own,   390
And better got, than *Bestia's*[64] from the throne.
Born to no Pride, inheriting no Strife,
Nor marrying Discord in a noble wife,[65]
Stranger to civil and religious rage,
The good man walk'd innoxious thro' his age.   395
Nor Courts he saw, no suits would ever try,
Nor dar'd an Oath, nor hazarded a Lie.
Un-learn'd, he knew no schoolman's subtle art,
No language, but the language of the heart.
By Nature honest, by Experience wise,   400
Healthy by temp'rance, and by exercise;
His life, tho' long, to sickness past unknown,
His death was instant, and without a groan.
O grant me, thus to live, and thus to die!
Who sprung from Kings shall know less joy than I.   405

    O Friend! may each domestic bliss be thine!
Be no unpleasing Melancholy mine:
Me, let the tender office long engage,
To rock the cradle of reposing Age,
With lenient arts extend a Mother's breath,   410
Make Languor smile, and smooth the bed of Death,
Explore the thought, explain the asking eye,
And keep a while one parent from the sky! [66]
On cares like these if length of days attend,
May Heav'n, to bless those days, preserve my friend,   415
Preserve him social, cheerful, and serene,
And just as rich as when he serv'd a QUEEN.
A. Whether that blessing be deny'd or giv'n,
Thus far was right, the rest belongs to Heav'n.   (1735)

[63] said to have been an illegitimate child   [64] one who receives bribes, perhaps here Horace Walpole, Sir Robert's brother   [65] Addison had unhappily married the Countess of Warwick.   [66] Pope's mother died in 1733.

The Universal Prayer

Father of all! in every age,
　　In every clime adored,
By saint, by savage, and by sage,
　　Jehovah, Jove, or Lord!

Thou Great First Cause, least understood:　　　5
　　Who all my sense confined
To know but this, that Thou art good,
　　And that myself am blind;

Yet gave me, in this dark estate,
　　To see the good from ill;　　　　　　　　10
And, binding nature fast in fate,
　　Left free the human will.

What conscience dictates to be done,
　　Or warns me not to do,
This, teach me more than hell to shun,　　　15
　　That, more than heaven pursue.

What blessings Thy free bounty gives,
　　Let me not cast away;
For God is paid when man receives;
　　T' enjoy is to obey.　　　　　　　　　　20

Yet not to earth's contracted span
　　Thy goodness let me bound,
Or think Thee Lord alone of man,
　　When thousand worlds are round.

Let not this weak, unknowing hand　　　　25
　　Presume Thy bolts to throw,
And deal damnation round the land,
　　On each I judge Thy foe.

If I am right, Thy grace impart,
　　Still in the right to stay;　　　　　　　　30
If I am wrong, Oh! teach my heart
　　To find that better way.

Save me alike from foolish pride
　　Or impious discontent,
At aught Thy wisdom has denied,　　　　35
　　Or aught Thy goodness lent.

Teach me to feel another's woe,
　　To hide the fault I see;
That mercy I to others show,
　　That mercy show to me.　　　　　　　　　　40

Mean though I am, not wholly so,
　　Since quickened by Thy breath;
Oh, lead me wheresoe'er I go,
　　Through this day's life or death.

This day, be bread and peace my lot;　　　　45
　　All else beneath the sun,
Thou know'st if best bestowed or not,
　　And let Thy will be done.

To Thee, whose temple is all space,
　　Whose altar earth, sea, skies,　　　　　　50
One chorus let all being raise,
　　All nature's incense rise!　　(1738)

ᴈ SAMUEL JOHNSON (1709–1784)

From *The Vanity of Human Wishes*

IN IMITATION OF THE TENTH SATIRE OF JUVENAL

.   .   .   .   .

When first the college rolls receive his name,   135
The young enthusiast quits his ease for fame;
Through all his veins the fever of renown
Spreads from the strong contagion of the gown;
O'er Bodley's dome [1] his future labours spread,
And Bacon's mansion trembles o'er his head. [2]   140
Are these thy views? proceed, illustrious youth,
And Virtue guard thee to the throne of Truth!
Yet should thy soul indulge the gen'rous heat,
Till captive Science yields her last retreat;
Should Reason guide thee with her brightest ray,   145
And pour on misty Doubt resistless day;
Should no false kindness lure to loose delight,
Nor praise relax, nor difficulty fright;
Should tempting Novelty thy cell refrain,
And Sloth effuse her opiate fumes in vain;   150
Should Beauty blunt on fops her fatal dart,
Nor claim the triumph of a letter'd heart;
Should no disease thy torpid veins invade,
Nor Melancholy's phantoms haunt thy shade;
Yet hope not life from grief or danger free,   155
Nor think the doom of man revers'd for thee:
Deign on the passing world to turn thine eyes,
And pause a while from letters, to be wise;
There mark what ills the scholar's life assail,
Toil, envy, want, the patron, and the jail.   160
See nations slowly wise, and meanly just,
To buried merit raise the tardy bust.
If dreams yet flatter, once again attend,
Hear Lydiat's life, [3] and Galileo's, end.
    Nor deem, when Learning her last prize bestows,   165
The glitt'ring eminence exempt from foes;

[1] the Bodleian, Oxford University library   [2] the tower in which Roger Bacon (1214–1294) lived; it would fall, it was said, on any man greater than he who might walk under it.   [3] suffered for his loyalty to Charles I

See when the vulgar 'scape, despis'd or aw'd,
Rebellion's vengeful talons seize on Laud.
From meaner minds, though smaller fines content
The plunder'd palace, or sequester'd rent;   170
Mark'd out by dang'rous parts he meets the shock,
And fatal Learning leads him to the block:
Around his tomb let Art and Genius weep,
But hear his death, ye blockheads, hear and sleep.
　　　The festal blazes, the triumphal show,   175
The ravish'd standard, and the captive foe,
The senate's thanks, the gazette's pompous tale,
With force resistless o'er the brave prevail.
Such bribes the rapid Greek [4] o'er Asia whirl'd,
For such the steady Romans shook the world;   180
For such in distant lands the Britons shine,
And stain with blood the Danube or the Rhine;
This pow'r has praise, that virtue scarce can warm,
Till fame supplies the universal charm.
Yet Reason frowns on War's unequal game,   185
Where wasted nations raise a single name,
And mortgag'd states their grandsires' wreaths regret
From age to age in everlasting debt;
Wreaths which at last the dear-bought right convey
To rust on medals, or on stones decay.   190
　　　On what foundation stands the warrior's pride,
How just his hopes, let Swedish Charles decide;
A frame of adamant, a soul of fire,
No dangers fright him, and no labours tire;
O'er love, o'er fear, extends his wide domain,   195
Unconquer'd lord of pleasure and of pain;
No joys to him pacific sceptres yield,
War sounds the trump, he rushes to the field;
Behold surrounding kings their pow'rs combine,
And one capitulate, and one resign;   200
Peace courts his hand, but spreads her charms in vain;
"Think nothing gain'd," he cries, "till naught remain,
On Moscow's walls till Gothic standards fly,
And all be mine beneath the polar sky."
The march begins in military state,   205
And nations on his eye suspended wait;
Stern famine guards the solitary coast,
And winter barricades the realms of frost;

[4] Alexander

He comes, not want and cold his course delay;—
Hide, blushing glory, hide Pultowa's [5] day: 210
The vanquish'd hero leaves his broken bands,
And shows his miseries in distant lands;
Condemn'd a needy suppliant to wait,
While ladies interpose, and slaves debate.
But did not chance at length her error mend?   215
Did no subverted empire mark his end?
Did rival monarchs give the fatal wound?
Or hostile millions press him to the ground?
His fall was destin'd to a barren strand,
A petty fortress, and a dubious hand;   220
He left the name at which the world grew pale,
To point a moral, or adorn a tale.

   . . . . .

Where then shall hope and fear their objects find?
Must dull suspense corrupt the stagnant mind?
Must helpless man, in ignorance sedate,   345
Roll darkling down the torrent of his fate?
Must no dislike alarm, no wishes rise,
No cries invoke the mercies of the skies?
Enquirer, cease, petitions yet remain,
Which heav'n may hear, nor deem religion vain.   350
Still raise for good the supplicating voice,
But leave to heav'n the measure and the choice.
Safe in His pow'r, whose eyes discern afar
The secret ambush of a specious pray'r.
Implore His aid, in His decisions rest,   355
Secure, whate'er He gives, He gives the best.
Yet when the sense of sacred presence fires,
And strong devotion to the skies aspires,
Pour forth thy fervors for a healthful mind,
Obedient passions, and a will resign'd;   360
For love, which scarce collective man can fill;
For patience sov'reign o'er transmuted ill;
For faith, that panting for a happier seat,
Counts death kind nature's signal of retreat:
These goods for man the laws of heav'n ordain,   365
These goods He grants, who grants the pow'r to gain;
With these celestial wisdom calms the mind,
And makes the happiness she does not find.   *(1749)*

[5] where Charles XII of Sweden was defeated

❧ THOMAS GRAY (1716–1771)

Elegy Written in a Country Church-Yard

The curfew tolls the knell of parting day,
    The lowing herd wind slowly o'er the lea,
The ploughman homeward plods his weary way,
    And leaves the world to darkness, and to me.

Now fades the glimmering landscape on the sight,   5
    And all the air a solemn stillness holds,
Save where the beetle wheels his droning flight,
    And drowsy tinklings lull the distant folds:

Save that from yonder ivy-mantled tower
    The moping owl does to the moon complain   10
Of such as, wandering near her secret bower,
    Molest her ancient solitary reign.

Beneath those rugged elms, that yew-tree's shade,
    Where heaves the turf in many a mouldering heap,
Each in his narrow cell for ever laid,   15
    The rude Forefathers of the hamlet sleep.

The breezy call of incense-breathing morn,
    The swallow twittering from the straw-built shed,
The cock's shrill clarion, or the echoing horn,
    No more shall rouse them from their lowly bed.   20

For them no more the blazing hearth shall burn,
    Or busy housewife ply her evening care:
No children run to lisp their sire's return,
    Or climb his knees the envied kiss to share,

Oft did the harvest to their sickle yield,   25
    Their furrow oft the stubborn glebe has broke;
How jocund did they drive their team afield!
    How bow'd the woods beneath their sturdy stroke!

Let not Ambition mock their useful toil,
    Their homely joys, and destiny obscure;   30
Nor Grandeur hear with a disdainful smile
    The short and simple annals of the Poor.

The boast of heraldry, the pomp of power,
    And all that beauty, all that wealth e'er gave,
Awaits alike th' inevitable hour:—   35
    The paths of glory lead but to the grave.

Nor you, ye Proud, impute to these the fault
    If Memory o'er their tomb no trophies raise,
Where through the long-drawn aisle and fretted vault
    The pealing anthem swells the note of praise.   40

Can storied urn or animated bust
    Back to its mansion call the fleeting breath?
Can Honour's voice provoke the silent dust,
    Or Flattery soothe the dull cold ear of Death?

Perhaps in this neglected spot is laid   45
    Some heart once pregnant with celestial fire;
Hands, that the rod of empire might have sway'd,
    Or waked to ecstasy the living lyre:

But Knowledge to their eyes her ample page,
    Rich with the spoils of time, did ne'er unroll;   50
Chill Penury repress'd their noble rage,[2]
    And froze the genial current of the soul.

Full many a gem of purest ray serene
    The dark unfathom'd caves of ocean bear:
Full many a flower is born to blush unseen,   55
    And waste its sweetness on the desert air.

Some village-Hampden,[3] that with dauntless breast
    The little tyrant of his fields withstood,
Some mute inglorious Milton here may rest,
    Some Cromwell, guiltless of his country's blood.   60

Th' applause of list'ning senates to command,
    The threats of pain and ruin to despise,
To scatter plenty o'er a smiling land,
    And read their history in a nation's eyes,

Their lot forbad: nor circumscribed alone   65
    Their growing virtues, but their crimes confined;
Forbad to wade through slaughter to a throne,
    And shut the gates of mercy on mankind,

[2] enthusiasm [3] John Hampden, enemy   in England
of Charles I when civil war broke out

The struggling pangs of conscious truth to hide,
    To quench the blushes of ingenuous shame,   70
Or heap the shrine of Luxury and Pride
    With incense kindled at the Muse's flame.

Far from the madding crowd's ignoble strife,
    Their sober wishes never learn'd to stray;
Along the cool sequester'd vale of life   75
    They kept the noiseless tenour of their way.

Yet e'en these bones from insult to protect
    Some frail memorial still erected nigh,
With uncouth rhymes and shapeless sculpture deck'd,
    Implores the passing tribute of a sigh.   80

Their name, their years, spelt by th' unletter'd Muse,
    The place of fame and elegy supply:
And many a holy text around she strews,
    That teach the rustic moralist to die.

For who, to dumb forgetfulness a prey,   85
    This pleasing anxious being e'er resign'd,
Left the warm precincts of the cheerful day,
    Nor cast one longing lingering look behind?

On some fond breast the parting soul relies,
    Some pious drops the closing eye requires;   90
E'en from the tomb the voice of Nature cries,
    E'en in our ashes live their wonted fires.

For thee, who, mindful of th' unhonour'd dead,
    Dost in these lines their artless tale relate;
If chance, by lonely contemplation led,   95
    Some kindred spirit shall inquire thy fate,

Haply some hoary-headed swain may say,
    'Oft have we seen him at the peep of dawn
Brushing with hasty steps the dews away,
    To meet the sun upon the upland lawn;   100

'There at the foot of yonder nodding beech
    That wreathes its old fantastic roots so high,
His listless length at noontide would he stretch,
    And pore upon the brook that babbles by.

'Hard by yon wood, now smiling as in scorn,   105
    Muttering his wayward fancies he would rove;

Now drooping, woeful wan, like one forlorn,
    Or crazed with care, or cross'd in hopeless love.

'One morn I miss'd him on the custom'd hill,
    Along the heath, and near his favourite tree;   110
Another came; nor yet beside the rill,
    Nor up the lawn, nor at the wood was he;

'The next with dirges due in sad array
    Slow through the church-way path we saw him borne,—
Approach and read (for thou canst read) the lay   115
    Graved on the stone beneath yon aged thorn.' [4]

THE EPITAPH

Here rests his head upon the lap of Earth
    A Youth, to Fortune and to Fame unknown;
Fair Science [5] frown'd not on his humble birth,
    And Melancholy mark'd him for her own.   120

Large was his bounty, and his soul sincere;
    Heaven did a recompense as largely send:
He gave to Misery all he had, a tear,
    He gain'd from Heaven, 'twas all he wish'd, a friend.

No farther seek his merits to disclose,   125
    Or draw his frailties from their dread abode,
(There they alike in trembling hope repose,)
    The bosom of his Father and his God.   (1751)

OLIVER GOLDSMITH (1730–1774)

When Lovely Woman Stoops to Folly

When lovely woman stoops to folly,
    And finds too late that men betray,
What charm can soothe her melancholy,
    What art can wash her guilt away?

The only art her guilt to cover,
    To hide her shame from every eye,
To give repentance to her lover,
    And wring his bosom—is to die.   (1766)

[4] hawthorn   [5] knowledge

WILLIAM COWPER (1731–1800)

Light Shining Out of Darkness

God moves in a mysterious way,
    His wonders to perform;
He plants His footsteps in the sea,
    And rides upon the storm.

Deep in unfathomable mines   5
    Of never failing skill,
He treasures up His bright designs,
    And works His sovereign will.

Ye fearful saints fresh courage take,
    The clouds ye so much dread   10
Are big with mercy, and shall break
    In blessings on your head.

Judge not the Lord by feeble sense,
    But trust Him for His grace;
Behind a frowning providence,   15
    He hides a smiling face.

His purposes will ripen fast,
    Unfolding ev'ry hour;
The bud may have a bitter taste,
    But sweet will be the flow'r.   20

Blind unbelief is sure to err,
    And scan His work in vain;
God is His own interpreter,
    And He will make it plain.   (1779)

Verses

*Supposed to be written by Alexander Selkirk, during his solitary
abode in the Island of Juan Fernandez*

I am monarch of all I survey,
    My right there is none to dispute;
From the centre all round to the sea
    I am lord of the fowl and the brute.

O solitude! where are the charms   5
    That sages have seen in thy face?
Better dwell in the midst of alarms
    Than reign in this horrible place.

I am out of humanity's reach.
    I must finish my journey alone,   10
Never hear the sweet music of speech;
    I start at the sound of my own.
The beasts that roam over the plain
    My form with indifference see;
They are so unacquainted with man,   15
    Their tameness is shocking to me.

Society, friendship, and love
    Divinely bestow'd upon man,
O had I the wings of a dove
    How soon would I taste you again!   20
My sorrows I then might assuage
    In the ways of religion and truth,
Might learn from the wisdom of age,
    And be cheer'd by the sallies of youth.

Religion! what treasure untold   25
    Resides in that heavenly world!
More precious than silver and gold,
    Or all that this earth can afford.
But the sound of the church-going bell
    These valleys and rocks never heard,   30
Ne'er sigh'd at the sound of a knell,
    Or smil'd when a sabbath appear'd.

Ye winds that have made me your sport,
    Convey to this desolate shore
Some cordial endearing report   35
    Of a land I shall visit no more:
My friends, do they now and then send
    A wish or a thought after me?
O tell me I yet have a friend,
    Though a friend I am never to see.   40

How fleet is a glance of the mind!
    Compared with the speed of its flight,
The tempest itself lags behind,
    And the swift-wingéd arrows of light.

When I think of my own native land 45
    In a moment I seem to be there;
But, alas! recollection at hand
    Soon hurries me back to despair.

But the seafowl is gone to her nest,
    The beast is laid down in his lair; 50
Even here is a season of rest,
    And I to my cabin repair.
There is mercy in every place,
    And mercy, encouraging thought!
Gives even affliction a grace 55
    And reconciles man to his lot.   (1782)

The Shrubbery

WRITTEN IN A TIME OF AFFLICTION

Oh, happy shades—to me unblest!
    Friendly to peace, but not to me!
How ill the scene that offers rest,
    And heart that cannot rest, agree!

This glassy stream, that spreading pine, 5
    Those alders quiv'ring to the breeze,
Might soothe a soul less hurt than mine,
    And please, if any thing could please.

But fix'd unalterable care
    Foregoes not what she feels within, 10
Shows the same sadness ev'ry where,
    And slights the season and the scene.

For all that pleas'd in wood or lawn,
    While peace posses'd these silent bow'rs,
Her animating smile withdrawn, 15
    Has lost its beauties and its pow'rs.

The saint or moralist should tread
    This moss-grown alley, musing, slow;
They seek, like me, the secret shade,
    But not, like me, to nourish woe! 20

Me fruitful scenes and prospects waste
    Alike admonish not to roam;
These tell me of enjoyments past,
    And those of sorrows yet to come.   (1782)

On The Receipt of My Mother's Picture, Out of Norfolk; The Gift of My Cousin, Ann Bodham

    Oh, that those lips had language! Life has passed
With me but roughly since I heard thee last.
Those lips are thine—thy own sweet smiles I see,
The same that oft in childhood solaced me;
Voice only fails, else how distinct they say,   5
"Grieve not, my child, chase all thy fears away!"
The meek intelligence of those dear eyes
(Blest be the art that can immortalize,
The art that baffles Time's tyrannic claim
To quench it) here shines on me, still the same.   10

    Faithful remembrancer of one so dear,
O welcome guest, though unexpected, here!
Who bidst me honor with an artless song,
Affectionate, a mother lost so long,
I will obey, not willingly alone,   15
But gladly, as the precept were her own.
And, while that face renews my filial grief,
Fancy shall weave a charm for my relief,
Shall steep me in Elysian reverie,
A momentary dream that thou art she.   20

    My mother! when I learned that thou wast dead,
Say, wast thou conscious of the tears I shed?
Hovered thy spirit o'er thy sorrowing son,
Wretch even then, life's journey just begun?
Perhaps thou gavest me, thou unfelt, a kiss;   25
Perhaps a tear, if souls can weep in bliss—
Ah, that maternal smile! It answers—Yes.
I heard the bell tolled on thy burial day,
I saw the hearse that bore thee slow away,

And, turning from my nursery window, drew 30
A long, long sigh, and wept a last adieu!
But was it such?—It was.—Where thou art gone,
Adieus and farewells are a sound unknown.
May I but meet thee on that peaceful shore,
The parting word shall pass my lips no more! 35
Thy maidens, grieved themselves at my concern,
Oft gave me promise of thy quick return.
What ardently I wished, I long believed,
And, disappointed still, was still deceived.
By expectation every day beguiled, 40
Dupe of *tomorrow* even from a child.
Thus many a sad tomorrow came and went,
Till, all my stock of infant sorrow spent,
I learned at last submission to my lot;
But, though I less deplored thee, ne'er forgot. 45

Where once we dwelt our name is heard no more,
Children not thine have trod my nursery floor;
And where the gardener, Robin, day by day,
Drew me to school along the public way,
Delighted with my bauble coach, and wrapped 50
In scarlet mantle warm, and velvet capped,
'Tis now become a history little known
That once we called the pastoral house our own.
Short-lived possession! But the record fair
That memory keeps, of all thy kindness there, 55
Still outlives many a storm that has effaced
A thousand other themes less deeply traced.
Thy nightly visits to my chamber made,
That thou might'st know me safe and warmly laid;
Thy morning bounties ere I left my home, 60
The biscuit, or confectionery plum;
The fragrant waters on my cheeks bestowed
By thy own hand, till fresh they shone and glowed;
All this, and more endearing still than all,
Thy constant flow of love that knew no fall, 65
Ne'er roughened by those cataracts and brakes
That humor, interposed, too often makes;
All this still legible in memory's page,
And still to be so to my latest age,
Adds joy to duty, makes me glad to pay 70
Such honors to thee as my numbers may;

Perhaps a frail memorial, but sincere,
Not scorned in heaven, though little noticed here.

    Could Time, his flight reversed, restore the hours
When, playing with thy vesture's tissued flowers,   75
The violet, the pink, and jessamine,
I pricked them into paper with a pin
(And thou wast happier than myself the while,
Wouldst softly speak, and stroke my head and smile),
Could those few pleasant days again appear,   80
Might one wish bring them, would I wish them here?
I would not trust my heart—the dear delight
Seems so to be desired, perhaps I might—
But no—what here we call our life is such
So little to be loved, and thou so much,   85
That I should ill requite thee to constrain
Thy unbound spirit into bonds again.

    Thou, as a gallant bark from Albion's coast
(The storms all weathered and the ocean crossed)
Shoots into port at some well-havened isle,   90
Where spices breathe, and brighter seasons smile,
There sits quiescent on the floods that show
Her beauteous form reflected clear below,
While airs impregnated with incense play
Around her, fanning light her streamers gay;   95
So thou, with sails how swift! hast reached the shore,
"Where tempest never beat nor billows roar,"
And thy loved consort on the dangerous tide
Of life long since has anchored by thy side.
But me, scarce hoping to attain that rest,   100
Always from port withheld, always distressed—
Me howling blasts drive devious, tempest tost,
Sails ripped, seams opening wide, and compass lost,
And day by day some current's thwarting force
Sets me more distant from a prosperous course.   105
Yet, oh, the thought that thou art safe, and he!
That thought is joy, arrive what may to me.
My boast is not that I deduce my birth
From loins enthroned, and rulers of the earth; [1]
But higher far my proud pretensions rise—   110

[1] Cowper's mother was descended from
Henry III.

The son of parents passed into the skies!
And now, farewell. Time unrevoked has run
His wonted course, yet what I wished is done.
By contemplation's help, not sought in vain,
I seem to have lived my childhood o'er again; 115
To have renewed the joys that once were mine,
Without the sin of violating thine.
And, while the wings of Fancy still are free
And I can view this mimic show of thee,
Time has but half succeeded in his theft— 120
Thyself removed, thy power to soothe me left. (*1798*)

Sonnet to William Wilberforce, Esq.[1]

Thy country, Wilberforce, with just disdain,
Hears thee, by cruel men and impious call'd
Fanatic, for thy zeal to loose th' enthrall'd
From exile, public sale, and slav'ry's chain.
Friend of the poor, the wrong'd, the fetter-gall'd,
Fear not lest labour such as thine be vain.
Thou hast achiev'd a part; hast gain'd the ear
Of Britain's senate to thy glorious cause;
Hope smiles, joy springs, and though cold caution pause
And weave delay, the better hour is near
That shall remunerate thy toils severe
By peace for Afric, fenced with British laws.
　　Enjoy what thou hast won, esteem and love
　　From all the Just on earth, and all the Blest above.
(*1815*)

[1] Wilberforce (1759–1833) sought to   the British Empire.
abolish the slave trade and slavery in

PHILIP FRENEAU (1752–1832)

The Indian Burying Ground

In spite of all the learned have said,
    I still my old opinion keep;
The posture, that we give the dead,
    Points out the soul's eternal sleep.

Not so the ancients of these lands—   5
    The Indian, when from life released,
Again is seated with his friends,
    And shares again the joyous feast.

His imaged birds, and painted bowl,
    And venison, for a journey dressed,   10
Bespeak the nature of the soul,
    Activity, that knows no rest.

His bow, for action ready bent,
    And arrows, with a head of stone,
Can only mean that life is spent,   15
    And not the old ideas gone.

Thou, stranger, that shalt come this way,
    No fraud upon the dead commit—
Observe the swelling turf, and say
    They do not lie, but here they sit.   20

Here still a lofty rock remains,
    On which the curious eye may trace
(Now wasted, half, by wearing rains)
    The fancies of a ruder race.

Here still an aged elm aspires,   25
    Beneath whose far-projecting shade
(And which the shepherd still admires)
    The children of the forest played!

There oft a restless Indian queen
    (Pale Shebah, with her braided hair)   30
And many a barbarous form is seen
    To chide the man that lingers there.

By midnight moons, o'er moistening dews;
    In habit for the chase arrayed,
The hunter still the deer pursues,   35
    The hunter and the deer, a shade!

And long shall timorous fancy see
    The painted chief, and pointed spear,
And Reason's self shall bow the knee
    To shadows and delusions here.   (1788)

The Wild Honeysuckle

Fair flower, that doest so comely grow,
Hid in this silent, dull retreat,
Untouched thy honied blossoms blow,
Unseen thy little branches greet:
    No roving foot shall crush thee here,   5
    No busy hand provoke a tear.

By Nature's self in white arrayed,
She bade thee shun the vulgar eye,
And planted here the guardian shade,
And sent soft waters murmuring by;   10
    Thus quietly thy summer goes,
    Thy days declining to repose.

Smit with those charms, that must decay,
I grieve to see your future doom;
They died—nor were those flowers more gay,   15
The flowers that did in Eden bloom;
    Unpitying frosts, and Autumn's power
    Shall leave no vestige of this flower.

From morning suns and evening dews
At first thy little being came: 20
If nothing once, you nothing lose,
For when you die you are the same;
    The space between, is but an hour,
    The frail duration of a flower.   (1788)

WILLIAM BLAKE (1757–1827)

From *Songs of Innocence*

Introduction

Piping down the valleys wild,
Piping songs of pleasant glee,
On a cloud I saw a child,
And he laughing said to me:

"Pipe a song about a Lamb!"   5
So I piped with merry cheer.
"Piper, pipe that song again";
So I piped: he wept to hear.

"Drop thy pipe, thy happy pipe;
Sing thy songs of happy cheer":   10
So I sang the same again,
While he wept with joy to hear.

"Piper, sit thee down and write
In a book, that all may read."
So he vanished from my sight,   15
And I plucked a hollow reed,

And I made a rural pen,
And I stained the water clear,
And I wrote my happy songs
Every child may joy to hear.   20

The Lamb

Little Lamb, who made thee?
Dost thou know who made thee;
Gave thee life and bid thee feed
By the stream and o'er the mead;
Gave thee clothing of delight,   5
Softest clothing, woolly, bright;
Gave thee such a tender voice
Making all the vales rejoice?
Little Lamb, who made thee?
Dost thou know who made thee?   10

Little Lamb, I'll tell thee,
Little Lamb, I'll tell thee:
He is called by thy name,
For He calls Himself a Lamb.
He is meek and He is mild: 15
He became a little child.
I a child and thou a lamb,
We are called by His name.
Little Lamb, God bless thee.
Little Lamb, God bless thee.   20

The Little Black Boy

My mother bore me in the southern wild,
And I am black, but O! my soul is white;
White as an angel is the English child,
But I am black, as if bereaved of light.

My mother taught me underneath a tree,   5
And, sitting down before the heat of day,
She took me on her lap and kisséd me,
And, pointing to the east, began to say:

"Look on the rising sun—there God does live,
And gives his light, and gives his heat away;   10
And flowers and trees and beasts and men receive
Comfort in morning, joy in the noon day.

"And we are put on earth a little space,
That we may learn to bear the beams of love;
And these black bodies and this sunburnt face   15
Is but a cloud, and like a shady grove.

"For when our souls have learned the heat to bear,
The cloud will vanish, we shall hear his voice,
Saying: 'Come out from the grove, my love and care,
And round my golden tent like lambs rejoice.'"   20

Thus did my mother say, and kisséd me;
And thus I say to little English boy.
When I from black, and he from white cloud free,
And round the tent of God like lambs we joy,

I'll shade him from the heat, till he can bear 25
To lean in joy upon our father's knee;
And then I'll stand and stroke his silver hair,
And be like him, and he will then love me.

The Chimney Sweeper

When my mother died I was very young,
And my father sold me while yet my tongue
Could scarcely cry " 'weep! 'weep! 'weep! 'weep!"
So your chimneys I sweep, and in soot I sleep.

There's little Tom Dacre, who cried when his head, 5
That curled like a lamb's back, was shaved: so I said
"Hush, Tom! never mind it, for when your head's bare
You know that the soot cannot spoil your white hair."

And so he was quiet, and that very night,
As Tom was a-sleeping, he had such a sight! 10
That thousands of sweepers, Dick, Joe, Ned, and Jack,
Were all of them locked up in coffins of black.

And by came an Angel who had a bright key,
And he opened the coffins and set them all free;
Then down a green plain leaping, laughing, they run, 15
And wash in a river, and shine in the Sun.

Then naked and white, all their bags left behind,
They rise upon clouds and sport in the wind;
And the Angel told Tom, if he'd be a good boy,
He'd have God for his father, and never want joy. 20

And so Tom awoke; and we rose in the dark,
And got with our bags and our brushes to work.
Tho' the morning was cold, Tom was happy and warm;
So if all do their duty they need not fear harm.

The Divine Image

To Mercy, Pity, Peace, and Love
All pray in their distress;
And to these virtues of delight
Return their thankfulness.

For Mercy, Pity, Peace, and Love   5
Is God, our father dear,
And Mercy, Pity, Peace, and Love
Is Man, his child and care.

For Mercy has a human heart,
Pity a human face,   10
And Love, the human form divine,
And Peace, the human dress.

Then every man, of every clime,
That prays in his distress,
Prays to the human form divine,   15
Love, Mercy, Pity, Peace.

And all must love the human form,
In heathen, turk, or jew;
Where Mercy, Love, and Pity dwell
There God is dwelling too.   20

Holy Thursday

'Twas on a Holy Thursday, their innocent faces clean,
The children walking two and two, in red and blue and green,
Grey-headed beadles walk'd before, with wands as white as snow,
Till into the high dome of Paul's they like Thames' waters flow.

O what a multitude they seem'd, these flowers of London town!
Seated in companies they sit with radiance all their own.
The hum of multitudes was there, but multitudes of lambs,
Thousands of little boys and girls raising their innocent hands.

Now like a mighty wind they raise to heaven the voice of song,
Or like harmonious thunderings the seats of Heaven among.
Beneath them sit the aged men, wise guardians of the poor;
Then cherish pity, lest you drive an angel from your door.   (1789)

From *Songs of Experience*

Holy Thursday

Is this a holy thing to see
In a rich and fruitful land,

Babes reduc'd to misery,
Fed with cold and usurous hand?

Is that trembling cry a song?   5
Can it be a song of joy?
And so many children poor?
It is a land of poverty!

And their sun does never shine,
And their fields are bleak and bare,   10
And their ways are fill'd with thorns:
It is eternal winter there.

For where-e'er the sun does shine,
And where-e'er the rain does fall,
Babe can never hunger there,   15
Nor poverty the mind appall.

The Chimney Sweeper

A little black thing among the snow,
Crying ' 'weep! 'weep!' in notes of woe!
"Where are thy father and mother? say?"
"They are both gone up to the church to pray.

"Because I was happy upon the hearth,
"And smil'd among the winter's snow,
"They clothed me in the clothes of death,
"And taught me to sing the notes of woe.

"And because I am happy and dance and sing,
"They think they have done me no injury,
"And are gone to praise God and his priest and king,
"Who make up a heaven of our misery."

The Sick Rose

O Rose, thou art sick!
The invisible worm
That flies in the night,
In the howling storm,

Has found out thy bed
Of crimson joy,
And his dark secret love
Does thy life destroy.

The Tyger

Tyger! Tyger! burning bright
In the forests of the night,
What immortal hand or eye
Could frame thy fearful symmetry?

In what distant deeps or skies   5
Burnt the fire of thine eyes?
On what wings dare he aspire?
What the hand dare seize the fire?

And what shoulder, and what art,
Could twist the sinews of thy heart?   10
And when thy heart began to beat,
What dread hand? and what dread feet?

What the hammer? what the chain?
In what furnace was thy brain?
What the anvil? what dread grasp   15
Dare its deadly terrors clasp?

When the stars threw down their spears
And watered heaven with their tears,
Did he smile his work to see?
Did he who made the Lamb make thee?   20

Tyger! Tyger! burning bright
In the forests of the night,
What immortal hand or eye
Dare frame thy fearful symmetry?

The Garden of Love

I went to the Garden of Love,
And saw what I never had seen:
A Chapel was built in the midst,
Where I used to play on the green.

And the gates of this Chapel were shut,
And "Thou shalt not" writ over the door;
So I turned to the Garden of Love
That so many sweet flowers bore;

And I saw it was filled with graves,
And tomb-stones where flowers should be;

And Priests in black gowns were walking their rounds,
And binding with briars my joys and desires.

London

I wander thro' each chartered street,
Near where the chartered Thames does flow,
And mark in every face I meet
Marks of weakness, marks of woe.

In every cry of every Man,   5
In every Infant's cry of fear,
In every voice, in every ban,
The mind-forged manacles I hear.

How the Chimney-sweeper's cry
Every black'ning Church appalls;   10
And the hapless Soldier's sigh
Runs in blood down Palace walls.

But most thro' midnight streets I hear
How the youthful Harlot's curse
Blasts the new born Infant's tear,   15
And blights with plagues the Marriage hearse.

A Little Boy Lost

"Nought loves another as itself,
"Nor venerates another so,
"Nor is it possible to Thought
"A greater than itself to know:

"And Father, how can I love you   5
"Or any of my brothers more?
"I love you like the little bird
"That picks up crumbs around the door."

The priest sat by and heard the child,
In trembling zeal he seiz'd his hair: 10
He led him by his little coat,
And all admir'd the priestly care.

And standing on the altar high,
"Lo! what a fiend is here!" said he,
"One who sets reason up for judge   15
"Of our most holy mystery."

The weeping child could not be heard,
The weeping parents wept in vain;
They stripp'd him to his little shirt,
And bound him in an iron chain;   20

And burn'd him in a holy place,
Where many had been burn'd before:
The weeping parents wept in vain.
Are such things done on Albion's shore?

A Divine Image

Cruelty has a human heart,
    And Jealousy a human face;
Terror the human form divine,
    And Secrecy the human dress.

The human dress is forgéd iron,
    The human form a fiery forge,
The human face a furnace seal'd,
    The human heart its hungry gorge.   (1794)

Eternity

He who bends to himself a joy
Does the winged life destroy;
But he who kisses the joy as it flies
Lives in eternity's sun rise.

Mock On, Mock On, Voltaire, Rousseau

Mock on, mock on, Voltaire, Rousseau,
    Mock on, mock on; 'tis all in vain;
You throw the sand against the wind
    And the wind blows it back again.

And every sand becomes a gem
    Reflected in the beams divine;
Blown back, they blind the mocking eye,
    But still in Israel's paths they shine.

> The atoms of Democritus
>   And Newton's particles of light
> Are sands upon the Red Sea shore,
>   Where Israel's tents do shine so bright.
>   *(c. 1800–1803)*

From *Milton*

PREFACE

> And did those feet in ancient time
> Walk upon England's mountains green?
> And was the Holy Lamb of God
> On England's pleasant pastures seen?
>
> And did the countenance divine   5
> Shine forth upon our clouded hills?
> And was Jerusalem builded here
> Among these dark satanic mills?
>
> Bring me my bow of burning gold!
> Bring me my arrows of desire!   10
> Bring me my spear! O clouds, unfold!
> Bring me my chariot of fire!
>
> I will not cease from mental fight,
> Nor shall my sword sleep in my hand,
> Till we have built Jerusalem   15
> In England's green and pleasant land.   *(1804)*

From *Jerusalem*

Chapter I:15

. . . . .

I see the Four-fold Man, The Humanity in deadly sleep
And its fallen Emanation, The Spectre and its cruel Shadow.
I see the Past, Present, and Future existing all at once
Before me. O Divine Spirit, sustain me on thy wings,

That I may awake Albion from his long and cold repose;   10
For Bacon and Newton, sheath'd in dismal steel, their terrors hang
Like iron scourges over Albion: Reasonings like vast Serpents
Infold around my limbs, bruising my minute articulations.

I turn my eyes to the Schools and Universities of Europe
And there behold the Loom of Locke, whose Woof rages dire,   15
Wash'd by the Water-wheels of Newton: black the cloth
In heavy wreathes folds over every Nation: cruel Works
Of many Wheels I view, wheel without wheel, with cogs tyrannic
Moving by compulsion each other, not as those in Eden, which
Wheel within Wheel, in freedom revolve in harmony and peace.   20

Chapter IV:90

. . . . .

But still the thunder of Los [1] peals loud, and thus the thunders cry:
"These beautiful Witchcrafts of Albion are gratifyd by Cruelty.

91

"It is easier to forgive an Enemy than to forgive a Friend.
"The man who permits you to injure him deserves your vengeance:
"He also will receive it; go Spectre; obey my most secret desire
"Which thou knowest without my speaking. Go to these Fiends of
    Righteousness,
"Tell them to obey their Humanities and not pretend Holiness   5
"When they are murderers as far as my Hammer and Anvil permit.
"Go, tell them that the Worship of God is honouring his gifts
In other men and loving the greatest men best, each according
"To his Genius which is the Holy Ghost in Man; there is no other
God than that God who is the intellectual fountain of Humanity.   10
He who envies or calumniates, which is murder and cruelty,
"Murders the Holy-one. Go, tell them this, and overthrow their cup,
"Their bread, their altar-table, their incense and their oath,
"Their marriage and their baptism, their burial and consecration.
"I have tried to make friends by corporeal gifts but have only   15
"Made enemies. I never made friends but by spiritual gifts,
"By severe contentions of friendship and the burning fire of thought.
"He who would see the Divinity must see him in his Children,

[1] Blake's personification of the poetic
spirit.

"One first, in friendship and love, then a Divine Family, and in the
    midst
"Jesus will appear; so he who wishes to see a Vision, a perfect Whole, 20
"Must see it in its Minute Particulars, Organized, and not as thou,
"O Fiend of Righteousness, pretendest; thine is a Disorganized
"And snowy cloud, brooder of tempests and destructive War.
"Your smile with pomp and rigor, you talk of benevolence and virtue;
"I act with benevolence and virtue and get murder'd time after time. 25
"You accumulate Particulars and murder by analyzing, that you
"May take the aggregate, and you call the aggregate Moral Law,
"And you call that swell'd and bloated Form a Minute Particular;
"But General Forms have their vitality in Particulars, and every
"Particular is a Man, a Divine Member of the Divine Jesus."   30

So Los cried at his Anvil in the horrible darkness weeping. (1804–1820)

🦢 ROBERT BURNS (1759–1796)

To a Mouse

ON TURNING HER UP IN HER NEST WITH THE PLOUGH,
NOVEMBER, 1785

Wee, sleekit, cow'rin', tim'rous beastie,
O what a panic's in thy breastie!
Thou need na start awa sae hasty,
    Wi' bickering brattle!
I wad be laith to rin an' chase thee   5
    Wi' murd'ring pattle! [1]

I'm truly sorry man's dominion
Has broken nature's social union,
An' justifies that ill opinion
    Which makes thee startle   10
At me, thy poor earth-born companion,
    An' fellow-mortal!

I doubt na, whiles, but thou may thieve;
What then? poor beastie, thou maun live!
A daimen-icker in a thrave [2]   15
    'S a sma' request:
I'll get a blessin' wi' the lave,[3]
    And never miss't!

Thy wee bit housie, too, in ruin!
Its silly wa's the win's are strewin':   20
And naething, now, to big [4] a new ane,
    O' foggage [5] green!
An' bleak December's winds ensuin'
    Baith snell an' keen!

Thou saw the fields laid bare and waste   25
An' weary winter comin' fast,
An' cozie here, beneath the blast,
    Thou thought to dwell,
Till, crash! the cruel coulter past
    Out thro' thy cell.   30

[1] paddle, spade   [2] an ear of corn in
a shock   [3] rest   [4] build   [5] coarse grass

That wee bit heap o' leaves an' stibble
Has cost thee mony a weary nibble!
Now thou's turn'd out, for a' thy trouble,
    But [6] house or hald,
To thole [7] the winter's sleety dribble   35
    An' cranreuch [8] cauld!

But, Mousie, thou art no thy lane [9]
In proving foresight may be vain:
The best laid schemes o' mice an' men
    Gang aft a-gley,[10]   40
An' lea'e us nought but grief an' pain,
    For promised joy.

Still thou art blest, compared wi' me!
The present only toucheth thee:
But, och! I backward cast my e'e   45
    On prospects drear!
An' forward, tho' I canna see,
    I guess an' fear!   (1786)

Man Was Made to Mourn, a Dirge

When chill November's surly blast
    Made fields and forests bare,
One ev'ning, as I wand'red forth,
    Along the banks of AIRE,
I spy'd a man, whose aged step   5
    Seem'd weary, worn with care;
His face was furrow'd o'er with years,
    And hoary was his hair.

Young stranger, whither wand'rest thou?
    Began the rev'rend Sage;   10
Does thirst of wealth thy step constrain,
    O youthful Pleasure's rage?
Or haply, prest with cares and woes,
    Too soon thou hast began,
To wander forth, with me, to mourn   15
    The miseries of Man.

[6] without   [7] suffer   [8] hoarfrost   [9] not
alone   [10] awry

The Sun that overhangs yon moors,
 Outspreading far and wide,
Where hundreds labour to support
 A haughty lordling's pride;   20
I've seen yon weary winter-sun
 Twice forty times return;
And ev'ry time has added proofs,
 That Man was made to mourn.

O Man! while in thy early years,   25
 How prodigal of time!
Mispending all thy precious hours,
 Thou glorious, youthful prime!
Alternate Follies take the sway;
 Licentious Passions burn;   30
Which tenfold force gives Nature's law,
 That Man was made to mourn.

Look not alone on youthful Prime,
 Or Manhood's active might;
Man then is useful to his kind,   35
 Supported is his right:
But see him on the edge of life,
 With Cares and Sorrows worn,
Then Age and Want, Oh! ill-match'd pair!
 Show Man was made to mourn.   40

A few seem favorites of Fate,
 In Pleasure's lap carest;
Yet think not all the Rich and Great,
 Are likewise truly blest.
But Oh! what crouds in ev'ry land,   45
 All wretched and forlorn,
Thro' weary life this lesson learn,
 That Man was made to mourn.

Many and sharp the num'rous Ills
 Inwoven with our frame!   50
More pointed still we make ourselves,
 Regret, Remorse and Shame!
And Man, whose heav'n-erected face,
 The smiles of love adorn,
Man's inhumanity to Man   55
 Makes countless thousands mourn!

See, yonder poor, o'erlabour'd wight,
    So abject, mean and vile,
Who begs a brother of the earth
    To give him leave to toil;   60
And see his lordly fellow-worm,
    The poor petition spurn,
Unmindful, tho' a weeping wife,
    And helpless offspring mourn.

If I'm design'd yon lordling's slave,   65
    By Nature's law design'd,
Why was an independent wish
    E'er planted in my mind?
If not, why am I subject to
    His cruelty, or scorn?   70
Or why has Man the will and pow'r
    To make his fellow mourn?

Yet, let not this too much, my Son,
    Disturb thy youthful breast:
This partial view of human-kind   75
    Is surely not the last!
The poor, oppressed, honest man
    Had never, sure, been born,
Had there not been some recompense
    To comfort those that mourn!   80

O Death! the poor man's dearest friend,
    The kindest and the best!
Welcome the hour, my aged limbs
    Are laid with thee at rest!
The Great, the Wealthy fear thy blow,   85
    From pomp and pleasure torn;
But Oh! a blest relief for those
    That weary-laden mourn!   (1786)

Green Grow the Rashes

Green grow the rashes, O,
    Green grow the rashes, O;
The sweetest hours that e'er I spend,
    Are spent amang the lasses, O!

There's nought but care on ev'ry han',   5
    In ev'ry hour that passes, O;
What signifies the life o' man,
    An' 'twere na for the lasses, O.

The warly ¹ race may riches chase,
    An' riches still may fly them, O;   10
An' tho' at last they catch them fast,
    Their hearts can ne'er enjoy them, O.

But gie me a canny hour at e'en,
    My arms about my dearie, O;
An' warly cares, an' warly men,   15
    May a' gae tapsalteerie,² O!

For you sae douce, ye sneer at this,
    Ye're nought but senseless asses, O:
The wisest man the warl' saw,
    He dearly lov'd the lasses, O.   20

Auld nature swears, the lovely dears
    Her noblest work she classes, O;
Her prentice han' she tried on man,
    An' then she made the lasses, O.   (1787)

John Anderson My Jo

John Anderson my jo,¹ John,
    When we were first acquent
Your locks were like the raven,
    Your bonnie brow was brent; ²
But now your brow is beld,³ John,   5
    Your locks are like the snow;
But blessings on your frosty pow,⁴
    John Anderson my jo.

John Anderson my jo, John,
    We clamb the hill thegither,   10
And mony a canty ⁵ day, John,
    We've had wi' ane anither:

¹ worldly   ² topsy-turvy

---

¹ darling   ² upright, with hair   ³ bald   ⁴ head   ⁵ happy

Now we maun totter down, John,
    But hand in hand we'll go,
And sleep thegither at the foot,   15
John Anderson my jo.   (*1790*)

Afton Water

Flow gently, sweet Afton! among thy green braes,
Flow gently, I'll sing thee a song in thy praise;
My Mary's asleep by thy murmuring stream,
Flow gently, sweet Afton, disturb not her dream.

Thou stock dove whose echo resounds through the gler   5
Ye wild whistling blackbirds in yon thorny den,
Thou green-crested lapwing, thy screaming forbear,
I charge you, disturb not my slumbering fair.

How loftly, sweet Afton, thy neighboring hills,
Far marked with the courses of clear, winding rills;   10
There daily I wander as noon rises high,
My flocks and my Mary's sweet cot in my eye.

How pleasant thy banks and green valleys below,
Where, wild in the woodlands, the primroses blow;
There oft, as mild ev'ning weeps over the lea,   15
The sweet-scented birk shades my Mary and me.

Thy crystal stream, Afton, how lovely it glides,
And winds by the cot where my Mary resides;
How wanton thy waters her snowy feet lave,
As, gathering sweet flowerets, she stems thy clear wave.   20

Flow gently, sweet Afton, among thy green braes,
Flow gently, sweet river, the theme of my lays;
My Mary's asleep by thy murmuring stream,
Flow gently, sweet Afton, disturb not her dream.   (*1792*)

A Red, Red Rose

O my luve is like a red, red rose,
    That's newly sprung in June:
O my luve is like the melodie,
    That's sweetly played in tune.

As fair art thou, my bonie lass,   5
    So deep in luve am I;
And I will luve thee still, my dear,
    Till a' the seas gang dry.

Till a' the seas gang dry, my dear,
    And the rocks melt wi' the sun;   10
And I will luve thee still, my dear,
    While the sands o' life shall run.

And fare thee weel, my only luve!
    And fare thee weel a while!
And I will come again, my luve,   15
    Tho' it were ten thousand mile.   (*1796*)

Bonnie Lesley

O saw ye bonnie Lesley
    As she gaed o'er the border?
She's gane, like Alexander,
    To spread her conquests farther.

To see her is to love her,   5
    And love but her for ever;
For nature made her what she is,
    And never made anither!

Thou art a queen, fair Lesley,
    Thy subjects we, before thee;   10
Thou art divine, fair Lesley,
    The hearts o' men adore thee.

The deil he couldna scaith thee,
    Or aught that wad belang thee;
He'd look into thy bonnie face,   15
    And say, "I canna wrang thee!"

The Powers aboon will tent thee;
    Misfortune sha'na steer thee;
Thou'rt like themsel' sae lovely,
    That ill they'll ne'er let near thee.   20

Return again, fair Lesley,
    Return to Caledonie!
That we may brag we hae a lass
    There's nane again sae bonnie.   (*1798*)

PART 5
The Nineteenth Century

WILLIAM WORDSWORTH (1770–1850)

Lines Composed a Few Miles above Tintern Abbey, On Revisiting the Banks of the Wye during a Tour, July 13, 1798

Five years have past; five summers, with the length
Of five long winters! and again I hear
These waters, rolling from their mountain springs
With a soft inland murmur.—Once again
Do I behold these steep and lofty cliffs,   5
That on a wild secluded scene impress
Thoughts of more deep seclusion; and connect
The landscape with the quiet of the sky.
The day is come when I again repose
Here, under this dark sycamore, and view   10
These plots of cottage-ground, these orchard tufts,
Which, at this season, with their unripe fruits,
Are clad in one green hue, and lose themselves
'Mid groves and copses. Once again I see
These hedgerows, hardly hedgerows, little lines   15
Of sportive wood run wild; these pastoral farms,
Green to the very door; and wreaths of smoke
Sent up, in silence, from among the trees!
With some uncertain notice, as might seem
Of vagrant dwellers in the houseless woods,   20
Or of some Hermit's cave, where by his fire
The Hermit sits alone.

                 These beauteous forms,
Through a long absence, have not been to me
As is a landscape to a blind man's eye:
But oft, in lonely rooms, and 'mid the din   25
Of towns and cities, I have owed to them,
In hours of weariness, sensations sweet,
Felt in the blood and felt along the heart,
And passing even into my purer mind
With tranquil restoration:—feelings too,   30
Of unremembered pleasure: such, perhaps,
As have no slight or trivial influence
On that best portion of a good man's life,

His little, nameless, unremembered acts
Of kindness and of love. Nor less, I trust,   35
To them I may have owed another gift
Of aspect more sublime; that blessed mood
In which the burthen of the mystery,
In which the heavy and the weary weight
Of all this unintelligible world   40
Is lightened:—that serene and blessed mood
In which the affections gently lead us on,—
Until, the breath of this corporeal frame
And even the motion of our human blood
Almost suspended, we are laid asleep   45
In body, and become a living soul:
While with an eye made quiet by the power
Of harmony, and the deep power of joy,
We see into the life of things.

                                      If this
Be but a vain belief, yet oh! how oft—   50
In darkness and amid the many shapes
Of joyless daylight; when the fretful stir
Unprofitable, and the fever of the world,
Have hung upon the beatings of my heart—
How oft in spirit have I turned to thee,   55
O sylvan Wye! thou wanderer through the woods,
How often has my spirit turned to thee!

And now, with gleams of half-extinguished thought,
With many recognitions sad and faint,
And somewhat of a sad perplexity,   60
The picture of the mind revives again;
While here I stand, not only with the sense
Of present pleasure, but with pleasing thoughts
That in this moment, there is life and food
For future years. And so I dare to hope,   65
Though changed, no doubt, from what I was when first
I came among these hills; when like a roe
I bounded o'er the mountains, by the sides
Of the deep rivers, and the lonely streams,
Wherever nature led: more like a man   70
Flying from something that he dreads than one
Who sought the thing he loved. For nature then
(The coarser pleasures of my boyish years,
And their glad animal movements all gone by)

To me was all in all.—I cannot paint   75
What then I was. The sounding cataract
Haunted me like a passion: the tall rock,
The mountain, and the deep and gloomy wood,
Their colours and their forms, were then to me
An appetite; a feeling and a love   80
That had no need of a remoter charm
By thought supplied, nor any interest
Unborrowed from the eye.—That time is past,
And all its aching joys are now no more,
And all its dizzy raptures. Not for this   85
Faint I, nor mourn nor murmur; other gifts
Have followed; for such loss, I would believe,
Abundant recompense. For I have learned
To look on nature, not as in the hour
Of thoughtless youth, but hearing oftentimes   90
The still sad music of humanity,
Nor harsh nor grating, though of ample power
To chasten and subdue. And I have felt
A presence that disturbs me with the joy
Of elevated thoughts; a sense sublime   95
Of something far more deeply interfused,
Whose dwelling is the light of setting suns,
And the round ocean and the living air,
And the blue sky, and in the mind of man:
A motion and a spirit, that impels   100
All thinking things, all objects of all thought,
And rolls through all things. Therefore am I still
A lover of the meadows and the woods,
And mountains; and of all that we behold
From this green earth; of all that mighty world   105
Of eye and ear,—both what they half create,
And what perceive; well pleased to recognise
In nature and the language of the sense
The anchor of my purest thoughts, the nurse,
The guide, the guardian of my heart, and soul   110
Of all my moral being.

                      Nor perchance,
If I were not thus taught, should I the more
Suffer my genial spirits to decay;
For thou art with me here upon the banks
Of this fair river; thou my dearest friend,   115

My dear, dear friend; and in thy voice I catch
The language of my former heart, and read
My former pleasures in the shooting lights
Of thy wild eyes. Oh! yet a little while
May I behold in thee what I was once,   120
My dear, dear sister! and this prayer I make,
Knowing that Nature never did betray
The heart that loved her; 'tis her privilege,
Through all the years of this our life, to lead
From joy to joy: for she can so inform   125
The mind that is within us, so impress
With quietness and beauty, and so feed
With lofty thoughts, that neither evil tongues,
Rash judgments, nor the sneers of selfish men,
Nor greetings where no kindness is, nor all   130
The dreary intercourse of daily life,
Shall e'er prevail against us, or disturb
Our cheerful faith, that all which we behold
Is full of blessings. Therefore let the moon
Shine on thee in thy solitary walk;   135
And let the misty mountain-winds be free
To blow against thee: and in after years,
When these wild ecstasies shall be matured
Into a sober pleasure; when thy mind
Shall be a mansion for all lovely forms,   140
Thy memory be as a dwelling-place
For all sweet sounds and harmonies; oh! then,
If solitude, or fear, or pain, or grief,
Should be thy portion, with what pleasing thoughts
Of tender joy wilt thou remember me,   145
And these my exhortations! Nor, perchance—
If I should be where I no more can hear
Thy voice, nor catch from thy wild eyes these gleams
Of past existence—wilt thou then forget
That on the banks of this delightful stream   150
We stood together; and that I, so long
A worshipper of Nature, hither came
Unwearied in that service: rather say
With warmer love—oh! with far deeper zeal
Of holier love. Nor wilt thou then forget   155
That after many wanderings, many years
Of absence, these steep woods and lofty cliffs,
And this green pastoral landscape, were to me
More dear, both for themselves, and for thy sake!   (1798)

The Two April Mornings

We walk'd along, while bright and red
    Uprose the morning sun;
And Matthew stopp'd, he look'd, and said,
    'The will of God be done!'

A village schoolmaster was he,   5
    With hair of glittering grey;
As blithe a man as you could see
    On a spring holiday.

And on that morning, through the grass
    And by the steaming rills   10
We travell'd merrily, to pass
    A day among the hills.

'Our work,' said I, 'was well begun;
    Then, from thy breast what thought,
Beneath so beautiful a sun,   15
    So sad a sigh has brought?'

A second time did Matthew stop;
    And fixing still his eye
Upon the eastern mountain-top,
    To me he made reply: 20

'Yon cloud with that long purple cleft
    Brings fresh into my mind
A day like this, which I have left
    Full thirty years behind.

'And just above yon slope of corn   25
    Such colours, and no other,
Were in the sky, that April morn,
    Of this the very brother.

'With rod and line I sued the sport
    Which that sweet season gave,   30
And, to the churchyard come, stopp'd short
    Beside my daughter's grave.

'Nine summers had she scarcely seen,
    The pride of all the vale;
And then she sang;—she would have been   35
    A very nightingale.

'Six feet in earth my Emma lay;
    And yet I loved her more—
For so it seem'd,—than till that day
    I e'er had loved before.   40

'And turning from her grave, I met
    Beside the churchyard yew
A blooming Girl, whose hair was wet
    With points of morning dew.

'A basket on her head she bare;
    Her brow was smooth and white: 45
To see a child so very fair,
    It was a pure delight!

'No fountain from its rocky cave
    E'er tripp'd with foot so free;
She seem'd as happy as a wave   50
    That dances on the sea.

'There came from me a sigh of pain
    Which I could ill confine;
I looked at her, and looked again: 55
    And did not wish her mine!'

—Matthew is in his grave, yet now
    Methinks I see him stand
As at that moment, with a bough
    Of wilding in his hand.   (1800)   60

Three Years She Grew

Three years she grew in sun and shower,
Then Nature said, "A lovelier flower
    On earth was never sown;
This child I to myself will take;
She shall be mine, and I will make   5
    A lady of my own.

"Myself will to my darling be
Both law and impulse: and with me
    The girl, in rock and plain,
In earth and heaven, in glade and bower,   10

Shall feel an overseeing power
    To kindle or restrain.

"She shall be sportive as the fawn
That wild with glee across the lawn,
    Or up the mountain springs;   15
And hers shall be the breathing balm,
And hers the silence and the calm
    Of mute insensate things.

"The floating clouds their state shall lend
To her; for her the willow bend;   20
    Nor shall she fail to see
Even in the motions of the storm
Grace that shall mould the maiden's form
    By silent sympathy.

"The stars of midnight shall be dear   25
To her; and she shall lean her ear
    In many a secret place
Where rivulets dance their wayward round,
And beauty born of murmuring sound
    Shall pass into her face.   30

"And vital feelings of delight
Shall rear her form to stately height,
    Her virgin bosom swell;
Such thoughts to Lucy I will give
While she and I together live   35
    Here in this happy dell."

Thus Nature spake—The work was done—
How soon my Lucy's race was run!
    She died, and left to me
This heath, this calm, and quiet scene;   40
The memory of what has been,
    And never more will be.   (1800)

She Dwelt among the Untrodden Ways

She dwelt among the untrodden ways
    Beside the springs of Dove,
A maid whom there were none to praise
    And very few to love:

A violet by a mossy stone
   Half hidden from the eye.
—Fair as a star, when only one
   Is shining in the sky.

She lived unknown, and few could know
   When Lucy ceased to be;
But she is in her grave, and, oh,
   The difference to me!   (*1800*)

A Slumber Did My Spirit Seal

A slumber did my spirit seal;
   I had no human fears:
She seemed a thing that could not feel
   The touch of earthly years.

No motion has she now, no force;
   She neither hears nor sees;
Rolled round in earth's diurnal course,
   With rocks, and stones, and trees.   (*1800*)

The Solitary Reaper

Behold her, single in the field,
Yon solitary highland lass!
Reaping and singing by herself;
Stop here, or gently pass!
Alone she cuts and binds the grain,   5
And sings a melancholy strain;
O listen! for the vale profound
Is overflowing with the sound.

No nightingale did ever chaunt
More welcome notes to weary bands   10
Of travelers in some shady haunt,
Among Arabian sands:
A voice so thrilling ne'er was heard
In spring-time from the cuckoo-bird,

Breaking the silence of the seas   15
Among the farthest Hebrides.

Will no one tell me what she sings?—
Perhaps the plaintive numbers flow
For old, unhappy, far-off things,
And battles long ago: 20
Or is it some more humble lay,
Familiar matter of today?
Some natural sorrow, loss, or pain,
That has been, and may be again?

Whate'er the theme, the maiden sang   25
As if her song could have no ending;
I saw her singing at her work,
And o'er the sickle bending;—
I listened, motionless and still;
And, as I mounted up the hill   30
The music in my heart I bore,
Long after it was heard no more.   (*1807*)

I *Wandered Lonely as a Cloud*

I wandered lonely as a cloud
That floats on high o'er vales and hills,
When all at once I saw a crowd,
A host of golden daffodils,
Beside the lake, beneath the trees   5
Fluttering and dancing in the breeze.

Continuous as the stars that shine
And twinkle on the Milky Way,
They stretched in never-ending line
Along the margin of a bay: 10
Ten thousand saw I at a glance
Tossing their heads in sprightly dance.

The waves beside them danced, but they
Outdid the sparkling waves in glee:
A poet could not but be gay   15
In such a jocund company!
I gazed—and gazed—but little thought
What wealth the show to me had brought:

For oft, when on my couch I lie
In vacant or in pensive mood,   20
They flash upon that inward eye
Which is the bliss of solitude;
And then my heart with pleasure fills,
And dances with the daffodils.   (1807)

The World Is Too Much with Us

The world is too much with us; late and soon,
Getting and spending, we lay waste our powers:
Little we see in Nature that is ours;
We have given our hearts away, a sordid boon!
The sea that bares her bosom to the moon;
The winds that will be howling at all hours,
And are up-gathered now like sleeping flowers;
For this, for everything, we are out of tune;
It moves us not.—Great God! I'd rather be
A pagan suckled in a creed outworn;
So might I, standing on this pleasant lea,
Have glimpses that would make me less forlorn;
Have sight of Proteus rising from the sea;
Or hear old Triton blow his wreathed horn.   (1807)

Composed Upon Westminster Bridge

SEPTEMBER 3, 1802

Earth has not anything to show more fair:
Dull would he be of soul who could pass by
A sight so touching in its majesty:
This city now doth, like a garment, wear
The beauty of the morning: silent, bare,
Ships, towers, domes, theaters, and temples lie
Open unto the fields, and to the sky;
All bright and glittering in the smokeless air.
Never did sun more beautifully steep
In his first splendor, valley, rock, or hill;

Ne'er saw I, never felt, a calm so deep!
The river glideth at his own sweet will:
Dear God! the very houses seem asleep;
And all that mighty heart is lying still!   (1807)

It Is a Beauteous Evening

It is a beauteous evening, calm and free;
The holy time is quiet as a nun
Breathless with adoration; the broad sun
Is sinking down in its tranquillity;
The gentleness of heaven broods o'er the sea:
Listen! the mighty Being is awake,
And doth with his eternal motion make
A sound like thunder—everlastingly.
Dear child! dear girl! that walkest with me here,
If thou appear untouched by solemn thought,
Thy nature is not therefore less divine:
Thou liest in Abraham's bosom all the year,
And worship'st at the Temple's inner shrine,
God being with thee when we know it not.   (1807)

London, 1802

Milton! thou shouldst be living at this hour:
England hath need of thee: she is a fen
Of stagnant waters: altar, sword, and pen,
Fireside, the heroic wealth of hall and bower,
Have forfeited their ancient English dower
Of inward happiness. We are selfish men;
Oh! raise us up, return to us again;
And give us manners, virtue, freedom, power.
Thy soul was like a star, and dwelt apart:
Thou hadst a voice whose sound was like the sea:
Pure as the naked heavens, majestic, free,
So didst thou travel on life's common way,
In cheerful godliness; and yet thy heart
The lowliest duties on herself did lay.   (1807)

Ode:

Intimations of Immortality from Recollections
of Early Childhood

> The Child is Father of the Man;
> And I could wish my days to be
> Bound each to each by natural piety.[1]

1

There was a time when meadow, grove, and stream,
    The earth, and every common sight,
        To me did seem
    Appareled in celestial light,
The glory and the freshness of a dream.   5
It is not now as it hath been of yore;—
        Turn whereso'er I may,
        By night or day,
The things which I have seen I now can see no more.

2

    The rainbow comes and goes,   10
    And lovely is the rose,
    The moon doth with delight
Look round her when the heavens are bare,
    Waters on a starry night
    Are beautiful and fair;   15
    The sunshine is a glorious birth;
    But yet I know, where'er I go,
That there hath passed away a glory from the earth.

3

Now, while the birds thus sing a joyous song,
    And while the young lambs bound   20
        As to the tabor's sound,
To me alone there came a thought of grief;
A timely utterance gave that thought relief,
        And I again am strong:
The cataracts blow their trumpets from the steep;   25
No more shall grief of mine the season wrong;
I hear the echoes through the mountains throng,

[1] Wordsworth, "My Heart Leaps Up
. . ."

The winds come to me from the fields of sleep,
> And all the earth is gay;
>> Land and sea   30
> Give themselves up to jollity
>> And with the heart of May
> Doth every beast keep holiday;—
>> Thou child of joy,
Shout round me, let me hear thy shouts, thou happy shepherd boy. 35

4

Ye blessed Creatures, I have heard the call
> Ye to each other make; I see
The heavens laugh with you in your jubilee;
> My heart is at your festival,
> My head hath its coronal,   40
The fullness of your bliss, I feel—I feel it all.
> Oh evil day! if I were sullen
> While Earth herself is adorning,
>> This sweet May-morning,
> And the children are culling   45
>> On every side,
> In a thousand valleys far and wide,
> Fresh flowers; while the sun shines warm,
And the babe leaps up on his mother's arm:—
> I hear, I hear, with joy I hear!   50
> —But there's a tree, of many, one,
A single field which I have looked upon,
Both of them speak of something that is gone:
> The pansy at my feet
> Doth the same tale repeat: 55
Whither is fled the visionary gleam?
Where is it now, the glory and the dream?

5

Our birth is but a sleep and a forgetting:
The soul that rises with us, our life's star,
> Hath had elsewhere its setting,   60
>> And cometh from afar;
> Not in entire forgetfulness,
> And not in utter nakedness,
But trailing clouds of glory do we come
>> From God, who is our home.   65
Heaven lies about us in our infancy;

Shades of the prison-house begin to close
      Upon the growing boy,
But he beholds the light, and whence it flows.
      He sees it in his joy;   70
The youth, who daily farther from the east
      Must travel, still is Nature's priest,
        And by the vision splendid
        Is on his way attended;
At length the man perceives it die away,   75
And fade into the light of common day.

6

Earth fills her lap with pleasures of her own;
Yearnings she hath in her own natural kind,
And, even with something of a mother's mind,
      And no unworthy aim,   80
      The homely nurse doth all she can
To make her foster-child, her inmate man,
      Forget the glories he hath known,
And that imperial palace whence he came.

7

Behold the child among his newborn blisses,   85
      A six years' darling of a pygmy size!
See, where 'mid work of his own hand he lies,
Fretted by sallies of his mother's kisses,
With light upon him from his father's eyes!
See, at his feet, some little plan or chart,   90
Some fragment from his dream of human life,
Shaped by himself with newly learned art;
      A wedding or a festival,
      A mourning or a funeral;
        And this hath now his heart,   95
      And unto this he frames his song:
        Then will he fit his tongue
To dialogues of business, love, or strife;
      But it will not be long
      Ere this be thrown aside,   100
      And with new joy and pride
The little actor cons another part;
Filling from time to time his "humorous stage" [2]

[2] Shakespeare, *As You Like It*, 2, 7,
139 ff.; humorous: set by moods

With all the persons, down to palsied age,
That life brings with her in her equipage;   105
  As if his whole vocation
  Were endless imitation.

8

Thou, whose exterior semblance doth belie
  Thy soul's immensity;
Thou best philosopher, who yet dost keep   110
Thy heritage, thou eye among the blind,
That, deaf and silent, read'st the eternal deep,
Haunted forever by the eternal mind—
  Mighty prophet! seer blest!
  On whom those truths do rest,   115
Which we are toiling all our lives to find,
In darkness lost, the darkness of the grave;
Thou, over whom thy immortality
Broods like the day, a master o'er a slave,
A presence which is not to be put by;   120
Thou little Child, yet glorious in the might
Of heaven-born freedom on thy being's height,
Why with such earnest pains dost thou provoke
The years to bring the inevitable yoke,
Thus blindly with thy blessedness at strife?   125
Full soon thy Soul shall have her earthly freight,
And custom lie upon thee with a weight,
Heavy as frost, and deep almost as life!

9

  O joy! that in our embers
  Is something that doth live,   130
  That nature yet remembers
  What was so fugitive!

The thought of our past years in me doth breed
Perpetual benediction: not indeed
For that which is most worthy to be blest—   135
Delight and liberty, the simple creed
Of childhood, whether busy or at rest,
With new-fledged hope still fluttering in his breast:—
  Not for these I raise
  The song of thanks and praise;   140
 But for those obstinate questionings

Of sense and outward things,
Falling from us, vanishings;
Blank misgivings of a creature
Moving about in worlds not realized,   145
High instincts before which our mortal nature
Did tremble like a guilty thing surprised:
      But for those first affections,
      Those shadowy recollections,
   Which, be they what they may,   150
Are yet the fountain-light of all our day,
Are yet a master-light of all our seeing;
   Uphold us, cherish, and have power to make
Our noisy years seem moments in the being
Of the eternal silence: truths that wake,   155
      To perish never;
Which neither listlessness, nor mad endeavor,
      Nor man nor boy,
Nor all that is at enmity with joy,
Can utterly abolish or destroy!   160
      Hence in a season of calm weather,
      Though inland far we be,
Our souls have sight of that immortal sea
      Which brought us hither,
      Can in a moment travel thither,   165
And see the children sport upon the shore,
And hear the mighty waters rolling evermore.

                  10

Then sing, ye birds! sing, sing a joyous song!
      And let the young lambs bound
      As to the tabor's sound!   170
   We in thought will join your throng,
      Ye that pipe and ye that play,
      Ye that through your hearts today
      Feel the gladness of the May!
What though the radiance which was once so bright   175
Be now forever taken from my sight,
      Though nothing can bring back the hour
Of splendor in the grass, or glory in the flower;
      We will grieve not, rather find
      Strength in what remains behind;   180
      In the primal sympathy
      Which having been must ever be;

In the soothing thoughts that spring
Out of human suffering;
In the faith that looks through death,   185
In years that bring the philosophic mind.

11

And oh, ye fountains, meadows, hills, and groves,
Forebode not any severing of our loves!
Yet in my heart of hearts I feel your might;
I only have relinquished one delight   190
To live beneath your more habitual sway.
I love the brooks which down their channels fret,
Even more than when I tripped lightly as they;
The innocent brightness of a new-born day
            Is lovely yet;   195
The clouds that gather round the setting sun
Do take a sober coloring from an eye
That hath kept watch o'er man's mortality;
Another race hath been, and other palms are won.
Thanks to the human heart by which we live,   200
Thanks to its tenderness, its joys, and fears,
To me the meanest flower that blows can give
Thoughts that do often lie too deep for tears.   (1807)

To a Skylark

Ethereal minstrel! pilgrim of the sky!
Dost thou despise the earth where cares abound?
Or, while the wings aspire, are heart and eye
Both with thy nest upon the dewy ground?
The nest which thou canst drop into at will,   5
Those quivering wings composed, that music still!

Leave to the nightingale her shady wood;
A privacy of glorious light is thine;
Whence thou dost pour upon the world a flood
Of harmony, with instinct more divine;   10
Types of the wise who soar, but never roam;
True to the kindred points of heaven and home!
                            (1827; rev. 1845)

SAMUEL TAYLOR COLERIDGE
(1772–1834)

Frost at Midnight

The frost performs its secret ministry,
Unhelped by any wind. The owlet's cry
Came loud—and hark, again! loud as before.
The inmates of my cottage, all at rest,
Have left me to that solitude, which suits⠀⠀⠀⠀⠀⠀⠀⠀5
Abstruser musings: save that at my side
My cradled infant slumbers peacefully.
'Tis calm indeed! so calm, that it disturbs
And vexes meditation with its strange
And extreme silentness. Sea, hill, and wood,⠀⠀⠀⠀⠀10
This populous village! Sea, and hill, and wood,
With all the numberless goings on of life
Inaudible as dreams! the thin blue flame
Lies on my low-burnt fire, and quivers not;
Only that film, which fluttered on the grate,[1]⠀⠀⠀⠀15
Still flutters there, the sole unquiet thing.
Methinks, its motion in this hush of nature
Gives it dim sympathies with me who live,
Making it a companionable form,
Whose puny flaps and freaks the idling Spirit⠀⠀⠀⠀20
By its own moods interprets, everywhere
Echo or mirror seeking of itself,
And makes a toy of Thought.
⠀⠀⠀⠀⠀⠀⠀⠀⠀⠀⠀⠀⠀⠀⠀But oh! how oft,
How oft, at school, with most believing mind,⠀⠀⠀⠀25
Presageful, have I gazed upon the bars,
To watch that fluttering stranger! and as oft
With unclosed lids, already had I dreamt
Of my sweet birth-place, and the old church-tower,
Whose bells, the poor man's only music, rang⠀⠀⠀⠀30
From morn to evening, all the hot Fairday,
So sweetly, that they stirred and haunted me

---

[1] films, called "strangers," which por-
tend a visitor

With a wild pleasure, falling on mine ear
Most like articulate sounds of things to come!
So gazed I, till the soothing things I dreamt   35
Lulled me to sleep, and sleep prolonged my dreams!
And so I brooded all the following morn,
Awed by the stern preceptor's face, mine eye
Fixed with mock study on my swimming book:
Save if the door half opened, and I snatched   40
A hasty glance, and still my heart leaped up
For still I hoped to see the stranger's face,
Townsman, or aunt, or sister more beloved,
My play-mate when we both were clothed alike!
　　Dear babe, that sleepest cradled by my side,   45
Whose gentle breathings, heard in this deep calm,
Fill up the interspersèd vacancies
And momentary pauses of the thought!
My babe so beautiful! it thrills my heart
With tender gladness, thus to look at thee,   50
And think that thou shalt learn far other lore
And in far other scenes! For I was reared
In the great city, pent 'mid cloisters dim,
And saw naught lovely but the sky and stars.
But thou, my babe! shalt wander like a breeze   55
By lakes and sandy shores, beneath the crags
Of ancient mountain, and beneath the clouds,
Which image in their bulk both lakes and shores
And mountain crags: so shalt thou see and hear
The lovely shapes and sounds intelligible   60
Of that eternal language, which thy God
Utters, who from eternity doth teach
Himself in all, and all things in himself.
Great universal Teacher! he shall mould
Thy spirit, and by giving make it ask.   65
　　Therefore all seasons shall be sweet to thee,
Whether the summer clothe the general earth
With greenness, or the redbreast sit and sing
Betwixt the tufts of snow on the bare branch
Of mossy apple-tree, while the nigh thatch   70
Smokes in the sun-thaw; whether the eavedrops fall
Heard only in the trances of the blast,
Or if the secret ministry of frost
Shall hang them up in silent icicles,
Quietly shining to the quiet moon.   (1798)   75

This Lime-Tree Bower My Prison

ADDRESSED TO CHARLES LAMB, OF THE
INDIA HOUSE, LONDON

In the June of 1797 some long-expected friends paid a visit to the author's cottage; and on the morning of their arrival, he met with an accident, which disabled him from walking during the whole time of their stay. One evening, when they had left him for a few hours, he composed the following lines in the garden-bower.

Well, they are gone, and here must I remain,
This lime-tree bower my prison! I have lost
Beauties and feelings, such as would have been
Most sweet to my remembrance even when age
Had dimm'd mine eyes to blindness! They, meanwhile,   5
Friends, whom I never more may meet again,
On springy [1] heath, along the hill-top edge,
Wander in gladness, and wind down, perchance,
To that still roaring dell, of which I told;
The roaring dell, o'erwooded, narrow, deep,   10
And only speckled by the mid-day sun;
Where its slim trunk the ash from rock to rock
Flings arching like a bridge;—that branchless ash,
Unsunn'd and damp, whose few poor yellow leaves
Ne'er tremble in the gale, yet tremble still,   15
Fann'd by the water-fall! and there my friends
Behold the dark green file of long lank weeds,[2]
That all at once (a most fantastic sight!)
Still nod and drip beneath the dripping edge
Of the blue clay-stone.   20

                    Now, my friends emerge
Beneath the wide wide Heaven—and view again
The many-steepled tract magnificent
Of hilly fields and meadows, and the sea,
With some fair bark, perhaps, whose sails light up
The slip of smooth clear blue betwixt two Isles   25
Of purple shadow! Yes! they wander on

[1] "Elastic, I mean," manuscript *Letter to Southey.* [2] The *Asplenium Scolopendrium,* called in some countries the Adder's Tongue, in others the Hart's Tongue, but Withering gives the Adder's Tongue as the trivial name of the *Ophioglossum* only.

In gladness all; but thou, methinks, most glad,
My gentle-hearted Charles! for thou hast pined
And hunger'd after Nature, many a year,
In the great City pent, winning thy way   30
With sad yet patient soul, through evil and pain
And strange calamity! Ah! slowly sink
Behind the western ridge, thou glorious Sun!
Shine in the slant beams of the sinking orb,
Ye purple heath-flowers! richlier burn, ye clouds!   35
Live in the yellow light, ye distant groves!
And kindle, thou blue Ocean! So my friend
Struck with deep joy may stand, as I have stood,
Silent with swimming sense; yea, gazing round
On the wide landscape, gaze till all doth seem   40
Less gross than bodily; and of such hues
As veil the Almighty Spirit, when yet he makes
Spirits perceive his presence.

                    A delight
Comes sudden on my heart, and I am glad
As I myself were there! Nor in this bower,   45
This little lime-tree bower, have I not mark'd
Much that has sooth'd me. Pale beneath the blaze
Hung the transparent foliage; and I watch'd
Some broad and sunny leaf, and lov'd to see
The shadow of the leaf and stem above   50
Dappling its sunshine! And that walnut-tree
Was richly ting'd, and a deep radiance lay
Full on the ancient ivy, which usurps
Those fronting elms, and now, with blackest mass
Makes their dark branches gleam a lighter hue   55
Through the late twilight: and though now the bat
Wheels silent by, and not a swallow twitters,
Yet still the solitary humble-bee
Sings in the bean-flower! Henceforth I shall know
That Nature ne'er deserts the wise and pure;   60
No plot so narrow, be but Nature there,
No waste so vacant, but may well employ
Each faculty of sense, and keep the heart
Awake to Love and Beauty! and sometimes
'Tis well to be bereft of promis'd good,   65
That we may lift the soul, and contemplate
With lively joy the joys we cannot share.

My gentle-hearted Charles! when the last rook
Beat its straight path along the dusky air
Homewards, I blest it! deeming its black wing   70
(Now a dim speck, now vanishing in light)
Had cross'd the mighty Orb's dilated glory,
While thou stood'st gazing; or, when all was still,
Flew creeking o'er thy head, and had a charm [3]
For thee, my gentle-hearted Charles, to whom   75
No sound is dissonant which tells of Life.   (1800)

Dejection: An Ode

Late, late yestreen I saw the new Moon,
With the old Moon in her arms;
And I fear, I fear, my Master dear!
We shall have a deadly storm.
                Ballad of Sir Patrick Spence.

I

Well! If the Bard was weather-wise, who made
    The grand old ballad of Sir Patrick Spence,
    This night, so tranquil now, will not go hence
Unroused by winds, that ply a busier trade
Than those which mould yon cloud in lazy flakes,   5
Or the dull sobbing draft, that moans and rakes
Upon the strings of this Æolian lute,
        Which better far were mute.
    For lo! the New-moon winter-bright!
    And overspread with phantom light,   10
    (With swimming phantom light o'erspread
    But rimmed and circled by a silver thread)
I see the old Moon in her lap, foretelling
    The coming-on of rain and squally blast.
And oh! that even now the gust were swelling,   15
    And the slant night-shower driving loud and fast!

[3] Some months after I had written this line, it gave me pleasure to find [to observe *An. Anth., S.L. 1828*] that Bartram had observed the same circumstance of the Savanna Crane: "When these Birds move their wings in flight, their strokes are slow, moderate and regular; and even when at a considerable distance or high above us, we plainly hear the quill-feathers: their shafts and webs upon one another creek as the joints or working of a vessel in a tempestuous sea."

Those sounds which oft have raised me, whilst they awed,
    And sent my soul abroad,
Might now perhaps their wonted impulse give,
Might startle this dull pain, and make it move and live!   20

2

A grief without a pang, void, dark, and drear,
    A stifled, drowsy, unimpassioned grief,
      Which finds no natural outlet, no relief,
        In word, or sigh, or tear—
O Lady! in this wan and heartless mood,   25
To other thoughts by yonder throstle woo'd,
    All this long eve, so balmy and serene,
Have I been gazing on the western sky,
    And its peculiar tint of yellow green:
And still I gaze—and with how blank an eye!   30
And those thin clouds above, in flakes and bars,
That give away their motion to the stars;
Those stars, that glide behind them or between,
Now sparkling, now bedimmed, but always seen:
Yon crescent Moon, as fixed as if it grew   35
In its own cloudless, starless lake of blue;
I see them all so excellently fair,
I see, not feel, how beautiful they are!

3

    My genial spirits fail;
      And what can these avail   40
To lift the smothering weight from off my breast?
    It were a vain endeavour,
      Though I should gaze for ever
On that green light that lingers in the west:
I may not hope from outward forms to win   45
The passion and the life, whose fountains are within.

4

O Lady! we receive but what we give,
And in our life alone does Nature live:
Ours is her wedding garment, ours her shroud!
    And would we aught behold, of higher worth,   50
Than that inanimate cold world allowed
To the poor loveless ever-anxious crowd,
    Ah! from the soul itself must issue forth

A light, a glory, a fair luminous cloud
        Enveloping the Earth—   55
And from the soul itself must there be sent
    A sweet and potent voice, of its own birth,
Of all sweet sounds the life and element!

                5

O pure of heart! thou need'st not ask of me
What this strong music in the soul may be!   60
What, and wherein it doth exist,
This light, this glory, this fair luminous mist,
This beautiful and beauty-making power.
        Joy, virtuous Lady! Joy that ne'er was given,
Save to the pure, and in their purest hour,   65
Life, and Life's effluence, cloud at once and shower,
Joy, Lady! is the spirit and the power,
Which wedding Nature to us gives in dower
        A new Earth and new Heaven,
Undreamt of by the sensual and the proud—   70
Joy is the sweet voice, Joy the luminous cloud—
        We in ourselves rejoice!
And thence flows all that charms or ear or sight,
    All melodies the echoes of that voice,
All colours a suffusion from that light.   75

                6

There was a time when, though my path was rough,
    This joy within me dallied with distress,
And all misfortunes were but as the stuff
    Whence Fancy made me dreams of happiness:
For hope grew round me, like the twining vine,   80
And fruits, and foliage, not my own, seemed mine.
But now afflictions bow me down to earth:
Nor care I that they rob me of my mirth;
        But oh! each visitation
Suspends what nature gave me at my birth,   85
    My shaping spirit of Imagination.
For not to think of what I needs must feel,
    But to be still and patient, all I can;
And haply by abstruse research to steal
    From my own nature all the natural man—   90
    This was my sole resource, my only plan:
Till that which suits a part infects the whole,
And now is almost grown the habit of my soul.

7

Hence, viper thoughts, that coil around my mind,
  Reality's dark dream!   95
I turn from you, and listen to the wind,
  Which long has raved unnoticed. What a scream
Of agony by torture lengthened out
That lute sent forth! Thou Wind, that rav'st without,
  Bare crag, or mountain-tairn,[1] or blasted tree, 100
Or pine-grove whither woodman never clomb,
Or lonely house, long held the witches' home,
  Methinks were fitter instruments for thee,
Mad Lutanist! who in this month of showers,
Of dark-brown gardens, and of peeping flowers, 105
Mak'st Devils' yule, with worse than wintry song,
The blossoms, buds, and timorous leaves among.
  Thou Actor, perfect in all tragic sounds!
Thou mighty Poet, e'en to frenzy bold!
    What tell'st thou now about?   110
    'Tis of the rushing of an host in rout,
  With groans, of trampled men, with smarting wounds—
At once they groan with pain, and shudder with the cold!
But hush! there is a pause of deepest silence!
  And all that noise, as of a rushing crowd, 115
With groans, and tremulous shudderings—all is over—
  It tells another tale, with sounds less deep and loud!
    A tale of less affright,
    And tempered with delight,
As Otway's self had framed the tender lay,— 120
    'Tis of a little child
    Upon a lonesome wild,
Not far from home, but she hath lost her way:
And now moans low in bitter grief and fear,
And now screams loud, and hopes to make her mother hear. 125

8

'Tis midnight, but small thoughts have I of sleep:
Full seldom may my friend such vigils keep!
Visit her, gentle Sleep! with wings of healing,
  And may this storm be but a mountain-birth,

[1] Tairn is a small lake, generally if not always applied to the lakes up in the mountains and which are the feeders of those in the valleys. This address to the Storm-wind will not appear extravagant to those who have heard it at night and in a mountainous country. [S.T.C.]

May all the stars hang bright above her dwelling,   130
    Silent as though they watched the sleeping Earth!
        With light heart may she rise,
        Gay fancy, cheerful eyes,
    Joy lift her spirit, joy attune her voice;
To her may all things live, from pole to pole,   135
Their life the eddying of her living soul!
    O simple spirit, guided from above,
Dear Lady! friend devoutest of my choice,
Thus mayest thou ever, evermore rejoice.   (1802)

Kubla Khan

In Xanadu did Kubla Khan
    A stately pleasure-dome decree:
Where Alph, the sacred river, ran
Through caverns measureless to man
    Down to a sunless sea.   5
So twice five miles of fertile ground
With walls and towers were girdled round:
And here were gardens bright with sinuous rills,
Where blossomed many an incense-bearing tree,
And here were forests ancient as the hills,   10
Enfolding sunny spots of greenery.

But oh! that deep romantic chasm which slanted
Down the green hill athwart a cedarn cover!
A savage place; as holy and enchanted
As e'er beneath a waning moon was haunted   15
By woman wailing for her demon-lover!
And from this chasm, with ceaseless turmoil seething,
As if this earth in fast thick pants were breathing,
A mighty fountain momently was forced,
Amid whose swift half-intermitted burst   20
Huge fragments vaulted like rebounding hail,
Or chaffy grain beneath the thresher's flail:
And 'mid these dancing rocks at once and ever
It flung up momently the sacred river.
Five miles meandering with a mazy motion   25
Through wood and dale the sacred river ran,
Then reached the caverns measureless to man,

And sank in tumult to a lifeless ocean:
And 'mid this tumult Kubla heard from far
Ancestral voices prophesying war!   30

    The shadow of the dome of pleasure
    Floated midway on the waves;
    Where was heard the mingled measure
    From the fountain and the caves.
It was a miracle of rare device,   35
A sunny pleasure-dome with caves of ice!

    A damsel with a dulcimer
    In a vision once I saw:
    It was an Abyssinian maid,
    And on her dulcimer she played,   40
    Singing of Mount Abora.
    Could I revive within me
    Her symphony and song,
    To such a deep delight 'twould win me,
That with music loud and long,   45
I would build that dome in air,
That sunny dome! those caves of ice!
And all who heard should see them there,
And all should cry, Beware! Beware!
His flashing eyes, his floating hair!   50
Weave a circle round him thrice,
And close your eyes with holy dread,
For he on honey-dew hath fed,
And drunk the milk of Paradise.   (*1816*)

WALTER SAVAGE LANDOR
(1775–1864)

Past Ruin'd Ilion

Past ruin'd Ilion Helen lives,
    Alcestis rises from the shades;
Verse calls them forth; 'tis verse that gives
    Immortal youth to mortal maids.

Soon shall Oblivion's deepening veil
    Hide all the peopled hills you see,
The gay, the proud, while lovers hail
    In distant ages you and me.

The tear for fading beauty check,
    For passing glory cease to sigh;
One form shall rise above the wreck,
    One name, Ianthe, shall not die.   *(1798)*

I Strove with None

I strove with none, for none was worth my strife.
    Nature I loved and, next to Nature, Art:
I warmed both hands before the fire of life;
    It sinks, and I am ready to depart.   *(1853)*

GEORGE GORDON, LORD BYRON
(1788–1824)

She Walks in Beauty

She walks in beauty, like the night
    Of cloudless climes and starry skies;
And all that's best of dark and bright
    Meet in her aspect and her eyes:
Thus mellowed to that tender light   5
    Which heaven to gaudy day denies.

One shade the more, one ray the less,
    Had half impaired the nameless grace
Which waves in every raven tress,
    Or softly lightens o'er her face;   10
Where thoughts serenely sweet express
    How pure, how dear, their dwelling-place.

And on that cheek, and o'er that brow,
    So soft, so calm, yet eloquent,
The smiles that win, the tints that glow,   15
    But tell of days in goodness spent,
A mind at peace with all below,
    A heart whose love is innocent!   (1815)

The Destruction of Sennacherib [1]

The Assyrian came down like the wolf on the fold,
And his cohorts were gleaming in purple and gold;
And the sheen of their spears was like stars on the sea,
When the blue wave rolls nightly on deep Galilee.

Like the leaves of the forest when Summer is green,   5
That host with their banners at sunset were seen:
Like the leaves of the forest when Autumn hath blown,
That host on the morrow lay withered and strown.

[1] Kings 2:18–19

For the Angel of Death spread his wings on the blast,
And breathed in the face of the foe as he passed;   10
And the eyes of the sleepers waxed deadly and chill,
And their hearts but once heaved, and for ever grew still!

And there lay the steed with his nostril all wide,
But through it there rolled not the breath of his pride;
And the foam of his gasping lay white on the turf,   15
And cold as the spray of the rock-beating surf.

And there lay the rider distorted and pale,
With the dew on his brow, and the rust on his mail:
And the tents were all silent, the banners alone,
The lances unlifted, the trumpet unblown.   20

And the widows of Ashur are loud in their wail,
And the idols are broke in the temple of Baal;
And the might of the Gentile, unsmote by the sword,
Hath melted like snow in the glance of the Lord!   (*1815*)

From *Childe Harold's Pilgrimage*

Canto IV

.   .   .   .   .

178

There is a pleasure in the pathless woods,
There is a rapture on the lonely shore,   1595
There is society, where none intrudes,
By the deep sea, and music in its roar:
I love not man the less, but Nature more,
From these our interviews, in which I steal
From all I may be, or have been before,   1600
To mingle with the Universe, and feel
What I can ne'er express, yet cannot all conceal.

179

Roll on, thou deep and dark blue Ocean—roll!
Ten thousand fleets sweep over thee in vain;

Man marks the earth with ruin; his control 1605
Stops with the shore; upon the watery plain
The wrecks are all thy deed, nor doth remain
A shadow of man's ravage, save his own,
When for a moment, like a drop of rain,
He sinks into thy depths with bubbling groan, 1610
Without a grave, unknelled, uncoffined and unknown.

180

His steps are not upon thy paths—thy fields
Are not a spoil for him—thou dost arise
And shake him from thee, the vile strength he wields
For earth's destruction thou dost all despise, 1615
Spurning him from thy bosom to the skies,
And sendst him, shivering in thy playful spray,
And howling, to his Gods, where haply lies
His petty hope in some near port or bay,
And dashest him again to earth—there let him lay. 1620

181

The armaments which thunderstrike the walls
Of rock-built cities, bidding nations quake,
And monarchs tremble in their capitals,
The oak leviathans, whose huge ribs make
Their clay creator the vain title take 1625
Of lord of thee, and arbiter of war:—
These are thy toys, and, as the snowy flake,
They melt into thy yeast of waves, which mar
Alike the Armada's pride, or spoils of Trafalgar.[1]

182

Thy shores are empires, changed in all save thee— 1630
Assyria, Greece, Rome, Carthage, what are they?
Thy waters washed them power while they were free,
And many a tyrant since: their shores obey
The stranger, slave or savage; their decay
Has dried up realms to deserts:—not so thou, 1635
Unchangeable save to thy wild waves' play—
Time writes no wrinkle on thine azure brow—
Such as creation's dawn beheld, thou rollest now.

[1] Sea storms destroyed the Spanish and the French fleet in 1805, at
fleet moving against England in 1588 Trafalgar.

183

Thou glorious mirror, where the Almighty's form
Glasses itself in tempests: in all time,   1640
Calm or convulsed—in breeze, or gale, or storm,
Icing the pole, or in the torrid clime
Dark-heaving; boundless, endless, and sublime—
The image of Eternity—the throne
Of the Invisible; even from out thy slime   1645
The monsters of the deep are made; each zone
Obeys thee; thou goest forth, dread, fathomless, alone.

184

And I have loved thee, Ocean! and my joy
Of youthful sports was on thy breast to be
Borne, like thy bubbles, onward; from a boy   1650
I wantoned with thy breakers—they to me
Were a delight; and if the freshening sea
Made them a terror—'twas a pleasing fear,
For I was as it were a child of thee,
And trusted to thy billows far and near,   1655
And laid my hand upon thy mane—as I do here.   (*1818*)

From *Don Juan*

Canto III

86

. . . . .

The isles of Greece, the isles of Greece!
   Where burning Sappho loved and sung,   690
Where grew the arts of war and peace—
   Where Delos rose, and Phoebus sprung!
Eternal summer gilds them yet,
But all, except their sun, is set.

The Scian and the Teian muse,[1]   695
   The hero's harp, the lover's lute,

---

[1] Homer   and   Anacreon

Have found the fame your shores refuse:
 Their place of birth alone is mute
To sounds which echo farther west
Than your sires' "Islands of the Blest." [2]   700

The mountains look on Marathon—
 And Marathon looks on the sea;
And musing there an hour alone,
 I dreamed that Greece might still be free;
For standing on the Persians' grave,   705
I could not deem myself a slave.

A king [3] sat on the rocky brow
 Which looks o'er sea-born Salamis;
And ships, by thousands, lay below,
 And men in nations—all were his!   710
He counted them at break of day—
And when the sun set, where were they?

And where are they? And where art thou,
 My country? On thy voiceless shore
The heroic lay is tuneless now—   715
 The heroic bosom beats no more!
And must thy lyre, so long divine,
Degenerate into hands like mine?

'Tis something, in the dearth of fame,
 Though linked among a fettered race,   720
To feel at least a patriot's shame,
 Even as I sing, suffuse my face;
For what is left the poet here?
For Greeks a blush—for Greece a tear.

Must *we* but weep o'er days more blest?   725
 Must *we* but blush?—Our fathers bled.
Earth! render back from out thy breast
 A remnant of our Spartan dead!
Of the three hundred grant but three,
To make a new Thermopylae!   730

What, silent still? and silent all?
 Ah! no—the voices of the dead

[2] Hesiod, *Works and Days,* 169
[3] Xerxes

Sound like a distant torrent's fall,
    And answer, "Let one living head,
But one arise—we come, we come!"   735
'Tis but the living who are dumb.

In vain—in vain: strike other chords;
    Fill high the cup with Samian wine!
Leave battles to the Turkish hordes,
    And shed the blood of Scio's vine!   740
Hark! rising to the ignoble call—
How answers each bold Bacchanal!

You have the Pyrrhic dance as yet;
    Where is the Pyrrhic phalanx gone?
Of two such lessons, why forget   745
    The nobler and the manlier one?
You have the letters Cadmus gave—
Think ye he meant them for a slave?

Fill high the bowl with Samian wine!
    We will not think of themes like these!   750
It made Anacreon's song divine;
    He served—but served Polycrates—
A tyrant; but our masters then
Were still, at least, our countrymen.

The tyrant of the Chersonese   755
    Was freedom's best and bravest friend;
That tyrant was Miltiades!
    Oh! that the present hour would lend
Another despot of the kind!
Such chains as his were sure to bind.   760

Fill high the bowl with Samian wine!
    On Suli's rock, and Parga's shore,
Exists the remnant of a line
    Such as the Doric mothers bore;
And there, perhaps, some seed is sown,   765
The Heracleidan blood might own.

Trust not for freedom to the Franks—
    They have a king who buys and sells;
In native swords and native ranks,
    The only hope of courage dwells: 770
But Turkish force, and Latin fraud,
Would break your shield, however broad.

Fill high the bowl with Samian wine!
    Our virgins dance beneath the shade—
I see their glorious black eyes shine;   775
    But gazing on each glowing maid,
My own the burning teardrop laves,
To think such breasts must suckle slaves.

Place me on Sunium's marbled steep,
    Where nothing, save the waves and I,   780
May hear our mutual murmurs sweep;
    There, swan-like, let me sing and die: [4]
A land of slaves shall ne'er be mine—
Dash down yon cup of Samian wine!   *(1819–1824)*

So We'll Go No More A-Roving

So we'll go no more a-roving
    So late into the night,
Though the heart be still as loving,
    And the moon be still as bright.

For the sword outwears its sheath,
    And the soul wears out the breast,
And the heart must pause to breathe,
    And Love itself have rest.

Though the night was made for loving,
    And the day returns too soon,
Yet we'll go no more a-roving
    By the light of the moon.   *(1807–1824)*

---

[4] The swan was said to sing when nearing death.

ᴥᴥᴥ PERCY BYSSHE SHELLEY (1792–1822)

Ozymandias

I met a traveler from an antique land
Who said: Two vast and trunkless legs of stone
Stand in the desert. Near them, on the sand,
Half sunk, a shattered visage lies, whose frown,
And wrinkled lip, and sneer of cold command,
Tell that its sculptor well those passions read
Which yet survive, stamped on these lifeless things,
The hand that mocked them and the heart that fed;
And on the pedestal these words appear:
"My name is Ozymandias, king of kings:
Look on my works, ye Mighty, and despair!"
Nothing beside remains. Round the decay
Of that colossal wreck, boundless and bare
The lone and level sands stretch far away.   (*1819*)

Love's Philosophy

The fountains mingle with the river
    And the rivers with the ocean,
The winds of heaven mix for ever
    With a sweet emotion;
Nothing in the world is single,   5
    All things by a law divine
In one another's being mingle—
    Why not I with thine?

See the mountains kiss high heaven
    And the waves clasp one another;   10
No sister-flower would be forgiven
    If it disdain'd its brother:
And the sunlight clasps the earth,
    And the moonbeams kiss the sea—
What are all these kissings worth,   15
    If thou kiss not me?   (*1819*)

The Cloud

I bring fresh showers for the thirsting flowers
    From the seas and the streams;
I bear light shade for the leaves when laid
    In their noonday dreams.
From my wings are shaken the dews that waken   5
    The sweet buds every one,
When rocked to rest on their mother's breast,
    As she dances about the sun.
I wield the flail of the lashing hail,
    And whiten the green plains under,   10
And then again I dissolve it in rain,
    And laugh as I pass in thunder.

I sift the snow on the mountains below,
    And their great pines groan aghast;
And all the night 'tis my pillow white,   15
    While I sleep in the arms of the blast.
Sublime on the towers of my skyey bowers,
    Lightning my pilot sits;
In a cavern under is fettered the thunder,
    It struggles and howls at fits;   20
Over earth and ocean, with gentle motion,
    This pilot is guiding me,
Lured by the love of the genii that move
    In the depths of the purple sea;
Over the rills, and the crags, and the hills,   25
    Over the lakes and the plains,
Wherever he dream, under mountain or stream,
    The spirit he loves remains;
And I all the while bask in heaven's blue smile,
    Whilst he is dissolving in rains.   30

The sanguine sunrise, with his meteor eyes,
    And his burning plumes outspread,
Leaps on the back of my sailing rack
    When the morning star shines dead,
As on the jag of a mountain crag,   35
    Which an earthquake rocks and swings,
An eagle alit one moment may sit
    In the light of its golden wings.

And when sunset may breathe, from the lit sea beneath,
    Its ardors of rest and of love,   40
And the crimson pall of eve may fall
    From the depth of heaven above,
With wings folded I rest, on mine airy nest,
    As still as a brooding dove.

That orbéd maiden with white fire laden,   45
    Whom mortals call the moon,
Glides glimmering o'er my fleece-like floor,
    By the midnight breezes strewn;
And wherever the beat of her unseen feet,
    Which only the angels hear,   50
May have broken the woof of my tent's thin roof,
    The stars peep behind her and peer;
And I laugh to see them whirl and flee,
    Like a swarm of golden bees,
When I widen the rent in my wind-built tent,   55
    Till the calm rivers, lakes, and seas,
Like strips of the sky fallen through me on high,
    Are each paved with the moon and these.

I bind the sun's throne with a burning zone,
    And the moon's with a girdle of pearl;   60
The volcanoes are dim, and the stars reel and swim,
    When the whirlwinds my banner unfurl.
From cape to cape, with a bridge-like shape,
    Over a torrent sea,
Sunbeam-proof, I hang like a roof—   65
    The mountains its columns be.
The triumphal arch through which I march
    With hurricane, fire, and snow,
When the powers of the air are chained to my chair,
    Is the million-colored bow;   70
The sphere-fire above its soft colors wove,
    While the moist earth was laughing below.

I am the daughter of earth and water,
    And the nursling of the sky;
I pass through the pores of the ocean and shores;   75
    I change, but I cannot die.
For after the rain when with never a stain
    The pavilion of heaven is bare,

And the winds and sunbeams with their convex gleams
    Build up the blue dome of air,   80
I silently laugh at my own cenotaph,
    And out of the caverns of rain,
Like a child from the womb, like a ghost from the tomb,
    I arise and unbuild it again.   (*1820*)

To a Skylark

Hail to thee, blithe spirit!
    Bird thou never wert—
That from heaven or near it
    Pourest thy full heart
In profuse strains of unpremeditated art.   5

Higher still and higher
    From the earth thou springest,
Like a cloud of fire;
    The blue deep thou wingest,
And singing still dost soar, and soaring ever singest.   10

In the golden light'ning
    Of the sunken sun,
O'er which clouds are bright'ning,
    Thou dost float and run,
Like an unbodied joy whose race is just begun.   15

The pale purple even
    Melts around thy flight;
Like a star of heaven,
    In the broad daylight
Thou art unseen, but yet I hear thy shrill delight—   20

Keen as are the arrows
    Of that silver sphere
Whose intense lamp narrows
    In the white dawn clear,
Until we hardly see, we feel that it is there.   25

All the earth and air
    With thy voice is loud,
As, when night is bare,
    From one lonely cloud
The moon rains out her beams, and heaven is overflow'd.   30

What thou art we know not;
    What is most like thee?
From rainbow clouds there flow not
    Drops so bright to see,
As from thy presence showers a rain of melody:—   35

Like a poet hidden
    In the light of thought,
Singing hymns unbidden,
    Till the world is wrought
To sympathy with hopes and fears it heeded not: 40

Like a high-born maiden
    In a palace tower,
Soothing her love-laden
    Soul in secret hour
With music sweet as love, which overflows her bower: 45

Like a glow-worm golden
    In a dell of dew,
Scattering unbeholden
    Its aërial hue
Among the flowers and grass which screen it from the view: 50

Like a rose embower'd
    In its own green leaves,
By warm winds deflower'd,
    Till the scent it gives
Makes faint with too much sweet those heavy-wingèd thieves.   55

Sound of vernal showers
    On the twinkling grass,
Rain-awaken'd flowers—
    All that ever was
Joyous and clear and fresh—thy music doth surpass.   60

Teach us, sprite or bird,
    What sweet thoughts are thine:
I have never heard
    Praise of love or wine
That panted forth a flood of rapture so divine.   65

Chorus hymeneal,
    Or triumphal chant,
Match'd with thine would be all
    But an empty vaunt—
A thing wherein we feel there is some hidden want.   70

What objects are the fountains
    Of thy happy strain
What fields, or waves, or mountains?
    What shapes of sky or plain?
What love of thine own kind? what ignorance of pain?   75

With thy clear keen joyance
    Languor cannot be:
Shadow of annoyance
    Never came near thee:
Thou lovest, but ne'er knew love's sad satiety.   80

Waking or asleep,
    Thou of death must deem
Things more true and deep
    Than we mortals dream,
Or how could thy notes flow in such a crystal stream?   85

We look before and after,
    And pine for what is not:
Our sincerest laughter
    With some pain is fraught;
Our sweetest songs are those that tell of saddest thought.   90

Yet, if we could scorn
    Hate and pride and fear,
If we were things born
    Not to shed a tear,
I know not how thy joy we ever should come near.   95

Better than all measures
    Of delightful sound,
Better than all treasures
    That in books are found,
Thy skill to poet were, thou scorner of the ground!   100

Teach me half the gladness
    That thy brain must know;
Such harmonious madness
    From my lips would flow,
The world should listen then, as I am listening now.   (1820)

From *Prometheus Unbound*

Act IV

. . . . .

Demogorgon: [1] This is the day, which down the void abysm
At the Earth-born's spell [2] yawns for Heaven's despotism,   555
    And Conquest is dragged captive through the deep:
Love, from its awful throne of patient power
In the wise heart, from the last giddy hour
    Of dead endurance, from the slippery, steep,
And narrow verge of crag-like agony, springs   560
And folds over the world its healing wings.

Gentleness, Virtue, Wisdom, and Endurance,
These are the seals of that most firm assurance
    Which bars the pit over Destruction's strength;
And if, with infirm hand, Eternity,   565
Mother of many acts and hours, should free
    The serpent that would clasp her with his length;
These are the spells by which to re-assume
An empire o'er the disentangled doom.

To suffer woes which Hope thinks infinite;   570
To forgive wrongs darker than death or night;
    To defy Power, which seems omnipotent;
To love, and bear; to hope till Hope creates
From its own wreck the thing it contemplates;
    Neither to change, nor falter, nor repent;   575
This, like thy glory, Titan, is to be
Good, great, and joyous, beautiful, and free;
This is alone Life, Joy, Empire, and Victory.   (1820)

Ode to the West Wind

I

O wild West Wind, thou breath of Autumn's being,
Thou, from whose unseen presence the leaves dead
Are driven, like ghosts from an enchanter fleeing,

---

[1] Shelley's personification of the eternal   theologies   [2] That of Prometheus
principles which oust the gods of false

Yellow, and black, and pale, and hectic red,
Pestilence-stricken multitudes: O thou,   5
Who chariotest to their dark wintry bed

The wingéd seeds, where they lie cold and low,
Each like a corpse within its grave, until
Thine azure sister of the spring shall blow

Her clarion o'er the dreaming earth, and fill   10
(Driving sweet buds like flocks to feed in air)
With living hues and odours plain and hill;

Wild Spirit, which art moving everywhere;
Destroyer and preserver; hear, Oh hear!

2

Thou on whose stream, 'mid the steep sky's commotion,   15
Loose clouds like earth's decaying leaves are shed,
Shook from the tangled boughs of Heaven and Ocean,

Angels of rain and lightning: there are spread
On the blue surface of thine airy surge,
Like the bright hair uplifted from the head   20

Of some fierce Mænad, even from the dim verge
Of the horizon to the zenith's height
The locks of the approaching storm. Thou dirge

Of the dying year, to which this closing night
Will be the dome of a vast sepulchre,   25
Vaulted with all thy congregated might

Of vapours, from whose solid atmosphere
Black rain, and fire, and hail will burst: Oh hear!

3

Thou who didst waken from his summer dreams
The blue Mediterranean, where he lay,   30
Lulled by the coil of his crystalline streams.

Beside a pumice isle in Baiæ's bay,
And saw in sleep old palaces and towers
Quivering within the wave's intenser day,

All overgrown with azure moss and flowers   35
So sweet, the sense faints picturing them! Thou
For whose path the Atlantic's level powers

Cleave themselves into chasms, while far below
The sea-blooms and the oozy woods which wear
The sapless foliage of the ocean, know   40

Thy voice, and suddenly grow gray with fear,
And tremble and despoil themselves: Oh hear!

4

If I were a dead leaf thou mightest bear;
If I were a swift cloud to fly with thee;
A wave to pant beneath thy power, and share   45

The impulse of thy strength, only less free
Than thou, O uncontrollable! If even
I were as in my boyhood, and could be

The comrade of thy wanderings over heaven,
As then, when to outstrip thy skiey speed   50
Scarce seemed a vision; I would ne'er have striven

As thus with thee in prayer in my sore need.
Oh lift me as a wave, a leaf, a cloud!
I fall upon the thorns of life! I bleed!

A heavy weight of hours has chained and bowed   55
One too like thee: tameless, and swift, and proud.

5

Make me thy lyre, even as the forest is:
What if my leaves are falling like its own!
The tumult of thy mighty harmonies

Will take from both a deep, autumnal tone,   60
Sweet though in sadness. Be thou, spirit fierce,
My spirit! Be thou me, impetuous one!

Drive my dead thoughts over the universe
Like withered leaves to quicken a new birth!
And, by the incantation of this verse,   65

Scatter, as from an unextinguished hearth
Ashes and sparks, my words among mankind!
Be through my lips to unawakened earth

The trumpet of a prophecy! O, wind,
If Winter comes, can Spring be far behind?   (1820)

From *Adonais*

AN ELEGY ON THE DEATH OF JOHN KEATS

1

I weep for Adonais—he is dead!
Oh weep for Adonais! though our tears
Thaw not the frost which binds so dear a head!
And thou, sad Hour, selected from all years
To mourn our loss, rouse thy obscure compeers,[1] 5
And teach them thine own sorrow! Say: 'With me
Died Adonais; till the Future dares
Forget the Past, his fate and fame shall be
An echo and a light unto Eternity!'

2

Where wert thou, mighty Mother,[2] when he lay, 10
When thy son lay, pierced by the shaft which flies
In darkness? where was lorn Urania
When Adonais died? With veilèd eyes,
'Mid listening Echoes, in her paradise
She sate, while one, with soft enamored breath, 15
Rekindled all the fading melodies,
With which, like flowers that mock the corse beneath,
He had adorned and hid the coming bulk of death.

3

Oh, weep for Adonais—he is dead!
Wake, melancholy Mother, wake and weep! 20
Yet wherefore? Quench within their burning bed
Thy fiery tears, and let thy loud heart keep
Like his, a mute and uncomplaining sleep;
For he is gone, where all things wise and fair
Descend. Oh, dream not that the amorous Deep 25
Will yet restore him to the vital air;
Death feeds on his mute voice, and laughs at our despair.

4

Most musical of mourners, weep again!
Lament anew, Urania!—He died,[3]

---

[1] later, less memorable hours [2] Urania, [3] Milton
Shelley's personification of lyric poetry

Who was the sire of an immortal strain,   30
Blind, old, and lonely, when his country's pride,
The priest, the slave, and the liberticide,
Trampled and mocked with many a loathèd rite
Of lust and blood; he went, unterrified,
Into the gulf of death; but his clear Sprite   35
Yet reigns o'er earth, the third among the sons of light.

5

Most musical of mourners, weep anew!
Not all to that bright station dared to climb;
And happier they their happiness who knew,
Whose tapers yet burn through that night of time   40
In which suns perished; others more sublime,
Struck by the envious wrath of man or God,
Have sunk, extinct in their refulgent prime;
And some yet live, treading the thorny road,
Which leads, through toil and hate, to Fame's serene abode.   45

.   .   .   .   .

39

Peace, peace! he is not dead, he doth not sleep—
He hath awakened from the dream of life—
'Tis we, who, lost in stormy visions, keep   345
With phantoms an unprofitable strife,
And in mad trance, strike with our spirit's knife
Invulnerable nothings. *We* decay
Like corpses in a charnel; fear and grief
Convulse us and consume us day by day,   350
And cold hopes swarm like worms within our living clay.

40

He has outsoared the shadow of our night;
Envy and calumny and hate and pain,
And that unrest which men miscall delight,
Can touch him not and torture not again;   355
From the contagion of the world's slow stain
He is secure, and now can never mourn
A heart grown cold, a head grown gray in vain;
Nor, when the spirit's self has ceased to burn,
With sparkless ashes load an unlamented urn.   360

41

He lives, he wakes—'tis Death is dead, not he;
Mourn not for Adonais.—Thou young Dawn,
Turn all thy dew to splendor, for from thee
The spirit thou lamentest is not gone;
Ye caverns and ye forests, cease to moan!   365
Cease, ye faint flowers and fountains, and thou air,
Which like a mourning veil thy scarf hadst thrown
O'er the abandoned Earth, now leave it bare
Even to the joyous stars which smile on its despair!

42

He is made one with Nature: there is heard   370
His voice in all her music, from the moan
Of thunder, to the song of night's sweet bird;
He is a presence to be felt and known
In darkness and in light, from herb and stone,
Spreading itself where'er that Power may move   375
Which has withdrawn his being to its own;
Which wields the world with never-wearied love,
Sustains it from beneath, and kindles it above.

43

He is a portion of the loveliness
Which once he made more lovely: he doth bear   380
His part, while the one Spirit's plastic stress
Sweeps through the dull dense world, compelling there
All new successions to the forms they wear,
Torturing the unwilling dross that checks its flight
To its own likeness, as each mass may bear;   385
And bursting in its beauty and its might
From trees and beasts and men into the Heaven's light,

44

The splendors of the firmament of time
May be eclipsed, but are extinguished not;
Like stars to their appointed height they climb,   390
And death is a low mist which cannot blot
The brightness it may veil. When lofty thought
Lifts a young heart above its mortal lair,
And love and life contend in it for what
Shall be its earthly doom, the dead live there   395
And move like winds of light on dark and stormy air.

45

The inheritors of unfulfilled renown
Rose from their thrones, built beyond mortal thought,
Far in the Unapparent. Chatterton
Rose pale,—his solemn agony had not   400
Yet faded from him; Sidney, as he fought
And as he fell and as he lived and loved
Sublimely mild, a Spirit without spot,
Arose; and Lucan, by his death approved:
Oblivion as they rose shrank like a thing reproved.   405

46

And many more, whose names on earth are dark,
But whose transmitted effluence cannot die
So long as fire outlives the parent spark,
Rose, robed in dazzling immortality.
"Thou art become as one of us," they cry,   410
"It was for thee yon kingless sphere has long
Swung blind in unascended majesty,
Silent alone amid an heaven of song.
Assume thy wingèd throne, thou Vesper of our throng!"

47

Who mourns for Adonais? Oh, come forth,   415
Fond wretch! and know thyself and him aright.
Clasp with thy panting soul the pendulous earth;
As from a center, dart by thy spirit's light
Beyond all worlds, until its spacious might
Satiate the void circumference: then shrink   420
Even to a point within our day and night;
And keep thy heart light lest it make thee sink
When hope has kindled hope, and lured thee to the brink.

48

Or go to Rome, which is the sepulcher,
Oh, not of him, but of our joy: 'tis nought   425
That ages, empires, and religions there
Lie buried in the ravage they have wrought;
For such as he can lend,—they borrow not
Glory from those who made the world their prey;
And he is gathered to the kings of thought   430
Who waged contention with their time's decay,
And of the past are all that cannot pass away.

49

Go thou to Rome,—at once the Paradise,
The grave, the city, and the wilderness;
And where its wrecks like shattered mountains rise,   435
And flowering weeds and fragrant copses dress
The bones of Desolation's nakedness,
Pass, till the Spirit of the spot shall lead
Thy footsteps to a slope of green access [4]
Where, like an infant's smile, over the dead   440
A light of laughing flowers along the grass is spread;

50

And gray walls molder round, on which dull Time
Feeds, like slow fire, upon a hoary brand;
And one keen pyramid [5] with wedge sublime,
Pavilioning the dust of him who planned   445
This refuge for his memory, doth stand
Like flame transformed to marble; and beneath,
A field is spread, on which a newer band
Have pitched in Heaven's smile their camp of death,
Welcoming him we lose with scarce extinguished breath.   450

51

Here pause: these graves [6] are all too young as yet
To have outgrown the sorrow which consigned
Its charge to each; and if the seal is set,
Here, on one fountain of a mourning mind,
Break it not thou! too surely shalt thou find   455
Thine own well full, if thou returnest home,
Of tears and gall. From the world's bitter wind
Seek shelter in the shadow of the tomb.
What Adonais is, why fear we to become?

52

The One remains, the many change and pass;   460
Heaven's light forever shines, Earth's shadows fly;
Life, like a dome of many-colored glass,
Stains the white radiance of Eternity,
Until Death tramples it to fragments.—Die,
If thou wouldst be with that which thou dost seek!   465
Follow where all is fled!—Rome's azure sky,

[4] Keats was buried in the Protestant cemetery at Rome.   [5] the tomb of Casius Cestius   [6] Shelley's son was also buried there

Flowers, ruins, statues, music, words, are weak
The glory they transfuse with fitting truth to speak.

53

Why linger, why turn back, why shrink, my heart?
Thy hopes are gone before: from all things here   470
They have departed; thou shouldst now depart!
A light is passed from the revolving year,
And man, and woman; and what still is dear
Attracts to crush, repels to make thee wither.
The soft sky smiles,—the low wind whispers near: 475
'Tis Adonais calls! oh, hasten thither,
No more let Life divide what Death can join together.

54

That Light whose smile kindles the Universe,
That Beauty in which all things work and move,
That Benediction which the eclipsing Curse   480
Of birth can quench not, that sustaining Love
Which through the web of being blindly wove
By man and beast and earth and air and sea,
Burns bright or dim, as each are mirrors of
The fire for which all thirst; now beams on me,   485
Consuming the last clouds of cold mortality.

55

The breath whose might I have invoked in song
Descends on me; my spirit's bark is driven,
Far from the shore, far from the trembling throng
Whose sails were never to the tempest given;   490
The massy earth and spherèd skies are riven!
I am borne darkly, fearfully, afar:
Whilst, burning through the inmost veil of Heaven,
The soul of Adonais, like a star,
Beacons from the abode where the Eternal are.   (*1821*)

From *Hellas*

The World's Great Age Begins Anew

The world's great age begins anew,
     The golden years return,
The earth doth like a snake renew
     Her winter weeds [1] outworn:

---

[1] garments

Heaven smiles, and faiths and empires gleam,   5
Like wrecks of a dissolving dream.

A brighter Hellas rears its mountains
   From waves serener far;
A new Peneus rolls his fountains
   Against the morning star.   10
Where fairer Tempes bloom, there sleep
Young Cyclads on a sunnier deep.

A loftier Argo cleaves the main,
   Fraught with a later prize;
Another Orpheus sings again,   15
   And loves, and weeps, and dies.
A new Ulysses leaves once more
Calypso for his native shore.

Oh, write no more the tale of Troy,
   If earth Death's scroll must be!   20
Nor mix with Laian rage the joy
   Which dawns upon the free:
Although a subtler Sphinx renew
Riddles of death Thebes never knew.

Another Athens shall arise,   25
   And to remoter time
Bequeath, like sunset to the skies,
   The splendor of its prime;
And leave, if naught so bright may live,
All earth can take or Heaven can give.   30

Saturn and Love their long repose
   Shall burst, more bright and good
Than all who fell,[2] than One who rose,[3]
   Than many unsubdued: [4]
Not gold, not blood, their altar dowers,   35
But votive tears and symbol flowers.

Oh, cease! must hate and death return?
   Cease! must men kill and die?
Cease! drain not to its dregs the urn
   Of bitter prophecy.   40
The world is weary of the past,
Oh, might it die or rest at last!   (1822)

[2] the gods of Egypt, Asia, and Greece before Jesus
[3] Jesus   [4] gods of the Orient

Hymn of Pan

1

From the forests and highlands
    We come, we come;
From the river-girt islands,
    Where loud waves are dumb
Listening to my sweet pipings.   5
The wind in the reeds and the rushes,
    The bees on the bells of thyme,
The birds on the myrtle bushes,
    The cicale [1] above in the lime,
And the lizards below in the grass,   10
Were as silent as ever old Timolus was,
Listening to my sweet pipings.

2

Liquid Peneus [2] was flowing,
    And all dark Tempe lay
In Pelion's shadow, outgrowing   15
    The light of the dying day,
Speeded by my sweet pipings.
The Sileni, and Sylvans, and Fauns,
    And the Nymphs of the woods and the waves,
To the edge of the moist river-lawns,   20
    And the brink of the dewy caves,
And all that did then attend and follow
Were silent with love, as you now, Apollo,
With envy of my sweet pipings.

3

I sang of the dancing stars,   25
    I sang of the daedal Earth,
And of Heaven—and the giant wars,
    And Love, and Death, and Birth,—
And then I changed my pipings,—
Singing how down the vale of Maenalus   30
    I pursued a maiden and clasped a reed:

---

[1] cicada, locust   [2] a river in Thessaly   in the high mountain range of Pelion
which flows through the vale of Tempe

Gods and men, we are all deluded thus!
    It breaks in our bosom and then we bleed:
All wept, as I think both ye now would,
If envy or age had not frozen your blood,   35
At the sorrow of my sweet pipings.   (*1824*)

To Night

Swiftly walk o'er the western wave,
    Spirit of Night!
Out of the misty eastern cave,
Where, all the long and lone daylight,
Thou wovest dreams of joy and fear,   5
Which make thee terrible and dear—
    Swift be thy flight!

Wrap thy form in a mantle gray,
    Star-inwrought!
Blind with thine hair the eyes of day;   10
Kiss her until she be wearied out,
Then wander o'er city, and sea, and land,
Touching all with thine opiate wand—
    Come, long-sought!

When I arose and saw the dawn,   15
    I sighed for thee;
When light rode high, and the dew was gone,
And noon lay heavy on flower and tree,
And the weary day turned to his rest,
Lingering like an unloved guest,   20
    I sighed for thee.

Thy brother Death came, and cried,
    Wouldst thou me?
Thy sweet child Sleep, the filmy-eyed,
Murmured like a noontide bee,   25
Shall I nestle near thy side?
Wouldst thou me?—And I replied,
    No, not thee!

Death will come when thou art dead,
    Soon, too soon—   30

Sleep will come when thou art fled;
Of neither would I ask the boon
I ask of thee, beloved Night—
Swift be thine approaching flight,
  Come soon, soon! (*1824*)

Time

Unfathomable Sea! whose waves are years,
 Ocean of Time, whose waters of deep woe
Are brackish with the salt of human tears !
 Thou shoreless flood, which in thy ebb and flow
Claspest the limits of mortality,   5
And sick of prey, yet howling on for more,
Vomitest thy wrecks on its inhospitable shore;
 Treacherous in calm, and terrible in storm,
  Who shall put forth on thee,
  Unfathomable Sea ? (*1824*)

JOHN CLARE (1793–1864)

Honey Dew Falls from the Tree

Honey dew falls from the tree
    Where my Julia walks with me
With her white arm held in mine;
    Luscious smells the eglantine;
In blushes sleeps the rosy briar   5
    Lit with tiny sparks of fire,
As the red hot sun goes down
    Like a ball to fire the town.

Glow worms fire the dark green grass
    Where my Julia's small feet pass,   10
And the kingcups rimm'd wi' dew,
    Gold, and white, and pearly blue,
Tap her on her evening track,
    Sandal shoes with ribbons black,
And woodbines with a crimson streak   15
    Nod against her bonnet peak.

The pearly west glowed golden charms
    While I held Julia in my arms,
Sweet Julia with the eye of dew,
    The heath-bell hasn't one so blue.   20
Her neck, the lily of the Vale
    Is not so fair and sweetly pale,
Her cheek—the rose cropt in the dew
    Is not so blushing in its hue.

I kissed—yes, I kissed her twice,   25
    While the little whistling mice
From the hedge ran in and out
    And bounced the silver dews about.
I leaned upon my Julia's cheek
    And could have rested there a week,   30
But we returned to our repose
    Just as the tall round moon arose.

The Winter's Spring

The winter comes; I walk alone,
    I want no bird to sing;
To those who keep their hearts their own,
    The winter is the spring.
No flowers to please—no bees to hum—   5
The coming spring's already come.

I never want the Christmas rose
    To come before its time;
The seasons, each as God bestows,
    Are simple and sublime.   10
I love to see the snowstorm hing;
 Tis but the winter garb of spring.

I never want the grass to bloom:
    The snowstorm's best in white.
I love to see the tempest come   15
    And love its piercing light.
The dazzled eyes that love to cling
O'er snow-white meadows sees the spring.

I love the snow, the crumpling snow
    That hangs on everything,   20
It covers everything below
    Like white dove's brooding wing,
A landscape to the aching sight,
A vast expanse of dazzling light.

It is the foliage of the woods   25
    That winters bring—the dress,
White Easter of the year in bud,
    That makes the winter Spring.
The frost and snow his posies bring,
Nature's white spirits of the spring.   30

I Am

I am; yet what I am none cares or knows,
    My friends forsake me like a memory lost;
I am the self-consumer of my woes,
    They rise and vanish in oblivious host,

Like shades in love and death's oblivion lost;   5
And yet I am, and live with shadows tost

Into the nothingness of scorn and noise,
  Into the living sea of waking dreams,
Where there is neither sense of life nor joys,
  But the vast shipwreck of my life's esteems;   10
And e'en the dearest—that I loved the best—
Are strange—nay, rather stranger than the rest.

I long for scenes where man has never trod;
  A place where woman never smiled or wept;
There to abide with my Creator, God,   15
  And sleep as I in childhood sweetly slept:
Untroubling and untroubled where I lie;
The grass below—above the vaulted sky.   (1848)

✑ JOHN KEATS (1795–1821)

On First Looking into Chapman's Homer

Much have I travell'd in the realms of gold,
And many goodly states and kingdoms seen;
Round many western islands have I been
Which bards in fealty to Apollo hold.
Oft of one wide expanse had I been told
That deep-brow'd Homer ruled as his demesne:
Yet did I never breathe its pure serene
Till I heard Chapman speak out loud and bold.
Then felt I like some watcher of the skies
When a new planet swims into his ken;
Or like stout Cortez when with eagle eyes [1]
He stared at the Pacific—and all his men
Look'd at each other with a wild surmise—
Silent, upon a peak in Darien.   (*1816*)

On Seeing the Elgin Marbles [1]

My spirit is too weak—mortality
Weighs heavily on me like unwilling sleep,
And each imagined pinnacle and steep
Of godlike hardship tells me I must die
Like a sick eagle looking at the sky.
Yet 'tis a gentle luxury to weep
That I have not the cloudy winds to keep,
Fresh for the opening of the morning's eye.
Such dim-conceived glories of the brain,
Bring round the heart an indescribable feud;
So do these wonders a most dizzy pain,
That mingles Grecian grandeur with the rude
Wasting of old Time—with a billowy main—
A sun—a shadow of a magnitude.   (*1817*)

[1] Keats's well-known error; Balboa was the first known European explorer to see the Pacific

[1] Lord Elgin had pieces of sculpture from the Parthenon moved to London in 1803.

On the Grasshopper and Cricket

The poetry of earth is never dead:
When all the birds are faint with the hot sun,
And hide in cooling tree, a voice will run
From hedge to hedge about the new-mown mead;
That is the grasshopper's—he takes the lead
In the summer luxury,—he has never done
With his delights, for when tired out with fun
He rests at ease beneath some pleasant weed.
The poetry of earth is ceasing never:
On a lone winter evening, when the frost
Has wrought a silence, from the stove there shrills
The cricket's song, in warmth increasing ever,
And seems to one, in drowsiness half-lost,
The grasshopper's among some grassy hills.   (1817)

When I Have Fears That I May Cease to Be

When I have fears that I may cease to be
Before my pen has gleaned my teeming brain,
Before high-piled books, in charactery,
Hold like rich garners the full ripened grain;
When I behold, upon the night's starred face,
Huge cloudy symbols of a high romance,
And think that I may never live to trace
Their shadows, with the magic hand of chance;
And when I feel, fair creature of an hour,
That I shall never look upon thee more,
Never have relish in the faery power
Of unreflecting love;—then on the shore
Of the wide world I stand alone, and think
Till love and fame to nothingness do sink.   (1848)

Bright Star, Would I Were Steadfast

Bright star, would I were steadfast as thou art—
Not in lone splendor hung aloft the night,
And watching, with eternal lids apart,

Like nature's patient sleepless Eremite,
The moving waters at their priestlike task
Of pure ablution round earth's human shores,
Or gazing on the new soft fallen mask
Of snow upon the mountains and the moors:
No—yet still steadfast, still unchangeable,
Pillowed upon my fair love's ripening breast
To feel for ever its soft fall and swell,
Awake for ever in a sweet unrest;
Still, still to hear her tender-taken breath,
And so live ever—or else swoon to death.   (1848)

Ode to a Nightingale

My heart aches, and a drowsy numbness pains
    My sense, as though of hemlock I had drunk,
Or emptied some dull opiate to the drains
    One minute past, and Lethe-wards had sunk:
'Tis not through envy of thy happy lot,   5
    But being too happy in thy happiness,—
        That thou, light-winged Dryad of the trees,
            In some melodious plot
    Of beechen green, and shadows numberless,
        Singest of summer in full-throated ease.   10

O for a draught of vintage, that hath been
    Cooled a long age in the deep-delved earth,
Tasting of Flora and the country green,
    Dance, and Provençal song, and sun-burnt mirth!
O for a beaker full of the warm South,   15
    Full of the true, the blushful Hippocrene,
        With beaded bubbles winking at the brim,
            And purple-stained mouth;
    That I might drink, and leave the world unseen,
        And with thee fade away into the forest dim: 20

Fade far away, dissolve, and quite forget
    What thou among the leaves hast never known,
The weariness, the fever, and the fret
    Here, where men sit and hear each other groan;

Where palsy shakes a few, sad, last gray hairs,   25
    Where youth grows pale, and spectre-thin, and dies;
        Where but to think is to be full of sorrow
           And leaden-eyed despairs;
Where beauty cannot keep her lustrous eyes,
    Or new love pine at them beyond tomorrow.   30

Away! away! for I will fly to thee,
    Not charioted by Bacchus and his pards,
But on the viewless [1] wings of Poesy,
    Though the dull brain perplexes and retards:
Already with thee! tender is the night,   35
    And haply the Queen-Moon is on her throne,
        Clustered around by all her starry fays;
           But here there is no light,
Save what from heaven is with the breezes blown
        Through verdurous glooms and winding mossy ways.   40

I cannot see what flowers are at my feet,
    Nor what soft incense hangs upon the boughs,
But, in embalmed darkness, guess each sweet
    Wherewith the seasonable month endows
The grass, the thicket, and the fruit-tree wild;   45
    White hawthorn, and the pastoral eglantine;
        Fast-fading violets covered up in leaves;
           And mid-May's eldest child,
The coming musk-rose, full of dewy wine,
        The murmurous haunt of flies on summer eves.   50

Darkling I listen; and for many a time
    I have been half in love with easeful Death,
Called him soft names in many a mused rhyme,
    To take into the air my quiet breath;
Now more than ever seems it rich to die,   55
    To cease upon the midnight with no pain,
        While thou art pouring forth thy soul abroad
           In such an ecstasy!
Still wouldst thou sing, and I have ears in vain—
        To thy high requiem become a sod.   60

Thou wast not born for death, immortal bird!
    No hungry generations tread thee down;

[1] invisible

The voice I hear this passing night was heard
  In ancient days by emperor and clown:
Perhaps the self-same song that found a path   65
    Through the sad heart of Ruth, when, sick for home,
      She stood in tears amid the alien corn;[3]
          The same that oft-times hath
  Charmed magic casements, opening on the foam
    Of perilous seas, in faery lands forlorn.   70

Forlorn! the very word is like a bell
  To toll me back from thee to my sole self!
Adieu! the fancy cannot cheat so well
  As she is famed to do, deceiving elf.
Adieu! adieu! thy plaintive anthem fades   75
    Past the near meadows, over the still stream,
      Up the hill-side; and now 'tis buried deep
        In the next valley-glades:
  Was it a vision, or a waking dream?
    Fled is that music:—do I wake or sleep?   *(1819)*   80

La Belle Dame Sans Merci[1]

O what can ail thee, knight-at-arms,
  Alone and palely loitering?
The sedge has wither'd from the lake,
  And no birds sing.

O what can ail thee, knight-at-arms!   5
  So haggard and so woe-begone?
The squirrel's granary is full,
  And the harvest's done.

I see a lily on thy brow
  With anguish moist and fever dew,   10
And on thy cheeks a fading rose
  Fast withereth too.

[3] wheat; Ruth:2

[1] The Beautiful Lady Without Pity.
Lord Houghton's 1848 version of the
poem

I met a lady in the meads,
    Full beautiful—a faery's child,
Her hair was long, her foot was light,   15
    And her eyes were wild.

I made a garland for her head,
    And bracelets too, and fragrant zone;
She look'd at me as she did love,
    And made sweet moan.   20

I set her on my pacing steed,
    And nothing else saw all day long,
For sidelong would she bend, and sing
    A faery's song.

She found me roots of relish sweet,   25
    And honey wild, and manna dew,
And sure in language strange she said—
    "I love thee true."

She took me to her elfin grot,
    And there she wept, and sigh'd full sore,   30
And there I shut her wild eyes
    With kisses four.

And there she lulled me asleep,
    And there I dream'd—Ah! woe betide!
The latest dream I ever dream'd   35
    On the cold hill's side.

I saw pale kings and princes too,
    Pale warriors, death-pale were they all;
They cried—"La Belle Dame sans Merci
    Hath thee in thrall!"   40

I saw their starved lips in the gloam,
    With horrid warning gaped wide,
And I awoke and found me here,
    On the cold hill's side.

And this is why I sojourn here,   45
    Alone and palely loitering,
Though the sedge is wither'd from the lake,
    And no birds sing.

Ode on a Grecian Urn

Thou still unravish'd bride of quietness,
Thou foster-child of silence and slow time,
Sylvan historian, who canst thus express
A flowery tale more sweetly than our rhyme:
What leaf-fring'd legend haunts about thy shape   5
Of deities or mortals, or of both,
In Tempe or the dales of Arcady?
What men or gods are these? What maidens loth?
What mad pursuit? What struggle to escape?
What pipes and timbrels? What wild ecstasy?   10

Heard melodies are sweet, but those unheard
Are sweeter; therefore, ye soft pipes, play on;
Not to the sensual ear, but, more endear'd,
Pipe to the spirit ditties of no tone:
Fair youth, beneath the trees, thou canst not leave   15
Thy song, nor ever can those trees be bare;
Bold lover, never, never canst thou kiss,
Though winning near the goal—yet, do not grieve;
She cannot fade, though thou hast not thy bliss,
For ever wilt thou love, and she be fair!   20

Ah, happy, happy boughs! that cannot shed
Your leaves, nor ever bid the spring adieu;
And, happy melodist, unwearièd,
For ever piping songs for ever new;
More happy love! more happy, happy love!   25
For ever warm and still to be enjoy'd,
For ever panting, and for ever young;
All breathing human passion far above,
That leaves a heart high-sorrowful and cloy'd,
A burning forehead, and a parching tongue.   30

Who are these coming to the sacrifice?
To what green altar, O mysterious priest,
Lead'st thou that heifer lowing at the skies,
And all her silken flanks with garlands drest?
What little town by river or sea shore,   35
Or mountain-built with peaceful citadel,
Is emptied of this folk, this pious morn?

And, little town, thy streets for evermore
    Will silent be; and not a soul to tell
        Why thou art desolate, can e'er return.   40

O Attic shape! Fair attitude! with brede [1]
    Of marble men and maidens overwrought,
With forest branches and the trodden weed;
    Thou, silent form, dost tease us out of thought
As doth eternity. Cold pastoral!   45
    When old age shall this generation waste,
        Thou shalt remain, in midst of other woe
Than ours, a friend to man, to whom thou say'st,
    "Beauty is truth, truth beauty," that is all
        Ye know on earth, and all ye need to know.   (*1819*)

To Autumn

Season of mists and mellow fruitfulness,
    Close bosom-friend of the maturing sun;
Conspiring with him how to load and bless
    With fruit the vines that round the thatch-eaves run;
To bend with apples the mossed cottage-trees,   5
    And fill all fruit with ripeness to the core;
        To swell the gourd, and plump the hazel shells
    With a sweet kernel; to set budding more,
And still more, later flowers for the bees,
Until they think warm days will never cease,   10
        For Summer has o'er-brimmed their clammy cells.

Who hath not seen thee oft amid thy store?
    Sometimes whoever seeks abroad may find
Thee sitting careless on a granary floor,
    Thy hair soft-lifted by the winnowing wind;   15
Or on a half-reaped furrow sound asleep,
    Drowsed with the fume of poppies, while thy hook
        Spares the next swath and all its twined flowers;
And sometimes like a gleaner thou dost keep
    Steady thy laden head across a brook;   20
    Or by a cider-press, with patient look,
        Thou watchest the last oozings, hours by hours.

[1] embroidery

Where are the songs of Spring? Ay, where are they?
   Think not of them, thou has thy music too,—
While barred clouds bloom the soft-dying day,   25
   And touch the stubble-plains with rosy hue;
Then in a wailful choir, the small gnats mourn
   Among the river sallows, borne aloft
      Or sinking as the light wind lives or dies;
And full-grown lambs loud bleat from hilly bourn;   30
   Hedge-crickets sing; and now with treble soft
   The redbreast whistles from a garden-croft,
      And gathering swallows twitter in the skies.   (1820)

Ode on Melancholy

No, no! go not to Lethe, neither twist
   Wolf's-bane,[1] tight-rooted, for its poisonous wine;
Nor suffer thy pale forehead to be kissed
   By nightshade, ruby grape of Proserpine;
Make not your rosary of yew-berries,   5
   Nor let the beetle [2] nor the death-moth be
      Your mournful Psyche, nor the downy owl
A partner in your sorrow's mysteries;
   For shade to shade will come too drowsily,
      And drown the wakeful anguish of the soul.   10

But when the melancholy fit shall fall
   Sudden from heaven like a weeping cloud,
That fosters the droop-headed flowers all,
   And hides the green hill in an April shroud;
Then glut thy sorrow on a morning rose,   15
   Or on the rainbow of the salt sand-wave,
      Or on the wealth of globed peonies;
Or if thy mistress some rich anger shows,
   Emprison her soft hand, and let her rave,
      And feed deep, deep upon her peerless eyes.   20

She dwells with Beauty—Beauty that must die;
   And Joy, whose hand is ever at his lips

[1] a poisonous plant   [2] Egyptian symbol
of resurrection. Replicas of the beetle
were placed in tombs.

Bidding adieu; and aching Pleasure nigh,
    Turning to poison while the bee-mouth sips:
Ay, in the very temple of delight   25
      Veiled Melancholy has her sovran shrine,
        Though seen of none save him whose strenuous tongue
    Can burst Joy's grape against his palate fine:
His soul shall taste the sadness of her might,
    And be among her cloudy trophies hung.   (*1820*)

The Eve of St. Agnes

St. Agnes' Eve—Ah, bitter chill it was!
The owl, for all his feathers, was a-cold;
The hare limp'd trembling through the frozen grass,
And silent was the flock in woolly fold:
Numb were the beadsman's fingers, while he told   5
His rosary, and while his frosted breath,
Like pious incense from a censer old,
Seem'd taking flight for heaven, without a death,
Past the sweet Virgin's picture, while his prayer he saith.

His prayer he saith, this patient, holy man;   10
Then takes his lamp, and riseth from his knees,
And back returneth, meager, barefoot, wan,
Along the chapel aisle by slow degrees:
The sculptur'd dead, on each side, seem to freeze,
Emprison'd in black, purgatorial rails: 15
Knights, ladies, praying in dumb orat'ries,
He passeth by; and his weak spirit fails
To think how they may ache in icy hoods and mails.

Northward he turneth through a little door,
And scarce three steps, ere Music's golden tongue   20
Flatter'd to tears this aged man and poor;
But no—already had his deathbell rung:
The joys of all his life were said and sung:
His was harsh penance on St. Agnes' Eve:
Another way he went, and soon among   25
Rough ashes sat he for his soul's reprieve,
And all night kept awake, for sinners' sake to grieve.

That ancient beadsman heard the prelude soft;
And so it chanc'd, for many a door was wide,
From hurry to and fro. Soon, up aloft,   30
The silver, snarling trumpets 'gan to chide:
The level chambers, ready with their pride,
Were glowing to receive a thousand guests:
The carved angels, ever eager-eyed,
Star'd, where upon their heads the cornice rests,   35
With hair blown back, and wings put cross-wise on their breasts.

At length burst in the argent revelry,
With plume, tiara, and all rich array,
Numerous as shadows haunting fairily
The brain, new stuff'd, in youth, with triumphs gay   40
Of old romance. These let us wish away,
And turn, sole-thoughted, to one lady there,
Whose heart had brooded, all that wintry day,
On love, and wing'd St. Agnes' saintly care,
As she had heard old dames full many times declare.   45

They told her how, upon St. Agnes' Eve,
Young virgins might have visions of delight,
And soft adorings from their loves receive
Upon the honey'd middle of the night,
If ceremonies due they did aright;   50
As, supperless to bed they must retire,
And couch supine their beauties, lily white;
Nor look behind, nor sideways, but require
Of Heaven with upward eyes for all that they desire.

Full of this whim was thoughtful Madeline: 55
The music, yearning like a god in pain,
She scarcely heard: her maiden eyes divine,
Fix'd on the floor, saw many a sweeping train
Pass by—she heeded not at all: in vain
Came many a tiptoe, amorous cavalier,   60
And back retir'd; not cool'd by high disdain,
But she saw not: her heart was otherwhere:
She sigh'd for Agnes' dreams, the sweetest of the year.

She danc'd along with vague, regardless eyes,
Anxious her lips, her breathing quick and short: 65
The hallow'd hour was near at hand: she sighs
Amid the timbrels, and the throng'd resort
Of whisperers in anger, or in sport;

'Mid looks of love, defiance, hate, and scorn,
Hoodwink'd with faery fancy; all amort,   70
Save to St. Agnes and her lambs unshorn,
And all the bliss to be before tomorrow morn.

So, purposing each moment to retire,
She linger'd still. Meantime, across the moors,
Had come young Porphyro, with heart on fire   75
For Madeline. Beside the portal doors,
Buttress'd from moonlight, stands he, and implores
All saints to give him sight of Madeline,
But for one moment in the tedious hours,
That he might gaze and worship all unseen;   80
Perchance speak, kneel, touch, kiss—in sooth such things have been.

He ventures in: let no buzz'd whisper tell:
All eyes be muffled, or a hundred swords
Will storm his heart, Love's fev'rous citadel:
For him, those chambers held barbarian hordes,   85
Hyena foemen, and hot-blooded lords,
Whose very dogs would execrations howl
Against his lineage: not one breast affords
Him any mercy, in that mansion foul,
Save one old beldame, weak in body and in soul.   90

Ah, happy chance! the aged creature came,
Shuffling along with ivory-headed wand,
To where he stood, hid from the torch's flame,
Behind a broad hall-pillar, far beyond
The sound of merriment and chorus bland: 95
He startled her; but soon she knew his face,
And grasp'd his fingers in her palsied hand,
Saying, "Mercy, Porphyro! hie thee from this place:
They are all here tonight, the whole blood-thirsty race!

"Get hence! get hence! there's dwarfish Hildebrand;   100
He had a fever late, and in the fit
He cursed thee and thine, both house and land:
Then there's that old Lord Maurice, not a whit
More tame for his gray hairs—Alas me! flit!
Flit like a ghost away."—"Ah, gossip dear,   105
We're safe enough; here in this armchair sit,
And tell me how"—"Good Saints! not here, not here;
Follow me, child, or else these stones will be thy bier."

He follow'd through a lowly arched way,
Brushing the cobwebs with his loftly plume,   110
And as she muttered, "Well-a—well-a-day!"
He found him in a little moonlight room,
Pale, lattic'd, chill, and silent as a tomb.
"Now tell me where is Madeline," said he,
"O tell me, Angela, by the holy loom   115
Which none but secret sisterhood may see,
When they St. Agnes' wool are weaving piously."

"St. Agnes! Ah! it is St. Agnes' Eve—
Yet men will murder upon holy days:
Thou must hold water in a witch's sieve,   120
And be liege-lord of all the elves and fays,
To venture so: it fills me with amaze
To see thee, Porphyro!—St. Agnes' Eve!
God's help! my lady fair the conjuror plays
This very night: good angels her deceive!   125
But let me laugh awhile, I've mickle time to grieve."

Feebly she laugheth in the languid moon,
While Porphyro upon her face doth look,
Like puzzled urchin on an aged crone
Who keepeth clos'd a wond'rous riddle-book,   130
As spectacled she sits in chimney nook.
But soon his eyes grew brilliant, when she told
His lady's purpose; and he scarce could brook
Tears, at the thought of those enchantments cold,
And Madeline asleep in lap of legends old.   135

Sudden a thought came like a full-blown rose,
Flushing his brow, and in his pained heart
Made purple riot: then doth he propose
A stratagem, that makes the beldame start:
"A cruel man and impious thou art: 140
Sweet lady, let her pray, and sleep, and dream
Alone with her good angels, far apart
From wicked men like thee. Go, go!—I deem
Thou canst not surely be the same that thou didst seem."

"I will not harm her, by all saints I swear,"   145
Quoth Porphyro: "O may I ne'er find grace
When my weak voice shall whisper its last prayer,
If one of her soft ringlets I displace,
Or look with ruffian passion in her face:

Good Angela, believe me by these tears;   150
Or I will, even in a moment's space,
Awake, with horrid shout; my foemen's ears,
And beard them, though they be more fang'd than wolves and bears."

"Ah! why wilt thou affright a feeble soul?
A poor, weak, palsy-stricken, churchyard thing,   155
Whose passing-bell may ere the midnight toll;
Whose prayers for thee, each morn and evening,
Were never miss'd."—Thus plaining, doth she bring
A gentler speech from burning Porphyro;
So woful, and of such deep sorrowing,   160
That Angela gives promise she will do
Whatever he shall wish, betide her weal or woe.

Which was, to lead him, in close secrecy,
Even to Madeline's chamber, and there hide
Him in a closet, of such privacy   165
That he might see her beauty unespied,
And win perhaps that night a peerless bride,
While legion'd fairies pac'd the coverlet,
And pale enchantment held her sleepy-eyed.
Never on such a night have lovers met,   170
Since Merlin paid his demon all the monstrous debt.

"It shall be as thou wishest," said the dame:
"All cates and dainties shall be stored there
Quickly on this feast-night: by the tambour frame
Her own lute thou wilt see: no time to spare,   175
For I am slow and feeble, and scarce dare
On such a catering trust my dizzy head.
Wait here, my child, with patience; kneel in prayer
The while. Ah! thou must needs the lady wed,
Or may I never leave my grave among the dead."   180

So saying, she hobbled off with busy fear.
The lover's endless minutes slowly pass'd;
The dame return'd, and whisper'd in his ear
To follow her; with aged eyes aghast
From fright of dim espial. Safe at last,   185
Through many a dusky gallery, they gain
The maiden's chamber, silken, hush'd, and chaste;
Where Porphyro took covert, pleas'd amain.
His poor guide hurried back with agues in her brain.

Her falt'ring hand upon the balustrade,   190
Old Angela was feeling for the stair,
When Madeline, St. Agnes' charmed maid,
Rose, like a mission'd spirit, unaware:
With silver taper's light, and pious care,
She turn'd, and down the aged gossip led   195
To a safe level matting. Now prepare,
Young Porphyro, for gazing on that bed;
She comes, she comes again, like ringdove fray'd [1] and fled.

Out went the taper as she hurried in;
Its little smoke, in pallid moonshine, died: 200
She clos'd the door, she panted, all akin
To spirits of the air, and visions wide:
No uttered syllable, or, woe betide!
But to her heart, her heart was voluble,
Paining with eloquence her balmy side;   205
As though a tongueless nightingale should swell
Her throat in vain, and die, heart-stifled, in her dell.

A casement high and triple-arch'd there was,
All garlanded with carven imag'ries
Of fruits, and flowers, and bunches of knot-grass,   210
And diamonded with panes of quaint device,
Innumerable of stains and splendid dyes,
As are the tiger-moth's deep-damask'd wings;
And in the midst, 'mid thousand heraldries,
And twilight saints, and dim emblazonings,   215
A shielded scutcheon blush'd with blood of queens and kings.

Full on this casement shone the wintry moon,
And threw warm gules on Madeline's fair breast,
As down she knelt for heaven's grace and boon;
Rose-bloom fell on her hands, together prest,   220
And on her silver cross soft amethyst,
And on her hair a glory, like a saint:
She seem'd a splendid angel, newly drest,
Save wings, for heaven:—Porphyro grew faint:
She knelt, so pure a thing, so free from mortal taint.   225

Anon his heart revives: her vespers done,
Of all its wreathed pearls her hair she frees;
Unclasps her warmed jewels one by one;
Loosens her fragrant bodice; by degrees

[1] frightened

Her rich attire creeps rustling to her knees: 230
   Half-hidden, like a mermaid in sea-weed,
   Pensive awhile she dreams awake, and sees
   In fancy, fair St. Agnes in her bed,
But dares not look behind, or all the charm is fled.

   Soon, trembling in her soft and chilly nest,   235
   In sort of wakeful swoon, perplex'd she lay,
   Until the poppied warmth of sleep oppress'd
   Her soothed limbs, and soul fatigued away;
   Flown, like a thought, until the morrow-day;
   Blissfully haven'd both from joy and pain;   240
   Clasp'd like a missal where swart Paynims pray;
   Blinded alike from sunshine and from rain,
As though a rose should shut, and be a bud again.

   Stol'n to this paradise, and so entranced,
   Porphyro gazed upon her empty dress,   245
   And listen'd to her breathing, if it chanced
   To wake into a slumbrous tenderness;
   Which when he heard, that minute did he bless,
   And breath'd himself: then from the closet crept,
   Noiseless as fear in a wide wilderness,   250
   And over the hush'd carpet, silent, stept,
And 'tween the curtain peep'd, where, lo!—how fast she slept.

   Then by the bed-side, where the faded moon
   Made a dim, silver twilight, soft he set
   A table, and, half anguish'd, threw thereon   255
   A cloth of woven crimson, gold, and jet:—
   O for some drowsy Morphean amulet!
   The boisterous, midnight, festive clarion,
   The kettle-drum, and far-heard clarinet,
   Affray his ears, though but in dying tone:—   260
The hall door shuts again, and all the noise is gone.

   And still she slept an azure-lidded sleep,
   In blanched linen, smooth, and lavender'd,
   While he from forth the closet brought a heap
   Of candied apple, quince, and plum, and gourd;   265
   With jellies soother than the creamy curd,
   And lucent syrups, tinct with cinnamon;
   Manna and dates, in argosy transferr'd
   From Fez; and spiced dainties, every one,
From silken Samarcand to cedar'd Lebanon.   270

These delicacies he heap'd with glowing hand
On golden dishes and in baskets bright
Of wreathed silver: sumptuous they stand
In the retired quiet of the night,
Filling the chilly room with perfume light.—   275
"And now, my love, my seraph fair, awake!
Thou art my heaven, and I thine eremite:
Open thine eyes, for meek St. Agnes' sake,
Or I shall drowse beside thee, so my soul doth ache."

Thus whispering, his warm, unnerved arm   280
Sank in her pillow. Shaded was her dream
By the dusk curtains:—'twas a midnight charm
Impossible to melt as iced stream:
The lustrous salvers in the moonlight gleam;
Broad golden fringe upon the carpet lies: 285
It seem'd he never, never could redeem
From such a steadfast spell his lady's eyes;
So mus'd awhile, entoil'd in woofed phantasies.

Awakening up, he took her hollow lute,—
Tumultuous,—and, in chords that tenderest be,   290
He play'd an ancient ditty, long since mute,
In Provence call'd, "La belle dame sans mercy:" [2]
Close to her ear touching the melody;—
Wherewith disturb'd, she utter'd a soft moan:
He ceased—she panted quick—and suddenly   295
Her blue affrayed eyes wide open shone:
Upon his knees he sank, pale as smooth-sculptured stone.

Her eyes were open, but she still beheld,
Now wide awake, the vision of her sleep:
There was a painful change, that nigh expell'd   300
The blisses of her dream so pure and deep
At which fair Madeline began to weep,
And moan forth witless words with many a sigh;
While still her gaze on Porphyro would keep;
Who knelt, with joined hands and piteous eye,   305
Fearing to move or speak, she look'd so dreamingly.

"Ah, Porphyro!" said she, "but even now
Thy voice was at sweet tremble in mine ear,
Made tuneable with every sweetest vow;

[2] a poem by Alain Chartier

And those sad eyes were spiritual and clear: 310
How chang'd thou art! how pallid, chill, and drear!
Give me that voice again, my Porphyro,
Those looks immortal, those complainings dear!
Oh leave me not in this eternal woe,
For if thou diest, my love, I know not where to go." 315

Beyond a mortal man impassion'd far
At these voluptuous accents, he arose,
Ethereal, flush'd, and like a throbbing star
Seen mid the sapphire heaven's deep repose;
Into her dream he melted, as the rose 320
Blendeth its odor with the violet,—
Solution sweet: meantime the frostwind blows
Like Love's alarum pattering the sharp sleet
Against the window-panes; St. Agnes' moon hath set.

'Tis dark: quick pattereth the flaw-blown sleet: 325
"This is no dream, my bride, my Madeline!"
'Tis dark: the iced gusts still rave and beat:
"No dream, alas! alas! and woe is mine!
Porphyro will leave me here to fade and pine.—
Cruel! what traitor could thee hither bring? 330
I curse not, for my heart is lost in thine,
Though thou forsakest a deceived thing;—
A dove forlorn and lost with sick unpruned wing."

"My Madeline! sweet dreamer! lovely bride!
Say, may I be for aye thy vassal blest? 335
Thy beauty's shield, heart-shap'd and vermeil-dyed?
Ah, silver shrine, here will I take my rest
After so many hours of toil and quest,
A famish'd pilgrim,—sav'd by miracle.
Though I have found, I will not rob thy nest 340
Saving of thy sweet self; if thou think'st well
To trust, fair Madeline, to no rude infidel.

"Hark! 'tis an elfin-storm from faery land,
Of haggard seeming,[3] but a boon indeed:
Arise—arise! the morning is at hand;— 345
The bloated wassaillers will never heed:—
Let us away, my love, with happy speed;
There are no ears to hear, or eyes to see,—

[3] appearance

Drown'd all in Rhenish and the sleepy mead:
Awake! arise! my love, and fearless be,   350
For o'er the southern moors I have a home for thee."

She hurried at his words, beset with fears,
For there were sleeping dragons all around,
At glaring watch, perhaps, with ready spears—
Down the wide stairs a darkling way they found.—   355
In all the house was heard no human sound.
A chain-droop'd lamp was flickering by each door;
The arras, rich with horseman, hawk, and hound,
Flutter'd in the besieging wind's uproar;
And the long carpets rose along the gusty floor.   360

They glide, like phantoms, into the wide hall;
Like phantoms, to the iron porch, they glide;
Where lay the porter in uneasy sprawl,
With a huge empty flagon by his side:
The wakeful bloodhound rose, and shook his hide,   365
But his sagacious eye an inmate owns:
By one and one, the bolts full easy slide:—
The chains lie silent on the footworn stones;—
The key turns, and the door upon its hinges groans.

And they are gone: aye, ages long ago   370
These lovers fled away into the storm.
That night the Baron dreamt of many a woe,
And all his warrior-guests, with shade and form
Of witch, and demon, and large coffin-worm,
Were long be-nightmar'd. Angela the old   375
Died palsy-twitch'd, with meager face deform;
The beadsman after thousand aves told,
For aye unsought-for slept among his ashes cold. (1820)

RALPH WALDO EMERSON (1803–1882)

Concord Hymn

By the rude bridge that arched the flood,
    Their flag to April's breeze unfurled,
Here once the embattled farmers stood,
    And fired the shot heard round the world.

The foe long since in silence slept;   5
    Alike the conqueror silent sleeps;
And time the ruined bridge has swept
    Down the dark stream that seaward creeps.

On this green bank, by this soft stream,
    We set to-day a votive stone;   10
That memory may their deed redeem,
    When, like our sires, our sons are gone.

Spirit, that made those heroes dare
    To die, and leave their children free,
Bid time and nature gently spare   15
    The shaft we raise to them and thee.   *(1837)*

Each and All

Little thinks, in the field, yon red-cloaked clown
Of thee from the hill-top looking down;
The heifer that lows in the upland farm,
Far-heard, lows not thine ear to charm;
The sexton, tolling his bell at noon,   5
Deems not that great Napoleon
Stops his horse, and lists with delight,
Whilst his files sweep round yon Alpine height;
Nor knowest thou what argument
Thy life to thy neighbor's creed has lent.   10
All are needed by each one;
Nothing is fair or good alone.
I thought the sparrow's note from heaven,
Singing at dawn on the alder bough;

343

I brought him home, in his nest, at even;   15
He sings the song, but it pleases not now,
For I did not bring home the river and sky;—
He sang to my ear,—they sang to my eye.
The delicate shells lay on the shore;
The bubbles of the latest wave   20
Fresh pearls to their enamel gave;
And the bellowing of the savage sea
Greeted their safe escape to me.
I wiped away the weeds and foam,
I fetch my sea-born treasures home;   25
But the poor, unsightly, noisome things
Had left their beauty on the shore
With the sun and the sand and the wild uproar.
The lover watched his graceful maid,
As 'mid the virgin train she strayed,   30
Nor knew her beauty's best attire
Was woven by the snow-white choir.
At last she came to his hermitage,
Like the bird from the woodlands to the cage;—
The gay enchantment was undone,   35
A gentle wife, but fairy none.
Then I said, "I covet truth;
Beauty is unripe childhood's cheat;
I leave it behind with the games of youth:"—
As I spoke, beneath my feet   40
The ground-pine curled its pretty wreath,
Running over the club-moss burrs;
I inhaled the violet's breath;
Around me stood the oaks and firs;
Pine-cones and acorns lay on the ground;   45
Over me soared the eternal sky,
Full of light and of deity;
Again I saw, again I heard,
The rolling river, the morning bird;
Beauty through my senses stole;   50
I yielded myself to the perfect whole.   (*1839*)

The Rhodora

ON BEING ASKED, WHENCE IS THE FLOWER?

In May, when sea-winds pierced our solitudes,
I found the fresh rhodora in the woods,
Spreading its leafless blooms in a damp nook,
To please the desert and the sluggish brook.
The purple petals, fallen in the pool,   5
Made the black water with their beauty gay;
Here might the red-bird come his plumes to cool,
And court the flower that cheapens his array.
Rhodora! if the sages ask thee why
This charm is wasted on the earth and sky,   10
Tell them, dear, that if eyes were made for seeing,
Then Beauty is its own excuse for being:
Why thou wert there, O rival of the rose!
I never thought to ask, I never knew:
But, in my simple ignorance, suppose   15
The self-same power that brought me there brought you.
                                                        (1839)

Days

Daughters of Time, the hypocritic Days,
Muffled and dumb like barefoot dervishes,
And marching single in an endless file,
Bring diadems and fagots in their hands.
To each they offer gifts after his will,   5
Bread, kingdoms, stars, and sky that holds them all.
I, in my pleached garden, watched the pomp,
Forgot my morning wishes, hastily
Took a few herbs and apples, and the Day
Turned and departed silently. I, too late,   10
Under her solemn fillet saw the scorn.   (1857)

Brahma

If the red slayer think he slays,
    Or if the slain think he is slain,
They know not well the subtle ways
    I keep, and pass, and turn again.

Far or forgot to me is near;   5
    Shadow and sunlight are the same;
The vanished gods to me appear;
    And one to me are shame and fame.

They reckon ill who leave me out;
    When me they fly, I am the wings;   10
I am the doubter and the doubt,
    And I the hymn the Brahmin sings.

The strong gods pine for my abode,
    And pine in vain the sacred Seven;
But thou, meek lover of the good!   15
    Find me, and turn thy back on heaven.   (1857)

Nemesis

Already blushes in thy cheek
The bosom-thought which thou must speak;
The bird, how far it haply roam
By cloud or isle, is flying home;
The maiden fears, and fearing runs   5
Into the charmed snare she shuns;
And every man, in love or pride,
Of his fate is never wide.

Will a woman's fan the ocean smooth?
Or prayers the stony Parcae soothe,   10
Or coax the thunder from its mark?
Or tapers light the chaos dark?
In spite of Virtue and the Muse,
Nemesis will have her dues,
And all our struggles and our toils   15
Tighter wind the giant coils.   (1867)

Terminus

It is time to be old,
To take in sail:—
The god of bounds,
Who sets to seas a shore,
Came to me in his fatal rounds,   5
And said: 'No more!
No farther shoot
Thy broad ambitious branches, and thy root,
Fancy departs: no more invent,
Contract thy firmament   10
To compass of a tent.
There's not enough for this and that,
Make thy option which of two;
Economize the failing river,
Nor the less revere the Giver,   15

Leave the many and hold the few.
Timely wise accept the terms,
Soften the fall with wary foot;
A little while
Still plan and smile,   20
And, fault of novel germs,
Mature the unfallen fruit.
Curse, if thou wilt, thy sires,
Bad husbands of their fires,
Who, when they gave thee breath,   25
Failed to bequeath
The needful sinew stark as once,
The Baresark marrow to thy bones,
But left a legacy of ebbing veins,
Inconstant heat and nerveless reins,—   30
Amid the Muses, left thee deaf and dumb,
Amid the gladiators, halt and numb.'

As the bird trims her to the gale,
I trim myself to the storm of time,
I man the rudder, reef the sail,   35
Obey the voice at eve obeyed at prime:
'Lowly faithful, banish fear,
Right onward drive unharmed;
The port well worth the cruise, is near,
And every wave is charmed.'   (*1867*)

JOHN GREENLEAF WHITTIER
(1807–1892)

Ichabod [1]

So fallen! so lost! the light withdrawn
    Which once he wore!
The glory from his gray hairs done
    Forevermore!

Revile him not, the Tempter hath   5
    A snare for all;
And pitying tears, not scorn and wrath,
    Befit his fall!

Oh, dumb be passion's stormy rage,
    When he who might   10
Have lighted up and led his age,
    Falls back in night.

Scorn! would the angels laugh, to mark
    A bright soul driven,
Fiend-goaded, down the endless dark,   15
    From hope and heaven!

Let not the land once proud of him
    Insult him now,
Nor brand with deeper shame his dim,
    Dishonored brow.   20

But let its humbled sons, instead
    From sea to lake,
A long lament, as for the dead,
    In sadness make.

Of all we loved and honored, naught   25
    Save power remains;
A fallen angel's pride of thought,
    Still strong in chains.

---

[1] Refers to Daniel Webster, whose support of the Compromise of 1850 and the Fugitive Slave Law Whittier here protests. Ichabod means "no glory."

All else is gone; from those great eyes
    The soul has fled:
When faith is lost, when honor dies,
    The man is dead!

Then pay the reverence of old days
    To his dead fame;
Walk backward, with averted gaze,   35
    And hide the shame!   (1850)

Telling the Bees [1]

Here is the place; right over the hill
    Runs the path I took;
You can see the gap in the old wall still,
    And the stepping-stones in the shallow brook.

There is the house, with the gate red-barred,   5
    And the poplars tall;
And the barn's brown length, and the cattle-yard,
    And the white horns tossing above the wall.

There are the beehives ranged in the sun;
    And down by the brink   10
Of the brook are her poor flowers, weed-o'errun,
    Pansy and daffodil, rose and pink.

A year has gone, as the tortoise goes,
    Heavy and slow;
And the same rose blows, and the same sun glows,   15
    And the same brook sings of a year ago.

There's the same sweet clover-smell in the breeze;
    And the June sun warm
Tangles his wings of fire in the trees,
    Setting, as then, over Fernside farm.   20

[1] "A remarkable custom, brought from the Old Country, formerly prevailed in the rural districts of New England. On the death of a member of the family, the bees were at once informed of the event, and their hives dressed in mourning. This ceremonial was supposed to be necessary to prevent the swarms from leaving their hives and seeking a new home." [WHITTIER]

I mind me how with a lover's care
    From my Sunday coat
I brushed off the burrs, and smoothed my hair,
    And cooled at the brookside my brow and throat.

Since we parted, a month had passed,—   25
    To love, a year;
Down through the beeches I looked at last
    On the little red gate and the well-sweep near.

I can see it all now,—the slantwise rain
    Of light through the leaves,   30
The sundown's blaze on her window-pane,
    The bloom of her roses under the eaves.

Just the same as a month before,—
    The house and the trees,
The barn's brown gable, the vine by the door,—   35
    Nothing changed but the hives of bees.

Before them, under the garden wall,
    Forward and back,
Went drearily singing the chore-girl small,
    Draping each hive with a shred of black.   40

Trembling, I listened: the summer sun
    Had the chill of snow;
For I knew she was telling the bees of one
    Gone on the journey we all must go!

Then I said to myself, "My Mary weeps   45
    For the dead to-day:
Haply her blind old grandsire sleeps
    The fret and the pain of his age away."

But her dog whined low; on the doorway sill,
    With his cane to his chin,   50
The old man sat; and the chore-girl still
    Sung to the bees stealing out and in.

And the song she was singing ever since
    In my ear sounds on:—
"Stay at home, pretty bees, fly not hence!   55
    Mistress Mary is dead and gone!"   (1858)

HENRY WADSWORTH LONGFELLOW
(1807–1882)

The Jewish Cemetery at Newport

How strange it seems! These Hebrews in their graves,
    Close by the street of this fair seaport town,
Silent beside the never-silent waves,
    At rest in all this moving up and down!

The trees are white with dust, that o'er their sleep   5
    Wave their broad curtains in the southwind's breath,
While underneath these leafy tents they keep
    The long, mysterious Exodus of Death.

And these sepulchral stones, so old and brown,
    That pave with level flags their burial-place,   10
Seem like the tablets of the Law, thrown down
    And broken by Moses at the mountain's base.[1]

The very names recorded here are strange,
    Of foreign accent, and of different climes;
Alvares and Rivera interchange   15
    With Abraham and Jacob of old times.

"Blessed be God! for he created Death!"
    The mourners said, "and Death is rest and peace";
Then added, in the certainty of faith,
    "And giveth Life that nevermore shall cease."   20

Closed are the portals of their Synagogue,
    No Psalms of David now the silence break,
No Rabbi reads the ancient Decalogue
    In the grand dialect the Prophets spake.

Gone are the living, but the dead remain,   25
    And not neglected; for a hand unseen,
Scattering its bounty, like a summer rain,
    Still keeps their graves and their remembrance green.

[1] Exodus 32:19.

How came they here? What burst of Christian hate,
    What persecution, merciless and blind,   30
Drove o'er the sea—that desert desolate—
    These Ishmaels and Hagars of mankind?[2]

They lived in narrow streets and lanes obscure,
    Ghetto and Judenstrass, in mirk and mire;
Taught in the school of patience to endure   35
    The life of anguish and the death of fire.

All their lives long, with the unleavened bread
    And bitter herbs of exile and its fears,
The wasting famine of the heart they fed,
    And slaked its thirst with marah [3] of their tears.   40

Anathema maranatha![4] was the cry
    That rang from town to town, from street to street;
At every gate the accursed Mordecai [5]
    Was mocked and jeered, and spurned by Christian feet.

Pride and humiliation hand in hand   45
    Walked with them through the world wher'er they went;
Trampled and beaten were they as the sand,
    And yet unshaken as the continent.

For in the background figures vague and vast
    Of patriarchs and of prophets rose sublime,   50
And all the great traditions of the Past
    They saw reflected in the coming time.

And thus forever with reverted look
    The mystic volume of the world they read,
Spelling it backward, like a Hebrew book,   55
    Till life became a Legend of the Dead.

But ah! what once has been shall be no more!
    The growing earth in travail and in pain
Brings forth its races, but does not restore,
    And the dead nations never rise again.   (1854)   60

[2] Genesis 16 and 21. [3] bitterness; Exodus 15:23–26. [4] *maran 'atha,* at the coming of the Lord; an anti-Semitic "burst of Christian hate." I Corinthians 16:22. [5] Esther 3.

Chaucer

An old man in a lodge within a park;
The chamber walls depicted all around
With portraitures of huntsman, hawk, and hound,
And the hurt deer. He listeneth to the lark,
Whose song comes with the sunshine through the dark   5
Of painted glass in leaden lattice bound;
He listeneth and he laugheth at the sound,
Then writeth in a book like any clerk.
He is the poet of the dawn, who wrote
The Canterbury Tales, and his old age   10
Made beautiful with song; and as I read
I hear the crowing cock, I hear the note
Of lark and linnet, and from every page
Rise odors of ploughed field or flowery mead.   (1873)

A Nameless Grave

"A soldier of the Union mustered out,"
Is the inscription on an unknown grave
At Newport News, beside the salt-sea wave,
Nameless and dateless; sentinel or scout
Shot down in skirmish, or disastrous rout   5
Of battle, when the loud artillery drave
Its iron wedges through the ranks of brave
And doomed battalions, storming the redoubt.
Thou unknown here sleeping by the sea
In thy forgotten grave! with secret shame   10
I feel my pulses beat, my forehead burn,
When I remember thou hast given for me
All that thou hadst, thy life, thy very name,
And I can give thee nothing in return.   (1874)

ᛰᣠ EDGAR ALLAN POE (1809–1849)

To Helen

Helen, thy beauty is to me
    Like those Nicean [1] barks of yore,
That gently, o'er a perfumed sea,
    The weary, way-worn wanderer bore
    To his own native shore.   5

On desperate seas long wont to roam,
    Thy hyacinth [2] hair, thy classic face,
Thy Naiad airs have brought me home
    To the glory that was Greece
And the grandeur that was Rome.   10

Lo! in yon brilliant window-niche
    How statue-like I see thee stand!
    The agate lamp within thy hand,
Ah! Psyche, from the regions which
    Are Holy Land!   (1831)   15

To One in Paradise

Thou wast that all to me, love,
    For which my soul did pine—
A green isle in the sea, love,
    A fountain and a shrine,
All wreathed with fairy fruits and flowers,   5
    And all the flowers were mine.

Ah, dream too bright to last!
    Ah, starry Hope! that didst arise
But to be overcast!
    A voice from out the Future cries,   10
"On! on!"—but o'er the Past
    (Dim gulf!) my spirit hovering lies
Mute, motionless, aghast!

[1] identity unknown, but suggestive of the Mediterranean, perhaps the journey of Catullus to Nicaea   [2] custers of curls, like young hyacinths

For, alas! alas! with me
    The light of Life is o'er!   15
No more—no more—no more—
    (Such language holds the solemn sea
To the sands upon the shore)
    Shall bloom the thunder-blasted tree,
Or the stricken eagle soar!   20

And all my days are trances,
    And all my nightly dreams
Are where thy grey eye glances,
    And where thy footstep gleams—
In what ethereal dances,   25
    By what eternal streams.   (1834)

The City in the Sea

Lo! Death has reared himself a throne
In a strange city lying alone
Far down within the dim West,
Where the good and the bad and the worst and the best
Have gone to their eternal rest.   5
There shrines and palaces and towers
(Time-eaten towers that tremble not!)
Resemble nothing that is ours.
Around, by lifting winds forgot,
Resignedly beneath the sky   10
The melancholy waters lie.

No rays from the holy heaven come down
On the long night-time of that town;
But light from out the lurid sea
Streams up the turrets silently—   15
Gleams up the pinnacles far and free—
Up domes—up spires—up kingly halls—
Up fanes—up Babylon-like walls—
Up shadowy long-forgotten bowers
Of sculptured ivy and stone flowers—   20
Up many and many a marvellous shrine
Whose wreathéd friezes intertwine
The viol, the violet, and the vine.

Resignedly beneath the sky
The melancholy waters lie.   25
So blend the turrets and shadows there
That all seem pendulous in air,
While from a proud tower in the town
Death looks gigantically down.

There open fanes and gaping graves   30
Yawn level with the luminous waves;
But not the riches there that lie
In each idol's diamond eye—
Not the gaily-jewelled dead
Tempt the waters from their bed;   35
For no ripples curl, alas!
Along that wilderness of glass—
No swellings tell that winds may be
Upon some far-off happier sea—
No heavings hint that winds have been   40
On seas less hideously serene.

But lo, a stir is in the air!
The wave—there is a movement there!
As if the towers had thrust aside,
In slightly sinking, the dull tide—   45
As if their tops had feebly given
A void within the filmy Heaven.
The waves have now a redder glow—
The hours are breathing faint and low—
And when, amid no earthly moans,   50
Down, down that town shall settle hence,
Hell, rising from a thousand thrones,
Shall do it reverence.   *(1845)*

Ulalume—A Ballad

The skies they were ashen and sober;
  The leaves they were crispéd and sere—
  The leaves they were withering and sere;
It was night, in the lonesome October
  Of my most immemorial year: 5

It was hard by the dim lake of Auber,
    In the misty mid region of Weir—
It was down by the dank tarn of Auber,
    In the ghoul-haunted woodland of Weir.

Here once, through an alley Titanic,   10
    Of cypress, I roamed with my Soul—
    Of cypress, with Psyche, my Soul.
These were days when my heart was volcanic
    As the scoriac rivers that roll—
    As the lavas that restlessly roll   15
Their sulphurous currents down Yaanek
    In the ultimate climes of the Pole—
That groan as they roll down Mount Yaanek
    In the realms of the Boreal Pole.

Our talk had been serious and sober,   20
    But our thoughts they were palsied and sere—
    Our memories were treacherous and sere;
For we knew not the month was October,
    And we marked not the night of the year
    (Ah, night of all nights in the year!)—   25
We noted not the dim lake of Auber
    (Though once we had journeyed down here)—
Remembered not the dank tarn of Auber,
    Nor the ghoul-haunted woodland of Weir.

And now, as the night was senescent   30
    And star-dials pointed to morn—
    As the star-dials hinted of morn—
At the end of our path a liquescent
    And nebulous lustre was born,
Out of which a miraculous crescent   35
    Arose with a duplicate horn—
Astarte's bediamonded crescent
    Distinct with its duplicate horn.

And I said: "She is warmer than Dian;
    She rolls through an ether of sighs—   40
    She revels in a region of sighs.
She has seen that the tears are not dry on
    These cheeks, where the worm never dies,
And has come past the stars of the Lion,
    To point us the path to the skies—   45
    To the Lethean peace of the skies—

Come up, in despite of the Lion,
    To shine on us with her bright eyes—
Come up through the lair of the Lion,
    With love in her luminous eyes."   50

But Psyche, uplifting her finger
    Said: "Sadly this star I mistrust—
    Her pallor I strangely mistrust:
Ah, hasten!—ah, let us not linger!
    Ah, fly!—let us fly!—for we must."   55
In terror she spoke, letting sink her
    Wings till they trailed in the dust—
In agony sobbed, letting sink her
    Plumes till they trailed in the dust—
    Till they sorrowfully trailed in the dust.   60

I replied: "This is nothing but dreaming:
    Let us on by this tremulous light!
    Let us bathe in this crystalline light!
Its Sibyllic splendor is beaming
    With Hope and in Beauty to-night!   65
    See!—it flickers up the sky through the night!
Ah, we safely may trust to its gleaming,
    And be sure it will lead us aright—
We safely may trust to a gleaming,
    That cannot but guide us aright,   70
    Since it flickers up to Heaven through the night."

Thus I pacified Psyche and kissed her,
    And tempted her out of her gloom—
    And conquered her scruples and gloom;
And we passed to the end of the vista,   75
    But were stopped by the door of a tomb—
    By the door of a legended tomb;
And I said: "What is written, sweet sister,
    On the door of this legended tomb?"
    She replied: "Ulalume—Ulalume!—   80
    'Tis the vault of thy lost Ulalume!"

Then my heart it grew ashen and sober
    As the leaves that were crispéd and sere—
    As the leaves that were withering and sere;
And I cried: "It was surely October   85
    On *this* very night of last year
    That I journeyed—I journeyed down here!—

That I brought a dread burden down here—
   On this night of all nights in the year,
   Ah, what demon has tempted me here?   90
Well I know, now, this dim lake of Auber—
   This misty mid region of Weir—
Well I know, now, this dank tarn of Auber,
   This ghoul-haunted woodland of Weir."

Said we, then—the two, then: "Ah can it   95
   Have been that woodlandish ghouls—
   The pitiful, the merciful ghouls—
To bar up our way and to ban it
   From the secret that lies in these wolds—
   From the thing that lies hidden in these wolds—   100
Have drawn up the spectre of a planet
   From the limbo of lunary souls—
This sinfully scintillant planet
   From the Hell of the planetary souls?   (1847)

EDWARD FITZGERALD (1809–1883)

From *The Rubáiyát of Omar Khayyám* [1]

1

Wake! for the Sun, who scattered into flight
The Stars before him from the Field of Night,
    Drives Night along with them from Heav'n, and strikes
The Sultán's Turret with a Shaft of Light.

2

Before the phantom of False morning died,   5
Methought a Voice within the Tavern cried,
    "When all the Temple is prepared within,
Why nods the drowsy Worshipper outside?"

3

And, as the cock crew, those who stood before
The Tavern shouted—"Open then the Door!   10
    You know how little while we have to stay,
And, once departed, may return no more."

4

Now the New Year reviving old Desires,
The thoughtful Soul to Solitude retires,
    Where the White Hand of Moses on the Bough [2]   15
Puts out, and Jesus from the Ground suspires.

5

Iram [3] indeed is gone with all his Rose,
And Jamshyd's [4] Sev'n-ring'd Cup where no one knows;
    But still a Ruby kindles in the Vine,
And many a Garden by the Water blows.   20

6

And David's lips are lockt; but in divine
High-piping Pehleví, with "Wine! Wine! Wine!
    Red Wine!"—the Nightingale cries to the Rose
That sallow cheek of hers to incarnadine.

[1] quatrians of Omar the Tentmaker, Persian poet of the eleventh century
[2] Exodus, 4:6   [3] ancient Persian garden, now lost   [4] legendary and ancient kings

7

Come, fill the Cup, and in the fire of Spring   25
Your Winter-garment of Repentance fling:
    The Bird of Time has but a little way
To flutter—and the Bird is on the Wing.

8

Whether at Naishápúr or Babylon,
Whether the Cup with sweet or bitter run,   30
    The Wine of Life keeps oozing drop by drop,
The Leaves of Life keep falling one by one.

9

Each morn a thousand Roses brings, you say;
Yes, but where leaves the Rose of Yesterday?
    And this first Summer month that brings the Rose   35
Shall take Jamshyd and Kaikobád [4] away.

10

Well, let it take them! What have we to do
With Kaikobád the Great, or Kaikhosrú? [4]
    Let Zál and Rustum [5] bluster as they will,
Or Hátim [6] call to Supper—heed not you.   40

11

With me along the strip of Herbage strown
That just divides the desert from the sown,
    Where name of Slave and Sultán is forgot—
And Peace to Mahmúd on his golden Throne!

12

A Book of Verses underneath the Bough,   45
A Jug of Wine, a Loaf of Bread—and Thou
    Beside me singing in the Wilderness—
Oh, Wilderness were Paradise enow!

13

Some for the Glories of This World; and some
Sigh for the Prophet's Paradise to come;   50
    Ah, take the Cash, and let the Credit go,
Nor heed the rumble of a distant Drum!

[5] Persian heroes   [6] generosity

14

Look to the blowing Rose about us—"Lo,
Laughing," she says, "into the world I blow,
    At once the silken tassel of my Purse   55
Tear, and its Treasure on the Garden throw."

15

And those who husbanded the Golden grain,[7]
And those who flung it to the winds like Rain,
    Alike to no such aureate Earth are turned
As, buried once, Men want dug up again.   60

16

The Worldly Hope men set their Hearts upon
Turns Ashes—or it prospers; and anon,
    Like Snow upon the Desert's dusty Face,
Lighting a little hour or two—is gone.

17

Think, in this battered Caravanserai [8]   65
Whose Portals are alternate Night and Day,
    How Sultán after Sultán with his Pomp
Abode his destined Hour, and went his way.

⋅　⋅　⋅　⋅　⋅

26

Why, all the Saints and Sages who discussed
Of the Two Worlds so wisely—they are thrust
    Like foolish Prophets forth; their Words to Scorn
Are scattered, and their Mouths are stopt with Dust.

27

Myself when young did eagerly frequent   105
Doctor and Saint, and heard great argument
    About it and about: but evermore
Came out by the same Door where in I went.

28

With them the seed of Wisdom did I sow,
And with mine own hand wrought to make it grow;   110
    And this was all the Harvest that I reaped—
"I came like Water, and like Wind I go."

[7] wealth   [8] inn

29

Into this Universe, and *Why* not knowing
Nor *Whence,* like Water willy-nilly flowing;
    And out of it, as Wind along the Waste,   115
I know not *Whither,* willy-nilly blowing.

30

What, without asking, hither hurried *Whence?*
And, without asking, *Whither* hurried hence!
    Oh, many a Cup of this forbidden Wine [9]
Must drown the memory of that insolence!   120

· · · · ·

63

O threats of Hell and Hopes of Paradise!
One thing at least is certain—*This* Life flies;   250
    One thing is certain and the rest is Lies;
The Flower that once has blown [10] for ever dies.

64

Strange, is it not? that of the myriads who
Before us passed the door of Darkness through,
    Not one returns to tell us of the Road,   255
Which to discover we must travel too.

65

The Revelations of Devout and Learned
Who rose before us, and as Prophets burned,
    Are all but Stories, which, awoke from Sleep
They told their comrades, and to Sleep returned.   260

66

I sent my soul through the Invisible,
Some letter of that After-life to spell:
    And by and by my Soul returned to me,
And answered "I Myself am Heav'n and Hell:"

67

Heav'n but the Vision of fulfilled Desire,   265
And Hell the Shadow from a Soul on fire

[9] Moslems were forbidden the use of
wine. [10] bloomed

Cast on the Darkness into which Ourselves,
So late emerged from, shall so soon expire.

68

We are no other than a moving row
Of Magic Shadow-shapes that come and go   270
   Round with the Sun-illumined Lantern held
In Midnight by the Master of the Show;

69

But helpless Pieces of the Game He plays
Upon this Chequer-board of Nights and Days;
   Hither and thither moves, and checks, and slays,   275
And one by one back in the Closet lays.

70

The Ball [11] no question makes of Ayes and Noes,
But Here or There as strikes the Player goes;
   And He that tossed you down into the Field,
He knows about it all—HE knows—HE knows!   280

71

The Moving Finger writes; and, having writ,
Moves on: nor all your Piety nor Wit
   Shall lure it back to cancel half a Line,
Nor all your Tears wash out a Word of it.

72

And that inverted Bowl they call the Sky,   285
Whereunder crawling cooped we live and die,
   Lift not your hands to *It* for help—for It
As impotently moves as you or I.

73

With Earth's first Clay They did the Last Man knead,
And there of the Last Harvest sowed the Seed: 290
   And the first Morning of Creation wrote
What the Last Dawn of Reckoning shall read.

74

Yesterday *This* Day's Madness did prepare;
To-morrow's Silence, Triumph, or Despair:

[11] in polo, of Persian origin

Drink for you know not whence you came nor why: 295
Drink! for you know not why you go, nor where.

．　．　．　．　．

96

Yet Ah, that Spring should vanish with the Rose!
That Youth's sweet-scented manuscript should close!
　　The Nightingale that in the branches sang,
Ah whence, and whither flown again, who knows!

97

Would but the desert of the Fountain yield   385
One glimpse—if dimly, yet indeed, revealed,
　　To which the fainting Traveller might spring,
As springs the trampled herbage of the field!

98

Would but some wingéd Angel ere too late
Arrest the yet unfolded Roll of Fate,   390
　　And make the stern Recorder otherwise
Enregister, or quite obliterate!

99

Ah Love! could you and I with Him conspire
To grasp this sorry Scheme of Things entire,
　　Would not we shatter it to bits—and then   395
Remould it nearer to the Heart's Desire!

100

Yon rising Moon that looks for us again—
How oft hereafter will she wax and wane;
　　How oft hereafter rising look for us
Through this same Garden—and for *one* in vain!   400

101

And when like her, O [12] Sákí, you shall pass
Among the Guests Star-scattered on the Grass,
　　And in your joyous errand reach the spot
Where I made One—turn down an empty Glass!   *(1879)*

[12] wine-bearer

✒️ ALFRED, LORD TENNYSON (1809–1892)

The Lotos-Eaters [1]

"Courage!" he said, and pointed toward the land,
"This mounting wave will roll us shoreward soon."
In the afternoon they came unto a land
In which it seeméd always afternoon.
All round the coast the languid air did swoon,   5
Breathing like one that hath a weary dream.
Full-faced above the valley stood the moon;
And, like a downward smoke, the slender stream
    Along the cliff to fall and pause and fall did seem.

A land of streams! some, like a downward smoke,   10
Slow-dropping veils of thinnest lawn, did go;
And some through wavering lights and shadows broke,
Rolling a slumbrous sheet of foam below.
They saw the gleaming river seaward flow
From the inner land; far off, three mountain-tops,   15
Three silent pinnacles of aged snow,
Stood sunset-flushed; and, dewed with showery drops,
    Up-clomb the shadowy pine above the woven copse.

The charméd sunset lingered low adown
In the red West; through mountain clefts the dale   20
Was seen far inland, and the yellow down
Bordered with palm, and many a winding vale
And meadow, set with slender galingale;
A land where all things always seemed the same!
And round about the keel with faces pale,   25
Dark faces pale against that rosy flame,
    The mild-eyed, melancholy Lotus-eaters came.

Branches they bore of that enchanted stem,
Laden with flower and fruit, whereof they gave
To each, but whoso did receive of them   30
And taste, to him the gushing of the wave
Far, far away did seem to mourn and rave
On alien shores; and if his fellow spake,
His voice was thin, as voices from the grave;

[1] Homer, *Odyssey,* Book IX

And deep-asleep he seemed, yet all awake,   35
    And music in his ears his beating heart did make.

They sat them down upon the yellow sand,
Between the sun and moon upon the shore;
And sweet it was to dream of Fatherland,
Of child, and wife, and slave; but evermore   40
Most weary seemed the sea, weary the oar,
Weary the wandering fields of barren foam.
Then some one said, "We will return no more";
And all at once they sang, "Our island home [2]
    Is far beyond the wave; we will no longer roam."   45

CHORIC SONG

   1

There is sweet music here that softer falls
Than petals from blown roses on the grass,
Or night-dews on still water between walls
Of shadowy granite, in a gleaming pass;
Music that gentlier on the spirit lies,   50
Than tired eyelids upon tired eyes;
Music that brings sleep down from the blissful skies
Here are cool mosses deep,
And through the moss the ivies creep,
And in the stream the long-leaved flowers weep,   55
And from the craggy ledge the poppy hangs in sleep.

   2

Why are we weighed upon with heaviness,
And utterly consumed with sharp distress,
While all things else have rest from weariness?
All things have rest; why should we toil alone,   60
We only toil, who are the first of things,
And make perpetual moan,
Still from one sorrow to another thrown;
Nor ever fold our wings,
And cease from wanderings,   65
Nor steep our brows in slumber's holy balm;
Nor harken what the inner spirit sings,
"There is no joy but calm!"—
Why should we only toil, the roof and crown of things?

[2] Ithaca

3

Lo! in the middle of the wood,   70
The folded leaf is wooed from out the bud
With winds upon the branch, and there
Grows green and broad, and takes no care,
Sun-steeped at noon, and in the moon
Nightly dew-fed; and turning yellow   75
Falls, and floats adown the air.
Lo! sweetened with the summer light,
The full-juiced apple, waxing over-mellow,
Drops in a silent autumn night.
All its allotted length of days   80
The flower ripens in its place,
Ripens and fades, and falls, and hath no toil,
Fast-rooted in the fruitful soil.

4

Hateful is the dark-blue sky,
Vaulted o'er the dark-blue sea.   85
Death is the end of life; ah, why
Should life all labour be?
Let us alone. Time driveth onward fast,
And in a little while our lips are dumb.
Let us alone. What is it that will last?   90
All things are taken from us, and become
Portions and parcels of the dreadful past.
Let us alone. What pleasure can we have
To war with evil? Is there any peace
In ever climbing up the climbing wave?   95
All things have rest, and ripen toward the grave
In silence—ripe, fall, and cease;
Give us long rest or death, dark death, or dreamful ease.

5

How sweet it were, hearing the downward stream
With half-shut eyes ever to seem   100
Falling asleep in a half-dream!
To dream and dream, like yonder amber light,
Which will not leave the myrrh-bush on the height;
To hear each other's whispered speech;
Eating the Lotos day by day,   105
To watch the crisping ripples on the beach,

And tender curving lines of creamy spray;
To lend our hearts and spirits wholly
To the influence of mild-minded melancholy;
To muse and brood and live again in memory,   110
With those old faces of our infancy
Heaped over with a mound of grass,
Two handfuls of white dust, shut in an urn of brass!

6

Dear is the memory of our wedded lives,
And dear the last embraces of our wives   115
And their warm tears; but all hath suffered change;
For surely now our household hearths are cold,
Our sons inherit us, our looks are strange,
And we should come like ghosts to trouble joy.
Or else the island princes over-bold   120
Have eat our substance, and the minstrel sings
Before them of the ten years' war in Troy,
And our great deeds, as half-forgotten things.
Is there confusion in the little isle?
Let what is broken so remain.   125
The gods are hard to reconcile;
'Tis hard to settle order once again.
There *is* confusion worse than death.
Trouble on trouble, pain on pain,
Long labour unto aged breath,   130
Sore task to hearts worn out by many wars
And eyes grown dim with gazing on the pilot-stars.

7

But, propped on beds of amaranth and moly,
How sweet—while warm airs lull us, blowing lowly—
With half-dropped eyelid still,   135
Beneath a heaven dark and holy,
To watch the long bright river drawing slowly
His waters from the purple hill—
To hear the dewy echoes calling
From cave to cave through the thick-twined vine—   140
To watch the emerald-coloured water falling
Through many a woven acanthus-wreath divine!
Only to hear and see the far-off sparkling brine,
Only to hear were sweet, stretched out beneath the pine.

8

The Lotos blooms below the barren peak,   145
The Lotos blows by every winding creek;
All day the wind breathes low with mellower tone;
Through every hollow cave and alley lone
Round and round the spicy downs the yellow Lotos-dust is blown.
We have had enough of action, and of motion we,   150
Rolled to starboard, rolled to larboard, when the surge was seething
      free,
Where the wallowing monster spouted his foam-fountains in the sea.
Let us swear an oath, and keep it with an equal mind,
In the hollow Lotos-land to live and lie reclined
On the hills like gods together, careless of mankind.   155
For they lie beside their nectar, and the bolts are hurled
Far below them in the valleys, and the clouds are lightly curled
Round their golden houses, girdled with the gleaming world;
Where they smile in secret, looking over wasted lands,
Blight and famine, plague and earthquake, roaring deeps and fiery
      sands,   160
Clanging fights, and flaming towns, and sinking ships, and praying
      hands.
But they smile, they find a music centered in a doleful song
Steaming up, a lamentation and an ancient tale of wrong,
Like a tale of little meaning though the words are strong;
Chanted from an ill-used race of men that cleave the soil,   165
Sow the seed, and reap the harvest with enduring toil,
Storing yearly little dues of wheat, and wine and oil;
Till they perish and they suffer—some, 'tis whispered—down in hell
Suffer endless anguish, others in Elysian valleys dwell,
Resting weary limbs at last on beds of asphodel,   170
Surely, surely, slumber is more sweet than toil, the shore
Than labour in the deep mid-ocean, wind and wave and oar;
O rest ye, brother mariners, we will not wander more.   (*1832*)

Ulysses [1]

It little profits that an idle king,
By this still hearth, among these barren crags,
Matched with an aged wife, I mete and dole

[1] Homer's Odysseus, but see Dante's
Inferno, canto 26

Unequal laws unto a savage race,
That hoard, and sleep, and feed, and know not me.   5
I cannot rest from travel: I will drink
Life to the lees: all times I have enjoyed
Greatly, have suffered greatly, both with those
That loved me, and alone; on shore, and when
Through scudding drifts the rainy Hyades   10
Vext the dim sea. I am become a name;
For always roaming with a hungry heart
Much have I seen and known: cities of men
And manners, climates, councils, governments,
Myself not least, but honored of them all,—   15
And drunk delight of battle with my peers,
Far on the ringing plains of windy Troy.
I am a part of all that I have met;
Yet all experience is an arch wherethrough
Gleams that untraveled world, whose margin fades   20
For ever and for ever when I move.
How dull it is to pause, to make an end,
To rust unburnished, not to shine in use!
As though to breathe were life. Life piled on life
Were all too little, and of one to me   25
Little remains: but every hour is saved
From that eternal silence, something more,
A bringer of new things; and vile it were
For some three suns to store and hoard myself,
And this gray spirit yearning in desire   30
To follow knowledge, like a sinking star,
Beyond the utmost bound of human thought.
    This is my son, mine own Telemachus,
To whom I leave the scepter and the isle—
Well-loved of me, discerning to fulfill   35
This labor, by slow prudence to make mild
A rugged people, and through soft degrees
Subdue them to the useful and the good.
Most blameless is he, centered in the sphere
Of common duties, decent not to fail   40
In offices of tenderness, and pay
Meet adoration to my household gods,
When I am gone. He works his work, I mine.
    There lies the port: the vessel puffs her sail:
There gloom the dark broad seas. My mariners,   45
Souls that have toiled, and wrought, and thought with me—

That ever with a frolic welcome took
The thunder and the sunshine, and opposed
Free hearts, free foreheads—you and I are old;
Old age hath yet his honor and his toil;   50
Death closes all: but something ere the end,
Some work of noble note, may yet be done,
Not unbecoming men that strove with Gods.
The lights begin to twinkle from the rocks:
The long day wanes: the slow moon climbs: the deep 55
Moans round with many voices. Come, my friends,
'Tis not too late to seek a newer world.
Push off, and sitting well in order smite
The sounding furrows; for my purpose holds
To sail beyond the sunset, and the baths   60
Of all the western stars, until I die.
It may be that the gulfs will wash us down:
It may be we shall touch the Happy Isles,
And see the great Achilles, whom we knew.
Though much is taken, much abides; and though   65
We are not now that strength which in old days
Moved earth and heaven, that which we are, we are,—
One equal temper of heroic hearts,
Made weak by time and fate, but strong in will
To strive, to seek, to find, and not to yield. (1842) 70

From *The Princess*

The Splendor Falls

The splendor falls on castle walls
  And snowy summits old in story:
The long light shakes across the lakes,
  And the wild cataract leaps in glory.
Blow, bugle, blow, set the wild echoes flying,   5
Blow, bugle; answer, echoes, dying, dying, dying.

  O hark, O hear! how thin and clear,
    And thinner, clearer, farther going!
  O sweet and far from cliff and scar
    The horns of Elfland faintly blowing!   10
Blow, let us hear the purple glens replying:
Blow, bugle; answer, echoes, dying, dying, dying.

O love, they die in yon rich sky,
    They faint on hill or field or river:
Our echoes roll from soul to soul,   15
    And grow for ever and for ever.
Blown, bugle, blow, set the wild echoes flying,
And answer, echoes, answer, dying, dying, dying.
                                        (*added in 1850*)

Tears, Idle Tears

Tears, idle tears, I know not what they mean,
Tears from the depth of some divine despair
Rise in the heart, and gather to the eyes,
In looking on the happy autumn-fields,
And thinking of the days that are no more.   5

Fresh as the first beam glittering on a sail,
That brings our friends up from the underworld,
Sad as the last which reddens over one
That sinks with all we love below the verge;
So sad, so fresh, the days that are no more.   10

Ah, sad and strange as in dark summer dawns
The earliest pipe of half-awakened birds
To dying ears, when unto dying eyes
The casement slowly grows a glimmering square;
So sad, so strange, the days that are no more.   15

Dear as remembered kisses after death,
And sweet as those by hopeless fancy feigned
On lips that are for others; deep as love,
Deep as first love, and wild with all regret;
O Death in Life, the days that are no more!   (1847)

Now Sleeps the Crimson Petal

Now sleeps the crimson petal, now the white;
Now waves the cypress in the palace walk;
Now winks the gold fin in the porphyry font.
The firefly wakens. Waken thou with me.

Now droops the milk-white peacock like a ghost,   5
And like a ghost she glimmers on to me.

Now lies the Earth all Danaë to the stars,
And all thy heart lies open unto me.

Now slides the silent meteor on, and leaves
A shining furrow, as thy thoughts in me.   10

Now folds the lily all her sweetness up,
And slips into the bosom of the lake;
So fold thyself, my dearest, thou, and slip
Into my bosom and be lost in me.   (1847)

From *In Memoriam A. H. H.* [1]

Obiit 1833

PROLOGUE

Strong Son of God, immortal Love,
     Whom we, that have not seen thy face,
     By faith, and faith alone, embrace,
Believing where we cannot prove;

Thine are these orbs of light and shade;   5
     Thou madest Life in man and brute;
     Thou madest Death; and lo, thy foot
Is on the skull which thou hast made.

Thou wilt not leave us in the dust;
     Thou madest man, he knows not why,   10
     He thinks he was not made to die;
And thou hast made him: thou art just.

Thou seemest human and divine,
     The highest, holiest manhood, thou.
     Our wills are ours, we know not how;   15
Our wills are ours, to make them thine.

Our little systems have their day;
     They have their day and cease to be;
     They are but broken lights of thee,
And thou, O Lord, art more than they.   20

We have but faith: we cannot know,
     For knowledge is of things we see;

[1] Arthur Henry Hallam, who died in
Vienna, in 1833

And yet we trust it comes from thee,
A beam in darkness: let it grow.

Let knowledge grow from more to more,   25
    But more of reverence in us dwell;
    That mind and soul, according well,
May make one music as before,

But vaster. We are fools and slight;
    We mock thee when we do not fear: 30
    But help thy foolish ones to bear;
Help thy vain worlds to bear thy light.

Forgive what seemed my sin in me;
    What seemed my worth since I began;
    For merit lives from man to man,   35
And not from man, O Lord, to thee.

Forgive my grief for one removed,
    Thy creature, whom I found so fair.
    I trust he lives in thee, and there
I find him worthier to be loved.   40

Forgive these wild and wandering cries,
    Confusions of a wasted youth;
    Forgive them where they fail in truth,
And in thy wisdom make me wise.

. . . . .

7

Dark house, by which once more I stand
    Here in the long unlovely street,
    Doors, where my heart was used to beat
So quickly, waiting for a hand,

A hand that can be clasped no more—   5
    Behold me, for I cannot sleep,
    And like a guilty thing I creep
At earliest morning to the door.

He is not here; but far away
    The noise of life begins again,   10
    And ghastly thro' the drizzling rain
On the bald street breaks the blank day.

. . . . .

54

Oh yet we trust that somehow good
   Will be the final goal of ill,
   To pangs of nature, sins of will,
Defects of doubt, and taints of blood;

That nothing walks with aimless feet;   5
   That not one life shall be destroyed,
   Or cast as rubbish to the void,
When God hath made the pile complete;

That not a worm is cloven in vain;
   That not a moth with vain desire   10
   Is shriveled in a fruitless fire,
Or but subserves another's gain.

Behold, we know not anything;
   I can but trust that good shall fall
   At last—far off—at last, to all,   15
And every winter change to spring.

So runs my dream: but what am I?
   An infant crying in the night:
   An infant crying for the light:
And with no language but a cry.   20

. . . . .

106

Ring out, wild bells, to the wild sky,
   The flying cloud, the frosty light:
   The year is dying in the night;
Ring out, wild bells, and let him die.

Ring out the old, ring in the new,   5
   Ring, happy bells, across the snow:
   The year is going, let him go;
Ring out the false, ring in the true.

Ring out the grief that saps the mind,
   For those that here we see no more;   10
   Ring out the feud of rich and poor,
Ring in redress to all mankind.

Ring out a slowly dying cause,
   And ancient forms of party strife;

Ring in the nobler modes of life,   15
With sweeter manners, purer laws.

Ring out the want, the care, the sin,
    The faithless coldness of the times;
    Ring out, ring out my mournful rhymes,
But ring the fuller minstrel in.   20

Ring out false pride in place and blood,
    The civic slander and the spite;
    Ring in the love of truth and right,
Ring in the common love of good.

Ring out old shapes of foul disease;   25
    Ring out the narrowing lust of gold;
    Ring out the thousand wars of old,
Ring in the thousand years of peace.

Ring in the valiant man and free,
    The larger heart, the kindlier hand;   30
    Ring out the darkness of the land,
Ring in the Christ that is to be.   (*1850*)

The Eagle

He clasps the crag with crooked hands:
Close to the sun in lonely lands,
Ringed with the azure world, he stands.

The wrinkled sea beneath him crawls;
He watches from his mountain walls,
And like a thunderbolt he falls.   (*1851*)

From *Maud*

Come Into the Garden, Maud

Come into the garden, Maud,
    For the black bat, night, has flown,
Come into the garden, Maud,
    I am here at the gate alone;

And the woodbine spices are wafted abroad,   5
   And the musk of the rose is blown.

For a breeze of morning moves,
   And the planet of love is on high,
Beginning to faint in the light that she loves
   On a bed of daffodil sky,   10
To faint in the light of the sun she loves,
   To faint in his light, and to die.

All night have the roses heard
   The flute, violin, bassoon;
All night has the casement jessamine stirred   15
   To the dancers dancing in tune;
Till a silence fell with the waking bird,
   And a hush with the setting moon.

I said to the lily, "There is but one,
   With whom she has heart to be gay.   20
When will the dancers leave her alone?
   She is weary of dance and play."
Now half to the setting moon are gone,
   And half to the rising day;
Low on the sand and loud on the stone   25
   The last wheel echoes away.

I said to the rose, "The brief night goes
   In babble and revel and wine.
O young lord-lover, what sighs are those,
   For one that will never be thine?   30
But mine, but mine," so I sware to the rose,
   "For ever and ever, mine."

And the soul of the rose went into my blood,
   As the music clashed in the Hall;
And long by the garden lake I stood,   35
   For I heard your rivulet fall
From the lake to the meadow and on to the wood,
   Our wood, that is dearer than all;

From the meadow your walks have left so sweet
   That whenever a March wind sighs   40
He sets the jewel-print of your feet
   In violets blue as your eyes,
To the woody hollows in which we meet
   And the valleys of Paradise.

The slender acacia would not shake   45
    One long milk-bloom on the tree;
The white lake-blossom fell into the lake
    As the pimpernel dozed on the lea;
But the rose was awake all night for your sake,
    Knowing your promise to me;   50
The lilies and roses were all awake,
    They sighed for the dawn and thee.

Queen rose of the rosebud garden of girls,
    Come hither, the dances are done,
In gloss of satin and glimmer of pearls,   55
    Queen lily and rose in one;
Shine out, little head, sunning over with curls,
    To the flowers, and be their sun.

There has fallen a splendid tear
    From the passion flower at the gate,   60
She is coming, my dove, my dear;
    She is coming, my life, my fate.
The red rose cries, "She is near, she is near";
    And the white rose weeps, "She is late";
The larkspur listens, "I hear, I hear";   65
    And the lily whispers, "I wait."

She is coming, my own, my sweet;
    Were it ever so airy a tread,
My heart would hear her and beat,
    Were it earth in an earthy bed;   70
My dust would hear her and beat,
    Had I lain for a century dead,
Would start and tremble under her feet,
    And blossom in purple and red.   (1855)

Flower in the Crannied Wall

    Flower in the crannied wall,
    I pluck you out of the crannies,
    I hold you here, root and all, in my hand,
    Little flower—but *if* I could understand
    What you are, root and all, and all in all,
    I should know what God and man is.   (1869)

OLIVER WENDELL HOLMES
(1809–1894)

The Last Leaf

I saw him once before,
As he passed by the door,
    And again
The pavement stones resound,
As he totters o'er the ground   5
    With his cane.

They say that in his prime,
Ere the pruning-knife of Time
    Cut him down,
Not a better man was found   10
By the Crier on his round
    Through the town.

But now he walks the streets,
And he looks at all he meets
    Sad and wan,   15
And he shakes his feeble head,
That it seems as if he said,
    "They are gone."

The mossy marbles rest
On the lips that he has prest   20
    In their bloom,
And the names he loved to hear
Have been carved for many a year
    On the tomb.

My grandmamma has said—   25
Poor old lady, she is dead
    Long ago—
That he had a Roman nose,
And his cheek was like a rose
    In the snow;   30

But now his nose is thin,
And it rests upon his chin
    Like a staff,

And a crook is in his back,
And a melancholy crack   35
  In his laugh.

I know it is a sin
For me to sit and grin
  At him here;
But the old three-cornered hat,   40
And the breeches, and all that,
  Are so queer!

And if I should live to be
The last leaf upon the tree
  In the spring,   45
Let them smile, as I do now,
At the old forsaken bough
  Where I cling. *(1830–1836)*

The Deacon's Masterpiece

The Wonderful One-Horse Shay

A Logical Story

Have you heard of the wonderful one-hoss shay,
That was built in such a logical way
It ran a hundred years to a day,
And then, of a sudden, it—ah, but stay,
I'll tell you what happened without delay,   5
Scaring the parson into fits,
Frightening people out of their wits,—
Have you ever heard of that, I say?

Seventeen hundred and fifty-five.
Georgius Secundus was then alive,—   10
Snuffy old drone from the German hive.
That was the year when Lisbon-town
Saw the earth open and gulp her down,
And Braddock's army was done so brown,
Left without a scalp to its crown.   15
It was on the terrible Earthquake-day
That the Deacon finished the one-hoss shay.[1]

[1] Holmes was a rationalist and an empiricist; the shay is commonly said to symbolize Calvinist doctrines which he believed to be outmoded.

Now in building of chaises, I tell you what,
There is always *somewhere* a weakest spot,—
In hub, tire, felloe, in spring or thill,   20
In panel, or crossbar, or floor, or sill,
In screw, bolt, thoroughbrace,—lurking still,
Find it somewhere you must and will,—
Above or below, or within or without,—
And that's the reason, beyond a doubt,   25
That a chaise *breaks down,* but doesn't *wear out.*

But the Deacon swore (as deacons do,
With an 'I dew vum,' or an 'I tell *yeou*')
He would build one shay to beat the taown
'N' the keounty 'n' all the kentry raoun';   30
It should be so built that it *could'n'* break daown:
'Fur,' said the Deacon, "t's mighty plain
Thut the weakes' place mus' stan' the strain;
'N' the way t' fix it, uz I maintain,
           Is only jest   35
T' make that place uz strong uz the rest.'

So the Deacon inquired of the village folk
Where he could find the strongest oak,
That could n't be split nor bent nor broke,—
That was for spokes and floor and sills;   40
He sent for lancewood to make the thills;
The crossbars were ash, from the straightest trees,
The panels of white-wood, that cuts like cheese,
But lasts like iron for things like these;
The hubs of logs from the 'Settler's ellum,'—   45
Last of its timber,—they could 'nt sell 'em,
Never an axe had seen their chips,
And the wedges flew from between their lips,
Their blunt ends frizzled like celery-tips;
Step and prop-iron, bolt and screw,   50
Spring, tire, axle, and linchpin too,
Steel of the finest, bright and blue;
Thoroughbrace bison-skin, thick and wide;
Boot, top, dasher, from tough old hide
Found in the pit when the tanner died.   55
That was the way he 'put her through.'
'There!' said the Deacon, 'naow she'll dew!'

Do! I tell you, I rather guess
She was a wonder, and nothing less!

Colts grew horses, beards turned gray,   60
Deacon and deaconess dropped away,
Children and grandchildren—where were they?
But there stood the stout old one-hoss shay
As fresh as on Lisbon-earthquake-day!

EIGHTEEN HUNDRED;—it came and found   65
The Deacon's masterpiece strong and sound.
Eighteen hundred increased by ten;—
'Hahnsum kerridge' they called it then.
Eighteen hundred and twenty came;—
Running as usual; much the same.   70
Thirty and forty at last arrive,
And then come fifty, and FIFTY-FIVE.

Little of all we value here
Wakes on the morn of its hundredth year
Without both feeling and looking queer.   75
In fact, there's nothing that keeps its youth,
So far as I know, but a tree and truth.
(This is a moral that runs at large;
Take it.—You're welcome.—No extra charge.)

FIRST OF NOVEMBER,—the earthquake-day,—   80
There are traces of age in the one-hoss shay,
A general flavor of mild decay,
But nothing local, as one may say.
There could n't be,—for the Deacon's art
Had made it so like in every part   85
That there was n't a chance for one to start.
For the wheels were just as strong as the thills,
And the floor was just as strong as the sills,
And the panels just as strong as the floor,
And the whipple-tree neither less nor more,   90
And the back crossbar as strong as the fore,
And spring and axle and hub *encore.*
And yet, *as a whole,* it is past a doubt
In another hour it will be *worn out!*

First of November, 'Fifty-five!   95
This morning the parson takes a drive.
Now, small boys, get out of the way!
Here comes the wonderful one-hoss shay,
Drawn by a rat-tailed, ewe-necked bay.
'Huddup!' said the parson.—Off went they.   100
The parson was working his Sunday's text,—

Had got to *fifthly*, and stopped perplexed
At what the—Moses—was coming next.
All at once the horse stood still,
Close by the meet'n'-house on the hill.   105
First a shiver, and then a thrill,
Then something decidedly like a spill,—
And the parson was sitting upon a rock,
At half past nine by the meet'n'-house clock,—
Just the hour of the Earthquake shock!   110
What do you think the parson found,
When he got up and stared around?
The poor old chaise in a heap or mound,
As if it had been to the mill and ground!
You see, of course, if you're not a dunce,   115
How it went to pieces all at once,—
All at once, and nothing first,—
Just as bubbles do when they burst.

End of the wonderful one-hoss shay
Logic is logic. That's all I say.   (*1857–1858*)

ROBERT BROWNING (1812–1889)

My Last Duchess

FERRARA

That's my last Duchess painted on the wall,
Looking as if she were alive. I call
That piece a wonder, now; Frà Pandolf's hands
Worked busily a day, and there she stands.
Will 't please you sit and look at her? I said   5
'Frà Pandolf' by design, for never read
Strangers like you that pictured countenance,
The depth and passion of its earnest glance,
But to myself they turned (since none puts by
The curtain I have drawn for you, but I)   10
And seemed as they would ask me, if they durst,
How such a glance came there; so, not the first
Are you to turn and ask thus. Sir, 'twas not
Her husband's presence only, called that spot
Of joy into the Duchess' cheek; perhaps   15
Frà Pandolf [1] chanced to say, "Her mantle laps
Over my lady's wrist too much," or "Paint
Must never hope to reproduce the faint
Half-flush that dies along her throat." Such stuff
Was courtesy, she thought, and cause enough   20
For calling up that spot of joy. She had
A heart—how shall I say?—too soon made glad,
Too easily impressed; she liked whate'er
She looked on, and her looks went everywhere.
Sir, 'twas all one! My favour at her breast,   25
The dropping of the daylight in the West,
The bough of cherries some officious fool
Broke in the orchard for her, the white mule
She rode with round the terrace—all and each
Would draw from her alike the approving speech,   30
Or blush, at least. She thanked men,—good! but thanked
Somehow—I know not how—as if she ranked

---

[1] an imaginary painter

My gift of a nine-hundred-years-old-name
With anybody's gift. Who'd stoop to blame
This sort of trifling? Even had you skill   35
In speech—which I have not—to make your will
Quite clear to such an one, and say, "Just this
Or that in you disgusts me; here you miss,
Or there exceed the mark"—and if she let
Herself be lessoned so, nor plainly set   40
Her wits to yours, forsooth, and made excuse—
E'en then would be some stooping; and I choose
Never to stoop. Oh, sir, she smiled, no doubt,
Whene'er I passed her; but who passed without
Much the same smile? This grew; I gave commands;   45
Then all smiles stopped together. There she stands
As if alive. Will 't please you rise? We'll meet
The company below, then. I repeat,
The Count your master's known munificence
Is ample warrant that no just pretense   50
Of mine for dowry will be disallowed;
Though his fair daughter's self, as I avowed
At starting, is my object. Nay, we'll go
Together down, sir. Notice Neptune, though,
Taming a sea-horse, thought a rarity,   55
Which Claus of Innsbruck cast in bronze for me!   (1842)

Soliloquy of the Spanish Cloister

Gr-r-r—there go, my heart's abhorrence!
    Water your damned flower-pots, do!
If hate killed men, Brother Lawrence,
    God's blood, would not mine kill you!
What? your myrtle-bush wants trimming?   5
    Oh, that rose has prior claims—
Needs its leaden vase filled brimming?
    Hell dry you up with its flames!

At the meal we sit together;
    Salve tibi! [1] I must hear   10
Wise talk of the kind of weather,
    Sort of season, time of year:

[1] hail to thee

Not a plenteous cork-crop: scarcely
    Dare we hope oak-galls, I doubt:
What's the Latin name for "parsley"?   15
    What's the Greek name for Swine's Snout?

Whew! We'll have our platter burnished,
    Laid with care on our own shelf!
With a fire-new spoon we're furnished,
    And a goblet for ourself,   20
Rinsed like something sacrificial
    Ere 'tis fit to touch our chaps—
Marked with L. for our initial!
    (He-he! There his lily snaps!)

Saint, forsooth! While brown Dolores   25
    Squats outside the Convent bank
With Sanchicha, telling stories,
    Steeping tresses in the tank,
Blue-black, lustrous, thick like horsehairs,
    —Can't I see his dead eye glow,   30
Bright as 'twere a Barbary corsair's?
    (That is, if he'd let it show!)

When he finishes refection,
    Knife and fork he never lays
Cross-wise, to my recollection,   35
    As do I, in Jesu's praise.
I, the Trinity illustrate,
    Drinking watered orange-pulp—
In three sips the Arian frustrate;
    While he drains his at one gulp!   40

Oh, those melons! If he's able
    We're to have a feast; so nice!
One goes to the Abbot's table,
    All of us get each a slice.
How go on your flowers? None double?   45
    Not one fruit-sort can you spy?
Strange!—And I, too, at such trouble,
    Keep them close-nipped on the sly!

There's a great text in Galatians,[2]
    Once you trip on it, entails   50

---

[2] Galatians 5:19–21, or possibly 3:10

Twenty-nine distinct damnations,
    One sure, if another fails;
If I trip him just a-dying,
    Sure of heaven as sure can be,
Spin him round and send him flying   55
    Off to hell, a Manichee?

Or, my scrofulous French novel
    On grey paper with blunt type!
Simply glance at it, you grovel
    Hand and foot in Belial's gripe;   60
If I double down its pages
    At the woeful sixteenth print,
When he gathers his greengages,
    Ope a sieve and slip it in't?

Or, there's Satan!—One might venture   65
    Pledge one's soul to him, yet leave
Such a flaw in the indenture
    As he'd miss, till, past retrieve,
Blasted lay that rose-acacia
    We're so proud of. *Hy, Zy, Hine* . . .   70
'St! There's Vespers! *Plena gratiâ*
    Ave, Virgo! Gr-r-r—you swine!   (1842)

The Bishop Orders His Tomb at Saint Praxed's Church [1]

Rome, 15–

Vanity, saith the preacher,[2] vanity!
Draw round my bed: is Anselm keeping back?
Nephews—sons mine . . . ah God, I know not! Well—
She, men would have to be your mother once,
Old Gandolf [3] envied me, so fair she was!   5
What's done is done, and she is dead beside,
Dead long ago, and I am Bishop since,
And as she died so must we die ourselves,
And thence ye may perceive the world's a dream.
Life, how and what is it? As here I lie   10
In this state-chamber, dying by degrees,

[1] St. Praxed's is in Rome, but the bishop and the tomb are imaginary.   [2] Ecclesiastes 1:2   [3] his predecessor

Hours and long hours in the dead night, I ask
"Do I live, am I dead?" Peace, peace seems all.
Saint Praxed's ever was the church for peace;
And so, about this tomb of mine. I fought   15
With tooth and nail to save my niche, ye know:
—Old Gandolf cozened me, despite my care;
Shrewd was that snatch from out the corner South
He graced his carrion with, God curse the same!
Yet still my niche is not so cramped but thence   20
One sees the pulpit o' the epistle-side,
And somewhat of the choir, those silent seats,
And up into the aery dome where live
The angels, and a sunbeam's sure to lurk:
And I shall fill my slab of basalt there,   25
And 'neath my tabernacle take my rest,
With those nine columns round me, two and two,
The odd one at my feet where Anselm stands:
Peach-blossom marble all, the rare, the ripe
As fresh-poured red wine of a mighty pulse   30
—Old Gandolf with his paltry onion-stone,
Put me where I may look at him! True peach,
Rosy and flawless: how I earned the prize!
Draw close: that conflagration of my church
—What then? So much was saved if aught were missed!   35
My sons, ye would not be my death? Go dig
The white-grape vineyard where the oil-press stood,
Drop water gently till the surface sinks,
And if ye find . . . ah God, I know not, I! . . .
Bedded in store of rotten fig-leaves soft,   40
And corded up in a tight olive-frail,[4]
Some lump, ah God, of *lapis lazuli,*
Big as a Jew's head cut off at the nape,
Blue as a vein o'er the Madonna's breast—
Sons, all have I bequeathed you, villas, all,   45
That brave Frascati villa with its bath—
So, let the blue lump poise between my knees,
Like God the Father's globe on both his hands
Ye worship in the Jesu Church so gay,
For Gandolf shall not choose but see and burst!   50
Swift as a weaver's shuttle fleet our years; [5]
Man goeth to the grave, and where is he?

[4] an olive basket   [5] Job 7:6

Did I say basalt for my slab, sons? Black—
'Twas ever antique-black I meant! How else
Shall ye contrast my frieze to come beneath?   55
The bas-relief in bronze ye promised me,
Those Pans and Nymphs ye wot of, and perchance
Some tripod, thyrsus, with a vase or so,
The Saviour at his sermon on the mount,
St. Praxed in a glory, and one Pan   60
Ready to twitch the Nymph's last garment off,
And Moses with the tables [6] . . . but I know
Ye mark me not! What do they whisper thee,
Child of my bowels, Anselm? Ah, ye hope
To revel down my villas while I gasp   65
Bricked o'er with beggar's moldy travertine
Which Gandolf from his tomb-top chuckles at!
Nay, boys, ye love me—all of jasper, then!
'Tis jasper ye stand pledged to, lest I grieve
My bath must needs be left behind, alas!   70
One block, pure green as a pistachio-nut,
There's plenty jasper somewhere in the world—
And have I not St. Praxed's ear to pray
Horses for ye, and brown Greek manuscripts,
And mistresses with great smooth marbly limbs?   75
—That's if ye carve my epitaph aright,
Choice Latin, picked phrase, Tully's every word,
No gaudy ware like Gandolf's second line—
Tully, my masters? Ulpian [7] serves his need!
And then how I shall lie through centuries,   80
And hear the blessèd mutter of the mass,
And see God made and eaten all day long,
And feel the steady candle-flame, and taste
Good strong thick stupefying incense-smoke!
For as I lie here, hours of the dead night,   85
Dying in state and by such slow degrees,
I fold my arms as if they clasped a crook,
And stretch my feet forth straight as stone can point
And let the bedclothes for a mortcloth drop
Into great laps and folds of sculptor's-work: 90
And as yon tapers dwindle, and strange thoughts
Grow, with a certain humming in my ears,

[6] Exodus 24–34   [7] a Roman jurist with
a fine Ciceronian style

About the life before I lived this life,
And this life too, popes, cardinals and priests,
Saint Praxed at his sermon on the mount,   95
Your tall pale mother with her talking eyes,
And new-found agate urns as fresh as day,
And marble's language, Latin pure, discreet,
—Aha, ELUCESCEBAT [8] quoth our friend?
No Tully, said I, Ulpian at the best!   100
Evil and brief hath been my pilgrimage.
All lapis, all, sons! Else I give the Pope
My villas: will ye ever eat my heart?
Ever your eyes were as a lizard's quick,
They glitter like your mother's for my soul,   105
Or ye would heighten my impoverished frieze,
Piece out its starved design, and fill my vase
With grapes, and add a vizor and a Term,
And to the tripod ye would tie a lynx
That in his struggle throws the thyrsus down,   110
To comfort me on my entablature
Whereon I am to lie till I must ask
"Do I live, am I dead?" There, leave me, there!
For ye have stabbed me with ingratitude
To death—ye wish it—God, ye wish it! Stone—   115
Gritstone, a-crumble! Clammy squares which sweat
As if the corpse they keep were oozing through—
And no more lapis to delight the world!
Well, go! I bless ye. Fewer tapers there,
But in a row: and, going, turn your backs   120
—Ay, like departing altar-ministrants,
And leave me in my church, the church for peace,
That I may watch at leisure if he leers—
Old Gandolf, at me, from his onion-stone,
As still he envied me, so fair she was!   (*1845*)

Home-Thoughts, from Abroad

Oh, to be in England
Now that April's there,
And whoever wakes in England

---

[8] "He was famous," but the bishop pre-
fers the classic form *elucebat*.

Sees some morning, unaware,
That the lowest boughs and the brush-wood sheaf   5
Round the elm-tree bole are in tiny leaf,
While the chaffinch sings on the orchard bough
In England—now!

And after April, when May follows,
And the whitethroat builds, and all the swallows!   10
Hark, where my blossomed pear-tree in the hedge
Leans to the field and scatters on the clover
Blossoms and dewdrops—at the bent-spray's edge—
That's the wise thrush; he sings each song twice over,
Lest you should think he never could recapture   15
The first fine careless rapture!
And though the fields look rough with hoary dew,
All will be gay when noontide wakes anew
The buttercups, the little children's dower,
—Far brighter than this gaudy melon-flower!   (1845)

Prospice [1]

Fear death?—to feel the fog in my throat,
    The mist in my face,
When the snows begin, and the blasts denote
    I am nearing the place,
The power of the night, the press of the storm,   5
    The post of the foe;
Where he stands, the Arch Fear in a visible form,
    Yet the strong man must go:
For the journey is done and the summit attained,
    And the barriers fall,   10
Though a battle's to fight ere the guerdon be gained,
    The reward of it all.
I was ever a fighter, so—one fight more,
    The best and the last!
I would hate that death bandaged my eyes, and forbore, 15
    And bade me creep past.
No! let me taste the whole of it, fare like my peers
    The heroes of old,

[1] look forward

Bear the brunt, in a minute pay glad life's arrears
    Of pain, darkness and cold.   20
For sudden the worse turns the best to the brave,
    The black minute's at end,
And the elements' rage, the fiend-voices that rave,
    Shall dwindle, shall blend,
Shall change, shall become first a peace out of pain,   25
    Then a light, then thy breast,
O thou soul of my soul! I shall clasp thee again,
    And with God be the rest!   (1864)

From *Asolando*

EPILOGUE

At the midnight in the silence of the sleep-time,
    When you set your fancies free,
Will they pass to where—by death, fools think, imprisoned—
Low he lies, who once so loved you, whom you loved so,
    —Pity me?   5

Oh to love so, be so loved, yet so mistaken!
    What had I on earth to do
With the slothful, with the mawkish, the unmanly?
Like the aimless, helpless, hopeless, did I drivel
    —Being—who?   10

One who never turned his back but marched breast forward,
    Never doubted clouds would break,
Never dreamed, though right were worsted, wrong would triumph,
Held we fall to rise, are baffled to fight better,
    Sleep to wake.   15

No, at noonday in the bustle of man's work-time
    Greet the unseen with a cheer!
Bid him forward, breast and back as either should be,
"Strive and thrive!" cry "Speed,—fight on, fare ever
    There as here!"   (1889)

JONES VERY (1813–1880)

The Presence

I sit within my room, and joy to find
That Thou who always lov'st art with me here,
That I am never left by Thee behind,
But by thyself Thou keep'st me ever near;
The fire burns brighter when with Thee I look,
And seems a kinder servant sent to me;
With gladder heart I read Thy holy book,
Because Thou art the eyes by which I see;
This aged chair, that table, watch and door
Around in ready service ever wait;
Nor can I ask of Thee a menial more
To fill the measure of my large estate,
For Thou thyself, with all a father's care,
Where'er I turn, art ever with me there.   (1839)

The Lost

The fairest day that ever yet has shone
Will be when thou the day within shalt see;
The fairest rose that ever yet has blown,
When thou the flower thou lookest on shalt be;
But thou art far away amidst Time's toys;
Thyself the day thou lookest for in them,
Thyself the flower that now thine eye enjoys;
But wilted now thou hang'st upon thy stem;
The bird thou hearest on the budding tree
Thou hast made sing with thy forgotten voice;
But when it swells again to melody,
The song is thine in which thou wilt rejoice;
And thou new risen 'midst these wonders live,
That now to them dost all thy substance give.   (1839)

The Created

There is nought for thee by thy haste to gain;
'Tis not the swift with Me that win the race;
Through long endurance of delaying pain,
Thine opened eye shall see thy Father's face;
Nor here nor there, where now thy feet would turn,
Thou wilt find Him who ever seeks for thee;
But let obedience quench desires that burn,
And where thou art, thy Father too will be!
Behold! as day by day the spirit grows,
Thou see'st by inward light things hid before;
Till what God is, thyself His image shows;
And thou dost wear the robe that first thou wore,
When, bright with radiance from His forming hand,
He saw the lord of all his creatures stand.   (*1839*)

Ship Rock

With a sudden sweet surprise
    Bursts the prospect on our eyes;
Far the city's spires are seen,
    Hills and fields and woods between.

Farther still, the ocean blue   5
    Fitly bounds the charming view;
Where, on the horizon clear,
    Noble ships their courses steer.

By the pond beneath the hill,
    Silent stands the noisy mill;   10
While the brook with laugh and song
    Through the meadow glides along.

Science may thy birth explore,
    On the far-off Arctic shore,
And thy various wanderings show   15
    In the ages long ago;

With more interest here I trace
    Backward my own name and race;

From thy top the scene behold
   Where they lived and toiled of old.   20

Here the wooded fields they cleared,
   And their humble homesteads reared;
Here they planted, gathered here
   Harvests ripe from year to year.

Here they worshiped Him, whose word   25
   In their father-land they heard;
Him, who o'er the ocean wide
   Was their Hope, their Strength, their Guide.

Here in sweet and holy trust
   They committed dust to dust;   30
Minding where the soul's conveyed
   More than where the body's laid.

Still their orchard-lot I see,
   Here and there a moss-grown tree;
Here their dwelling's site is known,   35
   Now by shrubs and vines o'ergrown.

Sacred is this spot to me,
   Rock and brook and lofty tree;
For amid the scenes I tread
   Rests the dust of kindred dead!   (1886)

CHRISTOPHER PEARSE CRANCH
(1815–1892)

Enosis [1]

Thought is deeper than all speech,
    Feeling deeper than all thought:
Souls to souls can never teach
    What unto themselves was taught.

We are spirits clad in veils;   5
    Man by man was never seen;
All our deep communing fails
    To remove the shadowy screen.

Heart to heart was never known;
    Mind with mind did never meet;   10
We are columns left alone
    Of a temple once complete.

Like the stars that gem the sky,
    For apart though seeming near,
In our light we scattered lie;   15
    All is thus but starlight here.

What is social company
    But a babbling summer stream?
What our wise philosophy
    But the glancing of a dream?   20

Only when the Sun of Love
    Melts the scattered stars of thought,
Only when we live above
    What the dim-eyed world hath taught,

Only when our souls are fed   25
    By the Fount which gave them birth,
And by inspiration led
    Which they never drew from earth,

We, like parted drops of rain,
    Swelling till they meet and run,   30
Shall be all absorbed again,
    Melting, flowing into one.

[1] Enosis: "flowing into one"; communion.

✒ EMILY BRONTË (1818–1848)

Remembrance

Cold in the earth, and the deep snow piled above thee!
Far, far removed, cold in the dreary grave!
Have I forgot, my only love, to love thee,
Severed at last by Time's all-wearing wave?

Now, when alone, do my thoughts no longer hover   5
Over the mountains on Angora's shore;
Resting their wings where heath and fern-leaves cover
That noble heart for ever, ever more?

Cold in the earth, and fifteen wild Decembers
From those brown hills have melted into spring—   10
Faithful indeed is the spirit that remembers
After such years of change and suffering!

Sweet Love of youth, forgive if I forget thee
While the world's tide is bearing me along:
Sterner desires and darker hopes beset me,   15
Hopes which obscure but cannot do thee wrong.

No other sun has lightened up my heaven;
No other star has ever shone for me:
All my life's bliss from thy dear life was given—
All my life's bliss is in the grave with thee.   20

But when the days of golden dreams had perished
And even despair was powerless to destroy,
Then did I learn how existence could be cherished,
Strengthened and fed without the aid of joy;

Then did I check the tears of useless passion,   25
Weaned my young soul from yearning after thine;
Sternly denied its burning wish to hasten
Down to that tomb already more than mine!

And even yet, I dare not let it languish,
Dare not indulge in memory's rapturous pain;   30
Once drinking deep of that divinest anguish,
How could I seek the empty world again?   (1846)

No Coward Soul Is Mine

No coward soul is mine,
No trembler in the world's storm-troubled sphere:
    I see Heaven's glories shine,
And faith shines equal, arming me from fear.

O God within my breast,   5
Almighty, ever-present Deity!
    Life, that in me hast rest
As I, undying life, have power in Thee!

Vain are the thousand creeds
That move men's hearts; unutterably vain;   10
    Worthless as withered weeds,
Or idlest froth amid the boundless main,

To waken doubt in one
Holding so fast by Thy infinity,
    So surely anchored on   15
The steadfast rock of immortality.

With wide embracing love
Thy spirit animates eternal years,
    Pervades and broods above,
Changes, sustains, dissolves, creates, and rears.   20

Though earth and moon were gone,
And suns and universes cease to be,
    And Thou wert left alone,
Every existence would exist in Thee.

There is not room for death,   25
Nor atom that his might could render void:
    Since Thou are Being and Breath
And what Thou art may never be destroyed.   (1850)

Often Rebuked

Often rebuked, yet always back returning
    To those first feelings that were born with me,
And leaving busy chase of wealth and learning
    For idle dreams of things which cannot be:

Today, I will not seek the shadowy region: 5
    Its unsustaining vastness waxes drear;
And visions rising, legion after legion,
    Bring the unreal world too strangely near.

I'll walk, but not in old heroic traces,
    And not in paths of high morality,   10
And not among the half-distinguished faces,
    The clouded forms of long-past history.

I'll walk where my own nature would be leading:
    It vexes me to choose another guide:
Where the gray flocks in ferny glens are feeding;   15
    Where the wild wind blows on the mountain-side.

What have those lonely mountains worth revealing?
    More glory and more grief than I can tell:
The earth that wakes *one* human heart to feeling
    Can centre both the worlds of Heaven and Hell.   (1850)

ARTHUR HUGH CLOUGH (1819–1861)

Qua Cursum Ventus [1]

As ships, becalmed at eve, that lay
    With canvas drooping, side by side,
Two towers of sail at dawn of day
    Are scarce long leagues apart descried;

When fell the night, upsprung the breeze,   5
    And all the darkling hours they plied,
Nor dreamt but each the self-same seas
    By each was cleaving, side by side:

E'en so, but why the tale reveal
    Of those, whom year by year unchanged,   10
Brief absence joined anew to feel,
    Astounded, soul from soul estranged?

At dead of night their sails were filled,
    And onward each rejoicing steered—
Ah, neither blame, for neither willed,   15
    Or wist, what first with dawn appeared!

To veer, how vain! On, onward strain,
    Brave barks! In light, in darkness, too,
Through winds and tides one compass guides—
    To that, and your own selves, be true.   20

But O blithe breeze! and O great seas,
    Though ne'er, that earliest parting past,
On your wide plain they join again,
    Together lead them home at last.

One port, methought, alike they sought,   25
    One purpose hold where'er they fare—
O bounding breeze, O rushing seas!
    At last, at last, unite them there!   (1849)

[1] as the wind sets the course

Say Not the Struggle Nought Availeth

Say not the struggle nought availeth,
 The labor and the wounds are vain,
The enemy faints not, nor faileth,
 And as things have been they remain.

If hopes were dupes, fears may be liars;   5
 It may be, in yon smoke concealed,
Your comrades chase e'en now the fliers,
 And, but for you, possess the field.

For while the tired waves, vainly breaking,
 Seem here no painful inch to gain,   10
Far back, through creeks and inlets making,
 Comes silent, flooding in, the main.

And not by eastern windows only,
 When daylight comes, comes in the light,
In front, the sun climbs slow, how slowly,   15
 But westward, look, the land is bright. (*1862*)

Where Lies the Land

Where lies the land to which the ship would go?
Far, far ahead, is all her seamen know.
And where the land she travels from? Away,
Far, far behind, is all that they can say.

On sunny noons upon the deck's smooth face,   5
Linked arm in arm, how pleasant here to pace;
Or, o'er the stern reclining, watch below
The foaming wake far widening as we go.

On stormy nights when wild northwesters rave,
How proud a thing to fight with wind and wave!   10
The dripping sailor on the reeling mast
Exults to bear, and scorns to wish it past.

Where lies the land to which the ship would go?
Far, far ahead, is all her seamen know.
And where the land she travels from? Away,   15
Far, far behind, is all that they can say. (*1862*)

The Latest Decalogue

Thou shalt have one God only; who
Would be at the expense of two?

No graven images may be
Worshipped, except the currency:

Swear not at all; for, for thy curse   5
Thine enemy is none the worse:

At church on Sunday to attend
Will serve to keep the world thy friend:

Honour thy parents; that is, all
From whom advancement may befall: 10

Thou shalt not kill; but need'st not strive
Officiously to keep alive:

Do not adultery commit;
Advantage rarely comes of it:

Thou shalt not steal; an empty feat,   15
When 'tis so lucrative to cheat:

Bear not false witness; let the lie
Have time on its own wings to fly:

Thou shalt not covet, but tradition
Approves all forms of competition.   20

The sum of all is, thou shalt love,
If any body, God above:
At any rate shall never labour
More than thyself to love thy neighbour.
(*1849*)

᪥ WALT WHITMAN (1819–1892)

From *Song of Myself*

1

I celebrate myself, and sing myself,
And what I assume you shall assume,
For every atom belonging to me as good belongs to you.

I loafe and invite my soul,
I lean and loafe at my ease observing a spear of summer grass.   5

My tongue, every atom of my blood, form'd from this soil, this air,
Born of parents born here from parents the same, and their parents the
    same,
I, now thirty-seven years old in perfect health begin,
Hoping to cease not till death.

Creeds and schools in abeyance,   10
Retiring back a while sufficed at what they are, but never forgotten,
I harbor for good or bad, I permit to speak at every hazard,
Nature without check with original energy.

. . . . .

3

I have heard what the talkers were talking, the talk of the beginning
    and the end,
But I do not talk of the beginning or the end.

There was never any more inception that there is now,
Nor any more youth or age than there is now,
And will never be any more perfection than there is now,   5
Nor any more heaven or hell than there is now.

Urge and urge and urge,
Always the procreant urge of the world.
Out of the dimness opposite equals advance, always substance and in-
    crease, always sex,
Always a knit of identity, always distinction, always a breed of life.   10

To elaborate is no avail, learn'd and unlearn'd feel that it is so.

Sure as the most certain sure, plumb in the uprights, well entretied,
    braced in the beams,

Stout as a horse, affectionate, haughty, electrical,
I and this mystery here we stand.

.   .   .   .   .

5

I believe in you my soul, the other I am must not abase itself to you,
And you must not be abased to the other.

Loafe with me on the grass, loose the stop from your throat,
Not words, not music or rhyme I want, not custom or lecture, not even
    the best,
Only the lull I like, the hum of your valvèd voice.   5

I mind how once we lay such a transparent summer morning,
How you settled your head athwart my hips and gently turn'd over
    upon me,
And parted the shirt from my bosom-bone, and plunged your tongue to
    my bare-stript heart,
And reach'd till you felt my beard, and reach'd till you held my feet.

Swiftly arose and spread around me the peace and knowledge that pass
    all the argument of the earth,   10
And I know that the hand of God is the promise of my own,
And I know that the spirit of God is the brother of my own,
And that all the men ever born are also my brothers, and the women
    my sisters and lovers,
And that a kelson of the creation is love,
And limitless are leaves stiff or drooping in the fields,   15
And brown ants in the little wells beneath them,
And mossy scabs of the worm fence, heap'd stones, elder, mullein and
    poke-weed.

.   .   .   .   .

20

Who goes there? hankering, gross, mystical, nude;
How is it I extract strength from the beef I eat?

What is a man anyhow? what am I? what are you?

All I mark as my own you shall offset it with your own,
Else it were time lost listening to me.   5

I do not snivel that snivel the world over,
That months are vacuums and the ground but wallow and filth.

Whimpering and truckling fold with powders for invalids, conformity goes to the fourth-remov'd,
I wear my hat as I please indoors or out.

Why should I pray? why should I venerate and be ceremonious?   10

Having pried through the strata, analyzed to a hair, counsel'd with doctors and calculated close,
I find no sweeter fat than sticks to my own bones.

In all people I see myself, none more and not one a barley-corn less,
And the good or bad I say of myself I say of them.

I know I am solid and sound,   15
To me the converging objects of the universe perpetually flow,
All are written to me, and I must get what the writing means.

I know I am deathless,
I know this orbit of mine cannot be swept by a carpenter's compass,
I know I shall not pass like a child's carlacue cut with a burnt stick at night.   20

I know I am august,
I do not trouble my spirit to vindicate itself or be understood,
I see that the elementary laws never apologize,
(I reckon I behave no prouder than the level I plant my house by, after all.)

I exist as I am, that is enough,   25
If no other in the world be aware I sit content,
And if each and all be aware I sit content.

One world is aware and by far the largest to me, and that is myself,
And whether I come to my own to-day or in ten thousand or ten million years,
I can cheerfully take it now, or with equal cheerfulness I can wait.   30

My foothold is tenon'd and mortis'd in granite,
I laugh at what you call dissolution,
And I know the amplitude of time.

21

I am the poet of the Body and I am the poet of the Soul,
The pleasures of heaven are with me and the pains of hell are with me,
The first I graft and increase upon myself, the latter I translate into a new tongue.

I am the poet of the woman the same as the man,
And I say it is as great to be a woman as to be a man,   5
And I say there is nothing greater than the mother of men.

I chant the chant of dilation or pride,
We have had ducking and deprecating about enough,
I show that size is only development.

Have you outstript the rest? are you the President?   10
It is a trifle, they will more than arrive there every one, and still pass on.

I am he that walks with the tender and growing night,
I call to the earth and sea half-held by the night.
Press close bare-bosom'd night—press close magnetic nourishing night!
Night of south winds—night of the large few stars!   15
Still nodding night—mad naked summer night.

Smile O voluptuous cool-breath'd earth!
Earth of the slumbering and liquid trees!
Earth of departed sunset—earth of the mountains misty-topt!
Earth of the vitreous pour of the full moon just tinged with blue!   20
Earth of shine and dark mottling the tide of the river!
Earth of the limpid grey of clouds brighter and clearer for my sake!
Far-swooping elbow'd earth—rich apple-blossom'd earth!
Smile, for your lover comes.

Prodigal, you have given me love—therefore I to you give love!   25
O unspeakable passionate love.

·   ·   ·   ·   ·

32

I think I could turn and live with animals, they're so placid and self-
  contain'd,
I stand and look at them long and long.

They do not sweat and whine about their condition,
They do not lie awake in the dark and weep for their sins,
They do not make me sick discussing their duty to God,   5
Not one is dissatisfied, not one is demented with the mania of owning
  things,
Not one kneels to another, nor to his kind that lived thousands of years
  ago,
Not one is respectable or unhappy over the whole earth.

So they show their relations to me and I accept them,
They bring me tokens of myself, they evince them plainly in their
  possession.   10

I wonder where they get those tokens,
Did I pass that way huge times ago and negligently drop them?

Myself moving forward then and now and forever,
Gathering and showing more always and with velocity,
Infinite and omnigenous, and the like of these among them, 15
Not too exclusive toward the reachers of my remembrancers,
Picking out here one that I love, and now go with him on brotherly
terms.

A gigantic beauty of a stallion, fresh and responsive to my caresses,
Head high in the forehead, wide between the ears,
Limbs glossy and supple, tail dusting the ground, 20
Eyes full of sparkling wickedness, ears finely cut, flexibly moving.

His nostrils dilate as my heels embrace him,
His well-built limbs tremble with pleasure as we race around and return.
I but use you a minute, then I resign you, stallion,
Why do I need your paces when I myself out-gallop them? 25
Even as I stand or sit passing faster than you.

. . . . .

48

I have said that the soul is not more than the body,
And I have said that the body is not more than the soul,
And nothing, not God, is greater to one than one's self is,
And whoever walks a furlong without sympathy walks to his own fu-
neral drest in his shroud,
And I or you pocketless of a dime may purchase the pick of the
earth, 5
And to glance with an eye or show a bean in its pod confounds the
learning of all times,
And there is no trade or employment but the young man following it
may become a hero,
And there is no object so soft but it makes a hub for the wheel'd
universe,
And I say to any man or woman, Let your soul stand cool and composed
before a million universes.

And I say to mankind, Be not curious about God, 10
For I who am curious about each am not curious about God,
(No array of terms can say how much I am at peace about God and
about death.)

I hear and behold God in every object, yet understand God not in the
    least,
Nor do I understand who there can be more wonderful than myself.

Why should I wish to see God better than this day?   15
I see something of God each hour of the twenty-four, and each moment
    then,
In the faces of men and women I see God, and in my own face in the
    glass,
I find letters from God dropt in the street, and every one is sign'd by
    God's name,
And I leave them where they are, for I know that wheresoe'er I go,
Others will punctually come for ever and ever.   20

    .   .   .   .   .

51

The past and present wilt—I have fill'd them, emptied them,
And proceed to fill my next fold of the future.

Listener up there! what have you to confide to me?
Look in my face while I snuff the sidle of evening.
(Talk honestly, no one else hears you, and I stay only a minute
    longer.)   5

Do I contradict myself?
Very well then I contradict myself,
(I am large, I contain multitudes.)

I concentrate toward them that are nigh, I wait on the door-slab.

Who has done his day's work? who will soonest be through with his
    supper?   10
Who wishes to walk with me?

Will you speak before I am gone? will you prove already too late?

52

The spotted hawk swoops by and accuses me, he complains of my gab
    and my loitering.

I too am not a bit tamed, I too am untranslatable,
I sound my barbaric yawp over the roofs of the world.

The last scud of day holds back for me,
It flings my likeness after the rest and true as any on the shadow'd
    wilds,   5
It coaxes me to the vapor and the dusk.

I depart as air, I shake my white locks at the runaway sun,
I effuse my flesh in eddies, and drift it in lacy jags.

I bequeath myself to the dirt to grow from the grass I love,
If you want me again look for me under your boot-soles.   10

You will hardly know who I am or what I mean,
But I shall be good health to you nevertheless,
And filter and fibre your blood.

Failing to fetch me at first keep encouraged,
Missing me one place search another,   15
I stop somewhere waiting for you.   (*1855*)

Crossing Brooklyn Ferry

1

Flood-tide below me! I see you face to face!
Clouds of the west—sun there half an hour high—I see you also face to
     face.
Crowds of men and women attired in the usual costumes, how curious
     you are to me!
On the ferry-boats the hundreds and hundreds that cross, returning
     home, are more curious to me than you suppose,
And you that shall cross from shore to shore years hence are more to me,
     and more in my meditations, than you might suppose.   5

2

The impalpable sustenance of me from all things at all hours of the day,
The simple, compact, well-join'd scheme, myself disintegrated, every
     one disintegrated yet part of the scheme,
The similitudes of the past and those of the future,
The glories strung like beads on my smallest sights and hearings, on the
     walk in the street and the passage over the river,
The current rushing so swiftly and swimming with me far away,   10
The others that are to follow me, the ties between me and them,
The certainty of others, the life, love, sight, hearing of others.

Others will enter the gates of the ferry and cross from shore to shore,
Others will watch the run of the flood-tide,
Others will see the shipping of Manhattan north and west, and the
     heights of Brooklyn to the south and east,   15
Others will see the islands large and small;

Fifty years hence, others will see them as they cross, the sun half an
hour high,
A hundred years hence, or ever so many hundred years hence, others
will see them,
Will enjoy the sunset, the pouring-in of the flood-tide, the falling-back
to the sea of the ebb-tide.

3

It avails not, time or place—distance avails not,   20
I am with you, you men and women of a generation, or ever so many
generations hence,
Just as you feel when you look on the river and sky, so I felt,
Just as any of you is one of a living crowd, I was one of a crowd,
Just as you are refresh'd by the gladness of the river and the bright flow,
I was refresh'd,
Just as you stand and lean on the rail, yet hurry with the swift current,
I stood yet was hurried,   25
Just as you look on the numberless masts of ships and the thick-stemm'd
pipes of steamboats, I look'd.

I too many and many a time cross'd the river of old,
Watched the Twelfth-month sea-gulls, saw them high in the air floating
with motionless wings, oscillating their bodies,
Saw how the glistening yellow lit up parts of their bodies and left the
rest in strong shadow,
Saw the slow-wheeling circles and the gradual edging toward the
south,   30
Saw the reflection of the summer sky in the water,
Had my eyes dazzled by the shimmering track of beams,
Look'd at the fine centrifugal spokes of light round the shape of my
head in the sunlit water,
Look'd on the haze on the hills southward and south-westward,
Look'd on the vapor as it flew in fleeces tinged with violet,   35
Look'd toward the lower bay to notice the vessels arriving,
Saw their approach, saw aboard those that were near me,
Saw the white sails of schooners and sloops, saw the ships at anchor,
The sailors at work in the rigging or out astride the spars,
The round masts, the swinging motion of the hulls, the slender serpen-
tine pennants,   40
The large and small steamers in motion, the pilots in their pilot-houses,
The white wake left by the passage, the quick tremulous whirl of the
wheels,
The flags of all nations, the falling of them at sunset,

The scallop-edged waves in the twilight, the ladled cups, the frolicsome
    crests and glistening,
The stretch afar growing dimmer and dimmer, the gray walls of the
    granite storehouses by the docks,   45
On the river the shadowy group, the big steam-tug closely flank'd on each
    side by the barges, the hay-boat, the belated lighter,
On the neighboring shore the fires from the foundry chimneys burning
    high and glaringly into the night,
Casting their flicker of black contrasted with wild red and yellow light
    over the tops of houses, and down into the clefts of streets.

    4

These and all else were to me the same as they are to you,
I loved well those cities, loved well the stately and rapid river,   50
The men and women I saw were all near to me,
Others the same—others who look back on me because I look'd forward
    to them,
(The time will come, though I stop here to-day and to-night.)

    5

What is it then between us?
What is the count of the scores or hundreds of years between us?   55

Whatever it is, it avails not—distance avails not, and place avails not,
I too lived, Brooklyn of ample hills was mine,
I too walk'd the streets of Manhattan island, and bathed in the waters
    around it,
I too felt the curious abrupt questionings stir within me,
In the day among crowds of people sometimes they came upon me,   60
In my walks home late at night or as I lay in my bed they came upon
    me,
I too had been struck from the float forever held in solution,
I too had receiv'd identity by my body,
That I was I knew was of my body, and what I should be I knew I
    should be of my body.

    6

It is not upon you alone the dark patches fall,   65
The dark threw its patches down upon me also,
The best I had done seem'd to me blank and suspicious,
My great thoughts as I supposed them, were they not in reality meagre?
Nor is it you alone who know what it is to be evil,
I am he who knew what it was to be evil,   70
I too knitted the old knot of contrariety,

Blabb'd, blush'd, resented, lied, stole, grudg'd,
Had guile, anger, lust, hot wishes I dared not speak,
Was wayward, vain, greedy, shallow, sly, cowardly, malignant,
The wolf, the snake, the hog, not wanting in me,   75
The cheating look, the frivolous word, the adulterous wish, not wanting,
Refusals, hates, postponements, meanness, laziness, none of these
    wanting,
Was one with the rest, the days and haps of the rest,
Was call'd by my nighest name by clear loud voices of young men as
    they saw me approaching or passing,
Felt their arms on my neck as I stood, or the negligent leaning of their
    flesh against me as I sat,   80
Saw many I loved in the street or ferry-boat or public assembly, yet
    never told them a word,
Lived the same life with the rest, the same old laughing, gnawing,
    sleeping,
Play'd the part that still looks back on the actor or actress,
The same old role, the role that is what we make it, as great as we like,
Or as small as we like, or both great and small.   85

7

Closer yet I approach you,
What thought you have of me now, I had as much of you—I laid in my
    stores in advance,
I consider'd long and seriously of you before you were born.
Who was to know what should come home to me?
Who knows but I am enjoying this?   90
Who knows, for all the distance, but I am as good as looking at you
    now, for all you cannot see me?
It is not you alone, nor I alone,
Not a few races, not a few generations, not a few centuries,
It is that each came, or comes, or shall come, from its due emission,
    without fail, either now, or then, or henceforth.

Everything indicates—the smallest does, and the largest does,   95
A necessary film envelops all, and envelops the soul for a proper time.

8

Ah, what can ever be more stately and admirable to me than mast-
    hemm'd Manhattan?
River and sunset and scallop-edg'd waves of flood-tide?
The sea-gulls oscillating their bodies, the hay-boat in the twilight, and
    the belated lighter?   100

What gods can exceed these that clasp me by the hand, and with
    voices I love call me promptly and loudly by my nighest name as
    I approach?
What is more subtle than this which ties me to the woman or man that
    looks in my face?
Which fuses me into you now, and pours my meaning into you?

We understand, then, do we not?
What I promis'd without mentioning it, have you not accepted?   105
What the study could not teach—what the preaching could not accom-
    plish is accomplish'd, is it not?
What the hush of reading could not start is started by me personally,
    is it not?

9

Flow on, river! flow with the flood-tide, and ebb with the ebb-tide!
Frolic on, crested and scallop-edg'd waves!
Gorgeous clouds of the sunset! drench with your splendor me, or the
    men and women generations after me!   110
Cross from shore to shore, countless crowds of passengers!
Stand up, tall masts of Mannahatta! stand up, beautiful hills of
    Brooklyn!
Throb, baffled and curious brain! throw out questions and answers!
Suspend here and everywhere, eternal float of solution!
Gaze, loving and thirsting eyes, in the house or street or public
    assembly!   115
Sound out, voices of young men! loudly and musically call me by my
    nighest name!
Live, old life! play the part that looks back on the actor or actress!
Play the old rôle, the rôle that is great or small according as one
    makes it!
Consider, you who peruse me, whether I may not in unknown ways be
    looking upon you;
Be firm, rail over the river, to support those who lean idly, yet haste
    with the hasting current;   120
Fly on, sea-birds! fly sideways, or wheel in large circles high in the air;
Receive the summer sky, you water, and faithfully hold it till all down-
    cast eyes have time to take it from you!
Diverge, fine spokes of light, from the shape of my head, or any one's
    head, in the sunlit water!
Come on, ships from the lower bay! pass up or down, white-sail'd
    schooners, sloops, lighters!
Flaunt away, flags of all nations! be duly lower'd at sunset!   125

Burn high your fires, foundry chimneys! cast black shadows at nightfall!
    cast red and yellow light over the tops of the houses!
Appearances, now or henceforth, indicate what you are,
You necessary film, continue to envelop the soul,
About my body for me, and your body for you, be hung our divinest
    aromas,
Thrive, cities—bring your freight, bring your shows, ample and sufficient
    rivers,   130
Expand, being than which none else is perhaps more spiritual,
Keep your places, objects than which none else is more lasting:
We descend upon you and all things, we arrest you all,
We realize the soul only by you, you faithful solids and fluids,
Through you color, form, location, sublimity, ideality,   135
Through you every proof, comparison, and all the suggestions and
    determinations of ourselves.

You have waited, you always wait, you dumb, beautiful ministers,
We receive you with free sense at last, and are insatiate henceforward,
Not you any more shall be able to foil us, or withhold yourselves
    from us,
We use you, and do not cast you aside—we plant you permanently
    within us,   140
We fathom you not—we love you—there is perfection in you also,
You furnish your parts toward eternity,
Great or small, you furnish your parts toward the soul.   *(1856)*

From *By Blue Ontario's Shore*

. . . . .

15

I swear I begin to see the meaning of these things,
It is not the earth, it is not America, who is so great,
It is I who am great or to be great, it is You up there, or any one,
It is to walk rapidly through civilisations, governments, theories,
Through poems, pageants, shows, to form individuals.   5

Underneath all, individuals.
I swear nothing is good to me now that ignores individuals,
The American compact is altogether with individuals.
The only government is that which makes minute of individuals,

The whole theory of the universe is directed unerringly to one single
    individual—namely to You.   10

(Mother! with subtle sense severe, with naked sword in your hand,
I saw you at last refuse to treat but directly with individuals.)

. . . . .

17

O I see flashing that this America is only you and me,
Its power, weapons, testimony, are you and me,
Its crimes, lies, thefts, defections, are you and me,
Its Congress is you and me, the officers, capitols, armies, ships, are you
    and me,
Its endless gestations of new States are you and me,   5
The war (that war so bloody and grim, the war I will henceforth
    forget), was you and me,
Natural and artificial are you and me,
Freedom, language, poems, employments are you and me,
Past, present, future, are you and me.

I dare not shirk any part of myself,   10
Not any part of America good or bad,
Not to build for that which builds for mankind,
Not to balance ranks, complexions, creeds, and the sexes,
Not to justify science nor the march of equality,
Nor to feed the arrogant blood of the brawn belov'd of time.   15

I am for those that have never been master'd,
For men and women whose tempers have never been master'd,
For those whom laws, theories, conventions, can never master.

I am for those who walk abreast with the whole earth,
Who inaugurate one to inaugurate all.   20

I will not be outfaced by irrational things,
I will penetrate what it is in them that is sarcastic upon me,
I will make cities and civilisations defer to me,
That is what I have learnt from America—it is the amount, and it I
    teach again.

(Democracy, while weapons were everywhere aim'd at your breast, 25
I saw you serenely give birth to immortal children, saw in dreams your
    dilating form,
Saw you with spreading mantle covering the world.)   (1856)

Lo, Victress on the Peaks

Lo, Victress on the peaks,
Where thou with mighty brow regarding the world,
(The world, O Libertad, that vainly conspired against thee),
Out of its countless beleaguering toils, after thwarting them all,
Dominant, with the dazzling sun around thee,
Flauntest now unharm'd in immortal soundness and bloom—lo, in these
    hours supreme,
No poem proud, I chanting bring to thee, nor mastery's rapturous verse,
But a cluster containing night's darkness and blood-dripping wounds,
And psalms of the dead.   (1865)

Chanting the Square Deific

1

Chanting the square deific, out of the One advancing, out of the sides,
Out of the old and new, out of the square entirely divine,
Solid, four-sided, (all the sides needed,) from this side Jehovah am I,
Old Brahm I, and I Saturnius am;
Not Time affects me—I am Time, old, modern as any,   5
Unpersuadable, relentless, executing righteous judgments,
As the Earth, the Father, the brown old Kronos, with laws,
Aged beyond computation, yet ever new, ever with those mighty laws
    rolling,
Relentless I forgive no man—whoever sins dies—I will have that man's
    life;
Therefore let none expect mercy—have the seasons, gravitation, the ap-
    pointed days, mercy? no more have I,   10
But as the seasons and gravitation, and as all the appointed days that
    forgive not,
I dispense from this side judgments inexorable without the least remorse.

2

Consolator most mild, the promis'd one advancing,
With gentle hand extended, the mightier God am I,
Foretold by prophets and poets in their most rapt prophecies and
    poems,   15

From this side, lo, the Lord Christ gazes—lo! Hermes I—lo! mine is
    Hercules' face,
All sorrow, labor, suffering, I, tallying it, absorb in myself,
Many times have I been rejected, taunted, put in prison, and crucified,
    and many times shall be again,
All the world have I given up for my dear brothers' and sisters' sake, for
    the soul's sake,
Wending my way through the homes of men, rich or poor, with the kiss
    of affection,   20
For I am affection, I am the cheer-bringing God, with hope and all
    enclosing charity,
With indulgent words as to children, with fresh and sane words, mine
    only,
Young and strong I pass knowing well I am destin'd myself to an early
    death;
But my charity has no death—my wisdom dies now, neither early nor
    late,
And my sweet love bequeath'd here and elsewhere never dies.   25

3

Aloof, dissatisfied, plotting revolt,
Comrade of criminals, brother of slaves,
Crafty, despised, a drudge, ignorant,
With sudra face and worn brow, black, but in the depths of my heart,
    proud as any,
Lifted now and always against whoever scorning assumes to rule me, 30
Morose, full of guile, full of reminiscences, brooding, with many wiles,
(Though it was thought I was baffled and dispel'd, and my wiles done,
    but that will never be,)
Defiant, I, Satan, still live, still utter words, in new lands duly appearing,
    (and old ones also,)
Permanent here from my side, warlike, equal with any, real as any,
Nor time nor change shall ever change me or my words.   35

4

Santa Spirita, breather, life,
Beyond the light, lighter than light,
Beyond the flames of hell, joyous, leaping easily above hell,
Beyond Paradise, perfumed solely with mine own perfume,
Including all life on earth, touching, including God, including Saviour
    and Satan,   40
Ethereal, pervading all, (for without me what were all? what were
    God?)

Essence of forms, life of real identities, permanent, positive, (namely
    the unseen,)
Life of the great round world, the sun and stars and of man, I, the
    general soul,
Here the square finishing, the solid, I the most solid,
Breathe my breath also through these songs.   (*1865*)   **45**

When Lilacs Last in the Dooryard Bloom'd

1

When lilacs last in the dooryard bloom'd,
And the great star early droop'd in the western sky in the night,
I mourn'd, and yet shall mourn with ever-returning spring.

Ever-returning spring, trinity sure to me you bring,
Lilac blooming perennial and drooping star in the west,   5
And thought of him I love.

2

O powerful western fallen star!
O shades of night—O moody, tearful night!
O great star disappear'd—O the black murk that hides the star!
O cruel hands that hold me powerless—O helpless soul of me!   10
O harsh surrounding cloud that will not free my soul.

3

In the dooryard fronting an old farm-house near the whitewash'd
    palings,
Stands the lilac-bush tall-growing with heart-shaped leaves of rich green,
With many a pointed blossom rising delicate, with the perfume strong
    I love,
With every leaf a miracle—and from this bush in the dooryard,   15
With delicate-color'd blossoms and heart-shaped leaves of rich green,
A sprig with its flower I break.

4

In the swamp in secluded recesses,
A shy and hidden bird is warbling a song.

Solitary the thrush,   20
The hermit withdrawn to himself, avoiding the settlements,
Sings by himself a song.

Song of the bleeding throat,
Death's outlet song of life, (for well dear brother I know,
If thou wast not granted to sing thou would'st surely die.)   25

5

Over the breast of the spring, the land, amid cities,
Amid lanes and through old woods, where lately the violets peep'd from
     the ground, spotting the gray débris,
Amid the grass in the fields each side of the lanes, passing the endless
     grass,
Passing the yellow-spear'd wheat, every grain from its shroud in the
     dark-brown fields uprisen,
Passing the apple-tree blows of white and pink in the orchards,   30
Carrying a corpse to where it shall rest in the grave,
Night and day journeys a coffin.

6

Coffin that passes through lanes and streets,
Through day and night with the great cloud darkening the land,
With the pomp of the inloop'd flags with the cities draped in black,   35
With the show of the States themselves as of crape-veil'd women
     standing,
With processions long and winding and the flambeaus of the night,
With the countless torches lit, with the silent sea of faces and the
     unbared heads,
With the waiting depot, the arriving coffin, and the somber faces,
With dirges through the night, with the thousand voices rising strong
     and solemn,   40
With all the mournful voices of the dirges pour'd around the coffin,
The dim-lit churches and the shuddering organs—where amid these you
     journey,
With the tolling tolling bells' perpetual clang,
Here, coffin that slowly passes,
I give you my sprig of lilac.   45

7

(Nor for you, for one alone,
Blossoms and branches green to coffins all I bring,
For fresh as the morning, thus would I chant a song for you O sane and
     sacred death.

All over bouquets of roses,
O death, I cover you over with roses and early lilies,   50
But mostly and now the lilac that blooms the first,

Copious I break, I break the sprigs from the bushes,
With loaded arms I come, pouring for you,
For you and the coffins all of you O death.)

8

O western orb sailing the heaven,   55
Now I know what you must have meant as a month since I walk'd,
As I walk'd in silence the transparent shadowy night,
As I saw you had something to tell as you bent to me night after night,
As you droop'd from the sky low down as if to my side, (while the other
    stars all look'd on,)
As we wander'd together the solemn night, (for something I know not
    what kept me from sleep,)   60
As the night advanced, and I saw on the rim of the west how full you
    were of woe,
As I stood on the rising ground in the breeze in the cool transparent
    night,
As I watch'd where you pass'd and was lost in the netherward black of
    the night,
As my soul in its trouble dissatisfied sank, as where you sad orb,
Concluded, dropt in the night, and was gone.   65

9

Sing on there in the swamp,
O singer bashful and tender, I hear your notes, I hear your call,
I hear, I come presently, I understand you,
But a moment I linger, for the lustrous star has detain'd me,
The star my departing comrade holds and detains me   70

10

O how shall I warble myself for the dead one there I loved?
And how shall I deck my song for the large sweet soul that has gone?
And what shall my perfume be for the grave of him I love?

Sea-winds blown from east and west,
Blown from the Eastern sea and blown from the Western sea, till there
    on the prairies meeting,   75
These and with these and the breath of my chant,
I'll perfume the grave of him I love.

11

O what shall I hang on the chamber walls?
And what shall the pictures be that I hang on the walls,
To adorn the burial-house of him I love?   80

Pictures of growing spring and farms and homes,
With the Fourth-month eve at sundown, and the gray smoke lucid and
  bright,
With floods of the yellow gold of the gorgeous, indolent, sinking sun,
  burning, expanding the air,
With the fresh sweet herbage under foot, and the pale green leaves of
  the trees prolific,
In the distance the flowing glaze, the breast of the river, with a wind-
  dapple here and there,   85
With ranging hills on the banks, with many a line against the sky, and
  shadows,
And the city at hand, with dwellings so dense, and stacks of chimneys,
And all the scenes of life and the workshops, and the workmen homeward returning.

  12

Lo, body and soul—this land,
My own Manhattan with spires, and the sparkling and hurrying tides,
  and the ships,   90
The varied and ample land, the South and the North in the light,
  Ohio's shores and flashing Missouri,
And ever the far-spreading prairies cover'd with grass and corn.

Lo, the most excellent sun so calm and haughty,
The violet and purple morn with just-felt breezes,
The gentle soft-born measureless light,   95
The miracle spreading bathing all, the fulfill'd noon,
The coming eve delicious, the welcome night and the stars,
Over my cities shining all, enveloping man and land.

  13

Sing on, sing on you gray-brown bird,
Sing from the swamps, the recesses, pour your chant from the
  bushes,   100
Limitless out of the dusk, out of the cedars and pines.

Sing on dearest brother, warble your reedy song,
Loud human song, with voice of uttermost woe.

O liquid and free and tender!
O wild and loose to my soul—O wondrous singer!   105
You only I hear—yet the star holds me, (but will soon depart,)
Yet the lilac with mastering odor holds me.

14

Now while I sat in the day and look'd forth,
In the close of the day with its light and the fields of spring, and the
    farmers preparing their crops,
In the large unconscious scenery of my land with its lakes and
    forests,   110
In the heavenly aerial beauty, (after the perturb'd winds and the storms,)
Under the arching heavens of the afternoon swift passing, and the voices
    of children and women,
The many-moving sea-tides, and I saw the ships how they sail'd,
And the summer approaching with richness, and the fields all busy with
    labor,
And the infinite separate houses, how they all went on, each with its
    meals and minutia of daily usages,   115
And the streets how their throbbings throbb'd, and the cities pent—lo,
    then and there,
Falling upon them all and among them all, enveloping me with the rest,
Appear'd the cloud, appear'd the long black trail,
And I knew death, its thought, and the sacred knowledge of death.

Then with the knowledge of death as walking one side of me,   120
And the thought of death close-walking the other side of me,
And I in the middle as with companions, and as holding the hands of
    companions,
I fled forth to the hiding receiving night that talks not,
Down to the shores of the water, the path by the swamp in the dimness,
To the solemn shadowy cedars and ghostly pines so still.   125

And the singer so shy to the rest receiv'd me,
The gray-brown bird I know receiv'd us comrades three,
And he sang the carol of death, and a verse for him I love.

From deep secluded recesses,
From the fragrant cedars and the ghostly pines so still,   130
Came the carol of the bird.

And the charm of the carol rapt me
As I held as if by their hands my comrades in the night,
And the voice of my spirit tallied the song of the bird.

Come lovely and soothing death,   135
Undulate round the world, serenely arriving, arriving,
In the day, in the night, to all, to each,
Sooner or later delicate death.

Prais'd be the fathomless universe,
For life and joy, and for objects and knowledge curious,   140
And for love, sweet love—but praise! praise! praise!
For the sure-enwinding arms of cool-enfolding death.

Dark mother always gliding near with soft feet,
Have none chanted for thee a chant of fullest welcome?
Then I chant it for thee, I glorify thee above all,   145
I bring thee a song that when thou must indeed come, come unfalter-
    ingly.

Approach strong deliveress,
When it is so, when thou hast taken them I joyously sing the dead,
Lost in the loving floating ocean of thee,
Laved in the flood of thy bliss O death.   150

From me to thee glad serenades,
Dances for thee I propose saluting thee, adornments and feastings for
    thee,
And the sights of the open landscape and the high-spread sky are fitting,
And life and the fields, and the huge and thoughtful night.

The night in silence under many a star,   155
The ocean shore and the husky whispering wave whose voice I know,
And the soul turning to thee O vast and well-veil'd death,
And the body gratefully nestling close to thee.

Over the tree-tops I float thee a song,
Over the rising and sinking waves, over the myriad fields and the prairies
    wide,   160
Over the dense-pack'd cities all and the teeming wharves and ways,
I float this carol with joy, with joy to thee O death.

    15

To the tally of my soul,
Loud and strong kept up the gray-brown bird,
With pure deliberate notes spreading filling the night.   165

Loud in the pines and cedars dim,
Clear in the freshness moist and the swamp-perfume,
And I with my comrades there in the night.

While my sight that was bound in my eyes unclosed,
As to long panoramas of visions.   170

And I saw askant the armies,
I saw as in noiseless dreams hundreds of battle-flags,

Borne through the smoke of the battles and pierc'd with missiles I saw
   them,
And carried hither and yon through the smoke, and torn and bloody,
And at last but a few shreds left on the staffs, (and all in silence,)   175
And the staffs all splinter'd and broken.

I saw battle-corpses, myriads of them,
And the white skeletons of young men, I saw them,
I saw the débris and débris of all the slain soldiers of the war,
But I saw they were not as was thought,   180
They themselves were fully at rest, they suffer'd not,
The living remain'd and suffer'd, the mother suffer'd,
And the wife and the child and the musing comrade suffer'd,
And the armies that remain'd suffer'd.

   16

Passing the visions, passing the night,   185
Passing, unloosing the hold of my comrades' hands,
Passing the song of the hermit bird and the tallying song of my soul,
Victorious song, death's outlet song, yet varying ever-altering song,
As low and wailing, yet clear the notes, rising and falling, flooding the
   night,
Sadly sinking and fainting, as warning and warning, and yet again
   bursting with joy,   190
Covering the earth and filling the spread of the heaven,
As that powerful psalm in the night I heard from recesses,
Passing, I leave thee lilac with heart-shaped leaves,
I leave thee there in the dooryard, blooming, returning with spring.

I cease from my song for thee,   195
From my gaze on thee in the west, fronting the west, communing with
   thee,
O comrade lustrous with silver face in the night

Yet each to keep and all, retrievements out of the night,
The song, the wondrous chant of the gray-brown bird,
And the tallying chant, the echo arous'd in my soul,   200
With the lustrous and drooping star with the countenance full of woe,
With the holders holding my hand nearing the call of the bird,
Comrades mine and I in the midst, and their memory ever to keep, for
   the dead I loved so well,
For the sweetest, wisest soul of all my days and lands—and this for his
   dear sake,
Lilac and star and bird twined with the chant of my soul,   205
There in the fragrant pines and the cedars dusk and dim.   (*1865*)

A Noiseless Patient Spider

A noiseless patient spider,
I mark'd where on a little promontory it stood isolated,
Mark'd how to explore the vacant vast surrounding,
It launch'd forth filament, filament, filament, out of itself.
Ever unreeling them, ever tirelessly speeding them.   5

And you O my soul where you stand,
Surrounded, detached, in measureless oceans of space,
Ceaselessly musing, venturing, throwing, seeking the spheres to connect
     them,
Till the bridge you will need be form'd, till the ductile anchor hold,
Till the gossamer thread you fling catch somewhere, O my soul.
                                                          (1862)

By Broad Potomac's Shore

By broad Potomac's shore—again old tongue!
(Still uttering, still ejaculating, canst never cease this babble?)
Again old heart so gay, again to you, your sense, the full flush spring
     returning;
Again the freshness and the odors, again Virginia's summer sky,
     pellucid blue and silver,
Again the forenoon purple of the hills,   5
Again the deathless grass, so noiseless, soft and green,
Again the blood-red roses blooming.

Perfume this book of mine, O blood-red roses!
Lave subtly with your waters every line, Potomac!
Give me of you, O spring, before I close, to put between its pages!   10
O forenoon purple of the hills, before I close, of you!
O smiling earth—O summer sun, give me of you!
O deathless grass, of you!   (1872)

HERMAN MELVILLE (1819–1891)

The Martyr

Indicative of the Passion of the People on the 15th Day of April, 1865

Good Friday was the day
  Of the prodigy and crime,
When they killed him in his pity,
  When they killed him in his prime
Of clemency and calm—   5
    When with yearning he was filled
    To redeem the evil-willed,
And, though conqueror, be kind;
  But they killed him in his kindness,
  In their madness and their blindness,   10
And they killed him from behind.

    There is sobbing of the strong,
      And a pall upon the land;
    But the People in their weeping
      Bare the iron hand: 15
    Beware the People weeping
      When they bare the iron hand.

He lieth in his blood—
  The father in his face;
They have killed him, the Forgiver—   20
  The Avenger takes his place,
The Avenger wisely stern,
    Who in righteousness shall do
    What the heavens call him to,
And the parricides remand;   25
  For they killed him in his kindness,
  In their madness and their blindness,
And his blood is on their hand.

    There is sobbing of the strong,
      And a pall upon the land;   30
    But the People in their weeping
      Bare the iron hand:
    Beware the People weeping
      When they bare the iron hand.   (1866)

The March into Virginia

Ending in the First Manassas, July 1861

Did all the lets and bars appear
    To every just or larger end,
Whence should come the trust and cheer?
    Youth must its ignorant impulse lend—
Age finds place in the rear.   5
    All wars are boyish, and are fought by boys,
The champions and enthusiasts of the state:
    Turbid ardors and vain joys
        Not barrenly abate—
    Stimulants to the power mature,   10
        Preparatives of fate.

Who here forecasteth the event?
What heart but spurns at precedent
And warnings of the wise,
Contemned foreclosures of surprise?   15
The banners play, the bugles call,
The air is blue and prodigal.
    No berrying party, pleasure-wooed,
No picnic party in the May,
Ever went less loth than they   20
    Into that leafy neighborhood.
In Bacchic glee they file toward Fate,
Moloch's uninitiate;
Expectancy, and glad surmise
Of battle's unknown mysteries.   25
All they feel is this: 'tis glory,
A rapture sharp, though transitory,
Yet lasting in belaureled story.
So they gaily go to fight,
Chatting left and laughing right.   30

But some who this blithe mood present,
    As on in lightsome files they fare,
Shall die experienced ere three days are spent—
    Perish, enlightened by the volleyed glare;
Or shame survive, and like to adamant,   35
    The throe of Second Manassas share.   (1866)

Monody

To have known him,[1] to have loved him
    After loneness long;
And then to be estranged in life,
    And neither in the wrong;
And now for death to set his seal—   5
    Ease me, a little ease, my song!

By wintry hills his hermit-mound
    The sheeted snow-drifts drape,
And houseless there the snow-bird flits
    Beneath the fir-trees' crape: 10
Glazed now with ice the cloistral vine
    That hid the shyest grape.   (1891)

Art

In placid hours well-pleased we dream
Of many a brave unbodied scheme.
But form to lend, pulsed life create,
What unlike things must meet and mate:
A flame to melt—a wind to freeze;   5
Sad patience—joyous energies;
Humility—yet pride and scorn;
Instinct and study; love and hate;
Audacity—reverence. These must mate
And fuse with Jacob's mystic heart,   10
To wrestle with the angel—Art.   (1891)

---

[1] Nathaniel Hawthorne

FREDERICK GODDARD TUCKERMAN
(1821–1873)

Sonnets

I:1

Sometimes, when winding slow by brook and bower,
Beating the idle grass,—of what avail,
I ask, are these dim fancies, cares, and fears?
What though from every bank I drew a flower,—
Bloodroot, king-orchis, or the pearlwort pale,—
And set it in my verse with thoughtful tears?
What would it count, though I should sing my death,
And muse and mourn with as poetic breath
As, in damp garden-walks, the autumn gale
Sighs o'er the fallen floriage? What avail
Is the swan's voice, if all the hearers fail,
Or his great flight, that no eye gathereth,
In the blending blue? And yet, depending so,
God were not God, whom knowledge cannot know.

I:4

Nor looks that backward life so bare to me,
My later youth, and ways I've wandered through;
But touched with innocent grace,—the early bee
On the maple log, the white-heaped cherry tree
That hummed all day in the sun, the April blue!
Yet hardly now one ray the Forward hath
To show where sorrow rests, and rest begins;
Although I check my feet, nor walk to wrath
Through days of crime, and grosser shadowings
Of evil done in the dark; but fearfully,
'Mid unfulfilled yet unrelinquished sins
That hedge me in, and press about my path,
Like purple-poison flowers of stramony,
With their dull opiate-breath, and dragon-wings.

I:5

And so the day drops by; the horizon draws
The fading sun, and we stand struck in grief;
Failing to find our haven of relief,—
Wide of the way, nor sure to turn or pause;
And weep to view how fast the splendour wanes,
And scarcely heed, that yet some share remains
Of the red after-light, some time to mark,
Some space between the sundown and the dark.
But not for him those golden calms succeed,
Who, while the day is high and glory reigns,
Sees it go by,—as the dim Pampas plain,
Hoary with salt, and gray with bitter weed,
Sees the vault blacken, feels the dark wind strain,
Hears the dry thunder roll, and knows no rain.

I:17

All men,—the preacher saith,—whate'er or whence
Their increase, walking through this world has been;
Both those that gather out, or after-glean,
Or hold in simple fee of harvests dense;
Or but perhaps a flowerless barren green,
Barren with spots of sorrel, knot-grass, spurge:—
See to one end their differing paths converge,
And all must render answer, here or hence.
"Lo, Death is at the doors," he crieth, "with blows!"
But what to him unto whose feverish sense
The stars tick audibly, and the wind's low surge
In the pine, attended, tolls, and throngs, and grows
On the dread ear,—a thunder too profound
For bearing,—a Niagara of sound!   (1860)

✒ MATTHEW ARNOLD (1822–1888)

Quiet Work

One lesson, Nature, let me learn of thee,
One lesson which in every wind is blown,
One lesson of two duties kept at one
Though the loud world proclaim their enmity—
Of toil unsevered from tranquillity!
Of labor, that in lasting fruit outgrows
Far noisier schemes, accomplished in repose,
Too great for haste, too high for rivalry!

Yes, while on earth a thousand discords ring,
Man's fitful uproar mingling with his toil,
Still do thy sleepless ministers move on,
Their glorious tasks in silence perfecting;
Still working, blaming still our vain turmoil,
Laborers that shall not fail, when man is gone.   (1849)

Shakespeare

Others abide our question. Thou art free.
We ask and ask—Thou smilest and art still,
Out-topping knowledge. For the loftiest hill,
Who to the stars uncrowns his majesty,
Planting his steadfast footsteps in the sea,
Making the heaven of heavens his dwelling-place,
Spares but the cloudy border of his base
To the foiled searching of mortality;
And thou, who didst the stars and sunbeams know,
Self-schooled, self-scanned, self-honored, self-secure,
Didst tread on earth unguessed at.—Better so!
All pains the immortal spirit must endure,
All weakness which impairs, all griefs which bow,
Find their sole speech in that victorious brow.   (1849)

In Harmony with Nature

TO A PREACHER

"In harmony with nature?" Restless fool,
Who with such heat dost preach what were to thee,
When true, the last impossibility—
To be like Nature strong, like Nature cool!
Know, man hath all which Nature hath, but more,
And in that *more* lie all his hopes of good.
Nature is cruel, man is sick of blood;
Nature is stubborn, man would fain adore;
Nature is fickle, man hath need of rest;
Nature forgives no debt, and fears no grave;
Man would be mild, and with safe conscience blest.
Man must begin, know this, where Nature ends;
Nature and man can never be fast friends.
Fool, if thou canst not pass her, rest her slave!   (*1849*)

Self-Dependence

Weary of myself, and sick of asking
What I am, and what I ought to be,
At this vessel's prow I stand, which bears me
Forward, forward, o'er the starlit sea.

And a look of passionate desire   5
O'er the sea and to the stars I send:
"Ye who from my childhood up have calmed me,
Calm me, ah, compose me to the end!

"Ah, once more," I cried, "ye stars, ye waters,
On my heart your mighty charm renew;   10
Still, still let me, as I gaze upon you,
Feel my soul becoming vast like you!"

From the intense, clear, star-sown vault of heaven,
Over the lit sea's unquiet way,
In the rustling night-air came the answer: 15
"Wouldst thou *be* as these are? *Live* as they.

"Unaffrighted by the silence round them,
Undistracted by the sights they see,
These demand not that the things without them
Yield them love, amusement, sympathy.   20

"And with joy the stars perform their shining,
And the sea its long, moon-silvered roll;
For self-poised they live, nor pine with noting
All the fever of some differing soul.

"Bounded by themselves, and unregardful,   25
In what state God's other works may be,
In their own tasks all their powers pouring,
These attain the mighty life you see."

O air-born voice! long since, severely clear,
A cry like thine in mine own heart I hear: 30
"Resolve to be thyself; and know that he,
Who finds himself, loses his misery!"   (1852)

Philomela

Hark! ah, the nightingale—
The tawny-throated!
Hark, from that moonlit cedar what a burst!
What triumph! hark!—what pain!

O wanderer from a Grecian shore,   5
Still, after many years, in distant lands,
Still nourishing in thy bewildered brain
That wild, unquenched, deep-sunken, old-world pain—
        Say, will it never heal?
And can this fragrant lawn   10
With its cool trees, and night,
And the sweet, tranquil Thames,
And moonshine, and the dew,
To thy racked heart and brain
        Afford no balm?   15

        Dost thou to-night behold
Here, through the moonlight on this English grass,
The unfriendly palace in the Thracian wild?

> Dost thou again peruse
> With hot cheeks and seared eyes   20
> The too clear web, and thy dumb sister's shame?
>   Dost thou once more assay
> Thy flight, and feel come over thee,
> Poor fugitive, the feathery change
> Once more, and once more seem to make resound   25
> With love and hate, triumph and agony,
> Lone Daulis,[1] and the high Cephissian [2] vale?
>   Listen, Eugenia [3]—
> How thick the bursts come crowding through the leaves!
>   Again—thou hearest?   30
> Eternal passion!
> Eternal pain!   (1853)

Dover Beach

> The sea is calm tonight,
> The tide is full, the moon lies fair
> Upon the straits;—on the French coast the light
> Gleams and is gone; the cliffs of England stand,
> Glimmering and vast, out in the tranquil bay.   5
> Come to the window, sweet is the night-air!
>
> Only, from the long line of spray
> Where the sea meets the moon-blanched land,
> Listen! you hear the grating roar
> Of pebbles which the waves draw back, and fling,   10
> At their return, up the high strand,
> Begin, and cease, and then again begin,
> With tremulous cadence slow, and bring
> The eternal note of sadness in.
>
> Sophocles long ago   15
> Heard it on the Aegean, and it brought
> Into his mind the turbid ebb and flow
> Of human misery; we
> Find also in the sound a thought,
> Hearing it by this distant northern sea.   20

[1] in Phocis, Greece, where Philomela was changed into a nightingale   [2] Cephissus is a river in Phocis.   [3] an imaginary person

The Sea of Faith
Was once, too, at the full, and round earth's shore
Lay like the folds of a bright girdle furled.
But now I only hear
Its melancholy, long, withdrawing roar,   25
Retreating, to the breath
Of the night-wind, down the vast edges drear
And naked shingles of the world.

Ah, love, let us be true
To one another! for the world, which seems   30
To lie before us like a land of dreams,
So various, so beautiful, so new,
Hath really neither joy, nor love, nor light,
Nor certitude, nor peace, nor help for pain;
And we are here as on a darkling plain   35
Swept with confused alarms of struggle and flight,
Where ignorant armies clash by night.   (1867)

GEORGE MEREDITH (1828–1909)

From *Modern Love*

. . . . .

13

"I play for Seasons: not Eternities!"
Says Nature, laughing on her way. "So must
All those whose stake is nothing more than dust!"
And lo, she wins, and of her harmonies
She is full sure! Upon her dying rose   5
She drops a look of fondness, and goes by,
Scarce any retrospection in her eye;
For she the laws of growth most deeply knows,
Whose hands bear, here, a seed-bag—there, an urn.
Pledged she herself to aught, 'twould mark her end!   10
This lesson of our only visible friend
Can we not teach our foolish hearts to learn?
Yes! yes!—but, oh, our human rose is fair
Surpassingly! Lose calmly Love's great bliss,
When the renewed for ever of a kiss   15
Whirls life within the shower of loosened hair!

. . . . .

50

Thus piteously Love closed what he begat:
The union of this ever-diverse pair!
These two were rapid falcons in a snare,
Condemned to do the flitting of the bat.
Lovers beneath the singing sky of May,   5
They wandered once; clear as the dew on flowers:
But they fed not on the advancing hours:
Their hearts held cravings for the buried day.
Then each applied to each that fatal knife,
Deep questioning, which probes to endless dole.   10
Ah, what a dusty answer gets the soul
When hot for certainties in this our life!—
In tragic hints here see what evermore,
Moves dark as yonder midnight ocean's force,
Thundering like ramping hosts of warrior horse,   15
To throw that faint thin line upon the shore!   (*1862*)

437

Lucifer in Starlight

On a starred night Prince Lucifer uprose.
Tired of his dark dominion swung the fiend
Above the rolling ball in cloud part screened,
Where sinners hugged their specter of repose.
Poor prey to his hot fit of pride were those.
And now upon his western wing he leaned,
Now his huge bulk o'er Afric's sands careened,
Now the black planet shadowed Arctic snows.
Soaring through wider zones that pricked his scars
With memory of the old revolt from Awe,
He reached a middle height, and at the stars,
Which are the brain of heaven, he looked, and sank.
Around the ancient track marched, rank on rank,
The army of unalterable law.   (*1883*)

Nature and Life

Leave the uproar! At a leap
Thou shalt strike a woodland path,
Enter silence, not of sleep,
Under shadows, not of wrath;
Breath which is the spirit's bath,   5
In the old Beginnings find,
And endow them with a mind,
Seed for seedling, swathe for swathe.
That gives Nature to us, this
Give we her, and so we kiss   10

Fruitful is it so—but hear
How within the shell thou art,
Music sounds; nor other near
Can to such a tremor start.
Of the waves our life is part;   15
They our running harvests bear—
Back to them for manful air,
Laden with the woodland's heart!
That gives Battle to us, this
Give we it, and good the kiss.   (*1888*)

DANTE GABRIEL ROSSETTI (1828–1882)

The Blessed Damozel

The blessed damozel leaned out
    From the gold bar of heaven;
Her eyes were deeper than the depth
    Of waters stilled at even;
She had three lilies in her hand,   5
    And the stars in her hair were seven.

Her robe, ungirt from clasp to hem,
    No wrought flowers did adorn,
But a white rose of Mary's gift,
    For service meetly worn;   10
Her hair that lay along her back
    Was yellow like ripe corn.

Herseemed she scarce had been a day
    One of God's choristers;
The wonder was not yet quite gone   15
    From that still look of hers;
Albeit, to them she left, her day
    Had counted as ten years.

(To one, it is ten years of years.
    . . . Yet now, and in this place,   20
Surely she leaned o'er me—her hair
    Fell all about my face. . . .
Nothing: the autumn fall of leaves.
  The whole year sets apace.)

It was the rampart of God's house   25
    That she was standing on;
By God built over the sheer depth
    The which is Space begun;
So high, that looking downward thence
    She scarce could see the sun.   30

It lies in heaven, across the flood
    Of ether, as a bridge.
Beneath the tides of day and night
    With flame and darkness ridge

The void, as low as where this earth 35
　　Spins like a fretful midge.

Around her, lovers, newly met
　　'Mid deathless love's acclaims,
Spoke evermore among themselves
　　Their heart-remembered names; 40
And the souls mounting up to God
　　Went by her like thin flames.

And still she bowed herself and stooped
　　Out of the circling charm;
Until her bosom must have made 45
　　The bar she leaned on warm,
And the lilies lay as if asleep
　　Along her bended arm.

From the fixed place of heaven she saw
　　Time like a pulse shake fierce 50
Through all the worlds. Her gaze still strove
　　Within the gulf to pierce
Its path; and now she spoke as when
　　The stars sang in their spheres.

The sun was gone now; the curled moon 55
　　Was like a little feather
Fluttering far down the gulf; and now
　　She spoke through the still weather.
Her voice was like the voice the stars
　　Had when they sang together. 60

(Ah sweet! Even now, in that bird's song,
　　Strove not her accents there,
Fain to be hearkened? When those bells
　　Possessed the mid-day air,
Strove not her steps to reach my side 65
　　Down all the echoing stair?)

"I wish that he were come to me,
　　For he will come," she said.
"Have I not prayed in Heaven?—on earth,
　　Lord, Lord, has he not prayed? 70
Are not two prayers a perfect strength?
　　And shall I feel afraid?

"When round his head the aureole clings,
　　And he is clothed in white,

I'll take his hand and go with him   75
    To the deep wells of light;
As unto a stream we will step down,
    And bathe there in God's sight.

"We two will stand beside that shrine,
    Occult, withheld, untrod,   80
Whose lamps are stirred continually
    With prayer sent up to God;
And see our old prayers, granted, melt
    Each like a little cloud.

"We two will lie i' the shadow of   85
    That living mystic tree [1]
Within whose secret growth the Dove
    Is sometimes felt to be,
While every leaf that His plumes touch
    Saith His Name audibly.   90

"And I myself will teach to him,
    I myself, lying so,
The songs I sing here; which his voice
    Shall pause in, hushed and slow.
And find some knowledge at each pause,   95
    Or some new thing to know."

(Alas! We two, we two, thou say'st!
    Yea, one wast thou with me
That once of old. But shall God lift
    To endless unity   100
The soul whose likeness with thy soul
    Was but its love for thee?)

"We two," she said, "will seek the groves
    Where the lady Mary is,
With her five handmaidens, whose names   105
    Are five sweet symphonies,
Cecily, Gertrude, Magdalen,
    Margaret and Rosalys. [2]

"Circlewise sit they, with bound locks
    And foreheads garlanded;   110
Into the fine cloth white like flame
    Weaving the golden thread,

[1] Revelation 22:2   [2] Christian saints

To fashion the birth-robes for them
    Who are just born, being dead.

"He shall fear, haply, and be dumb: 115
    Then will I lay my cheek
To his, and tell about our love,
    Not once abashed or weak:
And the dear Mother will approve
    My pride, and let me speak.   120

"Herself shall bring us, hand in hand,
    To Him round whom all souls
Kneel, the clear-ranged unnumbered heads
    Bowed with their aureoles:
And angels meeting us shall sing   125
    To their citherns and citoles.

"There will I ask of Christ the Lord
    Thus much for him and me:—
Only to live as once on earth
    With Love, only to be,   130
As then awhile, for ever now
    Together, I and he."

She gazed and listened and then said,
    Less sad of speech than mild:—
"All this is when he comes." She ceased.   135
    The light thrilled towards her, filled
With angels in strong level flight.
    Her eyes prayed, and she smiled.

(I saw her smile.) But soon their path
    Was vague in distant spheres: 140
And then she cast her arms along
    The golden barriers,
And laid her face between her hands,
    And wept. (I heard her tears.)   (*1850*)

The Woodspurge

The wind flapped loose, the wind was still,
Shaken out dead from tree and hill:
I had walked on at the wind's will,—
I sat now, for the wind was still.

Between my knees my forehead was,—   5
My lips, drawn in, said not Alas!
My hair was over in the grass,
My naked ears heard the day pass.

My eyes, wide open, had the run
Of some ten weeds to fix upon;   10
Among those few, out of the sun,
The woodspurge flowered, three cups in one.

From perfect grief there need not be
Wisdom or even memory:
One thing then learnt remains to me,—   15
The woodspurge has a cup of three.   (*1870*)

EMILY DICKINSON (1830–1886)

Success Is Counted Sweetest

Success is counted sweetest
By those who ne'er succeed.
To comprehend a nectar
Requires sorest need.

Not one of all the purple Host
Who took the Flag today
Can tell the definition
So clear of Victory

As he defeated—dying—
On whose forbidden ear
The distant strains of triumph
Burst agonized and clear!   (c. 1859 [1])

These Are the Days when Birds Come Back

These are the days when Birds come back—
A very few—a Bird or two—
To take a backward look.

These are the days when skies resume
The old—old sophistries of June—   5
A blue and gold mistake.

Oh fraud that cannot cheat the Bee—
Almost thy plausibility
Induces my belief.

Till ranks of seeds their witness bear—   10
And softly thro' the altered air
Hurries a timid leaf.

[1] The dates are those given by Thomas H. Johnson in *The Poems of Emily Dickinson,* The Belknap Press of Harvard University, with this qualification (p. lxi): "The poems have been given a chronological arrangement even though at best it is but an approximation. Since very few poems can be given exact dates, any chronology must be considered relative." Each poem, in form, is that given in the same edition.

Oh Sacrament of summer days,
Oh Last Communion in the Haze—
Permit a child to join.   15

Thy sacred emblems to partake—
Thy consecrated bread to take
And thine immortal wine!   (c. 1859)

Wild Nights—Wild Nights

Wild Nights—Wild Nights!
Were I with thee
Wild Nights should be
Our luxury!

Futile—the Winds—
To a Heart in port—
Done with the Compass—
Done with the Chart!

Rowing in Eden—
Ah, the Sea!
Might I but moor—Tonight—
In Thee!   (c. 1861)

After Great Pain

After great pain, a formal feeling comes—
The Nerves sit ceremonious, like Tombs—
The stiff Heart questions was it He, that bore,
And Yesterday, or Centuries before?

The Feet, mechanical, go round—   5
Of Ground, or Air, or Ought—
A wooden way
Regardless grown,
A Quartz contentment, like a stone—

This is the Hour of Lead—   10
Remembered, if outlived,
As Freezing persons, recollect the Snow—
First—Chill—then Stupor—then the letting go—   (1862)

The Heart Asks Pleasure First

The Heart asks Pleasure—first—
And then—Excuse from Pain—
And then—those little Anodynes
That deaden suffering—

And then—to go to sleep—
And then—if it should be
The will of it's Inquisitor
The privilege to die—   (c. 1862)

I Heard a Fly Buzz

I heard a Fly buzz—when I died—
The Stillness in the Room
Was like the Stillness in the Air—
Between the Heaves of Storm—

The Eyes around—had wrung them dry—   5
And Breaths were gathering firm
For that last Onset—when the King
Be witnessed—in the Room—

I willed my Keepsakes—Signed away
What portion of me be   10
Assignable—and then it was
There interposed a Fly—

With Blue—uncertain stumbling Buzz—
Between the light—and me—
And then the Windows failed—and then   15
I could not see to see—   (c. 1862)

The Soul Selects Her Own Society

The Soul selects her own Society—
Then—shuts the Door—
To her divine Majority—
Present no more—

Unmoved—she notes the Chariots—pausing—
At her low Gate—
Unmoved—an Emperor be kneeling
Upon her Mat—

I've known her—from an ample nation—
Choose One—
Then—close the Valves of her attention—
Like Stone—   (*c. 1862*)

I Cannot Live with You

I cannot live with You—
It would be Life—
And Life is over there—
Behind the Shelf

The Sexton keeps the Key to—   5
Putting up
Our Life—His Porcelain—
Like a Cup—

Discarded of the Housewife—
Quaint—or Broke—   10
A newer Sevres pleases—
Old Ones crack—

I could not die—with You—
For One must wait
To shut the Other's Gaze down—   15
You—could not—

And I—Could I stand by
And see You—freeze—
Without my Right of Frost—
Death's privilege?   20

Nor could I rise—with You—
Because Your Face
Would put out Jesus'—
That New Grace

Glow plain—and foreign   25
On my homesick Eye—
Except that You than He
Shone closer by—

They'd judge Us—How—
For You—served Heaven—You know,   30
Or sought to—
I could not—

Because You saturated Sight—
And I had no more Eyes
For sordid excellence   35
As Paradise

And were You lost, I would be—
Though My Name
Rang loudest
On the Heavenly fame—   40

And were You—saved—
And I—condemned to be
Where You were not—
That self—were Hell to Me—

So We must meet apart—   45
You there—I—here—
With just the Door ajar
That Oceans are—and Prayer—
And that White Sustenance—
Despair—   (c. 1862)

My Period Had Come for Prayer

My period had come for Prayer—
No other Art—would do—
My Tactics missed a rudiment—
Creator—Was it you?

God grows above—so those who pray   5
Horizons—must ascend—
And so I stepped upon the North
To see this Curious Friend—

His House was not—no sign had He—
By Chimney—nor by Door   10
Could I infer his Residence—
Vast Prairies of Air

Unbroken by a Settler—
Were all that I could see—
Infinitude—Had'st Thou no Face   15
That I might look on Thee?

The Silence condescended—
Creation stopped—for Me—
But awed beyond my errand—
I worshipped—did not "pray"—   (c. 1862)

Heaven Has Different Signs to Me

"Heaven" has different Signs—to me—
Sometimes, I think that Noon
Is but a symbol of the Place—
And when again, at Dawn,

A mighty look runs round the World   5
And settles in the Hills—
An Awe if it should be like that
Upon the Ignorance steals—

The Orchard, when the Sun is on—
The Triumph of the Birds   10
When they together Victory make—
Some Carnivals of Clouds—

The Rapture of a finished Day—
Returning to the West—
All these—remind us of the place   15
That Men call "Paradise"—

Itself be fairer—we suppose—
But how Ourself, shall be
Adorned, for a Superior Grace—
Not yet, our eyes can see—   (c. 1862)

Because I Could Not Stop for Death

Because I could not stop for Death—
He kindly stopped for me—
The Carriage held but just Ourselves—
And Immortality.

We slowly drove—He knew no haste   5
And I had put away
My labor and my leisure too,
For His Civility—

We passed the School, where Children strove
At Recess—in the Ring—   10
We passed the Fields of Gazing Grain—
We passed the Setting Sun—

Or rather—He passed Us—
The Dews drew quivering and chill—
For only Gossamer, my Gown—   15
My Tippet—only Tulle—

We paused before a House that seemed
A Swelling of the Ground—
The Roof was scarcely visible—
The Cornice—in the Ground—   20

Since then—'tis Centuries—and yet
Feels shorter than the Day
I first surmised the Horses Heads
Were toward Eternity—   (c. 1863)

One and One—Are One

One and One—are One—
Two—be finished using—
Well enough for Schools—
But for Minor Choosing—

Life—just—Or Death—
Or the Everlasting—
More—would be too vast
For the Soul's Comprising—   (c. 1863)

A Narrow Fellow in the Grass

A narrow Fellow in the Grass
Occasionally rides—
You may have met Him—did you not
His notice sudden is—

The Grass divides as with a Comb— 5
A spotted shaft is seen—
And then it closes at your feet
And opens further on—

He likes a Boggy Acre
A Floor too cool for Corn— 10
Yet when a Boy, and Barefoot—
I more than once at Noon
Have passed, I thought, a Whip lash
Unbraiding in the Sun
When stooping to secure it 15
It wrinkled, and was gone—

Several of Nature's People
I know, and they know me—
I feel for them a transport
Of cordiality— 20

But never met this Fellow
Attended, or alone
Without a tighter breathing
And Zero at the Bone—   (*1865*)

"Heavenly Father"—Take to Thee

"Heavenly Father"—take to thee
The supreme iniquity
Fashioned by thy candid Hand
In a moment contraband—
Though to trust us—seem to us
More respectful—"We are Dust"—
We apologize to thee
For thine own Duplicity—   (*c. 1879*)

Elysium Is as Far

Elysium is as far as to
The very nearest Room
If in that Room a Friend await
Felicity or Doom—

What fortitude the Soul contains,
That it can so endure
The accent of a coming Foot—
The opening of a Door—   (c. 1882)

There Came a Wind Like a Bugle

There came a Wind like a Bugle—
It quivered through the Grass
And a Green Chill upon the Heat
So ominous did pass
We barred the Windows and the Doors   5
As from an Emerald Ghost—
The Doom's electric Moccasin
That very instant passed—
On a strange Mob of panting Trees
And Fences fled away   10
And Rivers where the Houses ran
Those looked that lived—that Day—
The Bell within the steeple wild
The flying tidings told—
How much can come   15
And much can go,
And yet abide the World!   (c. 1883)

❧ LEWIS CARROLL [1] (1832–1898)

Jabberwocky

'Twas brillig, and the slithy toves
    Did gyre and gimble in the wabe:
All mimsy were the borogoves,
    And the mome raths outgrabe.

"Beware the Jabberwock, my son!   5
    The jaws that bite, the claws that catch!
Beware the Jubjub bird, and shun
    The frumious Bandersnatch!"

He took his vorpal sword in hand;
    Long time the manxome foe he sought—   10
So rested he by the Tumtum tree,
    And stood awhile in thought.

And, as in uffish thought he stood,
    The Jabberwock, with eyes of flame,
Came whiffling through the tulgey wood,   15
    And burbled as it came!

One, two! One, two! And through and through
    The vorpal blade went snicker-snack!
He left it dead, and with its head
    He went galumphing back.   20

"And hast thou slain the Jabberwock?
    Come to my arms, my beamish boy!
O frabjous day! Callooh, Callay!"
    He chortled in his joy.

'Twas brillig, and the slithy toves   25
    Did gyre and gimble in the wabe:
All mimsy were the borogoves,
    And the mome raths outgrabe.   *(1871)*

[1] Charles Lutwidge Dodgson

453

WILLIAM MORRIS (1834–1896)

Two Red Roses Across the Moon

There was a lady lived in a hall,
Large of her eyes and slim and tall;
And ever she sung from noon to noon,
Two red roses across the moon.

There was a knight came riding by   5
In early spring, when the roads were dry;
And he heard that lady sing at the noon,
Two red roses across the moon.

Yet none the more he stopped at all,
But he rode a-gallop past the hall;   10
And left that lady singing at noon,
Two red roses across the moon.

Because, forsooth, the battle was set,
And the scarlet and blue had got to be met,
He rode on the spur till the next warm noon;   15
Two red roses across the moon.

But the battle was scattered from hill to hill,
From the windmill to the watermill;
And he said to himself, as it neared the noon,
Two red roses across the moon.   20

You scarce could see for the scarlet and blue,
A golden helm or a golden shoe;
So he cried, as the fight grew thick at the noon,
Two red roses across the moon!

Verily then the gold bore through   25
The huddled spears of the scarlet and blue;
And they cried, as they cut them down at the noon,
Two red roses across the moon!

I trow he stopped when he rode again
By the hall, though draggled sore with the rain;   30
And his lips were pinched to kiss at the noon
Two red roses across the moon!

Under the may she stooped to the crown;
All was gold, there was nothing of brown,
And the horns blew up in the hall at noon,   35
Two red roses across the moon.   (1858)

From *The Earthly Paradise*

An Apology

Of Heaven or Hell I have no power to sing;
I cannot ease the burden of your fears,
Or make quick-coming death a little thing,
Or bring again the pleasure of past years,
Nor for my words shall ye forget your tears,   5
Or hope again for aught that I can say,—
The idle singer of an empty day.

But rather when, aweary of your mirth,
From full hearts still unsatisfied ye sigh,
And, feeling kindly unto all the earth,   10
Grudge every minute as it passes by,
Made the more mindful that the sweet days die:
Remember me a little then, I pray,—
The idle singer of an empty day.

The heavy trouble, the bewildering care   15
That weighs us down who live and earn our bread,
These idle verses have no power to bear;
So let me sing of names rememberéd,
Because they, living not, can ne'er be dead,
Or long time take their memory quite away   20
From us poor singers of an empty day.

Dreamer of dreams, born out of my due time,
Why should I strive to set the crooked straight?
Let it suffice me that my murmuring rhyme
Beats with light wing against the ivory gate,—   25
Telling a tale not too importunate
To those who in the sleepy region stay,
Lulled by the singer of an empty day.

Folk say, a wizard to a northern king
At Christmas-tide such wondrous things did show,   30

That through one window men beheld the spring,
And through another saw the summer glow,
And through a third the fruited vines a-row,—
While still, unheard, but on its wonted way,
Piped the drear wind of that December day.   35

So with this Earthly Paradise it is,
If ye will read aright, and pardon me,
Who strive to build a shadowy isle of bliss
Midmost the beating of the steely sea,
Where tossed about all hearts of men must be;   40
Whose ravening monsters mighty men shall slay—
Not the poor singer of an empty day.   (*1868–1870*)

ALGERNON CHARLES SWINBURNE
(1837–1909)

From *Atalanta in Calydon*

CHORUS

When the hounds of spring are on winter's traces,
    The mother of months [1] in meadow or plain
Fills the shadows and windy places
    With lisp of leaves and ripple of rain;
And the brown bright nightingale amorous   5
Is half assuaged for Itylus,[2]
For the Thracian ships and the foreign faces,
    The tongueless vigil, and all the pain.

Come with bows bent and with emptying of quivers,
    Maiden most perfect, lady of light,   10
With a noise of winds and many rivers,
    With a clamor of waters, and with might;
Bind on thy sandals, O thou most fleet,
Over the splendor and speed of thy feet;
For the faint east quickens, the wan west shivers,   15
    Round the feet of the day and the feet of the night.

Where shall we find her, how shall we sing to her,
    Fold our hands round her knees, and cling?
Oh, that man's heart were as fire and could spring to her,
    Fire, or the strength of the streams that spring!   20
For the stars and the winds are unto her
As raiment, as songs of the harp-player;
For the risen stars and the fallen cling to her,
    And the southwest wind and the west wind sing.

For winter's rains and ruins are over,   25
    And all the season of snows and sins;
The days dividing lover and lover,
    The light that loses, the night that wins;
And time remembered is grief forgotten,

---

[1] Artemis   [2] son of Procne, whom she
killed and served to his father, Tereus

And frosts are slain and flowers begotten,   30
And in green underwood and cover
   Blossom by blossom the spring begins.

The full streams feed on flower of rushes,
   Ripe grasses trammel a traveling foot,
The faint, fresh flame of the young year flushes   35
   From leaf to flower and flower to fruit;
And fruit and leaf are as gold and fire,
And the oat is heard above the lyre,
And the hoofèd heel of a satyr crushes
   The chestnut-husk at the chestnut-root.   40

And Pan by noon and Bacchus by night,
   Fleeter of foot than the fleet-foot kid,
Follows with dancing and fills with delight
   The Maenad and the Bassarid; [3]
And soft as lips that laugh and hide,   45
The laughing leaves of the trees divide,
And screen from seeing and leave in sight
   The god pursuing, the maiden hid.

The ivy falls with the Bacchanal's hair
   Over her eyebrows hiding her eyes;   50
The wild vine slipping down leaves bare
   Her bright breast shortening into sighs;
The wild vine slips with the weight of its leaves,
But the berried ivy catches and cleaves
To the limbs that glitter, the feet that scare   55
   The wolf that follows, the fawn that flies.   (*1865*)

The Garden of Proserpine

   Here, where the world is quiet,
      Here, where all trouble seems
   Dead winds' and spent waves' riot
      In doubtful dreams of dreams;
   I watch the green field growing   5
   For reaping folk and sowing,
   For harvest-time and mowing,
      A sleepy world of streams.

[3] a worshipper of Bacchus

I am tired of tears and laughter,
    And men that laugh and weep;   10
Of what may come hereafter
    For men that sow to reap:
I am weary of days and hours,
Blown buds of barren flowers,
Desires and dreams and powers   15
    And everything but sleep.

Here life has death for neighbor,
    And far from eye or ear
Wan waves and wet winds labor.
    Weak ships and spirits steer;   20
They drive adrift, and whither
They wot not who make thither;
But no such winds blow hither,
    And no such things grow here.

No growth of moor or coppice,   25
    No heather-flower or vine,
But bloomless buds of poppies,
    Green grapes of Proserpine,
Pale beds of blowing rushes,
Where no leaf blooms or blushes   30
Save this whereout she crushes
    For dead men deadly wine.

Pale, without name or number,
    In fruitless fields of corn,
They bow themselves and slumber   35
    All night till light is born;
And like a soul belated,
In hell and heaven unmated,
By cloud and mist abated
    Comes out of darkness morn.   40

Though one were strong as seven,
    He too with death shall dwell,
Nor wake with wings in heaven,
    Nor weep for pains in hell;
Though one were fair as roses,   45
His beauty clouds and closes;
And well though love reposes,
    In the end it is not well.

Pale, beyond porch and portal,
    Crowned with calm leaves, she stands   50
Who gathers all things mortal
    With cold immortal hands;
Her languid lips are sweeter
Than love's who fears to greet her,
To men that mix and meet her   55
    From many times and lands.

She waits for each and other,
    She waits for all men born;
Forgets the earth her mother,
    The life of fruits and corn;   60
And spring and seed and swallow
Take wing for her and follow
Where summer song rings hollow
    And flowers are put to scorn.

There go the loves that wither,   65
    The old loves with wearier wings;
And all dead years draw thither,
    And all disastrous things;
Dead dreams of days forsaken,
Blind buds that snows have shaken,   70
Wild leaves that winds have taken,
    Red strays of ruined springs.

We are not sure of sorrow;
    And joy was never sure;
To-day will die to-morrow;   75
Time stoops to no man's lure;
And love, grown faint and fretful,
With lips but half regretful
Sighs, and with eyes forgetful
    Weeps that no loves endure.   80

From too much love of living,
    From hope and fear set free,
We thank with brief thanksgiving
    Whatever gods may be
That no life lives for ever;   85
That dead men rise up never;
That even the weariest river
    Winds somewhere safe to sea.

Then star nor sun shall waken,
    Nor any change of light:
Nor sound of waters shaken,
    Nor any sound or sight:
Nor wintry leaves nor vernal,
Nor days nor things diurnal;
Only the sleep eternal   95
    In an eternal night.   (*1866*)

The Roundel

A roundel is wrought as a ring or a starbright sphere,
With craft of delight and with cunning of sound unsought,
That the heart of the hearer may smile if to pleasure his ear
    A roundel is wrought.

Its jewel of music is carven of all or of aught—
Love, laughter, or mourning—remembrance of rapture or fear—
That fancy may fashion to hang in the ear of thought.

As a bird's quick song runs round, and the hearts in us hear
Pause answer to pause, and again the same strain caught,
So moves the device whence, round as a pearl or tear
    A roundel is wrought.   (*1883*)

✍ SIDNEY LANIER (1842–1881)

The Marshes of Glynn

Glooms of the live-oaks, beautiful-braided and woven
With intricate shades of the vines that myriad-cloven
    Clamber the forks of the multiform boughs,—
        Emerald twilights,—
        Virginal shy lights,   5
Wrought of the leaves to allure to the whisper of vows,
When lovers pace timidly down through the green colonnades
Of the dim sweet woods, of the dear dark woods,
    Of the heavenly woods and glades,
That run to the radiant marginal sand-beach within   10
        The wide sea-marshes of Glynn;—

Beautiful glooms, soft dusks in the noonday fire,—
Wildwood privacies, closets of lone desire,
Chamber from chamber parted with wavering arras of leaves,—
Cells for the passionate pleasure of prayer to the soul that grieves,   15
Pure with a sense of the passing of saints through the wood,
Cool for the dutiful weighing of ill with good;—

O braided dusks of the oak and woven shades of the vine,
While the riotous noon-day sun of the June-day long did shine
Ye held me fast in your heart and I held you fast in mine;   20
But now when the noon is no more, and riot is rest,
And the sun is a-wait at the ponderous gate of the West,
And the slant yellow beam down the wood-aisle doth seem
Like a lane into heaven that leads from a dream,—
Ay, now, when my soul all day hath drunken the soul of the oak,   25
And my heart is at ease from men, and the wearisome sound of the stroke
    Of the scythe of time and the trowel of trade is low,
    And belief overmasters doubt, and I know that I know,
    And my spirit is grown to a lordly great compass within,
That the length and the breadth and the sweep of the Marshes of
        Glynn   30
Will work me no fear like the fear they have wrought me of yore
When length was fatigue, and when breadth was but bitterness sore,
And when terror and shrinking and dreary unnamable pain
Drew over me out of the merciless miles of the plain,—

Oh, now, unafraid, I am fain to face   35
    The vast sweet visage of space.
To the edge of the wood I am drawn, I am drawn,
Where the gray beach glimmering runs, as a belt of the dawn,
    For a mete and a mark
      To the forest-dark:—   40
        So:
Affable live-oak, leaning low,—
Thus—with your favor—soft, with a reverent hand
(Not lightly touching your person, Lord of the land!),
Bending your beauty aside, with a step I stand   45
On the firm-packed sand,
      Free
By a world of marsh that borders a world of sea.
    Sinuous southward and sinuous northward the shimmering band
    Of the sand-beach fastens the fringe of the marsh to the folds of the
        land.   50
Inward and outward to northward and southward the beach-lines linger
      and curl
As a silver-wrought garment that clings to and follows the firm sweet
      limbs of a girl.
Vanishing, swerving, evermore curving again into sight,
Softly the sand-beach wavers away to a dim gray looping of light.
And what if behind me to westward the wall of the woods stands
      high?   55
The world lies east: how ample, the marsh and the sea and the sky!
A league and a league of marsh-grass, waist-high, broad in the blade,
Green, and all of a height, and unflecked with a light or a shade,
Stretch leisurely off, in a pleasant plain,
To the terminal blue of the main.   60

Oh, what is abroad in the marsh and the terminal sea?
    Somehow my soul seems suddenly free
From the weighing of fate and the sad discussion of sin,
By the length and the breadth and the sweep of the marshes of Glynn.

Ye marshes, how candid and simple and nothing-withholding and
      free   65
Ye publish yourselves to the sky and offer yourselves to the sea!
Tolerant plains, that suffer the sea and the rains and the sun,
Ye spread and span like the catholic man who hath mightily won
God out of knowledge and good out of infinite pain
And sight out of blindness and purity out of a stain.   70

As the marsh-hen secretly builds on the watery sod,
Behold I will build me a nest on the greatness of God:
I will fly in the greatness of God as the marsh-hen flies
In the freedom that fills all the space 'twixt the marsh and the skies:
By so many roots as the marsh-grass sends in the sod   75
I will heartily lay me a-hold on the greatness of God:
Oh, like to the greatness of God is the greatness within
The range of the marshes, the liberal marshes of Glynn.

And the sea lends large, as the marsh: lo, out of his plenty the sea
Pours fast: full soon the time of the flood-tide must be: 80
Look how the grace of the sea doth go
About and about through the intricate channels that flow
  Here and there,
   Everywhere,
Till his waters have flooded the uttermost creeks and the low-lying
    lanes,   85
And the marsh is meshed with a million veins,
That like as with rosy and silvery essences flow
  In the rose-and-silver evening glow.
   Farewell, my lord Sun!
The creeks overflow: a thousand rivulets run   90
'Twixt the roots of the sod; the blades of the marsh-grass stir;
Passeth a hurrying sound of wings that westward whirr;
Passeth, and all is still; and the currents cease to run;
And the sea and the marsh are one.

How still the plains of the waters be!   95
The tide is in his ecstasy.
The tide is at his highest height:
  And it is night.

And now from the Vast of the Lord will the waters of sleep
Roll in on the souls of men,   100
But who will reveal to our waking ken
The forms that swim and the shapes that creep
  Under the waters of sleep?
And I would I could know what swimmeth below when the tide comes
   in
On the length and the breadth of the marvellous marshes of
   Glynn. (1878–9)   105

GERARD MANLEY HOPKINS
(1844–1889)

Spring and Fall

TO A YOUNG CHILD

Márgarét, are you gríeving
Over Goldengrove unleaving?
Leáves, líke the things of man, you
With your fresh thoughts care for, can you?
Áh! ás the heart grows older   5
It will come to such sights colder
By and by, nor spare a sigh
Though worlds of wanwood leafmeal lie;
And yet you wíll weep and know why.
Now no matter, child, the name: 10
Sórrow's spríngs áre the same.
Nor mouth had, no nor mind, expressed
What heart heard of, ghost guessed:
It ís the blight man was born for,
It is Margaret you mourn for.   15

The Windhover

TO CHRIST OUR LORD

I caught this morning morning's minion, king-
    dom of daylight's dauphin, dapple-dawn-drawn Falcon, in his riding
    Of the rolling level underneath him steady air, and striding
High there, how he rung upon the rein of a wimpling wing
In his ecstacy! then off, off forth on swing,
    As a skate's heel sweeps smooth on a bow-bend; the hurl and glid-
        ing   5
    Rebuffed the big wind. My heart in hiding
Stirred for a bird,—the achieve of, the mastery of the thing!

Brute beauty and valor and act, oh, air, pride, plume, here
    Buckle! And the fire that breaks from thee then, a billion
Times told lovelier, more dangerous, O my chevalier!   10

No wonder of it: shéer plód makes plough down sillion[1]
Shine, and blue-bleak embers, ah my dear,
 Fall, gall themselves, and gash gold-vermilion.

God's Grandeur

The world is charged with the grandeur of God.
 It will flame out, like shining from shook foil;
 It gathers to a greatness, like the ooze of oil
Crushed. Why do men then now not reck his rod?
Generations have trod, have trod, have trod;   5
 And all is seared with trade; bleared, smeared with toil;
 And wears man's smudge and shares man's smell: the soil
Is bare now, nor can foot feel, being shod.

And for all this, nature is never spent;
 There lives the dearest freshness deep down things;   10
And though the last lights off the black West went
 Oh, morning, at the brown brink eastward, springs—
Because the Holy Ghost over the bent
 World broods with warm breast and with ah! bright wings.

Hurrahing in Harvest

Summer ends now; now, barbarous in beauty, the stooks arise
 Around; up above, what wind-walks! what lovely behavior
 Of silk-sack clouds! has wilder, wilful-wavier
Meal-drift moulded ever and melted across skies?

I walk, I lift up, I lift up heart, eyes,   5
 Down all that glory in the heavens to glean our Saviour;
 And, éyes, heart, what looks, what lips yet gave you a
Rapturous love's greeting of realer, of rounder replies?

And the azurous hung hills are his world-wielding shoulder
 Majestic—as a stallion stalwart, very-violet-sweet!—   10
These things, these things were here and but the beholder
 Wanting; which two when they once meet,
The heart rears wings bold and bolder
 And hurls for him, O half hurls earth for him off under his feet.

[1] side of a furrow

The Habit of Perfection

Elected Silence, sing to me
And beat upon my whorlèd ear,
Pipe me to pastures still and be
The music that I care to hear.

Shape nothing, lips; be lovely-dumb: 5
It is the shut, the curfew sent
From there where all surrenders come
Which only makes you eloquent.

Be shellèd, eyes, with double dark
And find the uncreated light: 10
This ruck and reel which you remark
Coils, keeps, and teases simple sight.

Palate, the hutch of tasty lust,
Desire not to be rinsed with wine:
The can must be so sweet, the crust   15
So fresh that come in fasts divine!

Nostrils, your careless breath that spend
Upon the stir and keep of pride,
What relish shall the censers send
Along the sanctuary side!   20

O feel-of-primrose hands, O feet
That want the yield of plushy sward,
But you shall walk the golden street
And you unhouse and house the Lord.

And, Poverty, be thou the bride   25
And now the marriage feast begun, .
And lily-colored clothes provide
Your spouse not labored-at nor spun.

In the Valley of the Elwy

I remember a house where all were good
    To me, God knows, deserving no such thing:
    Comforting smell breathed at very entering,
Fetched fresh, as I suppose, off some sweet wood.
That cordial air made those kind people a hood
    All over, as a bevy of eggs the mothering wing
    Will, or mild nights the new morsels of spring:
Why, it seemed of course; seemed of right it should.

Lovely the woods, waters, meadows, combes, vales,
All the air things wear that build this world of Wales;
    Only the inmate does not correspond:
God, lover of souls swaying considerate scales,
Complete thy creature dear O where it fails,
    Being mighty a master, being a father and fond.

Inversnaid

This darksome burn, horseback brown,
His rollrock highroad roaring down,
In coop [1] and in comb [2] the fleece of his foam
Flutes and low to the lake falls home.

A windpuff-bonnet of fáwn-fróth   5
Turns and twindles [3] over the broth
Of a pool so pitchblack, féll-frówning,
It rounds and rounds Despair to drowning.

Degged [4] with dew, dappled with dew
Are the groins of the braes that the brook treads through,   10
Wiry heathpacks, flitches [5] of fern,
And the beadbonny ash that sits over the burn.

What would the world be, once bereft
Of wet and of wildness? Let them be left,
O let them be left, wildness and wet;   15
Long live the weeds and the wilderness yet.

[1] hollow or enclosed place   [2] crest, or and "dwindles"   [4] sprinkled   [5] tufts
water pouring over and through ob-   or clumps
stacles   [3] a combination of "twists"

IN HONOR OF

St. Alphonsus Rodriguez

LAYBROTHER OF THE SOCIETY OF JESUS

Honor is flashed off exploit, so we say;
And those strokes once that gashed flesh or galled shield
Should tongue that time now, trumpet now that field,
And, on the fighter, forge his glorious day.

On Christ they do and on the martyr may;   5
But be the war within, the brand we wield
Unseen, the heroic breast not outward-steeled,
Earth hears no hurtle then from fiercest fray.

    Yet God (that hews mountain and continent,
Earth, all, out; who, with trickling increment,   10
Veins violets and tall trees makes more and more)
Could crowd career with conquest while there went
Those years and years by of world without event
That in Majorca Alfonso watched the door.

To Him Who Ever Thought with Love of Me

To him who ever thought with love of me
Or ever did for my sake some good deed
I will appear, looking such charity
And kind compassion, at his life's last need
That he will out of hand and heartily
Repent he sinned and all his sins be freed.

Duns Scotus's Oxford

Towery city and branchy between towers;
Cuckoo-echoing, bell-swarmèd, lark-charmèd, rook-racked, river-rounded;
The dapple-eared lily below thee; that country and town did
Once encounter in, here coped and poisèd powers;

Thou hast a base and brickish skirt there, sours   5
That neighbor-nature thy grey beauty is grounded
Best in; graceless growth, thou hast confounded
Rural rural keeping—folk, flocks, and flowers.

Yet ah! this air I gather and I release
He lived on; these weeds and waters, these walls are what   10
He haunted who of all men most sways my spirits to peace;

Of realty the rarest-veinèd unraveller; a not
Rivalled insight, be rival Italy or Greece;
Who fired France for Mary without spot.

Carrion Comfort

Not, I'll not, carrion comfort, Despair, not feast on thee;
Not untwist—slack they may be—these last strands of man
In me ór, most weary, cry *I can no more.* I can;
Can something, hope, wish day come, not choose not to be.
But ah, but O thou terrible, why wouldst thou rude on me   5
Thy wring-world right foot rock? lay a lionlimb against me? scan
With darksome devouring eyes my bruisèd bones? and fan,
O in turns of tempest, me heaped there; me frantic to avoid thee and flee?

    Why? That my chaff might fly; my grain lie, sheer and clear.
Nay in all that toil, that coil, since (seems) I kissed the rod,   10
Hand rather, my heart lo! lapped strength, stole joy, would laugh, chéer.
Cheer whom though? the hero whose heaven-handling flung me, foót
      tród
Me? or me that fought him? O which one? is it each one?
    That night, that year
Of now done darkness I wretch lay wrestling with (my God!) my God.

No Worst, There Is None

No worst, there is none. Pitched past pitch of grief,
More pangs will, schooled at forepangs, wilder wring.
Comforter, where, where is your comforting?
Mary, mother of us, where is your relief?

My cries heave, herds-long; huddle in a main, a chief   5
Woe, world-sorrow; on an age-old anvil wince and sing—
Then lull, then leave off. Fury had shrieked 'No ling-
ering! Let me be fell: force I must be brief'.

O the mind, mind has mountains; cliffs of fall
Frightful, sheer, no-man fathomed. Hold them cheap   10
May who ne'er hung there. Nor does long our small
Durance deal with that steep or deep. Here! creep,
Wretch, under a comfort serves in a whirlwind: all
Life death does end and each day dies with sleep.

I Wake and Feel the Fell of Dark

I wake and feel the fell of dark, not day.
What hours, O what black hoürs we have spent
This night! what sights you, heart, saw; ways you went!
And more must, in yet longer light's delay.
    With witness I speak this. But where I say   5
Hours I mean years, mean life. And my lament
Is cries countless, cries like dead letters sent
To dearest him that lives alas! away.
    I am gall, I am heartburn. God's most deep decree
Bitter would have me taste: my taste was me;   10
Bones built in me, flesh filled, blood brimmed the curse.
    Selfyeast of spirit a dull dough sours. I see
The lost are like this, and their scourge to be
As I am mine, their sweating selves; but worse.

❧ WILLIAM ERNEST HENLEY (1849–1903)

Invictus

Out of the night that covers me,
  Black as the Pit from pole to pole,
I thank whatever gods may be
  For my unconquerable soul.

In the fell clutch of circumstance   5
  I have not winced nor cried aloud.
Under the bludgeonings of chance
  My head is bloody, but unbowed.

Beyond this place of wrath and tears
  Looms but the horror of the shade,   10
And yet the menace of the years
  Finds, and shall find me, unafraid.

It matters not how strait the gate,
  How charged with punishments the scroll,
I am the master of my fate: 15
  I am the captain of my soul.   (*1888*)

What Is to Come

What is to come we know not. But we know   23½
That what has been was good—was good to show,
Better to hide, and best of all to bear.
We are the masters of the days that were;
We have lived, we have loved, we have suffered . . . even so.   5

Shall we not take the ebb who had the flow?
Life was our friend. Now, if it be our foe—
Dear, though it spoil and break us!—need we care
  What is to come?

Let the great winds their worst and wildest blow,   10
Or the gold weather round us mellow slow;
We have fulfilled ourselves, and we can dare
And we can conquer, though we may not share
In the rich quiet of the afterglow
  What is to come.   (*1888*)

ROBERT LOUIS STEVENSON
(1850–1894)

The Wind

I saw you toss the kites on high
And blow the birds about the sky;
And all around I heard you pass,
Like ladies' skirts across the grass—
     O wind, a-blowing all day long,   5
     O wind, that sings so loud a song!

I saw the different things you did,
But always you yourself you hid.
I felt you push, I heard you call,
I could not see yourself at all—   10
     O wind, a-blowing all day long,
     O wind, that sings so loud a song!

O you that are so strong and cold,
O blower, are you young or old?
Are you a beast of field and tree,   15
Or just a stronger child than me?
     O wind, a-blowing all day long,
     O wind, that sings so loud a song!   (1885)

Requiem

Under the wide and stary sky
Dig the grave and let me lie:
Glad did I live and gladly die,
And I laid me down with a will.

This be the verse you grave for me: 5
Here he lies where he long'd to be;
Home is the sailor, home from the sea,
And the hunter home from the hill.   (1887)

473

⁓ FRANCIS THOMPSON (1859–1907)

The Hound of Heaven

I fled Him, down the nights and down the days;
　I fled Him, down the arches of the years;
I fled Him, down the labyrinthine ways
　　Of my own mind; and in the mist of tears
I hid from Him, and under running laughter. 5
　　　　Up vistaed hopes I sped;
　　　　And shot, precipitated,
Adown Titanic glooms of chasmèd fears,
　　From those strong Feet that followed, followed after.
　　　　But with unhurrying chase, 10
　　　　And unperturbèd pace,
Deliberate speed, majestic instancy,
　　　They beat—and a Voice beat
　　　More instant than the Feet—
　"All things betray thee, who betrayest Me." 15
　　　I pleaded, outlaw-wise,
By many a hearted casement, curtained red,
　Trellised with intertwining charities
(For, though I knew His love Who followèd,
　　　Yet was I sore adread 20
Lest, having Him, I must have naught beside);
But, if one little casement parted wide,
　The gust of His approach would clash it to:
　Fear wist not to evade, as Love wist to pursue.
Across the margent of the world I fled, 25
　And troubled the gold gateways of the stars,
　Smiting for shelter on their clangèd bars;
　　　Fretted to dulcet jars
And silvern chatter the pale ports o' the moon.
I said to Dawn: Be sudden—to Eve: Be soon; 30
　With thy young skiey blossoms heap me over
　　　From this tremendous Lover—
Float thy vague veil about me, lest He see!
　I tempted all His servitors, but to find
My own betrayal in their constancy, 35
In faith to Him their fickleness to me,
　Their traitorous trueness, and their loyal deceit.

To all swift things for swiftness did I sue;
    Clung to the whistling mane of every wind.
        But whether they swept, smoothly fleet,   40
      The long savannahs of the blue;
          Or whether, Thunder-driven,
         They clanged his chariot 'thwart a heaven,
Plashy with flying lightnings round the spurn o' their feet:—
    Fear wist not to evade as Love wist to pursue.   45
         Still with unhurrying chase,
         And unperturbéd pace,
      Deliberate speed, majestic instancy,
         Came on the following Feet,
         And a Voice above their beat—   50
    "Naught shelters thee, who wilt not shelter Me."

I sought no more that after which I strayed
         In face of man or maid;
But still within the little children's eyes
         Seems something, something that replies,   55
They at least are for me, surely for me!
I turned me to them very wistfully;
But just as their young eyes grew sudden fair
         With dawning answers there,
Their angel plucked them from me by the hair.   60
"Come then, ye other children, Nature's—share
With me" (said I) "your delicate fellowship;
        Let me greet you lip to lip,
        Let me twine with you caresses,
          Wantoning   65
        With our Lady-Mother's vagrant tresses,
          Banqueting
        With her in her wind-walled palace,
        Underneath her azured daïs,
        Quaffing, as your taintless way is,   70
          From a chalice
Lucent-weeping out of the dayspring."
         So it was done:
I in their delicate fellowship was one—
Drew the bolt of Nature's secrecies.   75
        I knew all the swift importings
        On the willful face of skies;
        I knew how the clouds arise
        Spumed of the wild sea-snortings;

All that's born or dies   80
Rose and drooped with; made them shapers
Of mine own moods, or wailful or divine;
With them joyed and was bereaven.
I was heavy with the even,
When she lit her glimmering tapers   85
Round the day's dead sanctities.
I laughed in the morning's eyes.
I triumphed and I saddened with all weather,
Heaven and I wept together,
And its sweet tears were salt with mortal mine;   90

Against the red throb of its sunset-heart
I laid my own to beat,
And share commingling heat;
But not by that, by that, was eased my human smart.
In vain my tears were wet on Heaven's gray cheek.   95
For ah! we know not what each other says,
These things and I; in sound I speak—
Their sound is but their stir, they speak by silences.
Nature, poor stepdame, cannot slake my drouth;
Let her, if she would owe me,   100
Drop yon blue bosom-veil of sky, and show me
The breasts o' her tenderness:
Never did any milk of hers once bless
My thirsting mouth.
Nigh and nigh draws the chase,   105
With unperturbéd pace,
Deliberate speed, majestic instancy;
And past those noiséd Feet
A Voice comes yet more fleet—
"Lo! naught contents thee, who content'st not Me."   110

Naked I wait Thy love's uplifted stroke!
My harness piece by piece Thou hast hewn from me,
And smitten me to my knee;
I am defenseless utterly.
I slept, methinks, and woke,   115
And, slowly gazing, find me stripped in sleep.
In the rash lustihead of my young powers,
I shook the pillaring hours
And pulled my life upon me; grimed with smears,
I stand amid the dust o' the mounded years—   120
My mangled youth lies dead beneath the heap.

My days have crackled and gone up in smoke,
Have puffed and burst as sun-starts on a stream.
       Yea, faileth now even dream
The dreamer, and the lute the lutanist;   125
Even the linked fantasies, in whose blossomy twist
I swung the earth a trinket at my wrist,
Are yielding; cords of all too weak account
For earth with heavy griefs so overpulsed.
       Ah! is Thy love indeed   130
A weed, albeit an amaranthine weed,
Suffering no flowers except its own to mount?
       Ah! must—
       Designer infinite!—
Ah! must Thou char the wood ere Thou canst limn with it?   135
My freshness spent its wavering shower i' the dust;
And now my heart is as a broken fount,
Wherein tear-drippings stagnate, split down ever
       From the dank thoughts that shiver
Upon the sighful branches of my mind.   140
       Such is; what is to be?
The pulp so bitter, how shall taste the rind?
I dimly guess what Time in mists confounds;
Yet ever and anon a trumpet sounds
From the hid battlements of Eternity;   145
Those shaken mists a space unsettle, then
Round the half-glimpsed turrets slowly wash again.
       But not ere him who summoneth
       I first have seen, enwound
With glooming robes purpureal, cypress-crowned;   150
His name I know, and what his trumpet saith.
Whether man's heart or life it be which yields
       Thee harvest, must Thy harvest-fields
       Be dunged with rotten death?

       Now of that long pursuit   155
       Comes on at hand the bruit;
       That Voice is round me like a bursting sea:
       "And is thy earth so marred,
       Shattered in shard on shard?
       Lo, all things fly thee, for thou fliest me!   160
       Strange, piteous, futile thing!
Wherefore should any set thee love apart?
Seeing none but I makes much of naught" (He said),

"And human love needs human meriting:
　　　How hast thou merited—　　　　　　　　　165
Of all man's clotted clay the dingiest clot?
　　　Alack, thou knowest not
How little worthy of any love thou art!
Whom wilt thou find to love ignoble thee
　　　Save Me, save only Me?　　　　　　　170
All which I took from thee I did but take,
　　　Not for thy harms,
But just that thou might'st seek it in My arms.
　　　All which thy child's mistake
Fancies as lost, I have stored for thee at home:　175
　　　Rise, clasp My hand, and come!"

　　　Halts by me that footfall:
　　　Is my gloom, after all,
　　Shade of His hand, outstretched caressingly?
　　　"Ah, fondest, blindest, weakest,　　　　180
　　　I am He Whom thou seekest!
Thou dravest love from thee, who dravest Me."

　　　　　　　　　　　　　　　　　(1890)

Desiderium Indesideratum [1]

O gain that lurk'st ungainèd in all gain!
O love we just fall short of in all love!
O height that in all heights art still above!
O beauty that dost leave all beauty pain!
Thou unpossessed that mak'st possession vain,　　5
See these strained arms which fright the simple air,
And say what ultimate fairness holds thee, Fair!
They girdle Heaven, and girdle Heaven in vain;
They shut, and lo! but shut in their unrest,
Thereat a voice in me that voiceless was:—　　10
'Whom seekest thou through the unmarged arcane,
And not discern'st to thine own bosom prest?'
I looked. My claspèd arms athwart my breast
Framed the august embraces of the Cross.　　(1893)

[1] Undesired desire

The Kingdom of God

IN NO STRANGE LAND [1]

O world invisible, we view thee,
O world intangible, we touch thee,
O world unknowable, we know thee,
Inapprehensible, we clutch thee!

Does the fish soar to find the ocean,   5
The eagle plunge to find the air—
That we ask of the stars in motion
If they have rumor of thee there?

Not where the wheeling systems darken,
And our benumbed conceiving soars!—   10
The drift of pinions, would we harken,
Beats at our own clay-shuttered doors.

The angels keep their ancient places;—
Turn but a stone, and start a wing!
'Tis ye, 'tis your estranged faces,   15
That miss the many-splendored thing.

But (when so sad thou canst not sadder)
Cry—and upon thy so sore loss
Shall shine the traffic of Jacob's ladder [2]
Pitched betwixt Heaven and Charing Cross. [3]   20

Yea, in the night, my Soul, my daughter,
Cry—clinging Heaven by the hems;
And lo, Christ walking on the water
Not of Gennesareth, [4] but Thames!   (1908)

[1] Exodus 2:22   [2] Genesis 28:12   [3] in
the center of London   [4] Galilee; Matthew 14:25–33

PART 6
The Twentieth Century

Afterwards

When the Present has latched its postern behind my tremulous stay,
  And the May month flaps its glad green leaves like wings,
Delicate-filmed as new-spun silk, will the neighbors say,
  "He was a man who used to notice such things"?

If it be in the dusk when, like an eyelid's soundless blink,   5
  The dewfall-hawk comes crossing the shades to alight
Upon the wind-warped upland thorn, a gazer may think,
  "To him this must have been a familiar sight."

If I pass during some nocturnal blackness, mothy and warm,
  When the hedgehog travels furtively over the lawn,   10
One may say, "He strove that such innocent creatures should come to no
    harm,
  But he could do little for them; and now he is gone."

If, when hearing that I have been stilled at last, they stand at the door,
  Watching the full-starred heavens that winter sees,
Will this thought rise on those who will meet my face no more,   15
  "He was one who had an eye for such mysteries"?

And will any say when my bell of quittance is heard in the gloom,
  And a crossing breeze cuts a pause in its outrollings,
Till they rise again, as they were a new bell's boom,
  "He hears it not now, but used to notice such things"?   20

The Darkling Thrush

I leant upon a coppice gate
    When Frost was spectre-gray,
And Winter's dregs made desolate
    The weakening eye of day.
The tangled bine-stems scored the sky   5
    Like strings of broken lyres,
And all mankind that haunted nigh
    Had sought their household fires.

The land's sharp features seemed to be
 The Century's corpse outleant,   10
His crypt the cloudy canopy,
 The wind his death-lament.
The ancient pulse of germ and birth
 Was shrunken hard and dry,
And every spirit upon earth   15
 Seemed fervorless as I.

At once a voice arose among
 The bleak twigs overhead
In a full-hearted evensong
 Of joy illimited;   20
An aged thrush, frail, gaunt, and small,
 In blast-beruffled plume,
Had chosen thus to fling his soul
 Upon the growing gloom.

So little cause for carolings   25
 Of such ecstatic sound
Was written on terrestrial things
 Afar or nigh around,
That I could think there trembled through
 His happy good-night air   30
Some blessed Hope, whereof he knew
 And I was unaware.   (*December 1900*)

The Man He Killed

"Had he and I but met
 By some old ancient inn,
We should have sat us down to wet
 Right many a nipperkin! [1]

"But ranged as infantry,   5
 And staring face to face,
I shot at him as he at me,
 And killed him in his place.

"I shot him dead because—
 Because he was my foe,   10

[1] a quantity of liquor

Just so: my foe of course he was;
    That's clear enough; although

  "He thought he'd 'list, perhaps,
    Off-hand like—just as I—
Was out of work—had sold his traps—   15
    No other reason why.

  "Yes; quaint and curious war is!
    You shoot a fellow down
You'd treat if met where any bar is,
    Or help to half-a-crown."   (1902)

Channel Firing

That night your great guns, unawares,
Shook all our coffins as we lay,
And broke the chancel window-squares,
We thought it was the Judgment-day

And sat upright. While drearisome   5
Arose the howl of wakened hounds:
The mouse let fall the altar-crumb,
The worms drew back into the mounds,

The glebe cow drooled. Till God called, "No;
It's gunnery practice out at sea   10
Just as before you went below:
The world is as it used to be:

"All nations striving strong to make
Red war yet redder. Mad as hatters
They do no more for Christés sake   15
Than you who are helpless in such matters.

"That this is not the judgment-hour
For some of them's a blessed thing,
For if it were they'd have to scour
Hell's floor for so much threatening. . . .   20

"Ha, ha. It will be warmer when
I blow the trumpet (if indeed
I ever do; for you are men,
And rest eternal sorely need)."

So down we lay again. "I wonder,   25
  Will the world ever saner be,"
Said one, "than when He sent us under
In our indifferent century!"

And many a skeleton shook his head.
  "Instead of preaching forty year,"   30
My neighbor Parson Thirdly said,
  "I wish I had stuck to pipes and beer."

Again the guns disturb the hour,
  Roaring their readiness to avenge,
As far inland as Stourton Tower,   35
  And Camelot, and starlit Stonehenge.   (*April 1914*)

Nature's Questioning

When I look forth at dawning, pool,
      Field, flock, and lonely tree,
      All seem to gaze at me
Like chastened children sitting silent in a school;

Their faces dulled, constrained, and worn,   5
      As though the master's ways
      Through the long teaching days
Had cowed them till their early zest was overborne.

Upon them stirs in lippings mere
      (As if once clear in call,   10
      But now scarce breathed at all)—
"We wonder, ever wonder, why we find us here!

"Has some Vast Imbecility,
      Mighty to build and blend,
      But impotent to tend,   15
Framed us in jest, and left us now to hazardry?

"Or come we of an Automaton
      Unconscious of our pains? . . .
      Or are we live remains
Of Godhead dying downwards, brain and eye now gone?   20

"Or is it that some high Plan betides,
      As yet not understood,

Of Evil stormed by Good,
We the Forlorn Hope over which Achievement strides?"

Thus things around. No answerer I. . . .   25
    Meanwhile the winds, and rains,
    And earth's old glooms and pains
Are still the same, and Life and Death are neighbors nigh.

The Oxen

Christmas Eve, and twelve of the clock.
    "Now they are all on their knees,"
An elder said as we sat in a flock
    By the embers in hearthside ease.

We pictured the meek mild creatures where   5
    They dwelt in their strawy pen,
Nor did it occur to one of us there
    To doubt they were kneeling then.

So fair a fancy few would weave
    In these years! Yet, I feel,   10
If someone said on Christmas Eve,
    "Come; see the oxen kneel,

"In the lonely barton [1] by yonder coomb
    Our childhood used to know,"
I should go with him in the gloom,   15
    Hoping it might be so.

Transformations

Portion of this yew
Is a man my grandsire knew,
Bosomed here at its foot:
This branch may be his wife,
A ruddy human life   5
Now turned to a green shoot.

[1] farmyard

These grasses must be made
Of her who often prayed,
Last century, for repose;
And the fair girl long ago   10
Whom I often tried to know
May be entering this rose.

So, they are not underground,
But as nerves and veins abound
In the growths of upper air,   15
And they feel the sun and rain,
And the energy again
That made them what they were!

During Wind and Rain

They sing their dearest songs—
He, she, all of them—yea,
Treble and tenor and bass,
       And one to play;
With the candles mooning each face. . . .   5
       Ah, no; the years O!
How the sick leaves reel down in throngs!

They clear the creeping moss—
Elders and juniors—aye,
Making the pathway neat   10
       And the garden gay;
And they build a shady seat. . . .
       Ah, no; the years, the years;
See, the white storm-birds wing across!

They are blithely breakfasting all—   15
Men and maidens—yea,
Under the summer tree,
       With a glimpse of the bay,
While pet fowl come to the knee. . . .
       Ah, no; the years O!   20
And the rotten rose is ript from the wall.

They change to a high new house,
He, she, all of them—aye.

Clocks and carpets, and chairs
 On the lawn all day,   25
And brightest things that are theirs. . . .
 Ah, no; the years, the years;
Down their carved names the rain-drop ploughs.

Weathers

1

This is the weather the cuckoo likes,
 And so do I;
When showers betumble the chestnut spikes,
 And nestlings fly:
And the little brown nightingale bills his best, 5
And they sit outside at "The Travellers' Rest,"
And maids come forth sprig-muslin drest,
And citizens dream of the south and west,
 And so do I;

2

This is the weather the shepherd shuns,   10
 And so do I;
When beeches drip in browns and duns,
 And thresh, and ply;
And hill-hid tides throb, throe on throe,
And meadow rivulets overflow,   15
And drops on gate-bars hang in a row,
And rooks in families homeward go,
 And so do I.

The Master and the Leaves

1

We are budding, Master, budding
 We of your favorite tree;
March drought and April flooding
 Arouse us merrily,
Our stemlets newly studding;   5
 And yet you do not see!

2

We are fully woven for summer
    In stuff of limpest green,
The twitterer and the hummer
    Here rest of nights, unseen,   10
While like a long-roll drummer
    The nightjar thrills the treen.[1]

3

We are turning yellow, Master,
    And next we are turning red,
And faster then and faster   15
    Shall seek our rooty bed,
All wasted in disaster!
    But you lift not your head.

4

—"I mark your early going,
    And that you'll soon be clay,   20
I have seen your summer showing
    As in my youthful day;
But why I seem unknowing
    Is too sunk in to say!"

The Dark-Eyed Gentleman

1

I pitched my day's leazings [1] in Crimmercrock Lane,
To tie up my garter and jog on again,
When a dear dark-eyed gentleman passed there and said,
In a way that made all o' me color rose-red,
    'What do I see—   5
    O pretty knee!'
And he came and he tied up my garter for me.

2

'Twixt sunset and moonrise it was, I can mind:
Ah, 'tis easy to lose what we nevermore find!—

[1] a section of land

---

[1] bundle of gleaned corn

Of the dear stranger's home, of his name, I knew nought,   10
But I soon knew his nature and all that it brought.
        Then bitterly
        Sobbed I that he
Should ever have tied up my garter for me!

    3
Yet now I've beside me a fine lissom lad,   15
And my slip's nigh forgot, and my days are not sad;
My own dearest joy is he, comrade, and friend,
He it is who safe-guards me, on him I depend;
        No sorrow brings he,
        And thankful I be   20
That his daddy once tied up my garter for me!

Epitaph on a Pessimist

I'm Smith of Stoke, aged sixty-odd,
    I've lived without a dame
From youth-time on; and would to God
    My dad had done the same.
               (From the French and Greek)

ROBERT BRIDGES (1844–1930)

London Snow

When men were all asleep the snow came flying,
In large white flakes falling on the city brown,
Stealthily and perpetually settling and loosely lying,
    Hushing the latest traffic of the drowsy town;
Deadening, muffling, stifling its murmurs failing;   5
Lazily and incessantly floating down and down:
    Silently sifting and veiling road, roof and railing;
Hiding difference, making unevenness even,
Into angles and crevices softly drifting and sailing.
    All night it fell, and when full inches seven   10
It lay in the depth of its uncompacted lightness,
The clouds blew off from a high and frosty heaven;
    And all woke earlier for the unaccustomed brightness
Of the winter dawning, the strange unheavenly glare:
The eye marvelled—marvelled at the dazzling whiteness;   15
    The ear harkened to the stillness of the solemn air;
No sound of wheel rumbling nor of foot falling,
And the busy morning cries came thin and spare.
    Then boys I heard, as they went to school, calling,
They gathered up the crystal manna to freeze   20
Their tongues with tasting, their hands with snowballing;
    Or rioted in a drift, plunging up to the knees;
Or peering up from under the white-mossed wonder,
'O look at the trees!' they cried, 'O look at the trees!'
    With lessened load a few carts creak and blunder,   25
Following along the white deserted way,
A country company long dispersed asunder:
    When now already the sun, in pale display
Standing by Paul's high dome, spread forth below
His sparkling beams, and awoke the stir of the day.   30

ΕΡΩΣ [1]

Why hast thou nothing in thy face?
Thou idol of the human race,
Thou tyrant of the human heart,
The flower of lovely youth that art;
Yea, and that standest in thy youth   5
An image of eternal Truth,
With thy exuberant flesh so fair,
That only Pheidias [2] might compare,
Ere from his chaste marmoreal form
Time had decayed the colors warm;   10
Like to his gods in thy proud dress,
Thy starry sheen of nakedness.

Surely thy body is thy mind,
For in thy face is nought to find,
Only thy soft unchristen'd smile,   15
That shadows neither love nor guile,
But shameless will and power immense,
In secret sensuous innocence.

O king of joy, what is thy thought?
I dream thou knowest it is nought,   20
And wouldst in darkness come, but thou
Makest the light where'er thou go.
Ah yet no victim of thy grace,
None who e'er long'd for thy embrace,
Hath cared to look upon thy face.   25

Low Barometer

The south-wind strengthens to a gale,
Across the moon the clouds fly fast,
The house is smitten as with a flail,
The chimney shudders to the blast.

[1] Eros   [2] often spelled Phidias

On such a night, when Air has loosed   5
Its guardian grasp on blood and brain,
Old terrors then of god or ghost
Creep from their caves to life again.

And Reason kens he herits in
A haunted house. Tenants unknown   10
Assert their squalid lease of sin
With earlier title than his own.

Unbodied presences, the pack'd
Pollution and remorse of Time,
Slipp'd from oblivion reenact   15
The horrors of unhouseld crime.

Some men would quell the thing with prayer
Whose sightless footsteps pad the floor,
Whose fearful trespass mounts the stair
Or bursts the lock'd forbidden door.   20

Some have seen corpses long interr'd
Escape from hallowing control,
Pale charnel forms—nay ev'n have heard
The shrilling of a troubled soul,

That wanders till the dawn hath cross'd   25
The dolorous dark, or Earth hath wound
Closer her storm-spredd cloke, and thrust
The baleful phantoms underground

ᴥᶚ A. E. HOUSMAN (1859–1936)

To an Athlete Dying Young

The time you won your town the race
We chaired you through the market-place;
Man and boy stood cheering by,
And home we brought you shoulder-high.

To-day, the road all runners come,   5
Shoulder-high we bring you home,
And set you at your threshold down,
Townsman of a stiller town.

Smart lad, to slip betimes away
From fields where glory does not stay   10
And early though the laurel grows
It withers quicker than the rose.

Eyes the shady night has shut
Cannot see the record cut,
And silence sounds no worse than cheers   15
After earth has stopped the ears:

Now you will not swell the rout
Of lads that wore their honors out,
Runners whom renown outran
And the name died before the man.   20

So set, before its echoes fade,
The fleet foot on the sill of shade,
And hold to the low lintel up
The still-defended challenge-cup.

And round that early-laurelled head   25
Will flock to gaze the strengthless dead,
And find unwithered on its curls
The garland briefer than a girl's.

'Farewell to Barn and Stack and Tree'

'Farewell to barn and stack and tree,
     Farewell to Severn shore.
Terence, look your last at me,
     For I come home no more.

'The sun burns on the half-mown hill,   5
     By now the blood is dried;
And Maurice amongst the hay lies still
     And my knife is in his side.

'My mother thinks us long away;
     'Tis time the field were mown.   10
She had two sons at rising day,
     To-night she'll be alone.

'And here's a bloody hand to shake,
     And oh, man, here's good-bye;
We'll sweat no more on scythe and rake,   15
     My bloody hands and I.

'I wish you strength to bring you pride,
     And a love to keep you clean,
And I wish you luck, come Lammastide,
     At racing on the green.   20

'Long for me the rick will wait,
     And long will wait the fold,
And long will stand the empty plate,
     And dinner will be cold.'

On Wenlock Edge the Wood's in Trouble

On Wenlock Edge the wood's in trouble;
     His forest fleece the Wrekin heaves;
The gale, it plies the saplings double,
     And thick on Severn snow the leaves.

'Twould blow like this through holt and hanger   5
     When Uricon the city stood:

'Tis the old wind in the old anger,
    But then it threshed another wood.

Then, 'twas before my time, the Roman
    At yonder heaving hill would stare: 10
The blood that warms an English yeoman,
    The thoughts that hurt him, they were there.

There, like the wind through woods in riot,
    Through him the gale of life blew high;
The tree of man was never quiet: 15
    Then 'twas the Roman, now 'tis I.

The gale, it plies the saplings double,
    It blows so hard, 'twill soon be gone:
To-day the Roman and his trouble
    Are ashes under Uricon.   20

Eight O'Clock

He stood, and heard the steeple
    Sprinkle the quarters on the morning town.
One, two, three, four, to market-place and people
    It tossed them down.

Strapped, noosed, nighing his hour,
    He stood and counted them and cursed his luck;
And then the clock collected in the tower
    Its strength, and struck.

Epitaph on an Army of Mercenaries

These, in the day when heaven was falling,
    The hour when earth's foundations fled,
Followed their mercenary calling
    And took their wages and are dead.

Their shoulders held the sky suspended;
    They stood, and earth's foundations stay;
What God abandoned, these defended,
    And saved the sum of things for pay.

✒ W. B. YEATS (1865–1939)

When You Are Old

When you are old and grey and full of sleep
And nodding by the fire, take down this book,
And slowly read, and dream of the soft look
Your eyes had once, and of their shadows deep;

How many loved your moments of glad grace,
And loved your beauty with love false or true,
But one man loved the pilgrim soul in you,
And loved the sorrows of your changing face;

And bending down beside the glowing bars,
Murmur, a little sadly, how Love fled
And paced upon the mountains overhead
And hid his face amid a crowd of stars.

Who Goes with Fergus?

Who will go drive with Fergus [1] now,
And pierce the deep wood's woven shade,
And dance upon the level shore?
Young man, lift up your russet brow,
And lift your tender eyelids, maid,   5
And brood on hopes and fear no more.

And no more turn aside and brood
Upon love's bitter mystery;
For Fergus rules the brazen cars,
And rules the shadows of the wood,   10
And the white breast of the dim sea
And all dishevelled wandering stars.

[1] a legendary king, who renounced his
kingdom for poetry

No Second Troy

Why should I blame her that she filled my days
With misery, or that she would of late
Have taught to ignorant men most violent ways,
Or hurled the little streets upon the great,
Had they but courage equal to desire?   5
What could have made her peaceful with a mind
That nobleness made simple as a fire,
With beauty like a tightened bow, a kind
That is not natural in an age like this,
Being high and solitary and most stern?   10
Why, what could she have done, being what she is?
Was there another Troy for her to burn?

September 1913

What need you, being come to sense,
But fumble in a greasy till
And add the halfpence to the pence
And prayer to shivering prayer, until
You have dried the marrow from the bone?   5
For men were born to pray and save:
Romantic Ireland's dead and gone,
It's with O'Leary [1] in the grave.

Yet they were of a different kind,
The names that stilled your childish play,   10
They have gone about the world like wind,
But little time had they to pray
For whom the hangman's rope was spun,
And what, God help us, could they save?
Romantic Ireland's dead and gone,   15
It's with O'Leary in the grave.

Was it for this the wild geese spread
The grey wing upon every tide;
For this that all that blood was shed,

[1] an Irish nationalist hero, like the men
listed later

For this Edward Fitzgerald died,   20
And Robert Emmet and Wolfe Tone,
All that delirium of the brave?
Romantic Ireland's dead and gone,
It's with O'Leary in the grave.

Yet could we turn the years again,   25
And call those exiles as they were
In all their loneliness and pain,
You'd cry, 'Some woman's yellow hair
Has maddened every mother's son':
They weighed so lightly what they gave   30
But let them be, they're dead and gone,
They're with O'Leary in the grave.

The Magi

Now as at all times I can see in the mind's eye,
In their stiff, painted clothes, the pale unsatisfied ones
Appear and disappear in the blue depth of the sky
With all their ancient faces like rain-beaten stones,
And all their helms of silver hovering side by side,
And all their eyes still fixed, hoping to find once more,
Being by Calvary's turbulence unsatisfied,
The uncontrollable mystery on the bestial floor.

The Wild Swans at Coole

The trees are in their autumn beauty,
The woodland paths are dry,
Under the October twilight the water
Mirrors a still sky;
Upon the brimming water among the stones   5
Are nine-and-fifty swans.

The nineteenth autumn has come upon me
Since I first made my count;
I saw, before I had well finished,
All suddenly mount   10

And scatter wheeling in great broken rings
Upon their clamorous wings.

I have looked upon those brilliant creatures,
And now my heart is sore.
All's changed since I, hearing at twilight,   15
The first time on this shore,
The bell-beat of their wings above my head,
Trod with a lighter tread.

Unwearied still, lover by lover,
They paddle in the cold   20
Companionable streams or climb the air;
Their hearts have not grown old;
Passion or conquest, wander where they will,
Attend upon them still.

But now they drift on the still water,   25
Mysterious, beautiful;
Among what rushes will they build,
By what lake's edge or pool
Delight men's eyes when I awake some day
To find they have flown away?   30

Easter 1916

I have met them at close of day
Coming with vivid faces
From counter or desk among grey
Eighteenth-century houses.
I have passed with a nod of the head   5
Or polite meaningless words,
Or have lingered awhile and said
Polite meaningless words
And thought before I had done
Of a mocking tale or a gibe   10
To please a companion
Around the fire at the club,
Being certain that they and I
But lived where motley is worn:
All changed, changed utterly: 15
A terrible beauty is born.

That woman's days were spent
In ignorant good-will,
Her nights in argument
Until her voice grew shrill.   20
What voice more sweet than hers
When, young and beautiful,
She rode to harriers?
This man had kept a school
And rode our wingèd horse;   25
This other his helper and friend
Was coming into his force;
He might have won fame in the end,
So sensitive his nature seemed,
So daring and sweet his thought.   30
This other man I had dreamed
A drunken, vainglorious lout.
He had done most bitter wrong
To some who are near my heart,
Yet I number him in the song;   35
He, too, has resigned his part
In the casual comedy;
He, too, has been changed in his turn,
Transformed utterly:
A terrible beauty is born.   40

Hearts with one purpose alone
Through summer and winter seem
Enchanted to a stone
To trouble the living stream.
The horse that comes from the road,   45
The rider, the birds that range
From cloud to tumbling cloud,
Minute by minute they change;
A shadow of cloud on the stream
Changes minute by minute;   50
A horse-hoof slides on the brim,
And a horse plashes within it;
The long-legged moor-hens dive,
And hens to moor-cocks call;
Minute by minute they live: 55
The stone's in the midst of all.

Too long a sacrifice
Can make a stone of the heart.

O when may it suffice?
That is Heaven's part, our part   60
To murmur name upon name,
As a mother names her child
When sleep at last has come
On limbs that had run wild.
What is it but nightfall?   65
No, no, not night but death;
Was it needless death after all?
For England may keep faith
For all that is done and said.
We know their dream; enough   70
To know they dreamed and are dead;
And what if excess of love
Bewildered them till they died?
I write it out in a verse—
MacDonagh and MacBride   75
And Connolly and Pearse [1]
Now and in time to be,
Wherever green is worn,
Are changed, changed utterly:
A terrible beauty is born.   80
                    (September 25, 1916)

The Second Coming

Turning and turning in the widening gyre
The falcon cannot hear the falconer;
Things fall apart; the centre cannot hold;
Mere anarchy is loosed upon the world,
The blood-dimmed tide is loosed, and everywhere   5
The ceremony of innocence is drowned;
The best lack all conviction, while the worst
Are full of passionate intensity.

Surely some revelation is at hand;
Surely the Second Coming is at hand.   10
The Second Coming! Hardly are those words out

[1] Irish nationalists killed in the 1916
uprising

When a vast image out of *Spiritus Mundi* [1]
Troubles my sight: somewhere in sands of the desert
A shape with lion body and the head of a man,
A gaze blank and pitiless as the sun,   15
Is moving its slow thighs, while all about it
Reel shadows of the indignant desert birds.
The darkness drops again; but now I know
That twenty centuries of stony sleep
Were vexed to nightmare by a rocking cradle,   20
And what rough beast, its hour come round at last,
Slouches towards Bethlehem to be born?

Sailing to Byzantium

1

That is no country for old men. The young
In one another's arms, birds in the trees
—Those dying generations—at their song,
The salmon-falls, the mackerel-crowded seas,
Fish, flesh, or fowl, commend all summer long   5
Whatever is begotten, born, and dies.
Caught in that sensual music all neglect
Monuments of unageing intellect.

2

An aged man is but a paltry thing,
A tattered coat upon a stick, unless   10
Soul clap its hands and sing, and louder sing
For every tatter in its mortal dress,
Nor is there singing school but studying
Monuments of its own magnificence;
And therefore I have sailed the seas and come   15
To the holy city of Byzantium.

3

O sages standing in God's holy fire
As in the gold mosaic of a wall,
Come from the holy fire, perne [1] in a gyre,

[1] the soul of the world

[1] spin

And be the singing-masters of my soul.   20
Consume my heart away; sick with desire
And fastened to a dying animal
It knows not what it is; and gather me
Into the artifice of eternity.

4

Once out of nature I shall never take   25
My bodily form from any natural thing,
But such a form as Grecian goldsmiths make
Of hammered gold and gold enamelling
To keep a drowsy Emperor awake;
Or set upon a golden bough to sing   30
To lords and ladies of Byzantium
Of what is past, or passing, or to come.   (*1927*)

Two Songs from a Play

1

I saw a staring virgin stand
Where holy Dionysus died,
And tear the heart out of his side,
And lay the heart upon her hand
And bear that beating heart away;   5
And then did all the Muses sing
Of Magnus Annus [1] at the spring,
As though God's death were but a play.

Another Troy must rise and set,
Another lineage feed the crow,   10
Another Argo's painted prow
Drive to a flashier bauble yet.
The Roman Empire stood appalled:
It dropped the reins of peace and war
When that fierce virgin and her Star   15
Out of the fabulous darkness called.

2

In pity for man's darkening thought
He walked that room and issued thence

[1] the Platonic "Great Year," which an-   death and rebirth of a god
nounces a new historical cycle by the

In Galilean turbulence;
The Babylonian starlight brought   20
A fabulous, formless darkness in;
Odor of blood when Christ was slain
Made all Platonic tolerance vain
And vain all Doric discipline.

Everything that man esteems   25
Endures a moment or a day.
Love's pleasure drives his love away,
The painter's brush consumes his dreams;
The herald's cry, the soldier's tread
Exhaust his glory and his might: 30
Whatever flames upon the night
Man's own resinous heart has fed.

Leda and the Swan

A sudden blow: the great wings beating still
Above the staggering girl, her thighs caressed
By the dark webs, her nape caught in his bill,
He holds her helpless breast upon his breast.

How can those terrified vague fingers push   5
The feathered glory from her loosening thighs?
And how can body, laid in that white rush,
But feel the strange heart beating where it lies?

A shudder in the loins engenders there
The broken wall, the burning roof and tower   10
And Agamemnon dead.
                              Being so caught up,
So mastered by the brute blood of the air,
Did she put on his knowledge with his power
Before the indifferent beak could let her drop?   (1923)

Among School Children

I

I walk through the long schoolroom questioning;
A kind old nun in a white hood replies;

The children learn to cipher and to sing,
To study reading-books and histories,
To cut and sew, be neat in everything   5
In the best modern way—the children's eyes
In momentary wonder stare upon
A sixty-year-old smiling public man.

2

I dream of a Ledaean body, bent
Above a sinking fire, a tale that she   10
Told of a harsh reproof, or trivial event
That changed some childish day to tragedy—
Told, and it seemed that our two natures blent
Into a sphere from youthful sympathy,
Or else, to alter Plato's parable,   15
Into the yolk and white of the one shell.

3

And thinking of that fit of grief or rage
I look upon one child or t'other there
And wonder if she stood so at that age—
For even daughters of the swan can share   20
Something of every paddler's heritage—
And had that color upon cheek or hair,
And thereupon my heart is driven wild:
She stands before me as a living child.

4

Her present image floats into the mind—   25
Did Quattrocento finger fashion it
Hollow of cheek as though it drank the wind
And took a mess of shadows for its meat?
And I though never of Ledaean kind
Had pretty plumage once—enough of that,   30
Better to smile on all that smile, and show
There is a comfortable kind of old scarecrow.

5

What youthful mother, a shape upon her lap
Honey of generation had betrayed,
And that must sleep, shriek, struggle to escape   35
As recollection or the drug decide,
Would think her son, did she but see that shape

With sixty or more winters on its head,
A compensation for the pang of his birth,
Or the uncertainty of his setting forth?   40

6

Plato thought nature but a spume that plays
Upon a ghostly paradigm of things;
Solider Aristotle played the taws
Upon the bottom of a king of kings; [1]
World-famous golden-thighed Pythagoras   45
Fingered upon a fiddle-stick or strings
What a star sang and careless Muses heard:
Old clothes upon old sticks to scare a bird.

7

Both nuns and mothers worship images,
But those the candles light are not as those   50
That animate a mother's reveries,
But keep a marble or a bronze repose.
And yet they too break hearts—O Presences
That passion, piety or affection knows,
And that all heavenly glory symbolize—   55
O self-born mockers of man's enterprise;

8

Labor is blossoming or dancing where
The body is not bruised to pleasure soul,
Nor beauty born out of its own despair,
Nor blear-eyed wisdom out of midnight oil.   60
O chestnut-tree, great-rooted blossomer,
Are you the leaf, the blossom or the bole?
O body swayed to music, O brightening glance,
How can we know the dancer from the dance?

Byzantium

The unpurged images of day recede;
The Emperor's drunken soldiery are abed;
Night resonance recedes, night-walkers' song

---

[1] Alexander

After great cathedral gong;
A starlit or a moonlit dome disdains   5
All that man is,
All mere complexities,
The fury and the mire of human veins.

Before me floats an image, man or shade,
Shade more than man, more image than a shade;   10
For Hades' bobbin bound in mummy-cloth
May unwind the winding path;
A mouth that has no moisture and no breath
Breathless mouths may summon;
I hail the superhuman;   15
I call it death-in-life and life-in-death.

Miracle, bird or golden handiwork,
More miracle than bird or handiwork,
Planted on the star-lit golden bough,
Can like the cocks of Hades crow,   20
Or, by the moon embittered, scorn aloud
In glory of changeless metal
Common bird or petal
And all complexities of mire or blood.

At midnight on the Emperor's pavement flit   25
Flames that no faggot feeds, nor steel has lit,
Nor storm disturbs, flames begotten of flame,
Where blood-begotten spirits come
And all complexities of fury leave,
Dying into a dance,   30
An agony of trance,
An agony of flame that cannot singe a sleeve.

Astraddle on the dolphin's mire and blood,
Spirit after spirit! The smithies break the flood,
The golden smithies of the Emperor!   35
Marbles of the dancing floor
Break bitter furies of complexity,
Those images that yet
Fresh images beget,
That dolphin-torn, that gong-tormented sea.   (1930)

Crazy Jane Talks with the Bishop

I met the Bishop on the road
And much said he and I.
'Those breasts are flat and fallen now,
Those veins must soon be dry;
Live in a heavenly mansion,   5
Not in some foul sty.'

'Fair and foul are near of kin,
And fair needs foul,' I cried.
'My friends are gone, but that's a truth
Nor grave nor bed denied,   10
Learned in bodily lowliness
And in the heart's pride.

'A woman can be proud and stiff
When on love intent;
But Love has pitched his mansion in   15
The place of excrement;
For nothing can be sole or whole
That has not been rent.'

Lapis Lazuli

(For Harry Clifton)

I have heard that hysterical women say
They are sick of the palette and fiddle-bow,
Of poets that are always gay,
For everybody knows or else should know
That if nothing drastic is done   5
Aeroplane and Zeppelin will come out,
Pitch like King Billy bomb-balls in
Until the town lie beaten flat.

All perform their tragic play,
There struts Hamlet, there is Lear,   10
That's Ophelia, that Cordelia;
Yet they, should the last scene be there,

The great stage curtain about to drop,
If worthy their prominent part in the play,
Do not break up their lines to weep.   15
They know that Hamlet and Lear are gay;
Gaiety transfiguring all that dread.
All men have aimed at, found and lost;
Black out; Heaven blazing into the head:
Tragedy wrought to its uttermost.   20
Though Hamlet rambles and Lear rages,
And all the drop-scenes drop at once
Upon a hundred thousand stages,
It cannot grow by an inch or an ounce.

On their own feet they came, or on shipboard,   25
Camel-back, horse-back, ass-back, mule-back,
Old civilizations put to the sword.
Then they and their wisdom went to rack:
No handiwork of Callimachus,[1]
Who handled marble as if it were bronze,   30
Made draperies that seem to rise
When sea-wind swept the corner, stands;
His long lamp-chimney shaped like the stem
Of a slender palm, stood but a day;
All things fall and are built again,   35
And those that build them again are gay.

Two Chinamen, behind them a third,
Are carved in lapis lazuli,
Over them flies a long-legged bird,
A symbol of longevity;   40
The third, doubtless a serving-man,
Carries a musical instrument.

Every discoloration of the stone,
Every accidental crack or dent,
Seems a water-course or an avalanche,   45
Or lofty slope where it still snows
Though doubtless plum or cherry-branch
Sweetens the little half-way house
Those Chinamen climb towards, and I
Delight to imagine them seated there;   50
There, on the mountain and the sky,

_____
[1] Athenian sculptor, 5th century B.C.

On all the tragic scene they stare.
One asks for mournful melodies;
Accomplished fingers begin to play.
Their eyes mid many wrinkles, their eyes,   55
Their ancient, glittering eyes, are gay.

Long-Legged Fly

That civilization may not sink,   20
Its great battle lost,
Quiet the dog, tether the pony
To a distant post;
Our master Caesar is in the tent   5
Where the maps are spread,
His eyes fixed upon nothing,
A hand under his head.
Like a long-legged fly upon the stream
His mind moves upon silence.   10

That the topless towers be burnt
And men recall that face,
Move most gently if move you must
In this lonely place.
She thinks, part woman, three parts a child,   15
That nobody looks; her feet
Practice a tinker shuffle
Picked up on a street.
Like a long-legged fly upon the stream
Her mind moves upon silence.   20

That girls at puberty may find
The first Adam in their thought,
Shut the door of the Pope's chapel,
Keep those children out.
There on that scaffolding reclines   25
Michael Angelo.
With no more sound than the mice make
His hand moves to and fro.
Like a long-legged fly upon the stream
His mind moves upon silence.   30

The Circus Animals' Desertion

1

I sought a theme and sought for it in vain,
I sought it daily for six weeks or so.
Maybe at last, being but a broken man,
I must be satisfied with my heart, although
Winter and summer till old age began   5
My circus animals were all on show,
Those stilted boys, that burnished chariot,
Lion and woman and the Lord knows what.

2

What can I but enumerate old themes?
First that sea-rider Oisin [1] led by the nose   10
Through three enchanted islands, allegorical dreams,
Vain gaiety, vain battle, vain repose,
Themes of the embittered heart, or so it seems,
That might adorn old songs or courtly shows;
But what cared I that set him on to ride,   15
I, starved for the bosom of his faery bride?

And then a counter-truth filled out its play,
The Countess Cathleen was the name I gave it;
She, pity-crazed, had given her soul away,
But masterful Heaven had intervened to save it.   20
I thought my dear must her own soul destroy,
So did fanaticism and hate enslave it,
And this brought forth a dream and soon enough
This dream itself had all my thought and love.

And when the Fool and Blind Man stole the bread   25
Cuchulain [2] fought the ungovernable sea;
Heart-mysteries there, and yet when all is said
It was the dream itself enchanted me:
Character isolated by a deed
To engross the present and dominate memory.   30
Players and painted stage took all my love,
And not those things that they were emblems of.

[1] legendary Irish hero, about whom Yeats wrote in "The Wanderings of Oisin," 1889 [2] legendary Irish hero

3

Those masterful images because complete
Grew in pure mind, but out of what began?
A mound of refuse or the sweepings of a street,   35
Old kettles, old bottles, and a broken can,
Old iron, old bones, old rags, that raving slut
Who keeps the till. Now that my ladder's gone,
I must lie down where all the ladders start,
In the foul-rag-and-bone shop of the heart.   40

The Apparitions

Because there is safety in derision
I talked about an apparition,
I took no trouble to convince,
Or seem plausible to a man of sense,
Distrustful of that popular eye   5
Whether it be bold or sly.
Fifteen apparitions have I seen;
The worst a coat upon a coat-hanger.

I have found nothing half so good
As my long-planned half solitude,   10
Where I can sit up half the night
With some friend that has the wit
Not to allow his looks to tell
When I am unintelligible.
Fifteen apparitions have I seen;   15
The worst a coat upon a coat-hanger.

When a man grows old his joy
Grows more deep day after day,
His empty heart is full at length,
But he has need of all that strength   20
Because of the increasing Night
That opens her mystery and fright.
Fifteen apparitions have I seen;
The worst a coat upon a coat-hanger.

E. A. ROBINSON (1869–1935)

Luke Havergal

Go to the western gate, Luke Havergal,
There where the vines cling crimson on the wall,
And in the twilight wait for what will come.
The leaves will whisper there of her, and some,
Like flying words, will strike you as they fall;   5
But go, and if you listen she will call.
Go to the western gate, Luke Havergal—
Luke Havergal.

No, there is not a dawn in eastern skies
To rift the fiery night that's in your eyes;   10
But there, where western glooms are gathering,
The dark will end the dark, if anything:
God slays Himself with every leaf that flies,
And hell is more than half of paradise.
No, there is not a dawn in eastern skies—   15
In eastern skies.

Out of a grave I come to tell you this,
Out of a grave I come to quench the kiss
That flames upon your forehead with a glow
That blinds you to the way that you must go.   20
Yes, there is yet one way to where she is,
Bitter, but one that faith may never miss.
Out of a grave I come to tell you this—
To tell you this.

There is the western gate, Luke Havergal,   25
There are the crimson leaves upon the wall.
Go, for the winds are tearing them away,—
Nor think to riddle the dead words they say,
Nor any more to feel them as they fall;
But go, and if you trust her she will call.   30
There is the western gate, Luke Havergal—
Luke Havergal.

The Dark Hills

Dark hills at evening in the west,
Where sunset hovers like a sound
Of golden horns that sang to rest
Old bones of warriors under ground,
Far now from all the bannered ways
Where flash the legions of the sun,
You fade—as if the last of days
Were fading, and all wars were done.

The Mill

The miller's wife had waited long,
    The tea was cold, the fire was dead;
And there might yet be nothing wrong
    In how he went and what he said:
"There are no millers any more,"   5
    Was all that she had heard him say;
And he had lingered at the door
    So long that it seemed yesterday.

Sick with a fear that had no form
    She knew that she was there at last;   10
And in the mill there was a warm
    And mealy fragrance of the past.
What else there was would only seem
    To say again what he had meant;
And what was hanging from a beam   15
    Would not have heeded where she went.

And if she thought it followed her,
    She may have reasoned in the dark
That one way of the few there were
    Would hide her and would leave no mark: 20
Black water, smooth above the weir
    Like starry velvet in the night,
Though ruffled once, would soon appear
    The same as ever to the sight.

The Poor Relation

No longer torn by what she knows
And sees within the eyes of others,
Her doubts are when the daylight goes,
Her fears are for the few she bothers.
She tells them it is wholly wrong   5
Of her to stay alive so long;
And when she smiles her forehead shows
A crinkle that had been her mother's.

Beneath her beauty, blanched with pain,
And wistful yet for being cheated,   10
A child would seem to ask again
A question many times repeated;
But no rebellion has betrayed
Her wonder at what she has paid
For memories that have no stain,   15
For triumph born to be defeated.

To those who come for what she was—
The few left who know where to find her—
She clings, for they are all she has;
And she may smile when they remind her,   20
As heretofore, of what they know
Of roses that are still to blow
By ways where not so much as grass
Remains of what she sees behind her.

They stay a while, and having done   25
What penance or the past requires,
They go, and leave her there alone
To count her chimneys and her spires.
Her lip shakes when they go away,
And yet she would not have them stay;   30
She knows as well as anyone
That Pity, having played, soon tires.

But one friend always reappears,
A good ghost, not to be forsaken;
Whereat she laughs and has no fears   35
Of what a ghost may reawaken,
But welcomes, while she wears and mends

The poor relation's odds and ends,
Her truant from a tomb of years—
Her power of youth so early taken.   40

Poor laugh, more slender than her song
It seems; and there are none to hear it
With even the stopped ears of the strong
For breaking heart or broken spirit.
The friends who clamored for her place,   45
And would have scratched her for her face,
Have lost her laughter for so long
That none would care enough to fear it.

None live who need fear anything
From her, whose losses are their pleasure;   50
The plover with a wounded wing
Stays not the flight that others measure;
So there she waits, and while she lives,
And death forgets, and faith forgives,
Her memories go foraging   55
For bits of childhood song they treasure.

And like a giant harp that hums
On always, and is always blending
The coming of what never comes
With what has past and had an ending,   60
The City trembles, throbs, and pounds
Outside, and through a thousand sounds
The small intolerable drums
Of Time are like slow drops descending.

Bereft enough to shame a sage   65
And given little to long sighing,
With no illusion to assuage
The lonely changelessness of dying,—
Unsought, unthought-of, and unheard,
She sings and watches like a bird,   70
Safe in a comfortable cage
From which there will be no more flying.

Eros Turannos [1]

She fears him, and will always ask
    What fated her to choose him;
She meets in his engaging mask
    All reasons to refuse him;
But what she meets and what she fears   5
Are less than are the downward years,
Drawn slowly to the foamless weirs
    Of age, were she to lose him.

Between a blurred sagacity
    That once had power to sound him,   10
And Love, that will not let him be
    The Judas that she found him,
Her pride assuages her almost,
As if it were alone the cost.—
He sees that he will not be lost,   15
    And waits and looks around him.

A sense of ocean and old trees
    Envelops and allures him;
Tradition, touching all he sees,
    Beguiles and reassures him;   20
And all her doubts of what he says
Are dimmed with what she knows of days—
Till even prejudice delays
    And fades, and she secures him.

The falling leaf inaugurates   25
    The reign of her confusion:
The pounding wave reverberates
    The dirge of her illusion;
And home, where passion lived and died,
Becomes a place where she can hide,   30
While all the town and harbor side
    Vibrate with her seclusion.

We tell you, tapping on our brows,
    The story as it should be,—
As if the story of a house   35
    Were told, or ever could be;

[1] Eros the tyrant

We'll have no kindly veil between
Her visions and those we have seen,—
As if we guessed what hers have been,
    Or what they are or would be.   40

Meanwhile we do no harm; for they
    That with a god have striven,
Not hearing much of what we say,
    Take what the god has given;
Though like waves breaking it may be,   45
Or like a changed familiar tree,
Or like a stairway to the sea
    Where down the blind are driven.

Hillcrest[1]

(To Mrs. Edward MacDowell)

No sound of any storm that shakes
Old island walls with older seas
Comes here where now September makes
An island in a sea of trees.

Between the sunlight and the shade   5
A man may learn till he forgets
The roaring of a world remade,
And all his ruins and regrets;

And if he still remembers here
Poor fights he may have won or lost,—   10
If he be ridden with the fear
Of what some other fight may cost,—

If, eager to confuse too soon,
What he has known with what may be,
He reads a planet out of tune   15
For cause of his jarred harmony,—

If here he venture to unroll
His index of adagios,

[1] the house at the MacDowell Colony
in New Hampshire where the poet spent his summers

And he be given to console
Humanity with what he knows,—   20

He may by contemplation learn
A little more than what he knew,
And even see great oaks return
To acorns out of which they grew.

He may, if he but listen well,   25
Through twilight and the silence here,
Be told what there are none may tell
To vanity's impatient ear;

And he may never dare again
Say what awaits him, or be sure   30
What sunlit labyrinth of pain
He may not enter and endure.

Who knows to-day from yesterday
May learn to count no thing too strange:
Love builds of what Time takes away,   35
Till Death itself is less than Change.

Who sees enough in his duress
May go as far as dreams have gone;
Who sees a little may do less
Than many who are blind have done;   40

Who sees unchastened here the soul
Triumphant has no other sight
Than has a child who sees the whole
World radiant with his own delight.

Far journeys and hard wandering   45
Await him in whose crude surmise
Peace, like a mask, hides everything
That is and has been from his eyes;

And all his wisdom is unfound,
Or like a web that error weaves   50
On airy looms that have a sound
No louder now than falling leaves.

RALPH HODGSON (1871–1962)

The Bells of Heaven

'Twould ring the bells of Heaven
The wildest peal for years,
If Parson lost his senses
And people came to theirs,
And he and they together   5
Knelt down with angry prayers
For tamed and shabby tigers
And dancing dogs and bears,
And wretched, blind pit ponies,
And little hunted hares.   10

Reason

Reason has moons, but moons not hers
    Lie mirrored on her sea,
Confusing her astronomers,
    But O! delighting me.

The Birdcatcher

When flighting time is on, I go
With clap-net and decoy,
A-fowling after goldfinches
And other birds of joy;

I lurk among the thickets of
The Heart where they are bred,
And catch the twittering beauties as
They fly into my Head.

The Hammers

Noise of hammers once I heard
Many hammers, busy hammers,
Beating, shaping night and day,
Shaping, beating dust and clay
To a palace; saw it reared;   5
Saw the hammers laid away.

And I listened, and I heard
Hammers beating, night and day,
In the palace newly reared,
Beating it to dust and clay: 10
Other hammers, muffled hammers,
Silent hammers of decay.

ROBERT FROST (1874–1963)

'Out, Out—'

The buzz-saw snarled and rattled in the yard
And made dust and dropped stove-length sticks of wood,
Sweet-scented stuff when the breeze drew across it.
And from there those that lifted eyes could count
Five mountain ranges one behind the other   5
Under the sunset far into Vermont.
And the saw snarled and rattled, snarled and rattled,
As it ran light, or had to bear a load.
And nothing happened: day was all but done.
Call it a day, I wish they might have said   10
To please the boy by giving him the half hour
That a boy counts so much when saved from work.
His sister stood beside them in her apron
To tell them 'Supper.' At the word, the saw,
As if to prove saws knew what supper meant,   15
Leaped out at the boy's hand, or seemed to leap—
He must have given the hand. However it was,
Neither refused the meeting. But the hand!
The boy's first outcry was a rueful laugh,
As he swung toward them holding up the hand   20
Half in appeal, but half as if to keep
The life from spilling. Then the boy saw all—
Since he was old enough to know, big boy
Doing a man's work, though a child at heart—
He saw all spoiled. 'Don't let him cut my hand off—   25
The doctor, when he comes. Don't let him, sister!'
So. But the hand was gone already.
The doctor put him in the dark of ether.
He lay and puffed his lips out with his breath.
And then—the watcher at his pulse took fright.   30
No one believed. They listened at his heart.
Little—less—nothing!—and that ended it.
No more to build on there. And they, since they
Were not the one dead, turned to their affairs.

524

Birches

When I see birches bend to left and right
Across the lines of straighter darker trees,
I like to think some boy's been swinging them.
But swinging doesn't bend them down to stay.
Ice-storms do that. Often you must have seen them   5
Loaded with ice a sunny winter morning
After a rain. They click upon themselves
As the breeze rises, and turn many-colored
As the stir cracks and crazes their enamel.
Soon the sun's warmth makes them shed crystal shells   10
Shattering and avalanching on the snow-crust—
Such heaps of broken glass to sweep away
You'd think the inner dome of heaven had fallen.
They are dragged to the withered bracken by the load,
And they seem not to break; though once they are bowed   15
So low for long, they never right themselves:
You may see their trunks arching in the woods
Years afterwards, trailing their leaves on the ground
Like girls on hands and knees that throw their hair
Before them over their heads to dry in the sun.   20
But I was going to say when Truth broke in
With all her matter-of-fact about the ice-storm
I should prefer to have some boy bend them
As he went out and in to fetch the cows—
Some boy too far from town to learn baseball,   25
Whose only play was what he found himself,
Summer or winter, and could play alone.
One by one he subdued his father's trees
By riding them down over and over again
Until he took the stiffness out of them,   30
And not one but hung limp, not one was left
For him to conquer. He learned all there was
To learn about not launching out too soon
And so not carrying the tree away
Clear to the ground. He always kept his poise   35
To the top branches, climbing carefully
With the same pains you use to fill a cup
Up to the brim, and even above the brim.
Then he flung outward, feet first, with a swish,
Kicking his way down through the air to the ground.   40

So was I once myself a swinger of birches.
And so I dream of going back to be.
It's when I'm weary of considerations,
And life is too much like a pathless wood
Where your face burns and tickles with the cobwebs   45
Broken across it, and one eye is weeping
From a twig's having lashed across it open.
I'd like to get away from earth awhile
And then come back to it and begin over.
May no fate willfully misunderstand me   50
And half grant what I wish and snatch me away
Not to return. Earth's the right place for love:
I don't know where it's likely to go better.
I'd like to go by climbing a birch tree,
And climb black branches up a snow-white trunk   55
Toward heaven, till the tree could bear no more,
But dipped its top and set me down again.
That would be good both going and coming back.
One could do worse than be a swinger of birches.

Tree at My Window

Tree at my window, window tree,
My sash is lowered when night comes on;
But let there never be curtain drawn
Between you and me.

Vague dream-head lifted out of the ground,   5
And thing next most diffuse to cloud,
Not all your light tongues talking aloud
Could be profound.

But tree, I have seen you taken and tossed,
And if you have seen me when I slept,   10
You have seen me when I was taken and swept
And all but lost.

That day she put our heads together,
Fate had her imagination about her,
Your head so much concerned with outer,   15
Mine with inner, weather.

Desert Places

Snow falling and night falling fast oh fast
In a field I looked into going past,
And the ground almost covered smooth in snow,
But a few weeds and stubble showing last.

The woods around it have it—it is theirs.   5
All animals are smothered in their lairs.
I am too absent-spirited to count;
The loneliness includes me unawares.

And lonely as it is that loneliness
Will be more lonely ere it will be less—   10
A blanker whiteness of benighted snow
With no expression, nothing to express.

They cannot scare me with their empty spaces
Between stars—on stars where no human race is.
I have it in me so much nearer home   15
To scare myself with my own desert places.

Design

I found a dimpled spider, fat and white,
On a white heal-all, holding up a moth
Like a white piece of rigid satin cloth—
Assorted characters of death and blight
Mixed ready to begin the morning right,
Like the ingredients of a witches' broth—
A snow-drop spider, a flower like froth,
And dead wings carried like a paper kite.

What had that flower to do with being white,
The wayside blue and innocent heal-all?
What brought the kindred spider to that height,
Then steered the white moth thither in the night?
What but design of darkness to appall?—
If design govern in a thing so small.

The Silken Tent

She is as in a field a silken tent
At midday when a sunny summer breeze
Has dried the dew and all its ropes relent,
So that in guys it gently sways at ease,
And its supporting central cedar pole,
That is its pinnacle to heavenward
And signifies the sureness of the soul,
Seems to owe naught to any single cord,
But strictly held by none, is loosely bound
By countless silken ties of love and thought
To everything on earth the compass round,
And only by one's going slightly taut
In the capriciousness of summer air
Is of the slightest bondage made aware.

To Earthward

Love at the lips was touch
As sweet as I could bear;
And once that seemed too much;
I lived on air

That crossed me from sweet things,   5
The flow of—was it musk
From hidden grapevine springs
Down hill at dusk?

I had the swirl and ache
From sprays of honeysuckle   10
That when they're gathered shake
Dew on the knuckle.

I craved strong sweets, but those
Seemed strong when I was young;
The petal of the rose   15
It was that stung.

Now no joy but lacks salt
That is not dashed with pain

And weariness and fault;
I crave the stain   20

Of tears, the aftermark
Of almost too much love,
The sweet of bitter bark
And burning clove.

When stiff and sore and scarred   25
I take away my hand
From leaning on it hard
In grass and sand,

The hurt is not enough:
I long for weight and strength   30
To feel the earth as rough
To all my length.

Come In

As I came to the edge of the woods,
Thrush music—hark!
Now if it was dusk outside,
Inside it was dark.

Too dark in the woods for a bird   5
By sleight of wing
To better its perch for the night,
Though it still could sing.

The last of the light of the sun
That had died in the west   10
Still lived for one song more
In a thrush's breast.

Far in the pillared dark
Thrush music went—
Almost like a call to come in   15
To the dark and lament.

But no, I was out for stars:
I would not come in.
I meant not even if asked,
And I hadn't been.   20

Acquainted with the Night

I have been one acquainted with the night.
I have walked out in rain—and back in rain.
I have outwalked the furthest city light.

I have looked down the saddest city lane.
I have passed by the watchman on his beat   5
And dropped my eyes, unwilling to explain.

I have stood still and stopped the sound of feet
When far away an interrupted cry
Came over houses from another street,

But not to call me back or say good-bye;   10
And further still at an unearthly height,
One luminary clock against the sky

Proclaimed the time was neither wrong nor right
I have been one acquainted with the night.

The Gift Outright

The land was ours before we were the land's.
She was our land more than a hundred years
Before we were her people. She was ours
In Massachusetts, in Virginia,
But we were England's, still colonials,   5
Possessing what we still were unpossessed by,
Possessed by what we now no more possessed.
Something we were withholding made us weak
Until we found out that it was ourselves
We were withholding from our land of living,   10
And forthwith found salvation in surrender.
Such as we were we gave ourselves outright
(The deed of gift was many deeds of war)
To the land vaguely realizing westward,
But still unstoried, artless, unenhanced,   15
Such as she was, such as she would become.

The Most of It

He thought he kept the universe alone;
For all the voice in answer he could wake
Was but the mocking echo of his own
From some tree-hidden cliff across the lake.
Some morning from the boulder-broken beach   5
He would cry out on life, that what it wants
Is not its own love back in copy speech,
But counter-love, original response.
And nothing ever came of what he cried
Unless it was the embodiment that crashed   10
In the cliff's talus on the other side,
And then in the far distant water splashed,
But after a time allowed for it to swim,
Instead of proving human when it neared
And someone else additional to him,   15
As a great buck it powerfully appeared,
Pushing the crumpled water up ahead,
And landed pouring like a waterfall,
And stumbled through the rocks with horny tread,
And forced the underbrush—and that was all.   20

Ends

Loud talk in the overlighted house
That made us stumble past.
Oh, there had once been night the first,
But this was night the last.

Of all the things he might have said,   5
Sincere or insincere,
He never said she wasn't young,
And hadn't been his dear.

Oh, some as soon would throw it all
As throw a part away.   10
And some will say all sorts of things,
But some mean what they say.

EDWARD THOMAS (1878–1917)

The Sign-Post

The dim sea glints chill. The white sun is shy,
And the skeleton weeds and the never-dry,
Rough, long grasses keep white with frost
At the hilltop by the finger-post;
The smoke of the traveller's-joy is puffed   5
Over hawthorn berry and hazel tuft.
I read the sign. Which way shall I go?
A voice says: You would not have doubted so
At twenty. Another voice gentle with scorn
Says: At twenty you wished you had never been born.   10

One hazel lost a leaf of gold
From a tuft at the tip, when the first voice told
The other he wished to know what 'twould be
To be sixty by this same post. 'You shall see,'
He laughed—and I had to join his laughter—   15
'You shall see; but either before or after,
Whatever happens, it must befall,
A mouthful of earth to remedy all
Regrets and wishes shall freely be given;
And if there be a flaw in that heaven   20
'Twill be freedom to wish, and your wish may be
To be here or anywhere talking to me,
No matter what the weather, on earth,
At any age between death and birth,—
To see what day or night can be,   25
The sun and the frost, the land and the sea,
Summer, Autumn, Winter, Spring,—
With a poor man of any sort, down to a king,
Standing upright out in the air
Wondering where he shall journey, O where?'   30

The Owl

Downhill I came, hungry, and yet not starved;
Cold, yet had heat within me that was proof
Against the North wind; tired, yet so that rest
Had seemed the sweetest thing under a roof.

Then at the inn I had food, fire, and rest,   5
Knowing how hungry, cold, and tired was I.
All of the night was quite barred out except
An owl's cry, a most melancholy cry

Shaken out long and clear upon the hill,
No merry note, nor cause of merriment,   10
But one telling me plain what I escaped
And others could not, that night, as in I went.

And salted was my food, and my repose,
Salted and sobered, too, by the bird's voice
Speaking for all who lay under the stars,   15
Soldiers and poor, unable to rejoice.

The Combe

The Combe was ever dark, ancient and dark.
Its mouth is stopped with bramble, thorn, and briar;
And no one scrambles over the sliding chalk
By beech and yew and perishing juniper
Down the half precipices of its sides, with roots   5
And rabbit holes for steps. The sun of Winter,
The moon of Summer, and all the singing birds
Except the missel-thrush that loves juniper,
Are quite shut out. But far more ancient and dark
The Combe looks since they killed the badger there,   10
Dug him out and gave him to the hounds,
That most ancient Briton of English beasts.

The Long Small Room

The long small room that showed willows in the west
Narrowed up to the end the fireplace filled,
Although not wide. I liked it. No one guessed
What need or accident made them so build.

Only the moon, the mouse and the sparrow peeped   5
In from the ivy round the casement thick.
Of all they saw and heard there they shall keep
The tale for the old ivy and older brick.

When I look back I am like moon, sparrow, and mouse
That witnessed what they could never understand   10
Or alter or prevent in the dark house.
One thing remains the same—this my right hand

Crawling crab-like over the clean white page,
Resting awhile each morning on the pillow,
Then once more starting to crawl on towards age.   15
The hundred last leaves stream upon the willow.

In Memoriam (Easter, 1915)

The flowers left thick at nightfall in the wood
This Eastertide call into mind the men,
Now far from home, who, with their sweethearts, should
Have gathered them and and will do never again.

⋙ CARL SANDBURG (1878–   )

Chicago

Hog Butcher for the World,
Tool Maker, Stacker of Wheat,
Player with Railroads and the Nation's Freight Handler;
Stormy, husky, brawling,
City of the Big Shoulders: 5
They tell me you are wicked and I believe them, for I have seen your
    painted women under the gas lamps luring the farm boys.
And they tell me you are crooked and I answer: Yes, it is true I have
    seen the gunman kill and go free to kill again.
And they tell me you are brutal and my reply is: On the faces of women
    and children I have seen the marks of wanton hunger.
And having answered so I turn once more to those who sneer at this my
    city, and I give them back the sneer and say to them:
Come and show me another city with lifted head singing so proud to be
    alive and coarse and strong and cunning.   10
Flinging magnetic curses amid the toil of piling job on job, here is a tall
    bold slugger set vivid against the little soft cities;
Fierce as a dog with tongue lapping for action, cunning as a savage
    pitted against the wilderness,
        Bareheaded,
        Shoveling,
        Wrecking,   15
        Planning,
        Building, breaking, rebuilding.
Under the smoke, dust all over his mouth, laughing with white teeth,
Under the terrible burden of destiny laughing as a young man laughs,
Laughing even as an ignorant fighter laughs who has never lost a
    battle,   20
Bragging and laughing that under his wrist is the pulse, and under his
    ribs the heart of the people,
                Laughing!
Laughing the stormy, husky, brawling laughter of Youth, half-naked,
    sweating, proud to be Hog Butcher, Tool Maker, Stacker of Wheat,
    Player with Railroads and Freight Handler to the Nation.

VACHEL LINDSAY (1879–1931)

The Flower-Fed Buffaloes

The flower-fed buffaloes of the spring
In the days of long ago,
Ranged where the locomotives sing
And the prairie flowers lie low:
The tossing, blooming, perfumed grass   5
Is swept away by wheat,
Wheels and wheels and wheels spin by
In the spring that still is sweet.
But the flower-fed buffaloes of the spring
Left us long ago.   10
They gore no more, they bellow no more,
They trundle around the hills no more:—
With the Blackfeet lying low,
With the Pawnees lying low.

Factory Windows Are Always Broken

Factory windows are always broken.
Somebody's always throwing bricks,
Somebody's always heaving cinders,
Playing ugly Yahoo tricks.

Factory windows are always broken.
Other windows are let alone.
No one throws through the chapel-window
The bitter, snarling derisive stone.

Factory windows are always broken.
Something or other is going wrong.
Something is rotten—I think, in Denmark.
End of the factory-window song.

✒ WALLACE STEVENS (1879–1955)

Disillusionment of Ten O'Clock

The houses are haunted
By white night-gowns.
None are green,
Or purple with green rings,
Or green with yellow rings,   5
Or yellow with blue rings.
None of them are strange,
With socks of lace
And beaded ceintures.[1]
People are not going   10
To dream of baboons and periwinkles.
Only, here and there, an old sailor,
Drunk and asleep in his boots,
Catches tigers
In red weather.   15

The Emperor of Ice-Cream

Call the roller of big cigars,
The muscular one, and bid him whip
In kitchen cups concupiscent curds.
Let the wenches dawdle in such dress
As they are used to wear, and let the boys   5
Bring flowers in last month's newspapers.
Let be be finale of seem.
The only emperor is the emperor of ice-cream.

Take from the dresser of deal,
Lacking the three glass knobs, that sheet   10
On which she embroidered fantails once
And spread it so as to cover her face.
If her horny feet protrude, they come
To show how cold she is, and dumb.
Let the lamp affix its beam.   15
The only emperor is the emperor of ice-cream.

[1] belts

The Snow Man

One must have a mind of winter
To regard the frost and the boughs
Of the pine-trees crusted with snow;

And have been cold a long time
To behold the junipers shagged with ice,   5
The spruces rough in the distant glitter

Of the January sun; and not to think
Of any misery in the sound of the wind,
In the sound of a few leaves,

Which is the sound of the land   10
Full of the same wind
That is blowing in the same bare place

For the listener, who listens in the snow,
And, nothing himself, beholds
Nothing that is not there and the nothing that is. 15

Sunday Morning

I

Complacencies of the peignoir, and late
Coffee and oranges in a sunny chair,
And the green freedom of a cockatoo
Upon a rug mingle to dissipate
The holy hush of ancient sacrifice.   5
She dreams a little, and she feels the dark
Encroachment of that old catastrophe,
As a calm darkens among water-lights.
The pungent oranges and bright, green wings
Seem things in some procession of the dead,   10
Winding across wide water, without sound.
The day is like wide water, without sound,
Stilled for the passing of her dreaming feet
Over the seas, to silent Palestine,
Dominion of the blood and sepulchre.   15

2

Why should she give her bounty to the dead?
What is divinity if it can come
Only in silent shadows and in dreams?
Shall she not find in comforts of the sun,
In pungent fruit and bright, green wings, or else   20
In any balm or beauty of the earth,
Things to be cherished like the thought of heaven?
Divinity must live within herself:
Passions of rain, or moods in falling snow;
Grievings in loneliness, or unsubdued   25
Elations when the forest blooms; gusty
Emotions on wet roads on autumn nights;
All pleasures and all pains, remembering
The bough of summer and the winter branch.
These are the measures destined for her soul.   30

3

Jove in the clouds had his inhuman birth.
No mother suckled him, no sweet land gave
Large-mannered motions to his mythy mind
He moved among us, as a muttering king,
Magnificent, would move among his hinds,   35
Until our blood, commingling, virginal,
With heaven, brought such requital to desire
The very hinds discerned it, in a star.
Shall our blood fail? Or shall it come to be
The blood of paradise? And shall the earth   40
Seem all of paradise that we shall know?
The sky will be much friendlier then than now,
A part of labor and a part of pain,
And next in glory to enduring love,
Not this dividing and indifferent blue.   45

4

She says, "I am content when wakened birds,
Before they fly, test the reality
Of misty fields, by their sweet questionings;
But when the birds are gone, and their warm fields
Return no more, where, then, is paradise?"   50
There is not any haunt of prophecy,
Nor any old chimera of the grave,

Neither the golden underground, nor isle
Melodious, where spirits gat them home,
Nor visionary south, nor cloudy palm   55
Remote on heaven's hill, that has endured
As April's green endures; or will endure
Like her remembrance of awakened birds,
Or her desire for June and evening, tipped
By the consummation of the swallow's wings.   60

5

She says, "But in contentment I still feel
The need of some imperishable bliss."
Death is the mother of beauty; hence from her,
Alone, shall come fulfilment to our dreams
And our desires. Although she strews the leaves   65
Of sure obliteration on our paths,
The path sick sorrow took, the many paths
Where triumph rang its brassy phrase, or love
Whispered a little out of tenderness,
She makes the willow shiver in the sun   70
For maidens who were wont to sit and gaze
Upon the grass, relinquished to their feet.
She causes boys to pile new plums and pears
On disregarded plate. The maidens taste
And stray impassioned in the littering leaves.   75

6

Is there no change of death in paradise?
Does ripe fruit never fall? Or do the boughs
Hang always heavy in that perfect sky,
Unchanging, yet so like our perishing earth,
With rivers like our own that seek for seas   80
They never find, the same receding shores
That never touch with inarticulate pang?
Why set the pear upon those river-banks
Or spice the shores with odors of the plum?
Alas, that they should wear our colors there,   85
The silken weavings of our afternoons,
And pick the strings of our insipid lutes!
Death is the mother of beauty, mystical,
Within whose burning bosom we devise
Our earthly mothers waiting, sleeplessly.   90

7

Supple and turbulent, a ring of men
Shall chant in orgy on a summer morn
Their boisterous devotion to the sun,
Not as a god, but as a god might be,
Naked among them, like a savage source.   95
Their chant shall be a chant of paradise,
Out of their blood, returning to the sky;
And in their chant shall enter, voice by voice,
The windy lake wherein their lord delights,
The trees, like serafin, and echoing hills,   100
That choir among themselves long afterward.
They shall know well the heavenly fellowship
Of men that perish and of summer morn.
And whence they came and whither they shall go
The dew upon their feet shall manifest.   105

8

She hears, upon that water without sound,
A voice that cries, "The tomb in Palestine
Is not the porch of spirits lingering.
It is the grave of Jesus, where he lay."
We live in an old chaos of the sun,   110
Or old dependency of day and night,
Or island solitude, unsponsored, free,
Of that wide water, inescapable.
Deer walk upon our mountains, and the quail
Whistle about us their spontaneous cries;   115
Sweet berries ripen in the wilderness;
And, in the isolation of the sky,
At evening, casual flocks of pigeons make
Ambiguous undulations as they sink,
Downward to darkness, on extended wings.   120

Anecdote of the Jar

I placed a jar in Tennessee,
And round it was, upon a hill.
It made the slovenly wilderness
Surround that hill.

The wilderness rose up to it,
And sprawled around, no longer wild.
The jar was round upon the ground
And tall and of a port in air.

It took dominion everywhere.
The jar was gray and bare.
It did not give of bird or bush,
Like nothing else in Tennessee.

The Idea of Order at Key West

She sang beyond the genius of the sea.
The water never formed to mind or voice,
Like a body wholly body, fluttering
Its empty sleeves; and yet its mimic motion
Made constant cry, caused constantly a cry,   5
That was not ours although we understood,
Inhuman, of the veritable ocean.

The sea was not a mask. No more was she.
The song and water were not medleyed sound
Even if what she sang was what she heard,   10
Since what she sang was uttered word by word.
It may be that in all her phrases stirred
The grinding water and the gasping wind;
But it was she and not the sea we heard.

For she was the maker of the song she sang.   15
The ever-hooded, tragic-gestured sea
Was merely a place by which she walked to sing.
Whose spirit is this? we said, because we knew
It was the spirit that we sought and knew
That we should ask this often as she sang.   20

If it was only the dark voice of the sea
That rose, or even colored by many waves;
If it was only the outer voice of sky
And cloud, of the sunken coral water-walled,
However clear, it would have been deep air,   25
The heaving speech of air, a summer sound
Repeated in a summer without end

And sound alone. But it was more than that,
More even than her voice, and ours, among
The meaningless plungings of water and the wind,　　　30
Theatrical distances, bronze shadows heaped
On high horizons, mountainous atmospheres
Of sky and sea.
　　　　　　　It was her voice that made
The sky acutest at its vanishing.　　　　　　　35
She measured to the hour its solitude.
She was the single artificer of the world
In which she sang. And when she sang, the sea,
Whatever self it had, became the self
That was her song, for she was the maker. Then we,　　40
As we beheld her striding there alone,
Knew that there never was a world for her
Except the one she sang and, singing, made.

Ramon Fernandez, tell me, if you know,
Why, when the singing ended and we turned　　　45
Toward the town, tell why the glassy lights,
The lights in the fishing boats at anchor there,
As the night descended, tilting in the air,
Mastered the night and portioned out the sea,
Fixing emblazoned zones and fiery poles,　　　50
Arranging, deepening, enchanting night.

Oh! Blessed rage for order, pale Ramon,
The maker's rage to order words of the sea,
Words of the fragrant portals, dimly-starred,
And of ourselves and of our origins,　　　55
In ghostlier demarcations, keener sounds.

Man Carrying Thing

The poem must resist the intelligence
Almost successfully. Illustration:

A brune figure in winter evening resists
Identity. The thing he carries resists

The most necessitous sense. Accept them, then,　　　5
As secondary (parts not quite perceived

Of the obvious whole, uncertain particles
Of the certain solid, the primary free from doubt,

Things floating like the first hundred flakes of snow
Out of a storm we must endure all night,   10

Out of a storm of secondary things),
A horror of thoughts that suddenly are real.

We must endure our thoughts all night, until
The bright obvious stands motionless in cold.

Final Soliloquy of the Interior Paramour

Light the first light of evening, as in a room
In which we rest and, for small reason, think
The world imagined is the ultimate good.

This is, therefore, the intensest rendezvous.
It is in that thought that we collect ourselves,   5
Out of all the indifferences, into one thing:

Within a single thing, a single shawl
Wrapped tightly round us, since we are poor, a warmth,
A light, a power, the miraculous influence.

Here, now, we forget each other and ourselves.   10
We feel the obscurity of an order, a whole,
A knowledge, that which arranged the rendezvous.

Within its vital boundary, in the mind.
We say God and the imagination are one . . .
How high that highest candle lights the dark.   15

Out of this same light, out of the central mind,
We make a dwelling in the evening air,
In which being there together is enough.

The Course of a Particular

Today the leaves cry, hanging on branches swept by wind,
Yct the nothingness of winter becomes a little less.
It is still full of icy shades and shapen snow.

The leaves cry . . . One holds off and merely hears the cry.
It is a busy cry, concerning someone else.   5
And though one says that one is part of everything,

There is a conflict, there is a resistance involved;
And being part is an exertion that declines:
One feels the life of that which gives life as it is.

The leaves cry. It is not a cry of divine attention,   10
Nor the smoke-drift of puffed-out heroes, nor human cry.
It is the cry of leaves that do not transcend themselves,

In the absence of fantasia, without meaning more
Than they are in the final finding of the air, in the thing
Itself, until, at last, the cry concerns no one at all.   15

Of Mere Being

The palm at the end of the mind,
Beyond the last thought, rises
In the bronze distance,

A gold-feathered bird
Sings in the palm, without human meaning,   5
Without human feeling, a foreign song.

You know then that it is not the reason
That makes us happy or unhappy.
The bird sings. Its feathers shine.

The palm stands on the edge of space.   10
The wind moves slowly in the branches.
The bird's fire-fangled feathers dangle down.

JAMES JOYCE (1882–1941)

Tilly

He travels after a winter sun,
Urging the cattle along a cold red road,
Calling to them, a voice they know,
He drives his beasts above Cabra.

The voice tells them home is warm.
They moo and make brute music with their hoofs.
He drives them with a flowering branch before him,
Smoke pluming their foreheads.

Boor, bond of the herd,
Tonight stretch full by the fire!
I bleed by the black stream
For my torn bough!

Ecce Puer

Of the dark past
A child is born
With joy and grief
My heart is torn

Calm in his cradle   5
The living lies.
May love and mercy
Unclose his eyes!

Young life is breathed
On the glass;   10
The world that was not
Comes to pass.

A child is sleeping:
An old man gone.
O, father forsaken,   15
Forgive your son!

Portrait of a Lady

Your thighs are appletrees
whose blossoms touch the sky.
Which sky? The sky
where Watteau hung a lady's
slipper. Your knees   5
are a southern breeze—or
a gust of snow. Agh! what
sort of man was Fragonard?
—as if that answered
anything. Ah, yes—below   10
the knees, since the tune
drops that way, it is
one of those white summer days,
the tall grass of your ankles
flickers upon the shore—   15
Which shore?—
the sand clings to my lips—
Which shore?
Agh, petals maybe. How
should I know?   20
Which shore? Which shore?
I said petals from an appletree.

To Waken an Old Lady

Old age is
a flight of small
cheeping birds
skimming
bare trees   5
above a snow glaze.
Gaining and failing
they are buffetted

547

by a dark wind—
But what?   10
On harsh weedstalks
the flock has rested,
the snow
is covered with broken
seedhusks   15
and the wind tempered
by a shrill
piping of plenty.

The Widow's Lament in Springtime

Sorrow is my own yard
where the new grass
flames as it has flamed
often before but not
with the cold fire   5
that closes round me this year.
Thirty-five years
I lived with my husband.
The plumtree is white today
with masses of flowers.   10
Masses of flowers
loaded the cherry branches
and color some bushes
yellow and some red
but the grief in my heart   15
is stronger than they
for though they were my joy
formerly, today I notice them
and turned away forgetting.
Today my son told me   20
that in the meadows,
at the edge of the heavy woods
in the distance, he saw
trees of white flowers.
I feel that I would like   25
to go there
and fall into those flowers
and sink into the marsh near them.

Spring and All

By the road to the contagious hospital
under the surge of the blue
mottled clouds driven from the
northeast—a cold wind. Beyond, the
waste of broad, muddy fields   5
brown with dried weeds, standing and fallen

patches of standing water
the scattering of tall trees

All along the road the reddish
purplish, forked, upstanding, twiggy   10
stuff of bushes and small trees
with dead, brown leaves under them
leafless vines—

Lifeless in appearance, sluggish
dazed spring approaches—   15

They enter the new world naked,
cold, uncertain of all
save that they enter. All about them
the cold, familiar wind—

Now the grass, tomorrow   20
the stiff curl of wildcarrot leaf

One by one objects are defined—
It quickens: clarity, outline of leaf

But now the stark dignity of
entrance—Still, the profound change   25
has come upon them: rooted they
grip down and begin to awaken

This Is Just to Say

I have eaten
the plums
that were in
the icebox

and which
you were probably
saving
for breakfast

Forgive me
they were delicious
so sweet
and so cold

A Sort of a Song

Let the snake wait under
his weed
and the writing
be of words, slow and quick, sharp
to strike, quiet to wait,   5
sleepless.

—through metaphor to reconcile
the people and the stones.
Compose. (No ideas
but in things) Invent!   10
Saxifrage is my flower that splits
the rocks.

A Unison

The grass is very green, my friend,
and tousled, like the head of—
your grandson, yes? And the mountain,
the mountain we climbed
twenty years since for the last   5
time (I write this thinking
of you) is saw-horned as then
upon the sky's edge—an old barn
is peaked there also, fatefully,
against the sky. And there it is   10
and we can't shift it or change

it or parse it or alter it
in any way. Listen! Do you not hear
them? the singing? There it is and
we'd better acknowledge it and   15
write it down that way, not otherwise.
Not twist the words to mean
what we should have said but to mean
—what cannot be escaped: the
mountain riding the afternoon as   20
it does, the grass matted green,
green underfoot and the air—
rotten wood. Hear! Hear them!
the Undying. The hill slopes away,
then rises in the middleground,   25
you remember, with a grove of gnarled
maples centering the bare pasture,
sacred, surely—for what reason?
I cannot say. Idyllic!
a shrine cinctured there by   30
the trees, a certainty of music!
a unison and a dance, joined
at this death's festival: Something
of a shed snake's skin, the beginning
goldenrod. Or, best, a white stone,   35
you have seen it: *Mathilda Maria
Fox*—and near the ground's lip,
all but undecipherable, *Aet Suae,
Anno 9*—still there, the grass
dripping of last night's rain—and   40
welcome! The thin air, the near,
clear brook water!—and could not,
and died, unable; to escape
what the air and the wet grass—
through which, tomorrow, bejeweled,   45
the great sun will rise—the
unchanging mountains, forced on them—
and they received, willingly!
Stones, stones of a difference
joining the others at pace. Hear!   50
Hear the unison of their voices. . . .

A Negro Woman

carrying a bunch of marigolds

       wrapped

              in an old newspaper:

She carries them upright,

       bare-headed,   5

             the bulk

of her thighs

       causing her to waddle

             as she walks

looking into   10

       the store window which she passes

             on her way.

What is she

       but an ambassador

              from another world   15

a world of pretty marigolds

       of two shades

              which she announces

not knowing what she does

       other   20

             than walk the streets

holding the flowers upright

       as a torch

             so early in the morning.

Cherry Robbers

Under the long dark boughs, like jewels red
 In the hair of an Eastern girl
Hangs strings of crimson cherries, as if had bled
 Blood-drops beneath each curl.

Under the glistening cherries, with folded wings
 Three dead birds lie:
Pale-breasted throstles and a blackbird, robberlings
 Stained with red dye.

Against the haystack a girl stands laughing at me,
 Cherries hung round her ears.
Offers me her scarlet fruit: I will see
 If she has any tears.

Piano

Softly, in the dusk, a woman is singing to me;
Taking me back down the vista of years, till I see
A child sitting under the piano, in the boom of the tingling strings
And pressing the small, poised feet of a mother who smiles as she sings.

In spite of myself, the insidious mastery of song
Betrays me back, till the heart of me weeps to belong
To the old Sunday evenings at home, with winter outside
And hymns in the cozy parlor, the tinkling piano our guide.

So now it is vain for the singer to burst into clamor
With the great black piano appassionato. The glamor
Of childish days is upon me, my manhood is cast
Down in the flood of remembrance, I weep like a child for the past.

Song of a Man Who Has Come Through

Not I, not I, but the wind that blows through me!
A fine wind is blowing the new direction of Time.
If only I let it bear me, carry me, if only it carry me!
If only I am sensitive, subtle, oh, delicate, a winged gift!
If only, most lovely of all, I yield myself and am borrowed   5
By the fine, fine wind that takes its course through the chaos of the
    world
Like a fine, an exquisite chisel, a wedge-blade inserted;
If only I am keen and hard like the sheer tip of a wedge
Driven by invisible blows,
The rock will split, we shall come at the wonder, we shall find the
    Hesperides.   10

Oh, for the wonder that bubbles into my soul,
I would be a good fountain, a good well-head,
Would blur no whisper, spoil no expression.

What is the knocking?
What is the knocking at the door in the night?   15
It is somebody wants to do us harm.

No, no, it is the three strange angels.
Admit them, admit them.

How Beastly the Bourgeois Is

How beastly the bourgeois is
especially the male of the species—
Presentable, eminently presentable—
shall I make you a present of him?

Isn't he handsome? isn't he healthy? isn't he a fine specimen?   5
doesn't he look the fresh clean englishman, outside?
Isn't it god's own image? tramping his thirty miles a day
after partridges, or a little rubber ball?
wouldn't you like to be like that, well off, and quite the thing?

Oh, but wait!   10
Let him meet a new emotion, let him be faced with another man's need,

let him come home to a bit of moral difficulty, let life face him with a
    new demand on his understanding
and then watch him go soggy, like a wet meringue.
Watch him turn into a mess, either a fool or a bully.
Just watch the display of him, confronted with a new demand on his
    intelligence,   15
a new life-demand.

How beastly the bourgeois is
especially the male of the species—
Nicely groomed, like a mushroom
standing there so sleek and erect and eyeable—   20
and like a fungus, living on the remains of bygone life
sucking his life out of the dead leaves of greater life than his own.
And even so, he's stale, he's been there too long.
Touch him, and you'll find he's all gone inside
just like an old mushroom, all wormy inside, and hollow   25
under a smooth skin and an upright appearance.

Full of seething, wormy, hollow feelings
rather nasty—
How beastly the bourgeois is!

Standing in their thousands, these appearances, in damp England   30
what a pity they can't all be kicked over
like sickening toadstools, and left to melt back, swiftly
into the soil of England.

Whales Weep Not!

They say the sea is cold, but the sea contains
the hottest blood of all, and the wildest, the most urgent.

All the whales in the wider deeps, hot are they, as they urge
on and on, and dive beneath the icebergs.
The right whales, the sperm-whales, the hammer-heads, the killers   5
there they blow, there they blow, hot wild white breath out of the sea!

And they rock, and they rock, through the sensual ageless ages
on the depths of the seven seas,
and through the salt they reel with drunk delight
and in the tropics tremble they with love   10
and roll with massive, strong desire, like gods.

Then the great bull lies up against his bride
in the blue deep of the sea.
as mountain pressing on mountain, in the zest of life:
and out of the inward roaring of the inner red ocean of whale blood   15
the long tip reaches strong, intense, like the maelstrom-tip, and comes to
    rest
in the clasp and the soft, wild clutch of a she-whale's fathomless body.

And over the bridge of the whale's strong phallus, linking the wonder of
    whales
the burning archangels under the sea keep passing, back and forth,
keep passing archangels of bliss   20
from him to her, from her to him, great Cherubim
that wait on whales in mid-ocean, suspended in the waves of the sea
great heaven of whales in the waters, old hierarchies.
And enormous mother whales lie dreaming suckling their whale-tender
    young
and dreaming with strange whale eyes wide open in the waters of the
    beginning and the end.   25

And bull-whales gather their women and whale-calves in a ring
when danger threatens, on the surface of the ceaseless flood
and range themselves like great fierce Seraphim facing the threat
encircling their huddled monsters of love.
and all this happiness in the sea, in the salt   30
where God is also love, but without words:
and Aphrodite is the wife of whales
most happy, happy she!
and Venus among the fishes skips and is a she-dolphin
she is the gay, delighted porpoise sporting with love and the sea   35
she is the female tunny-fish, round and happy among the males
and dense with happy blood, dark rainbow bliss in the sea.

Bavarian Gentians

Not every man has gentians in his house
In soft September, at slow, sad Michaelmas.

Bavarian gentians, tall and dark, but dark
Darkening the day-time torch-like with the smoking blueness of Pluto's
    gloom,

Ribbed hellish flowers erect, with their blaze of darkness spread blue   5
Blown into points, by the heavy white draught of the day.

Torch-flowers of the blue-smoking darkness, Pluto's dark blue blaze
Black lamps from the halls of Dio,[1] smoking dark blue
Giving of darkness, blue darkness, upon Demeter's yellow-pale day

Reach me a gentian, give me a torch!   10
Let me guide myself with the blue, forked torch of a flower
Down the darker and darker stairs, where blue is darkened on blueness
Down the way Persephone goes, just now, in first-frosted September.
To the sightless realm where darkness is married to dark
And Persephone herself is but a voice, as a bride   15
A gloom invisible enfolded in the deeper dark
Of the arms of Pluto as he ravishes her once again
And pierces her once more with his passion of the utter dark.

Among the splendor of black-blue torches, shedding fathomless darkness
    on the nuptials.

Give me a flower on a tall stem, and three dark flames,   20
For I will go to the wedding, and be wedding-guest
At the marriage of the living dark.   (MS. "A.")

[1] Dis (Pluto)

City Life

When I am in a great city, I know that I despair.
I know there is no hope for us, death waits, it is useless to care.

For oh the poor people, that are flesh of my flesh,
I, that am flesh of their flesh,
when I see the iron hooked into their faces   5
their poor, their fearful faces
I scream in my soul, for I know I cannot
take the iron hooks out of their faces, that make them so
    drawn,
nor cut the invisible wires of steel that pull them
back and forth, to work, back and forth to work,   10
like fearful and corpse-like fishes hooked and being played
by some malignant fisherman on an unseen shore
where he does not choose to land them yet, hooked fishes of
    the factory world.

⤛ EZRA POUND (1885–   )

Sestina: Altaforte

LOQUITUR: *En* Bertrans de Born.[1]
    Dante Alighieri put this man in hell for that he was a stirrer up
                                    of strife.
    Eccovi!
    Judge ye!
    Have I dug him up again?   5
The scene is at his castle, Altaforte. 'Papiols' is his jongleur.[2]
'The Leopard', the *device* of Richard Coeur de Lion.

    I

Damn it all! all this our South stinks peace.
You whoreson dog, Papiols, come! Let's to music!
I have no life save when the swords clash.   10
But ah! when I see the standards gold, vair, purple, opposing
And the broad fields beneath them turn crimson,
Then howls my heart nigh mad with rejoicing.

    2

In hot summer have I great rejoicing
When the tempests kill the earth's foul peace,   15
And the lightnings from black heav'n flash crimson,
And the fierce thunders roar me their music
And the winds shriek through the clouds mad, opposing,
And through all the riven skies God's swords clash.

    3

Hell grant soon we hear again the swords clash!   20
And the shrill neighs of destriers in battle rejoicing,
Spiked breast to spiked breast opposing!
Better one hour's stour [3] than a year's peace
With fat boards, bawds, wine and frail music!
Bah! there's no wine like the blood's crimson!   25

    4

And I love to see the sun rise blood-crimson.
And I watch his spears through the dark clash

[1] a troubador   [2] juggler   [3] combat

And it fills all my heart with rejoicing
And pries wide my mouth with fast music
When I see him so scorn and defy peace,   30
His lone might 'gainst all darkness opposing.

    5

The man who fears war and squats opposing
My words for stour, hath no blood of crimson,
But is fit only to rot in womanish peace
Far from where worth's won and the swords clash   35
For the death of such sluts I go rejoicing;
Yea, I fill all the air with my music.

    6

Papiols, Papiols, to the music!
There's no sound like to swords swords opposing,
No cry like the battle's rejoicing   40
When our elbows and swords drip the crimson
And our charges 'gainst 'The Leopard's' rush clash.
May God damn for ever all who cry 'Peace!'

    7

And let the music of the swords make them crimson!
Hell grant soon we hear again the swords clash!   45
Hell blot black for alway the thought 'Peace'!

Δώρια [1]

Be in me as the eternal moods
    of the bleak wind, and not
As transient things are—
    gaiety of flowers.
Have me in the strong loneliness
    of sunless cliffs
And of grey waters.
    Let the gods speak softly of us
In days hereafter,
    The shadowy flowers of Orcus
Remember thee.

[1] Doria

The River-Merchant's Wife: A Letter

While my hair was still cut straight across my forehead
I played about the front gate, pulling flowers.
You came by on bamboo stilts, playing horse,
You walked about my seat, playing with blue plums.
And we went on living in the village of Chokan: 5
Two small people, without dislike or suspicion.

At fourteen I married My Lord you.
I never laughed, being bashful.
Lowering my head, I looked at the wall.
Called to, a thousand times, I never looked back.   10

At fifteen I stopped scowling,
I desired my dust to be mingled with yours
For ever and for ever and for ever.
Why should I climb the look out?

At sixteen you departed,   15
You went into far Ku-to-yen, by the river of swirling eddies,
And you have been gone five months.
The monkeys make sorrowful noise overhead.

You dragged your feet when you went out.
By the gate now, the moss is grown, the different mosses,   20
Too deep to clear them away!
The leaves fall early this autumn, in wind.
The paired butterflies are already yellow with August
Over the grass in the West garden;
They hurt me. I grow older.   25
If you are coming down through the narrows of the river Kiang,
Please let me know beforehand,
And I will come out to meet you
                    As far as Cho-fu-Sa.   (By Rihaku [1])

In a Station of the Metro [1]

The apparition of these faces in the crowd;
Petals on a wet, black bough.

[1] a Japanese name for the Chinese poet Li Po

[1] the Parisian subway system

From *Langue d'Oc*

Alba

When the nightingale to his mate
Sings day-long and night late
My love and I keep state
In bower,
In flower,   5
 Till the watchman on the tower
Cry:
              "Up! Thou rascal, Rise,
              I see the white
                            Light   10
                            And the night
                                        Flies."

The Garden

En robe de parade [1]
—Samain [2]

Like a skein of loose silk blown against a wall
She walks by the railing of a path
            in Kensington Gardens,
And she is dying piece-meal
            of a sort of emotional anaemia.

And round about there is a rabble
Of the filthy, sturdy, unkillable infants of the very poor.   5
They shall inherit the earth.
In her is the end of breeding.
Her boredom is exquisite and excessive.
She would like some one to speak to her,
And is almost afraid that I
            will commit that indiscretion.   10

---

[1] parade dress [2] French symbolist poet

I Vecchi [1]

They will come no more,
The old men with beautiful manners.
Il était comme un tout petit garçon [2]
With his blouse full of apples
And sticking out all the way round;   5
Blagueur! [3] 'Con gli occhi onesti e tardi,' [4]

And he said:
           'Oh! Abelard!' as if the topic
Were much too abstruse for his comprehension,
And he talked about 'the Great Mary,'   10
And said: 'Mr. Pound is shocked at my levity.'
When it turned out he meant Mrs. Ward. [5]

And the other was rather like my bust by Gaudier, [6]
Or like a real Texas colonel,
He said: 'Why flay dead horses?   15
There was once a man called Voltaire.'
And he said they used to cheer Verdi,
In Rome, after the opera,
And the guards couldn't stop them,
And that was an anagram for Vittorio   20
Emanuele Re D' Italia, [7]
And the guards couldn't stop them.

      Old men with beautiful manners,
Sitting in the Row of a morning;
Walking on the Chelsea Embankment.   25

From Hugh Selwyn Mauberley

I

E. P. Ode Pour L'election De Son Sepulcre [1]

For three years, out of key with his time,   22
  He strove to resuscitate the dead art

---

[1] "the old men" [2] "He was like a very small boy." [3] "faker" [4] "with eyes honest and dull" [5] Mary Augusta Ward, a British novelist [6] French sculptor [7] Vittorio Emanuele, King of Italy

---

[1] Pound adapts Ronsard's title, "De l'Election de son Sepulchre" ("On the Choice of His Tomb")

Of poetry; to maintain 'the sublime'
In the old sense. Wrong from the start—

No, hardly, but seeing he had been born   5
In a half-savage country, out of date;
Bent resolutely on wringing lilies from the acorn;
Capaneus; [2] trout for factitious bait;

Ἴδμεν γάρ τοι πάνθ', ὅσ' ἐνὶ Τροίῃ [3]
Caught in the unstopped ear;   10
Giving the rocks small lee-way
The chopped seas held him, therefore, that year.

His true Penelope was Flaubert,
He fished by obstinate isles;
Observed the elegance of Circe's hair   .   15
Rather than the mottoes on sundials.

Unaffected by 'the march of events,'
He passed from men's memory in *l'an trentiesme
De son eage;* [4] the case presents
No adjunct to the Muses' diadem.   20

2

The age demanded an image
Of its accelerated grimace,
Something for the modern stage,
Not, at any rate, an Attic grace;

Not, not certainly, the obscure reveries   5
Of the inward gaze;
Better mendacities
Than the classics in paraphrase!

The 'age demanded' chiefly a mold in plaster,
Made with no loss of time,   10
A prose kinema,[5] not, not assuredly, alabaster
Or the 'sculpture' of rhyme.

.   .   .   .   .

[2] one of the seven against Thebes, struck down by Zeus because he defied him   [3] Homer: "For we know all things that are in Troy"—sung by the Sirens enticing Odysseus   [4] "the thirtieth year of his life," quoted from Villon's "Grand Testament"   [5] motion

4

These fought in any case,
and some believing,
        pro domo,[6] in any case . . .

Some quick to arm,
some for adventure,   5
some from fear of weakness,
some from fear of censure,
some for love of slaughter, in imagination,
learning later . . .
some in fear, learning love of slaughter;   10

Died some, pro patria,[7]
                non 'dulce' non 'et decor'[8] . . .
walked eye-deep in hell
believing in old men's lies, then unbelieving
came home, home to a lie,   15
home to many deceits,
home to old lies and new infamy;
usury age-old and age-thick
and liars in public places.

Daring as never before, wastage as never before.   20
Young blood and high blood,
fair cheeks, and fine bodies;

fortitude as never before

frankness as never before,
disillusions as never told in the old days,   25
hysterias, trench confessions,
laughter out of dead bellies.

5

There died a myriad,
And of the best, among them,
For an old bitch gone in the teeth,
For a botched civilization,

Charm, smiling at the good mouth,   5
Quick eyes gone under earth's lid,

[6] for home [7] for country [8] not 'sweet'   'dulce et decor' to die 'pro patria'—
not 'and fitting'; Horace said that it was   *Odes,* XII, ii, 13

For two gross of broken statues,
For a few thousand battered books.

. . . . .

10

Beneath the sagging roof
The stylist has taken shelter,
Unpaid, uncelebrated,
At last from the world's welter

Nature receives him;   5
With a placid and uneducated mistress
He exercises his talents
And the soil meets his distress.

The haven from sophistications and contentions
Leaks through its thatch;   10
He offers succulent cooking;
The door has a creaking latch.

. . . . .

Envoi (1919)

Go, dumb-born book,
Tell her that sang me once that song of Lawes: [9]
Hadst thou but song
As thou hast subjects known,
Then were there cause in three that should condone   5
Even my faults that heavy upon me lie,
And build her glories their longevity.

Tell her that sheds
Such treasure in the air,
Recking naught else but that her graces give   10
Life to the moment,
I would bid them live
As roses might, in magic amber laid,
Red overwrought with orange and all made
One substance and one color   15
Braving time.

Tell her that goes
With song upon her lips

[9] a variant on Edmund Waller's "Go,   1662), a composer of airs
Lovely Rose!" Henry Lawes (1596–

But sings not out the song, nor knows
The maker of it, some other mouth,   20
May be as fair as hers,
Might, in new ages, gain her worshippers,
When our two dusts with Waller's shall be laid,
Siftings on siftings in oblivion,
Till change hath broken down   25
All things save Beauty alone.

. . . . .

Canto I

And then went down to the ship,
Set keel to breakers, forth on the godly sea, and
We set up mast and sail on that swart ship,
Bore sheep aboard her, and our bodies also
Heavy with weeping, so winds from sternward   5
Bore us out onward with bellying canvas,
Circe's this craft, the trim-coifed goddess.
Then sat we amidships, wind jamming the tiller,
Thus with stretched sail, we went over sea till day's end.
Sun to his slumber, shadows o'er all the ocean,   10
Came we then to the bounds of deepest water,
To the Kimmerian lands,[1] and peopled cities
Covered with close-webbed mist, unpiercèd ever
With glitter of sun-rays
Nor with stars stretched, nor looking back from heaven   15
Swartest night stretched over wretched men there.
The ocean flowing backward, came we then to the place
Aforesaid by Circe.
Here did they rites, Perimedes and Eurylochus,[2]
And drawing sword from my hip   20
I dug the ell-square pitkin;[3]
Poured we libations unto each the dead,
First mead and then sweet wine, water mixed with white flour.
Then prayed I many a prayer to the sickly death's-heads;
As set in Ithaca, sterile bulls of the best   25
For sacrifice, heaping the pyre with goods,

---

[1] furthest point West for Homer, a land of darkness   [2] companions of Odysseus   [3] a small pit

A sheep to Tiresias only, black and a bell-sheep.
Dark blood flowed in the fosse,
Souls out of Erebus, cadaverous dead, of brides,
Of youths and of the old who had borne much;   30
Souls stained with recent tears, girls tender,
Men many, mauled with bronze lance heads,
Battle spoil, bearing yet dreory [4] arms,
These many crowded about me; with shouting,
Pallor upon me, cried to my men for more beasts;   35
Slaughtered the herds, sheep slain of bronze;
Poured ointment, cried to the gods,
To Pluto the strong, and praised Proserpine;
Unsheathed the narrow sword,
I sat to keep off the impetuous impotent dead,   40
Till I should hear Tiresias.
But first Elpenor [5] came, our friend Elpenor,
Unburied, cast on the wide earth,
Limbs that we left in the house of Circe,
Unwept, unwrapped in sepulchre, since toils urged other.   45
Pitiful spirit. And I cried in hurried speech:
'Elpenor, how art thou come to this dark coast?
'Cam'st thou afoot, outstripping seamen?'
          And he in heavy speech:
'Ill fate and abundant wine. I slept in Circe's ingle.   50
'Going down the long ladder unguarded,
'I fell against the buttress,
'Shattered the nape-nerve, the soul sought Avernus.
'But thou, O King, I bid remember me, unwept, unburied,
'Heap up mine arms, be tomb by sea-bord, and inscribed: 55
'*A man of no fortune, and with a name to come.*
'And set my oar up, that I swung mid fellows.'

And Anticlea came, whom I beat off, and then Tiresias Theban,
Holding his golden wand, knew me, and spoke first:
'A second time? why? man of ill star,   60
'Facing the sunless dead and this joyless region?
'Stand from the fosse, leave me my bloody bever [6]
'For soothsay.'
          And I stepped back,
And he strong with the blood, said then: 'Odysseus   65
'Shalt return through spiteful Neptune, over dark seas,

---

[4] bloody [5] a companion of Odysseus, accidentally killed in Circe's garden and left unburied when he was not missed [6] drink

'Lose all companions.' Then Anticlea came.
Lie quiet Divus.[7] I mean, that is Andreas Divus,
In officina Wecheli,[8] 1538, out of Homer.
And he sailed, by Sirens and thence outward and away   70
And unto Circe.
       Venerandam,[9]
In the Cretan's phrase, with the golden crown, Aphrodite,[10]
Cypri munimenta sortita est,[11] mirthful, oricalchi,[12] with golden
Girdles and breast bands, thou with dark eyelids   75
Bearing the golden bough of Argicida.[13] So that:

Canto XLV

With *Usura* [1]

With usura hath no man a house of good stone
each block cut smooth and well fitting
that design might cover their face,
with usura   5
hath no man a painted paradise on his church wall
harpes et luthes [2]
or where virgin receiveth message
and halo projects from incision,
with usura   10
seeth no man Gonzaga [3] his heirs and his concubines
no picture is made to endure nor to live with
but it is made to sell and sell quickly
with usura, sin against nature,
is thy bread ever more of stale rags   15
is thy bread dry as paper,
with no mountain wheat, no strong flour
with usura the line grows thick

---

[7] The foregoing lines were translated from the Divus' medieval Latin translation of Homer's Odyssey. [8] Christian Wechel was Divus' printer. [9] compelling admiration [10] "Venerandam" comes from Georgius Dartona Cretensis' Latin translation of *Homeric Hymn VI, To Aphrodite.* [11] "The citadels of Cyprus are her appointed realm." [12] "of copper" [13] Hermes

---

[1] usury [2] harps and lutes; from Villon [3] the princely family of Mantua, patrons of the arts

with usura is no clear demarcation
and no man can find site for his dwelling.   20
Stone cutter is kept from his stone
weaver is kept from his loom
WITH USURA
wool comes not to market
sheep bringeth no gain with usura   25
Usura is a murrain, usura
blunteth the needle in the maid's hand
and stoppeth the spinner's cunning. Pietro Lombardo [4]
came not by usura
Duccio [5] came not by usura   30
nor Pier della Francesca; [6] Zuan Bellin' [7] not by usura
nor was 'La Calunnia' [8] painted.
Came not by usura Angelico; [9] came not Ambrogio Praedis,[10]
Came no church of cut stone signed: *Adamo me fecit.*[11]
Not by usura St Trophime [12]   35
Not by usura Saint Hilaire,[13]
Usura rusteth the chisel
It rusteth the craft and the craftsman
It gnaweth the thread in the loom
None learneth to weave gold in her pattern;   40
Azure hath a canker by usura; cramoisi is unbroidered
Emerald findeth no Memling [14]
Usura slayeth the child in the womb
It stayeth the young man's courting
It hath brought palsey to bed, lyeth   45
between the young bride and her bridegroom
                CONTRA NATURAM.[15]
They have brought whores for Eleusis [16]
Corpses are set to banquet
at behest of usura.   50

[4] architect and sculptor; designer of Dante's tomb   [5] Sienese painter   [6] Umbrian painter   [7] Giovanni Bellini, Venetian painter   [8] painting by Botticelli   [9] Fra Angelico, Florentine painter   [10] Milanese painter   [11] "Adam made me."   [12] a church in Arles   [13] church in Poitiers   [14] Flemish painter   [15] against nature   [16] city in ancient Greece; scene of rites of initiation into religious mysteries

H. D.[1] (1886–1961)

Heat

O wind, rend open the heat,
cut apart the heat,
rend it to tatters.

Fruit cannot drop
through this thick air—   5
fruit cannot fall into heat
that presses up and blunts
the points of pears
and rounds the grapes.

Cut the heat—   10
plough through it,
turning it on either side
of your path.

---

[1] Hilda Doolittle

ROBINSON JEFFERS (1887–1962)

Shine, Perishing Republic

While this America settles in the mold of its vulgarity, heavily thicken-
    ing to empire,
And protest, only a bubble in the molten mass, pops and sighs out, and
    the mass hardens,

I sadly smiling remember that the flower fades to make fruit, the fruit
    rots to make earth.
Out of the mother; and through the spring exultances, ripeness and
    decadence; and home to the mother.

You making haste haste on decay: not blameworthy; life is good, be it
    stubbornly long or suddenly   5
A mortal splendor: meteors are not needed less than mountains: shine,
    perishing republic.

But for my children, I would have them keep their distance from the
    thickening center; corruption
Never has been compulsory, when the cities lie at the monster's feet
    there are left the mountains.

And boys, be in nothing so moderate as in love of man, a clever servant,
    insufferable master.
There is the trap that catches noblest spirits, that caught—they say—
    God, when he walked on earth.   10

MARIANNE MOORE (1887–   )

Poetry

I, too, dislike it: there are things that are important beyond all this
        fiddle.
   Reading it, however, with a perfect contempt for it, one discovers in
   it after all, a place for the genuine.
      Hands that can grasp, eyes
      that can dilate, hair that can rise   5
         if it must, these things are important not because a

high-sounding interpretation can be put upon them but because they
        are
   useful. When they become so derivative as to become unintelligible,
   the same thing may be said for all of us, that we
      do not admire what   10
      we cannot understand: the bat
         holding on upside down or in quest of something to

eat, elephants pushing, a wild horse taking a roll, a tireless wolf under
   a tree, the immovable critic twitching his skin like a horse that feels
        a flea, the base-
   ball fan, the statistician—   15
      nor is it valid
        to discriminate against 'business documents and

school-books'; all these phenomena are important. One must make a
        distinction
   however: when dragged into prominence by half poets, the result is
   not poetry,
   nor till the poets among us can be   20
      'literalists of
      the imagination'—above
        insolence and triviality and can present

for inspection, 'imaginary gardens with real toads in them,' shall we
        have
   it. In the meantime, if you demand on the one hand,   25
   the raw material of poetry in
      all its rawness and
      that which is on the other hand
        genuine, you are interested in poetry.

Silence

My father used to say,
'Superior people never make long visits,
have to be shown Longfellow's grave
or the glass flowers at Harvard.
Self-reliant like the cat—   5
that takes its prey to privacy,
the mouse's limp tail hanging like a shoelace from its mouth—
they sometimes enjoy solitude,
and can be robbed of speech
by speech which has delighted them.   10
The deepest feeling always shows itself in silence;
not in silence, but restraint.'
Nor was he insincere in saying, 'Make my house your inn.'
Inns are not residences.

Sojourn in the Whale

Trying to open locked doors with a sword, threading
        the points of needles, planting shade trees
        upside down; swallowed by the opaqueness of one whom
            the seas
love better than they love you, Ireland—   5

you have lived and lived on every kind of shortage.
        You have been compelled by hags to spin
        gold thread from straw and have heard men say: 'There
            is a feminine
temperament in direct contrast to   10

ours which makes her do these things. Circumscribed by a
        heritage of blindness and native
        incompetence, she will become wise and will be forced
            to give
in. Compelled by experience, she   15

will turn back; water seeks its own level': and you
        have smiled. 'Water in motion is far
        from level.' You have seen it, when obstacles happened
            to bar
the path, rise automatically.   20

Rigorists

'We saw reindeer
browsing,' a friend who'd been in Lapland, said:
'finding their own food; they are adapted

to scant *reino*
or pasture, yet they can run eleven   5
miles in fifty minutes; the feet spread when

the snow is soft,
and act as snow-shoes. They are rigorists,
however handsomely cutwork artists

of Lapland and   10
Siberia elaborate the trace
or saddle-girth with saw-tooth leather lace.

One looked at us
with its firm face part brown, part white,—a queen
of alpine flowers. Santa Claus' reindeer, seen   15

at last, had grey-
brown fur, with a neck like edelweiss or
lion's foot,—*leontopodium* more

exactly.' And
this candelabrum-headed ornament   20
for a place where ornaments are scarce, sent

to Alaska,
was a gift preventing the extinction
of the Esquimo. The battle was won

by a quiet man,   25
Sheldon Jackson,[1] evangel to that race
whose reprieve he read in the reindeer's face.

[1] who brought reindeer into Alaska, as
a source of food for the Eskimos

A Grave

Man looking into the sea,
taking the view from those who have as much right to it as you have to
    it yourself,
it is human nature to stand in the middle of a thing,
but you cannot stand in the middle of this;
the sea has nothing to give but a well excavated grave.   5
The firs stand in a procession, each with an emerald turkey-foot at the
    top,
reserved as their contours, saying nothing;
repression, however, is not the most obvious characteristic of the sea;
the sea is a collector, quick to return a rapacious look.
There are others besides you who have worn that look   10
whose expression is no longer a protest; the fish no longer investigate
    them
for their bones have not lasted:
men lower nets, unconscious of the fact that they are desecrating a
    grave,
and row quickly away—the blades of the oars
moving together like the feet of water-spiders as if there were no such
    thing as death.   15
The wrinkles progress among themselves in a phalanx—beautiful under
    networks of foam,
and fade breathlessly while the sea rustles in and out of the seaweed;
the birds swim through the air at top speed, emitting catcalls as
    heretofore—
the tortoise-shell scourges about the feet of the cliffs, in motion beneath
    them;
and the ocean, under the pulsation of lighthouses and noise of bell-
    buoys,   20
advances as usual, looking as if it were not that ocean in which dropped
    things are bound to sink—
in which if they turn and twist, it is neither with volition nor con-
    sciousness.

EDWIN MUIR (1887–1959)

The Three Mirrors

I looked in the first glass
And saw the fenceless field
And like broken stones in grass
The sad towns glint and shine.
The slowly twisting vine   5
Scribbled with wrath the stone,
The mountain summits were sealed
In incomprehensible wrath.
The hunting roads ran on
To round the flying hill   10
And bring the quarry home.
But the obstinate roots ran wrong,
The lumbering fate fell wrong,
The walls were askew with ill,
Askew went every path,   15
The dead lay askew in the tomb.

I looked in the second glass
And saw through the twisted scroll
In virtue undefiled
And new in eternity   20
Father and mother and child,
The house with its single tree,
Bed and board and cross,
And the dead asleep in the knoll.
But the little blade and leaf   25
By an angry law were bent
To shapes of terror and grief,
By a law the field was rent,
The crack ran over the floor,
The child at peace in his play   30
Changed as he passed through a door,
Changed were the house and the tree,
Changed the dead in the knoll,
For locked in love and grief
Good with evil lay.   35

If I looked in the third glass
I should see evil and good
Standing side by side
In the ever standing wood,
The wise king safe on his throne,   40
The rebel raising the rout,
And each so deeply grown
Into his own place
He'd be past desire or doubt.
If I could look I should see   45
The world's house open wide,
The million million rooms
And the quick god everywhere
Glowing at work and at rest,
Tranquillity in the air,   50
Peace of the humming looms
Weaving from east to west,
And you and myself there.

The Labyrinth

Since I emerged that day from the labyrinth,
Dazed with the tall and echoing passages,
The swift recoils, so many I almost feared
I'd meet myself returning at some smooth corner,
Myself or my ghost, for all there was unreal   5
After the straw ceased rustling and the bull
Lay dead upon the straw and I remained,
Blood-splashed, if dead or alive I could not tell
In the twilight nothingness (I might have been
A spirit seeking his body through the roads   10
Of intricate Hades)—ever since I came out
To the world, the still fields swift with flowers, the trees
All bright with blossom, the little green hills, the sea,
The sky and all in movement under it,
Shepherds and flocks and birds and the young and old, 15
(I stared in wonder at the young and the old,
For in the maze time had not been with me;
I had strayed, it seemed, past sun and season and change,
Past rest and motion, for I could not tell

At last if I moved or stayed; the maze itself   20
Revolved around me on its hidden axis
And swept me smoothly to its enemy,
The lovely world)—since I came out that day,
There have been times when I have heard my footsteps
Still echoing in the maze, and all the roads   25
That run through the noisy world, deceiving streets
That meet and part and meet, and rooms that open
Into each other—and never a final room—
Stairways and corridors and antechambers
That vacantly wait for some great audience,   30
The smooth sea-tracks that open and close again,
Tracks undiscoverable, indecipherable,
Paths on the earth and tunnels underground,
And bird-tracks in the air—all seemed a part
Of the great labyrinth. And then I'd stumble   35
In sudden blindness, hasten, almost run,
As if the maze itself were after me
And soon must catch me up. But taking thought,
I'd tell myself, 'You need not hurry. This
Is the firm good earth. All roads lie free before you.'   40
But my bad spirit would sneer, 'No, do not hurry.
No need to hurry. Haste and delay are equal
In this one world, for there's no exit, none,
No place to come to, and you'll end where you are,
Deep in the centre of the endless maze.'   45
I could not live if this were not illusion.
It is a world, perhaps; but there's another.
For once in a dream or trance I saw the gods
Each sitting on the top of his mountain-isle,
While down below the little ships sailed by,   50
Toy multitudes swarmed in the harbors, shepherds drove
Their tiny flocks to the pastures, marriage feasts
Went on below, small birthdays and holidays,
Ploughing and harvesting and life and death,
And all permissible, all acceptable,   55
Clear and secure as in a limpid dream.
But they, the gods, as large and bright as clouds,
Conversed across the sounds in tranquil voices
High in the sky above the untroubled sea,
And their eternal dialogue was peace   60
Where all these things were woven, and this our life
Was as a chord deep in that dialogue,

As easy utterance of harmonious words,
Spontaneous syllables bodying forth a world.

That was the real world; I have touched it once, 65
And now shall know it always. But the lie,
The maze, the wild-wood waste of falsehood, roads
That run and run and never reach an end,
Embowered in error—I'd be prisoned there
But that my soul has birdwings to fly free. 70

Oh these deceits are strong almost as life.
Last night I dreamt I was in the labyrinth,
And woke far on. I did not know the place.

The Incarnate One

The windless northern surge, the sea-gull's scream,
And Calvin's kirk crowning the barren brae.
I think of Giotto the Tuscan shepherd's dream,
Christ, man and creature in their inner day.
How could our race betray 5
The Image, and the Incarnate One unmake
Who chose this form and fashion for our sake?

The Word made flesh here is made word again,
A word made word in flourish and arrogant crook.
See there King Calvin with his iron pen, 10
And God three angry letters in a book,
And there the logical hook
On which the Mystery is impaled and bent
Into an ideological instrument.

There's better gospel in man's natural tongue, 15
And truer sight was theirs outside the Law
Who saw the far side of the Cross among
The archaic peoples in their ancient awe,
In ignorant wonder saw
The wooden cross-tree on the bare hillside, 20
Not knowing that there a God suffered and died.

The fleshless word, growing, will bring us down,
Pagan and Christian man alike will fall,
The auguries say, the white and black and brown,

The merry and sad, theorist, lover, all 25
Invisibly will fall:
Abstract calamity, save for those who can
Build their cold empire on the abstract man.

A soft breeze stirs and all my thoughts are blown
Far out to sea and lost. Yet I know well 30
The bloodless word will battle for its own
Invisibly in brain and nerve and cell.
The generations tell
Their personal tale: the One has far to go
Past the mirages and the murdering snow. 35

The Horses

Barely a twelvemonth after
The seven days war that put the world to sleep,
Late in the evening the strange horses came.
By then we had made our covenant with silence,
But in the first few days it was so still 5
We listened to our breathing and were afraid.
On the second day
The radios failed; we turned the knobs; no answer.
On the third day a warship passed us, heading north,
Dead bodies piled on the deck. On the sixth day 10
A plane plunged over us into the sea. Thereafter
Nothing. The radios dumb;
And still they stand in corners of our kitchens,
And stand, perhaps, turned on, in a million rooms
All over the world. But now if they should speak, 15
If on a sudden they should speak again,
If on the stroke of noon a voice should speak,
We would not listen, we would not let it bring
That old bad world that swallowed its children quick
At one great gulp. We would not have it again. 20
Sometimes we think of the nations lying asleep,
Curled blindly in impenetrable sorrow,
And then the thought confounds us with its strangeness.
The tractors lie about our fields; at evening
They look like dank sea-monsters couched and waiting. 25
We leave them where they are and let them rust:

'They'll moulder away and be like other loam.'
We make our oxen drag our rusty ploughs,
Long laid aside. We have gone back
Far past our fathers' land.   30
                              And then, that evening
Late in the summer the strange horses came.
We heard a distant tapping on the road,
A deepening drumming; it stopped, went on again
And at the corner changed to hollow thunder.   35
We saw the heads
Like a wild wave charging and were afraid.
We had sold our horses in our fathers' time
To buy new tractors. Now they were strange to us
As fabulous steeds set on an ancient shield   40
Or illustrations in a book of knights.
We did not dare go near them. Yet they waited,
Stubborn and shy, as if they had been sent
By an old command to find our whereabouts
And that long-lost archaic companionship.   45
In the first moment we had never a thought
That they were creatures to be owned and used.
Among them were some half-a-dozen colts
Dropped in some wilderness of the broken world,
Yet new as if they had come from their own Eden.   50
Since then they have pulled our ploughs and borne our loads
But that free servitude still can pierce our hearts.
Our life is changed; their coming our beginning.

The Island

Your arms will clasp the gathered grain
For your good time, and wield the flail
In merry fire and summer hail.
There stand the golden hills of corn
Which all the heroic clans have borne,   5
And bear the herdsmen of the plain,
The horseman in the mountain pass,
The archaic goat with silver horn,
Man, dog and flock and fruitful hearth.
Harvests of men to men give birth.   10

These the ancestral faces bred
And show as though a golden glass
Dances and temples of the dead.
Here speak through the transmuted tongue
The full grape bursting in the press,   15
The barley seething in the vat,
Which earth and man as one confess,
Babbling of what both would be at
In garrulous story and drunken song.
Though come a different destiny,   20
Though fall a universal wrong
More stern than simple savagery,
Men are made of what is made,
The meat, the drink, the life, the corn,
Laid up by them, in them reborn.   25
And self-begotten cycles close
About our way; indigenous art
And simple spells make unafraid
The haunted labyrinths of the heart,
And with our wild succession braid   3c
The resurrection of the rose.   (*Sicily*)

✑§ T. S. ELIOT (1888–   )

The Love Song of J. Alfred Prufrock

> *S'io credesse che mia risposta fosse*
> *A persona che mai tornasse al mondo,*
> *Questa fiamma staria senza piu scosse.*
> *Ma perciocche giammai di questo fondo*
> *Non torno vivo alcun, s'i'odo il vero,*
> *Senza tema d'infamia ti rispondo.*[1]

Let us go then, you and I,
When the evening is spread out against the sky
Like a patient etherized upon a table;
Let us go, through certain half-deserted streets,
The muttering retreats   5
Of restless nights in one-night cheap hotels
And sawdust restaurants with oyster-shells:
Streets that follow like a tedious argument
Of insidious intent
To lead you to an overwhelming question . . .   10
Oh, do not ask, "What is it?"
Let us go and make our visit.

In the room the women come and go
Talking of Michelangelo.

The yellow fog that rubs its back upon the window-panes,   15
The yellow smoke that rubs its muzzle on the window-panes
Licked its tongue into the corners of the evening,
Lingered upon the pools that stand in drains,
Let fall upon its back the soot that falls from chimneys,
Slipped by the terrace, made a sudden leap,   20
And seeing that it was a soft October night,
Curled once about the house, and fell asleep.

And indeed there will be time
For the yellow smoke that slides along the street,
Rubbing its back upon the window-panes;   25

[1] Guido da Montefeltro is speaking to Dante in the *Inferno,* XXVII, ll. 61–66: "If I thought my answer were to one who ever could return to the world, this flame would shake no more, but since none ever did return alive from this depth, if what I hear be true, without fear of infamy I may answer thee."

There will be time, there will be time
To prepare a face to meet the faces that you meet;
There will be time to murder and create,
And time for all the works and days of hands
That lift and drop a question on your plate;   30
Time for you and time for me,
And time yet for a hundred indecisions,
And for a hundred visions and revisions,
Before the taking of a toast and tea.

    In the room the women come and go   35
Talking of Michelangelo.

    And indeed there will be time
To wonder, "Do I dare?" and, "Do I dare?"
Time to turn back and descend the stair,
With a bald spot in the middle of my hair—   40
[They will say: "How his hair is growing thin!"]
My morning coat, my collar mounting firmly to the chin,
My necktie rich and modest, but asserted by a simple pin—
[They will say: "But how his arms and legs are thin!"]
Do I dare   45
Disturb the universe?
In a minute there is time
For decisions and revisions which a minute will reverse.

    For I have known them all already, known them all:—
Have known the evenings, mornings, afternoons,   50
I have measured out my life with coffee spoons;
I know the voices dying with a dying fall
Beneath the music from a farther room.
    So how should I presume?

    And I have known the eyes already, known them all—   55
The eyes that fix you in a formulated phrase,
And when I am formulated, sprawling on a pin,
When I am pinned and wriggling on the wall,
Then how should I begin
To spit out all the butt-ends of my days and ways?   60
    And how should I presume?

    And I have known the arms already, known them all—
Arms that are braceleted and white and bare
[But in the lamplight, downed with light brown hair!]
Is it perfume from a dress   65

That makes me so digress?
Arms that lie along a table, or wrap about a shawl.
    And should I then presume?
    And how should I begin?

          . . . . .

Shall I say, I have gone at dusk through narrow streets   70
And watched the smoke that rises from the pipes
Of lonely men in shirt-sleeves, leaning out of windows? . . .

    I should have been a pair of ragged claws
Scuttling across the floors of silent seas.

          . . . . .

And the afternoon, the evening, sleeps so peacefully!   75
Smoothed by long fingers,
Asleep . . . tired . . . or it malingers,
Stretched on the floor, here beside you and me.
Should I, after tea and cakes and ices,
Have the strength to force the moment to its crisis?   80
But though I have wept and fasted, wept and prayed,
Though I have seen my head [grown slightly bald] brought in upon a
       platter,
I am no prophet—and here's no great matter;
I have seen the moment of my greatness flicker,
And I have seen the eternal Footman hold my coat, and snicker,   85
And in short, I was afraid.

    And would it have been worth it, after all,
After the cups, the marmalade, the tea,
Among the porcelain, among some talk of you and me,
Would it have been worth while,   90
To have bitten off the matter with a smile,
To have squeezed the universe into a ball
To roll it toward some overwhelming question,
To say: "I am Lazarus, come from the dead,
Come back to tell you all, I shall tell you all"—   95
If one, settling a pillow by her head,
    Should say: "That is not what I meant at all.
    That is not it, at all."

    And would it have been worth it, after all,
Would it have been worth while,   100
After the sunsets and the dooryards and the sprinkled streets,
After the novels, after the teacups, after the skirts that trail along the
       floor—

And this, and so much more?—
It is impossible to say just what I mean!
But as if a magic lantern threw the nerves in patterns on a screen: 105
Would it have been worth while
If one, settling a pillow or throwing off a shawl,
And turning toward the window, should say:
    "That is not it at all,
    That is not what I meant, at all."   110

           .   .   .   .   .

No! I am not Prince Hamlet, nor was meant to be;
Am an attendant lord, one that will do
To swell a progress, start a scene or two,
Advise the prince; no doubt, an easy tool,
Deferential, glad to be of use,   115
Politic, cautious, and meticulous;
Full of high sentence, but a bit obtuse;
At times, indeed, almost ridiculous—
Almost, at times, the Fool.

    I grow old . . . I grow old . . .   120
I shall wear the bottoms of my trousers rolled.

    Shall I part my hair behind? Do I dare to eat a peach?
I shall wear white flannel trousers, and walk upon the beach.
I have heard the mermaids singing, each to each.

    I do not think that they will sing to me.   125

    I have seen them riding seaward on the waves
Combing the white hair of the waves blown back
When the wind blows the water white and black.

    We have lingered in the chambers of the sea
By sea-girls wreathed with seaweed red and brown   130
Till human voices wake us, and we drown.

La Figlia Che Piange [1]

O quam te memorem virgo . . . [2]

    Stand on the highest pavement of the stair—
    Lean on a garden urn—

---

[1] the weeping girl   [2] O maiden, how
may I speak of thee . . .

Weave, weave the sunlight in your hair—
Clasp your flowers to you with a pained surprise—
Fling them to the ground and turn   5
With a fugitive resentment in your eyes:
But weave, weave the sunlight in your hair.

    So I would have had him leave,
So I would have had her stand and grieve,
So he would have left   10
As the soul leaves the body torn and bruised,
As the mind deserts the body it has used.
I should find
Some way incomparably light and deft,
Some way we both should understand,   15
Simple and faithless as a smile and shake of the hand.

    She turned away, but with the autumn weather
Compelled my imagination many days,
Many days and many hours:
Her hair over her arms and her arms full of flowers.   20
And I wonder how they should have been together!
I should have lost a gesture and a pose.
Sometimes these cogitations still amaze
The troubled midnight and the noon's repose.

Gerontion

> *Thou hast nor youth nor age*
> *But as it were an after dinner sleep*
> *Dreaming of both.*[1]

Here I am, an old man in a dry month,
Being read to by a boy, waiting for rain.
I was neither at the hot gates
Nor fought in the warm rain
Nor knee deep in the salt marsh, heaving a cutlass,   5
Bitten by flies, fought.
My house is a decayed house,
And the jew squats on the window sill, the owner,

[1] from *Measure for Measure*

Spawned in some estaminet of Antwerp,
Blistered in Brussels, patched and peeled in London.   10
The goat coughs at night in the field overhead;
Rocks, moss, stonecrop, iron, merds.
The woman keeps the kitchen, makes tea,
Sneezes at evening, poking the peevish gutter.
                              I an old man,   15
A dull head among windy spaces.

    Signs are taken for wonders. "We would see a sign!"
The word within a word, unable to speak a word,
Swaddled with darkness. In the juvescence of the year
Came Christ the tiger   20

    In depraved May, dogwood and chestnut, flowering judas,
To be eaten, to be divided, to be drunk
Among whispers; by Mr. Silvero
With caressing hands, at Limoges
Who walked all night in the next room;   25

    By Hakagawa, bowing among the Titians;
By Madame de Tornquist, in the dark room
Shifting the candles; Fräulein von Kulp
Who turned in the hall, one hand on the door.
    Vacant shuttles   30
Weave the wind. I have no ghosts,
An old man in a draughty house
Under a windy knob.

    After such knowledge, what forgiveness? Think now
History has many cunning passages, contrived corridors   35
And issues, deceives with whispering ambitions,
Guides us by vanities. Think now
She gives when our attention is distracted
And what she gives, gives with such supple confusions
That the giving famishes the craving. Gives too late   40
What's not believed in, or if still believed,
In memory only, reconsidered passion. Gives too soon
Into weak hands, what's thought can be dispensed with
Till the refusal propagates a fear. Think
Neither fear nor courage saves us. Unnatural vices   45
Are fathered by our heroism. Virtues
Are forced upon us by our impudent crimes.
These tears are shaken from the wrath-bearing tree.

The tiger springs in the new year. Us he devours. Think at last
We have not reached conclusion, when I   50
Stiffen in a rented house. Think at last
I have not made this show purposelessly
And it is not by any concitation
Of the backward devils.
I would meet you upon this honestly.   55
I that was near your heart was removed therefrom
To lose beauty in terror, terror in inquisition.
I have lost my passion: why should I need to keep it
Since what is kept must be adulterated?
I have lost my sight, smell, hearing, taste and touch: 60
How should I use them for your closer contact?

These with a thousand small deliberations
Protract the profit of their chilled delirium,
Excite the membrane, when the sense has cooled,
With pungent sauces, multiply variety   65
In a wilderness of mirrors. What will the spider do,
Suspend its operations, will the weevil
Delay? De Bailhache, Fresca, Mrs. Cammel, whirled
Beyond the circuit of the shuddering Bear
In fractured atoms. Gull against the wind, in the windy straits   70
Of Belle Isle, or running on the Horn,
White feathers in the snow, the Gulf claims,
And an old man driven by the Trades
To a sleepy corner.

Tenants of the house,   75
Thoughts of a dry brain in a dry season.

Whispers of Immortality

Webster [1] was much possessed by death
And saw the skull beneath the skin;
And breastless creatures under ground
Leaned backward with a lipless grin.

Daffodil bulbs instead of balls   5
Stared from the sockets of the eyes!

[1] John Webster, Jacobean playwright

He knew that thought clings round dead limbs
Tightening its lusts and luxuries.

Donne, I suppose, was such another
Who found no substitute for sense,   10
To seize and clutch and penetrate;
Expert beyond experience,

He knew the anguish of the marrow
The ague of the skeleton;
No contact possible to flesh   15
Allayed the fever of the bone.

.   .   .   .   .

Grishkin is nice: her Russian eye
Is underlined for emphasis;
Uncorseted, her friendly bust
Gives promise of pneumatic bliss.   20

The couched Brazilian jaguar
Compels the scampering marmoset
With subtle effluence of cat;
Grishkin has a maisonette;

The sleek Brazilian jaguar   25
Does not in its arboreal gloom
Distil so rank a feline smell
As Grishkin in a drawing-room.

And even the Abstract Entities
Circumambulate her charm;   30
But our lot crawls between dry ribs
To keep our metaphysics warm.

Journey of the Magi

'A cold coming we had of it,
Just the worst time of the year
For a journey, and such a long journey:
The ways deep and the weather sharp,

The very dead of winter.'   5
And the camels galled, sore-footed, refractory,
Lying down in the melting snow.
There were times we regretted
The summer palaces on slopes, the terraces,
And the silken girls bringing sherbet.   10
Then the camel men cursing and grumbling
And running away, and wanting their liquor and women,
And the night-fires going out, and the lack of shelters,
And the cities hostile and the towns unfriendly
And the villages dirty and charging high prices: 15
A hard time we had of it.
At the end we preferred to travel all night,
Sleeping in snatches,
With the voices singing in our ears, saying
That this was all folly.   20

    Then at dawn we came down to a temperate valley,
Wet, below the snow line, smelling of vegetation;
With a running stream and a water-mill beating the darkness,
And three trees on the low sky,
And an old white horse galloped away in the meadow.   25
Then we came to a tavern with vine-leaves over the lintel,
Six hands at an open door dicing for pieces of silver,
And feet kicking the empty wine-skins.
But there was no information, and so we continued
And arrived at evening, not a moment too soon   30
Finding the place; it was (you may say) satisfactory.

    All this was a long time ago, I remember,
And I would do it again, but set down
This set down
This: were we led all that way for   35
Birth or Death? There was a Birth, certainly,
We had evidence and no doubt. I had seen birth and death,
But had thought they were different; this Birth was
Hard and bitter agony for us, like Death, our death.
We returned to our places, these Kingdoms,   40
But no longer at ease here, in the old dispensation,
With an alien people clutching their gods.
I should be glad of another death.

Marina [1]

Quis hic locus, quae regio, quae mundi plaga? [2]

What seas what shores what grey rocks and what islands
What water lapping the bow
And scent of pine and the woodthrush singing through the fog
What images return
O my daughter.   5

 Those who sharpen the tooth of the dog, meaning
Death
Those who glitter with the glory of the humming-bird, meaning
Death
Those who sit in the style of contentment, meaning   10
Death
Those who suffer the ecstasy of the animals, meaning
Death

 Are become unsubstantial, reduced by a wind,
A breath of pine, and the woodsong fog   15
By this grace dissolved in place

 What is this face, less clear and clearer
The pulse in the arm, less strong and stronger—
Given or lent? more distant than stars and nearer than the eye

 Whispers and small laughter between leaves and hurrying feet 20
Under sleep, where all the waters meet.

 Bowsprit cracked with ice and paint cracked with heat.
I made this, I have forgotten
And remember.
The rigging weak and the canvas rotten   25
Between one June and another September.
Made this unknowing, half conscious, unknown, my own.
The garboard strake leaks, the seams need caulking.
This form, this face, this life
Living to live in a world of time beyond me; let me   30
Resign my life for this life, my speech for that unspoken,
The awakened, lips parted, the hope, the new ships.

[1] the lost daughter in Shakespeare's *Pericles* [2] Seneca: "What place is this, what region, what part of the world?"

What seas what shores what granite islands towards my timbers
And woodthrush calling through the fog
My daughter.   35

Little Gidding [1]

I

Midwinter spring is its own season
Sempiternal though sodden towards sundown,
Suspended in time, between pole and tropic.
When the short day is brightest, with frost and fire,
The brief sun flames the ice, on pond and ditches,   5
In windless cold that is the heart's heat,
Reflecting in a watery mirror
A glare that is blindness in the early afternoon.
And glow more intense than blaze of branch, or brazier,
Stirs the dumb spirit: no wind, but pentecostal fire   10
In the dark time of the year. Between melting and freezing
The soul's sap quivers. There is no earth smell
Or smell of living thing. This is the spring time
But not in time's covenant. Now the hedgerow
Is blanched for an hour with transitory blossom   15
Of snow, a bloom more sudden
Than that of summer, neither budding nor fading,
Not in the scheme of generation.
Where is the summer, the unimaginable
Zero summer?   20

        If you came this way,
Taking the route you would be likely to take
From the place you would be likely to come from,
If you came this way in may time, you would find the hedges
White again, in May, with voluptuary sweetness.   25
It would be the same at the end of the journey,
If you came at night like a broken king,
If you came by day not knowing what you came for,
It would be the same, when you leave the rough road
And turn behind the pig-sty to the dull façade   30
And the tombstone. And what you thought you came for

[1] an Anglican religious community founded by Nicholas Ferrar, visited by Herbert and Crashaw, and eventually sacked by Cromwell. Charles I stopped at Little Gidding after Naseby.

Is only a shell, a husk of meaning
From which the purpose breaks only when it is fulfilled
If at all. Either you had no purpose
Or the purpose is beyond the end you figured   35
And is altered in fulfillment. There are other places
Which also are the world's end, some at the sea jaws,
Or over a dark lake, in a desert or a city—
But this is the nearest, in place and time,
Now and in England.   40

       If you came this way,
Taking any route, starting from anywhere,
At any time or at any season,
It would always be the same: you would have to put off
Sense and notion. You are not here to verify,   45
Instruct yourself, or inform curiosity
Or carry report. You are here to kneel
Where prayer has been valid. And prayer is more
Than an order of words, the conscious occupation
Of the praying mind, or the sound of the voice praying.   50
And what the dead had no speech for, when living,
They can tell you, being dead: the communication
Of the dead is tongued with fire beyond the language of the living.
Here, the intersection of the timeless moment
Is England and nowhere. Never and always.   55

    2

Ash on an old man's sleeve
Is all the ash the burnt roses leave.
Dust in the air suspended
Marks the place where a story ended.
Dust inbreathed was a house—   60
The wall, the wainscot and the mouse.
The death of hope and despair,
      This is the death of air.

    There are flood and drouth
Over the eyes and in the mouth,   65
Dead water and dead sand
Contending for the upper hand.
The parched eviscerate soil
Gapes at the vanity of toil,
Laughs without mirth.   70
      This is the death of earth.

Water and fire succeed
The town, the pasture and the weed.
Water and fire deride
The sacrifice that we denied.   75
Water and fire shall rot
The marred foundations we forgot,
Of sanctuary and choir.
      This is the death of water and fire.

In the uncertain hour before the morning   80
    Near the ending of interminable night
    At the recurrent end of the unending
After the dark dove with the flickering tongue
    Had passed below the horizon of his homing
    While the dead leaves still rattled on like tin   85
Over the asphalt where no other sound was
    Between three districts whence the smoke arose
    I met one walking, loitering and hurried
As if blown towards me like the metal leaves
    Before the urban dawn wind unresisting.   90
    And as I fixed upon the down-turned face
That pointed scrutiny with which we challenge
    The first-met stranger in the waning dusk
    I caught the sudden look of some dead master
Whom I had known, forgotten, half recalled   95
    Both one and many; in the brown baked features
    The eyes of a familiar compound ghost
Both intimate and unidentifiable.
    So I assumed a double part, and cried
    And heard another's voice cry: 'What are *you* here?'   100
Although we were not. I was still the same,
    Knowing myself yet being someone other—
    And he a face still forming; yet the words sufficed
To compel the recognition they preceded.
    And so, compliant to the common wind,   105
    Too strange to each other for misunderstanding,
In concord at this intersection time
    Of meeting nowhere, no before and after,
    We trod the pavement in a dead patrol.
I said: 'The wonder that I feel is easy,   110
    Yet ease is cause of wonder. Therefore speak:
    I may not comprehend, may not remember.'
And he: 'I am not eager to rehearse

My thought and theory which you have forgotten.
These things have served their purpose: let them be. 115
So with your own, and pray they be forgiven
By others, as I pray you to forgive
Both bad and good. Last season's fruit is eaten
And the fullfed beast shall kick the empty pail.
For last year's words belong to last year's language 120
And next year's words await another voice.
But, as the passage now presents no hindrance
To the spirit unappeased and peregrine
Between two worlds become much like each other,
So I find words I never thought to speak 125
In streets I never thought I should revisit
When I left my body on a distant shore.
Since our concern was speech, and speech impelled us
To purify the dialect of the tribe
And urge the mind to aftersight and foresight, 130
Let me disclose the gifts reserved for age
To set a crown upon your lifetime's effort.
First, the cold friction of expiring sense
Without enchantment, offering no promise
But bitter tastelessness of shadow fruit 135
As body and soul begin to fall asunder.
Second, the conscious impotence of rage
At human folly, and the laceration
Of laughter at what ceases to amuse.
And last, the rending pain of re-enactment 140
Of all that you have done, and been; the shame
Of motives late revealed, and the awareness
Of things ill done and done to others' harm
Which once you took for exercise of virtue.
Then fools' approval stings, and honor stains. 145
From wrong to wrong the exasperated spirit
Proceeds, unless restored by that refining fire
Where you must move in measure, like a dancer.'
The day was breaking. In the disfigured street
He left me, with a kind of valediction, 150
And faded on the blowing of the horn.

3

There are three conditions which often look alike
Yet differ completely, flourish in the same hedgerow:
Attachment to self and to things and to persons, detachment

From self and from things and from persons; and, growing between them,
     indifference   155
Which resembles the others as death resembles life,
Being between two lives—unflowering, between
The live and the dead nettle. This is the use of memory:
For liberation—not less of love but expanding
Of love beyond desire, and so liberation   160
From the future as well as the past. Thus, love of a country
Begins as attachment to our own field of action
And comes to find that action of little importance
Though never indifferent. History may be servitude,
History may be freedom. See, now they vanish,   165
The faces and places, with the self which, as it could, loved them,
To become renewed, transfigured, in another pattern.

    Sin is Behovely, but
All shall be well, and
All manner of thing shall be well.   170
If I think, again, of this place,
And of people, not wholly commendable,
Of no immediate kin or kindness,
But some of peculiar genius,
All touched by a common genius,   175
United in the strife which divided them;
If I think of a king at nightfall,
Of three men, and more, on the scaffold
And a few who died forgotten
In other places, here and abroad,   180
And of one who died blind and quiet,
Why should we celebrate
These dead men more than the dying?
It is not to ring the bell backward
Nor is it an incantation   185
To summon the spectre of a Rose.
We cannot revive old factions
We cannot restore old policies
Or follow an antique drum.
These men, and those who opposed them   190
And those whom they opposed
Accept the constitution of silence
And are folded in a single party.
Whatever we inherit from the fortunate
We have taken from the defeated   195

What they had to leave us—a symbol:
A symbol perfected in death.
And all shall be well and
All manner of thing shall be well
By the purification of the motive   200
In the ground of our beseeching.

          4

The dove descending breaks the air
With flame of incandescent terror
Of which the tongues declare
The one discharge from sin and error.   205
The only hope, or else despair
     Lies in the choice of pyre or pyre—
     To be redeemed from fire by fire.

     Who then devised the torment? Love.
Love is the unfamiliar Name   210
Behind the hands that wove
The intolerable shirt of flame
Which human power cannot remove.
     We only live, only suspire
     Consumed by either fire or fire.   215

          5

What we call the beginning is often the end
And to make an end is to make a beginning.
The end is where we start from. And every phrase
And sentence that is right (where every word is at home,
Taking its place to support the others,   220
The word neither diffident nor ostentatious,
An easy commerce of the old and the new,
The common word exact without vulgarity,
The formal word precise but not pedantic,
The complete consort dancing together)   225
Every phrase and every sentence is an end and a beginning,
Every poem an epitaph. And any action
Is a step to the block, to the fire, down the sea's throat
Or to an illegible stone: and that is where we start.
We die with the dying: 230
See, they depart, and we go with them.
We are born with the dead:
See, they return, and bring us with them.

The moment of the rose and the moment of the yew-tree
Are of equal duration. A people without history   235
Is not redeemed from time, for history is a pattern
Of timeless moments. So, while the light fails
On a winter's afternoon, in a secluded chapel
History is now and England.
With the drawing of this Love and the voice of this Calling   240

    We shall not cease from exploration
And the end of all our exploring
Will be to arrive where we started
And know the place for the first time.
Through the unknown, remembered gate   245
When the last of earth left to discover
Is that which was the beginning;
At the source of the longest river
The voice of the hidden waterfall
And the children in the apple-tree   250
Not known, because not looked for
But heard, half-heard, in the stillness
Between two waves of the sea.
Quick now, here, now, always—
A condition of complete simplicity   255
(Costing not less than everything)
And all shall be well and
All manner of thing shall be well
When the tongues of flame are in-folded
Into the crowned knot of fire   260
And the fire and the rose are one.

Bells for John Whiteside's Daughter

There was such speed in her little body
And such lightness in her footfall,
It is no wonder her brown study
Astonishes us all.

Her wars were bruited in our high window.   5
We looked among orchard trees and beyond,
Where she took arms against her shadow,
Or harried unto the pond

The lazy geese, like a snow cloud
Dripping their snow on the green grass,   10
Tricking and stopping, sleepy and proud,
Who cried in goose, Alas,

For the tireless heart within the little
Lady with rod that made them rise
From their noon apple-dreams and scuttle   15
Goose-fashion under the skies!

But now go the bells and we are ready,
In one house we are sternly stopped
To say we are vexed at her brown study,
Lying so primly propped.   20

Captain Carpenter

Captain Carpenter rose up in his prime
Put on his pistols and went riding out
But had got wellnigh nowhere at that time
Till he fell in with ladies in a rout.

It was a pretty lady and all her train   5
That played with him so sweetly but before
An hour she'd taken a sword with all her main
And twined him of his nose for evermore.

Captain Carpenter mounted up one day
And rode straightway into a stranger rogue   10
That looked unchristian but be that as may
The Captain did not wait upon prologue.

But drew upon him out of his great heart
The other swung against him with a club
And cracked his two legs at the shinny part   15
And let him roll and stick like any tub.

Captain Carpenter rode many a time
From male and female took he sundry harms
He met the wife of Satan crying "I'm
The she-wolf bids you shall bear no more arms."   20

Their strokes and counters whistled in the wind
I wish he had delivered half his blows
But where she should have made off like a hind
The bitch bit off his arms at the elbows.

And Captain Carpenter parted with his ears   25
To a black devil that used him in this wise
O Jesus ere his threescore and ten years
Another had plucked out his sweet blue eyes.

Captain Carpenter got up on his roan
And sallied from the gate in hell's despite   30
I heard him asking in the grimmest tone
If any enemy yet there was to fight?

"To any adversary it is fame
If he risk to be wounded by my tongue
Or burnt in two beneath my red heart's flame   35
Such are the perils he is cast among.

"But if he can he has a pretty choice
From an anatomy with little to lose
Whether he cut my tongue and take my voice
Or whether it be my round red heart he choose."   40

It was the neatest knave that ever was seen
Stepping in perfume from his lady's bower
Who at this word put in his merry mien
And fell on Captain Carpenter like a tower.

I would not knock old fellows in the dust   45
But there lay Captain Carpenter on his back

His weapons were the old heart in his bust
And a blade shook between rotten teeth alack.

The rogue in scarlet and grey soon knew his mind
He wished to get his trophy and depart   50
With gentle apology and touch refined
He pierced him and produced the Captain's heart.

God's mercy rest on Captain Carpenter now
I thought him Sirs an honest gentleman
Citizen husband soldier and scholar enow   55
Let jangling kites eat of him if they can.

But God's deep curses follow after those
That shore him of his goodly nose and ears
His legs and strong arms at the two elbows
And eyes that had not watered seventy years.   60

The curse of hell upon the sleek upstart
That got the Captain finally on his back
And took the red red vitals of his heart
And made the kites to whet their beaks clack clack.

Janet Waking

Beautifully Janet slept
Till it was deeply morning. She woke then
And thought about her dainty-feathered hen,
To see how it had kept.

One kiss she gave her mother,   5
Only a small one gave she to her daddy
Who would have kissed each curl of his shining baby;
No kiss at all for her brother.

"Old Chucky, old Chucky!" she cried,
Running across the world upon the grass   10
To Chucky's house, and listening. But alas,
Her Chucky had died.

It was a transmogrifying bee
Came droning down on Chucky's old bald head
And sat and put the poison. It scarcely bled,   15
But how exceedingly

And purply did the knot
Swell with the venom and communicate
Its rigor! Now the poor comb stood up straight
But Chucky did not.   20

So there was Janet
Kneeling on the wet grass, crying her brown hen
(Translated far beyond the daughters of men)
To rise and walk upon it.

And weeping fast as she had breath   25
Janet implored us, "Wake her from her sleep!"
And would not be instructed in how deep
Was the forgetful kingdom of death.

Painted Head

By dark severance the apparition head
Smiles from the air a capital on no
Column or a Platonic perhaps head
On a canvas sky depending from nothing;

Stirs up an old illusion of grandeur   5
By tickling the instinct of heads to be
Absolute and to try decapitation
And to play truant from the body bush;

But too happy and beautiful for those sorts
Of head (homekeeping heads are happiest)   10
Discovers maybe thirty unwidowed years
Of not dishonoring the faithful stem;

Is nameless and has authored for the evil
Historian headhunters neither book
Nor state and is therefore distinct from tart   15
Heads with crowns and guilty gallery heads;

So that the extravagant device of art
Unhousing by abstraction this once head
Was capital irony by a loving hand
That knew the no treason of a head like this;   20

Makes repentance in an unlovely head
For having vinegarly traduced the flesh

Till, the hurt flesh recusing, the hard egg
Is shrunken to its own deathlike surface;

And an image thus. The body bears the head   25
(So hardly one they terribly are two)
Feeds and obeys and unto please what end?
Not to the glory of tyrant head but to

The increase of body. Beauty is of body.
The flesh contouring shallowly on a head   30
Is a rock-garden needing body's love
And best bodiness to colorify

The big blue birds sitting and sea-shell flats
And caves, and on the iron acropolis
To spread the hyacinthine hair and rear   35
The olive garden for the nightingales.

Piazza Piece

—I am a gentleman in a dustcoat trying
To make you hear. Your ears are soft and small
And listen to an old man not at all,
They want the young men's whispering and sighing.
But see the roses on your trellis dying   5
And hear the spectral singing of the moon;
For I must have my lovely lady soon,
I am a gentleman in a dustcoat trying.

—I am a lady young in beauty waiting
Until my truelove comes, and then we kiss.   10
But what grey man among the vines is this
Whose words are dry and faint as in a dream?
Back from my trellis, Sir, before I scream!
I am a lady young in beauty waiting.

HUGH MacDIARMID (1892–   )

The Watergaw [1]

Ae weet [2] forenicht [3] i the yow-trummle [4]
I saw yon antrin [5] thing,
A watergaw wi its chitterin [6] licht [7]
Ayont [8] the on-ding; [9]
An I thocht o the last wild look ye gied [10]   5
Afore ye deed!

There was nae reek [11] i the laverock's [12] hoose
That nicht—an nane i mine;
But I hae thocht o that foolish licht
Ever sin syne; [13]   10
An I think that mebbe at last I ken [14]
What your look meant then.

Love

A luvin wumman is a licht
That shows a man his waefu' plicht, [1]
Bleezin steady on ilka bane, [2]
Wrigglin sinnen [3] an twinin vein,
Or fleerin [4] quick an gane again,   5
An the mair scunnersome [5] the sicht
The mair for luve an licht he's fain
Till clear an chitterin an nesh [6]
Move aa the miseries o his flesh.

---

[1] an indistinct rainbow [2] wet [3] early evening [4] cold spell at the end of July, after the sheep shearing (The phrase is, literally, "ewe-tremble.") [5] rare [6] shivering [7] light [8] beyond [9] downpour [10] gave [11] smoke [12] lark [13] afterwards [14] know

---

[1] woeful plight [2] each bone [3] sinews [4] flaring [5] disgusting [6] nervous, full of awareness

O Wha's the Bride

O wha's the bride that cairries the bunch
O' thistles blinterin [1] white?
Her cuckold bridegroom little dreids
What he sall ken this nicht.

For closer than gudeman can come   5
And closer to'r than hersel,
Wha didna need her maidenheid
Has wrocht his purpose fell.

O wha's been here afore me, lass,
And hoo did he get in?   10
—A man that deed or I was born
This evil thing has din.

And left, as it were on a corpse,
Your maidenheid to me?
—Nae lass, gudeman, sin Time began   15
'S hed ony mair to gie.

But I can gie ye kindness, lad,
And a pair o willin hands,
And ye sall hae my briests like stars,
My limbs like willow wands.   20

And on my lips ye'll heed nae mair,
And in my hair forget,
The seed o a' the men that in
My virgin womb hae met . . .

At My Father's Grave

The sunlicht still on me, you row'd [1] in clood,
We look upon each ither noo like hills
Across a valley. I'm nae mair your son.
It is my mind, nae son o yours, that looks,
And the great darkness o your death comes up
And equals it across the way.
A livin man upon a deid man thinks
And ony sma'er thocht's impossible.

---

[1] gleaming

---

[1] wrapped up

The End of the World

Quite unexpectedly as Vasserot
The armless ambidextrian was lighting
A match between his great and second toe
And Ralph the lion was engaged in biting
The neck of Madame Sossman while the drum
Pointed, and Teeny was about to cough
In waltz-time swinging Jocko by the thumb—
Quite unexpectedly the top blew off:

And there, there overhead, there, there, hung over
Those thousands of white faces, those dazed eyes,
There in the starless dark the poise, the hover,
There with vast wings across the canceled skies,
There in the sudden blackness the black pall
Of nothing, nothing, nothing—nothing at all.

You, Andrew Marvell

And here face down beneath the sun
And here upon earth's noonward height
To feel the always coming on
The always rising of the night;

To feel creep up the curving east   5
The earthy chill of dusk and slow
Upon those under lands the vast
And ever climbing shadow grow

And strange at Ecbatan the trees
Take leaf by leaf the evening strange   10
The flooding dark about their knees
The mountains over Persia change

And now at Kermanshah the gate
Dark empty and the withered grass
And through the twilight now the late   15
Few travelers in the westward pass

And Baghdad darken and the bridge
Across the silent river gone
And through Arabia the edge
Of evening widen and steal on   20

And deepen on Palmyra's street
The wheel rut in the ruined stone
And Lebanon fade out and Crete
High through the clouds and overblown

And over Sicily the air   25
Still flashing with the landward gulls
And loom and slowly disappear
The sails above the shadowy hulls

And Spain go under and the shore
Of Africa the gilded sand   30
And evening vanish and no more
The low pale light across that land

Nor now the long light on the sea:

And here face downward in the sun
To feel how swift how secretly   35
The shadow of the night comes on . . .

⮒ WILFRED OWEN (1893–1918)

Dulce Et Decorum Est

Bent double, like old beggars under sacks,
Knock-kneed, coughing like hags, we cursed through sludge,
Till on the haunting flares we turned our backs,
And towards our distant rest began to trudge.
Men marched asleep. Many had lost their boots,   5
But limped on, blood-shod. All went lame, all blind;
Drunk with fatigue; deaf even to the hoots
Of gas-shells dropping softly behind.

Gas! Gas! Quick, boys!—An ecstasy of fumbling,
Fitting the clumsy helmets just in time,   10
But someone still was yelling out and stumbling
And floundering like a man in fire or lime.—
Dim through the misty panes and thick green light,
As under a green sea, I saw him drowning.

In all my dreams before my helpless sight   15
He plunges at me, guttering, choking, drowning.

If in some smothering dreams, you too could pace
Behind the wagon that we flung him in,
And watch the white eyes writhing in his face,
His hanging face, like a devil's sick of sin;   20
If you could hear, at every jolt, the blood
Come gargling from the froth-corrupted lungs,
Bitter as the cud
Of vile, incurable sores on innocent tongues,—
My friend, you would not tell with such high zest   25
To children ardent for some desperate glory,
The old Lie: Dulce et decorum est
Pro patria mori.[1]

Strange Meeting

It seemed that out of battle I escaped
Down some profound dull tunnel, long since scooped

---

[1] Horace: "It is sweet and fitting to die
for one's country."

Through granites which titanic wars had groined.
Yet also there encumbered sleepers groaned,
Too fast in thought or death to be bestirred.   5
Then, as I probed them, one sprang up, and stared
With piteous recognition in fixed eyes,
Lifting distressful hands as if to bless.
And by his smile, I knew that sullen hall,
By his dead smile I knew we stood in Hell.   10
With a thousand pains that vision's face was grained;
Yet no blood reached there from the upper ground,
And no guns thumped, or down the flues made moan.
"Strange friend," I said, "here is no cause to mourn."
"None," said the other, "save the undone years,   15
The hopelessness. Whatever hope is yours,
Was my life also; I went hunting wild
After the wildest beauty in the world,
Which lies not calm in eyes, or braided hair,
But mocks the steady running of the hour,   20
And if it grieves, grieves richlier than here.
For by my glee might many men have laughed,
And of my weeping something had been left,
Which must die now. I mean the truth untold,
The pity of war, the pity war distilled.   25
Now men will go content with what we spoiled.
Or, discontent, boil bloody, and be spilled.
They will be swift with swiftness of the tigress,
None will break ranks, though nations trek from progress.
Courage was mine, and I had mystery,   30
Wisdom was mine, and I had mastery;
To miss the march of this retreating world
Into vain citadels that are not walled.
Then, when much blood had clogged their chariot-wheels
I would go up and wash them from sweet wells,   35
Even with truths that lie too deep for taint.
I would have poured my spirit without stint
But not through wounds; not on the cess of war.
Foreheads of men have bled where no wounds were.
I am the enemy you killed, my friend.   40
I knew you in this dark; for so you frowned
Yesterday through me as you jabbed and killed.
I parried; but my hands were loath and cold.
Let us sleep now. . . ."

✒ E. E. CUMMINGS (1894–1962)

Poem, or Beauty Hurts Mr. Vinal

take it from me kiddo
believe me
my country, 'tis of

you, land of the Cluett
Shirt Boston Garter and Spearmint   5
Girl With The Wrigley Eyes(of you
land of the Arrow Ide
and Earl &
Wilson
Collars)of you i   10
sing:land of Abraham Lincoln and Lydia E. Pinkham,
land above all of Just Add Hot Water And Serve—
from every B.V.D.

let freedom ring

amen. i do however protest, anent the un   15
-spontaneous and otherwise scented merde which
greets one(Everywhere Why)as divine poesy per
that and this radically defunct periodical. i would
suggest that certain ideas gestures
rhymes, like Gillette Razor Blades
having been used and reused
to the mystical moment of dullness emphatically are
Not To Be Resharpened. (Case in point

if we are to believe these gently O sweetly
melancholy trillers amid the thrillers   25
these crepuscular violinists among my and your
skyscrapers—Helen & Cleopatra were Just Too Lovely,
The Snail's On The Thorn enter Morn and God's
In His andsoforth

do you get me?)according   30
to such supposedly indigenous
throstles Art is O World O Life
a formula:example,Turn Your Shirttails Into
Drawers and If It Isn't An Eastman It Isn't A

Kodak therefore my friends let   35
us now sing each and all fortissimo A-
mer
i

ca, I
love,   40
You. And there're a
hun-dred-mil-lion-oth-ers, like
all of you successfully if
delicately gelded (or spaded)
gentlemen(and ladies)—pretty   45

littleliverpill-
hearted-Nujolneeding-There's-A-Reason
americans(who tensetendoned and with
upward vacant eyes, painfully
perpetually crouched, quivering, upon the   50
sternly allotted sandpile
—how silently
emit a tiny violetflavored nuisance: Odor?

ono.
comes out like a ribbon lies flat on the brush   55

next to of course god america i

"next to of course god america i
love you land of the pilgrims' and so forth oh
say can you see by the dawn's early my
country 'tis of centuries come and go
and are no more what of it we should worry   5
in every language even deafanddumb
thy sons acclaim your glorious name by gorry
by jingo by gee by gosh by gum
why talk of beauty what could be more beaut-
iful than these heroic happy dead   10
who rushed like lions to the roaring slaughter
they did not stop to think they died instead
then shall the voices of liberty be mute?"

He spoke. And drank rapidly a glass of water

i sing of Olaf glad and big

i sing of Olaf glad and big
whose warmest heart recoiled at war:
a conscientious object—or

his wellbelovéd colonel(trig
westpointer most succinctly bred)   5
took erring Olaf soon in hand;
but—though an host of overjoyed
noncoms(first knocking on the head
him(do through icy waters roll
that helplessness which others stroke   10
with brushes recently employed
anent this muddy toiletbowl,
while kindred intellects evoke
allegiance per blunt instruments—
Olaf(being to all intents   15
a corpse and wanting any rag
upon what God unto him gave)
responds,without getting annoyed
"Iwill not kiss your f.ing flag"

straightway the silver bird looked grave   20
(departing hurriedly to shave)
but—though all kinds of officers
(a yearning nation's blueeyed pride)
their passive prey did kick and curse
until for wear their clarion   25
voices and boots were much the worse,
and egged the firstclassprivates on
his rectum wickedly to tease
by means of skilfully applied
bayonets roasted hot with heat—   30
Olaf(upon what were once knees)
does almost ceaselessly repeat
"there is some s. I will not eat"

our president,being of which
assertions duly notified   35
threw the yellowsonofabitch
into a dungeon,where he died

Christ(of His mercy infinite)
i pray to see;and Olaf,too

preponderatingly because   40
unless statistics lie he was
more brave than me:more blond than you.

my father moved through dooms of love

my father moved through dooms of love
through sames of am through haves of give,
singing each morning out of each night
my father moved through depths of height

this motionless forgetful where   5
turned at his glance to shining here;
that if(so timid air is firm)
under his eyes would stir and squirm

newly as from unburied which
floats the first who,his april touch   10
drove sleeping selves to swarm their fates
woke dreamers to their ghostly roots

and should some why completely weep
my father's fingers brought her sleep:
vainly no smallest voice might cry   15
for he could feel the mountains grow.

Lifting the valleys of the sea
my father moved through griefs of joy;
praising a forehead called the moon
singing desire into begin   20

joy was his song and joy so pure
a heart of star by him could steer
and pure so now and now so yes
the wrists of twilight would rejoice

keen as midsummer's keen beyond   25
conceiving mind of sun will stand,
so strictly(over utmost him
so hugely)stood my father's dream

his flesh was flesh his blood was blood:
no hungry man but wished him food;   30

no cripple wouldn't creep one mile
uphill to only see him smile.

Scorning the pomp of must and shall
my father moved through dooms of feel;
his anger was as right as rain   35
his pity was as green as grain

septembering arms of year extend
less humbly wealth to foe and friend
than he to foolish and to wise
offered immeasurable is   40

proudly and(by octobering flame
beckoned)as earth will downward climb,
so naked for immortal work
his shoulders marched against the dark

his sorrow was as true as bread: 45
no liar looked him in the head;
if every friend became his foe
he'd laugh and build a world with snow.

My father moved through theys of we,
singing each new leaf out of each tree   50
(and every child was sure that spring
danced when she heard my father sing)

then let me kill which cannot share,
let blood and flesh be mud and mire,
scheming imagine,passion willed,   55
freedom a drug that's bought and sold

giving to steal and cruel kind,
a heart to fear,to doubt a mind,
to differ a disease of same,
conform the pinnacle of am   60

though dull were all we taste as bright,
bitter all utterly things sweet,
maggoty minus and dumb death
all we inherit,all bequeath

and nothing quite so least as truth   65
—i say though hate were why men breathe—
because my father lived his soul
love is the whole and more than all

ROBERT GRAVES (1895–)

Apples and Water

Dust in a cloud, blinding weather,
    Drums that rattle and roar!
A mother and daughter stood together
    By their cottage door.

'Mother, the heavens are bright like brass,   5
    The dust is shaken high,
With laboring breath the soldiers pass,
    Their lips are cracked and dry.

'Mother, I'll throw them apples down,
    I'll fetch them cups of water.'   10
The mother turned with an angry frown,
    Holding back her daughter.

'But, mother, see, they faint with thirst,
    They march away to war.'
'Ay, daughter, these are not the first   15
    And there will come yet more.

'There is no water can supply them
    In western streams that flow;
There is no fruit can satisfy them
    On orchard-trees that grow.   20

'Once in my youth I gave, poor fool,
    A soldier apples and water;
And may I die before you cool
    Such drouth as his, my daughter.'

Warning to Children

Children, if you dare to think
Of the greatness, rareness, muchness,
Fewness of this precious only
Endless world in which you say
You live, you think of things like this: 5

Blocks of slate enclosing dappled
Red and green, enclosing tawny
Yellow nets, enclosing white
And black acres of dominoes,
Where a neat brown paper parcel   10
Tempts you to untie the string.
In the parcel a small island,
On the island a large tree,
On the tree a husky fruit.
Strip the husk and pare the rind off: 15
In the kernel you will see
Blocks of slate enclosed by dappled
Red and green, enclosed by tawny
Yellow nets, enclosed by white
And black acres of dominoes,   20
Where the same brown paper parcel—
Children, leave the string alone!
For who dares undo the parcel
Finds himself at once inside it,
On the island, in the fruit,   25
Blocks of slate about his head,
Finds himself enclosed by dappled
Green and red, enclosed by yellow
Tawny nets, enclosed by black
And white acres of dominoes,   30
With the same brown paper parcel
Still untied upon his knee.
And, if he then should dare to think
Of the fewness, muchness, rareness,
Greatness of this endless only   35
Precious world in which he says
He lives—he then unties the string.

In Broken Images

He is quick, thinking in clear images;
I am slow, thinking in broken images.

He becomes dull, trusting to his clear images;
I become sharp, mistrusting my broken images.

Trusting his images, he assumes their relevance; 5
Mistrusting my images, I question their relevance.

Assuming their relevance, he assumes the fact;
Questioning their relevance, I question the fact.

When the fact fails him, he questions his senses;
When the fact fails me, I approve my senses. 10

He continues quick and dull in his clear images;
I continue slow and sharp in my broken images.

He in a new confusion of his understanding;
I in a new understanding of my confusion.

To Juan at the Winter Solstice

There is one story and one story only
That will prove worth your telling,
Whether as learned bard or gifted child;
To it all lines or lesser gauds belong
That startle with their shining 5
Such common stories as they stray into.

Is it of trees you tell, their months and virtues,
Or strange beasts that beset you,
Of birds that croak at you the Triple will?
Or of the Zodiac and how slow it turns 10
Below the Boreal Crown,
Prison of all true kings that ever reigned?

Water to water, ark again to ark,
From woman back to woman:
So each new victim treads unfalteringly 15
The never altered circuit of his fate,
Bringing twelve peers as witness
Both to his starry rise and starry fall.

Or is it of the Virgin's silver beauty,
All fish below the thighs? 20
She in her left hand bears a leafy quince;
When with her right she crooks a finger, smiling,
How may the King hold back?
Royally then he barters life for love.

Or of the undying snake from chaos hatched, 25
Whose coils contain the ocean,
Into whose chops with naked sword he springs,
Then in black water, tangled by the reeds,
Battles three days and nights,
To be spewed up beside her scalloped shore? 30

Much snow is falling, winds roar hollowly,
The owl hoots from the elder,
Fear in your heart cries to the loving-cup:
Sorrow to sorrow as the sparks fly upward.
The log groans and confesses: 35
There is one story and one story only.

Dwell on her graciousness, dwell on her smiling,
Do not forget what flowers
The great boar trampled down in ivy time.
Her brow was creamy as the crested wave, 40
Her sea-blue eyes were wild
But nothing promised that is not performed.

The White Goddess

All saints revile her, and all sober men
Ruled by the God Apollo's golden mean—
In scorn of which we sailed to find her
In distant regions likeliest to hold her
Whom we desired above all things to know, 5
Sister of the mirage and echo.

It was a virtue not to stay,
To go our headstrong and heroic way
Seeking her out at the volcano's head,
Among pack ice, or where the track had faded 10
Beyond the cavern of the seven sleepers:
Whose broad high brow was white as any leper's,
Whose eyes were blue, with rowan-berry lips,
With hair curled honey-colored to white hips.

Green sap of Spring in the young wood a-stir 15
Will celebrate the Mountain Mother,
And every song-bird shout awhile for her;

But we are gifted, even in November
Rawest of seasons, with so huge a sense
Of her nakedly worn magnificence   20
We forget cruelty and past betrayal,
Heedless of where the next bright bolt may fall.

Counting the Beats

You, love, and I,
(He whispers) you and I,
And if no more than only you and I
What care you or I?

Counting the beats,   5
Counting the slow heart beats,
The bleeding to death of time in slow heart beats,
Wakeful they lie.

Cloudless day,
Night, and a cloudless day,   10
Yet the huge storm will burst upon their heads one day
From a bitter sky.

Where shall we be,
(She whispers) where shall we be,
When death strikes home, O where then shall we be   15
Who were you and I?

Not there but here,
(He whispers) only here,
As we are, here, together, now and here,
Always you and I.   20

Counting the beats,
Counting the slow heart beats,
The bleeding to death of time in slow heart beats,
Wakeful they lie.

Repose of Rivers

The willows carried a slow sound,
A sarabande the wind mowed on the mead.
I could never remember
That seething, steady leveling of the marshes
Till age had brought me to the sea.   5

Flags, weeds. And remembrance of steep alcoves
Where cypresses shared the noon's
Tyranny; they drew me into hades almost.
And mammoth turtles climbing sulphur dreams
Yielded, while sun-silt rippled them   10
Asunder . . .

How much I would have bartered! the black gorge
And all the singular nestings in the hills
Where beavers learn stitch and tooth.
The pond I entered once and quickly fled—   .   15
I remember now its singing willow rim.

And finally, in that memory all things nurse;
After the city that I finally passed
With scalding unguents spread and smoking darts
The monsoon cut across the delta   20
At gulf gates . . . There, beyond the dykes
I heard wind flaking sapphire, like this summer,
And willows could not hold more steady sound.

At Melville's Tomb

Often beneath the wave, wide from this ledge
The dice of drowned men's bones he saw bequeath
An embassy. Their numbers as he watched,
Beat on the dusty shore and were obscured.

And wrecks passed without sound of bells,   5
The calyx of death's bounty giving back

A scattered chapter, livid hieroglyph,
The portent wound in corridors of shells.

Then in the circuit calm of one vast coil,
Its lashings charmed and malice reconciled,   10
Frosted eyes there were that lifted altars;
And silent answers crept across the stars.

Compass, quadrant and sextant contrive
No farther tides . . . High in the azure steeps
Monody shall not wake the mariner.   15
This fabulous shadow only the sea keeps.

Voyages

I

Above the fresh ruffles of the surf
Bright striped urchins flay each other with sand.
They have contrived a conquest for shell shucks,
And their fingers crumble fragments of baked weed
Gaily digging and scattering.   5

And in answer to their treble interjections
The sun beats lightning on the waves,
The waves fold thunder on the sand;
And could they hear me I would tell them:

O brilliant kids, frisk with your dog,   10
Fondle your shells and sticks, bleached
By time and the elements; but there is a line
You must not cross nor ever trust beyond it
Spry cordage of your bodies to caresses
Too lichen-faithful from too wide a breast.   15
The bottom of the sea is cruel.

2

And yet this great wink of eternity,
Of rimless floods, unfettered leewardings,
Samite sheeted and processioned where
Her undinal vast belly moonward bends,   20
Laughing the wrapt inflections of our love;

Take this Sea, whose diapason knells
On scrolls of silver snowy sentences,
The sceptred terror of whose sessions rends
As her demeanors motion well or ill,   25
All but the pieties of lovers' hands.

And onward, as bells off San Salvador
Salute the crocus lustres of the stars,
In these poinsettia meadows of her tides,—
Adagios of islands, O my Prodigal,   30
Complete the dark confessions her veins spell.

Mark how her turning shoulders wind the hours,
And hasten while her penniless rich palms
Pass superscription of bent foam and wave,—
Hasten, while they are true,—sleep, death, desire,   35
Close round one instant in one floating flower.

Bind us in time, O Seasons clear, and awe.
O minstrel galleons of Carib fire,
Bequeath us to no earthly shore until
Is answered in the vortex of our grave   40
The seal's wide spindrift gaze toward paradise.

        3
Infinite consanguinity it bears—
This tendered theme of you that light
Retrieves from sea plains where the sky
Resigns a breast that every wave enthrones;   45
While ribboned water lanes I wind
Are laved and scattered with no stroke
Wide from your side, whereto this hour
The sea lifts, also, reliquary hands.

And so, admitted through black swollen gates   50
That must arrest all distance otherwise,—
Past whirling pillars and lithe pediments,
Light wrestling there incessantly with light,
Star kissing star through wave on wave unto
Your body rocking!   55
                        and where death, if shed,
Presumes no carnage, but this single change,—
Upon the steep floor flung from dawn to dawn
The silken skilled transmemberment of song;

Permit me voyage, love, into your hands . . .   60

Royal Palm

FOR GRACE HART CRANE

Green rustlings, more than regal charities
Drift coolly from that tower of whispered light.
Amid the noontide's blazed asperities
I watched the sun's most gracious anchorite

Climb up as by communings, year on year   5
Uneaten of the earth or aught earth holds,
And the grey trunk, that's elephantine, rear
Its frondings sighing in aetherial folds.

Forever fruitless, and beyond that yield
Of sweat the jungle presses with hot love   10
And tendril till our deathward breath is sealed—
It grazes the horizons, launched above

Mortality—ascending emerald-bright,
A fountain at salute, a crown in view—
Unshackled, casual of its azured height   15
As though it soared suchwise through heaven too.

The Air Plant

GRAND CAYMAN

This tuft that thrives on saline nothingness,
Inverted octopus with heavenward arms
Thrust parching from a palm-bole hard by the cove—
A bird almost—of almost bird alarms,

Is pulmonary to the wind that jars   5
Its tentacles, horrific in their lurch.
The lizard's throat, held boated for a fly,
Balloons but warily from this throbbing perch.

The needles and hack-saws of cactus bleed
A milk of earth when stricken off the stalk;   10
But this,—defenseless, thornless, sheds no blood,
Almost no shadow—but the air's thin talk.

Angelic Dynamo! Ventriloquist of the Blue!
While beachward creeps the shark-swept Spanish Main
By what conjunctions do the winds appoint   15
Its apotheosis, at last—the hurricane!

The Broken Tower

The bell-rope that gathers God at dawn
Dispatches me as though I dropped down the knell
Of a spent day—to wander the cathedral lawn
From pit to crucifix, feet chill on steps from hell.

Have you not heard, have you not seen that corps   5
Of shadows in the tower, whose shoulders sway
Antiphonal carillons launched before
The stars are caught and hived in the sun's ray?

The bells, I say, the bells break down their tower;
And swing I know not where. Their tongues engrave   10
Membrane through marrow, my long-scattered score
Of broken intervals. . . . And I, their sexton slave!

Oval encyclicals in canyons heaping
The impasse high with choir. Banked voices slain!
Pagodas, campaniles with reveilles outleaping—   15
O terraced echoes prostrate on the plain! . . .

And so it was I entered the broken world
To trace the visionary company of love, its voice
An instant in the wind (I know not whither hurled)
But not for long to hold each desperate choice.   20

My word I poured. But was it cognate, scored
Of that tribunal monarch of the air
Whose thigh embronzes earth, strikes crystal Word
In wounds pledged once to hope—cleft to despair?

The steep encroachments of my blood left me   25
No answer (could blood hold such a lofty tower
As flings the question true?)—or is it she
Whose sweet mortality stirs latent power?—

And through whose pulse I hear, counting the strokes
My veins recall and add, revived and sure   30

The angelus of wars my chest evokes:
What.I hold healed, original now, and pure . . .

And builds, within, a tower that is not stone
(Not stone can jacket heaven)—but slip
Of pebbles—visible wings of silence sown   35
In azure circles, widening as they dip

The matrix of the heart, lift down the eye
That shrines the quiet lake and swells a tower . . .
The commodious, tall decorum of that sky
Unseals her earth, and lifts love in its shower.   40

From *The Bridge*

To Brooklyn Bridge

How many dawns, chill from his rippling rest
The seagull's wings shall dip and pivot him,
Shedding white rings of tumult, building high
Over the chained bay waters Liberty—

Then, with inviolate curve, forsake our eyes   5
As apparitional as sails that cross
Some page of figures to be filed away;
—Till elevators drop us from our day . . .

I think of cinemas, panoramic sleights
With multitudes bent toward some flashing scene   10
Never disclosed, but hastened to again,
Foretold to other eyes on the same screen;

And Thee, across the harbor, silver-paced
As though the sun took step of thee, yet left
Some motion ever unspent in thy stride,—   15
Implicitly thy freedom staying thee!

Out of some subway scuttle, cell or loft
A bedlamite speeds to thy parapets,
Tilting there momently, shrill shirt ballooning,
A jest falls from the speechless caravan.   20

Down Wall, from girder into street noon leaks,
A rip-tooth of the sky's acetylene;

All afternoon the cloud-flown derricks turn . . .
Thy cables breathe the North Atlantic still.

And obscure as that heaven of the Jews,   25
Thy guerdon . . . Accolade thou dost bestow
Of anonymity time cannot raise:
Vibrant reprieve and pardon thou dost show.

O harp and altar, of the fury fused,
(How could mere toil align thy choiring strings!)   30
Terrific threshold of the prophet's pledge,
Prayer of pariah, and the lover's cry,—

Again the traffic lights that skim thy swift
Unfractioned idiom, immaculate sigh of stars,
Beading thy path—condense eternity: 35
And we have seen night lifted in thine arms.

Under thy shadow by the piers I waited;
Only in darkness is thy shadow clear.
The City's fiery parcels all undone,
Already snow submerges an iron year . . .   40

O Sleepless as the river under thee,
Vaulting the sea, the prairies' dreaming sod,
Unto us lowliest sometime sweep, descend
And of the curveship lend a myth to God.

Ode to the Confederate Dead

Row after row with strict impunity
The headstones yield their names to the element,
The wind whirrs without recollection;
In the riven troughs the splayed leaves
Pile up, of nature the casual sacrament   5
To the seasonal eternity of death;
Then driven by the fierce scrutiny
Of heaven to their election in the vast breath,
They sough the rumor of mortality.

Autumn is desolation in the plot   10
Of a thousand acres where these memories grow
From the inexhaustible bodies that are not
Dead, but feed the grass row after rich row.
Think of the autumns that have come and gone!—
Ambitious November with the humors of the year,   15
With a particular zeal for every slab,
Staining the uncomfortable angels that rot
On the slabs, a wing chipped here, an arm there:
The brute curiosity of an angel's stare
Turns you, like them, to stone,   20
Transforms the heaving air
Till plunged to a heavier world below
You shift your sea-space blindly
Heaving, turning like the blind crab.

　　Dazed by the wind, only the wind   25
　　The leaves flying, plunge

You know who have waited by the wall
The twilight certainty of an animal,
Those midnight restitutions of the blood
You know—the immitigable pines, the smoky frieze   30
Of the sky, the sudden call: you know the rage,
The cold pool left by the mounting flood,
Of muted Zeno and Parmeinides.
You who have waited for the angry resolution
Of those desires that should be yours tomorrow,   35

You know the unimportant shrift of death
And praise the vision
And praise the arrogant circumstance
Of those who fall
Rank upon rank, hurried beyond decision—   40
Here by the sagging gate, stopped by the wall.

    Seeing, seeing only the leaves
    Flying, plunge and expire

Turn your eyes to the immoderate past,
Turn to the inscrutable infantry rising   45
Demons out of the earth—they will not last.
Stonewall, Stonewall, and the sunken fields of hemp,
Shiloh, Antietam, Malvern Hill, Bull Run.
Lost in that orient of the thick-and-fast
You will curse the setting sun.   50

    Cursing only the leaves crying
    Like an old man in a storm

You hear the shout, the crazy hemlocks point
With troubled fingers to the silence which
Smothers you, a mummy, in time.   55

                  The hound bitch
Toothless and dying, in a musty cellar
Hears the wind only.

            Now that the salt of their blood
Stiffens the saltier oblivion of the sea,   60
Seals the malignant purity of the flood,
What shall we who count our days and bow
Our heads with a commemorial woe
In the ribboned coats of grim felicity,
What shall we say of the bones, unclean,   65
Whose verdurous anonymity will grow?
The ragged arms, the ragged heads and eyes
Lost in these acres of the insane green?
The gray lean spiders come, they come and go;
In a tangle of willows without light   70
The singular screech-owl's tight
Invisible lyric seeds the mind
With the furious murmur of their chivalry.

    We shall say only the leaves
    Flying, plunge and expire   75

We shall say only the leaves whispering
In the improbable mist of nightfall
That flies on multiple wing;
Night is the beginning and the end
And in between the ends of distraction   80
Waits mute speculation, the patient curse
That stones the eyes, or like the jaguar leaps
For his own image in a jungle pool, his victim.
What shall we say who have knowledge
Carried to the heart? Shall we take the act   85
To the grave? Shall we, more hopeful, set up the grave
In the house? The ravenous grave?

                                        Leave now
The shut gate and the decomposing wall:
The gentle serpent, green in the mulberry bush,   90
Riots with his tongue through the hush—
Sentinel of the grave who counts us all!

YVOR WINTERS (1900–   )

Sir Gawaine and the Green Knight

Reptilian green the wrinkled throat,
Green as a bough of yew the beard;
He bent his head, and so I smote;
Then for a thought my vision cleared.

The head dropped clean; he rose and walked;   5
He fixed his fingers in the hair;
The head was unabashed and talked;
I understood what I must dare.

His flesh, cut down, arose and grew.
He bade me wait the season's round,   10
And then, when he had strength anew,
To meet him on his native ground.

The year declined; and in his keep
I passed in joy a thriving yule;
And whether waking or in sleep,   15
I lived in riot like a fool.

He beat the woods to bring me meat.
His lady, like a forest vine,
Grew in my arms; the growth was sweet;
And yet what thoughtless force was mine!   20

By practice and conviction formed,
With ancient stubbornness ingrained,
Although her body clung and swarmed,
My own identity remained.

Her beauty, lithe, unholy, pure,   25
Took shapes that I had never known;
And had I once been insecure,
Had grafted laurel in my bone.

And then, since I had kept the trust,
Had loved the lady, yet was true,   30
The knight withheld his giant thrust
And let me go with what I knew.

I left the green bark and the shade,
Where growth was rapid, thick, and still;
I found a road that men had made   35
And rested on a drying hill.

A Fragment

I cannot find my way to Nazareth.
I have had enough of this. Thy will is death,
And this unholy quiet is thy peace.
Thy will be done; and let discussion cease.

To the Holy Spirit

*from a deserted graveyard
in the Salinas Valley*

Immeasurable haze:
The desert valley spreads
Up golden river-beds
As if in other days.
Trees rise and thin away,   5
And past the trees, the hills,
Pure line and shade of dust,
Bear witness to our wills:
We see them, for we must;
Calm in deceit, they stay.   10

High noon returns the mind
Upon its local fact:
Dry grass and sand; we find
No vision to distract.
Low in the summer heat,   15
Naming old graves, are stones
Pushed here and there, the seat
Of nothing, and the bones
Beneath are similar:
Relics of lonely men,   20
Brutal and aimless, then,
As now, irregular.

These are thy fallen sons,
Thou whom I try to reach.
Thou whom the quick eye shuns,   25
Thou dost elude my speech.
Yet when I go from sense
And trace thee down in thought,
I meet thee, then, intense,
And know thee as I ought.   30
But thou art mind alone,
And I, alas, am bound
Pure mind to flesh and bone,
And flesh and bone to ground.

These had no thought: at most   35
Dark faith and blinding earth.
Where is the trammeled ghost?
Was there another birth?
Only one certainty
Beside thine unfleshed eye,   40
Beside the spectral tree,
Can I discern: these die.
All of this stir of age,
Though it elude my sense
Into what heritage   45
I know not, seems to fall,
Quiet beyond recall,
Into irrelevance.

ROBERT FRANCIS (1901–   )

Farm Boy after Summer

A seated statue of himself he seems.
A bronze slowness becomes him. Patently
The page he contemplates he doesn't see.

The lesson, the long lesson, has been summer.
His mind holds summer as his skin holds sun.   5
For once the homework, all of it, was done.

What were the crops, where were the fiery fields
Where for so many days so many hours
The sun assaulted him with glittering showers?

Expect a certain absence in his presence.   10
Expect all winter long a summer scholar,
For scarcely all its snows can cool that color.

Hide-and-Seek

Here where the dead lie hidden
Too well ever to speak,
Three children unforbidden
Are playing hide-and-seek.

What if for such a hiding
These stones were not designed?
The dead are far from chiding;
The living need not mind.

Too soon the stones that hid them
Anonymously in play
Will learn their names and bid them
Come back to hide to stay.

Epitaph

Believer he and unbeliever both
For less than both would have been less than truth.
His creed was godliness and godlessness.
His credit had been cramped with any less.

Freedom he loved and order he embraced.   5
Fifty extremists called him Janus-faced.
Though cool centrality was his desire,
He drew the zealot fire and counter-fire.

Baffled by what he deeply understood,
He found life evil and he found life good.   10
Lover he was, unlonely, yet alone—
Esteemed, belittled, nicknamed, and unknown.

Hogwash

The tongue that mothered such a metaphor
Only the purest purist could despair of.

Nobody ever called swill sweet but isn't
Hogwash a daisy in a field of daisies?

What beside sports and flowers could you find   5
To praise better than the American language?

Bruised by American foreign policy
What shall I soothe me, what defend me with

But a handful of clean unmistakable words—
Daisies, daisies, in a field of daisies?   10

Dirge

1–2–3 was the number he played but today the number came 3–2–1;
Bought his Carbide at 30 and it went to 29; had the favorite at Bowie
    but the track was slow—

O executive type, would you like to drive a floating-power, knee-action,
    silk-upholstered six? Wed a Hollywood star? Shoot the course in 58?
    Draw to the ace, king, jack?
O fellow with a will who won't take no, watch out for three cigarettes on
    the same, single match; O democratic voter born in August under
    Mars, beware of liquidated rails—

Denouement to denouement, he took a personal pride in the certain,
    certain way he lived his own, private life,   5
But nevertheless, they shut off his gas; nevertheless, the bank foreclosed;
    nevertheless, the landlord called; nevertheless, the radio broke,

And twelve o'clock arrived just once too often,
Just the same he wore one gray tweed suit, bought one straw hat, drank
    one straight Scotch, walked one short step, took one long look, drew
    one deep breath,
Just one too many,

And wow he died as wow he lived,   10
Going whop to the office and blooie home to sleep and biff got married
    and bam had children and oof got fired,
Zowie did he live and zowie did he die,

With who the hell are you at the corner of his casket, and where the
    hell're we going on the right-hand silver knob, and who the hell
    cares walking second from the end with an American Beauty wreath
    from why the hell not,

Very much missed by the circulation staff of the New York Evening
    Post; deeply, deeply mourned by the B.M.T.
Wham, Mr. Roosevelt; pow, Sears Roebuck; awk, big dipper; bopy,
    summer rain;   15
Bong, Mr., bong, Mr., bong, Mr., bong.

RICHARD EBERHART (1904–   )

The Groundhog

In June, amid the golden fields,
I saw a groundhog lying dead.
Dead lay he; my senses shook,
And mind outshot our naked frailty.
There lowly in the vigorous summer   5
His form began its senseless change,
And made my senses waver dim
Seeing nature ferocious in him.
Inspecting close his maggots' might
And seething cauldron of his being,   10
Half with loathing, half with a strange love,
I poked him with an angry stick.
The fever arose, became a flame
And Vigour circumscribed the skies,
Immense energy in the sun,   15
And through my frame a sunless trembling.
My stick had done nor good nor harm.
Then stood I silent in the day
Watching the object, as before;
And kept my reverence for knowledge   20
Trying for control, to be still,
To quell the passion of the blood;
Until I had bent down on my knees
Praying for joy in the sight of decay.
And so I left; and I returned   25
In Autumn strict of eye, to see
The sap gone out of the groundhog,
But the bony sodden hulk remained.
But the year had lost its meaning,
And in intellectual chains   30
I lost both love and loathing,
Mured up in the wall of wisdom.
Another summer took the fields again
Massive and burning, full of life,
But when I chanced upon the spot   35
There was only a little hair left,
And bones bleaching in the sunlight

Beautiful as architecture;
I watched them like a geometer,
And cut a walking stick from a birch.   40
It has been three years, now.
There is no sign of the groundhog.
I stood there in the whirling summer,
My hand capped a withered heart,
And thought of China and of Greece,   45
Of Alexander in his tent;
Of Montaigne in his tower,
Of Saint Theresa in her wild lament.

I Walked Out to the Graveyard to See the Dead

I walked out to the graveyard to see the dead
The iron gates were locked, I couldn't get in,
A golden pheasant on the dark fir boughs
Looked with fearful method at the sunset,

Said I, Sir bird, wink no more at me
I have had enough of my dark eye-smarting,
I cannot adore you, nor do I praise you,
But assign you to the rafters of Montaigne.

Who talks with the Absolute salutes a Shadow,
Who seeks himself shall lose himself;
And the golden pheasants are no help
And action must be learned from love of man.

The Fury of Aerial Bombardment

You would think the fury of aerial bombardment
Would rouse God to relent; the infinite spaces
Are still silent. He looks on shock-pried faces.
History, even, does not know what is meant.

You would feel that after so many centuries   5
God would give man to repent; yet he can kill
As Cain could, but with multitudinous will,
No farther advanced than in his ancient furies.

Was man made stupid to see his own stupidity?
Is God by definition indifferent, beyond us all?   10
Is the eternal truth man's fighting soul
Wherein the Beast ravens in its own avidity?

Of Van Wettering I speak, and Averill,
Names on a list, whose faces I do not recall
But they are gone to early death, who late in school   15
Distinguished the belt feed lever from the belt holding pawl.

The Enigma

Mine will last though others fall to dust.
He began to row across the flaming lake.
Acrid fumes were sweet as the unexplained.
Tears ran down his face all day
As on the whirling came, as come they must.   5
In his gutted heart bell's memories would break.

Mine will stay though others live in hate.
The lake was vile with forms tormenting mind,
The fumes through tears were dear reality.
They came believing but they faded in the maze   10
As he rode on time's mystery of fate.
Change as they would, there was no other kind.

Mine will survive though others fall to dust.
He neared the dark escarpment and white pall,
Crying in a wilderness of forms,   15
His head fiery, his heart hearing ancient bells.
They came to judgment, as come all must,
He thought he felt the meaning of the fall.

It had to do with struggles in the night,
With breakless Adam and still breakless Eve,   20
The ever oncome, the will to row in fire,
Bells bringing memories of helps long gone.
Though he hailed them, hurled them out of sight,
His would survive, though never to him cleave.

WILLIAM EMPSON (1906–   )

Villanelle

It is the pain, it is the pain, endures.
Your chemic beauty burned my muscles through.
Poise of my hands reminded me of yours.

What later purge from this deep toxin cures?
What kindness now could the old salve renew?   5
It is the pain, it is the pain, endures.

The infection slept (custom or change inures)
And when pain's secondary phase was due
Poise of my hands reminded me of yours.

How safe I felt, whom memory assures,   10
Rich that your grace safely by heart I knew.
It is the pain, it is the pain, endures.

My stare drank deep beauty that still allures.
My heart pumps yet the poison draught of you.
Poise of my hands reminded me of yours.   15

You are still kind whom the same shape immures.
Kind and beyond adieu. We miss our cue.
It is the pain, it is the pain, endures.
Poise of my hands reminded me of yours.

Missing Dates

Slowly the poison the whole blood stream fills
It is not the effort nor the failure tires.
The waste remains, the waste remains and kills.

It is not your system or clear sight that mills
Down small to the consequence a life requires;   5
Slowly the poison the whole blood stream fills.

They bled an old dog dry yet the exchange rills
Of young dog blood gave but a month's desires;
The waste remains, the waste remains and kills.

It is the Chinese tombs and the slag hills 10
Usurp the soil, and not the soil retires.
Slowly the poison the whole blood stream fills.

Not to have fire is to be a skin that shrills.
The complete fire is death. From partial fires
The waste remains, the waste remains and kills. 15

It is the poems you have lost, the ills
From missing dates, at which the heart expires.
Slowly the poison the whole blood stream fills.
The waste remains, the waste remains and kills.

Let It Go

It is this deep blankness is the real thing strange.
  The more things happen to you the more you can't
    Tell or remember even what they were.

The contradictions cover such a range.
  The talk would talk and go so far aslant.
    You don't want madhouse and the whole thing there.

❧ VERNON WATKINS (1906–   )

Discoveries

The poles are flying where the two eyes set:
America has not found Columbus yet.

Ptolemy's planets, playing fast and loose,
Foretell the wisdom of Copernicus.

Dante calls Primum Mobile, the First Cause: 5
'Love that moves the world and the other stars.'

Great Galileo, twisted by the rack,
Groans the bright sun from heaven, then breathes it back.

Blake, on the world alighting, holds the skies,
And all the stars shine down through human eyes.   10

Donne sees those stars, yet will not let them lie:
'We're tapers, too, and at our own cost die.'

The shroud-lamp catches. Lips are smiling there.
'Les flammes—déjà?' [1]—The world dies, or Voltaire.

Swift, a cold mourner at his burial-rite,   15
Burns to the world's heart like a meteorite.

Beethoven deaf, in deafness hearing all,
Unwinds all music from sound's funeral.

Three prophets fall, the litter of one night:
Blind Milton gazes in fixed deeps of light.   20

Beggar of those Minute Particulars,
Yeats lights again the turmoil of the stars.

Motionless motion! Come, Tiresias,
The eternal flies, what's passing cannot pass.

'Solace in flight,' old Heraclitus cries;   25
Light changing to Von Hügel's butterflies.

Rilke bears all, thinks like a tree, believes,
Sinks in the hand that bears the falling leaves.

---

[1] "The flames—already?"

The stars! The signs! Great Angelo hurls them back.
His whirling ceiling draws the zodiac.   30

The pulse of Keats testing the axiom;
The second music when the sound is dumb.

The Christian Paradox, bringing its great reward
By loss; the moment known to Kierkegaard.

The Strangled Prayer

Look down at midnight when my strangled prayer
Calls through night-leaves the shades of ancestors,
Midsummer night, Eden of windless air,
Coiled with strange creepers where the moth-wing stirs.
Conscience fights echoes, footprints on worn stairs,   5
And my ten fingers separate the stars.
Bless my strained heels. I drown in a child's hair.

The boards are full of voices. Through my vow
Insects run out. The cricket chirps Amen.
Plumb on the floor I kneel. Stark moonlight now   10
Touches the skin and pricks desirous men;
They dance, they leap, they gratify the moon.
Bones make a circle round my naked moan.
Above this sheet the Pleiads and the Plough

Are white with ancient music. Mars is red   15
With violent fury, glowing with vine-must.
The crested darkness hovering overhead
Has eyes of serpents. My great prayer is crossed
By all the travelling beasts. My proud loins lust.
Snatch up, untwist me, twelve-tongued Pentecost,   20
For Nature makes me mortal in her bed.

W. H. AUDEN (1907–   )

Petition

Sir, no man's enemy, forgiving all
But will its negative inversion, be prodigal:
Send to us power and light, a sovereign touch
Curing the intolerable neural itch,
The exhaustion of weaning, the liar's quinsy,   5
And the distortions of ingrown virginity.
Prohibit sharply the rehearsed response
And gradually correct the coward's stance;
Cover in time with beams those in retreat
That spotted, they turn though the reverse were great;   10
Publish each healer that in city lives
Or country houses at the end of drives;
Harrow the house of the dead; look shining at
New styles of architecture, a change of heart.

Musée des Beaux Arts [1]

About suffering they were never wrong,
The Old Masters: how well they understood
Its human position; how it takes place
While someone else is eating or opening a window or just walking dully
    along;
How, when the aged are reverently, passionately waiting   5
For the miraculous birth, there always must be
Children who did not specially want it to happen, skating
On a pond at the edge of the wood:
They never forgot
That even the dreadful martyrdom must run its course   10
Anyhow in a corner, some untidy spot
Where the dogs go on with their doggy life and the torturer's horse
Scratches its innocent behind on a tree.

[1] Fine Arts Museum

644

In Brueghel's *Icarus,* for instance: how everything turns away
Quite leisurely from the disaster; the ploughman may   15
Have heard the splash, the forsaken cry,
But for him it was not an important failure; the sun shone
As it had to on the white legs disappearing into the green
Water; and the expensive delicate ship that must have seen
Something amazing, a boy falling out of the sky,   20
Had somewhere to get to and sailed calmly on.

In Memory of W. B. Yeats

(d. Jan. 1939)

I

He disappeared in the dead of winter:
The brooks were frozen, the airports almost deserted,
And snow disfigured the public statues;
The mercury sank in the mouth of the dying day.
O all the instruments agree   5
The day of his death was a dark cold day.

Far from his illness
The wolves ran on through the evergreen forests,
The peasant river was untempted by the fashionable quays;
By mourning tongues   10
The death of the poet was kept from his poems.

But for him it was his last afternoon as himself,
An afternoon of nurses and rumors;
The provinces of his body revolted,
The squares of his mind were empty,   15
Silence invaded the suburbs,
The current of his feeling failed: he became his admirers.

Now he is scattered among a hundred cities
And wholly given over to unfamiliar affections;
To find his happiness in another kind of wood   20
And be punished under a foreign code of conscience.
The words of a dead man
Are modified in the guts of the living.

But in the importance and noise of tomorrow
When the brokers are roaring like beasts on the floor of the Bourse,   25
And the poor have the sufferings to which they are fairly accustomed,
And each in his cell of himself is almost convinced of his freedom;
A few thousand will think of this day
As one thinks of a day when one did something slightly unusual.
O all the instruments agree   30
The day of his death was a dark cold day.

2

You were silly like us: your gift survived it all;
The parish of rich women, physical decay,
Yourself; mad Ireland hurt you into poetry.
Now Ireland has her madness and her weather still,   35
For poetry makes nothing happen: it survives
In the valley of its saying where executives
Would never want to tamper; it flows south
From ranches of isolation and the busy griefs,
Raw towns that we believe and die in; it survives,   40
A way of happening, a mouth.

3

Earth, receive an honored guest;
William Yeats is laid to rest:
Let the Irish vessel lie
Emptied of its poetry.   45

Time that is intolerant
Of the brave and innocent,
And indifferent in a week
To a beautiful physique,

Worships language and forgives   50
Everyone by whom it lives;
Pardons cowardice, conceit,
Lays its honors at their feet.

Time that with this strange excuse
Pardoned Kipling and his views,   55
And will pardon Paul Claudel,
Pardons him for writing well.

In the nightmare of the dark
All the dogs of Europe bark,

And the living nations wait,   60
Each sequestered in its hate;

Intellectual disgrace
Stares from every human face,
And the seas of pity lie
Locked and frozen in each eye.   65

Follow, poet, follow right
To the bottom of the night,
With your unconstraining voice
Still persuade us to rejoice;

With the farming of a verse   70
Make a vineyard of the curse,
Sing of human unsuccess
In a rapture of distress;

In the deserts of the heart
Let the healing fountain start,   75
In the prison of his days
Teach the free man how to praise.

O Where Are You Going?

"O where are you going?" said reader to rider,
"That valley is fatal when furnaces burn,
Yonder's the midden whose odors will madden,
That gap is the grave where the tall return."

"O do you imagine," said fearer to farer,   5
"That dusk will delay on your path to the pass,
Your diligent looking discover the lacking
Your footsteps feel from granite to grass?"

"O what was that bird," said horror to hearer,
"Did you see that shape in the twisted trees?   10
Behind you swiftly the figure comes softly,
The spot on your skin is a shocking disease?"

"Out of this house"—said rider to reader,
"Yours never will"—said farer to fearer,
"They're looking for you"—said hearer to horror,   15
As he left them there, as he left there.

In Praise of Limestone

If it form the one landscape that we the inconstant ones
    Are consistently homesick for, this is chiefly
Because it dissolves in water. Mark these rounded slopes
    With their surface fragrance of thyme and beneath
A secret system of caves and conduits; hear these springs   5
    That spurt out everywhere with a chuckle
Each filling a private pool for its fish and carving
    Its own little ravine whose cliffs entertain
The butterfly and the lizard; examine this region
    Of short distances and definite places: 10
What could be more like Mother or a fitter background
    For her son, for the nude young male who lounges
Against a rock displaying his dildo, never doubting
    That for all his faults he is loved, whose works are but
Extensions of his power to charm? From weathered outcrop   15
    To hill-top temple, from appearing waters to
Conspicuous fountains, from a wild to a formal vineyard,
    Are ingenious but short steps that a child's wish
To receive more attention than his brothers, whether
    By pleasing or teasing, can easily take.   20

Watch, then, the band of rivals as they climb up and down
    Their steep stone gennels in twos and threes, sometimes
Arm in arm, but never, thank God, in step; or engaged
    On the shady side of a square at midday in
Voluble discourse, knowing each other too well to think   25
    There are any important secrets, unable
To conceive a god whose temper-tantrums are moral
    And not to be pacified by a clever line
Or a good lay: for, accustomed to a stone that responds,
    They have never had to veil their faces in awe   30
Of a crater whose blazing fury could not be fixed;
    Adjusted to the local needs of valleys
Where everything can be touched or reached by walking,
    Their eyes have never looked into infinite space
Through the lattice-work of a nomad's comb; born lucky,   35
    Their legs have never encountered the fungi
And insects of the jungle, the monstrous forms and lives
    With which we have nothing, we like to hope, in common.

So, when one of them goes to the bad, the way his mind works
    Remains comprehensible: to become a pimp   40
Or deal in fake jewelry or ruin a fine tenor voice
    For effects that bring down the house could happen to all
But the best and the worst of us . . .
                        That is why, I suppose,
    The best and worst never stayed here long but sought   45
Immoderate soils where the beauty was not so external,
    The light less public and the meaning of life
Something more than a mad camp. "Come!" cried the granite wastes,
    "How evasive is your humor, how accidental
Your kindest kiss, how permanent is death." (Saints-to-be   50
    Slipped away sighing.) "Come!" purred the clays and gravels.
"On our plains there is room for armies to drill; rivers
    Wait to be tamed and slaves to construct you a tomb
In the grand manner: soft as the earth is mankind and both
    Need to be altered." (Intendant Caesars rose and   55
Left, slamming the door." But the really reckless were fetched
    By an older colder voice, the oceanic whisper:
"I am the solitude that asks and promises nothing;
    That is how I shall set you free. There is no love;
There are only the various envies, all of them sad."   60
    They were right, my dear, all those voices were right
And still are; this land is not the sweet home that it looks,
    Nor its peace the historical calm of a site
Where something was settled once and for all: A backward
    And delapidated province, connected   65
To the big busy world by a tunnel, with a certain
    Seedy appeal, is that all it is now? Not quite:
It has a worldly duty which in spite of itself
    It does not neglect, but calls into question
All the Great Powers assume; it disturbs our rights. The poet,   70
    Admired for his earnest habit of calling
The sun the sun, his mind Puzzle, is made uneasy
    By these solid statues which so obviously doubt
His antimythological myth; and these gamins,
    Pursuing the scientist down the tiled colonnade   75
With such lively offers, rebuke his concern for Nature's
    Remotest aspects: I, too, am reproached, for what
And how much you know. Not to lose time, not to get caught,
    Not to be left behind, not, please! to resemble
The beasts who repeat themselves, or a thing like water   80
    Or stone whose conduct can be predicted, these

Are our Common Prayer, whose greatest comfort is music
    Which can be made anywhere, is invisible,
And does not smell. In so far as we have to look forward
    To death as a fact, not doubt we are right: But if   85
Sins can be forgiven, if bodies rise from the dead,
    These modifications of matter into
Innocent athletes and gesticulating fountains,
    Made solely for pleasure, make a further point:
The blessed will not care what angle they are regarded from,   90
    Having nothing to hide. Dear, I know nothing of
Either, but when I try to imagine a faultless love
    Or the life to come, what I hear is the murmur
Of underground streams, what I see is a limestone landscape.

At the Party

Unrhymed, unrhythmical, the chatter goes:
Yet no one hears his own remarks as prose.

Beneath each topic tunelessly discussed
The ground-bass is reciprocal mistrust.

The names in fashion shuttling to and fro   5
Yield, when deciphered, messages of woe.

You cannot read me like an open book.

I'm more myself than you will ever look.

Will no one listen to my little song?

Perhaps I shan't be with you very long.   10

A howl for recognition, shrill with fear,
Shakes the jam-packed apartment, but each ear
Is listening to its hearing, so none hear.

The Sunlight on the Garden

The sunlight on the garden
Hardens and grows cold,
We cannot cage the minute
Within its nets of gold,
When all is told   5
We cannot beg for pardon.

Our freedom as free lances
Advances towards its end;
The earth compels, upon it
Sonnets and birds descend;   10
And soon, my friend,
We shall have no time for dances.

The sky was good for flying
Defying the church bells
And every evil iron   15
Siren and what it tells:
The earth compels,
We are dying, Egypt, dying

And not expecting pardon,
Hardened in heart anew,   20
But glad to have sat under
Thunder and rain with you,
And grateful too
For sunlight on the garden.

Wessex Guidebook

Hayfoot; strawfoot; the illiterate seasons
Still clump their way through Somerset and Dorset
While George the Third still rides his horse of chalk
From Weymouth and the new salt water cure
Towards Windsor and incurable madness. Inland   5
The ghosts of monks have grown too fat to walk
Through bone-dry ruins plugged with fossil sea-shells.

Thou shalt! Thou shalt not! In the yellow abbey
Inscribed beneath the crossing the Ten Commandments
Are tinted red by a Fifteenth Century fire;   10
On one round hill the yews still furnish bows
For Agincourt while, equally persistent,
Beneath another, in green-grassed repose,
Arthur still waits the call to rescue Britain.

Flake-tool; core-tool; in the small museum   15
Rare butterflies, green coins of Caracalla,
Keep easy company with the fading hand
Of one who chronicled a fading world;
Outside, the long roads, that the Roman ruler
Ruled himself out with, point across the land   20
To lasting barrows and long vanished barracks.

And thatchpoll numskull rows of limestone houses,
Dead from the navel down in plate glass windows,
Despise their homebrewed past, ignore the clock
On the village church in deference to Big Ben   25
Who booms round china dog and oaken settle
Announcing it is time and time again
To plough up tumuli, to damn the hindmost.

But hindmost, topmost, those illiterate seasons
Still smoke their pipes in swallow-hole and hide-out   30
As scornful of the tractor and the jet
As of the Roman road, or axe of flint,
Forgotten by the mass of human beings
Whom they, the Seasons, need not even forget
Since, though they fostered man, they never loved him. 35

The Wall

Face to the wall and behind him
The room full of well-wishers.
But what, they said, can we do?
He has abdicated, his life is behind him.

The bed had known birth and death;   5
Where was the wall had once been a window.
Now all the light is behind him.
The wall is a blind end.

No, they said, no doctor.
Nor priest. What is the use?   10
There is not even a window
For body or soul to look through.

But, as they spoke, their voices
Faded away while the wall
Grew nearer so that he heard   15
Different voices beyond it,

Singing. And there was light
Before him as through a window
That opens on to a garden.
The first garden. The last.   20

The Truisms

His father gave him a box of truisms
Shaped like a coffin, then his father died;
The truisms remained on the mantelpiece
As wooden as the playbox they had been packed in
Or that other his father skulked inside.   5

Then he left home, left the truisms behind him
Still on the mantelpiece, met love, met war,
Sordor, disappointment, defeat, betrayal,
Till through disbeliefs he arrived at a house
He could not remember seeing before.   10

And he walked straight in; it was where he had come from
And something told him the way to behave.
He raised his hand and blessed his home;
The truisms flew and perched on his shoulders
And a tall tree sprouted from his father's grave.   15

Spell of Creation

Within the flower there lies a seed,
Within the seed there springs a tree,
Within the tree there spreads a wood.

In the wood there burns a fire,
And in the fire there melts a stone,   5
Within the stone a ring of iron.

Within the ring there lies an O
Within the O there looks an eye,
In the eye there swims a sea,

And in the sea reflected sky,   10
And in the sky there shines the sun,
Within the sun a bird of gold.

Within the bird there beats a heart,
And from the heart there flows a song,
And in the song there sings a word.   15

In the word there speaks a world,
A word of joy, a world of grief,
From joy and grief there springs my love.

Oh love, my love, there springs a world
And on the world there shines a sun   20
And in the sun there burns a fire,

Within the fire consumes my heart
And in my heart there beats a bird,
And in the bird there wakes an eye,

Within the eye, earth, sea and sky,   25
Earth, sky and sea within an O
Lie like the seed within the flower.

✌ THEODORE ROETHKE (1908–   )

Cuttings (Later)

This urge, wrestle, resurrection of dry sticks,
Cut stems struggling to put down feet,
What saint strained so much,
Rose on such lopped limbs to a new life?

I can hear, underground, that sucking and sobbing,   5
In my veins, in my bones I feel it,—
The small waters seeping upward,
The tight grains parting at last.
When sprouts break out,
Slippery as fish,   10
I quail, lean to beginnings, sheath-wet.

My Papa's Waltz

The whiskey on your breath
Could make a small boy dizzy;
But I hung on like death:
Such waltzing was not easy.

We romped until the pans   5
Slid from the kitchen shelf;
My mother's countenance
Could not unfrown itself.

The hand that held my wrist
Was battered on one knuckle;   10
At every step you missed
My right ear scraped a buckle.

You beat time on my head
With a palm caked hard by dirt,
Then waltzed me off to bed   15
Still clinging to your shirt.

Dolor

I have known the inexorable sadness of pencils,
Neat in their boxes, dolor of pad and paper-weight,
All the misery of manila folders and mucilage,
Desolation in immaculate public places,
Lonely reception room, lavatory, switchboard,   5
The unalterable pathos of basin and pitcher,
Ritual of multigraph, paper-clip, comma,
Endless duplication of lives and objects.
And I have seen dust from the walls of institutions,
Finer than flour, alive, more dangerous than silica,   10
Sift, almost invisible, through long afternoons of tedium,
Dropping a fine film on nails and delicate eyebrows,
Glazing the pale hair, the duplicate grey standard faces.

The Visitant

1

A cloud moved close. The bulk of the wind shifted.
A tree swayed over water.
A voice said:
Stay. Stay by the slip-ooze. Stay.

Dearest tree, I said, may I rest here?   5
A ripple made a soft reply.
I waited, alert as a dog.
The leech clinging to a stone waited;
And the crab, the quiet breather.

2

Slow, slow as a fish she came,   10
Slow as a fish coming forward,
Swaying in a long wave;
Her skirts not touching a leaf,
Her white arms reaching towards me.

She came without sound,   15
Without brushing the wet stones;

In the soft dark of early evening,
She came,
The wind in her hair,
The moon beginning.   20

    3
I woke in the first of morning.
Staring at a tree, I felt the pulse of a stone.
Where's she now, I kept saying.
Where's she now, the mountain's downy girl?
But the bright day had no answer.   25
A wind stirred in a web of appleworms;
The tree, the close willow, swayed.

I Knew a Woman

I knew a woman, lovely in her bones,
When small birds sighed, she would sigh back at them;
Ah, when she moved, she moved more ways than one:
The shapes a bright container can contain!
Of her choice virtues only gods should speak,   5
Or English poets who grew up on Greek
(I'd have them sing in chorus, cheek to cheek).

How well her wishes went! She stroked my chin,
She taught me Turn, and Counter-turn, and Stand;
She taught me Touch, that undulant white skin;   10
I nibbled meekly from her proffered hand;
She was the sickle; I, poor I, the rake,
Coming behind her for her pretty sake
(But what prodigious mowing we did make).

Love likes a gander, and adores a goose: 15
Her full lips pursed, the errant note to seize;
She played it quick, she played it light and loose;
My eyes, they dazzled at her flowing knees;
Her several parts could keep a pure repose,
Or one hip quiver with a mobile nose   20
(She moved in circles, and those circles moved).

Let seed be grass, and grass turn into hay:
I'm martyr to a motion not my own;
What's freedom for? To know eternity.
I swear she cast a shadow white as stone.   25
But who would count eternity in days?
These old bones live to learn her wanton ways:
(I measure time by how a body sways).

The Rose

I

There are those to whom place is unimportant,
But this place, where sea and fresh water meet,
Is important—
Where the hawks sway out into the wind,
Without a single wingbeat,   5
And the eagles sail low over the fir trees,
And the gulls cry against the crows
In the curved harbors,
And the tide rises up against the grass
Nibbled by sheep and rabbits.   10

A time for watching the tide,
For the heron's hieratic fishing,
For the sleepy cries of the towhee,
The morning birds gone, the twittering finches,
But still the flash of the kingfisher, the wingbeat of the scoter,   15
The sun a ball of fire coming down over the water,
The last geese crossing against the reflected afterlight,
The moon retreating into a vague cloud-shape
To the cries of the owl, the eerie whooper.
The old log subsides with the lessening waves,   20
And there is silence.

I sway outside myself
Into the darkening currents,
Into the small spillage of driftwood,
The waters swirling past the tiny headlands.   25
Was it here I wore a crown of birds for a moment

While on a far point of the rocks
The light heightened,
And below, in a mist out of nowhere,
The first rain gathered?   30

2

As when a ship sails with a light wind—
The waves less than the ripples made by rising fish,
The lacelike wrinkles of the wake widening, thinning out,
Sliding away from the traveler's eye,
The prow pitching easily up and down,   35
The whole ship rolling slightly sideways,
The stern high, dipping like a child's boat in a pond—
Our motion continues.

But this rose, this rose in the sea-wind,
Stays,   40
Stays in its true place,
Flowering out of the dark,
Widening at high noon, face upward,
A single wild rose, struggling out of the white embrace of the morning-
     glory,
Out of the briary hedge, the tangle of matted underbrush,   45
Beyond the clover, the ragged hay,
Beyond the sea pine, the oak, the wind-tipped madrona,
Moving with the waves, the undulating driftwood,
Where the slow creek winds down to the black sand of the shore
With its thick grassy scum and crabs scuttling back into their glistening
     craters.   50

And I think of roses, roses,
White and red, in the wide six-hundred-foot greenhouses,
And my father standing astride the cement benches,
Lifting me high over the four-foot stems, the Mrs. Russells, and his own
     elaborate hybrids,
And how those flowerheads seemed to flow toward me, to beckon me,
     only a child, out of myself.   55

What need for heaven, then,
With that man, and those roses?

3

What do they tell us, sound and silence?
I think of American sounds in this silence:
On the banks of the Tombstone, the wind-harps having their say,   60
The thrush singing alone, that easy bird,
The killdeer whistling away from me,
The mimetic chortling of the catbird
Down in the corner of the garden, among the raggedy lilacs,
The bobolink skirring from a broken fencepost,   65
The bluebird, lover of holes in old wood, lilting its light song,
And that thin cry, like a needle piercing the ear, the insistent cicada,
And the ticking of snow around oil drums in the Dakotas,
The thin whine of telephone wires in the wind of a Michigan winter,
The shriek of nails as old shingles are ripped from the top of a roof,   70
The bulldozer backing away, the hiss of the sandblaster,
And the deep chorus of horns coming up from the streets in early
    morning.
I return to the twittering of swallows above water,
And that sound, that single sound,
When the mind remembers all,   75
And gently the light enters the sleeping soul,
A sound so thin it could not woo a bird,

Beautiful my desire, and the place of my desire.

I think of the rock singing, and light making its own silence,
At the edge of a ripening meadow, in early summer,   80
The moon lolling in the close elm, a shimmer of silver,
Or that lonely time before the breaking of morning
When the slow freight winds along the edge of the ravaged hillside,
And the wind tries the shape of a tree,
While the moon lingers,   85
And a drop of rain water hangs at the tip of a leaf
Shifting in the wakening sunlight
Like the eye of a new-caught fish.

4

I live with the rocks, their weeds,
Their filmy fringes of green, their harsh   90

Edges, their holes
Cut by the sea-slime, far from the crash
Of the long swell,
The oily, tar-laden walls
Of the toppling waves,   95
Where the salmon ease their way into the kelp beds,
And the sea rearranges itself among the small islands.

Near this rose, in this grove of sun-parched, wind-warped madronas,
Among the half-dead trees, I came upon the true ease of myself,
As if another man appeared out of the depths of my being,   100
And I stood outside myself,
Beyond becoming and perishing,
A something wholly other,
As if I swayed out on the wildest wave alive,
And yet was still.   105
And I rejoiced in being what I was:
In the lilac change, the white reptilian calm,
In the bird beyond the bough, the single one
With all the air to greet him as he flies,
The dolphin rising from the darkening waves;   110

And in this rose, this rose in the sea-wind,
Rooted in stone, keeping the whole of light,
Gathering to itself sound and silence—
Mine and the sea-wind's.

The Meadow Mouse

I

In a shoe box stuffed in an old nylon stocking
Sleeps the baby mouse I found in the meadow,
Where he trembled and shook beneath a stick
Till I caught him up by the tail and brought him in,
Cradled in my hand,   5
A little quaker, the whole body of him trembling,
His absurd whiskers sticking out like a cartoon-mouse,
His feet like small leaves,
Little lizard-feet,

Whitish and spread wide when he tried to struggle away,   10
Wriggling like a miniscule puppy.

Now he's eaten his three kinds of cheese and drunk from his bottle-cap
  watering-trough—
So much he just lies in one corner,
His tail curled under him, his belly big
As his head; his bat-like ears   15
Twitching, tilting toward the least sound.

Do I imagine he no longer trembles
When I come close to him?
He seems no longer to tremble.

  2

But this morning the shoe-box house on the back porch is empty.   20
Where has he gone, my meadow mouse,
My thumb of a child that nuzzled in my palm?—
To run under the hawk's wing,
Under the eye of the great owl watching from the elm-tree,
To live by courtesy of the shrike, the snake, the tom-cat.   25

I think of the nestling fallen into the deep grass,
The turtle gasping in the dusty rubble of the highway,
The paralytic stunned in the tub, and the water rising,—
All things innocent, hapless, forsaken.

STEPHEN SPENDER (1909–   )

What I Expected, Was

What I expected, was
Thunder, fighting,
Long struggles with men
And climbing.
After continual straining   5
I should grow strong;
Then the rocks would shake,
And I rest long.

What I had not foreseen
Was the gradual day   10
Weakening the will
Leaking the brightness away,
The lack of good to touch,
The fading of body and soul
—Smoke before wind,   15
Corrupt, unsubstantial.

The wearing of Time,
And the watching of cripples pass
With limbs shaped like questions
In their odd twist,   20
The pulverous grief
Melting the bones with pity,
The sick falling from earth—
These, I could not foresee.

Expecting always   25
Some brightness to hold in trust,
Some final innocence
Exempt from dust,
That, hanging solid,
Would dangle through all,   30
Like the created poem,
Or faceted crystal.

I Think Continually of Those Who Were Truly Great

I think continually of those who were truly great.
Who, from the womb, remembered the soul's history
Through corridors of light where the hours are suns,
Endless and singing. Whose lovely ambition
Was that their lips, still touched with fire,   5
Should tell of the Spirit, clothed from head to foot in song.
And who hoarded from the Spring branches
The desires falling across their bodies like blossoms.

What is precious, is never to forget
The essential delight of the blood drawn from ageless springs   10
Breaking through rocks in worlds before our earth.
Never to deny its pleasure in the morning simple light
Nor its grave evening demand for love.
Never to allow gradually the traffic to smother
With noise and fog, the flowering of the Spirit.   15

Near the snow, near the sun, in the highest fields,
See how these names are fêted by the waving grass
And by the streamers of white cloud
And whispers of wind in the listening sky.
The names of those who in their lives fought for life,   20
Who wore at their hearts the fire's centre.
Born of the sun, they travelled a short while toward the sun,
And left the vivid air signed with their honor.

August Hail

In late summer the wild geese
In the white draws are flying.
The grain beards in the blue peace.
The weeds are drying.

The hushed sky breeds hail.
Who shall revenge unreason?
Wheat headless in the white flail
Denies the season.

Montana Pastoral

I am no shepherd of a child's surmises.
I have seen fear where the coiled serpent rises,

Thirst where the grasses burn in early May
And thistle, mustard, and the wild oat stay.

There is dust in this air. I saw in the heat   5
Grasshoppers busy in the threshing wheat.

So to this hour. Through the warm dusk I drove
To blizzards sifting on the hissing stove,

And found no images of pastoral will,
But fear, thirst, hunger, and this huddled chill.   10

On the Calculus

From almost naught to almost all I flee,
And *almost* has almost confounded me,
Zero my limit, and infinity.

In Whose Will Is Our Peace?

In whose will is our peace? Thou happiness,
Thou ghostly promise, to thee I confess
Neither in thine nor love's nor in that form
Disquiet hints at have I yet been warm;
And if I rest not till I rest in thee
Cold as thy grace, whose hand shall comfort me?

On a Cold Night

On a cold night I came through the cold rain
And false snow to the wind shrill on your pane
With no hope and no anger and no fear:
Who are you? and with whom do you sleep here

Horoscope

Out of one's birth
The magi chart his worth;
They mark the influence
Of hour and day, and weigh what thence

Will come to be.
I in their cold sky see
Neither Venus nor Mars;
It is the past that cast the stars

That guide me now.
In winter when the bough
Has lost its leaves, the storm
That piled them deep will keep them warm.

The Monument

Now can you see the monument? It is of wood
built somewhat like a box. No. Built
like several boxes in descending sizes
one above the other.
Each is turned half-way round so that   5
its corners point toward the sides
of the one below and the angles alternate.
Then on the topmost cube is set
a sort of fleur-de-lys of weathered wood,
long petals of board, pierced with odd holes,   10
four-sided, stiff, ecclesiastical.
From it four thin, warped poles spring out,
(slanted like fishing-poles or flag-poles)
and from them jig-saw work hangs down,
four lines of vaguely whittled ornament   15
over the edges of the boxes
to the ground.
The monument is one-third set against
a sea; two-thirds against a sky.
The view is geared   20
(that is, the view's perspective)
so low there is no "far away,"
and we are far away within the view.
A sea of narrow, horizontal boards
lies out behind our lonely monument,   25
its long grains alternating right and left
like floor-boards—spotted, swarming-still,
and motionless. A sky runs parallel,
and it is palings, coarser than the sea's:
splintery sunlight and long-fibred clouds.   30
"Why does that strange sea make no sound?
Is it because we're far away?
Where are we? Are we in Asia Minor,
or in Mongolia?"

                     An ancient promontory,   35
an ancient principality whose artist-prince
might have wanted to build a monument
to mark a tomb or boundary, or make

a melancholy or romantic scene of it . . .
"But that queer sea looks made of wood,   40
half-shining, like a driftwood sea.
And the sky looks wooden, grained with cloud.
It's like a stage-set; it is all so flat!
Those clouds are full of glistening splinters!
What is that?"   45

                    It is the monument.
"It's piled-up boxes,
outlined with shoddy fret-work, half-fallen off,
cracked and unpainted. It looks old."
—The strong sunlight, the wind from the sea,   50
all the conditions of its existence,
may have flaked off the paint, if ever it was painted,
and made it homelier than it was.
"Why did you bring me here to see it?
A temple of crates in cramped and crated scenery,   55
what can it prove?
I am tired of breathing this eroded air,
this dryness in which the monument is cracking."

It is an artifact
of wood. Wood holds together better   60
than sea or cloud or sand could by itself,
much better than real sea or sand or cloud.
It chose that way to grow and not to move.
The monument's an object, yet those decorations,
carelessly nailed, looking like nothing at all,   65
give it away as having life, and wishing;
wanting to be a monument, to cherish something.
The crudest scroll-work says "commemorate,"
while once each day the light goes around it
like a prowling animal,   70
or the rain falls on it, or the wind blows into it.
It may be solid, may be hollow.
The bones of the artist-prince may be inside
or far away on even dryer soil.
But roughly but adequately it can shelter   75
what is within (which after all
cannot have been intended to be seen).
It is the beginning of a painting,
a piece of sculpture, or poem, or monument,
and all of wood. Watch it closely.   80

KARL SHAPIRO (1913–   )

Buick

As a sloop with a sweep of immaculate wing on her delicate spine
And a keel as steel as a root that holds in the sea as she leans,
Leaning and laughing, my warm-hearted beauty, you ride, you ride,
You tack on the curves with parabola speed and a kiss of goodbye,
Like a thoroughbred sloop, my new high-spirited spirit, my kiss.   5

As my foot suggests that you leap in the air with your hips of a girl,
My finger that praises your wheel and announces your voices of song,
Flouncing your skirts, you blueness of joy, you flirt of politeness,
You leap, you intelligence, essence of wheelness with silvery nose,
And your platinum clocks of excitement stir like the hairs of a fern.   10

But how alien you are from the booming belts of your birth and the
        smoke
Where you turned on the stinging lathes of Detroit and Lansing at
        night
And shrieked at the torch in your secret parts and the amorous tests,
But now with your eyes that enter the future of roads you forget;
You are all instinct with your phosphorous glow and your streaking
        hair.   15

And now when we stop it is not as the bird from the shell that I leave
Or the leathery pilot who steps from his bird with a sneer of delight,
And not as the ignorant beast do you squat and watch me depart,
But with exquisite breathing you smile, with satisfaction of love,
And I touch you again as you tick in the silence and settle in sleep.   20

Glass Poem

The afternoon lies glazed upon the wall
And on the window shines the scene-like bay,
And on the dark reflective floor a ray
Falls, and my thoughts like ashes softly fall.

And I look up as one who looks through glass   5
And sees the thing his soul clearly desires,
Who stares until his vision flags and tires,
But from whose eye the image fails to pass;

Until a wish crashes the vitreous air
And comes to your real hands across this space,　　　　10
Thief-like and deeply cut to touch your face,
Dearly, most bitterly to touch your hair.

And I could shatter these transparent lights,
Could thrust my arms and bring your body through,
Break from the subtle spectrum the last hue　　　　15
And change my eyes to dark soft-seeing nights.

But the sun stands and the hours stare like brass
And day flows thickly into permanent time,
And toward your eyes my threatening wishes climb
Where you move through a sea of solid glass.　　　　20

A Garden in Chicago

In the mid-city, under an oiled sky,
I lay in a garden of such dusky green
It seemed the dregs of the imagination.
Hedged round by elegant spears of iron fence
My face became a moon to absent suns.　　　　5
A low heat beat upon my reading face;
There rose no roses in that gritty place
But blue-gray lilacs hung their tassels out.
Hard zinnias and ugly marigolds
And one sweet statue of a child stood by.　　　　10

A gutter of poetry flowed outside the yard,
Making me think I was a bird of prose;
For overhead, bagged in a golden cloud,
There hung the fatted souls of animals,
While at my eyes bright dots of butterflies　　　　15
Turned off and on like distant neon signs.

Assuming that this garden still exists,
One ancient lady patrols the zinnias
(She looks like George Washington crossing the Delaware),
The janitor wanders to the iron rail,　　　　20
The traffic mounts bombastically out there,
And across the street in a pitch-black bar
With midnight mirrors, the professional
Takes her first whiskey of the afternoon—

Ah! It is like a breath of country air.　　　　25

Epistle I

Meeting a monster of mourning wherever I go
Who crosses me at morning and evening also,
For whom are you miserable I ask and he murmurs
I am miserable for innumerable man: for him
Who wanders through Woolworth's gazing at tin stars;   5
I mourn the maternal future tense, Time's mother,
Who has him in her lap, and I mourn also her,
Time whose dial face flashes with scars.

I gave the ghost my money and he smiled and said,
Keep it for the eyeballs of the dead instead.   10
Why here, I asked, why is it here you come
Breaking into the evening line going to another,
Edging your axe between my pencil fingers,
Twisting my word from a comedy to a crime?
I am the face once seen never forgotten,   15
Whose human look your dirty page will smother.

I know what it was, he said, that you were beginning;
The rigmarole of private life's belongings.
Birth, boyhood, and the adolescent baloney. So I say
Good go ahead, and see what happens then.   20
I promise you horror shall stand in your shoes,
And when your register of youth is through
What will it be but about the horror of man?
Try telling about birth and observe the issue.

Epping Forest where the deer and girls   25
Mope like lost ones looking for Love's gaols—
Among the dilapidated glades my mother wandered
With me as kid, and sadly we saw
The deer in the rain near the trees, the leaf-hidden shit,
The Sunday papers, and the foliage's falling world;   30
I not knowing nothing was our possession,
Not knowing Poverty my position.

Epping Forest glutted with the green tree
Grew up again like a sweet wood inside me.
I had the deer browsing on my heart,   35

This was my mother; and I had the dirt.
Inside was well with the green well of love,
Outside privation, poverty, all dearth.
Thus like the pearl I came from hurt,
Like the prize pig I came from love.   40

Now I know what was wanting in my youth,
It was not water or a loving mouth.
It was what makes the apple-tree grow big,
The mountain fall, and the minnow die.
It was hard cash I needed at my root.   45
I now know that how I grew was due
To echoing guts and the empty bag—
My song was out of tune for a few notes.

Oh, my ghost cried, the charming chimes of coincidence!
I was born also there where distress collects the rents.   50
Guttersnipe gutless, I was planted in your guts there,
The tear of time my sperm. I rose from
The woe-womb of the want-raped mind,
Empty hunger cracked with stomach's thunder.
Remember the rags that flattered your frame   55
Froze hard and formed this flesh my rind.

So close over the chapter of my birth,
Blessed by distress, baptized by dearth.
How I swung myself from the tree's bough
Demonstrating death in my gay play: 60
How the germ of the sperm of this ghost like a worm
I caught from the cold comfort of never enough.
How by being miserable for myself I began,
And now am miserable for the mass of man.

Epitaph for the Poet

The single sleeper lying here
    Is neither lying nor asleep.
Bend down your nosey parker ear
    And eavesdrop on him. In the deep
Conundrum of the dirt he speaks
    The one word you will never hear.

Death of a Peasant

You remember Davies? He died, you know,
With his face to the wall, as the manner is
Of the poor peasant in his stone croft
On the Welsh hills. I recall the room
Under the slates, and the smirched snow   5
Of the wide bed in which he lay,
Lonely as an ewe that is sick to lamb
In the hard weather of mid-March.
I remember also the trapped wind
Tearing the curtains, and the wild light's   10
Frequent hysteria upon the floor,
The bare floor without a rug
Or mat to soften the loud tread
Of neighbors crossing the uneasy boards
To peer at Davies with gruff words   15
Of meaningless comfort, before they turned
Heartless away from the stale smell
Of death in league with those dank walls.

The Country Clergy

I see them working in old rectories
By the sun's light, by candlelight,
Venerable men, their black cloth
A little dusty, a little green
With holy mildew. And yet their skulls,   5
Ripening over so many prayers,
Toppled into the same grave
With oafs and yokels. They left no books,
Memorial to their lonely thought
In grey parishes; rather they wrote   10
On men's hearts and in the minds
Of young children sublime words
Too soon forgotten. God in his time
Or out of time will correct this.

ROBERT HAYDEN (1913–   )

Approximations

1

In dead of winter
wept beside your open grave.
   Falling snow.

2

Darkness, darkness.
I grope and falter. Flare   5
   of a match.

3

Not sunflowers, not
roses, but rocks in patterned
   sand grow here. And bloom.

4

On the platform at   10
dawn, grey mailbags waiting;
   a crated coffin.

"Summertime and the Living . . ."

Nobody planted roses, he recalls,
but sunflowers gangled there sometimes,
tough-stalked and bold
and like the vivid children there unplanned.
There circus-poster horses curveted   5
in trees of heaven
above the quarrels and shattered glass,
and he was bareback rider of them all.

674

No roses there in summer—
oh, never roses except when people died—   10
and no vacations for his elders,
so harshened after each unrelenting day
that they were shouting-angry.
But summer was, they said, the poor folks' time
of year. And he remembers   15
how they would sit on broken steps amid

The fevered tossings of the dusk, the dark,
wafting hearsay with funeral-parlor fans
or making evening solemn by
their quietness. Feels their Mosaic eyes   20
upon him, though the florist roses
that only sorrow could afford
long since have bidden them Godspeed.

Oh, summer summer summertime—

Then grim street preachers shook   25
their tambourines and Bibles in the face
of tolerant wickedness;
then Elks parades and big splendiferous
Jack Johnson in his diamond limousine
set the ghetto burgeoning   30
with fantasies
of Ethiopia spreading her gorgeous wings.

DYLAN THOMAS (1914–1953)

The Force That Through the Green Fuse Drives the Flower

The force that through the green fuse drives the flower
Drives my green age; that blasts the roots of trees
Is my destroyer.
And I am dumb to tell the crooked rose
My youth is bent by the same wintry fever.   5

The force that drives the water through the rocks
Drives my red blood; that dries the mouthing streams
Turns mine to wax.
And I am dumb to mouth unto my veins
How at the mountain spring the same mouth sucks.   10

The hand that whirls the water in the pool
Stirs the quicksand; that ropes the blowing wind
Hauls my shroud sail.
And I am dumb to tell the hanging man
How of my clay is made the hangman's lime.   15

The lips of time leech to the fountain head;
Love drips and gathers, but the fallen blood
Shall calm her sores.
And I am dumb to tell a weather's wind
How time has ticked a heaven round the stars.   20

And I am dumb to tell the lover's tomb
How at my sheet goes the same crooked worm.

This Bread I Break

This bread I break was once the oat,
This wine upon a foreign tree
Plunged in its fruit;
Man in the day or wind at night
Laid the crops low, broke the grape's joy.   5

Once in this wind the summer blood
Knocked in the flesh that decked the vine,
Once in this bread
The oat was merry in the wind;
Man broke the sun, pulled the wind down.   10

This flesh you break, this blood you let
Make desolation in the vein,
Were oat and grape
Born of the sensual root and sap;
My wine you drink, my bread you snap.   15

And Death Shall Have No Dominion

And death shall have no dominion.
Dead men naked they shall be one
With the man in the wind and the west moon;
When their bones are picked clean and the clean bones gone,
They shall have stars at elbow and foot;   5
Though they go mad they shall be sane,
Though they sink through the sea they shall rise again;
Though lovers be lost love shall not;
And death shall have no dominion.

And death shall have no dominion.   10
Under the windings of the sea
They lying long shall not die windily;
Twisting on racks when sinews give way,
Strapped to a wheel, yet they shall not break;
Faith in their hands shall snap in two,   15
And the unicorn evils run them through;
Split all ends up they shan't crack;
And death shall have no dominion.

And death shall have no dominion.
No more may gulls cry at their ears   20
Or waves break loud on the seashores;
Where blew a flower may a flower no more
Lift its head to the blows of the rain;
Though they be mad and dead as nails,
Heads of the characters hammer through daisies;   25
Break in the sun till the sun breaks down,
And death shall have no dominion.

After the Funeral

(In memory of Ann Jones)

After the funeral, mule praises, brays,
Windshake of sailshaped ears, muffle-toed tap
Tap happily of one peg in the thick
Grave's foot, blinds down the lids, the teeth in black,
The spittled eyes, the salt ponds in the sleeves,   5
Morning smack of the spade that wakes up sleep,
Shakes a desolate boy who slits his throat
In the dark of the coffin and sheds dry leaves,
That breaks one bone to light with a judgment clout,
After the feast of tear-stuffed time and thistles   10
In a room with a stuffed fox and a stale fern,
I stand, for this memorial's sake, alone
In the snivelling hours with dead, humped Ann
Whose hooded, fountain heart once fell in puddles
Round the parched worlds of Wales and drowned each sun   15
(Though this for her is a monstrous image blindly
Magnified out of praise; her death was a still drop;
She would not have me sinking in the holy
Flood of her heart's fame; she would lie dumb and deep
And need no druid of her broken body).   20
But I, Ann's bard on a raised hearth, call all
The seas to service that her wood-tongued virtue
Babble like a bellbuoy over the hymning heads,
Bow down the walls of the ferned and foxy woods
That her love sing and swing through a brown chapel,   25
Bless her bent spirit with four, crossing birds.
Her flesh was meek as milk, but this skyward statue
With the wild breast and blessed and giant skull
Is carved from her in a room with a wet window
In a fiercely mourning house in a crooked year.   30
I know her scrubbed and sour humble hands
Lie with religion in their cramp, her threadbare
Whisper in a damp word, her wits drilled hollow,
Her fist of a face died clenched on a round pain;
And sculptured Ann is seventy years of stone.   35
These cloud-sopped, marble hands, this monumental
Argument of the hewn voice, gesture and psalm,
Storm me forever over her grave until
The stuffed lung of the fox twitch and cry Love
And the strutting fern lay seeds on the black sill.   40

Twenty-Four Years

Twenty-four years remind the tears of my eyes.
(Bury the dead for fear that they walk to the grave in labor.)
In the groin of the natural doorway I crouched like a tailor
Sewing a shroud for a journey
By the light of the meat-eating sun.   5
Dressed to die, the sensual strut begun,
With my red veins full of money,
In the final direction of the elementary town
I advance for as long as forever is.

A Refusal to Mourn the Death, by Fire,
of a Child in London

Never until the mankind making
Bird beast and flower
Fathering and all humbling darkness
Tells with silence the last light breaking
And the still hour   5
Is come of the sea tumbling in harness

And I must enter again the round
Zion of the water bead
And the synagogue of the ear of corn
Shall I let pray the shadow of a sound   10
Or sow my salt seed
In the least valley of sackcloth to mourn

The majesty and burning of the child's death.
I shall not murder
The mankind of her going with a grave truth   15
Nor blaspheme down the stations of the breath
With any further
Elegy of innocence and youth.

Deep with the first dead lies London's daughter,
Robed in the long friends,   20
The grains beyond age, the dark veins of her mother,
Secret by the unmourning water
Of the riding Thames.
After the first death, there is no other.

Poem in October

It was my thirtieth year to heaven
Woke to my hearing from harbor and neighbor wood
   And the mussel pooled and the heron
      Priested shore
     The morning beckon   5
With water praying and call of seagull and rook
And the knock of sailing boats on the net webbed wall
   Myself to set foot
      That second
In the still sleeping town and set forth.   10

My birthday began with the water-
Birds and the birds of the winged trees flying my name
   Above the farms and the white horses
      And I rose
     In rainy autumn   15
And walked abroad in a shower of all my days.
High tide and the heron dived when I took the road
   Over the border
      And the gates
     Of the town closed as the town awoke.   20

A springful of larks in a rolling
Cloud and the roadside bushes brimming with whistling
   Blackbirds and the sun of October
      Summery
     On the hill's shoulder,   25
Here were fond climates and sweet singers suddenly
Come in the morning where I wandered and listened
   To the rain wringing
      Wind blow cold
     In the wood faraway under me.   30

Pale rain over the dwindling harbor
And over the sea wet church the size of a snail
   With its horns through mist and the castle
      Brown as owls
     But all the gardens   35
Of spring and summer were blooming in the tall tales
Beyond the border and under the lark full cloud.

                There could I marvel
                    My birthday
            Away but the weather turned around.   40

            It turned away from the blithe country
        And down the other air and the blue altered sky
                Streamed again a wonder of summer
                        With apples
                    Pears and red currants   45
        And I saw in the turning so clearly a child's
        Forgotten mornings when he walked with his mother
                    Through the parables
                        Of sun light
            And the legends of the green chapels   50

            And the twice told fields of infancy
        That his tears burned my cheeks and his heart moved in mine.
                These were the woods the river and sea
                        Where a boy
                    In the listening   55
        Summertime of the dead whispered the truth of his joy
        To the trees and the stones and the fish in the tide.
                    And the mystery
                        Sang alive
            Still in the water and singingbirds.   60

            And there could I marvel my birthday
        Away but the weather turned around. And the true
                Joy of the long dead child sang burning
                        In the sun.
                    It was my thirtieth   65
        Year to heaven stood there then in the summer noon
        Though the town below lay leaved with October blood.
                    O may my heart's truth
                        Still be sung
            On this high hill in a year's turning.   70

The Hunchback in the Park

            The hunchback in the park
            A solitary mister
            Propped between trees and water

From the opening of the garden lock
That lets the trees and water enter   5
Until the Sunday sombre bell at dark

Eating bread from a newspaper
Drinking water from the chained cup
That the children filled with gravel
In the fountain basin where I sailed my ship   10
Slept at night in a dog kennel
But nobody chained him up.

Like the park birds he came early
Like the water he sat down
And Mister they called Hey mister   15
The truant boys from the town
Running when he had heard them clearly
On out of sound

Past lake and rockery
Laughing when he shook his paper   20
Hunchbacked in mockery
Through the loud zoo of the willow groves
Dodging the park keeper
With his stick that picked up leaves.

And the old dog sleeper   25
Alone between nurses and swans
While the boys among willows
Made the tigers jump out of their eyes
To roar on the rockery stones
And the groves were blue with sailors   30

Made all day until bell time
A woman figure without fault
Straight as a young elm
Straight and tall from his crooked bones
That she might stand in the night   35
After the locks and chains

All night in the unmade park
After the railings and shrubberies
The birds the grass the trees the lake
And the wild boys innocent as strawberries   40
Had followed the hunchback
To his kennel in the dark.

ROBERT LOWELL (1917–   )

The Quaker Graveyard in Nantucket

(For Warren Winslow, Dead at Sea)

Let man have dominion over the fishes of the sea and the fowls of the air and the beasts and the whole earth, and every creeping creature that moveth upon the earth.

I

A brackish reach of shoal off Madaket,—
The sea was still breaking violently and night
Had steamed into our North Atlantic Fleet,
When the drowned sailor clutched the drag-net. Light
Flashed from his matted head and marble feet,   5
He grappled at the net
With the coiled, hurdling muscles of his thighs:
The corpse was bloodless, a botch of reds and whites,
Its open, staring eyes
Were lustreless dead-lights   10
Or cabin-windows on a stranded hulk
Heavy with sand. We weight the body, close
Its eyes and heave it seaward whence it came,
Where the heel-headed dogfish barks its nose
On Ahab's [1] void and forehead; and the name   15
Is blocked in yellow chalk.
Sailors, who pitch this portent at the sea
Where dreadnoughts shall confess
Its hell-bent deity,
When you are powerless   20
To sand-bag this Atlantic bulwark, faced
By the earth-shaker, green, unwearied, chaste
In his steel scales: ask for no Orphean lute
To pluck life back. The guns of the steeled fleet
Recoil and then repeat   25
The hoarse salute.

[1] captain of the *Pequod,* in Melville's *Moby Dick*

683

2

Whenever winds are moving and their breath
Heaves at the roped-in bulwarks of this pier,
The terns and sea-gulls tremble at your death
In these home waters. Sailor, can you hear   30
The Pequod's sea wings, beating landward, fall
Headlong and break on our Atlantic wall
Off 'Sconset, where the yawing S-boats splash
The bellbuoy, with ballooning spinnakers,
As the entangled, screeching mainsheet clears   35
The blocks: off Madaket, where lubbers lash
The heavy surf and throw their long lead squids
For blue-fish? Sea-gulls blink their heavy lids
Seaward. The winds' wings beat upon the stones,
Cousin, and scream for you and the claws rush   40
At the sea's throat and wring it in the slush
Of this old Quaker graveyard where the bones
Cry out in the long night for the hurt beast
Bobbing by Ahab's whaleboats in the East.

3

All you recovered from Poseidon died   45
With you, my cousin, and the harrowed brine
Is fruitless on the blue beard of the god,
Stretching beyond us to the castles in Spain,
Nantucket's westward haven. To Cape Cod
Guns, cradled on the tide,   50
Blast the eelgrass about a waterclock
Of bilge and backwash, roil the salt and sand
Lashing earth's scaffold, rock
Our warships in the hand
Of the great God, where time's contrition blues   55
Whatever it was these Quaker sailors lost
In the mad scramble of their lives. They died
When time was open-eyed,
Wooden and childish; only bones abide
There, in the nowhere, where their boats were tossed 60
Sky-high, where mariners had fabled news
Of IS, the whited monster. What it cost
Them is their secret. In the sperm-whale's slick
I see the Quakers drown and hear their cry:
"If God himself had not been on our side,   65

If God himself had not been on our side,
When the Atlantic rose against us, why,
Then it had swallowed us up quick."

4

This is the end of the whaleroad and the whale
Who spewed Nantucket bones on the thrashed swell   70
And stirred the troubled waters to whirlpools
To send the Pequod packing off to hell:
This is the end of them, three-quarters fools,
Snatching at straws to sail
Seaward and seaward on the turntail whale,   75
Spouting out blood and water as it rolls,
Sick as a dog to these Atlantic shoals:
Clamavimus, [2] O depths. Let the sea-gulls wail

For water, for the deep where the high tide
Mutters to its hurt self, mutters and ebbs.   80
Waves wallow in their wash, go out and out,
Leave only the death-rattle of the crabs,
The beach increasing, its enormous snout
Sucking the ocean's side.
This is the end of running on the waves;   85
We are poured out like water. Who will dance
The mast-lashed master of Leviathans
Up from this field of Quakers in their unstoned graves?

5

When the whale's viscera go and the roll
Of its corruption overruns this world   90
Beyond tree-swept Nantucket and Wood's Hole
And Martha's Vineyard, Sailor, will your sword
Whistle and fall and sink into the fat?
In the great ash-pit of Jehoshaphat
The bones cry for the blood of the white whale,   95
The fat flukes arch and whack about its ears,
The death-lance churns into the sanctuary, tears
The gun-blue swingle, heaving like a flail,
And hacks the coiling life out: it works and drags
And rips the sperm-whale's midriff into rags,   100
Gobbets of blubber spill to wind and weather,
Sailor, and gulls go round the stoven timbers

---

[2] we called out

Where the morning stars sing out together
And thunder shakes the white surf and dismembers
The red flag hammered in the mast-head. Hide,   105
Our steel, Jonas Messias, in Thy side.

6

Our Lady of Walsingham [3]

There once the penitents took off their shoes
And then walked barefoot the remaining mile;
And the small trees, a stream and hedgerows file
Slowly along the munching English lane,   110
Like cows to the old shrine, until you lose
Track of your dragging pain.
The stream flows down under the druid tree,
Shiloah's whirlpools gurgle and make glad
The castle of God. Sailor, you were glad   115
And whistled Sion by that stream. But see:

Our Lady, too small for her canopy,
Sits near the altar. There's no comeliness
At all, or charm in that expressionless
Face with its heavy eyelids. As before,   120
This face, for centuries a memory,
Non est species, neque decor, [4]
Expressionless, expresses God: it goes
Past castled Sion. She knows what God knows,
Not Calvary's Cross nor crib at Bethlehem   125
Now, and the world shall come to Walsingham.

7

The empty winds are creaking and the oak
Splatters and splatters on the cenotaph,
The boughs are trembling and a gaff
Bobs on the untimely stroke   130
Of the greased wash exploding on a shoal-bell
In the old mouth of the Atlantic. It's well;
Atlantic, you are fouled with the blue sailors,
Sea-monsters, upward angel, downward fish:
Unmarried and corroding, spare of flesh   135
Mart once of supercilious, wing'd clippers,

[3] chapel in Walsingham Priory, Nor-   [4] "He had no form or comeliness,"
folk, England, destroyed in 1538   Isaiah 53:2.

Atlantic, where your bell-trap guts its spoil
You could cut the brackish winds with a knife
Here in Nantucket, and cast up the time
When the Lord God formed man from the sea's slime   140
And breathed into his face the breath of life,
And blue-lung'd combers lumbered to the kill.
The Lord survives the rainbow of His will.

Skunk Hour

(For Elizabeth Bishop)

Nautilus Island's hermit
heiress still lives through winter in her Spartan cottage;
her sheep still graze above the sea.
Her son's a bishop. Her farmer
is first selectman in our village;   5
she's in her dotage.

Thirsting for
the hierarchic privacy
of Queen Victoria's century,
she buys up all   10
the eyesores facing her shore,
and lets them fall.

The season's ill—
we've lost our summer millionaire,
who seemed to leap from an L. L. Bean   15
catalogue. His nine-knot yawl
was auctioned off to lobstermen.
A red fox stain covers Blue Hill.

And now our fairy
decorator brightens his shop for fall;   20
his fishnet's filled with orange cork,
orange, his cobbler's bench and awl;
there is no money in his work,
he'd rather marry.

One dark night,   25
my Tudor Ford climbed the hill's skull;

I watched for love-cars. Lights turned down,
they lay together, hull to hull,
where the graveyard shelves on the town. . . .
My mind's not right.   30

A car radio bleats,
"Love, O careless Love. . . ." I hear
my ill-spirit sob in each blood cell,
as if my hand were at its throat. . . .
I myself am hell;   35
nobody's here—

only skunks, that search
in the moonlight for a bite to eat.
They march on their soles up Main Street:
white stripes, moonstruck eyes' red fire   40
under the chalk-dry and spar spire
of the Trinitarian Church.

I stand on top
of our back steps and breathe the rich air—
a mother skunk with her column of kittens swills the garbage pail. 45
She jabs her wedge-head in a cup
of sour cream, drops her ostrich tail,
and will not scare.

Storm Windows

People are putting up storm windows now,
Or were, this morning, until the heavy rain
Drove them indoors. So, coming home at noon,
I saw storm windows lying on the ground,
Frame-full of rain; through the water and glass   5
I saw the crushed grass, how it seemed to stream
Away in lines like seaweed on the tide
Or blades of wheat leaning under the wind.
The ripple and splash of rain on the blurred glass
Seemed that it briefly said, as I walked by,   10
Something I should have liked to say to you,
Something . . . the dry grass bent under the pane
Brimful of bouncing water . . . something of
A swaying clarity which blindly echoes
This lonely afternoon of memories   15
And missed desires, while the wintry rain
(Unspeakable, the distance in the mind!)
Runs on the standing windows and away.

RICHARD WILBUR (1921–   )

Museum Piece

The good grey guardians of art
Patrol the halls on spongy shoes,
Impartially protective, though
Perhaps suspicious of Toulouse.

Here dozes one against the wall,   5
Disposed upon a funeral chair.
A Degas dancer pirouettes
Upon the parting of his hair.

See how she spins! The grace is there,
But strain as well is plain to see.   10
Degas loved the two together:
Beauty joined to energy.

Edgar Degas purchased once
A fine El Greco, which he kept
Against the wall beside his bed   15
To hang his pants on while he slept.

Juggler

A ball will bounce, but less and less. It's not
A light-hearted thing, resents its own resilience.
Falling is what it loves, and the earth falls
So in our hearts from brilliance,
Settles and is forgot.   5
It takes a sky-blue juggler with five red balls

To shake our gravity up. Whee, in the air
The balls roll round, wheel on his wheeling hands,
Learning the ways of lightness, alter to spheres
Grazing his finger ends,   10
Cling to their courses there,
Swinging a small heaven about his ears.

690

But a heaven is easier made of nothing at all
Than the earth regained, and still and sole within
The spin of worlds, with a gesture sure and noble   15
He reels that heaven in,
Landing it ball by ball,
And trades it all for a broom, a plate, a table.

Oh, on his toe the table is turning, the broom's
Balancing up on his nose, and the plate whirls   20
On the tip of the broom! Damn, what a show, we cry:
The boys stamp, and the girls
Shriek, and the drum booms
And all comes down, and he bows and says good-bye.

If the juggler is tired now, if the broom stands   25
In the dust again, if the table starts to drop
Through the daily dark again, and though the plate
Lies flat on the table top,
For him we batter our hands
Who has won for once over the world's weight.   30

Year's-End

Now winter downs the dying of the year,
And night is all a settlement of snow;
From the soft street the rooms of houses show
A gathered light, a shapen atmosphere,
Like frozen-over lakes whose ice is thin   5
And still allows some stirring down within.

I've known the wind by water banks to shake
The late leaves down, which frozen where they fell
And held in ice as dancers in a spell
Fluttered all winter long into a lake;   10
Graved on the dark in gestures of descent,
They seemed their own most perfect monument.

There was perfection in the death of ferns
Which laid their fragile cheeks against the stone
A million years. Great mammoths overthrown   15
Composedly have made their long sojourns,
Like palaces of patience, in the grey
And changeless lands of ice. And at Pompeii

The little dog lay curled and did not rise
But slept the deeper as the ashes rose   20
And found the people incomplete, and froze
The random hands, the loose unready eyes
Of men expecting yet another sun
To do the shapely thing they had not done.

These sudden ends of time must give us pause.   25
We fray into the future, rarely wrought
Save in the tapestries of afterthought.
More time, more time. Barrages of applause
Come muffled from a buried radio.
The New-year bells are wrangling with the snow.   30

Mind

Mind in its purest play is like some bat
That beats about in caverns all alone,
Contriving by a kind of senseless wit
Not to conclude against a wall of stone.

It has no need to falter or explore;   5
Darkly it knows what obstacles are there,
And so may weave and flitter, dip and soar
In perfect courses through the blackest air.

And has this simile a like perfection?
The mind is like a bat. Precisely. Save   10
That in the very happiest intellection
A graceful error may correct the cave.

PHILIP LARKIN (1922–)

Next, Please

Always too eager for the future, we
Pick up bad habits of expectancy.
Something is always approaching; every day
Till then we say,

Watching from a bluff the tiny, clear,   5
Sparkling armada of promises draw near.
How slow they are! And how much time they waste,
Refusing to make haste!

Yet still they leave us holding wretched stalks
Of disappointment, for, though nothing balks   10
Each big approach, leaning with brasswork prinked,
Each rope distinct,

Flagged, and the figurehead with golden tits
Arching our way, it never anchors; it's
No sooner present than it turns to past.   15
Right to the last

We think each one will heave to and unload
All good into our lives, all we are owed
For waiting so devoutly and so long.
But we are wrong: 20

Only one ship is seeking us, a black-
Sailed unfamiliar, towing at her back
A huge and birdless silence. In her wake
No waters breed or break.

Church Going

Once I am sure there's nothing going on
I step inside, letting the door thud shut.
Another church: matting, seats, and stone,
And little books; sprawlings of flowers, cut
For Sunday, brownish now; some brass and stuff   5

Up at the holy end; the small neat organ;
And a tense, musty, unignorable silence,
Brewed God knows how long. Hatless, I take off
My cycle-clips in awkward reverence,

Move forward, run my hand around the font.   10
From where I stand, the roof looks almost new—
Cleaned, or restored? Someone would know: I don't.
Mounting the lectern, I peruse a few
Hectoring large-scale verses, and pronounce
'Here endeth' much more loudly than I'd meant.   15
The echoes snigger briefly. Back at the door
I sign the book, donate an Irish sixpence,
Reflect the place was not worth stopping for.

Yet stop I did: in fact I often do,
And always end much at a loss like this,   20
Wondering what to look for; wondering, too,
When churches fall completely out of use
What we shall turn them into, if we shall keep
A few cathedrals chronically on show,
Their parchment, plate and pyx in locked cases,   25
And let the rest rent-free to rain and sheep.
Shall we avoid them as unlucky places?

Or, after dark, will dubious women come
To make their children touch a particular stone;
Pick simples for a cancer; or on some   30
Advised night see walking a dead one?
Power of some sort or other will go on
In games, in riddles, seemingly at random;
But superstition, like belief, must die,
And what remains when disbelief has gone?   35
Grass, weedy pavement, brambles, buttress, sky,

A shape less recognizable each week,
A purpose more obscure. I wonder who
Will be the last, the very last, to seek
This place for what it was; one of the crew   40
That tap and jot and know what rood-lofts were?
Some ruin-bibber, randy for antique,
Or Christmas-addict, counting on a whiff
Of gown-and-bands and organ-pipes and myrrh?
Or will he be my representative,   45

Bored, uninformed, knowing the ghostly silt
Dispersed, yet tending to this cross of ground
Through suburb scrub because it held unspilt
So long and equably what since is found
Only in separation—marriage, and birth,   50
And death, and thoughts of these—for whom was built
This special shell? For, though I've no idea
What this accoutred frowsty barn is worth,
It pleases me to stand in silence here;

A serious house on serious earth it is,   55
In whose blent air all our compulsions meet,
Are recognized, and robed as destinies.
And that much never can be obsolete,
Since someone will forever be surprising
A hunger in himself to be more serious,   60
And gravitating with it to this ground,
Which, he once heard, was proper to grow wise in,
If only that so many dead lie round.

Mr. Bleaney

'This was Mr. Bleaney's room. He stayed
The whole time he was at the Bodies, till
They moved him.' Flowered curtains, thin and frayed,
Fall to within five inches of the sill,

Whose window shows a strip of building land,   5
Tussocky, littered. 'Mr. Bleaney took
My bit of garden properly in hand.'
Bed, upright chair, sixty-watt bulb, no hook

Behind the door, no room for books or bags—
'I'll take it.' So it happens that I lie   10
Where Mr. Bleaney lay, and stub my fags
On the same saucer-souvenir, and try

Stuffing my ears with cotton-wool, to drown
The jabbering set he egged her on to buy.
I know his habits—what time he came down,   15
His preference for sauce to gravy, why

He kept on plugging at the four aways—
Likewise their yearly frame: the Frinton folk
Who put him up for summer holidays,
And Christmas at his sister's house in Stoke.   20

But if he stood and watched the frigid wind
Tousling the clouds, lay on the fusty bed
Telling himself that this was home, and grinned,
And shivered, without shaking off the dread

That how we live measures our own nature,   25
And at his age having no more to show
Than one hired box should make him pretty sure
He warranted no better, I don't know.

Behold the Lilies of the Field

for Leonard Baskin

And now. An attempt.
Don't tense yourself; take it easy.
Look at the flowers there in the glass bowl.
Yes, they are lovely and fresh. I remember
Giving my mother flowers once, rather like those   5
(Are they narcissus or jonquils?)
And I hoped she would show some pleasure in them
But got that mechanical enthusiastic show
She used on the telephone once in praising some friend
For thoughtfulness or good taste or whatever it was,   10
And when she hung up, turned to us all and said,
"God, what a bore she is!"
I think she was trying to show us how honest she was,
At least with us. But the effect
Was just the opposite, and now I don't think   15
She knows what honesty is. "Your mother's a whore,"
Someone said, not meaning she slept around,
Though perhaps this was part of it, but
Meaning she had lost all sense of honor,
And I think this is true.   20

But that's not what I wanted to say.
What was it I wanted to say?
When he said that about Mother, I had to laugh,
I really did, it was so amazingly true.
Where was I?   25
Lie back. Relax.
Oh yes. I remember now what it was.
It was what I saw them do to the emperor.
They captured him, you know. Eagles and all.
They stripped him, and made an iron collar for his neck,   30
And they made a cage out of our captured spears,
And they put him inside, naked and collared,
And exposed to the view of the whole enemy camp.
And I was tied to a post and made to watch

When he was taken out and flogged by one of their generals   35
And then forced to offer his ripped back
As a mounting block for the barbarian king
To get on his horse;
And one time to get down on all fours to be the royal throne
When the king received our ambassadors   40
To discuss the question of ransom.
Of course, he didn't want ransom.
And I was tied to a post and made to watch.
That's enough for now. Lie back. Try to relax.
No, that's not all.   45
They kept it up for two months.
We were taken to their outmost provinces.
It was always the same, and we were always made to watch,
The others and I. How he stood it, I don't know.
And then suddenly   50
There were no more floggings or humiliations,
The king's personal doctor saw to his back,
He was given decent clothing, and the collar was taken off,
And they treated us all with a special courtesy.
By the time we reached their capital city   55
His back was completely healed.
They had taken the cage apart—
But of course they didn't give us back our spears.
Then later that month, it was a warm afternoon in May,
The rest of us were marched out to the central square.   60
The crowds were there already, and the posts were set up,
To which we were tied in the old watching positions.
And he was brought out in the old way, and stripped,
And then tied flat on a big rectangular table
So that only his head could move.   65
Then the king made a short speech to the crowds,
To which they responded with gasps of wild excitement,
And which was then translated for the rest of us.
It was the sentence. He was to be flayed alive,
As slowly as possible, to drag out the pain.   70
And we were made to watch. The king's personal doctor,
The one who had tended his back,
Came forward with a tray of surgical knives.
They began at the feet.
And we were not allowed to close our eyes   75
Or to look away. When they were done, hours later,
The skin was turned over to one of their saddle-makers

To be tanned and stuffed and sewn. And for what?
A hideous life-sized doll, filled out with straw,
In the skin of the Roman Emperor, Valerian,   80
With blanks of mother-of-pearl under the eyelids,
And painted shells that had been prepared beforehand
For the fingernails and toenails,
Roughly cross-stitched on the inseam of the legs
And up the back to the center of the head,   85
Swung in the wind on a rope from the palace flag-pole;
And young girls were brought there by their mothers
To be told about the male anatomy.
His death had taken hours.
They were very patient.   90
And with him passed away the honor of Rome.

In the end, I was ransomed. Mother paid for me.
You must rest now. You must. Lean back.
Look at the flowers.
Yes. I am looking. I wish I could be like them.   95

DENISE LEVERTOV (1923–   )

To the Snake

Green Snake, when I hung you round my neck
and stroked your cold, pulsing throat
    as you hissed to me, glinting
arrowy gold scales, and I felt
    the weight of you on my shoulders,   5
and the whispering silver of your dryness
    sounded close at my ears—

Green Snake—I swore to my companions that certainly
    you were harmless! But truly
I had no certainty, and no hope, only desiring   10
    to hold you, for that joy,
                    which left

a long wake of pleasure, as the leaves moved
and you faded into the pattern
of grass and shadows, and I returned   15
smiling and haunted, to a dark morning.

Love Song

Your beauty, which I lost sight of once
for a long time, is long,
not symmetrical, and wears
the earth colors that make me see it.

A long beauty, what is that?   5
A song
that can be sung over and over,
long notes or long bones.

Love is a landscape the long mountains
define but don't   10

shut off from the
unseeable distance.

In fall, in fall,
your trees stretch
their long arms in sleeves   15
of earth-red and

sky-yellow. I take
long walks among them. The grapes
that need frost to ripen them

are amber and grow deep in the   20
hedge, half-concealed,
the way your beauty grows in long tendrils
half in darkness.

Song for Ishtar

The moon is a sow
and grunts in my throat
Her great shining shines through me
so the mud of my hollow gleams
and breaks in silver bubbles   5

She is a sow
and I a pig and a poet

When she opens her white
lips to devour me I bite back
and laughter rocks the moon   10

In the black of desire
we rock and grunt, grunt and
shine

LOUIS SIMPSON (1923–   )

Early in the Morning

Early in the morning
The dark Queen said,
'The trumpets are warning
There's trouble ahead.'
Spent with carousing,   5
With wine-soaked wits,
Antony drowsing
Whispered, 'It's
Too cold a morning
To get out of bed.'   10

The army's retreating,
The fleet has fled,
Caesar is beating
His drums through the dead.
'Antony, horses!   15
We'll get away,
Gather our forces
For another day . . .'
'It's a cold morning,'
Antony said.   20

Caesar Augustus
Cleared his phlegm.
'Corpses disgust us.
Cover them.'
Caesar Augustus   25
In his time lay
Dying, and just as
Cold as they,
On the cold morning
Of a cold day.   30

Birch

Birch tree, you remind me
Of a room filled with breathing,
The sway and whisper of love.

She slips off her shoes;
Unzips her skirt; arms raised,   5
Unclasps an earring, and the other.

Just so the sallow trunk
Divides, and the branches
Are pale and smooth.

In the Suburbs

There's no way out.
You were born to waste your life
You were born to this middleclass life

As others before you
Were born to walk in procession   5
To the temple, singing.

Mementos, 1

Sorting out letters and piles of my old
    Canceled checks, old clippings, and yellow note cards
That meant something once, I happened to find
    Your picture. *That* picture. I stopped there cold,
Like a man raking piles of dead leaves in his yard   5
      Who has turned up a severed hand.

Still, that first second, I was glad: you stand
    Just as you stood—shy, delicate, slender,
In that long gown of green lace netting and daisies
    That you wore to our first dance. The sight of you stunned   10
Us all. Well, our needs were different, then,
      And our ideals came easy.

Then through the war and those two long years
    Overseas, the Japanese dead in their shacks
Among dishes, dolls, and lost shoes; I carried   15
    This glimpse of you, there, to choke down my fear,
Prove it had been, that it might come back.
      That was before we got married.

Before we drained out one another's force
    With lies, self-denial, unspoken regret   20
And the sick eyes that blame; before the divorce
    And the treachery. Say it: before we met. Still,
I put back your picture. Someday, in due course,
      I will find that it's still there.

Lobsters in the Window

First, you think they are dead.
Then you are almost sure
One is beginning to stir.
Out of the crushed ice, slow

As the hands of a schoolroom clock,   5
He lifts his one great claw
And holds it over his head;
Now, he is trying to walk.

But like a run-down toy;
Like the backward crabs we boys   10
Splashed after in the creek,
Trapped in jars or a net,
And then took home to keep.
Overgrown, retarded, weak,
He is fumbling yet   15
From the deep chill of his sleep

As if, in a glacial thaw,
Some ancient thing might wake
Sore and cold and stiff
Struggling to raise one claw   20
Like a defiant fist;
Yet wavering, as if
Starting to swell and ache
With that thick peg in the wrist.

I should wave back, I guess.   25
But still in his permanent clench
He's fallen back with the mass
Heaped in their common trench
Who stir, but do not look out
Through the rainstreaming glass,   30
Hear what the newsboys shout,
Or see the raincoats pass.

✑ ALLEN GINSBERG (1926–   )

America

America I've given you all and now I'm nothing.
American two dollars and twentyseven cents January 17, 1956.
I can't stand on my own mind.
America when will we end the human war?
Go fuck yourself with your atom bomb.   5
I don't feel good don't bother me.
I won't write my poem till I'm in my right mind.
America when will you be angelic?
When will you take off your clothes?
When will you look at yourself through the grave?   10
When will you be worthy of your million Trotskyites?
America why are your libraries full of tears?
America when will you send your eggs to India?
I'm sick of your insane demands.
When can I go into the supermarket and buy what I need with my
    good looks?   15
America after all it is you and I who are perfect not the next world.
Your machinery is too much for me.
You made me want to be a saint.
There must be some other way to settle this argument.
Burroughs is in Tangiers I don't think he'll come back it's sinister.   20
Are you being sinister or is this some form of practical joke?
I'm trying to come to the point.
I refuse to give up my obsession.
America stop pushing I know what I'm doing.
America the plum blossoms are falling.   25
I haven't read the newspapers for months, everyday somebody goes on
    trial for murder.
America I feel sentimental about the Wobblies.
America I used to be a communist when I was a kid I'm not sorry.
I smoke marijuana every chance I get.
I sit in my house for days on end and stare at the roses in the closet. 30
When I go to Chinatown I get drunk and never get laid.
My mind is made up there's going to be trouble.
You should have seen me reading Marx.
My psychoanalyst thinks I'm perfectly right.
I won't say the Lord's Prayer.   35

I have mystical visions and cosmic vibrations.
America I still haven't told you what you did to Uncle Max after he
    came over from Russia.

I'm addressing you.
Are you going to let your emotional life be run by Time Magazine?
I'm obsessed by Time Magazine.   40
I read it every week.
Its cover stares at me every time I slink past the corner candystore.
I read it in the basement of the Berkeley Public Library.
It's always telling me about responsibility. Businessmen are serious.
    Movie producers are serious. Everybody's serious but me.   45
It occurs to me that I am America.
I am talking to myself again.

Asia is rising against me.
I haven't got a chinaman's chance.
I'd better consider my national resources.   50
My national resources consist of two joints of marijuana millions of
    genitals an unpublishable private literature that goes 1400 miles
    an hour and twentyfive-thousand mental institutions.
I say nothing about my prisons nor the millions of underprivileged who
    live in my flowerpots under the light of five hundred suns.
I have abolished the whorehouses of France, Tangiers is the next to go.
My ambition is to be President despite the fact that I'm a Catholic.

America how can I write a holy litany in your silly mood?   55
I will continue like Henry Ford my strophes are as individual as his
    automobiles more so they're all different sexes.
America I will sell you strophes $2500 apiece $500 down on your old
    strophe
America free Tom Mooney
America save the Spanish Loyalists
America Sacco & Vanzetti must not die   60
America I am the Scottsboro boys.
America when I was seven momma took me to Communist Cell meet-
    ings they sold us garbanzos a handful per ticket a ticket costs a
    nickel and the speeches were free everybody was angelic and senti-
    mental about the workers it was all so sincere you have no idea
    what a good thing the party was in 1835 Scott Nearing was a grand
    old man a real mensch Mother Bloor made me cry I once saw
    Israel Amter plain. Everybody must have been a spy.
America you don't really want to go to war.

America it's them bad Russians.

Them Russians them Russians and them Chinamen. And them
   Russians.   65

The Russia wants to eat us alive. The Russia's power mad. She wants
   to take our cars from out our garages.

Her wants to grab Chicago. Her needs a Red Readers' Digest. Her
   wants our auto plants in Siberia. Him big bureaucracy running our
   fillingstations.

That no good. Ugh. Him make Indians learn read. Him need big
   black niggers. Hah. Her make us all work sixteen hours a day. Help.

America this is quite serious.

America this is the impression I get from looking in the television
   set.   70

America is this correct?

I'd better get right down to the job.

It's true I don't want to join the Army or turn lathes in precision parts
   factories, I'm nearsighted and psychopathic anyway.

America I'm putting my queer shoulder to the wheel.

A Man Writes to a Part of Himself

What cave are you in, hiding, rained on?
Like a wife, starving, without care,
Water dripping from your head, bent
Over ground corn . . .

  You raise your face into the rain   5
That drives over the valley—
Forgive me, your husband,
On the streets of a distant city, laughing,
With many appointments,
Though at night going also   10
To a bare room, a room of povetry,
To sleep beside a bare pitcher and basin
In a room with no heat—

  Which of us two then is the worse off?
And how did this separation come about?   15

"Taking the Hands"

Taking the hands of someone you love,
You see they are delicate cages . . .
Tiny birds are singing
In the secluded prairies
And in the deep valleys of the hand.

Romans Angry About the Inner World

What shall the world do with its children?
There are lives the executives
Know nothing of,

A leaping of the body,
The body rolling—and I have felt it—   5
And we float
Joyfully on the dark places;
But the executioners
Move toward Drusia. They tie her legs
On the iron horse. "Here is a woman   10
Who has seen our mother
In the other world!" Next they warm
The hooks. The two Romans had put their trust
In the outer world. Irons glowed
Like teeth. They wanted her   15
To assure them. She refused. Finally they took burning
Pine sticks, and pushed them
Into her sides. Her breath rose
And she died. The executioners
Rolled her off onto the ground.   20
A light snow began to fall
And covered the mangled body,
And the executives, astonished, withdrew.
The other world is like a thorn
In the ear of a tiny beast!   25
The fingers of the executives are too thick
To pull it out!
It is like a jagged stone
Flying toward them out of the darkness.

CHARLES TOMLINSON (1927–   )

Paring the Apple

There are portraits and still-lifes.

And there is paring the apple.

And then? Paring it slowly,
From under cool-yellow
Cold-white emerging. And . . .?   5

The spring of concentric peel
Unwinding off white,
The blade hidden, dividing.

There are portraits and still-lifes
And the first, because 'human'   10
Does not excel the second, and
Neither is less weighted
With a human gesture, than paring the apple
With a human stillness.

The cool blade   15
Severs between coolness, apple-rind
Compelling a recognition.

The Bear

1

In late winter
I sometimes glimpse bits of steam
coming up from
some fault in the old snow
and bend close and see it is lung-colored   5
and put down my nose
and know
the chilly, enduring odor of bear.

2

I take a wolf's rib and whittle
it sharp at both ends   10
and coil it up
and freeze it in blubber and place it out
on the fairway of the bears.

And when it has vanished
I move out on the bear tracks,   15
roaming in circles
until I come to the first, tentative, dark
splash on the earth.

And I set out
running, following the splashes   20
of blood wandering over the world.
At the cut, gashed resting places
I stop and rest,
at the crawl-marks
where he lay out on his belly   25
to overpass some stretch of bauchy ice
I lie out
dragging myself forward with bear-knives in my fists.

3

On the third day I begin to starve,
at nightfall I bend down as I knew I would   30
at a turd sopped in blood,
and hesitate, and pick it up,
and thrust it in my mouth, and gnash it down,
and rise
and go on running.   35

4

On the seventh day,
living by now on bear blood alone,
I can see his upturned carcass far out ahead, a scraggled,
steamy hulk,
the heavy fur riffling in the wind.   40

I come up to him
and stare at the narrow spaced, petty eyes,
the dismayed
face laid back on the shoulder, the nostrils
flared, catching   45
perhaps the first taint of me as he
died.

I hack
a ravine in his thigh, and eat and drink,
and tear him down his whole length   50
and open him and climb in
and close him up after me, against the wind,
and sleep

5

And dream
of lumbering flatfooted   55
over the tundra,
stabbed twice from within,
splattering a trail behind me,
splattering it out no matter which way I lurch
no matter which parabola of bear-transcendence,   60
which dance of solitude I attempt,

which gravity-clutched leap,
which trudge, which groan.

6

Until one day I totter and fall—
fall on this   65
stomach that has tried so hard to keep up,
to digest the blood as it leaked in,
to break up
and digest the bone itself: and now the breeze
blows over me, blows off   70
the hideous belches of ill-digested bear blood
and rotted stomach
and the ordinary, wretched odor of bear,

blows across
my sore, lolled tongue a song   75
or screech, until I think I must rise up
and dance. And I lie still.

7

I awaken I think. Marshlights
reappear, geese
come trailing again up the flyway.   80
In her ravine under old snow the dam-bear
lies, licking
lumps of smeared fur
and drizzly eyes into shapes
with her tongue. And one   85
hairy soled trudge stuck out before me,
the next groaned out,
the next,
the next,
the rest of my days I spend   90
wandering: wondering
what, anyway,
was that sticky infusion, that rank flavor of blood, that poetry, by which
    I lived?

W. S. MERWIN (1927–   )

The Iceberg

It is not its air but our own awe
That freezes us. Hardest of all to believe
That so fearsome a destroyer can be
Dead, with those lights moving in it,
With the sea all around it charged   5
With its influence. It seems that only now
We realize the depth of the waters, the
Abyss over which we float among such
Clouds. And still not understanding
The coldness of most elegance, even   10
With so vast and heartless a splendor
Before us, stare, caught in the magnetism
Of great silence, thinking: this is the terror
That cannot be charted, this is only
A little of it. And recall how many   15
Mariners, watching the sun set, have seen
These peaks on the horizon and made sail
Through the darkness for islands that no map
Had promised, floating blessèd in
The west. These must dissolve   20
Before they can again grow apple trees.

It Is March

It is March and black dust falls out of the books
Soon I will be gone
The tall spirit who lodged here has
Left already
On the avenues the colorless thread lies under   5
Old prices

When you look back there is always the past
Even when it has vanished

But when you look forward
With your dirty knuckles and the wingless   10
Bird on your shoulder
What can you write

The bitterness is still rising in the old mines
The fist is coming out of the egg
The thermometers out of the mouths of the corpses   15

At a certain height
The tails of the kites for a moment are
Covered with footsteps

Whatever I have to do has not yet begun

New Moon in November

I have been watching crows and now it is dark
Together they led night into the creaking oaks
Under them I hear the dry leaves walking
That blind man
Gathering their feathers before winter
By the dim road that the wind will take
And the cold
And the note of the trumpet

THOM GUNN (1929–   )

In Santa Maria Del Popolo

Waiting for when the sun an hour or less
Conveniently oblique makes visible
The painting on one wall of this recess
By Caravaggio, of the Roman School,
I see how shadow in the painting brims   5
With a real shadow, drowning all shapes out
But a dim horse's haunch and various limbs,
Until the very subject is in doubt.

But evening gives the act, beneath the horse
And one indifferent groom, I see him sprawl,   10
Foreshortened from the head, with hidden face,
Where he has fallen, Saul becoming Paul.
O wily painter, limiting the scene
From a cacophany of dusty forms
To the one convulsion, what is it you mean   15
In that wide gesture of the lifting arms?

No Ananias croons a mystery yet,
Casting the pain out under name of sin.
The painter saw what was, an alternate
Candor and secrecy inside the skin.   20
He painted, elsewhere, that firm insolent
Young whore in Venus' clothes, those pudgy cheats,
Those sharpers; and was strangled, as things went,
For money, by one such picked off the streets.

I turn, hardly enlightened, from the chapel   25
To the dim interior of the church instead,
In which there kneel already several people,
Mostly old women: each head closeted
In tiny fists holds comfort as it can.
Their poor arms are too tired for more than this   30
—For the large gesture of solitary man,
Resisting, by embracing, nothingness.

Thrushes

Terrifying are the attent sleek thrushes on the lawn,
More coiled steel than living—a poised
Dark deadly eye, those delicate legs
Triggered to stirrings beyond sense—with a start, a bounce, a stab
Overtake the instant and drag out some writhing thing.   5
No indolent procrastinations and no yawning stares,
No sighs or head-scratchings. Nothing but bounce and stab
And a ravening second.

Is it their single-mind-sized skulls, or a trained
Body, or genius, or a nestful of brats   10
Gives their days this bullet and automatic
Purpose? Mozart's brain had it, and the shark's mouth
That hungers down the blood-smell even to a leak of its own
Side and devouring of itself: efficiency which
Strikes too streamlined for any doubt to pluck at it   15
Or obstruction deflect.

With a man it is otherwise. Heroisms on horseback,
Outstripping his desk-diary at a broad desk,
Carving at a tiny ivory ornament
For years: his act worships itself—while for him,   20
Though he bends to be blent in the prayer, how loud and above what
Furious spaces of fire do the distracting devils
Orgy and hosannah, under what wilderness
Of black silent waters weep.

The Retired Colonel

Who lived at the top end of our street
Was a Mafeking stereotype, ageing.
Came, face pulped scarlet with kept rage,
For air past our gate.

Barked at his dog knout and whipcrack   5
And cowerings of India: five or six wars
Stiffened in his reddened neck;
Brow bull-down for the stroke.

Wife dead, daughters gone, lived on
Honouring his own caricature.   10
Shot through the heart with whisky wore
The lurch like ancient courage, would not go down
While posterity's trash stood, held
His habits like a last stand, even
As if he had Victoria rolled   15
In a Union Jack in that stronghold.

And what if his sort should vanish?
The rabble starlings roar upon
Trafalgar. The man-eating British lion
By a pimply age brought down.   20
Here's his head mounted, though only in rhymes,
Beside the head of the last English
Wolf (those starved gloomy times!)
And the last sturgeon of Thames.

Wodwo

What am I? Nosing here, turning leaves over
Following a faint stain on the air to the river's edge
I enter water. What am I to split
The glassy grain of water looking upward I see the bed
Of the river above me upside down very clear   5
What am I doing here in mid-air? Why do I find
this frog so interesting as I inspect its most secret
interior and make it my own? Do these weeds
know me and name me to each other have they
seen me before, do I fit in their world? I seem   10
separate from the ground and not rooted but dropped
out of nothing casually I've no threads
fastening me to anything I can go anywhere
I seem to have been given the freedom
of this place what am I then? And picking   15

bits of bark off this rotten stump gives me
no pleasure and it's no use so why do I do it
me and doing that have coincided very queerly
But what shall I be called am I the first
have I an owner what shape am I what   20
shape am I am I huge if I go
to the end on this way past these trees and past these trees
till I get tired that's touching one wall of me
for the moment if I sit still how everything
stops to watch me I suppose I am the exact centre   25
but there's all this what is it roots
roots roots roots and here's the water
again very queer but I'll go on looking

GEOFFREY HILL (1932–)

Orpheus and Eurydice

Though there are wild dogs
    Infesting the roads
We have recitals, catalogues
    Of protected birds;

And the rare pale sun   5
    To water our days.
Men turn to savagery now or turn
    To the laws'

Immutable black and red.
    To be judged for his song,   10
Traversing the still-moist dead,
    The newly-stung,

Love goes, carrying compassion
    To the rawly-difficult;
His countenance, his hands' motion,   15
    Serene even to a fault.   *(1958)*

INDEX

A

A ball will bounce, but less and less. It's not, 690
A brackish reach of shoal off Madaket, 683
A cloud moved close. The bulk of the wind shifted, 656
'A cold coming we had of it, 590
A God and yet a man?, 35
A little black thing among the snow, 251
A luvin wumman is licht, 605
A narrow Fellow in the Grass, 451
A noiseless patient spider, 426
A roundel is wrought as a ring or a starbright sphere, 461
A seated statue of himself he seems, 634
A set of phrases learnt by rote, 200
A slumber did my spirit seal, 274
"A soldier of the Union mustered out," 353
A Sonnet upon a Stolen Kiss, 141
A sudden blow: the great wings beating still, 506
A sweet disorder in the dress, 142
About suffering they were never wrong, 644
Above the fresh ruffles of the surf, 622
Accurst be Love, and those that trust his trains, 90
Acquainted with the Night, 530
Adam lay i-bowndyn, 34
ADDISON, JOSEPH, 202
Adieu! farewell earth's bliss, 112
from *Adonais,* 311
Ae weet forenicht i the yow-trummle, 605
After great pain, a formal feeling comes, 445
After the funeral, mule praises, brays, 678
Afterwards, 483
Afton Water, 263
Ah how sweet it is to love, 187
Ah, sweet Content! where is thy mild abode, 117
Ah, what can ail thee, wretched wight, 328
Air Plant, The, 624
Alba (from *Langue d'Oc*), 561
All human things are subject to decay, 178
All men,—the preacher saith,—whate'er or whence, 431
All saints revile her, and all sober men, 619
All the flowers of the spring, 139

C

D

E

F

G

H

I

M

O

P

Q

R

S

T

Y